MOON HANDBOOKS

DOMINICAN REPUBLIC

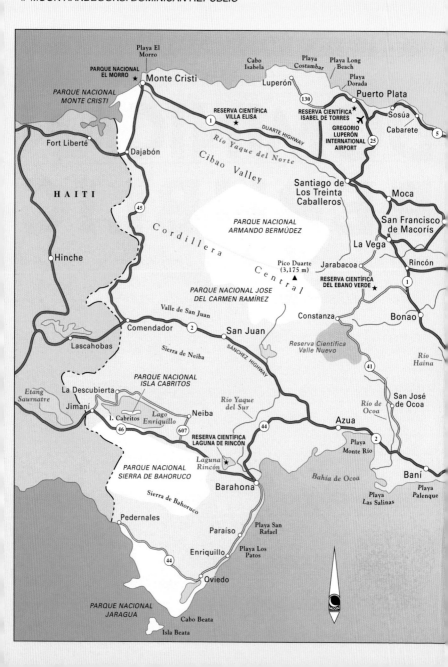

DOMINICAN REPUBLIC

★ SANTUARIO DE BALLENAS JOROBADAS
DEL BANCO DE LA PLATA

Playa Grande

Cabo Francis
Viejo

PARQUE NACIONAL
CABO FRANCES VIEJO

Río San
Juan

Playa
El Bretón

Playa
Diamante

Bahía Escocesa

Playa Boza
De Bojolo

Nagua

Las Terrenas

Playa Rincón

Playa
Las Galeras

Samaná
Peninsula

Samaná

Cabo
Samaná

A T L A N T I C   O C E A N

Sánchez

5

Contuí

Río Yuna

Bahía de Samaná

Playa
Los Cacaos

Sabana
de la Mar

Reserva Científica
Lagunas Redonda
Y Limón

PARQUE NACIONAL
LOS HAITISES

Miches

Santo Domingo

Monte Plata

Bayaguana

73

Hato
Mayor

75

El Seíbo

Sierra   Orientale

Río Chavón

Playa Macao

Playa Bavara

Playa Cabeza
de Toro

Coastal Plain

Río Ozama

DUARTE
HIGHWAY

1

Santo
Domingo

4

La Caleta

Río Magua

Río Soco

4

San Pedro
de Macorís

MELLA HIGHWAY

LAS AMÉRICAS HIGHWAY

Higüey

Playa
Punta Cana

4

Punta Cana

San
Cristóbal

PARQUE NACIONAL
SUBMARINO LA
CALETA

★

Playa
La Caleta

LAS AMÉRICAS
INTERNATIONAL
AIRPORT

Playa Boca
Chica

Playa
Caribe

Playa
Guayacanes

Playa Juan
Dolio

La
Romana

3

Isla
Catalina

Playa
Bayahibe

Playa
Dominicus

Boca de
Yuma

Playa
Juanillo

PARQUE NACIONAL
DE ESTE

Isla Saona

C a r i b b e a n   S e a

0	20 mi
0	20 km

MOON HANDBOOKS

DOMINICAN REPUBLIC

SECOND EDITION

GAYLORD DOLD

AVALON
TRAVEL

MOON HANDBOOKS:
DOMINICAN REPUBLIC
SECOND EDITION

Gaylord Dold

Published by
Avalon Travel Publishing
5855 Beaudry St.
Emeryville, CA 94608, USA

Please send all comments,
corrections, additions,
amendments, and critiques to:

**MOON HANDBOOKS:
DOMINICAN REBUBLIC
AVALON TRAVEL PUBLISHING
5855 BEAUDRY ST.
EMERYVILLE, CA, USA**
email: info@travelmatters.com
www.travelmatters.com

Printing History
1st edition—1997
2nd edition—September 2001
5 4 3 2 1

ISBN: 1-56691-340-3
ISSN: 1533-8924

Editor: Marisa Solís
Series Manager: Erin Van Rheenen
Copy Editor: Lynne Lipkind
Proofreaders: Valerie Blanton, Michele Back
Graphics Coordinator: Melissa Sherowski
Production: Darren Alessi, Susan Jacobs
Map Editor: Naomi Dancis
Cartography: Kat Kalamaras, Mike Morgenfeld, Bob Race
Index: Valerie Blanton

"Visa para un Sueño," words and music by Juan Luis Guerra used by permission of Karen Publishing Co.
Recipes courtesy *Américas* magazine.

Front cover photo: *Casa de Campo, Altos de Chavon* © MCMXCIV Len Kaufman

Distributed in the United States by Publishers Group West

Printed in China through Colorcraft Ltd., Hong Kong

This book is for Megumi, with love.

CONTENTS

ON THE ROAD . . . . 114~182

Swimming; Scuba Diving; Snorkeling; Whale-watching; Windsurfing, Parasailing, Surfing, Sailing; Sportfishing; Golf; Tennis; Horses; Casino Gaming; Spectator Sports
Festivals and Celebrations; Arts and Crafts; Shopping
Traditional Fare; Dominican Meals; What To Eat; Where To Eat; Buying Groceries; Drinks
Airports; Airlines; Internet Resources; Couriers; Other Options
By Air; By Car; By Bus; By Taxi and *Público*; By Train; Tours
Visas and Officialdom; Special Interests; Maps and Tourist Information; Conduct and Courtesy; What To Take; Film and Photography; Weights and Measures; Money
Postal Services; Telephones; Media
Caribbean Disease History; Before You Go; Common Health Problems and Diseases; Doctors and Emergency Care; Medicine; Insurance; Crime; To Haiti

SPECIAL TOPICS

SANTO DOMINGO . . . . 181~237

SPECIAL TOPICS

THE ARID SOUTHWEST. . . . . 238~255

SPECIAL TOPICS

SPECIAL TOPICS

MAPS

MAP SYMBOLS

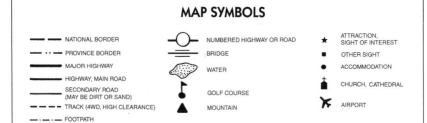

— — NATIONAL BORDER

— ·· — PROVINCE BORDER

▬▬ MAJOR HIGHWAY

▬▬ HIGHWAY, MAIN ROAD

▬▬ SECONDARY ROAD
       (MAY BE DIRT OR SAND)

– – – TRACK (4WD, HIGH CLEARANCE)

— · — · — FOOTPATH

—◯— NUMBERED HIGHWAY OR ROAD

═══ BRIDGE

WATER

GOLF COURSE

▲ MOUNTAIN

★ ATTRACTION,
    SIGHT OF INTEREST

■ OTHER SIGHT

● ACCOMMODATION

✝ CHURCH, CATHEDRAL

✗ AIRPORT

DOMINICAN REPUBLIC.
HANDBOOK DIVISIONS

(Map labels: CIBAO VALLEY, NORTH COAST, THE CENTRAL MOUNTAINS, SAMANA PENINSULA, SANTO DOMINGO, THE ARID SOUTHWEST, THE EAST COAST)

ABBREVIATIONS

a/c—air conditioning/air-conditioned
C—centigrade/Celsius
CDT—Confederación Dominicano del Trabajo
CEBSE—Centro para la Conservación y
  Ecodesarrollo de la Bahía de Samaná (Center
  for the Conservation and Ecodevelopment of
  Samaná Bay)
CMC—Center for Marine Conservation
CSRP—Christian Social Revolutionary Party
d—double
EST—Eastern Standard Time
F—Fahrenheit
IIEE—Instituto Internacional de Español para
  Extranjeros (International Institute of Spanish for
  Foreigners)
IMF—International Monetary Fund
km—kilometer(s)

m—meter(s)
OAS—Organization of American States
PLD—Partido de la Liberación Dominicana
  (Dominican Liberation Party)
PRD—Partido Reformista Dominicano
  (Dominican Reformist Party), led by Joaquín
  Balaguer
PRD—Partido Revolucionario Domincano
  (Domican Revolutionary Party, which later
  became the PLD), led by Juan Bosch
PST—Pacific Standard Time
s—single
tel.—telephone
UASD—Universidad Autónomo de Santo
  Domingo (Autonomous University of Santo
  Domingo)

ACKNOWLEDGMENTS

None of us is alone, and no person labors without help—least of all a writer, and especially a writer who travels. So I would like to thank some special people who made my travel in the Dominican Republic enjoyable and meaningful, and who, by dint of their own effort, assisted me in understanding their wonderful country.

First of all, there is Ana Green, who helped me see her land with Dominican eyes. In addition, I must thank Juan Batista, an architect of distinguished skills, who taught me about Santo Domingo, Puerta Plata, and how the people live in the buildings they've built. Cesar Namnún offered me his music—for which I am grateful—while Marisol Ortiz at the Tourism Promotion Council was more than generous with her time and her organization's materials. In matters of art, especially painting, I was in the good hands of Marcos Manzueta and Señor Colombo at María del Carmen art shop; they were always there at the outdoor café with coffee and conversation. It would be unthinkable not to mention Dagoberto Tejeda, professor of sociology, who gave freely of his time to tell me about folklore, Carnaval, and medicine, and shared his guava velí with me on more than one occasion.

And finally, and perhaps most important of all, I wish to express my profound thanks to Roosevelt, at Hostál Nader, and his compatriot Martin Bolanco, who were there with rum and baseball at night and coffee and philosophy in the morning, both with courtesy bordering on true friendship.

PLEASE HELP KEEP THIS BOOK CURRENT

The world of international travel and regional development is a world of rapid change. The Dominican Republic is only now being discovered by more and more travelers, who appreciate its beaches, mountains, and people. You—the reader—are a valuable resource in ensuring that future editions contain the most up-to-date and accurate information. Please let us know about any price changes, new accommodations or restaurants, map errors or updates, travel tips, and any other corrections.

Your correspondence may be addressed to:

> *Moon Handbooks: Dominican Republic,* second edition
> Avalon Travel Publishing
> 5855 Beaudry Street
> Emeryville, CA 94608 USA
>
> website: www.moon.com
> email: info@travelmatters.com

ACCOMMODATIONS RATINGS

Under US$30	Inexpensive
US$30–80	Moderate
US$80–100	Expensive
US$100+	Luxury

FOOD RATINGS

Under US$5	Inexpensive
US$5–10	Moderate
US$10–25	Expensive
Prices are per person.	

THE ESSENCE OF THE DOMINICAN REPUBLIC

As the twentieth century nears its end, the Dominican Republic faces the world as a democratic country that has survived hurricanes, colonization, foreign invasion, and brutal dictatorship. Its original inhabitants, the Taínos, have long since disappeared in the welter of bloodshed and disease brought on by the original Spanish conquest. The very landscape of the Dominican Republic, once dominated by lush tropical and deciduous mountain forests, roaring torrents of streams, and rich meadowlands, has been drastically altered by the hand of man.

And yet the Dominican Republic's people are one of the country's great attractions. Taíno, Spanish, African, French, and English traditions have woven together to create a complex cultural fabric that not only survives but flourishes as we begin the next millennium.

In some ways, the Dominican Republic is a typical Latin American country, with stark contrasts between wealth and poverty, modernity and antiquity, rural agricultural regions and crowded cities, mountainous vistas and tropical beaches. The Dominican people themselves very much resemble other Latin American peoples in their love of music, poetry, and dance; their dignified bearing; their fertile sense of humor; and a resigned but undespairing spirit in the face of much trouble and unemployment.

But no country is really a *typical* Latin American country, any more than a single person is typical. How, then, is it possible for a humble writer to communicate the essence of this multifaceted place?

I suppose I might first try to explain the country's unique geography. Along with Haiti, the Dominican Republic occupies the island of Hispaniola—the second largest of the Greater Antilles. The first European to visit Hispaniola was Christopher Columbus. In a letter to Ferdinand and Isabella written just after he'd set foot on the island's northern shore, he exclaimed, "*Es esta la tierra más bella bajo los cielos!*"—"This is the fairest land under Heaven!" Columbus had encountered a spectacle beyond compare: a vast system of double mountain ranges enclosing an impossibly fertile valley now known as the Cibao. Unfortunately for the admiral, he and his men had neither the time nor the energy to cross every mountain system on the island—the convoluted Cordillera Central, the graceful eastern mountains, or the sharp Sierra de Neiba and Bahoruco Mountains of the arid southwest. Nor could they traverse to the source of some very mighty rivers—the famous Yaque del Norte, the Yuna, or the southwest's spectacular Yaque del Sur.

Today, over a network of roads, anyone willing to make the effort can reach places hidden to the world until a few short years ago. Sometimes hopelessly and forever "under repair," choked by traffic, or wandering ghostlike without a hint of a traffic sign, the Dominican Republic's roads and highways beckon the adventurous. Consequently, all it takes to really get out and away from the hustle of modern tourism is a rental car, a spirit of adventure, and a simple willingness to stop, ask directions, have a *coco frío*, and enjoy whatever comes next. In all my travels in the Dominican Republic, I've become lost dozens, if not hundreds, of times and have always been set straight with a hearty smile and sincere best wishes.

Certainly, the rewards awaiting those who explore the Dominican Republic are great. The country holds the highest peaks in the Caribbean, including the sometimes snow-dusted Pico Duarte, which stands 10,319 feet (3,175 meters) high. With a car, you can access most of the mountain towns, where warm clothes and blankets are a nighttime necessity even in summer. Yet only half a day's journey away from the high peaks lies Lake Enriquillo, 135 feet below sea level, surrounded by salt marshes and an arid coral desert. Far to the east lie the graceful sugar provinces of El Seibo and Higüey—presided over by the gentle Cordillera Oriental—where farmers tend cane and cattle graze in well-kept fields.

Part of the Dominican Republic's beauty lies in this surprising diversity. In Samaná, huge mangroves, coral reefs, and nearly deserted tropical beaches await visitors. Santo Domingo is home to a vibrant art scene and the most exuberant, expressive people you'll ever meet. In Santiago Carnaval is held, and in La Vega the famous Yellow House market offers an abundance of fruits, medicines, crafts, clothing, musical instruments, animals, grains, and the services of wandering astrologers. Every night, all through the winter, most major Dominican cities offer baseball second in quality only to the American major leagues. And everywhere, on every evening, you'll find merengue.

Of course, not every star above the Dominican Republic shines down on a romantic seascape. Many Dominicans are poor. As in most developing countries, the birth rate here is high and the countryside overpopulated, the land tenure laws are disjointed, and the land ownership too narrowly divided. Many of the agriculturally dispossessed have fled the rural regions and surfaced in Santo Domingo or other large cities, where they find a scarcity of jobs and inadequate sanitation and medical care. The results are shantytowns, political distress, and a poverty that grinds down the spirit.

Overpopulation and deforestation go hand in hand as well. Where once the land was primarily tropical and deciduous (montane) forest, only about 15% remains so. As in North America and Europe, land once forest is now under cultivation, grazed by cattle or goats, or no longer arable. Fortunately, the Dominican people seem to possess a new consciousness of the need to preserve what's left of their precious resources and to improve what's gone bad. The men and women I've met in my visits to the offices of the national parks administrators and the new wildlife bureaus show a true devotion to setting aside parts of the country for preservation and conservation. However, a country like the Dominican Republic has little money to spend on projects that seem to offer scant direct benefit to people in immediate need.

Politically, too, all is not well. To be sure, the days of the Trujillo dictatorship are long gone—no longer do soldiers prowl the streets nor police arrest without justification. But while organized, peaceful political demonstrations are common and the press enjoys a level of freedom unknown at any time in the nation's history, the power remains narrowly distributed. Perhaps 200 wealthy families own or control most of the manufacturing, agricultural, and service-sector economic firms. The political parties pretending to compete really don't but rather joust for power without much ideological difference. The country has the face of a democracy and the soul of an oligarchy. Fortunately, the large-scale geopolitical effects of cable TV, video, and film offer some hope that foreign influences may alter the political landscape in the country.

What is the essence of this place? Perhaps one Dominican Republic is the country artfully presented to tourists by official government agencies, travel bureaus, major hotel chains, airlines, and car rental agencies. Blessed by a year-round mean temperature in the upper 70s F and summer and winter trade winds that sweep the island from north to south, the country might sound like a perfect place for visitors. And, in many ways, it is. It's a country of sun and fun, of white beaches and friendly, outgoing people, a place available to those who desire a carefree week in a single location. It's a Dominican Republic whose fascinating capital is the oldest city in the western hemisphere, a city where one can savor shopping, sophisticated art, music, theater, and exclusive hotels along an oceanfront bristling with fine restaurants and new construction.

But a second Dominican Republic dwells along the north coast beyond Puerto Plata east and west, all the way to the Samaná Peninsula. It hides in the desert southwest, near the Sierra de Bahoruco, on the shores of Lake Enriquillo, and in the provinces of La Altagracia and El Seibo. It is a country you have to reach for but which rewards you when you do with views of mountain valleys swept by cool winds or acacia forests dominated by 10-foot-tall cacti. It's a place where you can enjoy a leisurely drive along well-maintained roads, wake to a good breakfast of strong coffee and fresh mango, take a hike, ride a horse, or fish for dorado.

And, finally, there is a third Dominican Republic, a truly wild land—a place for adventurers. This is a country of high peaks, sunken lakes, offshore islands, uncharted coral reefs, karst caves, savannah-like grasslands, sun-blistered deserts, and whale sanctuaries on the open seas. It is a country difficult but not impossible to visit—and worth every bit of extra effort to the exploring soul open to new experiences and willing to learn.

I remember one early evening along El Conde, Santo Domingo's main shopping street. For nearly a city block, young chess players lined the street, sitting at tables in white shirts and clean clothes, organized as part of a spontaneous exhibition by a famous Dominican expert. The setting sun, in its particularly beautiful Caribbean way, bathed everything in an unearthly pink glow. It was near Christmas, and the light standards were ablaze with colored bulbs.

Suddenly, the billowing purple and rose clouds opened up, and down fell a cooling torrent of rain. Nevertheless, the boys and girls happily played on as the expert toured the tables. The rain continued to pour. Proud parents and interested onlookers kept watching, undeterred. Down the street, above the din of merengue from record-store jam-boxes, the Firemen's Band played Christmas songs. It all seemed entirely appropriate: the dignity of the children in their school clothes, the tropical downpour, the music, the color.

It's just these kinds of moments that can lead visitors away from the ordinary and into the extraordinary travel experience. Whether you're a tourist, a traveler, or adventurer, may this book guide you to many such sacred moments.

BOB RACE

INTRODUCTION

LAND

One main factor in the upward trend of animal life has been the power of wandering. Animals wander into new conditions. They have to adapt themselves or die. Mankind has wandered from the trees to the plains, from the plains to the seacoast, from climate to climate, from continent to continent, and from habit of life to habit of life. Other nations of different habits are not enemies; they are godsends.

— Alfred North Whitehead

Size and Area

The Dominican Republic occupies the eastern two-thirds of the island of Hispaniola, the second-largest island in the Caribbean, with an area of 29,979 square miles (77,945 square km). Formerly a colony of Spain, it shares the island with Creole-French–speaking Haiti, located at the western end of the island. Hispaniola is part of the Greater Antilles island group in the Caribbean

and lies between Cuba to the northwest and Puerto Rico to the east.

While Hispaniola is the second-largest island in the Caribbean, the Dominican Republic is the second-largest country in the region, occupying 18,700 square miles (48,620 square km). It includes 977 miles of coastline, with the Caribbean Sea to its south, the Atlantic Ocean to the north, and the deep, current-driven Mona Passage separating its eastern tip from Puerto Rico.

The Dominican Republic's geography doesn't lend itself to easy classification. Its complicated blend of relief, weather, and vegetation makes for a varied topography and diverse land-use strategies. For travelers, it's best to think of the Dominican Republic as a combination of highlands, lowlands, and highland valleys, but professional geographers have actually divided the country into more than *twenty* distinct regions. This diversity means you can visit numerous different kinds of places, all on one large island.

If you pressed a professional geographer to characterize the Dominican Republic in a few words, he or she would probably tell you it resembles a Central American country tugged into the middle of the Caribbean Sea. Sounds interesting, doesn't it?

THE PLATES

Eurasian Plate

South East Asian Plate

Phillippine Plate

Pacific Plate

Cocos Plate

North American Plate

Nazca Plate

Caribbean Plate

African Plate

Eurasian Plate

Indian Plate

South American Plate

Antarctic Plate

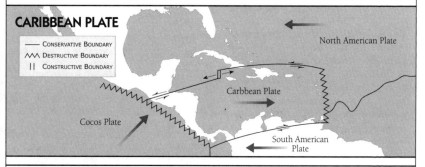

CARIBBEAN PLATE

— CONSERVATIVE BOUNDARY
∧∧∧ DESTRUCTIVE BOUNDARY
|| CONSTRUCTIVE BOUNDARY

North American Plate

Cocos Plate

Carbbean Plate

South American Plate

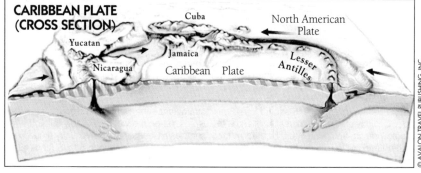

CARIBBEAN PLATE (CROSS SECTION)

Cuba

North American Plate

Yucatan

Jamaica

Nicaragua

Caribbean Plate

Lesser Antilles

PLATE TECTONICS
AND THE CARIBBEAN

A plausible account of the history of Dominican geology had to wait for a mature theory of Plate Tectonics, a theory that did not come of age until the 1960s. Even now, there are relatively few "experts" on Dominican geology, but one of those, English-born Dr. Grenville Draper, Professor of Geology and expert in Caribbean ecology at Florida International University in Miami, Florida, has provided this author with a detailed explanation of regional and local geology, based in part on his own field work in the West Indies. According to Dr. Draper, studies utilizing ultrasound waves to "X-ray" the Earth reveal that it has a structure reminiscent of a peeled coconut, with a liquid core, a solid, but soft "flesh," and a thin, rigid outer shell. The liquid core is about 6000km in diameter and composed of swirling molten metallic iron and nickel. This core is surrounded by a solid region called the mantle that makes up almost all of the remaining 12,000km of the diameter of the Earth. Although solid, the material is hot, and so like heated glass or metal, flows like a thick liquid. The outer shell is about 100km thick. Here, Draper says, the coconut analogy fails. The shell of the Earth is not intact, but is cracked to form a series of curved plates. Some of the plates have continents embedded in them, and this continental crust is lighter (less dense) than most of the underlying plate.

Though the ins and outs of the 160-million-year geologic history of the Hispaniola area are complicated, Dr. Draper has provided a capsule analysis of Dominican geology in his own words:

The Greater Antilles, with the exception of Cuba, lie atop what geologists call the Caribbean Plate. The Caribbean Plate is just one of a dozen or so of 100km-thick rigid shells that make up the outer part of the Earth. These plates are constantly moving with respect to each other at rates averaging a few centimeters per year (about the same rate as your fingernails grow).

The Caribbean Plate lies between the much bigger plates of North and South America and is moving eastward with respect to each at about 2cms (1 inch) per year. The present boundaries of the plate form an approximate oblong shape that includes, in addition to the Greater Antilles, much of Central America in the west, the Lesser Antilles in the east, and a sliver of the northern part of South America. The northern boundary runs east-west through Guatemala, between Jamaica and Cuba, north of Hispaniola and Puerto Rico, before joining the eastern boundary.

The eastern (Lesser Antilles) and western boundaries (Central America) are examples of convergent boundaries, also called subduction zones, where one plate slides (subducts) under the other back into the Earth's interior. Chemical reactions in the downgoing plate cause melting of the Earth's interior, producing a string of volcanoes on the edge of the overriding plate. In the east, part of the Atlantic Ocean floor dips under the volcanic islands of the Lesser Antilles, and in the west the Cocos Plate dips under Central America.

On the northern boundary, the islands of Jamaica, Hispaniola, and Puerto Rico are sliding past the Bahamas region, which forms the southern margin of North America (Cuba is part of the North American Plate and has been for 50 million years).

Most geologists now agree that the Caribbean region was born about 170 million years ago when the huge supercontinent of Pangea began to break up. North America split from Europe and Africa, creating the early North Atlantic Ocean and the gap between North and South America that we now call the Caribbean. The Greater Antilles was later created when the Pacific Ocean floor descended under the early Caribbean and produced a chain of volcanic islands that occupied the same position as modern-day Central America. About 110 million years ago, when South America began to split from Africa, this whole system changed, causing deformation and faulting of the volcanic chain. Instead of the Caribbean overriding the Pacific, the Pacific began to override the early Caribbean and drift into the Atlantic. This change in subduction produced another set of volcanic islands that built up and over the distorted remains of the first island chain. The part of the Pacific that moved into the gap between the Americas contained a huge submarine plateau that eventually became the sea floor of the present Caribbean and created what is now the Caribbean Plate.

Around 50 million years ago the leading edge of the Caribbean Plate collided with the Bahama region and the Caribbean Plate was deflected eastwards. As it has scraped by the Bahamas, the northern Caribbean Plate has splintered along numerous geologic faults, many of which are still moving. One of these eventually broke eastern Cuba off from Hispaniola and transferred it to the North American Plate. Some splinters were pushed up, and still others were pushed down to form undersea basins in which sediments were laid down and eventually hardened into rock.

About 12 million years ago, a final collision event began which is still occurring and which defines the character of the present geologic structure of the island. In eastern Hispaniola and Puerto Rico, the northern edge of the Caribbean Sea floor was pushed under the islands, causing relatively gentle uplift and the modest mountains of those regions. Some geologists even think that this region has become disconnected from the main Caribbean Plate to form a sliver or "microplate" on the Caribbean's northeastern

boundary. In southwestern Hispaniola, the northern edge of the Caribbean Sea floor was thrust upward and onto Hispaniola, and now forms the mountainous massif of the Southern Peninsula of Haiti and Baharona. The whole of the area to the north was squeezed and uplifted to form the lofty peaks of the Cordillera Central and Cordillera Septentrional.

Earthquakes

The plate tectonic motion causes earthquakes on the boundaries of the Caribbean Plate. Most of the countries of the Caribbean, situated as they are on the plate, have suffered earthquakes. The Dominican Republic is no exception. Two main active zones exist: One is around the Cibao Valley in the north of the island, and the other runs from Santo Domingo through the Enriquillo Valley to Port-au-Prince in Haiti. The original site of Santiago de los Caballeros was destroyed (along with La Vega) in 1562 and severely damaged in 1842 and again in 1897. Santo Domingo was damaged several times in the seventeenth century and again in 1751 and 1761.

Volcanoes

Volcanoes and earthquakes do not always go together. The present plate boundary in the northern Caribbean is the type known as a transform boundary (like that in California), which produces little volcanic activity. This contrasts with the convergent boundary of the Lesser Antilles, where there are many active volcanoes, notably on the island of Montserrat. Plate boundaries change, however, and from about 130 million years until about 50 million years ago the Dominican Republic was part of a convergent plate boundary made up of huge volcanoes like those of the present-day Lesser Antilles. Later movements on the plate boundary squeezed, uplifted, and eroded these volcanoes. The present-day Cordillera Central, including the rocks underneath Pico Duarte, is made up of the roots of those ancient volcanoes.

Some complicated stretching of the plate boundary did produce volcanoes in Hispaniola during the period between six million and one million years ago (quite recently, geologically speaking!). On the southern flanks of the Cordillera Central, south of Constanza, some volcanic domes, flows, and ash cones can still be seen.

PRESENT CHANGE

Most of the more recent geologic changes have come from waves, wind, and river action. You won't find very severe marine erosion on Hispaniola. For one thing, the tidal action isn't great over much of the island, and this limits areas exposed to waves. Secondly, coral reefs shelter many coastal areas and provide a source of much-needed beach-building material.

Cliffs
All over Hispaniola you can see where waves have cut into narrow platforms of rock, shaving off shelves and terraces until all that's left is a cliff dramatically dropping straight to the ocean. These cliffs are what make the Dominican Republic's beaches so spectacular and, in a way, surprising: Hidden between these high cliffs, white-sand beaches suddenly appear, seemingly out of nowhere.

DOMINICAN REPUBLIC NATURAL FEATURES

River Terraces

More common in Hispaniola than wave- and wind-caused landforms are river terraces. You can spot them everywhere in the Dominican Republic. They form as river water runs down steep grades. As gravity causes the flow to cut deeper into the riverbed, the river's former banks—composed of floodplain sediment—are left stranded along the edges of the valley. The sides of mountains literally fall into the sea as the river undercuts the terraces and then carries their soil toward the river mouth and, eventually, into the sea.

New Coastal Lands

Since the end of the last ice age—a few thousand years ago—new land has come into being in Hispaniola. This kind of thing is possible only in the tropics, where coral and mangroves grow. Trade winds throw sand into the shallow coral reefs and cause the upsurgence of small cays; mangroves trap mud, silt, and sediment, along with sand carried in by tides and wind, creating new coastal lands.

Karst Regions

In the West Indies, rain, river action, wind, and the sea constantly combine to create new landforms. Especially in the eastern parts of islands—and dramatically so in the Dominican Republic—the low-lying limestone rocks are subjected to many years of heavy rainfall. Though these areas begin as wide plateaus, over eons they become riddled with caves and sinkholes, until the hills are cone-shaped and studded with intervening pits. Geologists call these kinds of landscapes karst regions, which provide some of the most dramatic wilderness experiences in the Dominican Republic.

MOUNTAINS

According to a well-worn story, when England's King George III asked one of his admirals to describe the island of Hispaniola, the naval commander crumpled a piece of paper, tossed it on the table, and said, "Thus looks Hispaniola." No other island in the Caribbean possesses Hispaniola's mountainous terrain. And with the resulting 20-plus distinct geographical regions and eco-zones, the Dominican Republic is one of the most ecologically diverse countries in the whole world.

The remarkable dual chains of mountains running east to west through the Dominican Republic are actually continued ranges traceable to Central America. One axis runs from Central America to Cuba and beyond, the other through Jamaica eastward. The two merge on Hispaniola, lending it a unique character.

Despite the complexity of the mountain systems, a topographical map clearly reveals four main ranges on the island: one in the north, one in the south, and two sub-chains directly in between. A fifth, minor chain extends throughout the province of La Altagracia in the eastern part of the country.

Cordillera Septentrional

The most northerly range of mountains is the Cordillera Septentrional, with modestly precipitous slopes and deeply etched valleys. This range rises near the coastal town of Monte Cristi (it's locally called the Sierra de Monte Cristi) and runs north-northwest to east-southeast, parallel to the Dominican coast, for nearly 200km. Never far from the ocean, it gradually rises west to east, reaching its apex at Pico Diego de Ocampo, 1,249m (about 4,000 feet) above sea level.

With the exception of Pico Diego de Ocampo, most mountains in the eastern part of the Cordillera Septentrional rise 600–900 meters. Most amazing about the Septentrional is how suddenly its southern end descends into the Cibao Valley—almost without transition. Standing in gentle Santiago and looking north, you see the magnificent Septentrional range rise abruptly from the green Cibao and shoot almost straight up to its highest point—a very dramatic view indeed.

The Septentrional continues east until it encounters the Gran Estero swamps, from which it emerges as a series of low hills on the Samaná Peninsula (once an island, until fault blocking smashed it into the mainland). The southeastern end of the Septentrional descends in hilly and gentle declines into what's called the Vega Real, really the eastern end of the Cibao Valley. The mountain range itself is composed mainly of Miocene and Oligocene limestone and has karst formations in some places.

As you can imagine, the north-facing parts of the Septentrional experience strong trade winds and heavy precipitation. Sosúa, a town on the north coast, endures regular downpours. Tropical rainforests and semi-evergreen seasonal forests predominate on the lower altitudes of the Septentrional's north face, while evergreen and semi-evergreen montane forests grow at the middle altitudes. The little primeval first growth left on Hispaniola lies within the Septentrional. Few paved roads exist here.

The Cordillera Central

The dissected and highly convoluted Cordillera Central divides the Dominican Republic nearly in half. It's composed of at least two highly defined branches (the lower of which lies farther north) and stretches east across the island, forming what's actually a spur of the Cordillera Oriental. The southern branch of the Cordillera Central, locally called the Sierra de Ocoa, makes a southerly turn and comes out near the Caribbean coast at the town of Azua. The entire mountain chain of the Central features precipitous and rugged slopes, with gradients as high as 40 degrees. It is the principal watershed for the country and, taken together with Haiti's Massif du Nord (connected to the Central), constitutes about one-third of the landmass of the entire bulk of Hispaniola. Its canyons, streams, gulches, barrancas, and peaks make it largely inaccessible to regular passenger vehicles. The Cordillera Central includes by far the highest peaks in all the Caribbean, with the sometimes snow-dusted Pico Duarte rising to 3,175 meters.

The Cordillera Central is so high in altitude that it has 12 rainy months. Impressively, the mountains are still covered by much forest—mostly pine. Since workers carved out a road into the mountains near Constanza, many wood-cutters have set up camps and begun taking timber out of the forest. Nevertheless, the Central's steep slopes and heavy forest have continued to prove a barrier to settlement, exploitation, and communication. In most areas, you still won't find actual roads, only localized paths and unimproved dirt tracks.

Way back in the early colonial period, Columbus and his men found gold in the Central, but the few deposits were quickly exhausted. These days, while there is still some chrome and nickel to be found, mining plays a very minor role in the exploitation of the Central.

A relatively old mountain range, the Cordillera Central has undergone century upon century of rain and wind erosion, and this erosion has created alluvial slopes, valleys, and hills where agriculture can get a foothold. The best example of this topography is the town of Constanza, where cultivated fields of tomatoes, cabbage, onions, beans, strawberries, and fresh flowers lie in a block. Standing in the valley of Constanza, surrounded by fields of colorful flowers, with the rugged, all-encompassing peaks of the Cordillera Central in the distance, is an experience not to be missed.

The Sierra de Neiba

In the southwestern part of the Dominican Republic, south of the Central, stand the double ranges of the Sierra de Neiba and the Sierra de Bahoruco. The Sierra de Neiba rises to 2,249 meters at its highest point. The Río Yaque del Sur cuts a gap in the eastern part of the range, and the mountains that continue on after the gap are locally called the Sierra Martín García (they end at the Azua coastal plain). The south face of the Sierra de Neiba is very dry and rocky, cut by gullies and watersheds that carry occasional rains south. Semi-evergreen seasonal forests largely cover the northern slopes. In these very remote regions with few roads, some *conuqueros* eke out an existence by cultivating small fields. You'll find some market-oriented coffee plantations here, but they're few and far between. Communication in this remote range is undeveloped.

The Sierra de Bahoruco

The Sierra de Bahoruco, south of the Sierra de Neiba, is a continuation of the Haitian mountains called the Massif de la Selle. Like the Sierra de Neiba, the Sierra de Bahoruco is semi-arid at lower elevations. Rising to 2,420 meters, though averaging around 1,600 meters in the east, this mountain range resembles something straight out of a spaghetti Western. Imagine Mexico or northern Spain, add some pine trees, rocks, and heavily eroded surfaces, and you've got the Sierra de Bahoruco. The Bahoruco's very highest elevations receive rain throughout the year—enough at any rate to grow good forests of *Pinus occidentalis.* Farmers cultivate coffee on the northern slopes, but the southern slopes are dry, sometimes rather barren, and heavily eroded.

One road leads from the Pedernales Peninsula up the southern slope of the Bahoruco. From the top of the mountains, you can look north out on the salt sea called Lake Enriquillo and across the lake to the Sierra de Neiba. Encompassing as many as five or six land types, including acacia and cactus desert, pine forest, and salt sea, the Sierra de Bahoruco is fascinating—even magical.

The mountains are a great place for sunsets. And, as remote and rugged as it is, the range has achieved some economic importance to the Dominican Republic because of the coffee grown there and because companies have begun to mine the area's bauxite deposits, mainly for shipment to the United States.

Cordillera Oriental

Last, but not least, comes the Cordillera Orientale, a range less of mountains than of sharp hills extending west about 120km from the Atlantic Coast along the southern shore of Samaná Bay to the foothills of the Cordillera Central, about 50km north of Santo Domingo. Much of the range is rolling, not rugged, occasionally cut by streams, and covered by tropical deciduous forest and savannah. From a distance, these mountains may remind you of Asian landscapes. Near Samaná Bay, however, the range becomes slightly more craggy and remote, and more streams cut through the region's abundant limestone, creating a karst-like topography.

This is good cattle country, and in the provinces of La Altagracia and El Seibo, fields are neatly tended, interspersed with coconut trees and sugar plantations.

HIGHLAND VALLEYS

The Cibao

It was in part the highland valley Dominicans call the *Cibao* that caused Columbus to believe he had stumbled into paradise. Perhaps he thought first about gold, but he could not help being impressed by the overall loveliness of the valley itself, the pleasant climate, and the fertility of the soil. Indeed, the Cibao is the breadbasket of the Dominican Republic.

Fifteen to 40km wide and approximately 225km long, this highland valley stretches between the peaks of the Cordillera Septentrional and those of the Cordillera Central, giving it sharp definition and steep banks. The Samaná Peninsula lies to the valley's east, and the city of Santiago lies at its midpoint, between the westward-flowing Río Yaque del Norte and the eastward-flowing Río Yuna. To the west, near Monte Cristi, the valley turns somewhat dry (reminiscent of California's San Joaquin Valley) but in a few short kilometers becomes humid.

The Cibao was originally a rift valley, meaning that it was formed by fault-block movement. In most places, erosion and alluvial movement have filled the originally very deep chasm. Both the Río Yaque del Norte and the Río Yuna have created wide river terraces and have cut deep down into the valley floor. Everywhere, the soil lies at least three meters deep and is very easy to plow and cultivate. Some call it the highest-yielding soil anywhere in the Greater Antilles. Driving through the valley on any of its well-maintained roads, you can see why this is probably true. Along the river courses, banana plantations and rice fields abound. The rice fields of the western Cibao supply most of the country's rice, and what the rice crop is in the west, tobacco is in the east.

Everything in the Cibao—rice, bananas, and tobacco—is grown on large plantations, with many, if not most, of the plantations depending directly on irrigation to maintain productivity.

The western end of the Cibao is mainly dry and dusty scrub savannah. Here the original Spanish conquerors raised draft animals and supplied them to the French of Haiti, who were raising sugarcane. The region continues to be known for the livestock raised there—today it's famed for its cattle ranches.

At the eastern end of the Cibao is the **Vega Real,** another distinct highland valley. The site of the largest concentration of original Amerindian populations, the Vega Real was a center of culture and agriculture for native peoples. Here, too, Columbus—and, later, his brother and son—wandered, fought, killed, and subdued, making the Vega Real the oldest economic center on Hispaniola. During colonial times, most of the population lived in the Vega Real for its healthful climate and fertile land. Even today, the area is home to nearly one-third of the Dominican Republic's population.

Driving through the Vega Real is a real eye-opener. Nowhere else in the Caribbean will you find a more mixed group of crops or a higher proportion of small and medium-size farms. Farmers here grow cacao, coffee, bananas, maize, sweet potatoes, manioc, and dry rice. Most fields contain one or more of these crops, some of which are grown for subsistence, others for export. The fields themselves are quite beautiful, too, with young cacao and coffee plants protected from the sun first by maize, then by bananas. Often, farmers plant sweet potatoes and taro between rows of cacao and coffee. To put exclamation points on this kaleidoscope of field patterns, royal palms tower everywhere, many of them growing in impressive clumps of a half-dozen trees.

Busy, small, provincial market towns like La Vega, Moca, and San Francisco de Macorís carry out the regional functions of the Vega Real. Way back in colonial times, during the period 1495–1865, most of the eastern Cibao's produce went overland—first by mule track, then by wagon road—from these towns (and Santiago) to Puerto Plata on the north coast. In 1888, a British company built a railroad to Sánchez on Samaná Bay in order to expedite crop export. Now, roads connect all of the Cibao with Puerto Plata to the north and Santo Domingo to the south, leaving Santiago as the principal market and economic town in the valley.

Valle de San Juan

South of the Cordillera Central's high mountains lies the Valle de San Juan, extending westward into Haiti, where it is that country's central plateau. About 130km in length, with an average width

of about 65km, the valley is uniformly semiarid because of its position in the lee of the Cordillera Central. Originally, *conqueros* used the valley for extensive cattle operations, but now those same cattle operations are interspersed with small areas of maize and bean farming. As the valley eases and narrows toward the east, and before it finally funnels down to the Caribbean Sea in a space not five km wide, some of the farmers grow tobacco and coffee. You can see tobacco farmers walking their long, sausage-shaped tobacco rolls to market.

The Valle de San Juan is also known for its many beekeepers and fine stores of honey and beeswax—sold at roadside stalls along the highway into the valley. With its large cactus and cholla stands, modern apple farms, and iguana-carrying children, the Valle de San Juan is a special surprise.

Valle de Neiba

The last of the three parallel valleys in the western Dominican Republic really can't be called a "highland" valley at all. In fact, with many parts of this *Valle de Neiba* lying below sea level, it deserves the name many geographers have given it: the **Enriquillo Depression.** About 20km wide and about 100km long, this hot, low valley lies between the Sierra de Neiba to the north and the Sierra de Bahoruco to the south. Once, in the recent geological past, it was an inlet of the Caribbean Sea. After the Río Yaque del Sur enters the depression, you'll begin to see the many alluvial cones it's created—similar to, if less dramatic than, the mesas and pinnacles of the American Southwest. They give the Valle de Neiba its haunting feel.

It's also a hot, dry place, giving rise to enormous stands of bayahonda *(Prosopis julifloria),* columnar kinds of cactus and agaves that valley residents often use as hedges and borders. The Neiba's population, even today, remains extremely sparse, and settlements like Jimaní and Neiba contain only a few thousand people. However, with irrigation, small farmers raise grapes, produce some wine, and grow rice. Driving into the depths of the Enriquillo Depression, it's a real treat to stop in the shade of an acacia and buy fresh grapes, grape juice, and apples from a roadside vendor—usually a group of farmers' wives and daughters. With its flat, white-roofed houses, the area looks in parts like Morocco, while other settlements boast colorful Victorian gingerbread buildings.

The largest town of the Valle de Neiba is Barahona, near the coast. During the 1930s, the Trujillo regime began a program eventually dubbed *Dominicación fronteriza,* a system of internal colonization designed to build up population, settlement, and cultivation along the Haitian border—for obvious political reasons. It was during this time that plantation-style sugar farming began along the Caribbean coast, despite the area's aridity and salinity. The port of Barahona also exports some rock salt and gypsum, mined in the hills.

With the Valle de Neiba's stands of cactus and cholla, long rocky vistas, and heat, you can almost imagine Clint Eastwood riding in from the distance. It's that kind of compelling country.

LOWLANDS

Lowland plains dominate the south and southeastern parts of the island. Elsewhere, the lowlands are small and isolated from each other by the ridges, karst areas, and barrancas that dominate the landscape.

Coastal Plain of Santo Domingo

Of the four main coastal lowland plains in the Dominican Republic, the largest and most economically important is the coastal plain of Santo Domingo. Commencing just west of Santo Domingo, at the mouth of Río Ocoa, it stretches eastward as the plain of Baní, where it's only about 10km wide, then expands to 60km near Santo Domingo and continues east at this width all the way across the island to the Atlantic Ocean. The entire eastern section of this vast coastal plain is called the **Llano de Seibo** and contains some of the most idyllic scenery in the country.

All of this plain is composed of limestone made up of Pleistocene corals, added to the island after relatively recent uplifting action. With the limestone comes karst formations.

The climate of Santo Domingo's coastal plain ranges from semiarid in the Baní plain to subhumid in the areas east of Santo Domingo. From the southern coast, a series of marine terraces climbs up and up until the plain reaches an altitude

of about 100 meters just before reaching the Cordillera Oriental in El Seibo province. Handsome savannah, royal palms, and ceiba trees originally covered all of the coastal plain. Now, however, the huge sugarcane monoculture dominates most of the region, while cattle graze much of the remaining land. Geographers commonly compare this vast coastal plain—with its savannah, sugarcane, and cattle—to Cuba's Camagüey plains, which were settled in roughly the same part of the late 18th century, when large amounts of American capital poured into the country.

The areas around La Romana and the south coast island of Saona differ slightly from the rest of the plain in that tropical deciduous and semi-evergreen seasonal forest sporadically stud the savannah. Many dairy farms operate here, but as you proceed west past Santo Domingo you'll notice that the Baní coast becomes progressively the domain of coconut palms and wet rice fields, until it finally gives way to increasing aridity and scrub savannah. Except in Santo Domingo itself, not too many people have settled in the coastal plain—at least not compared to areas like the Vega Real and Cibao.

Starting with the Río Ocoa near Baní, a procession of impressive rivers strikes south from the Cordillera Oriental, cutting down through the limestone and draining into the Caribbean Sea. Some of these rivers are navigable for a number of miles, and sugar companies use some of them to transport their products. As you cross many of these rivers on the main highway east of Santo Domingo and see their wide expanses and pleasant tree-lined banks, it makes you wonder what kinds of fishing and boating possibilities they might hold.

Other Lowlands

Other lowlands are scattered throughout the country but are much smaller than the huge plain of Santo Domingo. Near the northern coastal town of Puerto Plata is a small coastal plain, squashed onto a few kilometers of land under the rise of the Cordillera Septentrional. Most of this small plain is taken up by sugarcane production, the rest by fields of pasture and forest. In a narrow strip, right against the ocean, grow banana trees, and copra is produced in considerable amounts. The soil on this small coastal plain is very good but, because of the suddenness of the rise of the mountains and the lack of roads, this part of the plain has always been relatively isolated from the rest of the country.

Another isolated coastal plain is at the southern tip of the Pedernales Peninsula, in the far southwest of the country. Others surround the towns of Baní and Azua. They are arid but, with irrigation, moderately fertile. An extremely narrow strip of what is technically coastal plain surrounds Samaná Bay, particularly at Los Haitises—a wild karst region holding a vast and beautiful national park.

RIVERS

Dozens of rivers, streams, and creeks drain the island's monumental mountain systems. Most rivers in the Dominican Republic are shallow and seasonal. During the dry season, from December through April, many of the waterways dry up altogether and disappear—especially in areas with heavy limestone concentrations in the north, west, and northeast. Most are also too short and steep to be of much use for navigation, and only in the last few years has anyone thought much about using them for recreational purposes.

In a few places, engineers have harnessed the major rivers to generate electrical power: on Haiti's Artibonite River gorge, for example, and at Jimenoa Falls in the Dominican Republic's central mountains, Coadillera Central. A regular series of rivers flows south from the central lowlands, draining the eastern mountains and forming a chain that slides east all the way to the coast. Farmers use these rivers for irrigation.

It's useful to think of the systems as either mountain rivers or coastal plain rivers. In the far north, two rivers drain the mighty Cibao Valley. The Yaque del Norte, the country's longest river and the only one currently used much for pleasure and recreation, drains west and north. In the Vega Real, the Río Yuna flows east into first a swamp, then an estuary, and finally Samaná Bay.

South of the Cibao, the Valle de San Juan also has two drainage systems—east and west. In the west, a small tributary of the Río Artibonito crosses the Haitian border. To the east, the Yaque del Sur flows south and finally empties into the Caribbean near Neiba Bay. Most of the surface water in the Bahoruco mountain sys-

tem, south of Valle de San Juan, tends to evaporate or is used by irrigators.

To the east of Santo Domingo, the Río Magua, Río Soco, and impressive Río Chavón cut the plain in regular succession. The major Río Ozama flows through Santo Domingo. Engineers have created some artificial lakes by damming the Yaque del Norte at Tavera and the Río Nizao at Valdesia.

Many of the rivers of the Dominican Republic—especially in the mountains and valleys of the east—seem quite beautiful and serene from a distance, glistening in the sunshine and lined as they are by dense subtropical and tropical growth. Upon closer inspection, sadly, they often turn up rather dirty and misused, serving many times as garbage and sewage dumps for the local population. No one uses the artificial lakes much for sport or recreation.

LAKES AND MARSHES

The largest natural lake in the Dominican Republic is Lake Enriquillo, in the Neiba Valley. This huge depression, once a strait of the Caribbean Sea, is now 114m below sea level and three times saltier than the ocean. Drained by 10 minor river systems in the mountains surrounding it to the north (the Sierra de Neiba) and south (the Sierra de Bahoruco), the lake has no present outlet to the sea and suffers constantly falling levels. The only other sizable body of natural water is the Laguna de Rincón, near Barahona at Neiba Bay.

Given the dramatic clifflike coasts of most of the Dominican Republic, marshlands are few and far between. However, an extensive area of lowland marsh exists in the delta of the Río Yuna on Samaná Bay, and is a great place for bird-watching. Some salt marshes also lie near the town of Monte Cristi, in the far northwest of the country, where the Yaque del Norte empties.

SEA

Coasts

With all the travel posters fairly screaming about the Dominican Republic's fabulous beaches, boasting of their beckoning sunshine and gir-

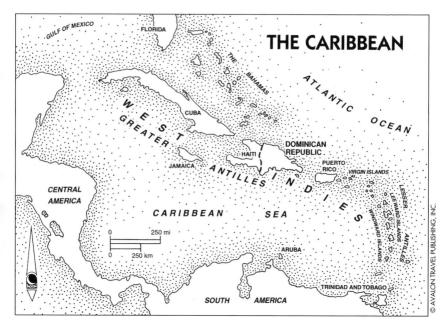

THE CARIBBEAN

GULF OF MEXICO · FLORIDA · THE BAHAMAS · ATLANTIC OCEAN · WEST GREATER ANTILLES · CUBA · DOMINICAN REPUBLIC · HAITI · JAMAICA · PUERTO RICO · VIRGIN ISLANDS · WEST INDIES · LEEWARD ISLANDS · LESSER ANTILLES · CENTRAL AMERICA · CARIBBEAN SEA · WINDWARD ISLANDS · ARUBA · SOUTH AMERICA · TRINIDAD AND TOBAGO

0   250 mi
0   250 km

© AVALON TRAVEL PUBLISHING, INC.

dles of palm trees, you'd think the whole place was lined with white sand. While there are many, many stretches of fine white-sand beaches, the predominant motif along the Dominican coast is the rocky shelf and the limestone cliff.

In fact, Hispaniola—both Haiti and the Dominican Republic—sits on top of a rock platform. On the northern coast of the Dominican Republic, this platform is rather extensive, reaching anywhere from a few hundred meters to 50km and more out into the surrounding Atlantic. Numerous ragged coral reefs sit atop this rocky shelf, as do lots of tiny islands. In fact, this rocky shelf is responsible for the widespread series of banks that provide such excellent cover and breeding grounds for humpback whales. Given the strong seas, heavy trade winds, frequent rains, and sudden dropoffs into great depths here and there, it's easy to see why the majority of historic Spanish shipwrecks lie along this dangerous north coast.

Strangely enough, along this same north coast, arguably the most beautiful beaches in the country pop up amid the craggy escarp-ments and high cliffs. Perhaps remoteness, or the suddenness of their appearance, makes these beaches so appealing. But appealing they are—expanses of white sand, palms, and sun, all whisked by a nice trade wind.

The rocky shelf along the south Caribbean coast is much deeper than the shelf along the north coast. Hence, you'll find fewer coral reefs there and fewer small islands. However, the presence of deeper water gives the Caribbean coast an advantage when it comes to ports. Deep water is the main reason why the Spanish founded Santo Domingo where they did—to take advantage of its river harbor and its relatively good weather. However, no matter where you go around the coasts of the Dominican Republic, the shallow rock platform makes fishing for sport species a good bet.

Islands
Off the southwestern coast of the Dominican Republic lie the uninhabited Isla Beata and Alto Vela. Off the southeastern coast, large Isla Saona is maintained as a bird sanctuary and contains a few poorly marked hiking trails.

Oceanography

The sea surrounding the island is itself unique. For example, to the north of Hispaniola rest three coral bank shallows: Navidad Bank, The Ambrosias, and Silver Bank. Lying just north of the province of Samaná, Navidad sits, oddly enough, beside the Brownson Trough—one of the deepest valleys in the Atlantic Ocean. Plunging to a depth of 9,000 meters (29,500 feet) beneath the surface, this sea valley is the second deepest place in the oceanic world. A band of mostly unexplored coral reefs extends along the north coast all the way from Puerto Plata to Monte Cristi, and several reef systems edge along the south coast near La Romana. The north-Atlantic coast is often wild and unpredictable, with strong tides and uncertain weather. It's no accident that the windsurfing capital of the world (or so say the thousands of Germans and Canadians who go there to surf) is the little resort town of Cabarete, on the northeast coast.

On the other hand, the southern shore of Hispaniola, washed by the Caribbean Sea, is composed of weathered sea cliffs, gentle tides, and calm seas.

Waters and Currents

The relatively high surface temperature of the waters near Hispaniola results in great heat loss into the atmosphere, which in turn produces profound climatic effects in the surrounding air. During the warmest months of the year, water temperatures around Hispaniola average about 25.6°C. Seasonal changes, while they do occur, are minimal, amounting to only about 3°C—and even less the farther seaward you go.

High surface temperatures lead to relatively high rates of evaporation, which in turn lead to a high proportion of surface salinity. It's a salty sea, the Caribbean. Due to the water exchange between the Atlantic and the Caribbean, however, it's not nearly so salty as the Mediterranean. During the high rainy season, between June and November, the surface salinity decreases.

The ocean currents in the Caribbean are particularly pronounced, due mainly to the earth's rotation and atmospheric circulation. Secondary causes of ocean currents include interruptions in current flows caused by islands—even by large land masses like Hispaniola itself.

One thing is certain: The entire Caribbean is swept by a strong westward flow called the North Equatorial Current. Near the south coast of Hispaniola, a northwest-flowing current merges into the western flow, called the Guayana Current. These currents converge to sweep around the Greater Antilles, both north and south. The southern half of the current is squeezed between Cuba and the Yucatán Peninsula, gaining speed along the way, until it becomes very swift indeed. In fact, this rooster tail of the North Equatorial Current gains so much speed that it gives impetus to the Gulf Stream off the coast of Florida.

Depending upon the time of year, the speed of the North Equatorial Current off Hispaniola ranges from one to three knots. The existence of such powerful currents, running in such predictable patterns, led to the establishment of numerous sea routes during the early days of exploration by sailing vessels.

Topographical features in the Greater Antilles, especially on Hispaniola, create countercurrents, or eddies, flowing clockwise. One such countercurrent develops on the southern edge of Hispaniola and flows back eastward along the south coast of the Dominican Republic. A similar clockwise eddy develops along the southern coast of Cuba, for the same topographical reasons.

The waters of the Caribbean—both on the surface and at depth—come mainly from subtropical areas in the Atlantic Ocean. What this means is that the waters around Hispaniola are constantly being renewed at all levels. Unlike the Mediterranean, the Caribbean Sea is typified by shallow basins as well as deep troughs, all open to the facing Atlantic. Located wholly in the tropical zone, and thus subject to heavy wind pressure, the water around Hispaniola is always fresh, moving, lively, and colorful.

CLIMATE

The Tropic of Cancer is a line of latitude located at 23 degrees 27 minutes north. Called the line of the Torrid Zone on many old maps and charts, this latitude describes the limit of the sun's northward journey during summer in the northern hemisphere. Most Caribbean islands are situated in the tropics; the Dominican Republic ranges in latitude from 17 degrees 40 minutes to 19 degrees 53 minutes north. Its position in the tropics, along with the fact that the temperature of the surrounding waters never falls much below 25°C, go a long way toward determining Caribbean environmental factors.

The other factor in determining Caribbean environment is relief. In a mountainous country such as the Dominican Republic, it's sometimes the *major* factor. Fortunately, since the altitude of a given Dominican city, village, or beach is likely to remain a constant, you as a traveler have a pretty good chance of predicting the weather.

TRAVEL SEASONS, LOCALES, AND WEATHER

It doesn't matter when you go to the Dominican Republic, because you'll find the temperature pretty much the same from month to month. The great thing is that you can pick your climate just by picking your altitude, although with the moderate trade winds and maritime environment, it's never really unpleasant anywhere in the country. On average, the temperatures in most of the Dominican Republic fall in the high 20s C, dropping a few degrees during the night. Fairly typical is Santo Domingo—the capital of the south coast—and most towns and villages at the bottom of the Cibao Valley, including Santiago.

In many mountainous regions of the Dominican Republic, the temperatures are much more moderate. In addition, there is a greater daily variation in temperature in the Dominican Republic's mountains than along the coast or in the valleys. In the mountain town of Jarabacoa (675 meters), the average temperature is 26°C during the day. In Constanza (1,110 meters), the temperature average is several degrees cooler, and nighttime temperatures often fall below 10°C. In the beautiful mountain town of San Juan, the average temperature is in the mid-20s C, and in the higher elevations of the Pico Duarte system of the Cordillera Central, frost is very common.

On the other hand, several places in the Dominican Republic are very, very hot indeed. Due to its special location in the southwest rain shadow, the region around Barahona and Lake Enriquillo (below sea level) can see temperatures in excess of 40°C (104°F). In this semiarid region, rain is rare and humidity is low. Keep in mind that with its relatively high temperatures and high humidity, Santo Domingo is pretty typical of the coastal areas—although for all of that, it's still a pleasant place because of winds and breezes and huge cumulus clouds that hide the sun for long periods (not to mention the lovely avenues of old mahogany trees).

TEMPERATURE AND PRESSURE

Temperature Variation

High temperature comes at low latitude: The closer to the equator one goes, the hotter it gets. That's simple enough, but it's not the whole story. At sea level in the Caribbean, the average temperature throughout the year is above 25°C. That average slowly rises as you go toward the equator. At the same time, the difference between the hottest and coolest months decreases. Therefore, seasonal differences in temperature are unknown in the Dominican Republic and elsewhere throughout the Caribbean. In the words of climatologists, Caribbean islands have not seasonal climates but *daily* ones.

In the Caribbean, the average difference between a given day's high and low temperatures is only 8°C. It's coolest just before sunrise, which, because of the uniform length of the day, always comes around 6 A.M. If you're up that early, you'll notice a very sudden temperature rise; the rate of increase slows as the sun comes up. As you'd suspect, the day is hottest at noon, when the sun reaches its zenith. In the Caribbean, noon is also the time of day when there are few shadows (at least in the cities); the sun, nearly directly overhead, shines straight down.

Depending on your altitude, noon and the couple of hours thereafter are good times to stay out of the direct sunlight, take a nap indoors, or sit under a mango tree and rest. Surprisingly, the temperature in the Caribbean falls rather rapidly during the afternoon. It continues to fall at night, but more slowly, as the land radiates heat back into the atmosphere. This is especially true in cities like Santo Domingo, where radiated heat from concrete buildings and streets keeps the temperature relatively high for hours after the sun has set.

For the most part, extremes of temperature don't exist in the Caribbean. However, this isn't true of the Dominican Republic, with dramatic contrasts between lowland plains and high mountainous valleys.

In the mountainous islands, daily climate zones are defined by altitude. You can count on an average decrease in temperature of 0.6°C per 100-meter increase in altitude. Climatologists have a word for these zones, which correspond to the same zones on the South and Central American mainlands. The lowest zone, up to about 900 meters in elevation, is called the *tierra caliente* ("hot land"—clever people, these climatologists), with an average temperature exceeding 21°C. Beyond this is the *tierra templada*, with average temperatures of 16–21°C.

The zone highest in altitude is the *tierra fría*. Including all land above 2,000 meters, this zone's temperatures average less than 16°C. Such zones exist only in the Greater Antilles, and in particular in the Dominican Republic, which has the highest mountains in the whole Caribbean. It's a great treat to visit the *tierra fría*, with its profusion of both subtropical and deciduous plants, its warm clear days, and its crisp cold nights (when you'll need a fire to keep warm).

Atmospheric Pressure

It may sound funny, but atmospheric pressure accounts for a lot of the Caribbean's climate. The Dominican Republic sits smack between two dominating areas of pressure differences, the first being an area of low pressure that characterizes the equator, and the second being an area of high pressure that dominates the subtropics (around the latitude of Florida). If you're on the Samaná Peninsula of the Dominican Republic's northeast coast, you can see the direct effects of this difference in pressure—wind-bowed trees all along the shore.

This pressure gradient produces the trade winds that blow from the east steadily throughout the year. Studies have revealed that there isn't any variation in speed and direction even worth mentioning! Above the trade winds, high in the atmosphere, a counter trade wind blows, similar to the jet stream in temperate latitudes.

However, when you're on the south or southwest sides of islands, or in places blocked or sheltered by high mountains, the regular flow of the trade winds is replaced by the daily effect of the rhythmic land and sea breezes. It's this combination of breezes and winds that makes the Caribbean's relatively high temperatures so bearable, even pleasurable.

HUMIDITY AND CLOUDS

It's sticky in the Dominican Republic, except, of course, when you're at higher elevations. As with other climatic factors, humidity tends to remain unaffected by seasonal variances and fluctuates more during the day than during the year.

At lower altitudes throughout the country, humidity can reach around 90% at sunrise. As you'd expect, this high humidity can result in veils of mist or fog, especially in low-lying areas such as mangrove swamps. As the temperature rises during the day, the relative humidity falls—although not below about 50%, and tends to hover most times around 70%. Because the humidity is high, the air doesn't seem to have that sparkling transparency it does in places like the Mexican deserts. It is this high humidity that makes the air of the Dominican Republic seem wooly and diffuse and that makes for such spectacular colors in the sunsets.

Why is the air so moist? Because the prevalent trade winds have to make a long journey across subtropical oceans. When this air arrives in the Caribbean, it's very wet, and as it encounters the relatively dry counter trade winds (which are higher up), huge banks of cumulus clouds form, with their tops at around

1,500–1,800 meters during winter and 300–600 meters during summer. First thing in the morning, the hot, moist, unstable trade air rises and smashes into the warm, dry high air. This morning accumulation of cumulus is quite beautiful, like big white and black dahlias over the shores and mountain peaks.

Over the sea, cloud formation is greatest at night and reaches its peak at dawn. Nothing is quite so impressive as a moonlit night off one of the Dominican Republic's southern beaches, when occasional lightning cracks through huge balls of cumulus and isolated squalls drop rain on a perfect blue sea.

PRECIPITATION

You'll find the Dominican Republic's rainfall patterns a little more complex than its temperatures. In line with regular Caribbean patterns, the country enjoys two rainy seasons—usually in late spring and early fall—with the island's northern and eastern parts receiving the most rain. Most of the time, the showers occur very suddenly and are accompanied by strong gusts of wind. Extremely heavy rains follow, often stopping traffic.

In the Dominican Republic, it can be raining on one side of a highway but not on the other. One day, as I attended the horse races at the new V Centenario track in Santo Domingo, a squall caught and began to follow the horses just as they began their sprint toward home. The crowd, meanwhile, basked in bright sunshine. By the time the horses crossed the finish line, however, they were dry, and it was the crowd that was getting soaked. Then the whole squall moved away, toward the center of the city.

Average Rainfall

In general, mountainous islands like Hispaniola receive more rain than such lower-lying islands as the Bahamas, which depend only upon squalls and can't count on the wringing effect of the mountains. Rainfall levels also vary more widely on mountainous islands: Their windward sides receive the most rain. This holds especially true in the Dominican Republic, where the northern mountains rise suddenly out of the coastal plain. In the area around Puerto Plata

on the north coast, the mountains seemingly shoot up right out of the sea, to a height of several thousand meters, and the rain comes down in cool buckets, often many times a day during the rainy season. However, precipitation decreases as you travel southwest in the Dominican Republic, until you reach true cactus-acacia desert in the country's most southwestern parts.

Santo Domingo annually averages around 140mm (55 inches) of rain. The rainiest region in the country is the Cordillera Oriental, with one weather station reporting an average of 280mm (110 inches) over a 15-year period. In the northeast, the Samaná province, on a peninsula jutting into the Atlantic, also receives a great deal of rainfall, averaging about 250mm (100 inches). Moving west from Samaná along the north coast to Puerto Plata, you'll find the weather getting slightly drier (180mm), until things become genuinely arid (80mm) at dusty Monte Cristi, in the northwest corner of the nation.

Due to a slight anomaly caused by a combination of pressure and relief factors, the north coast's dry season falls during the summer. Along the coast between Puerto Plata and Luperón, most of the rain falls from November to December; what little rain falls in the desert southwest usually does so in January, May, and October.

As a rule of thumb, the country's rainy season runs from May to November. In Santo Domingo, two-thirds of the capital's rain falls during this period. Showers, occasionally frequent during the rainy season, occur often at night, some-

---

WATER, WATER, EVERYWHERE

Many Caribbean islands suffer water shortages, partly because they are low lying and receive only sporadic squall rainfall. On other islands, like Hispaniola, deforestation has increased runoff and decreased the land's ability to store rainfall adequately. Most of the original inhabitants of Hispaniola caught rainwater from their roofs. Even today, water is in short supply on the island, and some expensive desalinization projects have been undertaken to make salt water usable for daily consumption. With everything on Hispaniola pegged to the price of sugar, water is an expensive commodity.

times very late, leaving the days sunny and mild. Sometimes in Santo Domingo's long rainy summer, the steady humidity and occasional nighttime cloudbursts combine to cause mildew, mold, and fungus, which can contribute to respiratory ailments and skin irritations. And, of course, there's the problem of rust.

Aguaceros

Most rain showers are short and warm. However, isolated *aguaceros* (cloudbursts) can last an hour or more and may dump several inches of rain at a time. When one hits, stop at a café and load up on coffee and sweets, just as the Dominicans do.

Orographic Rainfall

Because of the tremendous mountain relief features on the Greater Antilles, and especially on Hispaniola, much of the area's rain is called relief rain. Relief rain occurs when the trade winds force warm moist air onto mountain slopes where it rises rapidly, thus cooling it, producing rain. Clouds commonly cover the windward sides of the mountains, overlap the summits, and extend for a short distance to leeward. Sometimes a mountain chain in the Antilles will be high enough to cause clouds to form but low enough so that the trade winds blow the clouds all the way across the summits to the leeward sides. In this unusual circumstance, some highland areas may actually show more rainfall on the leeward side, which would ordinarily be in a rain shadow. However, the Dominican Republic's mountains are very high, and much more rain falls to windward than to leeward. The land in the wind and rain shadows of the mountains can be quite dry.

Convectional Rain

The other kind of rainfall in the Greater Antilles is called "convectional." Land heats and cools quickly (much more quickly than the surrounding water). In the early morning in the Dominican Republic, the rapidly heating land sends hot currents of air (convections) into the atmosphere; there, they cool rapidly (just like trade winds, which rise on the sides of mountains), causing the moisture in the convections to condense and form those huge cumulus clouds so characteristic of the Caribbean. If the air is really wet, the clouds mushroom and grow until they cover the

sun, which causes cooling, which in turn causes the moisture in the clouds to fall. *Voilà*—convectional rainfall!

Throughout the Caribbean, there are seasons of great rain and seasons of little. But in the Greater Antilles, including the Dominican Republic, something even more curious happens with rainy seasons. There is actually a double rainy season here, during the warmer months of summer—meaning the six months from spring to fall. Twice a year, the dominant subtropical high-pressure system shifts north, allowing troughs of low pressure to interrupt the flow of the trade winds and create rain.

Storms

Once in a blue moon, a norther—the tail ends of a North America cold front leaving snow in Bismarck—will strike Cuba and the northern and western sections of Hispaniola, bringing temperatures down to a cool 18°C (65°F).

Much more common than northers are hurricanes. Usually cropping up from June to November, hurricanes come in two types. One develops over the western Caribbean and affects mainly Cuba and the Bahamas. The other develops over the Atlantic Ocean and sweeps westward with an average diameter of about 600–800 km. The Dominican Republic is directly in the path of these huge storms, which are like great Coriolis holes in the sky. These are dangerous and destructive storms; exercise caution when you're around them.

WIND

Land and Sea Breezes

Another very typical, and very pleasant, occurrence in the Greater Antilles is the everyday phenomenon of land and sea breezes. Along with the trade winds, the ever-present land and sea breezes serve as natural air-conditioning, making it much cooler and pleasant than it would be otherwise. Daytimes, a strong sea breeze usually blows inland to replace the air that's rising from convection. At night, the reverse happens—the cooler air over land sinks and pushes the warmer air out to sea. Thus, over the coastal plains of the Dominican Republic, the normal trade winds are interrupted by an alternating set of day and night breezes.

Squalls

The season of tropical disturbances extends from June through early November. Squalls occur frequently, some of them generating swift winds of around 30 to 45mph. During these months, you should be especially careful in venturing out for windsurfing, snorkeling, diving, and fishing, and pay close attention to the signs of squall: cumulus clouds, freshening winds, and turbid water. Weather reports aren't of much value, because squall weather tends to be strictly local, coming and going unpredictably.

Hurricanes

As far as hurricanes are concerned, pay attention to the old island folkloric ditty:

> *June too soon*
> *July pass by*
> *August we must*
> *Remember September*
> *October all over*

Every hurricane starts its life as an isolated zone of tropical low pressure, a storm that circles in a counterclockwise direction. Cyclones, as they're called, develop energy by feeding on the warm surface water of the Caribbean and are impelled forward by the trade winds on a generally easterly path. At 118kph (74mph), a cyclone is upgraded to hurricane status. In really unusual circumstances, hurricane winds can reach 320kph (200mph).

Although nobody really understands down to the minutest detail how hurricanes develop, we know they start when a powerful upward air current creates a nearly circular low-pressure system. If this particular system is far enough north (at least 10 degrees N), the effect of the Coriolis rotation spins these low-pressure systems in a counterclockwise direction. The energy produced is actually latent heat and is released as water vapor and then as rain. Hurricanes begin life quite small—only a dozen or so kilometers in diameter—but they may eventually cover 1,000 km or more.

The average hurricane has a life span of nine days, travels at around 15mph, and usually results in little or no damage. However, when a hurricane strikes land, it can be tremendously destructive. After all, a small hurricane releases energy in the same amount as six atom bombs per second. As a hurricane is pushed slightly north by the trades, cooler and drier air invades it and causes it to head farther north, usually toward the Gulf of Mexico or the American East Coast. Oddly, every hurricane has a sky-blue eye in its center, usually about 15 miles in diameter, a center that is utterly calm.

If you've never been through a hurricane (I saw Hurricane David in 1979 from the beach at Ft. Lauderdale), the first indication, other than TV and radio alarms, is the sea swell, which is both long and slow. A thin gauze of clouds draws across the sky, and the sun glows very red at sunrise and sunset, while the air grows sultry. The wind rises, its speed increases, and the first rain appears along with a growing

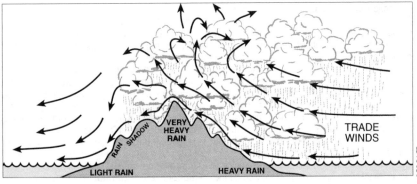

cover of low, dark clouds. Pretty soon, there are very strong winds and buckets of rain. Much of the damage from hurricanes comes from a storm surge of water that washes in over the beach and can cover low-lying inland areas. The wind, if it's strong enough, can tear roofs off houses and send glass and debris roaring through the streets and across fields at high enough speeds to skewer humans and animals alike. During Hurricane David, I remember seeing trash cans and lids, plate glass, hubcaps, and debris blown through the streets about five feet off the ground. I was glad I was safe inside.

The people of the Dominican Republic have been victimized by more than one killer hurricane. For example, a massive storm struck the island in 1930, killing 2,000. This same storm changed history by allowing the dictator Trujillo to consolidate his power under the guise of a state of emergency. More recently, David in 1979 killed 1,000 and did a billion dollars worth of damage, leaving 10,000 people homeless. This terrible storm was followed shortly by Hurricane Frederick. In late September of 1998, Hurricane Georges killed several thousand and destroyed crops in the east and north-central parts of Hispaniola.

As damaging and unpredictable as they are, hurricanes can be tracked by modern weather satellites, which take some of the anxiety out of the summer season in the Caribbean. If you visit

HURRICANE GEORGES

During the evening of September 23, 1998, a powerful Force 4 hurricane struck the south-eastern tip of the Dominican Republic and swept across the center of the island of Hispaniola for hours. The hurricane passed over the port city of San Pedro de Macoris, battered the agricultural-ly rich central valley, then proceeded to cross the Cordillera Central into Haiti.

The unusually high winds of Georges did substantial damage in the eastern sections of the island, destroying almost the entire rice crop, uprooting fruit trees, and killing livestock. In the Cordillera Central however, thousands were killed—no accurate count of the dead has ever been made—as walls of water rushed down mountainsides, sweeping away entire villages, and depositing dead bodies as far away as 50km from their homes. As long as two months later, towns in the west of the Dominican Republic had no electricity or running water.

the Dominican Republic in summer, when prices are low and tourists not so prevalent, listen carefully to AM radio and follow instructions. Odds are in your favor for enjoying a storm-free holiday. After all, the combined average for all the Caribbean is only six hurricanes per season (just don't think about 1933, when 21 storms raked the area).

ISLAND ECOSYSTEMS

Because the Dominican Republic is located on the second-largest island in the Caribbean, it enjoys a larger number of plant and animal species than most other islands. The island's wide variations in relief and climate also provide visitors with a unique opportunity to experience several kinds of ecosystems in the course of one day. From the warm, low, moist coast near Puerto Plata, with its seabirds, marine life, and offshore reefs, you can ascend in 10 minutes by cable car to the mountains of Isabel de Torres Reserve, where clouds surround tropical forest and make it cool enough to require a jacket.

Deep in the Bahoruco Mountains on the Pedernales Peninsula, you can view both iguanas

and a profusion of orchids—a unique experience. On the coasts, mangroves, coral reefs, and offshore banks teem with wildlife. Gamefish, including dorado, tarpon, bonito, mackerel, red snapper, and even trophy species like marlin thrive in the waters off the Dominican Republic. The Caribbean Sea to the south abounds with gamefish, lobster, and the ever-present shark. Lake Enriquillo, in the Neiba Valley, is home to the endangered American crocodile.

Although the island of Hispaniola has a long history of exploitation by man, it remains a nature-lover's paradise. Thanks in part to its proximity to Haiti, Dominican consciousness about the value of conserving natural resources, maintaining ecological balance, preserving species, and improving forest areas is growing.

ISLAND HOPPING

Some islands are oceanic, some continental. Continental islands were once connected to a mainland by land bridges, which eventually disappeared under the sea, probably as a result of flooding at the end of an ice age. Trinidad, once attached to South America, is a good example of this type of island. The plants and animals you'll encounter there look much like their mainland counterparts in, say, Venezuela.

Oceanic islands, on the other hand, were never connected to a mainland. The island of Hispaniola was once part of an underwater mountain chain, uplifted in the recent geologic past. So, you may ask, how did plants and animals come to inhabit a barren rock in the middle of the ocean? Well, scientists have wondered such things, too. The most widely accepted explanation is called the "island dispersal" theory.

Floating and Rafting

In addition to thinking about how species organize, develop, and adapt, Charles Darwin thought a lot about island dispersal. He was perhaps the first rigorous scientist to develop theories about such matters and to test his theories against his observations. For example, Darwin theorized that plants—at least some of them—could come to their island homes by floating seeds on ocean currents. To test his theory, he soaked seeds in salt water to see if they would sprout. He found many species that would—particularly the hardy red mangrove; its bean-like seed case, about eight inches long, is capable of floating for long periods and the seeds can sprout after many months of partial immersion. This probably accounts for the presence of red mangrove on most of the world's tropical islands.

Darwin further theorized that another phenomenon, called "rafting," could also be responsible for transference of seeds—and of animals, too. Rafting occurs when species hitch rides on floating debris like branches of trees, leaves, lumber, and the like. Seeds ride easily. Reptiles, especially lizards and geckos (snakes

are less adaptable to raft riding), are fairly successful raft riders. Mammals and amphibians, needing a steady supply of fresh water, aren't very successful raft riders.

Birds make up far and away the largest group of species of fauna on most Caribbean islands. In a process not unlike rafting, hurricanes and storms can blow birds onto islands, or the birds can stay aloft and drift there themselves. Among mammals, bats are very common on oceanic islands, probably because they can both float *and* raft. Frogs and toads, likely to slip off a raft and try to swim for home, are understandably rare in the Caribbean.

Like ocean currents and storms, wind currents in general are responsible for island dispersals. Insects, being light in weight, can drift for miles and miles. Birds, sometimes carrying seeds, snails, or snail eggs, drift with air currents. In one famous experiment, Darwin fed the seeds of some freshwater plants to fish, then fed the fish to some birds. Later, he found that the expelled seeds would still sprout, obviously unharmed by the digestive processes.

Human Influences

Everywhere on Hispaniola, the hand of man has altered the landscape in many, sometimes drastic, ways—including cultivation, deforestation, and salinization. The most ancient people on Hispaniola, the pre-Arawaks (arriving perhaps 2000 B.C.), disturbed the natural flora and fauna very little. They hardly practiced agriculture, being mostly hunters and gatherers, and subsisting largely on shellfish. They also hunted iguana and agouti and did some fishing. Later, the Taínos, an Arawak people with an advanced civilization and political structure, brought barkless dogs to Hispaniola from the South American mainland. They practiced agriculture around what is now the Dominican Republic, especially in the Cibao and Vega Real. They grew squash, beans, and melons, raised parrots as pets, and fished out certain shallow coves and lagoons.

However, it was Christopher Columbus and the colonists who followed him who changed Hispaniola forever. What Columbus saw when he landed on Hispaniola in 1492 exists nowhere today except perhaps on the isolated mountains of Dominicana. Colonists brought cows and goats, which grazed the natural vegetation to a nub. Mostly, however, they brought sugarcane, radically changing Hispaniola's ecology as well as its economy and dooming the island to a troubled sociopolitical history. Later, more colonists, immigrants, and African slaves brought new waves of plants and animals along with them. What few land mammals had existed on Hispaniola before the colonial period were soon almost hunted out.

FLORA

With its 20 distinct geographical regions and numerous tropical, subtropical, and semi-arid zones, the Dominican Republic has it all. You'd have to be a dedicated botanist to spot and catalogue most of the 5,600 plant species on Hispaniola, of which fewer than half are endemic. However, a little foreknowledge can allow the inquisitive visitor to start identifying the major kinds of flora regions and then the plants that live and grow in each.

Native to the Dominican Republic are many kinds of cultivated plants used by the pre-Columbian inhabitants, the Taínos. Among these are papaya, tobacco, manioc, and many types of pepper. The Taínos also cultivated the *higuero,* or calabash, tree, the wood from which they used to make eating utensils and formal ceremonial masks.

Many distinguished and readily identifiable trees are native to Hispaniola; most common among them are the Dominican magnolia, the *mamón* tree, and the lovely ceiba (also called the silk-cotton) tree. In the countryside, you'll often see absolutely enormous ceiba trees, which live as long as 300 years. Creolian pines cover the high mountain slopes.

Spanish colonizers introduced other cultivated plants, including mangos, bananas, cacao, coffee, and sugarcane. They imported trees as well, including the coral tree, the African tulip, the flamboyant, and the poinciana. Orchids and Hawaiian ornamentals abound. On the average shady street in any middle-class neighborhood in Santo Domingo, the shade comes from the stately mahogany trees that used to cover the island in abundance. Fruit is readily available and cheap in the Dominican Republic, and almost nothing is better than one of the local milkshakes made from either mango or *lechosa* (papaya) or a fresh fruit drink made from *chinola* (passion fruit), orange, or grapefruit. Whole fresh pineapples can be purchased from vendors or roadside stands for a few pesos per slice. For the equivalent of less than $1, you can get a whole pineapple, sliced and cored. The banana, the plantain, the *guayaba* (guava), and the guanábana are just a few of the dozens of fruits to choose from.

The plains, mainly in the south and east, grow sugarcane, rice, cotton, pineapple, citrus, coconut, and melons. Just recently, Dominican farmers have discovered that they can grow grapes and even a strain of red apples. Fruit stands in the major cities abound in both types of fruit, which can be purchased at very reasonable prices. In the fields near the eastern mountains, which are not fertile enough for intensive crops like cotton and rice, cattle graze in well-tended fields.

On Hispaniola, plants are influenced by elevation—shelter from trade winds—and rainfall. Because there is such a sharp contrast in these conditions, and because soils vary so greatly on the island, a bewildering array of plants can be found. Scientists identify about nine basic and seven transitional vegetation zones on Hispaniola, but merely understanding the five basic types will give you a good grasp of the Dominican Republic's flora.

VEGETATION ZONES

Subtropical Forest
Although you'll find many zones and regions in the Dominican Republic, the most common type of landscape is moist subtropical forest. You can see it everywhere, but especially on the dominant Santo Domingan lowland that sweeps from near Azua on the southwest coast all the way to the Atlantic Ocean. In the northwest, this kind of landscape covers the floors and slopes of most valleys, including the Cibao. It covers much of the Samaná Peninsula. It's a lovely landscape: easy on the eye, tranquilly majestic. Of course,

this isn't the *natural* landscape. What Columbus saw on his first visit to the Cibao, we'll never know.

The species most characteristic of a moist subtropical forest are the mahogany and the royal palm. Also common is the capa tree, a nonindigenous West Indian tree that colonists used extensively in shipbuilding. Second growth occurs in pastures and along the courses of many streams; it includes the jagua palm, lancewood, cashew (the roasted nuts are sold in small jars along the roadsides), ground oak, and yellowwood. The Dominican savannah consists of wide open grasslands. You'll find it in slightly drier areas, or, as in eastern La Altagracia, on the lee slope of mountains, interspersed with royal palms, ground oaks, or malpighia.

You can't drive through the Dominican Republic without noticing and admiring the royal palm. It usually grows in clumps, and it grows everywhere except at the highest elevations. Dominicans use its nuts to feed pigs, its fronds for thatch, and its trunk for the soft, easily sawn lumber. The whisk of the trade winds in the fronds of the royal palm is one of the most soothing sounds in all of nature. Other types of palms evident are cana, guano, and yarey, all native to Hispaniola and still used for brooms and shelter. No portrait of the Dominican Republic is complete without reference to the towering coconut palm, which lines the beaches of the island. It was supposedly brought by African slaves in the 16th and 17th centuries.

The typical Dominican cactus is the meloncactus *(Melocactus communis)*. After about 20 or 30 years, this unusual cactus ceases its growth, creates a woolly cover, and sprouts tiny red flowers. The deserts of the southwest are full of it. Columbus was so taken with the plant that he transferred meloncactus back to Europe after his first voyage.

Tropical Rainforest

It would be nice to report that tropical rainforest, the kind of evergreen forest found in areas receiving more than 2,000mm of rain every year and more than 10 humid months, is abundant on Hispaniola. It is not. For one thing, of the original forest on the island, around 85% has been lost to man. Even if this were not the case, the specific conditions for the occurrence of tropical rainforest are rare in the Dominican Republic. However, this kind of humid forest can be found in the eastern Cibao, and particularly the Vega Real, as it borders on the Samaná region.

The rainforest comes in stories. The upper story, a treetop canopy, spreads out about 40 meters above the ground. Evergreen, because the many trees of different species lose their leaves at different times during the year, these dense, damp forests host orchids and bromeliads at higher places, ferns nearer the earth, and a luxurious ground-level growth of lianas and epiphytes. This lush growth hides the fact that the plants themselves and not-yet-decomposed plant material store most of the forest's nutrients; the soil itself holds little nourishment for plants. When woodcutters clear a tropical rainforest, the soil's few nutrients are soon leached away and exhausted. Any secondary growth, emerging from eroded and leached soil, does not thrive. That's why chopping and burning a rainforest is more harmful than chopping and burning a temperate woodland—though both do much damage.

Subhumid Forests

Any area with seven to nine months of rain each year and 1,250–2,000mm of precipitation is called a semievergreen seasonal forest region. Trees in these forests lose their leaves during the three-month dry season. This is the case for probably four-fifths of all the species in the upper tree levels, so if you're in this kind of forest during the dry season, it can appear rather bare. Likewise, the tropical deciduous seasonal forest grows in areas with less than 1,250mm of rain and five to seven humid months each year. Trees in this forest are usually less than 10 meters in height, and the tree cover is rather open. Often, the open spaces are shrubby, with several kinds of thorny species present, as well as bromeliads on the ground. Lianas, epiphytes, lichens, and moss are rare. In many places, this kind of deciduous forest can appear as an impenetrable thicket of trees, shrubs, and thorn bushes.

Finally, savannah is a subhumid region, consisting of grasslands interspersed with forest growth, along with clumps of royal palm.

Mountain Forests

The physical geography of the Dominican Republic's mountains is characterized, oddly, by the palm and the pine. Drive through any of the central or northern mountain chains and you'll witness a profusion of ferns, bromeliads, orchids, and heliconias growing near pines, palms, and coffee plantations. Unusual, indeed. In these regions, the sloping farmland—some of it cleared and grazed as well—grows cacao, bamboo, bananas, flowers, and vegetables.

The interesting thing about being in the Dominican mountains is that you can see every type of forest found on the island, sometimes within only a few miles. The slope, elevation, position, and rainfall of the mountain areas determine the kind of forest you encounter.

For example, in the *tierra caliente* region, you might pass through semidesert, thorny woods, and finally semievergreen forest as you climb a mountainside on its leeward slope. On the same mountain's windward side, facing clouds and rain, you might encounter tropical rainforest and deciduous seasonal forest. In the *tierra templada,* montane pine forests grow on the windward side, tropical forests on the leeward. Only the *tierra fría* has montane pine forest throughout, and, at the highest elevations, elfin woodland on all slopes, consisting of smaller, hardier varieties of tree.

Some Dominican experiences can't be matched anywhere in the Caribbean. For example, you can spend an early morning snorkeling on coral reefs on the northwest coast, then hustle up into the mountains (if you're a fast driver with a good car) for an afternoon of horseback riding in a dense pine forest. Barbados to Colorado in three hours!

Thorn and Succulent Forests

Thorns and succulents grow in areas that receive less than 750mm of precipitation and fewer than four humid months a year. This kind of region is typified by thorny woodland (more than 500mm of rain) and cactus scrub (less than 500mm). Cacti in these regions are oddly shaped indeed, in the form of spheres, columns, even candelabras. Agaves abound, and, combined with thorn trees like acacias, make the ground cover nearly impenetrable.

Thorn and succulent forest make up most of the arid desert southwest of the island as well as the dry and/or overgrazed western ends of most upland valleys.

MANGROVES

Fabulous red mangroves cluster around the edges of Samaná Bay and in Parque Nacional Los Haitises. In Parque Nacional Jaragua, at the far southwest end of the Pedernales Peninsula, you'll find the white mangrove, a less hardy species than the red. It grows farther from the sea and produces beautiful white blossoms.

You'll find mangroves growing everywhere in the world's tropical regions. There are about 55 varieties, and their reach extends well into the temperate zone, though northern Florida's mangroves, for example, are much smaller than their tropical brothers and sisters. In general, though, biologists are amazed at the remarkable similarity of the plants from species to species, and some theorize that they may spring from a common ancestor. About 25% of the Caribbean coastline is colonized by mangroves, though in the Dominican Republic that figure is certainly lower, given the clifflike coastline of much of the country and the deep water and strong tides that strike the north coast.

Mangroves establish colonies close to shore, usually in shallow water, where they take root and gradually build outward toward the sea. The roots interlace, forming a thick, nearly impenetrable mass, and biologic activity inside this aerial network is intense as numerous flocks of storks, pelicans, herons, and migrating ducks compete to feed on the abundant sealife the mangroves and shallow water attract. In the shallow, muddy water, crabs abound, as do many species of grunt, snapper, grouper, tarpon, and sea trout, along with dozens of smaller species like sponges, algae, and mollusks. Mangroves provide an ecological service for the coastlines they shelter, helping to filter high winds and waves, thus preventing erosion.

Mangroves are unlike most other plants in the way they extract oxygen from the surrounding air. Plants usually accomplish this necessary task by taking air from between slightly compacted soil particles underground. In the thickly compacted mud that is home to the mangrove, though, there is no space between soil particles, and thus little oxygen. Mangroves must extract air directly, by having aboveground roots which breathe for the plant through tiny pores.

Red mangroves, like those found around Samaná Bay, tolerate very salty water and high tides by maintaining massive sets of aerial roots. In fact, scientists call them halophytes precisely because of this ability to survive salty conditions. White or buttonwood mangroves, like those found around the Pedernales Peninsula in the desert southwest of the Dominican Republic, grow farther inland, in tranquil conditions. You can identify these plants by white blossoms or pinecone-like buttons, which sprout on their thick leaves and branches.

The most amazing thing about mangroves is that these hardy plants serve as the biological starting point for a chain of ecological miracles. The mangrove's broad, drought-resistant leaves fall from the plants and settle to the bottom of the shallow swamps in which the plants live. In some mangroves, the leaf droppings account for as much as three tons of detritus accumulation each year and can form up to 90% of the food eaten by bottom-feeding species like crabs, worms, shellfish, insect larvae, and many small fish. In a short while after the leaf falls, these scavengers will have eaten about a third of the fallen leaves. The scavengers eventually become food themselves for large species like barracuda, snook, and tarpon. However, this productivity in terms of biomass isn't strictly limited to the mangrove's immediate area. Tides and currents wash away many nutrients, and these become part of the food chain on distant shores and in seaward areas.

It's one of the ironies of nature—and probably one we should think long and hard about—that the mangrove, so hardy and perfectly adapted to its circumstances, is also one of the life forms most susceptible to the negative effects of modern civilization. It's not just that mangroves—especially in places like Florida and its Keys—are regularly bulldozed to make room for shopping centers and parking lots; mangroves are affected in many more subtle ways as well. For example, once a developer clears beachfront near a mangrove, the concrete and clearing produces unnaturally high amounts of runoff from shore. Runoff washes nutrients into the sea, resulting in increased algae growth, which in turn clogs the mangrove's delicately balanced root system, impairing its capacity to extract air from its surroundings. The soil carried by the runoff also clouds the water, blocking the sunlight and upsetting the biological balance even further. And sediment can kill—just like spilled oil.

For now, the red and white mangroves of Samaná, Los Haitises, and Jaragua are protected mainly by their isolation. It remains to be seen whether isolation will be enough.

Consider exploring the mangroves. You'll find it a challenge, due to their generally remote locations, dense aerial root system, and subjection to tides and swamps. It's hot down by the sea, and you'll have to combat mud and insects, but a trip through the mangroves of Los Haitises is worth every bit of trouble it takes.

ORCHIDS

Orchids love light. And in the Dominican Republic, wherever there is an abundance of light (and that is almost everywhere, except in the thickest mountain forest), orchids thrive. Indeed, while it's somewhat difficult to get out to see mangroves, orchid-watching is as easy as taking a walk in Santo Domingo's National Botanic Garden or a stroll along a mountain path in the early freshness of a tropical morning. The Dominican Republic doesn't have a "national flower," but if it did, it would almost certainly be the beautiful orchid. In the Sierra de Bahoruco, in deep southwestern Pedernales, you'll find

BOB RACE

more than 50% of all the native orchids in the Dominican Republic.

Classification

All plants belong to families, which are distinguished from one another by differences in the structure of their flowers, stems, leaves, and roots. Families are further split up into genera, and each genus is divided into species. This system of classification was first put into place by the great botanist Carl Linnaeus, the "father of modern botany," in the 18th century. His system focused on six differences and used the "binary system," whereby the scientific name for a plant gives its genus, then species. For example, the orchid Linnaeus studied primarily is called *Cattleya* (genus) *dowiana* (species). In Linnaeus' book *Species Plantarum*, published in 1743, he identified eight genera and 60 species of orchid.

Orchids came to be noticed by people with a scientific bent as early as ancient Greece, when wandering philosophers made a listing of southern European species. Later, medieval herbalists used orchids in their healing rites and further identified many plants. By the mid-18th century, Victorian John Lindley, a professor at the University of London, gave 10 years of his life to the classification of orchids, including them in his huge *Botanical Register*. Now we know that there are at least 20,000 species of orchid, and new ones are constantly being discovered—most in tropical latitudes where forests predominate.

banana plant

Orchid Distinctions

All orchids, whether they are the European types or ones growing in tropical jungles, share characteristics that differentiate them from all other plants. Orchids have three sepals (outer whorls of leaves at the base of the stems), with the sepals frequently conforming to the color of the petals, of which there are also three. One petal is always different from the other two as well, frequently larger or more brightly colored or patterned, and may be in the form of a tube, lip, or pouch. A column containing the sex organs projects from the center of the flower. At the tip of the column is pollen, which must be transferred to the female part of the column for fertilization to take place. Then a seed develops at the base of the column. The seeds are so small that there may be as many as a million of them at the base of each column.

Adaptability

Orchids are wonderfully adaptable plants. They are ancient and have had plenty of time to adjust to a broad range of growing conditions, although four-fifths of the known types grow in tropical and subtropical regions. The farther north the range of orchids extends, the smaller the variety. However, orchids have penetrated even into the subarctic zones. Subarctic orchids retreat into the ground during harsh winters, with the aboveground sections of the plant dying off while its tubers, or rhizomes, survive to send up new shoots when the weather warms in spring.

Orchids are perennial—meaning that they return year after year. Most European orchids, and some tropical ones, are called terrestrial, because they grow in the ground and take nourishment from soil. In the tropics, terrestrial orchids are in the minority. Many tropical orchids are epiphytes, which means they grow on trees, usually high up in the forest canopy, sending out long, tough aerial roots which anchor the plant to the tree. Epiphytes get nourishment directly from the air, usually through leaves that absorb minute particles of organic matter. Other orchids, called lithophytes, have a similar method of growing and transpiring, but they attach themselves to rocks. The less common saprophytic orchids are practically rootless and leafless and feed on top of the soil, mainly on dead organic matter.

Terrestrial orchids develop root systems that allow them to take advantage of deep soils and to weather extremes of temperature and drought because they can store both moisture and nutrients. Epiphytic orchids, however, have no such system. Living disattached from soil, high in trees, on rocks, or on trunks at medium heights, epiphytic orchids rely on steady amounts of moisture, spread evenly over the months, and retain moisture by cupping it in the folds of the plant itself. For many years, scientists were at a loss to explain how orchids could survive without roots (or with meager systems), until a small fungus was found growing in conjunction with most epiphytic varieties and many terrestrial ones as well. The fine filaments of the fungus push through the meager root of the orchid and spread, eating away at the root. The orchid responds, and feeds on the fungus, deriving mineral salts and moisture. At some point, a perfect balance is reached between fungus and orchid root, each providing the other with essentials for its continued life, without going beyond a boundary that would cause mutual death. In this delicate symbiosis, orchid and fungus thrive.

Nobody is quite certain how many species grow in the Dominican Republic, but the National Botanical Gardens in Santo Domingo displays 350 different species across a sunny and lovely hillside. Because orchids love light, the edges of forest and savannah provide them with a perfect habitat. You'll commonly find epiphytic orchids growing on forested windward sides of mountains. Look for woodland terrestrial orchids in the northern valleys.

For me, being inside a field of orchids is much like being inside a coral reef system—so beautiful it takes away my breath.

FURTHER READING

University libraries, as well as better public ones, are filled with books about mangroves, palm trees, tropical forestry and agriculture, orchids, and other tropical plants. You probably don't need to spend a lot of time on details, but consulting a few basic guidebooks ahead of time can increase your traveling pleasure.

The Macmillan Caribbean library publishes a series of volumes about the natural history of the islands called the Pocket Natural History Series. It includes books about the trees, flowers, fruits and vegetables, and native orchids of the Caribbean. For information, write to Sales, Macmillan Caribbean, Houndmills, Basingstoke, Hampshire, RG21, 2XS, England.

When in Santo Domingo, nature lovers should be sure to stop at the Museo Nacional de Historia Natural (Plaza de la Cultura, Calle Cesár Nicolás Pensón, tel. 809/689-0106), which has excellent displays as well as a bookstore where you'll find many Spanish-language books and pamphlets. The Dominican Republic's National Parks Department is located in Santo Domingo at Avenue Independence, no. 359 (tel. 809/221-5340). The times I've visited to chat, I've found the personnel friendly and open to discussion. There is a small library upstairs, where pamphlets can be purchased. (They're often out of stock or unavailable, so, if you speak Spanish, call ahead and find out what they have on hand.)

The Jardín Botánico Nacional (National Botanical Gardens) (Avenida Colombia at Avenida República de Los Próceres, tel. 809/567-6211) conducts tours through its marvelous orchid hills and huge, magnificent collection of palms and tropical and aquatic plants. Look for the small cubicle bookstore about 200 yards inside the entrance to the gardens—where the train tours commence. This store sells numerous books and pamphlets on Dominican flora, a few of which are in English. Also, the Smithsonian Institution publishes the field guide, *Marine Plants of the Caribbean,* available through bookstores or in many university libraries.

FAUNA

In the Caribbean, only Trinidad abounds in land species, and that's because it was once (nearly 8,000 years ago) connected to the South American mainland. Because they were never joined to a continent, oceanic islands like Hispaniola can't boast many native mammals or reptiles. Of the 33 identified species of land mammals present on Hispaniola, for instance, only four are indigenous to the island. Though there are 13 reported species of marine mammals, only the humpback whale is present in any quantity; the rest are rare or endangered species like porpoises, manatees, and beaked whales. On the other hand, though reptiles and amphibians are uncommon on Hispaniola, 60 species of amphibians and 141 species of reptiles—most of them endemic—do live here. These are high numbers for a Caribbean island—or any other.

Much of the Dominican Republic's beauty lies in its birdlife. With 258 species—20 endemic—of exotic birds present, even casual and inexperienced bird-watchers can have a field day (so to speak) in the Dominican Republic. Some spots, like Isla Beata, Saona Island, and Samaná Bay, are paradises for anyone interested in exotic birds. If you look carefully enough, you'll spot parakeets, parrots, cuckoos, siskins, and palm crows, along with the very rare and odd tody.

Overall, somewhere around 5,600 species of fauna call the Dominican Republic home. In the typical subtropical landscape of pastures, savannahs, royal palms, and mahogany trees, the most common sights are cattle, goats, pigs, chickens, and horses, none of which are endemic to the country. Like cats, dogs are uncommon as pets in the Dominican Republic. The ones you do see will have a narrow, pointed shape, much like a greyhound's. These dogs are direct descendants of the canine hordes used by conquerors to terrorize the original native inhabitants.

Most of the native fauna immigrated from mainland areas. Like Darwin, we're left only with theories as to how they accomplished the feat. According to some scientists, most fauna reached the Antilles and Hispaniola from South America, by chance, carried by ocean currents and by people.

In terms of species diversity, and in sheer numbers, the sea creatures of the Caribbean far outnumber the land fauna. For one thing, many of the islands contain shoreward structures of reef-building corals, and this complex weave automatically leads to dense biotypes, where hundreds of species create diverse colonies. Snails, urchins, sponges, oysters, and fish also live in mangrove areas. Both coastal and pelagic fish species are common, including tuna, bonito, swordfish, snapper, mackerel, and dolphin. Plenty of sharks cruise these waters as well, including at least two species that are dangerous to man—the blue shark and the great barracuda *(Sphyraena barracuda)*.

It may be true that in terms of diversity, the Caribbean area lacks something the mainland has. Yet, while it may seem poor in animal species compared with, say, the Central American mainland, the Dominican Republic's isolated beaches, mangroves, and coral reefs can provide ideal opportunities to observe exotic birds and littoral fishes, along with rare and endangered species.

MAMMALS

Mammals are few and far between in the Dominican Republic. There are a few mammalian insectivores, and a few rodents that live in brackish—or freshwater—environments. Probably the most common mammal in the Caribbean is the bat, which feeds on insects, fruit, and fish. In the areas of Los Haitises, Samaná Bay, and the desert southwest, bats live in shoreline caves and can be seen in great numbers during early evening.

Aside from introducing the typical goats, horses, and dogs to Hispaniola, Europeans were also responsible for mice, rats, and that later arrival, the mongoose—imported from India to catch the rats. These imports brought about the worst of natural disasters: mongeese wreaked havoc on the food chain, devouring not only rats and mice but everything in their path and thriving in the near-absence of natural enemies on the island. This is perhaps a major reason why there are really only two endemic land mammals on Hispaniola.

Unfortunately, it's highly unlikely that you'll see either one on a visit to Hispaniola. First, there's the solenodon, found, they say, only on Cuba and Hispaniola. This small insectivore looks something like a friendly-faced rat, and has an odd gait, pacing on the edges of its feet. By day, it sleeps in small caves or hollow tree trunks; at night, it feeds on a wide variety of insects, worms, and small vertebrates. Habitat destruction and the mongoose are mainly responsible for the present downfall of the solenodon. Although natural historians in the Dominican Republic, and many guidebooks, tout this small creature as the sole surviving example of insectivorous mammals living in the Dominican Republic, there are others who believe it may already be extinct. So don't get your hopes up for seeing solenodons in any nightly explorations.

The hutia is touted as Hispaniola's second endemic mammal. This rodent is small—about 30cm in length. Like the solenodon, it lives in caves and tree trunks and emerges to hunt and eat only at night.

Two species of marine mammals—manatees and humpback whales—dwell in Samaná Bay and its estuarial environs. Sometimes called the sea cow, the gentle manatee used to be common along the coasts of South America and as far north as the Carolinas in North America, but hunting and other man-made dangers like motorboat propellers and pesticides have drastically reduced its numbers. In adulthood, the pudgy, ungainly manatee can reach four meters in length and weigh anywhere from 225 to 500kg. Manatees cruise the ocean floor searching for aquatic plants to eat, sheltering their young with a flipper, and sometimes traveling and cavorting in small groups, often nestling with or seeming to affectionately kiss other manatees.

Because the manatee cruises in shallow water, the drastic increase in boat traffic in Samaná Bay, particularly among tourists looking for manatees and whales, has caused an increase in mortality. On some days during February and March, peak whale-watching months in Samaná Bay, hundreds of small boats—many unregulated—cruise the water. Hence, what passes for love of nature recklessly damages and endangers these gentle creatures, which have few natural protections. Once, manatees were hunted for their hides and oil, just like whales. Now hordes of tourists in pleasure boats represent just as great a threat.

Humpback whales *(Megaptera novaengliae)* are truly huge and magnificent. They have, at adulthood, stocky rounded bodies and massive heads marked with protuberances containing hair follicles, which shelter barnacles and whale lice. The body tapers to a slender tail stock. One of the distinguishing characteristics of the majestic humpback is its pectoral fin (the genus name *Megaptera* means "great wing"), which may measure as much as a third of the whale's total body length. The leading edge of the pectoral fin is serrated, and the body is black, except for white patches on the chin, throat, belly, and flukes. Up close, you can see scars, barnacles, and shark bites on the body. Fourteen to 22 deep throat grooves sweep up toward the gullet.

At birth, humpback whales average five meters in length; they reach 20 meters as adults and weigh up to 40 tons at maturity. These whales are found in most waters up to the Arctic ice pack and feed in cold water only—mostly on krill, sardines, mackerel, anchovies, and other small schooling fish. Humpback whales migrate, which brings them in winter to the north shore of the Dominican Republic, especially around the shallow banks and to the calm waters of the Samaná Bay. Humpbacks run in groups of between four to twelve adult animals and their young. Females give birth to calves every two or three winters, which makes whale viewing especially exciting in the Dominican Republic.

For more whale information on the Internet, see www.samana.org.do or coastalstudies.org/research/titles.htm. Or call Victoria Marine at 809/538-2494.

TURTLES

Freshwater Turtles

Freshwater turtles are not common in the Dominican Republic, and the ones that are present are highly endangered, because of both habitat destruction and predation by man. The so-called "slider" turtle is endemic to the fresh waters of the Dominican Republic and Haiti, and you'll find it in lakes, bogs, and brackish rivers in the far southwestern Pedernales. Dominicans have long prized these little turtles for their meat and eggs and hunt them with dogs trained, believe it or not, for the selective capture of females during the egg-laying season. Specially designed traps also capture adults of both sexes. Scientists at the aquarium in Santo Domingo have begun breeding the turtles in captivity, but, like most such efforts, this is really a stopgap. It remains to be seen if the slider can survive human overpopulation and predation.

Sea Turtles

The four types of sea turtles living off the Dominican coast—the green sea turtle, the leatherback, the hawksbill, and the loggerhead—are doing better than their freshwater brothers and sisters, but not much. They're often captured (intentionally and accidentally) in nets, and hunted for their meat, eggs, and shells (which folk artists use for design work).

Ocean contamination and beach pollution destroy the turtles' habitat and nesting areas. If you've been down to the beaches in Florida lately, you know that plastics, nets, rope, and other refuse are common sights. Ocean dumping of garbage, which the turtles tend to eat, causes respiratory and intestinal diseases, which often leads to turtle death. Sand waste by construction crews, the erosion of beaches caused by all-terrain vehicles, the construction of wave breaks, and poor coastal planning all combine to further imperil these creatures. If you think the picture sounds bleak for the wonderful marine turtle, you're absolutely right.

The Network for Caribbean Environment reports that marine turtles are among the oldest living reptiles, originating about 180 million years ago. These animals are cold blooded, breathe air, lay eggs, and live in tropical and subtropical oceans. Adults of different species vary in weight between 35 and 650kg. In general, adult females nest every two or three years, and some scientists believe they lay eggs on the beaches where they themselves hatched. The number of eggs depends upon the species. The eggs lie under the sand incubating for between 50 and 70 days. Upon hatching, newborn turtles emerge at night and make for the ocean, guided by ambient light reflected off of sea foam. The presence of lights on the beach, from nearby development or tourists with flashlights, may confuse the baby turtles and cause their deaths. Once in the water, the little turtles face many predators. Only one in a thousand hatched marine turtles survives to reproduce—and that's under optimum natural conditions, minus people.

The largest marine turtle is called the leatherback, from the fact that it has a leathery hide on its back instead of a shell. Dominicans call the leatherback the tinglar, and it can weigh up to 775kg and measure two meters in length. It is chiefly endangered because of poaching. Second in size (really in weight) to the leatherback is the loggerhead turtle, which Dominicans call *caguama* or *cabezona*, meaning "big head." The loggerhead has a long, narrow, birdlike head, and its body is usually about 1.3 meters in length, compared to the average two-meters of the leatherback. The loggerhead dines on urchins, jellyfish, crabs, and starfish and is threatened by coastal development, egg gathering, and predation.

The hawksbill is, sadly, probably condemned to extinction because of its beautiful shell, which has a translucent layer of gelatin that can be peeled from its back. For this reason, and consequent high prices for shells in places like Japan, this turtle has been hunted and slaughtered everywhere in its range. If a lovely hawksbill can achieve maturity, it is less than 90cm in length but weighs up to 100kg.

Intermediate in weight among marine turtles, the herbivorous green sea turtle, called *peje blanco* by Dominicans, can weigh between 160 and 250kg. The green turtle has a large fin and lays its eggs every two or three years. Females swarm onto beaches in groups, laying eggs together in what are called *barricadas*.

OTHER MARINE SPECIES

The relatively shallow coastal shelves and coral reefs that surround much of the Dominican Republic host large numbers of crustaceans, echinoderms, cnidrarians, and sponges. In addition, the coral-reef systems—both natural and man-made—that dot much of the south coast east of Santo Domingo, the east coast north from Punta Cana, and the northwest coast from Puerto Plata to Monte Cristi, play host to colorful reef dwellers like trumpet fish, French angelfish, yellowtail snapper, blue chromis, and blue-headed wrasse. Of course, many non-picturesque species call the reefs home as well, including the barracuda, hermit crab, and spiny lobster, among many, many other creatures.

Crustaceans

Everybody knows about crustaceans, especially people who like good seafood. Crustaceans are a class of arthropods, a group identified by their complex outer skeletons and jointed legs. Decapods, those with five pairs of legs, include shrimp, crabs, and lobsters. Crabs abound on the beaches of the Dominican Republic, especially the aptly named ghost crab, which tunnels beneath beach sand and emerges at night to forage for food. The hermit crab carries around a mollusk shell to protect its otherwise vulnerable underbelly. As it grows larger, it must find another, larger shell.

Enchinoderms

Echinoderms, on the other hand, aren't much good to eat. This group of spiny or bumpy-skinned creatures includes starfish, sea urchins, sea cucumbers, and sea stars. All are propelled through the sand and along the surface of shallower waters by tube feet. Sea cucumbers actually ingest sand, filter it, extract whatever organic matter they find, and then spit out the rest from a tube-like mouth. The sea urchin's many spines pose a danger to bathers. Covered by brown barbs, the urchin uses its mouth—located on the underside of its spine—to scrape algae from rocks. Actually, the sea cucumber is one echinoderm that is edible, and in some societies it is prized for its claimed aphrodisiacal properties. Sea cucumbers are delicacies in both France and Spain and fetch prices comparable to those for sushi in Japan.

It's better not to come into contact with the spines of the sea urchin. If you do, remember that you cannot remove a spine with your hand. Instead, carefully crumple up the spine while it's still in your skin and let nature take its course, all the while applying an antibiotic salve, and keeping the wound dry and cov-

ered. Some people say that urine helps take away the sting, perhaps because of the ammonia, which spurs disintegration of the spine. Best of all, be careful.

Cnidarians

Cnidarians are very simple animals, distinguished by cup-shaped bodies and mouth-anus openings at one end, all encircled by tentacles. Hydroids, anemones, coral, and jellyfish are either colonial (living in clustered groups) or individual. Hydroids (meaning, simply, "water forms") are those creatures that look like plants or ferns, commonly seen swaying in and around onshore areas and reefs. One well-known hydroid, the Portuguese man-of-war, has tentacles that extend or retract as needed. The Portuguese man-of-war can lengthen its tentacles to up to 50 feet. You can identify the jellyfish, on the other hand, by its cap dome or, in some cases, by its box-like dome, which floats just above the water line. From each corner of this dome protrudes a tentacle housing a stinging nematocyst, used for both defense and the capture of prey. Finally, the sea anemone isn't even distinguished by an outer skeleton. It's simply a polyp with tentacles that lives singly on the sea bottom, mostly buried in sand. The tentacles stun prey and shove the barely alive being into a simple polyp mouth.

Sponges

Last but not least are sponges, which look and act like plants; they have a corrugated or pleated sheath that (almost alone among animals) does not react when touched. The sponges come in an infinite variety of colors, though most are brown or reddish. The sponge is a very old, simple life-form, having been on earth for at least half a billion years. Because of pollution and overharvesting, even this most ancient of life-forms is having a hard time living with human beings.

CROCODILES

You might see the warty, 12-foot-long American crocodile *(Crocodylus acutus)* in its home at Lake Enriquillo National Park. This highly endangered species lives only in the West Indies, Mexico, and the mangrove-lined estuaries of southern Florida. Habitat destruction and hunting have led to decreasing numbers of the creature. In the United States, the number of American crocodiles had shrunk to fewer than 100 in the early 1970s, though, under the Endangered Species Act, their numbers in the United States have climbed back to around 400.

Adventuresome travelers to the Dominican Republic can take a small boat out to Isla Cabritos in Lake Enriquillo and perhaps catch a glimpse of this reclusive fellow, which is much less aggressive than its cousin, the alligator. The American crocodile has an extremely pointed nose and an elongated fourth tooth on its bottom jaw. In the Dominican Republic, it is protected by law directly and also because its habitat is located within the confines of a national park. Exact calculations of its present numbers in the island nation are not available.

MORE AMPHIBIANS, REPTILES, AND INSECTS

Amphibians are rare in the Caribbean, with 30 frog and toad genera and only one frog genus in the entire region. Reptiles in the Dominican Republic include the rhinoceros iguana and the ricard iguana, which can be seen in Isla Cabritos and in the desert southwest. Because of the dynamics of rafting and floating, there are more lizards than snakes among the reptiles. You'll see lots of lizards in the Dominican Republic (21 species), as well as a handful of colorful butterflies and moths. A small, relatively harmless scorpion is common in desert areas, as is a small type of tarantula. Finally, what would life be without large brown cockroaches, mosquitoes, flies, and ants?

BIRDS

Bird species are multitudinous. Oddly, quite a few mainland species are entirely absent, while indigenous species abound in many areas. Wintering birds from the North American mainland are common, as are recent permanent immigrants like the small white Ardeola ibis, which came over from the mainland in 1952, presumably bypassing customs and immigration. Parrots, parakeets, hummingbirds, and aquatic birds provide accents of color across the island.

The Dominican Republic is a veritable riot of bird species. The beaches, coves, estuaries, mountains, deserts, and offshore islands everywhere offer both the avid birdwatcher and the more casual enthusiast an opportunity to identify and enjoy a broad variety of shorebirds, forest dwellers, and larger oceangoing species as well. While the symbol-bird, chosen by most Dominican tourist agencies as a kind of mascot—the *cotorra,* nicknamed *cotica,* or "little parrot"—began its long descent into near oblivion when the Taínos made presents of them to the original Spanish conquerors, the lovely Hispaniolan parakeet serves as a noble substitute and can be seen everywhere in the more forested sections of the Santo Dominigan coastal plain. Characteristic of the more open royal palm savannahs on these same coastal plains and upland valleys is the palmchat (sometimes called the palm thrush), which flocks in open areas. This interesting bird builds a large, multistoried nest high on the trunks of the royal palm, into which it cuts apartments.

All of the national parks and scientific reserves in the Dominican Republic are havens for many species. At least 20 distinctive species of birds, some found nowhere else in the Antilles, reside in the Sierra de Bahoruco alone. In these dry desert mountains, you can see the Antillean siskin, LeSelle's thrush, the narrow-billed tody, white-winged warbler, the rare Hispaniolan trogon, the white-winged dove, rufous solitaire, the Greater Antillean pewee, and the list goes on and on. On the shores of the Parque Nacional Los Haitises and the Parque Nacional de Este, larger species like frigates, masked and ruddy ducks, flamingos, herons, ibis, crakes, blue herons, and roseate spoonbills live in forest and shore habitats. Crows, especially the palm crow and the white-necked crow (which resides only on Hispaniola), are common in the savannahs.

Beata Island, off the southern tip of Parque Nacional Jaragua in the Pedernales region; Saona Island, off Parque Nacional de Este; and Catalina Island, near La Romana, are veritable bird sanctuaries. A hike in the high mountains could be rewarded by visions of butterflies, warblers, nighthawks, and jacanas. Goat Island, in the middle of Lake Enriquillo, again in the far southwestern desert, is host to over 62 species of birds, including the tiny manuelito, the great hummingbird, the curious querebebe (which is best heard at dusk), and the cu-cu, which produces its lovely song at night and at dawn and which burrows in the desert for a nest.

Suffice it to say that every region in the Dominican Republic offers its own pleasures for the bird lover. I'll never forget the lovely half hour of conversation I had with a pair of colorful *cotica-parrots* kept as pets by two Dominican kids in the seaside village of Bayahibe. The parrots would talk and gambol and the kids would laugh. It was one of the most pleasant conversations imaginable.

CORAL KINGDOMS

Once upon a time, in the very dim geologic past, the coral reef was the dominant ecological lifeform on the face of the planet. In many ways, the coral reef was more dominant in scope and activity than we imagine when we think of great carboniferous fern forests and huge reptiles. Rising from the sea bottom in underwater sparkles, shapes, and forms, the coral reef is a vast community, not a single creature or even group of creatures. In fact, the coral reef is one of the most complex and dynamic structures biologists can study and one of the most beautiful for us to view. Reefs are also very delicate and depend upon a limited, and highly impervious, set of circumstances to survive. The history of the emergence and decline of the coral reef lifeform goes back to the time when the earth was home to but a single continent surrounded by a single sea and enveloped by a single climate.

Continents and Oceans

As I've always said, a little geology and a little oceanography never hurt anybody. Besides, knowing where coral reefs come from makes exploring them all the more fascinating.

The first glimmer of a theory about the coral reefs' existence emerged accidentally from Sir Francis Bacon in 1620, when he suggested that the continents of the Western Hemisphere, Europe, and Africa had all once been joined. Modern maps had just made a picture of the landmasses on earth clear, and he probably took a look and drew the obvious, if heretical, conclusion. The argument, quiet at first, raged on, commencing in the mid-18th century. By the end of the century, the scientist Edward Suess postulated the existence of a single huge continent called Gondwanaland. By 1966, research on magnetic fields in seabed floors culminated in a widely accepted theory of continental drift and plate tectonics. Computer studies showed how a single huge continent called Pangaea began to break apart about 300 million years ago. Breakage increased until today's continents migrated to their present positions. When scientists finally understood how the original single continent broke apart and drifted, they began to understand findings that had puzzled them in every sphere of biology.

For example, scientists have found samples of desert soil on the bottom of Atlantic seabeds and palm tree fossils in Canada, Siberia, and New Zealand—evidence of a widespread tropical climate. In fact, such discoveries, and the theory of continental drift, do much to explain the emergence of coral reefs as dominant lifeforms about 500 million years ago. Even as little as 65 million years ago, huge reefs dominated landmasses in places that are now Texas and New Mexico, North Africa, Central Europe, and southern China.

But 500 million years ago, Pangaea had not broken apart. The earth was covered by a single sea, called the Tethys Sea, which connected areas such as the central Pacific, Atlantic, and Indian Oceans, and the Mediterranean Sea—all now departmentalized. The water of this sea was shallow from pole to pole and of a uniform and very warm temperature. Such conditions were perfect for the rise of the dominant coral reef, which spread throughout the world.

Unfortunately for the reef system, plate tectonics—the shifting, cracking, and moving of continental crust—became responsible for complicated rises and falls in the fortunes of reef communities. Before continental drift set in, there were no biogeographical zones as there are today, but only a single tropical zone, dominated by coral reefs. Then the continents began to drift, cracks formed in the earth's crust, and oceans spread, deepened, and were divided.

BASIC CORAL TYPES

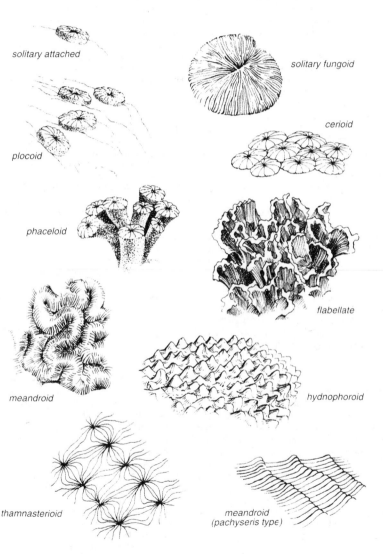

solitary attached

solitary fungoid

plocoid

cerioid

phaceloid

flabellate

meandroid

hydnophoroid

thamnasterioid

meandroid
(pachyseris type)

BOB RACE

Much of this history of drift was hostile to extant life-forms. Starting with the original shallow sea and single continent, the seabed began to spread, driving continental movement, and the water in the oceans grew deeper and colder. As landmasses emerged, the shallow coral seas drained off them and into the ever-deepening oceans. With the emergence of several landmasses, another astonishing feature emerged in the world: ocean currents. Where once shallow, motionless coral seas were prevalent, now landmasses created tides, then deflection currents, and finally a worldwide system of currents and movement of water. As a result, both terrestrial and marine climates changed dramatically. Research suggests that the temperature of water deep in the world's oceans has dropped from around 57°F during the early Cretaceous period (75 million years ago) to only about 37°F today. During the same period, surface water temperatures have dropped from 75°F to 59°F.

Thus, in the relatively short period since the commencement of continental drift 150 million years ago, dozens of shifts in temperature and ocean currents, and several ice ages, have affected coral reefs. Tropical weather, which once prevailed all over the earth, has been replaced by extremes in climate from pole to pole, with tropical bands limited to about 30 degrees on either side of the equator. Compared to the times of the immense tropical seas and single biospheres, today's coral kingdoms are tiny, and shrinking, enclaves surviving only because of the warm equatorial currents that feed them.

Currents

Plate tectonics, continental drift, and changing climate—including the arrival of several long ice ages—served to eliminate the worldwide dominance of coral reefs. After the separation of the continents, a complex circulatory system generated fast currents in some places, diverting polar water to tropical latitudes, which in turn led to the development of powerful weather systems replacing the placid tropical weather which had typified Pangaea. It's because of ocean currents that you can see penguins in the Galápagos Islands and palm trees on the coast of Cornwall in southwest England.

Unobstructed by any landmass, the oceans would have simple currents. The rotation of the earth would produce a global wind system. Along the equator, winds would move west. Around the poles, winds would move west as well. In both northern and southern middle latitudes, winds and currents would move east. This pattern of winds holds true for an earth subdivided into landmasses, except that the landmasses create obstructions, thus causing what are called gyres, currents which, complicated by the Coriolis force, deflect them to the right in the Northern Hemisphere and to the left in the Southern Hemisphere.

Because the climate of the earth is so much cooler than at the time corals dominated life, and because the oceans are so much deeper, with few exceptions coral reefs cannot exist without the equatorial and western boundary currents that sweep warm, enriched water into the Caribbean Sea and other tropical reef zones. It's the subtropical gyres that feed these kingdoms.

Commencing with the late Cretaceous period, perhaps 65 million years ago, there have been four great sweepings-away of life-forms on earth—all probably caused by plate tectonics, deepening oceans, and changing climates. The eons of unchanging climate, shallow seas, and little wind formed coral reefs, and ill-equipped them even for temperate winters. Today's reef-building coral polyps can survive only in a temperature range of 70°F to 85°F. Severe changes in temperature or salinity kill them quickly.

Corals

"Coral" is a general term used to describe many forms of life belonging to the phylum *Coelenterata*. A stony coral polyp is a living animal tissue with skeletal material which is either embedded in its living tissues or encloses the animal altogether. When people think of corals, they most often think of "hard" corals, the kind that enclose animal tissue with a hard covering of limestone. However, there are many "soft" corals as well, which resemble plants, in that their texture is fleshy.

Many people believe that the coral polyp is mainly responsible for building the reef. However, in reality, more than 90% of a reef mass consists of sandy detritus, most of it skeletal mass of dead marine organisms that aren't polyps, all converted into limestone and bonded by animals and plants which anchor there. In fact, many organisms help to build and maintain a coral reef, of which several types of algae are most important. Red algae grows as nodules, which help bind the reef frame, especially on windward reefs, where they help solidify the reef against the action of wind and waves. Green algae is also present on reefs, and, while not directly binding the reef together, releases coarse sediments which helps to consolidate the reef as well. Other organisms like mollusks, crustaceans, bryozoans, echinoderms, and many other animals with microscopic limestone skeletons add calcareous material to the reef platform.

The living part of a coral is relatively simple and looks much like an anemone. It is generally cylindrical in shape and varies from less than a millimeter to several centimeters in diameter. Tentacles surround its polyp mouth at the top. The mouth leads down to a short pharynx, which opens into a "stomach," where gastration takes place. A series of radial partitions—some of which bear gonads and others of which play roles in digestion—divide the cavity of the coral polyp. The skeleton of a polyp is called a "corallum." Suffice it to say that the accretions, variations, and divisions of skeletal material in coral polyps are very complicated and have been the subject of much scientific research. At any rate, the structural diversity of coral skeletal forms is staggering, ranging from solitary cylindrical shapes to branching, foliaceous, encrusting, and massive. Some of the things that determine coral structure are shelter, light, wave action, and general weather.

Most of the time, color indicates coral type, but not always, as in the case of dying coral colonies, which are always white once algae is ejected. Many corals are brown, blue, green, yellow, pink, red, and even black. Many reds and greens come from algae which bore into skeletal coral, thus lending additional color to natural ones already present.

It's probably best, and more polite, not to discuss the private sex lives of coral polyps. However, many corals are hermaphroditic, although some are either male or female. Some even seem to change sex as they grow. It seems that the animals produce eggs, which are in turn fertilized, become larvae, and are sometimes brooded within an adult colony.

The Coral Colony

The reefs around the Dominican Republic, and those in the rest of the world, are formed by a common process. Coral larvae are carried by vast oceanic currents to places far from their originating polyps. Many larvae don't survive, instead becoming food for their other planktonic organisms or simply dying and falling to the ocean floor. But if a larvae survives and finds some shallow water of warm temperature, it can take up residence. Gradually, limestone structures are built which become coral heads, then later more massed structures shelter and nourish other creatures. Coral polyps feed on other zooplankton and phytoplankton, which are caught up in passing currents and snagged by the polyp tentacles.

But there are other important biological interactions taking place as well. For example, inside the coral tissue itself tiny creatures called zooxanthellae reside, nourished by the polyps' nitrogen waste. This symbiosis produces added oxygen to the surrounding water, which allows further species access to and use of the coral structure. It has been proven experimentally that the zooxanthellae promote the production of calcium by the polyp. It is this basic symbiosis which drives the dynamic involved in forming reef societies.

Also, numerous small crabs and shrimp have permanent relationships with corals. Sometimes a particular species of crustacean evolves a symbiotic relationship with a particular coral species. One crab, called the gall crab, actually lives its entire life inside the limestone coral skeleton. Shrimps, usually very small, inhabit enclosed surroundings as well, and many live in interconnected chambers within the coral. Several types of worms are associated with reefs, as are barnacles, which filter-feed in the reef environment. Many fish use a reef's holes, ledges, and cliffs to hide themselves while looking for prey.

While there are many passive, nondestructive coral residents, others are more like parasites to coral, including some sponges which bore into coral skeletons and take a toll on the health of the reef. Some mollusks burrow in as well. Some crustaceans and gastropods feed on the living tissue of the polyp. One kind of snail lacks both a jaw and radulae (teeth), happily sucking out the tissue instead of biting it. It may be hard to believe, but many of the beautifully colorful fishes that reside in the reef do so to feed on the flesh of the polyp. Perhaps the most notorious of these fishes is the parrot fish. Butterflyfish and angelfish are more delicate browsers of coral but munch away nonetheless. If you sometimes observe a white scar on a coral surface, it might be the result of the voracious crown-of-thorns starfish, which feeds by enveloping living polyps in its out-thrusted stomach. Sometimes, and for reasons scientists don't yet fully understand, starfish suffer population explosions, which in turn cause plagues to sweep across the reef.

Conservation

A healthy coral reef is a beautiful place. A healthy coral reef is also an exotic and complicated biological structure, worth studying and appreciating. However, even healthy coral reefs far from human influence can suffer disasters and be affected by natural occurrences like hurricanes, temperature and salinity changes, sedimentation, and a host of other factors including predation. Most of the time, a coral reef that's healthy suffers for a while, then weathers the storm and makes a comeback.

With people on the scene, it's a different story. Throughout the Caribbean, coral reefs have been torn down to provide limestone building material for structures on shore. Some reefs are crushed to build airport runways. Some are destroyed when fishermen use dynamite to kill fish. Some are choked by silt washed offshore by dredging or sand extraction operations. And that's not to mention pollution in general, from garbage dumping to oil spills, pesticides, warm-water outflow, and industrial waste.

Unfortunately, the Dominican Republic has few laws directly protecting coral reefs, so it's up to you to use common sense. Don't touch coral, don't break off coral arms for souvenirs, and, if you really care, don't buy coral jewelry or trinkets.

FURTHER READING

These days, reading about coral reefs, tropical fish, and other tropical animals is easy. Almost any public or university library worth its salt has a large selection of books available. Before you head to the Dominican Republic—or any tropical destination for that matter—taking just a few days to study your destination's geology, geography, and biology can pay off in greatly increased pleasure.

If you'd like to own your own, and travel with a handbook or two, again the Macmillan Caribbean Library has a pocket natural history series, with books about seashells, birds, butterflies, and insects. The classic *Birds of the West Indies,* by James Bond, published by Houghton-Mifflin, remains in print, and you can also find it at most libraries. *Butterflies of the West Indies,* by Norman Riley, published by Collins in London, isn't in print but may be available at used-book stores or in good libraries.

When in Santo Domingo, nature lovers should be sure to stop at the Museo Nacional de Historia Natural (Plaza de la Cultura, Calle Cesár Nicolás Pensón, tel. 809/689-0106), which has excellent displays, as well as a bookstore where you'll find many Spanish-language books and pamphlets. In particular, the museum sells a volume called *Aves de la República Dominicana,* edited by Annabelle Stockton de Dod. This volume is published in both an expensive hardbound version and a smaller fieldbook edition suitable for stuffing in backpacks and luggage. You'll find the National Parks Department in Santo Domingo at Av. Independence, no. 359 (tel. 809/221-5340). Finally, there's a small bookstore at the Parque Zoológico Nacional (National Zoo), in the northern part of the city.

Peterson guides are pretty good if you're interested in reef fishes, as is Idaz and Greenberg's *Guide to Corals and Fishes of Florida, the Bahamas, and the Caribbean,* available from Seahawk Press, 6840 S.W. 92nd Street, Miami, Florida. I hate to say it, but field guides to reefs and reef fishes are pretty much a dime a dozen, so scout local bookstores and libraries and find one that suits you.

NATIONAL PARKS AND RESERVES

Many of us hailing from larger, wealthier countries think of "national parks" as special reserves, set aside for public use and enjoyment, upon which we lavish a special care and fondness. These places are national heritages, which we expect our governments to support and cultivate by protecting them forever, preserving them against all comers. In addition, we probably expect our governments to spend healthy sums of money to maintain the parks in good condition and to see that most everyone who wants to visit may do so expeditiously and with maximum enjoyment. In tropical areas, the Costa Rican park system springs to mind as a good example: these parks are the pride of the Costa Rican population, and hundreds of thousands of visitors enjoy them each year.

And while it's true that the Dominican national park system and the associated scientific reserve areas are indeed vast, comprising as they do nearly 10% of the land area of the country, making up an area larger than the state of Rhode Island, the parks' infrastructure can best be described as raw. Transportation to and from the parks is strictly self-service, and inside the borders of almost all the parks, roads and trails are few and far between. In addition, there are no services in most of the wilder areas. Visitors must carry their own water. In the large karst parks of the east, and in the mountainous parks of central Hispaniola, services don't exist at all. Of course, the so-called urban parks are really more like recreational areas, and, located in Santo Domingo and near Puerto Plata, they're well served. At least two brand-new scientific reserves have just been established—Villa Elisa, in the northwest Cibao, and del Ebano Verde, southeast of Jarabacoa in the Cordillera Central moutains.

In every office I have visited in Santo Domingo—whether part of the National Parks Department, an ecotourism group, or a marine mammal preservation society—I have detected a sense of pride and an eagerness to please. Just as obvious was a lack of money to maintain the parks and to see to adequate protection and development. In fact, this aspect of things points to one

of the great differences between national parks in wealthier countries and those in the Dominican Republic: most of the people in the Dominican Republic don't have the leisure to devote themselves to travel, nor does the government have spare change with which to build roads, concession stands, or water systems.

Thus, it struck me that those of us fortunate enough to be able to enjoy travel should welcome the opportunity to support national parks in any way possible, with our fees, payments to local guides, and the use of local transportation and support services. And, finally, if you've been to Yellowstone or Yosemite lately, you know what "development" can do. The lovely and wild Dominican national parks remain ungroomed, and for this we should be thankful.

According to government sources and the private Tourism Promotion Council, there are 14 national parks in the Dominican Republic. Other agencies identify 13 national parks. And a large number of highway, tourist, and government maps identify only nine major national parks. This kind of sliding factual scale isn't something out of Gabriel García Márquez's *One Hundred Years of Solitude* but rather represents a difference of opinion about what constitutes a national park. For example, in the capital city of Santo Domingo, you'll find several urban recreational areas which certainly constitute "parks" in their own way, being either manicured and sculpted green areas near the beach or containing caves and sinkholes which constitute major tourist attractions. Some officials and tourist organizations refer to them as national parks simply because they're "nationally owned" and are undeniably parks—pleasant places where people can picnic and hike. The government also maintains two "historic" parks: the La Vega Vieja, outside La Vega, and La Isabela, outside Puerto Plata, both of which are often referred to as "national parks."

Perhaps I'm myopic, but to me a "national park" is a wild area away from cities, traffic, and smog. By that definition, there are nine major national parks in the Dominican Republic, and taken together they constitute some of the most dramatic and spectacular scenery in the entire Caribbean. They are somewhat hard to visit, but that only increases the pleasure for those making the effort.

In a country that has lost nearly 85% of its virgin forest, the national parks under consideration here help to preserve a great deal of what is left of the Dominican countryside. The topography of the parks ranges from offshore areas to semiarid deserts and high mountains, and serves as home to 254 species of birds, 300 varieties of orchids, and endangered species like crocodiles and turtles. The national parks represent ecospheres ranging from below–sea-level islands in the middle of salt-choked inland seas to windward slopes of tropical forested mountainsides and even snow-covered peaks.

For more information on any of the parks discussed below, see the appropriate regional section. What follows is intended only as an overview of the parks and scientific reserves, something to whet your interest in getting adventuresome and leaving the beaten track.

MOUNTAIN PARKS

Since the arrival of Christopher Columbus, most of the virgin forests in the mountains of the Dominican Republic have disappeared due to fire, logging, and clearing by landless peasants seeking to agriculturalize marginal areas. In 1973, it was gloomily predicted that by the mid-1990s, the forests would be entirely gone. However, through the establishment of mountain parks, this fate has been avoided. In fact, a pilot reforestation project called Plan Sierra has begun near the town of San José de las Matas. If you're ever able to fly back and forth across the border between the Dominican Republic and Haiti, the difference is immediately, and horribly, clear. Haiti is brown and barren, almost worn to bedrock; by contrast, the Dominican side seems pleasantly, almost Edenically, green.

Of course, the Dominican side is far from Edenic in reality. Some mountainsides are in fact a pleasantly green mix of pine and royal palm, along with deep grass and running streams. Other hillsides have been logged, cleared, grazed by goats, and overcultivated, which dramatizes the effect of erosion from tropical rain. Although there seems to be a heightened public consciousness about the need to protect the environment, both mountainous and marine, the Dominican Republic is still in a footrace between overpopulation and poverty on one side and conservation on the other. The winner is yet to be decided.

Parque Nacional Armando Bermúdez

The granddaddy of all the mountain parks in the Dominican Republic, Parque Nacional Armando Bermúdez was founded in 1956. Making up most of the northern and windward slopes of the Cordillera Central, this huge national park is sometimes called the Dominican Alps, though it really looks nothing like an alpine place at all. In fact, these slopes are heavily pined and slashed by gulleys. But always in the windblown distance is the highest peak in the Caribbean, Pico Duarte (known during the dictatorship as Pico Trujillo), which, at 3,175m, is a strenuous climb requiring a commitment of at least four to six days, depending on conditions and routes. Climbing and hiking in this spectacular region represents a logistical challenge, given the sparsity of services—but the rewards are great. Along the path are hundreds of species of orchids and many native birds, including the Hispaniolan parrot and the palmchat. Here also, believe it or not, the temperatures often drop below freezing—sometimes significantly below—so excellent gear is required for safety. If you're adamant about climbing Pico Duarte, plan on hiring a local guide with mules and food, and plan on going during the cold months of winter, when rain isn't a problem.

Parque Nacional José del Carmen Ramírez

A large part of the southern Cordillera Central was declared a protected national park in 1958. It contains several of the highest peaks in the central range and the Yaque del Sur, San Juan, and Miro Rivers, all of which drain to the Valle de San Juan. Due to its position on the leeward side of the mountains, the temperatures are somewhat warmer than elsewhere in the high mountains. Nevertheless, in some places rainfall surpasses 250cm each year, which makes it a rainy place, second only to its brother park to the north. It's a toss-up as to which of these central mountain parks is the most isolated.

This one gets my vote, but reasonable minds can differ!

Parque Nacional Sierra de Bahoruco

Located in the arid southwestern region of the Dominican Republic, this very isolated park is perhaps the nation's most idiosyncratic. Near the rugged Haitian border, some of these mountains reach 2,367m in elevation, and their relief is steep and abrupt. Because these mountains are as tall as they are, they manage to catch a little more rain than the surrounding countryside, which is near-desert. Thus, the vegetation ranges from wet and pine forest to dry forest, and supports many different types of animals and trees. As mentioned before, the Sierra de Bahoruco is known for its many species of orchids and for a wide variety of birdlife. Getting there, getting outfitted, and getting up into the mountains is a large task but something adventurers can look forward to with relish.

DESERT PARKS

Parque Nacional Jaragua

It isn't quite fair to call Jaragua, in the extreme southwestern tip of the Barahona Peninsula (sometimes referred to as the Pedernales Peninsula), a desert park, because this largest of all national parks in the country includes shoreline areas and two offshore islands, including Isla Beata (which might as well be one big bird sanctuary). Encompassed in this huge, somewhat hot and arid region are mangroves, lagoons, beaches, and vast areas of dry and semi-dry forest and thorn jungle, all of which provide perfect habitat for turtles, reptiles, and many species of birds. The country's biologists report that 60% of bird species in the Dominican Republic can be found in Jaragua, including a large collection of flamingos. As in the Sierra de Bahoruco, getting there, getting outfitted, and getting back can be something of a chore, especially for do-it-yourselfers.

Parque Nacional Isla Cabritos

Like Jaragua, the Isla Cabritos is a hybrid—not exactly desert and not exactly marine, but a fascinating mixture of both. Located in the middle of steamy, salty Lake Enriquillo, in the Neiba Valley,

Isla Cabritos is the smallest of the country's national parks, ranging in elevation from four to 40 meters below sea level. All of the park's natural vegetation has been lost to razing, or to grazing of goats and cattle. In its dry, thorn-scrub second growth are many types of bizarrely shaped cactus, many birds (including some rare aquatic types and endemic species), and the rare American crocodile, which finds the heat and salty water very hospitable. I'm happy to report that getting to and from the island isn't too tough. There's a decent national park office right on the shore of the lake, staffed by reasonably helpful personnel.

KARST AND SHORE PARKS

Parque Nacional Los Haitises

There aren't enough superlatives in the dictionary to describe Los Haitises, located on the south side of lovely Samaná Bay. The mainland portion of the park is quite warm and humid and consists exclusively of karst formations (there are few natural trails and no facilities). Shoreward, the park consists of rock formations (called *mongones*), which jut out of the sea along the cliffs, and large mangrove stands everywhere you look. Pelicans, herons, and parakeets populate the humid tropical forests, bays, and lagoons. Also in Los Haitises are three cave systems which can be enjoyed by the adventuresome traveler. These caves feature Taíno petroglyphs and lots of bats, making them spectacular locales for discovery. Just now the national park department has gotten around to publishing pamphlets describing certain of the trails in the national park, along with diagrams of the caves, though when I visited the office, the pamphlets were just about gone. Visiting Los Haitises requires a boat and a strong constitution but rewards the effort abundantly.

Parque Nacional de Este

Traveling east from Santo Domingo along the coast almost to the Atlantic Ocean, you reach the Parque Nacional de Este, south of the town of San Rafael de Yuma. The park itself, on the mainland, is almost entirely flat, composed of limestone terraces which rise, one after the other, to the limits of the park. Predominately dry forest,

KARST

The presence of karst in the Dominican Republic, along with rainfall and unique plants and animals, makes Los Haitises one of the most exciting national parks to visit in the Caribbean.

Karst develops when rain falls on permeable limestone, forming holes, rounded forms, and deeply entrenched hollows sometimes called cockpits, and later combining with underground water tables to create deep caves and subterranean streams. The karst experience can be had in many places in the Caribbean, but it isn't anywhere as wild and exotic as in the Dominican Republic. Karst describes a very special landscape, and once you see karst, you'll never forget it.

Three things are needed for the development of karst landscape. First, you need a limestone surface that has plenty of calcium carbonate in its composition. Next, you need a warm, rainy climate. Finally, you need a relatively high water table, which allows undercutting of the surface by streams. When these three elements combine, karst can develop rapidly, creating weird and fantastic terrestrial shapes.

While the main area of karst in the Dominican Republic is in Parque Nacional Los Haitises, on the southern shore of Samaná Bay, other areas are found—in the Parque Nacional de Este and along the north coast. This karst is called Dinaric karst (after the Yugoslavian Dinaric Alps, where it is prevalent) and features dolines (barrel shapes) and cone karst, as well as "haystack hills" and cockpits. Much of the Samaná Peninsula itself is karst, but less dramatic in form.

Given its wide range of natural features, the Dominican Republic is a good place to roam and practice a little amateur geography and geology. Being able to recognize the natural forces that combine to produce primitive land and water forms can bring great pleasure on even a casual visit.

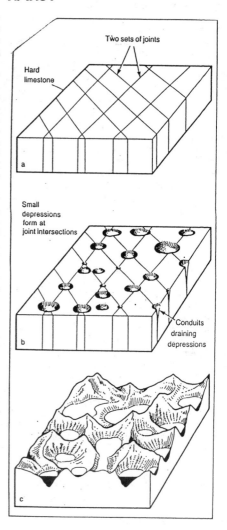

it contains regions of mesquite, some very isolated beaches, cliffs, coves, and caves. Some of the caves contain ancient petroglyphs. The extreme porosity of the soil accounts for the fact that there are no streams or brooks in the whole region. Be forewarned—it's very hot in this park, and the lack of water makes travel difficult. Still, the birdlife here is magnificent, and the offshore Isla Saona—part of the park—is itself a virtual bird sanctuary that can be hiked along some unimproved trails.

Parque Nacional Monte Cristi

This park is situated in the extreme northwest part of the Dominican Republic, in and around the town of Monte Cristi, which contains hotels and tourist facilities. The park itself borders Haiti and is located in one of the driest regions of the country, with an average rainfall of only 60mm each year—on top of which, it's usually hot and windy. Nevertheless, it has some pretty spots, especially shoreward lagoons and coves and, behind the coves and lagoons, lots of salt marsh, where egrets and herons roam and you can also spot canaries and a few American crocodiles if you're lucky.

The area around Monte Cristi is generally flat, although some hills rise up to 300 meters. At the headland of Monte Cristi is the striking mesa called El Morro, which can be hiked on goat paths if you're headquartered in town. Although hot and dry, it's a colorful region of frangipani and wild sage (hot days smell good here).

Parque Nacional Submarino La Caleta

This park undertakes to combine ethnology and oceanography in an area about 22km east of Santo Domingo, along the main highway that skirts the coast and the major holiday resort beaches. Originally, La Caleta encompassed only some original Taíno sites and some caves with interesting petroglyphs. Around 1984, however, a group involving itself in submarine investigations received government permission to sink a vessel called the *Hickory* just offshore, with the goal of creating a man-made reef with which to attract fish and replenish an area which had been overfished by locals years before. Now the park is a haven for divers, within easy reach of Santo Domingo. There are many local hotels and independent dive shops nearby, all catering to day-trippers as well as experienced independents.

RESERVES AND SANCTUARIES

There are seven scientific reserves (one of them officially a sanctuary) in operation in the Dominican Republic. Two of the reserves are new, just up and running, so there isn't much information available about them. However, the other five are long established. To hear the national parks people tell it, scientific reserves are exclusively for use by the scientific community, their purpose being to advance science. I was told that those planning to use these reserves should file a plan with the national park administration and apply for permission to enter well in advance. However, driving through a reserve isn't that difficult. One way is just to show up and be nice. On the other hand, one of the reserves—the Isabel de Torres, located high on a peak above Puerto Plata in the north—serves the public exclusively and is appointed with paths. So, think of the reserves as very special setasides and plan on visiting one when you're in the area, even if just for a drive through and look around.

Banco de la Plata Sanctuary

The most spectacular reserve is the Banco de la Plata Sanctuary, located about 140km off the north coast of the Dominican Republic. The main jumping-off point for the Silver Bank is Samaná, though several tours jump off at Puerto Plata. In many places, the Silver Bank is barely 20m deep, although parts of the sanctuary achieve depths of more than 1,800 meters. A reef protects the northern part of the sanctuary. Every year from November through March, humpback whales congregate here, thousands of them, bringing their calves from the cold Arctic waters which serve as their summer home. The water, as indicated, is shallow and lined with reefs, so it is somewhat dangerous to navigate. You must join an organized and responsible tour, which can get fairly expensive. However, the whale-watching, diving, and snorkeling are superb, and it's a once-in-a-lifetime experience to visit the Silver Bank.

Lagunas Redonda and Limón Scientific Reserve

Two lagoon areas in the Dominican Republic have been made into special scientific reserves and may be visited by the general public. Just go. One area, the Lagunas Redonda and Limón Scientific Reserve, is located on the northeast coast, about 20km from the village of Miches. These lagoons are reachable by bad but passable road. As you'd expect, mangroves line the shore here, and a wide variety of seabirds abound, along with marine fauna such as crabs.

Laguna Rincón

Also called the de Cabral Scientific Reserve, this second lagoon area is located at the eastern end of the Neiba Valley, in the dry southwestern part of the country. It's the second-largest lagoon in the Dominican Republic and the largest spot of freshwater in inland Dominicana. The lagoon is reachable by good paved road from Santo Domingo. Here you'll find the largest population of endemic freshwater turtles called sliders. If you want to try to see turtles, you might spend an enjoyable afternoon at the beautiful National Aquarium in Santo Domingo, where a large display on sliders is available, and then head to Laguna Rincón for an afternoon. Many kinds of shallow-water wading birds also make the lagoon their home.

Valle Nuevo Scientific Reserve

You'd almost have to describe the Valle Nuevo Scientific Reserve as being in the center of the center of the center. This mountain reserve is located in the center of the Dominican Republic, and in the center of the Cordillera Central. It is mainly pine country but is also famous for huge Dominican magnolias and tree ferns, all on an alpine plateau at an elevation of about 2,600 meters. Much of the reserve burned over in 1983, so it's still in the process of recovery. However, there are many bird species present. Temperatures vary greatly, from hot in summer to cold in winter. The Yuna and Nizao Rivers rise in this country, which can be quite beautiful and pleasing to the eye.

Isabel de Torres Scientific Reserve

Probably the most accessible of all the scientific reserves is the Isabel de Torres, sited on an 800m-tall mountain south of the town of Puerto Plata on the north coast of the Dominican Republic. Most tourists in Puerto Plata, or in transit through Puerto Plata for resorts on the north coast, find their way to this lovely park-like area, which is reached from the flatlands by a steep (and, for me, nerve-wracking) ride on a safe and well-maintained cable car. Most people seem to love the ride, which takes you from warm and balmy coast conditions, through cloud, to a rain-scoured mountain peak from which you can see much of the beautiful north coast. The park itself has paths, a snack bar, and a souvenir shop. Throughout, the flora is mainly subtropical low-mountain forest; palms, tamarinds, and mahoganies abound, as do many species of birds. It's a particularly beautiful place for a quiet lunch and to escape the humidity of the coast for an afternoon. Take your camera!

URBAN AND HISTORIC PARKS

As I explained before, many government officials include several nationally owned urban parks in the general category of national parks. Many also include at least two "historical areas." And while these areas have their own special

flamingos

BOB RACE

charms and allures, I just don't think of them as national parks in the same way I think of Los Haitises as one.

Paseo de los Indios and Parque Mirador

In Santo Domingo, there is the Paseo de los Indios and the Parque Mirador, actually a beautiful, tree-lined boulevard which commences in the central residential area of Mirador and runs to the industrial outskirts. Many city residents find relief from the afternoon sun in its shady environs, and there are several Taíno caves for exploration along the coast.

Parque Mirador Este and Parque Los Tres Ojos

At the other end of Santo Domingo is Parque Mirador Este, whose major attraction is Parque Los Tres Ojos. Mirador Este, like its counterpart, is along tree-lined green space, with a facing boulevard that is used by residents for recreation. The eponymous *tres ojos* (three eyes) are a series of deep limestone caverns dug by wave action and frequented by tourists. Often included under the general rubric of "national park" are the Parque Zoológico Nacional, the Jardín Botánico Nacional, and the Museo Nacional de Historia Natural, all urban attractions and all well worth a visit.

La Isabela

A historic park, La Isabela is the site of Columbus' first New World establishment. Located west of Puerto Plata, it is reached by rough dirt track. There are few improvements on the site, and it's mainly a sentimental attraction at this point. See the North Coast chapter for more on La Isabela.

Vieja Vega

The Vieja Vega, outside the town of La Vega in the eastern Cibao, is the site of one of the oldest religious establishments on the island—fascinating for visitors.

VISITOR INFORMATION

As I've said before, visiting the national parks of the Dominican Republic isn't like going to a movie. You can't just buy a ticket, walk in, and sit down to enjoy the show. Because of the isolation of many parks, and the lack of roads and trails, visitors who wish to see these wild and natural places might wish to join an organized tour. Many tour operators serve the parks and can make some of the more backbreaking logistical problems disappear. Know, too, that some parks require visitors to bring along guides—especially in the mountains and when the visit involves a climb. Besides, it would be impossible to climb most of the peaks of the Cordillera Central without making advance arrangements for food, water, and transport. But it isn't impossible to visit many parks on your own; just use common sense, advance planning, and a few simple preparations.

For individuals or groups who wish to participate in an organized tour, an outfit called **Ecoturisa** is a good bet. Located at Calle Santiago, No. 203-B, in the Gazcue neighborhood of Santo Domingo (tel. 809/221-4104; fax 809/685-1544), they can organize something suitable. There are many private tour companies in Santo Domingo, Puerto Plata, and elsewhere that handle tour requests for major parks and scientific reserves. In addition, private tour leaders have their own organization, and many of them can lead you into and out of national parks. Contact them at Avenue Central No. 32, Apto. 5, Ens. Carolina (tel. 809/532-7920; fax 809/532-8323). The private **Tourism Promotion Council,** Calle Desiderio Arias #24, Bella Vista, Santo Domingo (tel. 809/534-3276), is very helpful in regard to tours, maps, information, and guidance.

In addition to these general tour services, there are others that specialize. **Iguana Mama** (U.S. tel. 800/849-4720; fax 809/541-0734) is based in Cabarete and offers a number of adventures from biking and hiking to Pico Duarte climbs. Try also **Extra Tours** (tel. 809/571-3106) in Sosúa for specialized ecotourism with no more than eight people. Finally, **Rancho Baiguate** (tel. 809/696-0318 or 809/563-8005; fax 574-4940) is a nice hotel in the mountains near Jarabacoa. It offers climbs of Pico Duarte, rafting on the Yaque del Norte, canyoning, riding, tubing, the whole mountain-adventure ball of wax.

Be sure to stop by the **National Parks Department** office to pick up the appropriate permissions. In addition to the main office in Santo Domingo, you'll find a smaller office located at

Calle Las Damas, #6, Colonial City (tel. 809/685-1316). Government offices are open 7:30 A.M.–2:30 P.M. except Saturday, Sunday, and religious holidays. The **Wildlife Office** of the Secretary of State for Agriculture can give you permission to collect specimens. See Division de Vida Silvestre, Secretaria de Estado de Agricultura, La Feria (tel. 809/533-0049).

Just a word of warning about expecting to collect permissions from government agencies.

Most Dominicans only speak Spanish. If you write or fax, try to do it in Spanish—and try to polish up a little Spanish before you go, just enough to make a good-faith effort. I have found officials uniformly pleasant and hopeful to please, but the Dominican culture operates differently from what you may be used to.

Finally, most parks charge a small fee for admission, usually no more than RD$50, which amounts to about US$4.

HISTORY

For millions of years, the continents of Asia and North America were connected by a land bridge across what is now the Bering Strait. About 10,000 years ago, ice sheets sucked huge amounts of salt water out of the shallow oceans around Alaska and Siberia, and grass began growing on what is now the cold ocean floor. For a time, animals and people could walk from the Siberian East Cape to the Seward Peninsula of Alaska. Most anthropologists and archaeologists concur that humans and animals alike poured across that frontier onto the North American continent. Today, the bones of ice-age caribou and the fires and flints and ancient campsites of the tribes who hunted them can be found strung along the Yukon River, into Canada, and farther south.

During the Ice Age, the North American continent had summers little colder than those in the north today. Even when the ice sheets pushed south toward Ohio and shoved a muck of cold mud into the current American midwest, the whole west coast of North America was free of ice, and much of the basin of what is now Utah and Nevada was dotted with lakes. During the high period of the ice ages, people and game animals covered the north and were beginning to find their way south as well.

By around 3000 B.C., primitive tribes began leaving the South American mainland, around what is now Venezuela and the Orinoco basin, in dugout crafts bound for the Caribbean islands. On Hispaniola, there is some evidence of these very early people, who had no agriculture and were apparently not particularly well organized politically. They hunted and gathered, relying mainly on shellfish and mollusks for food. Scientists have found their caves and shell mounds at several places on Hispaniola's shores. There's even evidence that these early people fished and hunted out certain coves and were forced to move on.

ANCIENT MIGRATIONS

Before Europeans came to Hispaniola, the Caribbean area had been settled and resettled by at least three distinct peoples. The most numerous were the Arawaks. They inhabited the Greater Antilles, the Bahamas, and the islands of the Leeward chain. Farther south were the Caribs in the Windward Islands. Pushed far away, to the extremities of Cuba and the southwest peninsula of Hispaniola, lived a primitive group known as the Ciboney. The Ciboney, who disappeared not long after Arawaks developed their culture and became known as Taínos, lived near the coast and were fishermen and sometimes hunters and gatherers.

Archaeologists point to two different pre-Columbian migration waves. Both waves commenced on the South American mainland. The Arawaks are thought to have first reached the Caribbean Islands around the time of Christ, while the Caribs didn't begin arriving until about A.D. 500. Both groups continued their migrations until roughly A.D. 800, when their settlement patterns were complete. Obviously, these types of migrations were only possible because both the Arawak and Carib were highly skilled seafarers. They built and manned huge canoes carrying up to 80 people, and though not familiar with the art of sailing, they successfully used these vessels for trade and migration.

Arawaks

The Arawaks forced the Ciboney to retreat to less fertile land because the Arawak made their livings from agriculture. Given the similarity of spoken Arawak from island to island over a large area, scientists have concluded that their expansion, forcing out the Ciboney, occurred shortly before the discovery of the islands by Europeans.

For the eight centuries leading up to about A.D. 800, these mixtures of people generally called Arawak were making their long, slow sea journeys, drifting through the islands, perhaps across open ocean from Venezuela to Tobago, then up the chain of islands that constitute the Antilles, through Hispaniola, Jamaica, Cuba, and finally to the Bahamas. At each stop, they left behind small populations that grew and flourished and evolved in their own culturally distinct ways.

Because of the importance of fish and shellfish as a source of protein in their diet, most of these early Arawaks tended to live near coasts. Nevertheless, small family groups did live by other means, including raising root plants. The early Arawaks borrowed this form of agriculture from their South American relatives, and it is well suited to the fragile soils of Hispaniola. Near the end of the dry season, the Arawaks would clear brush and forest ground by burning it. This released the limited nutrients in the soil, which was heaped into mounds three or four feet across and perhaps knee high. Using sticks to scratch and poke, the Arawaks planted cuttings from several types of roots—the most important of which was cassava (called "manioc" in South America). The cassava was an ideal source of starch and sugar. The plant was suited to Hispaniola and could be grown in lowlands and on slopes—and the mounds prevented erosion. Also, the mounds didn't require much tending and could be used in one spot for about 10 or 15 years. Because the cassava's root is poisonous, Arawaks shredded the root, drained its juice, and then baked the flour into flat unleavened bread.

Early Arawak also grew yams, sweet potatoes, sweet cassava, arrowroot, peanuts, peppers, and gourds. They harvested local fruits, including pineapple, guava, and perhaps the cashew. For variety, they hunted iguanas, several kinds of birds, and sometimes snakes, worms, and even insects. Still, the Arawaks depended a lot on the sea, hunting large sea turtles, manatees, crabs, and fish.

Mightier traders than the Caribs, who preferred conquest to commerce, the Arawaks roamed from the Bahamas to Trinidad, exchanging goods.

Caribs

The Caribs, in contrast to the Arawaks, were extremely warlike. Caribs, who lived on islands closer to mainland South America, frequently raided the islands to the north, killing whatever Arawak men they didn't capture and take away as slaves. Most scientists agree that Caribs had only been in the Windward Islands for a few hundred years when Columbus appeared, but in that time the Caribs had earned a fearsome reputation. The term "cannibal" is derived from the Spanish name for Caribs, *Caníbal*.

TAÍNO PERIOD

Gradually, over a thousand years, the early Arawak culture, based on primitive agriculture and gathering, evolved into something more complex. The Arawaks in what is now the Dominican Republic gave birth to a culture with complex agriculture, systematic politics, leisure activities, rituals, and art. It was a society at peace with itself, living in a bountiful land. Its heyday lasted from around A.D. 900 until a man named Columbus landed on its northern boundary in 1492. Thirty years later, it had completely disappeared in a mighty holocaust.

The Caribbean expert Carl Sauer has said that "the tropical idyll of the accounts of Columbus and Peter Martyr was largely true." The people Columbus found on Hispaniola were called, in their own language, the Taíno (tie-EE-no), meaning "good" or "noble" (perhaps to distinguish themselves from the savage and warlike Caribs to the south). According to Sauer, the Taíno people suffered no want. They took care of their plantings and were dexterous fishermen and bold canoeists and swimmers. They designed attractive houses and kept them clean. They found aesthetic expression in woodworking. They had leisure to enjoy diversion in ball games, dances, and music. They lived in peace and amity.

Of great importance in their encounter with the Europeans in the years after 1492, they had no endemic scourge diseases, no concept of private property, and no slavery.

The real Taíno people—the people and culture Columbus found when he arrived on the north coast of Hispaniola—were made possible because of agricultural surpluses (and ways of storing those surpluses), which gave rise to the development of rituals surrounding death, leisure activities, and music. In the Museo del Hombre Dominicano (Museum of Dominican Man), located on the Plaza de la Cultura in Santo Domingo, and at the Regional Archaeological Museum of Altos de Chavón, located outside La Romana, you'll find truly extraordinary collections of Arawak-Taíno artifacts. These collections are a must for anyone interested in the pre-European history of the Dominican Republic.

Taíno Society

Experts disagree on how many Taínos lived in Hispaniola when Columbus arrived. There were at least 100,000, and maybe as many as a million. Many Taínos also made Puerto Rico their home, and there's ample evidence of visitations between the islands among kinsmen. Anthropologists often refer to the Taínos of Hispaniola and Puerto Rico as "classic Taínos," simply because most of the anthropological and archaeological information about Taíno society comes from these islands, rather than, say, Jamaica and Cuba, where Taínos also lived. The Spanish never did colonize the Bahamas, the Virgins, or the lesser Antilles, and by the time they settled on Cuba and Jamaica, Taíno culture was already disintegrating under the pressure of

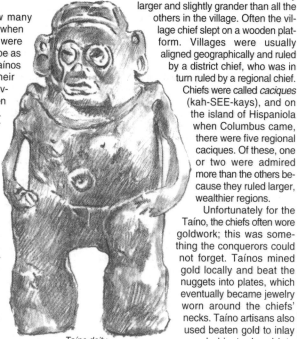

Taíno deity

Spanish dominion.

The Taínos Columbus encountered had no written language. They lived in large, permanent villages of as many as 2,000. Sometimes, a small village had only two or three houses, but most villages had 50 to 80 houses, made of wood and thatch, with several related families living in each large house. These houses were arranged haphazardly around a central plaza or square. The houses were generally of two types. Most were round with conical roofs, called *caneys.* Some, however, were thatched rectangular structures called *bohios.* (Today, in many rural parts of the Dominican Republic, one can see the literal descendants of *bohios.*) There were dirt floors in the homes, and no partitions to separate families. People slept in hammocks and stored their goods in baskets hung from roofs and trees.

A system of chiefs governed villages, districts, and regions. The chief of the village lived in the central square, in a house usually larger and slightly grander than all the others in the village. Often the village chief slept on a wooden platform. Villages were usually aligned geographically and ruled by a district chief, who was in turn ruled by a regional chief. Chiefs were called *caciques* (kah-SEE-kays), and on the island of Hispaniola when Columbus came, there were five regional caciques. Of these, one or two were admired more than the others because they ruled larger, wealthier regions.

Unfortunately for the Taíno, the chiefs often wore goldwork; this was something the conquerors could not forget. Taínos mined gold locally and beat the nuggets into plates, which eventually became jewelry worn around the chiefs' necks. Taíno artisans also used beaten gold to inlay wood objects, bead into

BOB RACE

clothing, and create ritual ornaments. Of course the Taínos could not cast the metals, but they did trade with South American Arawaks for a gold-copper alloy, which chiefs wore as *guanín.* When Columbus and his men, greedy for spoil, saw the few hammered gold objects the Taíno possessed, they went into a frenzy.

Local Taínos were experienced artisans in other ways as well. They worked wood, made ceramic pots, wove cotton, and carved stone, bone, and shell. Though anthropologists don't believe full-time craftsmen existed in Taíno culture, the part-timers were highly skilled.

Men went naked or covered their bodies with cotton loincloths. Unmarried women went naked, though married women wore headbands and short skirts, the lengths of which indicated rank. Both sexes used body paint for ceremonies, and the men also donned it for their infrequent battles. Red was their favorite color (which may be what gave the Spanish their ideas about "redskins"). Villagers were divided into two ranks—the nobility and commoners. Commoners farmed but were not slaves or feudal toilers.

The Taínos had their own fashion styles. It was not uncommon for a Taíno parent to flatten a child's forehead by binding a rock against it while the skull was still soft. Adults pierced their ears and noses for the insertion of feathers. They decorated their necks and waists with feathered belts, and the chiefs wore headdresses of brightly arrayed parrot feathers and some gold.

Once Taíno agriculture got going, it provided ample food. Cassava thrived in local conditions, but even in arid southwestern Hispaniola Taínos developed complex irrigation systems to produce big crops. Maize was less important, being grown on forest floors and generally eaten right off the cob—not hammered into meal and bread, as in Central America. This was probably because the grain, unlike cassava, could not be stored in such humid conditions. The typical Taíno house kept a pot boiling, into which women would toss sweet potatoes, peppers, and fish. Over the same fire, Taínos would roast fish, turtles, and birds.

The Taínos smoked tobacco cigars for pleasure. Unlike their mainland relatives, they did not indulge in beer fermented from cassava or corn, nor did they chew coca. Later Spanish

---

COLUMBUS ON THE TAINOS

I assure Your Highness that I believe that in all the world there is no better people nor better country. They love their neighbors as themselves, and they have the sweetest talk in the world, and are gentle and always laughing.

They bear no arms, and are all naked and of no skill in arms, and so very cowardly that a thousand would not stand against three. They are fit to be ordered about and made to work, to sow and do everything else that may be needed.

— December 16, 1492

---

chroniclers say that the Taínos seined for fish, speared them, and stored them along with turtles in weirs until ready to eat. They also organized hunting expeditions, drove the native hutia into corrals by burning prairie regions, and kept non-barking dogs, eating them when need be. They plucked iguanas off trees and trapped wild parrots.

Once the Taínos were agriculturally secure, they established stable village populations and further developed their arts and ceremonies.

Religion

Anthropologists know more about Taíno religion than any other aspect of the culture. This is largely because Columbus commissioned a priest named Father Ramón Pané to study Taíno religion. Also, many stone and ceramic artifacts have survived for later generations to study and place in museums.

Taíno religion centered on two supreme deities—Yucahu, lord of cassava and the sea, and Atabey, his mother, goddess of fresh water and fertility. All other spiritual beings were less important; they were called *zemis. Zemis* lived in trees, on rocks, or on other natural features. Some *zemis* were spirits of ancestors and were represented by a host of fetishes and idols produced in an array of forms in wood, bone, shell, or ceramics. Each Taíno could have as many as 10 *zemi* fetishes and kept some in niches in their houses, or on tables. Chiefs kept their *zemis* in separate temples. Some *zemis* have been found in Dominican coastal caves, but it is likely that Taínos took them there to save them from the Spanish, who considered them heathen artifacts. *Zemis* were greatly prized by the Taíno, and each thought his best and most powerful.

When a male chief died, one or two of his wives might be buried with him. He was usually flexed into a fetal position and bound with cotton, then placed in the ground with his most prized possessions. Sometimes body parts were preserved in hollow *zemis* or caves.

Zemis were commonly used as decorations on pottery, ornaments, and rocks. Individual Taínos communed with their *zemis* through an interesting ritual in which a person first inserted a stick down his or her throat to induce vomiting for purification purposes. With an empty stomach, the Taíno would ingest crushed seeds from the piptadenia tree. The seeds caused hallucinations, through which the *zemi* would make known a will or prediction of the future.

Once a year, whole villages gathered for a gigantic religious ceremony. Chiefs presided, but priests attended as well. The ceremony consisted of a procession of villagers bedecked with their best ornaments, then ritual vomiting and ingestion of seeds, then offerings of cassava to *zemis,* then dancing, followed by prayers and the distribution of bread to heads of families as protection against accidents. Poorer villages had dance grounds in the central plaza, while richer ones had "courts" with walls surrounding the ritual or dance grounds. Certain Taínos became shamans, who cured the sick and communicated directly with *zemis* in trances, then ritualized over the ailing person.

Leisure
Classic Taínos loved to play ball (just like modern Dominicans!). Even Arawaks played simple ball games on unstructured grounds. However, the Taínos themselves played a game called *batey*

in large formal courts surrounded by stone embankments. Most spectators sat on the ground, chiefs on large stools. Games were played among villagers but were also organized between villages. In Puerto Rico, *batey* was even more popular, the courts were larger, and the game was a form of politics as well as a leisure activity.

Men and women both played ball, though separately. Each team had between 10 and 30 players, who stood at opposite ends of the court and attempted to keep the ball in motion back and forth, much as in tennis. The ball was made of rubber (a fact which amazed the Spanish, who had never seen the substance). Courts seem to have been used constantly, and Taínos commonly bet on games. Chiefs often offered prizes to good players and winners. You can find the remains of Arawak ball fields all the way from eastern Cuba to St. Croix in the Virgin Islands.

Other leisure activities included swimming and competitive hunting and running.

Politics and Trade
The Taínos traveled the seas in canoes made from hollowed-out logs. They made their canoes by alternately charring the wood and chopping it out with stone axes. Once in the water, Taínos propelled the canoes with spade-shaped paddles. The chiefs owned the largest canoes, which were often housed in special boathouses. The chief's canoe was carved stylistically, then painted, and could hold up to 150 people. They remind anthropologists of Polynesian vessels. On land, chiefs traveled by carried litter. Commoners walked, carrying goods suspended between poles.

Chiefs could be male or female; both were eligible to live in the "big house," sit on high stools, and wear appropriate clothing and feathers. Chiefs were responsible for organizing food storage, distribution of surplus food to those who needed it, and upkeep of village houses. They acted as hosts when visitors called at the village. They also served as music directors and provided public transportation in their large canoes.

Chiefs also held the power of life and death over villagers (district and regional chiefs did not dispense local justice). Regional chiefs were responsible for larger matters, like military service and emergency. Everything important was inherited and traced through matrilineal lines, including goods, status, and *zemis*. A man resided in the village of his mother's lineage, and polygyny was common.

Trade was prevalent, with individuals and parties making voyages. It is even said that Taínos on Puerto Rico and Hispaniola exchanged daily visits across the narrow Mona Passage.

Taínos fought, to avenge murders, resolve fishing and hunting disputes, or force someone to deliver a bargained-for bride. War was not common, but it did happen, and when it did the chief was elected to lead an attack with the nobles serving as bodyguards. They painted themselves, carried their *zemis*, and fought with clubs, spears, and bows and arrows. Anthropologists claim that the most warlike Arawaks were Ciguayan and Borinquen, on the eastern shores of Hispaniola and Puerto Rico. It is thought that they had to be more warlike because they were often subject to Carib raids.

Art and Ritual

Increased leisure gave Taínos the time to practice decorative arts, apart from works of religious significance. Artisans carved many simple objects from natural products like bone and shell, but they also made beautiful and complex pottery, utilizing motifs which denote artistic expression and manifest marked magical and mythological symbolism. Many parts of their homes were elaborately decorated, and they made special hammocks, polished axes, and mortars and pestles, all with decorative elements. The Taínos used a great variety of bowls with characteristic engraved motifs, including heart-shaped jars engraved with abstractions of bats and owls, both of which were associated with the spirits of the dead.

The Taínos enjoyed music and used a primitive musical instrument called the *areyto* in communal dances. On special occasions, Taínos decorated their bodies elaborately with vegetable tints extracted from the jagua plant; they smeared themselves with juice, then used clay stampers to make a kind of tattoo on themselves. They wore necklaces, anklets, and many kinds of amulets and beads. Chiefs often wore distinctive masks, called *guaizas*, made from conch shells

and etched into haunting expressions. Even Columbus was impressed with the *guaizas* and mentions them in his journal, perhaps because some of these masks were lined with gold or laminated with gold inside the ocular or oral cavities. Of marked artistic and ritualistic importance were the commonly used, three-sided, wooden fertility idols called *cohoba*, used in the inhalation of hallucinogenic seed grains.

Many idol heads have been found in the Dominican Republic. Carved of stone, these effigies have wide eyes and shallow mouths that together form expressions as haunting as they are spiritual. They must have been very beautiful when laminated with shiny conch and gold, as they once were.

Anthropologists conclude that the Taínos did not separate art, death, and ritual. Death among the Taínos was a fundamental metaphysical as well as social phenomenon. The *cohoba* ceremony was ultimately related to death as a trip to the beyond, and all the artifacts related to the ceremony—the rattles, inhalers, and wooden benches for priests—give a rich, ritualistic tenor to Taíno culture. Other items, like the *cohoba*, were actually used in rituals for the planting of cassava mounds, when the idols were placed in the mounds to appease the gods of agriculture. In fact, art, death, ritual, agriculture, life, and sex were all fields for symbolic expression in Taíno life. Perhaps the culture was not fully theocratic, but it was on its way to becoming so when Columbus and his men came ashore, fatefully, in 1492.

On October 12 of that year, Columbus reached the Bahama island chain (San Salvador, according to lore). He had been carried there by eastern trade winds. In three small ships, his party made the voyage of 2,400 miles in only 36 days. He believed then that he had reached Asia, and he continued to believe he had reached Asia until his death in 1506. For the next 450 years, the history of the Dominican Republic was inseparable from that of Europe.

The Taíno were not to be part of this history.

UNDER COLUMBUS

In his journal on October 13, 1492, Columbus wrote, "I was attentive, and took trouble to ascertain if there was gold." In four separate voyages of discovery, extending until 1504, he continued to seek gold. He wrote of gold endlessly in his journals and in letters to the Spanish king and queen, who looked on hopefully from their European perch. He speculated repeatedly about the gold and riches he could obtain from the lands he was exploring. Thinking them part of China and perhaps even mainland Japan, he expected that gold would be his reward and that riches and glory would cover him and his family.

As Columbus coasted among the islands of the Bahamas during that first voyage, and, later, as he sailed along Cuba's northern coast (and still later, in mid-December, when he first sighted what he called Ysla Española), he continued to write, speculate, and dream about gold "as big as a hand. . . and signs there would be more." Later, someone on his crew wrote that "the Admiral believed that he was very near the source, and that our Lord would show him where the gold came from." As the *Santa María* and the *Niña* continued to run east along the northern coast of Hispaniola, the crews spied Indians and bartered for some gold.

All at once, on Christmas Eve, 1492, the *Santa María* ran aground on a coral reef near what is now the border between the Dominican Republic and Haiti. One of the great caciques of the Taínos greeted Columbus, helped his men ashore, and presented the Admiral with a belt and mask with large features of hammered gold—a gift, he was told. The sailors bartered for more small gold pieces. These presents of gold were finally given, the sailors reported, "as freely as. . . a calabash of water." How could Columbus not conclude that "there was a tremendous quantity of gold" and that he "could get it for nothing"?

At the same time, Columbus wrote in a letter to King Ferdinand and Queen Isabella: "In all the world there can be no better people (than the Taíno). You should take great joy as they will soon become Christians. . . . [A]ll are the most singular loving people and speak pleasantly and are of good stature, men and women, and not black, and the houses and buildings are pretty."

For Columbus, however, it was not to be. For him, it was the end, not the beginning, of the gold rush; in fact, there was little gold on Hispaniola, and the few deposits that did exist in the Cordillera Central were soon exhausted by the period's primitive mining methods. The Spaniards went away seeking new deposits. "God take me to Peru!" was the universal cry in Puerto Rico in 1534.

Soon after his arrival, Columbus sailed from Hispaniola for Spain, leaving behind a small settlement of Spaniards called La Navidad (in honor of its Christmas founding). In just a few months, the history of exploration and discovery was to become the history of slavery, holocaust, and warfare. Hispaniola was to become the cradle of a sugar economy that depended upon slavery just as the original searches for gold had depended upon forced labor of a different kind. The gentle people that Columbus had written of were to be transformed into subhumans.

The Four Voyages

After the *Santa María* ran aground, Columbus had his men take all the equipment and goods off the ship and reduce her to boards, which they used to make a fort. Leaving behind 39 men, he sailed on as the remains of the *Santa María* gradually broke up under the pounding of the surf. In this whole project, Columbus and his men were assisted by a friendly cacique named Guacanagarí, and Columbus recorded in his diary that not so much as a nail was stolen. He sailed away, and in early January of 1493 came to Monte Cristi, in what is now the Dominican Republic, where he was windbound for two weeks. He spent this time exploring the mouth of the Río Yaque del Norte and reported (erroneously) that its sands were full of gold grains, some as big as lentils. On January 9, he continued east and found the lovely and sheltered harbor of Puerto Plata. Three days later, he happened upon the anchorage of Samaná Bay, where he encountered the first hostile natives. These people were Carib, not Taíno, but they did not attack. Instead, they commenced bartering with some sailors for their weapons. Things turned sour somehow, and when the Caribs turned to their bows and arrows, the Spanish fell upon them, wounding two and routing the rest. Two days later, Columbus sailed for Spain, his first voyage complete.

The second voyage commenced at Cadiz on September 25, 1493. Encouraged by stories of gold, there were, this time, 17 vessels filled with 1,500 men. The king instructed the

the exterior of the Columbus home in Santo Domingo

LEO DE WYS

Admiral to treat the Indians "lovingly" and convert them to Christianity. In the official government instructions given to him, the matter of gold was played down.

The ships crossed in 39 days, touched at Guadeloupe, raided Carib settlements, and carried off 15 or 16 "plump beautiful girls." The ships discovered the Virgin Islands and coasted south along Puerto Rico, sailed through the Mona Passage, then took on provisions and water at the eastern tip of Hispaniola. They then proceeded west along the north coast, looking for La Navidad. But La Navidad was gone, and the story the Indians told was that the Spaniards had fought and killed each other and the survivors had left of their own accord. Columbus believed they had been massacred, and his attitude hardened.

The truth is probably that the colonists had split into gangs and had gone willy-nilly looking for gold but had run into a cacique named Caonabo, who put the Spaniards he caught to death. The rest probably died of disease. Chief Guacanagarí protested his innocence and was believed, though the Spaniards were, from then on, set against the Taíno.

The colonists began to look for a site to build. They bypassed the good anchorage and fruitful visage of what is now Cap Haitien (in Haiti), because they had heard that the source of gold in Hispaniola was a valley called Cibao, farther east. So it was that Columbus established La Isabela on January 2, 1494, at one of the least promising spots on the whole north coast—low, hot, disease-ridden, and unprotected. Though it was a horrible place, and nothing of it remains, for two years—until the founding of Santo Domingo on the south coast in 1496—La Isabela was the focal point of a ruthless search for gold.

In only two months, the colonists pursued gold wherever they could find it, demanding it of the Taínos, searching for it themselves. Early in February, 12 of the ships sailed for Spain, taking 30,000 ducats worth of gold, 60 parrots, and scores of slaves (most of whom died on the voyage). Columbus remained to explore the inland valleys, the Cibao, and the Vega Real (royal plain). He visited the source of the Yaque del Norte, now the city of Santiago, and founded Santo Tomás, near the present village of Jánico. Of course he also collected more gold, even though many of his men were sick. On a second expedition out of La Isabela in April 1494, one of the Admiral's lieutenants cut off an Indian's ear for thievery (or so he said) and nearly beheaded a local cacique over the incident. "This was the first injustice," the humanist priest Las Casas wrote later, "and the beginning of the shedding of blood, which has since flowed so copiously in this island."

Columbus sailed away, leaving his brother Diego in charge of La Isabela. He sailed around Cuba, discovered Jamaica, then returned to investigate the entire southern coast of the Dominican Republic. He sighted Saona Island, which he described in his journal as large and well populated, and presented the island as a present to one of his men, who promptly built a cross and a gallows.

Five months after he had left La Isabela, Columbus returned, sick with fever, to find the colony wracked by disease, confusion, and strife. The famous biographer Morrison called this period "hell on Hispaniola," because the Spanish had been turned loose—they were eating the Indians' food, demanding tribute, killing hostages, and working the Taínos with whips and dogs. Columbus's brother Bartholomew had arrived, but he was able to do nothing to quell the disturbances. There was even a small revolt, and several of the Spanish ships were taken back to Spain, where Columbus was roundly slandered.

At this point, Columbus had his chance to stop the terror, but he did not. Instead, he joined it. Taínos were hunted on horseback, tribute was demanded, food was expropriated, and several important regional caciques were executed. Finally, in March 1495, a huge battle with the Taínos began in the valley of La Vega, and the united Indians were killed, enslaved, or routed by the Spaniards. As usual, it was horses and dogs that tipped the balance, with the Indians assuming that the horse and its rider were

one magical enemy. By early 1496, the Taínos were thoroughly "pacified," and the Spaniards enjoyed free food, women, and even piggy-back rides.

Columbus prepared to return to Spain when a hurricane destroyed his ships, which had to be rebuilt. In the interval, he devised a system of tribute, described by Las Casas as "irrational and impossible," which would contribute to the extinction of the Taíno. Each Indian was to give, on pain of death, a "Flander's hawk's bell full of gold dust" each year. Since most of the meager supply was already gone, and many Taínos lived nowhere near the source of what gold there was in the Cibao, Columbus allowed each Taíno to substitute 25 pounds of woven cotton. The Taínos were incapable of supplying either. By now, there were only 630 Spaniards left on Hispaniola, and despite the very fertile soil and splendid growing conditions, they could not feed themselves.

As day broke on March 10, 1496, a small remnant of ships returned to Spain, with Columbus, 225 Christians, and 30 slaves. They left behind other Taínos, who fled into the mountains, were captured and forced to work, took cassava poison, or died of disease and starvation. One-third of the Taínos were gone by this time.

The third voyage commenced on May 30, 1498. Columbus sailed with six caravels, taking many

CHIEF CAONABO

The story of Chief Caonabo, one of the great caciques who met Columbus on Hispaniola, is exemplary of the troubled relationship between natives and conquistadors. Caonabo, of Caribbean (not Taíno) origin, greeted Columbus with friendship at first. In time, he came to see the dangers in cooperating with the rapacious foreigners and openly opposed them. After Caonabo had formed his opposition to the Spaniards, a royal delegation invited him as a guest of honor to La Isabela, the Spaniards' first settlement on Hispaniola. Caonabo came to the meeting and was told that important Spanish dignitaries wear "bracelets" to confirm their status. Once Caonabo was in handcuffs, they never came off his

wrists; he became a Spanish prisoner. Columbus took him aboard ship on March 10, 1496, for the express purpose of taking him to Spain. For weeks, Caonabo refused food, eventually starving himself to death as an act of defiance. He was buried at sea by the Spanish.

Caonabo's wife, the graceful and dignified Anacaona, ruled in his place. She tried to maintain good relations with the Spanish, despite their treachery. But she, too, became a Spanish victim. During a celebration sponsored by Anacaona, the Spanish used false pretexts and lies to overpower the queen and her bodyguard and took her in chains to Santo Domingo, where she was publicly hanged in the plaza, near the cathedral.

priests and many criminals who had been let out of Spanish prisons to become "colonists." He discovered Trinidad and the coast of Venezuela, then dropped anchor in the Ozama River, now in Santo Domingo, in August, where his brother Bartholomew had founded a city. Internally, another Spanish revolt had arisen, led by a blackguard named Roldan. Taínos all over the island were being hunted down and killed, with much blood shed on the Samaná Peninsula. One-third of the Spanish colonists were ill with syphillis.

But Columbus, aging and sick, failed to deal with the revolt and allowed the rebels to sail for Spain with gold and slaves. Finally, Ferdinand and Isabella were fed up and sent a royal investigator, Francisco de Bobadilla, to the scene. Considered ugly and martinetish by some, de Bobadilla landed in Santo Domingo, promptly clapped all of Columbus's men in chains, and sent them back to Spain.

Before long, the Admiral and his brothers were released, but all were disgraced. Back in Hispaniola, a system of land tenure called *encomiendas* (also *repartimientos*) was instituted, calling for every Spanish colonist to own large parcels of land, along with the Indians that lived on the land, in perpetuity. To escape the intolerable gold tribute, the remaining Taíno caciques, tired and sick, agreed. It was a system of slavery and it governed all the Indies, and Mexico, for hundreds of years.

The last voyage was a bit of an anticlimax. Columbus left Cádiz on May 9, 1502, with the intention of sailing around the world. He had four small caravels and sailed along the coast of Honduras, then put in, just before a hurricane struck, at the Río Haina, just west of Santo Domingo. He was not in favor and soon was put aboard a ship chartered back to Spain, where he arrived November 7, 1504. Spanish Governor Ovando, who ignored the warnings about the hurricane that had forced Columbus to harbor in June, was lost at sea during the storm. By this time, the fate of Hispaniola was sealed. It was to be run corruptly by Spanish colonials, exploited for sugar and slaves, and turned into an entrepôt of despotism.

Holocaust

It can be said of Christopher Columbus that he was not the worst. He found the Taínos' naked-ness appalling and debated with himself their "civilizedness." But, in light of the other colonists' behavior on Hispaniola, Columbus tried to do his best by the Indians. Of course, he knew nothing about antibodies, bacteria, and viruses, or the effects the introduction of the latter two could have on a population unprotected by the first.

But die the Taíno did, and in large numbers. Whether the 1492 Taíno population in Hispaniola was a million or as little as 300,000, a 1508 census revealed only 60,000 survivors. By 1548, the Spanish colonial historian Fernández de Oviedo believed there were fewer than 500 left. How did it happen?

The great Italian Renaissance historian Peter Martyr wrote in his *De Orbe Novo* (The New World) that the men who eventually controlled Hispaniola were "debauchees, profligates, thieves, seducers, ravishers, vagabonds, given over to violence and rapine." According to Martyr, in the first 50 years of Spanish colonialism in what is now the Dominican Republic, Spaniards spared no Taíno. They worked the natives as miners and camp servants and even forced them to carry the Spaniards on their shoulders. After the institution of the *encomienda*, the remaining Taínos had been reduced to a condition of chattel slavery.

By 1510, some members of the Dominican priesthood were beginning to rebel against the horrid treatment of the Taínos. A company of missionaries arrived in Santo Domingo and immediately waged a campaign against slavery. By 1512, on paper at least, the treatment of Taínos as "dogs," and their beating, was forbidden by King Ferdinand. But hard labor continued to kill Taínos—until the Spanish began to steal Arawaks from the Bahamas and bring *them* to the mines and cane fields of Hispaniola to work. These Arawaks, called Lucayans, were exterminated completely, too.

In addition to overwork, cruelty and massacre killed many Taínos as well. While Columbus was marooned on Jamaica in 1496, Governor Ovando "pacified" the native population by burning alive or hanging 80 recalcitrant Taíno caciques. Some, like the noble cacique Enriquillo, fled to the Sierra de Bahoruco, to continue a rebellion from afar. The beautiful Taíno queen Anacaona, of the Xaraguas, was invited by Diego Velasquez, conqueror of Cuba, to witness a military drill. She and her people were watching the spectacle when, at a signal from trumpets, the Christians turned on them and killed them. Anacaona was seized, then later executed for not being a sufficiently "sincere" Christian. Massacres continued. The Spanish killed 50,000 natives that year, 20,000 in a slaughter at the village of Zucayo alone. Those who ran were hunted with huge mastiffs and Spaniards on horseback.

As Las Casas wrote, "The Spaniards found pleasure in inventing all kinds of odd cruelties, the more cruel the better." In *De Orbe Novo,* Peter Martyr wrote that the Spaniards:

> *spared nobody; and having been brought to the island of Hispaniola originally to do the work of miners or of camp servants, they now never moved a step from their houses on foot, but insisted upon being carried about the island on the shoulders of the unfortunate natives, as though they were dignitaries of the State. Not to lose practice in the shedding of blood, and to exercise the strength of their arms, they invented a game in which they drew their swords, and amused themselves in cutting off the heads of innocent victims with one sole blow. Whoever succeeded in more quickly landing the head of an unfortunate islander on the ground with one stroke, was proclaimed the bravest, and as such was honored.*

Even more deadly than the Spaniards' overwork and cruelty towards the Taínos were the diseases they brought with them from Europe. In 1494, a tremendous epidemic swept through Spanish colonists and Taínos alike, though the Taínos suffered immeasurably more than the Spanish. Epidemic historians speculate that the plague was a combination of influenza, smallpox, and measles, with measles being perhaps the most deadly killer of all. "So many Indians died," wrote the historian Fernández de Oviedo, that "all through the land the Indians lay dead everywhere. The stench was very great and pestiferous."

PRAYER FOR THE TAINOS

Las Casas transcribed this sermon delivered by the Dominican friar Antonio de Montesinos in Santo Domingo, on the last Sunday of Advent, 1511:

> *Tell me, by what right or justice do you hold these Indians in such cruel and horrible servitude? On what authority have you waged such detestable wars against these peoples, who dwelt quietly and peacefully on their own land? Wars in which you have destroyed such infinite numbers of them by homicides and slaughters never before heard of? Why do you keep them so oppressed and exhausted, without giving them enough to eat, without giving them enough to drink, or curing them of the sicknesses they incur from the excessive labor you give them? And they die, or rather, you kill them, in order to extract and acquire gold every day.*
>
> *And what care do you take that they should be instructed in religion? Are these not men? Do they not have rational souls? Are you not bound to love them as you love yourselves? Don't you understand this? Don't you feel this? Why are you sleeping in such profound and lethargic slumber?*

Taínos who were not enslaved, murdered, or ill often died by their own hands. Many refused to have children or were too ill to do so. In less than the lifetime of an average human being, an entire culture of hundreds of thousands of people disappeared forever. Within a few years, the same fate befell the Arawaks of the surrounding islands.

SPANISH COLONIAL PERIOD

Spain ruled Hispaniola, with a few politically caused interruptions, until 1865. Many Dominican historians refer to this period as the reign of *España boba* ("foolish Spain"), when colonial administrators—many corrupt, many simply inept—oversaw a disintegrating social and economic structure based on slavery and sugar and adrift in the sea of European war and piracy. But this three-century drift was really a kind of limbo. In the years immediately after Columbus, the colony was relatively rich. Then it went downhill, and, finally, became a backwater.

The Slave Trade

Agents of the Spanish conquistadors brought the first slaves from Africa to the Caribbean around 1505. This horrid trade in human beings did not officially end until the liberation in Brazil, in 1888, though many think slaving still exists in parts of the Middle East and Africa. In 400 years of slaving, the trade saw around 10 million Africans brought to the New World (with perhaps two million dying at sea). Half of these went to the Caribbean as workers on sugar plantations. Between 1720 and 1820—a period sometimes called the Dark Century—perhaps seven million slaves went west. In total, there were probably 20,000 Atlantic crossings, and in each ship approximately 500 slaves were kept in fetid holds. Approximately 10 slave ships docked each month in the New World, with the slaves sold and parceled out to plantation owners. A slave sent to Haiti had an average life expectancy there of seven years.

The Portuguese were the main traders, though plenty of British, French, and Dutch traders were involved as well. Numerous revolts took place on the Caribbean Islands, most of them small, disorganized, and easily put down. However, the Haitian revolt succeeded—and caused terror in the European mind.

Royal taxes, monopolies, and harsh trading rules made plantation operations on Hispaniola and Puerto Rico unprofitable for many years, so slaving was never lucrative on these islands. Ironically, the corruption and backwardness of those years perhaps saved the Dominican Republic from the worst abuses of the chattel system.

Beginnings of Colonialism

After Columbus's death, his son Diego served as one of the island's first governors. His handsome imperial house still stands along the banks of the Ozama River in Santo Domingo and is a main tourist attraction. In 1524, Diego left Santo Domingo; there followed a succession of 50 governors, each dealing with a colony and a city in decline, suffering from economic stagnation, disease, and political calamity. The only constant during these first decades of colonial administration was the steadily increasing importation of African slaves to do the hard labor that sugarcane farming involved.

Perhaps the only governor to really accomplish anything worthwhile was Alonso de Fuenmayor, who governed between 1533 and 1556 (and also became an archbishop). He was something of a builder—and fair-minded to boot—and in his tenure constructed the main cathedral of Santo Domingo and erected the walls of the city and the major forts around the capital, many of which are still standing. The "Colonial City" of Santo Domingo, which is so beautiful and such a rich source of pleasure to tourists and Dominicans alike, is in existence thanks to Fuenmayor. Fuenmayor also built a decent military force and navy and managed to repel pirates, who were beginning to infest the Caribbean and raid coastal cities.

But it wasn't as if during this time the Spanish Emperor Charles V let the colony of Santo Domingo govern itself. In order to block Columbus's family from taking over the colony independent of the crown, King Ferdinand had established the *Audencia,* a council with jurisdiction over civil, military, and even criminal matters, which oversaw each governor's acts. Consequently, there developed a constant power struggle between Spain and the governors and colonists.

The Trade Triangle

In order to maximize their profits from trade with the New World, European merchants devised a system of triangular sailings. The first leg of the triangle saw ships sail from ports in Portugal, England, and Holland, loaded with tile and brick as ballast, making for Africa to pick up slaves and African merchandise. Generally, the Europeans needed only copper bangles and glass beads to trade for slaves. To replace the bangles and beads as ballast, traders collected coconuts. These were also good for eating and drinking while at sea. Once the trading vessels arrived in the Caribbean, coconut shells would be thrown overboard to wash ashore, and these seeded the present West Indian coconut groves.

At first, European traders sent agricultural supplies and equipment to the colonies, as well as animals such as horses, cows, pigs, and chickens. Then they sent seeds and, later, clay smoking pipes, which had become a European fad. The list of other trade goods is almost endless—barrels of wine, cheeses, cured hams and bacon, garlic, tools, mercury to refine gold, gunpowder, buttons, needles, scissors, jewelry, religious paraphernalia, and kitchenware.

No ship on the return voyage could be loaded to the gunwales with gold and silver, so there was plenty of room on each trading ship for goods like pearls and emeralds, sugar, rum, silk, carpets, porcelain, and fabrics.

Beginning of the Slide
Though fabulous fortunes were made on all sides of the trade triangle, within a decade of Governor Fuenmayor's departure, two disasters overtook Hispaniola and propelled the island's long downhill slide. First, in 1564, a huge earthquake destroyed the main inland cities of Santiago and La Vega, both agricultural and colonial centers, and damaged Santo Domingo as well.

Second, since Charles V needed cash for Spain's ongoing war with England, his efforts to conquer Italy, and to keep the Dutch colonies in line, he began to bleed all of Spain's colonies dry, Hispaniola not excepted. As part of the Spanish-English War, the English privateer Sir Francis Drake, in command of 18 ships, appeared in Santo Domingo in 1586. At anchor in the river of Río Haina, he laid siege to the capital, sacked and looted it for a month, then held it for ransom. When the payment was delayed, he burned and reduced to rubble nearly one-third of the city. Once the ransom was delivered, Drake took the city's cannon and everything of any worth in the churches, hanged several churchmen, and left.

Pirates and War
In 1530, an anguished Frenchman from Dieppe named Pierre le Grand had sailed into Hispan-

iolan waters looking for a Spanish treasure ship. When he found one, he took it with a crew of 28 men. These were the first pirates.

The religious and imperial wars waged by Spain during the 17th and 18th centuries kept the country in turmoil and contributed to the continuing descent of Hispaniola into chaos. Because Spain was fighting most of the Atlantic European countries while also instituting the Inquisition, designed to burn heresy from the heart of Europe, many patriots and religiously persecuted people hated Spain with a passion, and took it out on its colonies.

Around 1620, a society of pirates congregated on Tortuga. They called themselves either the Brethren of the Goat—*frei-boots* in Dutch, which actually means "free boats" but was translated into English as freebooters. Most of the original brethren were French Huguenots led by Pierre d'Esnambuc, and initially they fought everybody, including the English. They set up shop on the island of Tortuga (now part of Haiti), because it sat directly astride the Windward Passage, between Cuba and Hispaniola, through which Spanish treasure ships regularly passed on their way to Puerto Plata and Spain. They built *ajoupas* (palm-thatched huts) and cultivated maize, tobacco, manioc, yams, mangos, coconuts, oranges, and bananas. They also raised cattle on the island and roasted meat over open pits called *boucans,* which some Arawaks (who hid out there, too) called *boucaniers.* Thus was born the term "buccaneer."

As the 17th century progressed, the original French and Dutch were joined by Scots and Irish driven from their homes by the same poverty and religious persecution that had brought their French counterparts. Some came at first to the West Indies as indentured servants but ran away from the brutal mistreatments there and joined the other refugees on Tortuga.

Gradually, a self-governing "free" colony grew up, which shared a common goal with common responsibilities. One group of men and women stayed on the island to tend the crops. Another group manned longboats and ships and preyed on passing galleons, bringing the booty back to Tortuga for division. A third group left for Hispaniola on yearlong hunting trips. Some hunted wild cattle with dogs, while others hunted boar. Hunting with huge French guns four feet long, the buccaneers would head back to the Hispaniolan coast with all the meat and hides they could carry.

Though rapacious towards others, the buccaneers lived a strictly ethical life in their relationships with one another. It was considered highly unethical to cheat a partner, and the brethren shared the group's wealth equally.

The buccaneers formed partnerships, intermarried, and eventually spilled over into mainland Hispaniola, where they established farms and hideouts. They also went into the business of smuggling in order to best the Spanish monopoly on trade in the Caribbean. Beginning in 1630, the pirates, busy all over the Caribbean, began sporadic raids on all the coastal ports of Hispaniola as well. In fact, Spanish authorities were so intent on monopolizing the remainder of Hispaniola's trade that they burned Puerto Plata, Monte Cristi, and several other cities just to prevent smuggling. In the history of piracy, privateering, and freebooting, the French dominated the entire 16th century, while the English were more important in later years. With war erupting again between France and Spain in the 18th century, the French once again became preeminent.

Thwarted British Invasion

One unique event interrupted this jumble of confusion and constant piracy. During the middle of the 1600s, a popular revolution put Oliver Cromwell in charge of the English government. The Protestant Cromwell hated the Spanish and the French, governed as they were by Catholic monarchies. Besides, the English were jealous of the territorial acquisitions made by both Spain and France in the West Indies. As a result, Cromwell, the First Lord of England, ordered an attack on Hispaniola, in order to add that important island to England's colonial possessions.

In 1655, Cromwell sent 34 warships and 15,000 men against tiny Santo Domingo, then with a non-slave population of only 15,000. Defending Santo Domingo was a Spanish force of 2,300 soldiers, armed with perhaps 1,300 lances. Led by William Penn (the elder), the English ships anchored about 20km west of the city, de-

THE SILVER FLEETS

The Spanish gold and silver mines in the New World poured forth an unimaginable quantity of the precious metals. From mines like Monte Cerro, near Potosí in the Bolivian Andes, enough silver was mined to bridge the Atlantic Ocean. Silver from the Andes was minted into ingots and coins on the spot, then carried by mule across Panama to Portobelo on the Caribbean coast, where it awaited the arrival of the annual Spanish silver fleet. The fabulous mines of Mexico produced astonishing quantities of gold and silver also, most of which was minted in Mexico City into doubloons, pieces of eight, and ingots before being hauled by mule to Veracruz—where *it* awaited the silver fleet. In typical Spanish fashion, every ounce of metal mined in the New World was meticulously accounted for by a complex system of administration, requiring many bureaucrats and government officials. At the same time, the Spanish Pacific fleet was gathering spices and silks in the Orient for delivery to the Mexican Pacific coast, where the goods would be hauled, again by mule, overland to Veracruz, for shipment to Spain.

The annual silver fleet was taking on trade goods in Spain, which it sold at inflated prices to Spanish colonists in the New World. After sailing from Spain, the fleet would split up in the Caribbean—some ships going to Cartagena and Portobelo, others to Veracruz—and reunite in two or three months in Havana.

The New World's gold and silver was loaded in Havana, with every ingot, coin, and doubloon counted and recorded. A copy of the cargo records was kept in Havana, another copy was delivered independently to Spain, and a third copy went with the gold and silver.

The silver fleet consisted of about 20 overloaded galleons. From Havana the fleet went through the Florida Straits, then crossed from Bermuda to the Azores, and finally sailed to Spain. In the early days, the fleet made a stop at Puerto Plata as well. Although the route was the most practical one, it was still dangerous. Pitch between the ships' planking would melt in the sun, and worms would feast on the wood. Tropical storms were a constant hazard. And there was piracy and privateering.

Romantic? Certainly. Dangerous? Absolutely.

ciding to march overland and surprise the Spanish—perhaps recalling Drake's strategy. However, after five months at sea and 12 miles of rugged hiking, the English suffered heavily from the heat and insects. When they arrived at Santo Domingo, to their surprise they found the city abandoned. The Spanish attacked them from behind. Suffering 1,500 casualties in short order, the demoralized English fled to their ships.

The English captains decided not to return to England empty-handed. They sailed to Port Royal on Jamaica, attacked it instead, and claimed that island for England.

French Arrival and Dominican Resurgence

More importantly for Hispaniola, in 1664, the French, well-established on Tortuga, sent an expedition to the western end of Hispaniola and, with the support of the English, took it for France. This explains why the island of Hispaniola is today divided between French-speaking Haiti and the Spanish-speaking Dominican Republic. Thereafter, for years, the French on the western end of the island would periodically raid the Spanish in the east, and vice-versa. For example, in 1674, the French captured both Puerto Plata and Santiago and briefly held them. Later, in 1685 and 1697, the Spanish marched west and sacked Cap Haitien and Port-de-Paix, while the French retook Santiago and burned it to the ground. Finally, in 1697, the Treaty of Ryswick officially ceded the western end of the island to France. From that day on, Haiti was to become the richest colony in the New World, while the Spanish side only sank further into poverty and neglect. Oddly, part of the reason was Spain's inability to procure slaves to work its plantations there. Ultimately, that was to be one of the saving graces for the country.

By 1730, the population on the Spanish side of Hispaniola had dropped to 6,000, slaves and freemen included. Most of the land was held by absentee landlords, and there were few roads to the Cibao, which hindered agriculture. The Spanish monopoly on trade destroyed business. All seemed bleak, indeed.

During the course of the 18th century, population revived on both sides of Hispaniola, and the slave trade added to the numbers of slaves as well. In the 1790s, the French colony of Saint-Domingue (modern Haiti) had a slave population of more than 500,000, outnumbering their French masters eight to one. These slaves were miserably overworked and dangerously angry. In Spanish Hispaniola, however, even after large increases in slaving throughout the 1700s, the latter part of the century found only about 40,000 slaves in the country. Under Spanish law, they were treated with relative lenience and could

---

THE ARTICLES OF PIRACY

Men who signed on with a pirate ship were part of a criminal partnership with very specific understandings. Captain Kidd, for example, issued written agreements. Some of the articles were as follows:

(1) Captain Kidd and his ships to have forty shares and any man that would come aboard the said ships should have shares of such treasure as should be taken.

(2) If any man should loose a leg or arm in ye said service, he should have sex (six) hundred pieces of eight, or sex able slaves.

(3) If any man should loose a joynt in ye said service, he should have a hundred pieces of 8.

(4) If any man shipped himself aboard ye said ships and should offer to go away from her, he shall suffer what punishment ye Capt. and ye Company Quartermaster shall think fitt, and shall have no share.

The contract also dealt with cowardice, mutiny, drunkenness, and the chain of command. A piece of eight mentioned in the contract was worth the equivalent of an American dollar (at a time when the buying power of a dollar was quite large). Slaves meant prisoners from prize vessels. Often these "slaves" were held for ransom or worked in the fields. The systems for sharing a payout were varied and complex, but almost everybody abided by the rules.

easily buy their freedom. The harsh racial laws of the French side of the island were largely unknown; black freemen in Spanish Hispaniola already outnumbered the slaves and soon formed a mulatto society integrated with the Spanish one. By the beginning of the 19th century, life in Santo Domingo had developed a Spanish insouciance, dominated by religion, music, and food, all overseen by a laziness of mood commented upon by contemporary observers. The ruling class in Santo Domingo ate dried corned beef sprinkled with lime juice, cassava, plantains, and cornmeal, drank chocolate smuggled from Saint-Domingue, and chewed local tobacco, which turned their teeth black. Sugar was generally cane syrup. There was lots of rum (also smuggled in from Saint-Domingue). Almost all of the tobacco, cotton, cacao, and cane produced at that time in Spanish Hispaniola was consumed locally. The only export was beef, because cattle were raised extensively in the highland valleys.

Haitian Occupation and Terror

In 1789, the French Revolution changed everything. In the first place, the colony of Saint-Domingue was the richest in the world, and the republicans in France, as well as the English—who perceived France's moment of weakness—were covetous of controlling it. The English invaded the colony and took Port-au-Prince. Meanwhile, black slaves, free mulattos, and certain fearful whites all conspired to control the colony. Finally, under the black general Toussaint Louverture, an outbreak freed the French slaves. Later, with the rise of Napoleon and his victories against Spain in the imperial wars that followed, Spain was forced to cede Spanish Hispaniola to France.

Upon hearing this, Toussaint drove the English out of Haiti and then began to occupy Spanish Hispaniola. Along with his senior general, Dessalines, and aided by the English—who were eager to break both French and Spanish power in the Caribbean—Toussaint went on a murderous war of conquest against all Hispaniola, killing, raping, and butchering. It soon became clear to Napoleon, who had forbidden Toussaint to capture Hispaniola, that the "gilded African" (as Napoleon called him) was out to free the entire island from French rule. In early 1802, it was also

clear to Napoleon that he would have to fight to retain Hispaniola against Toussaint. This war, between France and Haiti (led by Toussaint and Dessalines), was to be won by Haitians, partly because of logistics, partly because of disease, and partly because of fierce resistance. However, for 10 years, the entire island of Hispaniola was a terror house of murder.

For 20 years, until 1844, the Haitians occupied Spanish Hispaniola. Under the mulatto general Jean-Pierre Boyer, this occupation was anarchic and degrading.

Brief Liberation and Drift

The Haitian occupation was probably doomed from its start. There was a vast gulf in language and tradition, but the matter of race was vital. Dessalines himself was committed to racial domination by black former slaves. Besides, Boyer's army had come to exploit the Spanish colony, not improve it. Although the slaves of Hispaniola were freed, production was paralyzed. Soldiers seized church property, and the bureaucracy plundered everything in sight. Boyer's all-black army, angry after many decades of slavery, took graft and robbed cultivators. During these years, too, Latin America was rife with liberation movements, which the Haitian army carefully kept isolated from Spanish Hispaniola. For one man, however, that new sense of liberation, based upon philosophical romanticism, had already become plainly clear. Born in Santo Domingo, Juan Pablo Duarte journeyed to New York and Europe in 1830, when he was 17 years old. It was a voyage that would open his eyes. Duarte, raised in Hispaniola's stifling oppression, encountered the romantic character then so popular in French theater—a stranger to men, an opponent of tyranny, and a republican in spirit.

Returning home in 1833 after a visit to Catalonia in Spain, Duarte announced to his friends that Santo Domingo would soon be free. Thereafter, he began to rouse his countrymen and eventually formed La Trinitaria, a secret society organized into small self-contained groups replete with passwords, codes, and declarations signed in blood. They conducted demonstrations in the guise of religious observances. A flag was devised with a white, red, and green color scheme and a cross. Dominicans residing in Venezuela began to give financial help to the movement. Arms began to filter into the occupied zone. Duarte contacted dissident groups in Haiti to organize against Boyer, which they did.

Finally, Duarte was forced into hiding in Santo Domingo and later had to flee to Venezuela. Nevertheless, on the night of February 27, 1844, armed conspirators struck with force, taking the El Conde gate in Santo Domingo, then the Ozama fort—already abandoned by the Haitians. By March 14, it was all over and Duarte returned in triumph. His triumph was, however, to be short lived.

Though Duarte was back in Santo Domingo, the dangers were not over. Haitian troops were camped just west of the capital, in Azua, and various conspiracies for power abounded on the island. Several "big men" in the country, especially Pedro Santana, were organizing armies to take power. Buenaventura Baez wanted the country to become a protectorate of France. A wealthy landowner named Sanchez was also prominent. It was he who, temporarily, emerged as the leader of a junta which controlled the city of Santo Domingo. He appointed Duarte Governor of Cibao, and Duarte was cheered by crowds in Santo Domingo. The Spanish army of the north succeeded in driving the Haitians out of that part of the country. Finally, Duarte agreed that a vote should take place to decide the fate of the country, provided that it was "a free election, by majority vote, and without pressure." He believed that such a vote would make him president.

Nothing of the kind happened. On July 12, 1844, Santana marched into Santo Domingo and declared himself dictator. He threw opposition leaders into jail and deposed Sánchez. He also threatened Duarte with the death penalty unless he left the colony. Duarte had lost. He reluctantly boarded a vessel for Germany, never to see Santo Domingo again. After wandering in Europe for some years, he immersed himself in an ascetic life, traveling to a remote village on the Rio Negro, a tributary of the Amazon in northern Brazil, where he stayed for 15 years.

During Duarte's exile in Brazil, the semi-independent but still partially feudal country of Santo Domingo (as it was then called) was ruled by Santana and Baez, who seemed to take turns pillaging the people. Santana himself tried to offer the beautiful Samaná Peninsula to the highest bidder, but the international bidders were so fumbling that nothing came of this effort. Santana and Baez were deceptively dissimilar in personality and appearance. Santana was burly, brutish, and brazen, lacking principles and intelligence. He was always able to command when survival was at stake, then retire to his *estancia* near El Seibo when there was a lull of peace. Baez, on the other hand, was suave and clever, more cruel than Santana, but lacking Santana's ability to lead peasants into battle. Baez was utterly money-hungry and without character. Baez came from Azua, which he used as his base of operations, gliding between the courts of Spain, France, England, Haiti, and the United States with the adaptability of a chameleon, then seizing power when the need arose.

During almost 20 years of alternating presidencies, Santana and Baez managed to bankrupt the country. During that same time there were constant threats from Haiti, now ruled by the strange and corrupt hand of a man called Soulouque. Then, during the early 1860s, Duarte was suddenly back in Santiago, where a liberal northern party had risen to prominence. Now, surrounding himself with cronies, Santana got rid of Duarte for the last time, liquidated the liberal party, and took advantage of this opportunity to accomplish his lifelong ambition of making Santo Domingo a protectorate of Spain.

On March 17, 1861, the citizens of Santo Domingo woke to find billboards all over the capital proclaiming a grand reincorporation of the country into Spain. The red and gold flag of Spain flew above the old fort in Santo Domingo. At the same time, Santana negotiated timber and mineral concessions with the French and Spanish. The French even considered a return to Haiti, a part of the then-European drive for colonies.

In Spanish Hispaniola, ferment was brewing against this return to Spanish domination. When Spain finally took over, disastrous tax levies impoverished the middle class. Merchants and farmers faced ruin. Spain substituted its own medieval legal code for the more enlightened Napoleonic Code that the country had received from Haiti. The new Spanish archbishop annulled freedom of worship, alienating Methodists and Masons. Then, an outbreak of yellow fever began to devastate the Spanish garrisons, and what had been a token opposition began to grow. Half a dozen local generals operated armies against the Spaniards in 1863. In 1864, the Spanish lost half of their 20,000-man garrison to warfare and disease, mainly smallpox and yellow fever. Then, on June 14 of that year, Santana himself died, removing the last obstacle to the final removal of the Spanish.

BOB RACE

INDEPENDENCE AND TYRANNY

The Dominican Republic became a fully independent country again in March 1865. It would be nice to report that it enjoyed peace and prosperity, but the reverse is true. The principal cities were devastated by warfare. Fields were ruined, the treasury was empty, and the masses were in poverty. Into this horrid vacuum stepped Baez again, who came back from overseas and resumed power. He immediately began looking around for sources of money and tried to find it in odd places, indeed.

In the spring of 1869, Baez managed to secure a loan for a staggering amount of money from a New York commercial company on the pledge to build and develop the Samaná Peninsula. The loan was backed by bonds redeemable at six months' notice. By this device, Baez had secured funds, but he had mortgaged his country's entire future, saddling it with enormous debt and surrendering part of its sovereignty. At the same time, Baez negotiated with the Grant administration in the United States to annex the country and make it a state. In the years after the American Civil War, the United States had become more interested in keeping European countries out of the Western Hemisphere by authority of the Monroe Doc-

Juan Pablo Duarte

trine; therefore, Grant took the offer seriously. American warships appeared off Samaná Bay, and Baez put the annexation to a rigged popular vote. However, the U.S. Senate, sniffing a rat, refused annexation, leaving Baez to twist. On January 2, 1874, he fled the country, yielding to a revolution led by generals Luperón and González.

For five years, 1874–79, these generals selected reformist Ulises Espaillat to act as president of the Dominican Republic. Espaillat tried to make democracy work but could not. He issued money which had no backing and became worthless. Insurrections by generals plagued his government, until the reformer was forced to retire, only to be replaced by Baez. Even Baez was forced out of power after a short time, leaving for Puerto Rico with $300,000 of government money in his suitcase.

Out of all this confusion came a truly unique and terrible dictator named Ulises Heureaux, a black general who ruled the Dominican Republic mercilessly for the last two decades of the 19th century. Heureaux possessed reckless courage, an heroic stature, and military genius. He shared with Baez and Santana an interest in packing the bureaucracy with frightened toadies and issuing worthless paper money. Unlike his predecessors, Heureaux's aim was neither money nor pleasure. Instead, he seems to have been interested solely in the exercise of naked power. To that end, he exiled his military rivals, kept legions of spies throughout the country, employed assassins abroad, and exercised his prodigious promiscuity freely. It is said that one day Heureaux took a dinner guest for a stroll. The guest spied some men digging a hole by the side of the road and asked its purpose. Heureaux supposedly replied, "They are digging your grave." Whereupon soldiers appeared and murdered the guest.

As a black, Heureaux was able to play upon the sympathies of the black and mulatto peasants. He also took the opportunity to increase racial tensions and hatred whenever this benefited him.

After putting down several insurrections, Heureaux found himself short of money and began to negotiate loans against, once again, a concession on Samaná Bay. When American companies balked, he finally found a Dutch company that loaned him money against a lien on the country's customs revenues. By now, the country was also hampered by foreign concessions elsewhere, as the economy fell more and more into hock to German, French, and American interests. The last seven years of Heureaux's rule became a reign of terror as the dictator withdrew into paranoia. The fortress prison of Santo Domingo was overcrowded with political prisoners. Enemies were thrown to the sharks from cliffs. Despite all these deterrents, an opposition formed against Heureaux.

All told, Heureaux survived five coup attempts, but the sixth spelled his end. Finally, in 1899, a young man named Ramón Cáceres, accompanied only by a 16-year-old boy named Jacobito Lara, assassinated Heureaux. In the provincial city of Moca, Cáceres stepped in front of the dictator and fired several shots into him. The dictator squeezed off one shot spasmodically, killing a beggar on the outskirts of the crowd.

His death brought a dual legacy to the Dominican Republic. Heureaux indeed built some modern wharves and buildings, created an efficient army and navy, allowed some newspapers to thrive, and revived the bureaucracy. He also stifled national agriculture, laying the foundations for a monopolistic economy that exists even today. He set the standards for imprisonment of political opponents and forced political parties to disintegrate.

Cáceres became provisional president and was followed to power by Juan Jiménez, and later by Horacio Vásquez, who collectively governed until civil war and chaos intervened at the outbreak of World War I. But the dawn of the 20th century brought a new player to the table: the United States. In 1904, Theodore Roosevelt proclaimed his corollary to the Monroe Doctrine, which in effect made the United States a kind

of policeman of the hemisphere. Roosevelt negotiated a deal with the Dominican Republic that allowed the United States to administer the country's export customs duties (virtually the only cash flow available), returning less than half to the country and applying the rest to its external debt. This was the famous "receivership of 1905," which supposedly saved the Dominican Republic from bankruptcy. The treaty was ratified in 1907. In 1908, Cáceres became president.

It was to be a brief interlude of reform under Cáceres. He was himself murdered in 1911, after which full-scale civil war broke out between the adherents of Jiménez and those of Vásquez. It was now, within the administration of Woodrow Wilson in the United States, that serious thoughts about occupying the Dominican Republic first bloomed.

REVOLUTION AND U.S. OCCUPATION

Invasion

In March 1913, a contest for power between two major factions broke out in the Dominican Republic. The United States looked on "with interest," especially since the Dominican Republic owed much of its foreign debt to the United States and because the country's continuing chaos "threatened the security" of America. The Jiménez and Vásquez factions battled for two years. Meanwhile, in Europe, of course, World War I broke out in August 1914. With German influence at a high point in Haiti—German marines had actually landed at Port-au-Prince in February 1914—and Germans angling for influence in the Dominican Republic, it wasn't long before Americans landed in Haiti. Then, in June 1915, French troops took over Port-au-Prince. On July 27, a Haitian mob lynched President V.G. Sam, following his butchery of 167 political prisoners, and the United States sent a brigade of marines to restore order in the country.

In 1916, the Americans came to the Dominican Republic after President Jiménez was impeached by both houses of the Dominican Congress "for violation of the Constitution." Marines landed at the principal ports; the group landing at Monte Cristi bought up all 12 Model T Fords at the local Ford dealership for transportation. Another group landed at Puerto Plata, installed a machine gun on a railroad flatcar, and ran the flatcar from Puerto Plata to Santiago.

The Dominicans responded by closing ranks and defying the Americans. Incidents of violence escalated. The Americans retaliated by demanding that the Dominicans hand over full control of their nation's treasury and disband their Army, replacing it with a civilian "constabulary." The Dominican press fanned resentment against the occupation. Finally, Wilson proclaimed that the Dominican Republic would be placed under American military rule.

The occupation lasted eight years. The Americans were worried about a chaotic country directly on the line of the Panama Canal. They were also concerned about the debts owed them by the Dominicans. On the surface, the occupation actually accomplished a great deal in the way of public works, limited economic growth, and military reform. However, there were many serious problems, including acts of pillage and rape committed by frustrated U.S. Marines. Placed in charge of the American operation, Captain (later Rear Admiral) Harry S. Knapp was an able governor. Still, most of his staff could not speak the Spanish language and did not understand the customs and mores of the Dominicans. The war in Europe deprived Knapp of some of his ablest and most sensitive officers. In addition, his forces were constantly overstretched, as the native "constabulary" never materialized (qualified Dominicans refusing to serve as "puppets" for the Americans).

Especially in the eastern provinces of El Seibo and San Pedro de Macorís, rebellion was chronic. Called *gavilleros,* local guerrillas roamed the countryside. In and around the village of Hato Mayor, the fighting was often savage. One marine captain, Charles F. Merkel, instigated "counter-terror." Hato Mayor was not pacified until nearly 1921, just as the occupation was coming to an end.

Still, Knapp's military government established a beginning civil service and responsible control of public-works projects, helped farmers vary crops with modern implements, formed a land-title system to impose order on the chaos of land ownership, and made a start on a sanitation system for the towns. Education was drastically overhauled, schools built, and new students enrolled. Roads were also built: Monte Cristi was linked for the first time with Santiago, and an east-west road along the south coast was constructed. Nothing was done, however, about the problem of absentee land ownership or peasants who lived on nothing. The national debt was gradually reduced.

Withdrawal and Transition

As the Americans were preparing to leave in 1921, their problem was to find a group of sincere people to whom they could hand power. The slogan of the Dominicans was, "Evacuation, pure and simple!" However, evacuation was not so simple, as the Americans would leave the thousands of economic contracts and concession agreements in limbo if they simply withdrew without some kind of legal understanding. The new American secretary of state, Charles Evans Hughes, campaigned in the Dominican Republic all through 1922, attempting to form political parties and find emerging candidates. The Americans appointed a provisional president in October 1922, and by March 1924, an election was held in an uncoerced and orderly fashion. General Vásquez was elected president of the Dominican Republic, and on July 13, the American flag was lowered over the Ozama fortress in Santo Domingo. The Americans concluded that "a new era of liberty and independence" had commenced.

There was only a little truth in the pronouncement. Vásquez did rule quietly, though he unilaterally extended his term of office from four to six years. By that time it was 1930, and a worldwide political movement called fascism had swept like a tide throughout Europe. Parties in Germany, Italy, eastern Europe, France, Spain, and Portugal were infected. In the Dominican Republic, a group of rebels led by a thug named Rafael Trujillo began an insurrection against the government with the tacit approval of the head of the National Guard. The rebels, full of military bravado and fascistic machismo, toppled the government. Trujillo, one of the leaders, encouraged a man named Ureña to run for president, then convinced him to step aside and run as Trujillo's vice-president.

Trujillo won the election with more votes than there were voters. This former telegraph operator, sugar weigher, and gang member had been given a chance by the American occupation to join the National Guard in 1918 and had quickly risen to the rank of lieutenant colonel, and then to chief of staff, an appointment made by Vásquez himself. By 1927, he was Chief of the National Army. Now, in 1930, this strutting, blustering rooster was president, and he'd remain so for the next 31 years.

Trujillo, however, would prove to be far more than just another in a line of brutal Dominican dictators. During the 31 years that Rafael Leonidas Trujillo Molina held power, he turned the Dominican Republic into his private fiefdom, running it for personal aggrandizement, economic control, and systematic repression. The self-proclaimed *Benefactor de la Patria y Padre de la Patria Nueva* had brought fascist totalitarianism to the long-suffering Dominican people.

FASCISM UNDER TRUJILLO

The September after Trujillo took power in a rigged election, a powerful hurricane struck Santo Domingo and nearly leveled it. Using this emergency as a pretext, Trujillo swept all economic power into his hands and ruled by decree, destroying the constitution. The Great Depression allowed him further opportunities to take over most industry, crush trade unions, and imprison opponents. Because the country was so poor, when the economy began to recover, Trujillo became popular, despite his repressions. In just a few years, Trujillo, his family, and his inner circle managed to gain control of over 60% of the country's economy, including sugar, cement, airlines, shipping, tobacco, and banking. Later, he posed as the hemisphere's foremost anticommunist, assuring himself of U.S. congressional support during the virulent anticommunist years.

Master Dictator
Trujillo ran one of the tightest dictatorships the world has ever seen. His web controlled the military, education, and all political thought. His picture was everywhere. The capital was renamed Ciudad Trujillo. What is now Pico Duarte, the Caribbean's highest peak, became Pico Trujillo. His vast police state sent spies and agents into many foreign countries in order to stamp out

any possible resistance movements. His fortune during the 1950s was estimated at one billion dollars, with his friends and family enjoying huge fortunes as well. He was called El Jefe (the Boss), and his form in busts, statues, and photos became the symbol of the regime. Public buildings had his speeches engraved on their walls, signs on village water wells claimed "Only Trujillo Gives Us a Drink," and sick people were told, "Only Trujillo cures us." In fact, Trujillo did wind up employing, directly and indirectly, more than half of all Dominican workers, in part because he had bought up hurricane-ravaged lands and become a landlord of sugar plantations, and partly because he controlled most of the country's industry and processing. Other Latin and South American dictators emerged during that era, many of them becoming incredibly wealthy—like Batista in Cuba and Perón in Argentina—but Trujillo, in terms of wealth, put them all to shame with his billions. Of course, the money, procured through fraud and monopoly, went straight into Swiss accounts.

United States Support
How did he do it for so long? For one thing, Trujillo got lots of help from the United States. For many years, he lobbied U.S. congressmen to maintain the sugar quota for the Dominican Republic, which assured the regime of a continuing source of cash. He met with Franklin Roosevelt and many other business and political leaders on a regular basis, showering them with cash and gifts. The American secretary of state praised Trujillo as "a splendid President, who is outstanding among all those in the American nations." He had public-relations people in the United States working tirelessly on his behalf and paid Mutual Broadcasting nearly a million dollars to broadcast propaganda as news. To promote travel, Pan Am World Airways took out full-page ads featuring his picture.

Shortly after World War II ended, the United States, overcome by an irrational wave of anticommunist sentiment, began supporting the militaries of many repressive regimes with arms and training. Beneficiaries included Honduras, Guatemala, and El Salvador, but perhaps the foremost recipient of military aid was Trujillo's army. The Mutual Security Act of 1951 devoted nearly six million dollars of U.S. military equipment and weapons to the Dominican Army. In 1953, the United States and the Dominican Republic signed a mutual defense agreement, designed as a "bulwark" against communism in the hemisphere.

"Trujillismo"

On the domestic front, Trujillo was a genius at social control and personal manipulation. He spread his relatives widely throughout the armed services; his son Ramfis (Rafael Trujillo Martínez), for example, became an Air Force chief of staff.

Trujillo maintained a staff of phone-tapping informants. An Army fort stood in every town. Roadblocks and checkpoints lay every 20 miles on the roads. Each citizen was required to possess an identity card, without which it was impossible to marry, work, drive, vote, or travel. Trujillo also created his own "labor union," the Confederación Dominicano del Trabajo (CDT), and forced all the serfs on his sugar plantations to join, which was another way to keep track of their activities.

Trujillo controlled all broadcasting and made sure Dominican radio and television devoted most of their efforts to filtering the news, promoting the regime, and propagandizing the new Dominican Policy, called "Trujillismo." Trujillismo identified all social good as the harmonization of an individual's life into the "whole," which meant, effectively, into the totalitarian state.

Not surprisingly, the dictator also carefully indoctrinated the Dominican youth from an early age into this cult of personality. Trujillo himself claimed authorship of all elementary school texts, and his wife penned a weekly "moral" newspaper column. Even artists conformed to the needs of the regime, producing poems, plays, stories, and paintings extolling the virtues of Trujillo, representing him as God, Pegasus, an eagle, the sun, and Plato. Popular musicians wrote merengues in his honor, and these, too, circulated throughout the country.

Dominican Exodus

The expansion of the bureaucracy during the Trujillo years, as well as the increase in commerce, succeeded in fostering a growing middle class, people lacking favorable family backgrounds but who prospered nonetheless.

Many upper-class Dominicans, however, fled the country under Trujillo, having seen their own economic power eroded and their freedom destroyed. Many opposed the government, but others were forced to flee simply because they owned enterprises which Trujillo coveted.

Ominously, some émigrés from the Dominican Republic drifted to the United States, Cuba, or Venezuela and began to form opposition groups. At the same time, during the mid-1950s, the entire regime began to sag a bit, as the Caribbean's political and economic winds began to turn against most Latin dictators.

The End

The beginning of Trujillo's end came on March 12, 1956, in New York City, when a Dominican émigré named Jesús Galíndez was kidnapped by Trujillo's agents and flown to Santo Domingo. Galíndez was a well-known professor at Columbia University and a Dominican social critic. A private plane piloted by alleged CIA man Gerald Murphy took Galíndez to prison, where Galíndez was brutally murdered. Murphy, who had piloted the plane with the assistance of Dominican Air Force officer Octavio de la Maza, was later murdered in Santo Domingo in December, 1956, and de la Maza was arrested for the murder. In January, de la Maza was killed in prison, his death proclaimed a suicide by the regime.

Unfortunately for Trujillo, Octavio de la Maza was himself the member of a prominent Dominican family of businesspeople and officers, and one of them, Antonio de la Maza, swore vengeance on Trujillo. As a result of the scandal, tourism from the United States plummeted. By pure coincidence, sugar prices fell disastrously on the world market, and the Dominican Republic entered a recession.

In the late 1950s, world tensions had increased enormously, with most areas of the Caribbean involved peripherally in the struggle between the great powers. Trujillo himself watched as Castro's rebellion against Batista gained steam in Cuba and as other revolutionary movements heated up in South America and Central America. Trujillo then launched three major efforts to assassinate Venezuela's President Rómulo Betancourt, a relatively liberal man whom Trujillo accused of harboring émigré Dominicans. In retaliation, the Organization of American States (OAS) attempted to isolate Trujillo by placing a trade embargo on the Dominican Republic. Hypocritically, the United States then increased the sugar quota four times. Because of criticism, the Eisenhower administration finally imposed an excise tax on Dominican sugar, which cost the Trujillo regime $30 million.

On January 1, 1959, Fidel Castro's Cuban revolution succeeded, and the dictator Batista fled the country. Many Dominican Air Force officers were in Cuba at the time, came into contact with new democratic and left-wing ideas, and formed their own revolutionary group with a view to overturning the regime of Trujillo. On June 14, 1959, they acted, and hundreds of rebels were helicoptered to the Cordillera Central of the Dominican Republic, in hopes of stirring a popular revolt. These men, known officially as the *Catorce de Junio,* or 14J, failed to get the necessary popular support and by December and January had been rounded up and tortured by the Dominican secret police. The American government registered its official disapproval, and in August 1960, the OAS formally severed diplomatic relations with the Dominican Republic. At the same time, the Eisenhower administration closed its embassy and began to establish secret ties to other dissident groups, using the CIA as a go-between. The groups began to consider killing Trujillo with U.S.-supplied arms.

Thereafter, things moved quickly. The de la Maza group began serious efforts to further their plot to kill Trujillo for personal reasons. Then, in November 1960, three sisters—Minerva, María, and Patricia Mercedes—were ambushed and murdered by Trujillo's agents on a lonely highway. Some said they were murdered because they resisted Trujillo's sexual advances. Others said it was because they were married to dissidents. At any rate, this brutal act crystallized several groups' efforts to bring their assassination plans to fruition.

On May 30, 1961, accompanied only by his personal chauffeur, Rafael Trujillo left Santo Domingo for his hometown of San Cristóbal after a hard week of work. Headed west on the coast highway, the ocean in view, his custom Cadillac was forced to the roadside by at least two vehicles containing seven men, most of them members of the de la Maza clan. They had been coached and armed by the CIA. Always armed, Trujillo leapt out and attempted to shoot his way free. He was hit by several shots, and died on the highway in a pool of blood.

In the next six months, hundreds and hundreds of people would be imprisoned, tortured, and murdered as Trujillo's son Ramfis and the secret police orchestrated the "counter-terror."

The next few years would see vast changes in the Dominican Republic, but as a popular merengue put it:

> *They've killed the goat*
> *On the highway*
> *They've killed the goat*
> *On the highway.*
>
> *Let's laugh*
> *Let's dance*

GERMAN SUBS

While at one point during WorldWar II, Trujillo did declare war on Hitler for the publicity value, rumor has it that the dictator clandestinely assisted the Germans.

Numerous German subs cruised off the coast of the Dominican Republic, looking for American supply ships loaded with goods and fuel on their way to Europe. German freighters used these waters also, supplying the submarine fleet with diesel fuel and ammunition. For the subs, though, fresh food and water were a particular problem. Some say the subs would arrive at Las Salinas, west of Santo Domingo, to pick up food and supplies, while others claim the pickup point was Playa Grande, where the subs would arrive in 4,000m of water, surface, and be gone by sunrise. It is possible that numerous German accomplices resident in the country assisted in this secret operation, including a German photographer who had a studio on the Calle Comercio, known today as the Avenida John F. Kennedy.

German subs may have inadvertently introduced soccer to the Dominican Republic as well. One British supply ship was sunk off the north coast, leaving its crew stranded in Puerto Plata for several months. Having nothing better to do, the men organized football matches for the locals until they were rescued by blockade runners.

A TRUJILLO CHRONOLOGY

1918——The U.S. Marine Corps Occupying Force in the Dominican Republic recruits Rafael Leonidas Trujillo Molina into the National Guard.

1924—The marines depart. Trujillo is now in command of the armed forces.

1930—Trujillo leads a coup against President Horacio Vásquez and installs himself as president.

1955—Vice-President Richard Nixon, in a gesture of goodwill, visits the Dominican Republic. The CIA establishes a base there.

March 12, 1956—Jesús Galíndez is murdered at Trujillo's orders.

December 3, 1956—Gerald Murphy is murdered in the Dominican Republic. Fellow pilot Octavio de la Maza is arrested for the murder.

January 7, 1957—Octavio de la Maza is murdered in prison; his death is called a suicide. Antonio de la Maza swears revenge.

December 1958—CIA Chief of Station Lear B. Reed offers aid to dissident Dominicans who plotted the assassination of Trujillo.

January 1, 1959—President Fulgencio Batista, the dictator of Cuba, flees before Fidel Castro's forces seize power there.

June 14, 1959—Dominican émigré invaders launched from Cuba are killed or captured in the Dominican Republic. From the date of their landing in the Dominican Republic, domestic support cells take the name *Catorce de Junio,* abbreviated 14J.

January 1960—Hundreds of 14J members are rounded up and tortured by the Dominican secret police.

The United States registers official disapproval.

May 1960—Trujillo expels U.S. embassy press officer Carl Davis. President Eisenhower approves a contingency plan to aid a domestic coup against Trujillo. First request for arms by Dominican dissidents to the U.S. embassy.

June 1960—Trujillo directs assassination attempt against President Rómulo Betancourt of Venezuela, which fails.

August 1960—OAS member states vote to sever diplomatic relations with the Dominican Republic and to impose economic sanctions. The United States downgrades its embassy to a consulate general. Consul General Henry Dearborn also becomes de facto CIA chief of station. The United States makes contact with the group of dissidents of which Antonio de la Maza and General Juan Tomás Días form the core.

November 25, 1960—Trujillo's agents murder three sisters (Minerva, María Theresa, and Patricia Mercedes Mirabal), all of whom are married to 14J leaders.

January 12, 1961—United States "Special Group" approves arms delivery to Dominican dissidents.

January 20, 1961—President John F. Kennedy inaugurated.

February 1961—General Pupo Román, Trujillo's nephew by marriage, enlisted by the de la Maza group.

April 17, 1961—The Bay of Pigs invasion of Cuba, sponsored by the United States, fails.

May 30, 1961—Trujillo is assassinated.

Let's enjoy
The Thirtieth of May
Day of Liberty.

MODERN ERA

American Intervention (Again)

No doubt the CIA and the U.S. State Department hoped that a conservative anticommunist government would inherit Trujillo's power and exercise it in a slightly less brutal and conspicuous way. Unfortunately, the months and years after the assassination were chaotic, and the power structure, essentially, did not change. Ramfis Trujillo immediately took power and, as a

military officer, ruled through Joaquín Balaguer, a politician in the Trujillo camp. The United States, however, was not eager to see a repressive right-wing military regime remain in power and pressured the Dominican government for reform, especially since Castro was on the prowl in the Caribbean.

Balaguer allowed émigrés to return and even allowed the formation of several "independent" political parties, including the National Union (UCN), which represented businessmen, and the Revolutionary Party (PRD), led by the popular Juan Bosch, oriented towards students and workers. Then came a series of strikes and disturbances aimed against the regime. Finally, in November 1961, Ramfis and the rest of the Trujillo family fled the country, emptying the treasury to the tune of $90 million. Balaguer shared power with a seven-man council of businessmen, clergy, and politicians from the UCN. Two weeks later, a military coup restored the officers; then a counter-coup restored the council. It was obvious that the chaos was damaging United States "interests," and finally the OAS and the United States pressured the government into allowing elections. Balaguer himself went into exile in New York.

The election was scheduled for December 1962. As election day neared, it became clear that the Dominican people favored Juan Bosch and the PRD by a large margin. In Bosch, the people had found a fiery, articulate leader, ostensibly dedicated to democracy and reform. The election was indeed won by Bosch and represented a victory by the masses over the country's military and the traditional ruling elite. Bosch came to office on a platform of economic reform and social justice but recognized the necessity of dealing amicably with the conservative clergy, military, and upper middle class.

Bosch went about his business, parceling out Trujillo's estates to peasants, refusing to declare the Catholic Church the state church, and seeking aid from Europe as an antidote to United States domination. Conservative elements opposed the government at every step, raising the hue and cry of anticommunism and fear of Cuban invasion. In September 1963, after only seven months in office, Bosch was ousted in a bloodless military coup led by Colonel—soon to become General—Elias Wessin y Wessin. Bosch went into Puerto Rican exile, and soon the government was led by a cabal of three people, including the unpopular businessman Donald Cabral, whom the people viewed as a front for the military and an interloper.

In the United States, President Kennedy began to consider supporting the constitutionalist rebels, if only to the extent of stopping the fighting and formally backing Bosch. Unfortunately, in November, before he could do much more than stop American aid to the conservatives, Kennedy was assassinated. His successor, Lyndon Johnson, restored the aid and seemed dead set against Bosch.

Plotting and antigovernment intrigue continued unabated, by both rightists and leftists. Some in the military wanted a stronger anticommunist government; some businessmen wanted power, solely to accumulate wealth. The PRD began actively plotting to restore Bosch and constitutional government. Even Balaguer began scheming a comeback. Then, on April 24, 1965, the PRD moved to seize power. Led by PRD veterans and younger military officers favoring reform, the revolutionists took the Santo Domingo radio station and urged thousands into the streets of the capital. Soon, "constitutional troops" occupied the presidential palace, and Bosch made preparations for his return. The people began to rejoice.

Then, with the U.S. embassy encouraging them, the conservatives counterattacked. Air Force jets strafed the palace. The constitutionalists suffered losses but persevered. Finally, just as they seemed about to drive the military out of Santo Domingo, the United States acted decisively against the constitutionalists, providing support and aid to the conservatives. The American embassy spread rumors of communist influence in the PRD. Even with United States support and aid, however, the conservatives failed to reverse the tide, and on April 28, the military seemed about to crumble. Then Lyndon Johnson sent in American troops to defeat the Dominican people.

At first, Johnson claimed that American intervention was intended to save American lives and property. Neither the press nor most politicians accepted this explanation, so Johnson changed it: by intervening in the Dominican Republic, the United States would "prevent another Cuba," and "send a message to the North Vietnamese." Soon, someone produced a list of the PRD's communist members, despite the fact that communist influence in the PRD was actually quite minimal. The United States also pressured the OAS into a vote to send "peacekeeping" troops, but only right-wing military dictatorships actually responded. American troops fought in the streets of Santo Domingo to subdue the PRD and prevent Bosch's return. All told, about 2,000 Dominicans died in the fighting. In August, a cease-fire was arranged and an "act of reconciliation" signed. The agreements named a provisional president and called for elections.

And what about the revolution? Having fallen prey to Cold War dogma and anticommunism, the United States had effectively crushed a movement not so much about communism as about democracy. In the rise and fall of the revolution, the weak of the Dominican Republic had had their hopes raised, then dashed. Dominicans believed the revolution involved their destiny as a nation, their right to self-determination, dignity, sovereignty, and national pride. Certainly, the "crisis" of 1964–1965 had begun long before the Wessin coup. As one Dominican historian writes, "In a deeper sense, the Dominican crisis began with the arrival of Christopher Columbus at the fair island of Hispaniola." In 1965, the Dominicans attempted to break free from foreign dependence and intervention but were prevented from doing so by the United States.

Balaguer

In the months before the election, Bosch was allowed to return to the country, but death threats forced him to keep a very low profile. Though nearly 40% of the electorate risked their lives (literally) to vote for Bosch, Balaguer—Trujillo's old sidekick—spent $13 million on his campaign, a huge sum by Dominican standards, and won the election with 57% of the vote. Oddly, 25% more votes were cast in 1966 than in 1963— *exactly* Balaguer's margin of victory.

Suspicious election or no, Balaguer set out in his presidency to get some things done. He'd go on to rule as a kind of civilian dictator from 1966 to 1978, in one continuous streak of graft and abuse of power, though more subtly than Trujillo. In fact, although some people saw Balaguer as a "neo-Trujillo," he was actually more complicated. He pledged to return the country to normalcy, order, and reconstruction. He tried to play the part of a benevolent father figure, and in some regions, like the conservative Cibao, where most of the population still lived, this image worked well. In some ways, his first presidency was quite successful. He ruled in a quiet way, outside the eye of cameras and publicity, and he did a lot of his work with United States help. The Congress gave the Dominican Republic $132 million during Balaguer's first two years, and he spent millions building dams, roads, and tourist facilities, creating what he called a Dominican "miracle." He built bridges, housing projects, schools, clinics, and irriga-

tion canals—using his own construction companies, of course. Multinational corporations were given virtual carte blanche and began gold-mining, ferronickel, and bauxite operations. Still, unemployment continued to hover around 25%, and price controls on agricultural products were an effective tax on the peasants.

At the same time, a small band of ultra-rightists called La Banda roamed the country, murdering and "disappearing" leftists, students, and labor leaders. On February 3, 1973, the constitutionalists, led by Francisco Deno, tried another invasion, but Balaguer crushed it by sending troops to the streets and campuses, arresting 1,400 labor and student leaders. Later in 1973, Balaguer formed his own party, the Partido Reformista Dominicano (PRD) (Reformist Party), to oppose the old Bosch party, now called the Partido de la Liberación Dominicana (PLD) (Dominican Liberation Party). The PLD nominated prosperous rancher Antonio Guzmán as its candidate. During this election, one could see troops in the streets carrying Balaguer posters on their bayonets, and PRD flags on their jeeps. Balaguer won.

During Balaguer's first 12-year stint as president, the hyperbole of his "miracle" hid the facts. Poverty was epidemic in the countryside and on the outskirts of major cities. Illiteracy remained rampant. The distribution of income continued to be greatly inequitable. Although per capita income rose, this was mainly due to United States aid, which tended to fall into the hands of the rich, or the upper-middle classes, both of which favored Balaguer. Malnutrition was widespread, and the social conditions of the poor deteriorated. At election time, many people, confronted with their options, chose to vote for nobody.

Finally, in 1974, the bubble burst. The oil price hike hurt the country badly, as did a further decline in sugar prices. High inflation plagued the economy, and increased balance-of-payments problems threatened the stability of Balaguer's government. By 1978, Balaguer, aging and ill, was unable to assuage public dissatisfaction with the situation by announcing another "project." Now, a sizable number of the emerging middle class were demanding reform, joining forces with the urban poor.

New Presidents

In 1978, the rusting PRD revived its grassroots organization and once again nominated Guzmán for president. It looked as if this would be the first meaningful election in 12 years, especially for the middle class and the poor. Guzmán was also acceptable to the Dominican oligarchy and to the U.S. embassy. During the election, the military seized the ballots for Santo Domingo, but when the Carter administration and the OAS sent U.S. Secretary of State Cyrus Vance and a major U.S. military leader to Santo Domingo, the ballot boxes were returned. With the help of the recovered votes, Guzmán won the election.

Although major concessions were granted to the old Balagueristas, Guzmán was finally installed as president. The Carter administration sent 30 representatives to his inauguration as a show of support. The new president castigated the military and promised reform, justice, and freedom.

Once in office, Guzmán moved away from the practices of Balaguer, allowing more political freedom and human rights, stressing health care and rural development, and placing tighter controls on foreign development projects. Still, Guzmán faced horrid economic realities in high oil prices and low sugar prices along with steadily declining export revenues. Despite his good intentions, the problems remained.

As the economy failed to turn around, Guzmán struggled with growing unpopularity. He managed to professionalize the military and release political prisoners, but the people and the press clamored for a return of the "miracle days" of Balaguer.

The election of 1982 saw the electorate split. Juan Bosch and his PLD returned to the country, although Bosch himself had been absent from politics for most of Balaguer's three terms in office. The ruling PRD chose a moderate lawyer named Salvador Blanco, which alienated its own left wing. Balaguer jumped into the fray, promising a return to "normalcy." Eventually, the power of the PRD's promise of social change allowed Blanco to become president with just 47% of the vote. The lame-duck president Guzmán killed himself in office, worried over reports of corruption and bribery. It cast a pall over the country and caused many to worry about future democratic reforms.

Blanco's presidency was marked by austerity, urban violence, widening corruption scandals, and a factionalized governing party. The International Monetary Fund (IMF) began to involve itself in Dominican economics. Sugar prices had collapsed to four cents a pound, and the public debt soared to $4 billion. When the IMF agreed to loan the country $599 million, it also imposed a currency devaluation, import restrictions, and budget cuts. When the Blanco government raised oil prices as promised in April 1984, riots broke out in Santo Domingo and rapidly spread to 20 cities. Many died and many more were arrested by the U.S.–trained Cazadores de Montaña. Although order was restored, the Blanco government had lost the support of the people. Blanco was seen to have bowed to IMF pressure and to have used excessive force in putting down the unrest.

The Blanco years were not good ones for the people. On February 11, 1985, a general strike shut down Santo Domingo and affected many other cities. Blanco attempted to license journalists. He detained labor leaders and repressed many left-wing activities. The government's bureaucracy ballooned to nearly 250,000 workers, and corruption reached dizzying new heights. About the only positives were the administration's seemingly successful literacy campaign and the construction of some new low-income housing units. Five years after leaving office in 1986, Blanco was convicted of embezzling government funds. He's presently serving a 20-year sentence, though his conviction is under appeal—Blanco claims Balaguer orchestrated his imprisonment for political reasons.

Back to Balaguer

The 1986 election was one of the most controversial in the history of the Dominican Republic. Three ex-presidents ran for office, and with many predicting a close race, tensions ran very high. Juan Bosch was back again, trying to speak for the poor. The former interim president Jacobo Jajluta ran under the banner of the PRD. And Balaguer fused his "reform" party into a Christian Democratic organization, running on a platform of "normalcy." Votes were cast, and in the summer a long election turned into a period of uncertainty, a period of power negotiations among various conservative groups. Finally, Joaquín

Balaguer returned to power.

Balaguer went back to work in good, old-style caudillo form, pouring huge amounts of public money into housing, roads, hydroelectric plants, and other infrastructure projects. He reintroduced efforts to build up the country's tourist industry and inaugurated "industrial free zones" to lure offshore manufacturing by foreign companies, promising them low taxes and cheap labor. By now nearly 79 years old and nearly blind, the old caudillo ran a "moralization campaign," which focused on the PRD opposition. But the late 1980s and early 1990s did not go well for the country. Given Balaguer's massive public spending, inflation once again raged out of control. Dominicans suffered from shortages of food, along with frequent brownouts. Public transportation hardly operated. Rioting began in early 1988, led by something called the Coordinator of Popular Struggles. Labor unions began calling for strikes again.

To no one's surprise, Balaguer ran again in 1990. He stressed his managerial capabilities and continued to hint at an ultimate societal breakdown if the people chose Bosch. Then Bosch played into the old caudillo's hand by attacking the Catholic Church. Balaguer talked openly and proudly about the part the Dominican Republic would play in the Columbus festival in 1992. The election of 1990 was won by Balaguer with only 35% of the possible vote. Many Dominicans simply refused to vote or stayed home, and Bosch claimed fraud.

Then, for the first time in six presidential terms, Balaguer seemed to falter. Inflation doubled, the foreign debt mounted, power blackouts became frequent. Beans, rice, and bread grew scarce. In the face of all this, Balaguer spent millions of dollars on the Columbus Lighthouse, which many Dominicans considered absurd and wasteful. Other huge new public structures were built as well, while the poor were ground further down. Hardly anyone could predict what the president would do when new elections came around again.

In 1994, Balaguer once again announced himself as a candidate. Eighty-six years old and now completely blind, the old caudillo had drifted more and more out of the spotlight, though he continued to maintain a tight rein on politics from behind the scenes. Bosch and Antonio Reynoso, an outspoken priest representing several grassroots minority parties, were the other candidates. The Catholic Church took away Reynoso's parish, but he ran anyway. In near-daily rallies, Balaguer appeared on television, and when election day came around, he appeared to have won, though the other candidates claimed fraud. There were certainly irregularities in the vote, but Balaguer remained in office.

Balaguer ruled under the rubric of his own Partido Reformista Social Cristiano, representing a fusion of parties backed mainly by conservatives. Today, they are opposed by the PRD—the Partido Revolucionario Dominicano, a distinctly social-democratic party which is a member of the Socialist International party—and the old PLD of Bosch.

Recent Elections

A much-anticipated round of democratic elections to replace Balaguer took place in early 1996, with a runoff election in May 1996. The returns from the early elections showed Jose Francisco Peña Gómez holding a plurality, and the country faced the real possibility that a social democrat would once again become president, replacing the long line of conservatives—mainly Balaguer—who have occupied the seat. However, on July 2, 1996, Leonel Fernández, an attorney raised in the United States, edged out Gómez in the runoffs. Balaguer used his support to help Fernández come from behind to win.

After finishing second in the first round on May 16th, Fernández received 51% in the July vote, compared to 49% for Gómez. There was little violence at the polls, and Dominicans seemed to accept the election results without rancor.

Fernández himself pursued a rigorously reformist course of action, a course of action that seemed to shock even the most left-leaning of liberals of his own party. For starters, Fernández retired two dozen generals and asked his defense minister to accept an inquisition by civilian authorities in the government, then fired the defense minister, actions taken all in one week of hectic activity. During that week, most Dominicans expected a military backlash, including some king of martial action, but nothing much happened.

During 1997, Fernández increased the country's teacher salaries by nearly double. Unfortunately, during that same year the performance of the economy did not match Fernández's expectations. Inflation soared as the price of imported oil increased, rice rose above 50 cents a pound, and poor harvests drove prices of onions through the roof. There were many power blackouts, a constant source to frustration for Dominicans, especially those too poor to own their own generators. Political demonstrations by the poor erupted in the towns of Naguabo and Salcedo, where hundreds of demonstrators hurled bombs and one policeman was shot. Demonstrators themselves were pelted with pellets.

Another unfortunate circumstance hampered the well-intentioned Fernández. During the 1998 local and congressional elections, the popular Peña Gómez was running for mayor of Santo Domingo, but died of cancer before the vote. As the lower classes were swept by nostalgia for Gómez, they tended to cast their vote for the PRD, which ultimately took control of Congress, driving a wedge between the executive branch and the ruling legislative party. Thus, the centrist party of Fernández found itself looking for partners in Congress, simply in order to find a majority to pass legislation. In fact, for much of his time in office, Fernández was stymied by the PRD, leaving the country with its longtime problems—lack of a social security system, inadequate schools, poor health care, poor transportation networks.

On the positive side, the elections of 2000 went off without a hitch, and without fraud or violence. Early in the campaign it became clear that the conservative groups and centrists had no genuinely popular or strong candidate to replace the likes of Balaguer. In May 2000, left-leaning populist Hipólito Mejía was declared the winner of the Dominican presidential race after his opponents had withdrawn from a run-off election. Both Danilo Medino of the Dominican Liberation Party and Joaquín Balaguer announced that they were leaving the race because a second round would cause instability and damage the economy. This in itself is a rather amazing change for a country that not so long ago was ruled by a fascist dictator named Trujillo.

Sadly, however, the classes and castes that ultimately make the most important decisions in the Dominican Republic are still mostly blind to its major problems—stratified inequality, environmental damage, low wages, a sugar monoculture, growing drug subcultures (Hispaniola has become a transit point for Colombian cocaine), and sex discrimination. Even in all-inclusive tourism, wages for Dominicans are low and hours long. Haitians are still hated and mistreated badly.

On the positive side, the military is finally under civilian control and Mejía seems to be willing to use his position as president as a bully-pulpit for change. There is still gridlock in Congress, but there is an air of change.

So today the Dominican Republic is a country at peace, and almost at peace with itself. Though there is much concern about prices, brownouts, and poverty, political demonstrations take place openly on Santo Domingo's main streets, politicians campaign freely, and newspapers provide a comparatively open and uncensored flow of information. The country, however, is still watched over very carefully by the police and the army, acting in the interests of those who hold power.

GOVERNMENT

ORGANIZATION

The Dominican Republic adopted a new constitution in 1966, and it remains in place today. At least in theory, the country is a representative democracy, with the customary three branches of government. Of course, the executive is the most important branch of the government, especially given the long tradition of caudillismo. Nominally, the president is elected for a four-year term and is eligible for one more term. The legislature is a bicameral one, consisting of a 27-member senate and a 120-member chamber of deputies. There is a supreme court with nine justices. The judicial branch also includes an attorney general, three courts of appeal, 30 federal courts, and a judge or justice of the peace for each municipality. In the small towns and villages, the local hall houses the justice of the peace—generally a respected elder or lawyer in the community. Disputes are often resolved by town meetings presided over by the justice of the peace, and formal resolutions of these disputes are readily accepted. In these instances, there are no resorts to lawsuits or other kinds of administrative action. It is truly local justice, based on convention and mutual respect.

Administratively, the country is divided into 26 provinces, most of which retain their historical identities from years past. Governors of the districts are appointed by the president. Keep in mind that when a Dominican speaks of "La Vega" or "El Seibo," he more likely means the province than the city itself. These terms for provinces carry a great deal of historical and social weight and mean very specific things to Dominicans. Being from "La Vega" carries much the same kind of social and political freight that being a "Southerner" does for an American or a "Welshman" does for somebody in the United Kingdom. The national district includes the capital city of Santo Domingo. The provinces are further divided into 96 municipalities.

Congress and Elections

The legislature is called the National Assembly. It's housed in an impressive government building in downtown Santo Domingo. A single senator represents each province (plus one from Santo Domingo), and each is elected by direct vote to a four-year term. The members of the Chamber of Deputies come from districts apportioned in accordance with population. The National Assembly meets for two 90-day sessions and has, by law, broad legislative powers, including the right to levy taxes, regulate the debt, approve treaties, and proclaim a national emergency. The provincial governments don't have much power. The nine members of the Supreme Court of Justice are appointed by the Senate for four-year terms, and, in practice, have little judicial independence.

Citizens of age 18 and over can vote, and so can any married person under 18. Voting is supposedly compulsory, though the law isn't much enforced. Elections are held in May and supervised by a three-member Central Electoral Board elected by the Senate.

"STRONG MAN" POLITICS

Historically, the Dominican Republic has been led by strong men, some of whom were megalomaniacal and self serving, others simply corrupt, inefficient, or both. But the truth remains that today Dominican politics is shaped largely by the figure of the president. From the time of Duarte, the "dual caudillos" and Heureaux, Trujillo, Bosch, and Balaguer, the country has been formed not so much by its various constitutions and external relations as by the personality and character of its strong men. Although the Dominican Republic today has a rigid constitution and an increasingly large and entrenched bureaucracy, the president still makes all the decisions, passes on all appointments, and functions as the central authority figure. The president usually proposes formalistic legislation and monitors its enactment.

Balaguer, like most other leaders in Dominican

history, learned to survive in a hostile environment and managed through a system of family, military, and bureaucratic favors. These leaders are almost always masters of public relations, being either brilliant showmen like Trujillo or clever tacticians like Balaguer. Most of the successful big men of the Dominican Republic survived not only by repressing opposition (which they certainly did), but also by being shrewd manipulators, paternalistic benefactors, providers of goods and services to special interest groups, and guardians of Catholic culture.

But it cannot be denied that the old political reality of the Dominican "big man" is rapidly changing. In fact, it may already be a thing of the past. Increasingly, modern authoritarians like Balaguer have gradually realized that democracy is becoming more and more institutionalized and requires greater accountability from its politicians. In his final years in power, Balaguer was forced to recognize that he could no longer run the government as if it were his own private business.

President Mejía, and future presidents of the Dominican Republic, can also look forward to dealing with a host of other, formerly unthinkable pressures—from the International Monetary Fund, labor unions, opposition parties, and the like. More and more, the Dominican people demand that the police and army not exceed their legal mandates for maintaining public order. Though you can still expect to encounter the police and army everywhere you go in the Dominican Republic, it is no longer the threatening experience it once was.

PRESENT-DAY POLITICAL DIVISIONS

The real tension in present-day Dominican politics involves, on one side, the old school of conservative interests and some elements of the emerging middle class (all represented more or less by Balaguer and his like) and, on the other side, the rural and urban poor, students, intellectuals, and labor. Generally speaking, the U.S. embassy sides with the conservative groups. Balaguer's party, an amalgamation of his former reform party and the Christian Social Revolutionary Party (CSRP), has never truly developed a cohesive or ideologically well-defined

organization. Although the Christian party did have a well-defined platform and some hazy goals, after its merger with Balaguer's party, these dwindled until the modern CSRP really only became a vehicle for the election of a strong president who represents old interests.

On the other hand, the PRD, which held power twice during the 1980s, is one of the earliest social-democratic reform parties in Latin America, with a proud heritage of opposition to Trujillo. Once Juan Bosch left this party to form his own PLD, the PRD quickly veered towards a more traditionally Dominican political philosophy, seeking power for power's sake rather than as a tool for social improvement. Although Juan Bosch continues to champion the poor, he is aging and no longer a satisfactory alternative for the many Dominicans who long for change.

There are perhaps 18 or 19 other recognized political parties in the country, including a small communist party. The real struggle in party politics involves developing a true party organization with commitment to principles and programs, to serve ends and means, and not just as a vehicle for the advancement of a single politician's career.

Outlook

In the recent past, the poor and laboring classes in urban areas have begun to demonstrate increasing dissatisfaction with politics as usual. During the early 1990s, corruption seemed to have reached its peak, forcing an austerity plan which hit consumers and laborers particularly hard. In the fall of 1990, and again in July 1991, the population showed its general disgust by staging strikes and stoppages, but Balaguer brutally put these down. The social situation that produces this epidemic dissatisfaction is all too common in Latin America: a wide divergence between the rich and poor. Many Dominicans have trouble obtaining basic necessities, while a small minority enjoys fabulous wealth. This marginalization presents a major roadblock to democratization, and all of this uncertainty places an emerging middle class, particularly in major cities like Santo Domingo and Santiago, in a delicate and increasingly untenable position.

The political problems confronting Dominicans today include not only democratization, wealth distribution, pollution, and social stability, but also the "Haitian problem." For many years, the international community has expressed concern over the treatment of Haitian *braceros*—sugarcane workers—many of whom are imported to work in fields and held in virtual bondage. At first, Balaguer promised to rectify the problem. Then, in June 1991, he deported all the workers back to Haiti, attempting to turn the problem of illegal bondage into the problem of illegal immigration. Today, many illegal-immigrant Haitians continue to work in the Dominican Republic, usually in low-paying menial or agricultural jobs.

Lest this sound rather grim, keep in mind that the Dominican Republic has come a long way from the darkness of the Trujillo regime, a mere 35 years ago. Although many of the political parties have no broad support or structure, they operate with relative freedom and are beginning to widen their ideological stances. The Dominican people are an industrious lot with great integrity and cultural grit, who have worked their way out of tough situations before. There is a widespread love of learning and art, which bodes well for the future of any country. As the octogenarians who have dominated politics for 40 years pass on, new and more vigorous leaders have emerged—leaders who represent not only their own families of followers, but wider groups as well.

ECONOMY

Columbus introduced sugarcane to Hispaniola. Today, sugar—once cultivated by slaves, owned by largely absent plantaon landlords, and exported under strictly monopolistic trade policies to Spanish interests—is the dominant agricultural product of the Dominican Republic. Traditionally, the nation has so depended upon sugar that any price fluctuation—usually down—has caused unimpeded ripples throughout the economy. The United States, along with Puerto Rico, buys fully two-thirds of Dominican exports, and so in addition to its sugar dependence, the Dominican Republic's economy also suffers from an extreme sensitivity to the fortunes and whims of the United States.

Now that the country is moving away from one-man rule and into multiparty democracy, many forward-looking people believe it's time for the Republic to grow out of its status as an underdeveloped nation with a single-crop economy and into a new one allowing more diverse production modes and sources of income.

Toward the end of diversifying the economy, Dominicans are working to create a mixture of light manufacturing, mining, tourism, and modern agriculture, which will lessen foreign dependence and vulnerability to frequent price fluctuations. Still, the per capita income of the Dominican Republic is US$1,000, compared to about US$5,000 in Puerto Rico and nearly US$20,000 in the United States itself. Anywhere from 500,000 to one million Dominicans live abroad, escaping to America and Puerto Rico—aspirations manifest in both popular song and widespread visa fraud.

AGRICULTURE

Once you get away from the swirling traffic of Santo Domingo, or the fashionable and crowded shopping streets of Santiago, you'll see the real Dominican Republic, the country where nearly half the population toils as rural farmers who own or sharecrop small parcels of land. Production per acre on these small parcels is extremely low, and wages are shameful. Most laborers and field hands operate without the benefit of any modern forms of labor regulations, insurance, or minimum wage. In the mountains of the Cordillera Central, in the hinterlands of eastern La Altagracia, and all up and down the western borderlands, you can see these farmers struggling on their tiny parcels.

But small farms are only part of the story of agriculture in the Dominican Republic. Nearly half of the agricultural land is divided into 100-hectare parcels, but these constitute less than one percent of all enterprises. Three-quarters of all agricultural enterprises cover less than five hectares, but together these do not amount to 10% of the agricultural land. These statistics tell a simple story: the richest 10% of farmers control 70% of the land. This concentration of land ownership was stimulated by the creation of the modern sugar industry late in the 19th century and increased considerably during the United States occupation of 1916–22. During the Trujillo regime, large farmers got larger and richer. Although this agrarian structure is not as imbalanced as in pre-revolutionary Cuba, land reform is still an urgent necessity.

Agriculture dominates almost every geographical area of the country, save for the zone around Santo Domingo and the wild regions south of Samaná Bay. Most of the Cibao and the south coast are parceled for humid crops; the Valle de San Juan, the Enriquillo Depression, and the Baní Plain are all irrigated. The Trujillo regime encouraged the development of agricultural colonies along the Haitian border and in the Cordillera Central. Foreigners—particularly Japanese, Hungarian, and Spanish immigrants—populated some of these colonies.

Sugarcane

The most important export crop in the Dominican Republic is sugarcane. Amazingly, this wasn't always so, mainly because the Spanish colonists had no effective means of bringing in the large number of slaves needed to cultivate the crop on massive plantations. Modern production began in the late 19th century, when wars forced many Cuban planters to move to Hispaniola. In 1921, sugar exports exceeded all other exports by over 400%. At the same time, the number of plantations steadily decreased, while their acreage increased, until by 1925, only 21 estates remained, with 12 of those U.S.-owned. In the early Trujillo years, sugar made up 67% of exports by itself. Modern sugar exports constitute less than 50%, and that fraction is falling. The downside of sugar dependence includes foreign domination of the economy, extreme fluctuations in prices, and the inability of locals to produce subsistence foods. In addition, many small farmers have been forced from land ownership or sharecropping into peonage. In the 1920s, when sugar was king of the island, large estates would sometimes forcibly drive village landholders off their land or cheat them out of vague land titles by legal hoodwinkery.

Lately, the practice of importing labor from Haiti and the Windward Islands has led to lower wages and decreased standards of living for sugar workers. Quotas established by the United States have been dropping every year, and in 1988, they reached their lowest level since 1875.

Now, wherever you drive along the coastal plain east and west of Santo Domingo or into the eastern provinces of El Seibo and La Altagracia, you'll see miles of sugarcane, with *braceros* on horseback riding to and from their work. Cane cutters, many of them illegal Haitian immigrants, make about US$1.50 a day for cutting approximately one ton of cane. They bathe in irrigation ditches, wash their clothes and defecate in those same ditches, and live in shanty towns. All of this takes place in a tranquil, dramatically beautiful country.

Coffee

Coffee is the second-largest export crop, cultivated mainly on small peasant holdings. Introduced in 1715, coffee farms are usually located on steep or rolling hills on the slopes of upland valleys. The mountains of the Bahoruco and the Cordillera Central, and the slopes of the Cibao, produce a variety of high-quality arabica coffee.

Cacao production, which is mainly from the Vega Real and the humid lowlands near Sabana del Mar, constitutes the third most valuable crop of the Dominican Republic and is also cultivated mainly on small holdings.

Food Crops

The Dominican Republic is very lucky to be able to produce most of its own food. Mainly because of colonization efforts on the interior of the island, rice, bananas, maize, and peanuts all constitute significant crops, and many small farmers grow sweet potatoes, peas, red beans, and cassava (or manioc). The bananas are usually grown on medium-size to large plantations, while vegetable crops remain the province of small farmers. Many of the upland valleys produce significant crops of cabbage, tomatoes, onions, radishes, and garlic. Fruit abounds in the Dominican Republic, and stands on every corner and on every highway abound in pineapples, oranges, mangos, and even apples and grapes.

Tobacco

Of great importance in the Cibao is the tobacco industry. Tobacco cultivation began there in 1531, and today Dominican tobacco and the cigars produced around Santiago are world famous.

Industrial Agriculture

Industrial agriculture has recently shown its face in the Dominican Republic, with foreign companies now growing pineapples, melons, oranges, olives, and cashews. The American company Dole has taken the lead in producing pineapples, investing $41 million in the nation so far.

Livestock

Livestock-raising has always constituted an important activity in the Dominican Republic. In fact, until the rise of the sugar industry in the late 19th century, the raising of stock was the most important branch of the economy. Though extensive cattle farming is no longer the rule in all parts of the country, cattle ranches still dominate the upland ranges of El Seibo, La Altagracia, and the Cibao. The million cattle still roaming Dominican pastures descend from a small original variety called the *crillo,* although now many ranchers also raise Holstein, Zebu, Jersey, and brown Swiss cattle. Dairy farmers currently use the milk to make cheese.

Although few commercial farms raise pigs, pork also constitutes an important food product. Pigs swarm in small villages, eating refuse and royal palm nuts.

Last come the ubiquitous goats, roaming the farms and barrios. Dominicans milk goats and eat them, using their delicious meat in many Creole stews and soups.

INDUSTRY

For much of Dominican history, the country has been predominantly rural. The average Dominican worked a parcel of land or was involved in the food industry at the village level. Hence, the main industry was sugar. During the Trujillo era, however, industrialization took a great step forward. Sugar and its related processing industries are still major players in the Dominican economy, but there has been a lot of diversification recently into consumer goods, flour milling, brewing, and textiles. The cement and construction industries are growing, and the Dominican Republic produces clothes, footwear,

sugarcane

processed food, and soft drinks. Millions of bottles of rum are produced here each year, though none are exported.

Balaguer hoped that so-called duty-free zones would help develop the economy, and indeed, in almost every provincial town you'll find such a zone. Located in La Romana, San Pedro de Macorís, Puerto Plata, Santiago, Azua, Barahona, El Seibo, Higüey, La Vega, and Baní, these zones use tax exemptions, cheap labor, low customs duties, and an absence of unions to entice foreign corporations to manufacture textiles, footwear, electronic components, and leather goods. Multinational firms operating out of these zones must pay all rent and salaries in U.S. dollars through the Central Bank. Even so, these zones have only slightly reduced the pressing problem of external debt and underemployment.

Mineral Deposits

Although the fantasies of Columbus dwarfed the actual realized gold production on Hispaniola, the island was, in fact, once an important source of the precious metal. For many years, a state-run gold mine generated significant revenue for the Dominican Republic and, as late as 1983, produced nearly $450 million in foreign cash— the top industry after tourism. Unfortunately for the government, the mine is now closed, awaiting new technology. Gold deposits still exist near Miches, Villa Altagracia, and in the Cordillera Central. The one major gold mine in the country, located near Pueblo Viejo, has been nationalized for many years and is operated by the state-run Rosario Dominicana. Prior to 1994, this mine produced oxide ores in open pits. Apparently there are vast reserves locked inside sulfide ores, such ores being much harder to smelt than simple oxide ores. President Balaguer stopped investment in expensive equipment to unlock sulfide ores because he feared such investment would stop the flow of cash coming from the mine, thus preventing him from raking in its profit. Thus, for five years, 1994–1999, the mine lost considerable money from its failure to upgrade equipment and from consistent mismanagement. When Fernández became president, he talked about privatizing the mine and finding a foreign company to invest in new equipment. However, the opposition parties opposed privatization, and foreign companies are reluctant to enter a heavy capital system where political accountability, stability, and a favorable tax climate are absent.

However, Pueblo Viejo is still one of the richest gold mines in the world. The problem is that sulfide ores are difficult to extract, expensive, and dirty. At present, three of the world's biggest names in gold mining are waiting for a resolution of this problem. But even more important, perhaps, is the ecological situation. Pueblo Viejo isn't very far from the Samaná Bay and peninsula, and all rivers from there flow north and east into the bay. Mine drainage is heavily laden with metals and is very acidic. Right now the operation has no money for pollution control. If the day comes when sulfide ores are mined at Pueblo Viejo, expect major damage to Samaná.

Other mineral deposits were not surveyed in the Dominican Republic until after World War II.

Today, however, there is a considerable amount of mining of other deposits. A Canadian company currently mines nickel around Bonao. Nickel is, in fact, the nation's most significant mineral deposit today. A major salt deposit is located in the southwest in the Valle de Neiba, and salt is reclaimed from seawater along the coast between Santo Domingo and Barahona. Miners also extract granite and marble in the desert southwest, and the Dominican soil continues to yield ornamental stones like onyx and travertine. Amber and larimar are the most significant gemstones. The Sierra de Bahoruco's bauxite deposits have been exploited off and on since 1959. Dominican officals harbor hope of finding oil off the coastal town of Azua, and search concessions have been let.

Although manufacturing, mining, and sugar refining continue to grow as constituent elements in the Dominican economy, progressive labor laws and higher wages have not followed. Very few workers belong to organized labor unions, and the minimum wage stands at RD$1,450 a month. Current labor laws prohibit public workers from striking. Labor unions are currently very divided and often allied to a political party, making them hardly independent. A third of all Dominicans are underemployed, and just as many are unemployed. Given that about 40% of the present population is between the ages of 18 and 29, and many of these are educated and literate, the lack of job opportunities makes for considerable unhappiness and social tension.

The lack of funds for government programs needed to develop the economy is partly due to a lax tax policy, which allows many wealthy business owners to avoid annual land, property, and capital-gains taxes. In a growing economy, where educational levels and social expectations continue to increase, this lack of a responsible tax and fiscal policy has contributed to a visible malaise.

Fishing and Forestry

The relatively minor fishing and forestry industries round out the Dominican economic picture. For many years, logging went unrestricted in the Dominican Republic, leading to massive deforestation, consequent degradation of the environment, and eventual destruction of the forestry industry itself. Tree cutting has been illegal since

1967, but clandestine logging still occurs. Goats and cattle are now the prime deforesters, but the Dominican people seem to have a good understanding of the need for trees on mountain slopes and upland valleys.

Most fishing is small in scale and not very commercial. Samaná Bay and Monte Cristi are the prime commercial fishing areas, with shrimp, mackerel, and red snapper the major catches.

Foreign Investment

Foreign investment, mostly from the United States, has proved a mixed blessing for the Dominican economy. Many United States multinationals operate here, including Esso, Alcoa, 3M, Xerox, Gillette, Colgate-Palmolive, and Phillip Morris, mostly in Balaguer's "economic free zones." Dominicans in and out of government fear the power of these huge industrial and consumer manufacturing firms, especially in the areas of labor exploitation and political influence. Perhaps part of the problem stems from Gulf and Western's reign as prime developer of resort and sugar property in the La Romana region. For decades, Gulf and Western operated resorts and refineries in the Dominican Republic with wily and brutal tactics, including, some believed, union busting and bribery.

While it operated its far-flung operation and invested over $200 million, the corporation's annual sales soon exceeded the nation's GNP. In 1966, the company moved to replace the sugar cutters' union with a nationally controlled union. At one point, the company owned 2 percent of the land in the Dominican Republic. This was especially galling to a nation where 75 percent of the population was landless. Besides owning its own resorts of Casa de Campo and Altos de Chavón, Gulf and Western operated virtually restriction-free in its own industrial zone and ran major resort hotels in Santo Domingo.

In 1985, the corporation sold its holdings to the notorious Fanjul family of Cuba and south Florida. Part of a long bloodline of Cuban sugar and real estate tycoons, the Fanjul brothers, Alfonso and José, today control Gulf and Western's old properties, though they keep a much lower profile. Even so, when Balaguer was in office, the owners would occasionally loan him their Learjet, while holding their laborers in virtual bondage through low wages and bad conditions.

Public Sector

The public sector problems in the Dominican economy continue to cripple the country's surge to development. When the Trujillo regime fell in 1961, the governments that followed sometimes pledged to distribute Trujillo's holdings to the people. In reality, they generally wound up practicing a kind of ugly socialism. One branch, called the Consejo Estatal de Azúcar (State Sugar Council), operates sugarcane refineries, while another, the Corporación de Fomento Industrial (State Enterprises Corporation), operates a variety of companies. Perhaps the biggest white elephant is the state-owned Dominican Electricity Corporation, which causes many brownouts and blackouts in major metropolitan areas.

When you added together all state enterprises (including a few tourist hotels), the public sector accounted for nearly 20% of the Dominican GNP during the 1980s. Despite promises to the contrary, almost every government—including those of Blanco and Guzmán—have increased the size of the Dominican "civil service," a bureaucracy which is often a haven for the president's friends, family, and loyal party followers.

The Oil Problem

Oil dependency is a persistent problem in the Dominican Republic. Though world oil prices have plummeted since 1983, sugar prices have dropped even more dramatically, so that the amount of sugar necessary to buy a barrel of oil has steadily increased. Consequently, the Dominican Republic has a hard time buying the oil it needs to run its transport industry and generate its electricity.

Foreign Dependence

Moreover, because the United States buys two-thirds of Dominican exports, any recession or change in taste in the United States severely impacts the Dominican deficit. In order to maintain the cash accounts necessary to purchase needed imports and service its debt, the Dominican government is forced to rely on a number of international and bilateral sources for loans. The World Bank and the Inter-American Development Bank have loaned the country money, as have the United States, Italy, Japan, and Germany. Given remittances by the many Dominicans living abroad and foreign exchange generated by tourism, the problem of the balance of payments is always an extremely delicate one.

Outlook

It's easy to be pessimistic about prospects for growth and responsible development in the Dominican Republic. Transportation is underdeveloped, with many bad roads and no superior airline service from city to city. While some argue that the country has been hampered by its relatively small population (eight million), others view the recent population boom as a liability, creating a strain on educational and agricultural resources in a country that can barely afford what it has, let alone provide for many more mouths yearly.

Nevertheless, there is some room for optimism as well. The prospect of improved agriculture bodes well, as does the increasing world impetus toward free trade and regional trade pacts. Tourism could act as a catalyst for growth in other areas. Already, young people are training themselves for jobs in airlines, travel agencies, and education—jobs that require advanced skills and know-how. Nearly half of all Dominicans are under age 14, and if these young people can obtain decent educations, their prospects may improve. As many as 500 Dominicans a week, most of them young, flee across the Mona Passage to Puerto Rico in search of better opportunities.

It seems to me that people are perhaps the Dominican economy's greatest asset. Everywhere you go in the Dominican Republic, you meet young people who are intelligent, able, and ambitious. Many of them are students with diverse interests in business, literature, and travel. They carry expanding hopes and ever-widening horizons in which they see themselves as integral members of a democratic country actively involved in self-development. Right now, the Dominican Republic is walking a tightrope. Though the margin for error is small, the mood seems confident and determined.

TOURISM

Talk about the tourism industry with Dominicans and you'll find them deeply divided. Some see tourism as the new sugar industry, binding the people to a single source of income heavily dependent upon foreign sources. There are now 28,000 hotel rooms in the Dominican Republic, and the government touts the country as the "best-kept secret in the Caribbean." Tourism accounts for more than 13% of the GNP and employs thousands of Dominicans as baggage handlers, cab drivers, maids, waiters, groundskeepers, and cashiers—not high-paying positions, it's true, but jobs nonetheless. And this is where opinion divides. Some argue that such jobs are demeaning and dead end. Others argue that tourism promotes civil stability and encourages government officials to try to solve problems peacefully rather than through force and violence, which scares away the tourist dollar.

To monitor the tourist industry and plan its growth, the government has created the Department of Tourist Investment and Infrastructure (INFRATUR), a Central Bank agency, designed to invest in tourist-related infrastructure such as roads, sewers, water systems, and airports. Maintaining a visible tourist-information service in places like New York, Toronto, Montreal, and at Dominican embassies throughout Europe and Latin America, the government has devoted itself to tourism regardless of the social consequences. There is also a Tourist Incentive Law, which allows companies a tax exemption on construction, licenses, and capital gains.

Dominicans themselves are a reserved but friendly people, with great integrity and charm. They seem aware that the tourist dollar, mark, and franc are whimsical at best, and that tourism is a mixed blessing.

PEOPLE

Let's say you're spending a lovely afternoon in Santo Domingo, the Dominican Republic's dynamic metropolitan capital. You've been walking for an hour in one of the busy neighborhoods like Gazcue, spending time looking in one or two of the many shops selling antiques or serious art, and you've had lunch in a busy and excellent restaurant, then continued your walk beneath the shade of the old mahogany trees lining the narrow streets. As you pass well-appointed homes with Japanese and American cars in the driveways, you may well see a political gathering on the street, watched over by soldiers and police. All around you, people of many colors go about their daily chores: businesspersons, street vendors, shoeshine boys, and government officials. On almost every corner, you pass a busy open-air grocery or small bar bursting with merengue music. Lines of uniformed schoolchildren pass by on their way to class. Many of the stone walls surrounding larger houses and public buildings are hung with political signs in Spanish, each urging the reader to vote or think a certain way. You walk by a music conservatory, an art gallery, more shops, and middle-class homes. In all this, what never leaves you is the music and the smell of delicious food.

The name for this culture is "Creole," from a Spanish word, criar, meaning "to rear." During the time of the Mexican conquest, the term came to apply to any person of Spanish descent born in the New World, which meant that, somehow, the person was not quite authentic. As time went on, "Creole" was distinguished from "mulatto," which meant a person with African blood. Creole culture, especially in Mexico, came to be a very rigid kind of social structure, based primarily upon race and color. As time went on, however, the colors and races became more and more mixed, until whole new cultures grew up in place of the old rigid structures, and a completely new kind of culture came to be. African slaves, brought to the Caribbean against their will, synthesized Catholicism with their own religion and invented new musical forms from the raw materials of Spanish ballads and their own African music. Europeans,

too, after many years of separation from Europe, had to invent a new culture. Thus, whole new languages, crafts, music, art, and religions arose in the Caribbean.

First inhabited by Taínos, then conquered by Spaniards, fought over by French and Haitians, bombarded by Dutch and English, and later settled by Arabs and Lebanese, the Dominican Republic has a fully developed, eclectic Creole culture like nowhere else in the Caribbean. Of course, most people know that Dominicans play their own music, called merengue, and have adopted American baseball with a passion. But in the Cibao, French ballads and dances are also common. English Victorian gingerbread architecture abounds in rural districts, and open-air restaurants throughout the country serve up Cuban sandwiches. Nowadays, you can even buy allegedly Italian pizza that's no different from the fast-food varieties found anywhere else.

Creole culture is exciting because it is genuine. American cable and satellite television threaten it today, as American cultural imperialism threatens just about everything, but for now anyway, going to the Dominican Republic remains a truly distinct social and cultural experience.

ETHNIC DIVISIONS

Just as Dominican society is divided sharply between rich and poor, so is it divided along racial lines. And while race divides Dominicans less sharply than wealth, skin color tends to distinguish upper class from lower class, a reflection of historical realities inherited from the earliest days of Spanish rule.

A recent census counted 7,300,000 people in the Dominican Republic. That figure is probably low, given the fact that, as with all of its Latin neighbors, the country has a very high birth rate. Most Dominicans live either in Santo Domingo, with its bustling and near-to-bursting population approaching two million, or in the fruitful and lush Cibao Valley, where a clutch of towns runs along the valley floor from Santiago to La Vega and San Francisco de Macorís. The population density has reached 150 people per kilometer.

Light-skinned Dominicans call themselves white and may be of unmixed European ancestry. They constitute about 16% of the population, while blacks make up about 11%. The majority of Dominicans—about 73% overall—are of mixed ancestry and may call themselves Indians or mulattos. Many other peoples live in the Dominican Republic as well, including immigrants from Haiti, Lebanon, China, Italy, France, Japan, and the United States. The Asian communities in the Dominican Republic are small but viable; mountainous Constanza is a particularly strong Japanese farming enclave. Descendants of European Jews still live in Sosúa on the north coast.

Race and Class

Trujillo called his national ideology *hispanidad,* which defined Dominicans as the most Spanish people in the Americas. The practical result of this ideology was a pyramidal social system in which the primary division separates the gentility, called *la gente buena* or *la gente culta,* from the common people. The elites strive to adhere to traditional Hispanic ideals—dignity, leisure, grandeur, and generosity—while the common people struggle for day-to-day existence. Historically, about the only opening for the common people has been the military, where it is still possible for a black or mulatto to have a respectable career.

The blacks of the Dominican Republic are descended from either Haiti or America. In fact, many Dominican blacks can trace their ancestry to former American slaves who immigrated from Philadelphia and Baltimore in the early 19th century and settled in the Samaná Bay region, forming a small and very compact Protestant minority. Today, many of the descendents of those ex-slaves still live in Samaná (though many more have migrated to Santo Domingo) and are intermarrying with other Dominicans.

The descendents of white colonists form the original landed gentry and civilian leadership. They'll tell you that Santiago de los Caballeros (Santiago of the Gentlemen) is one of the purest Hispanic cities in America. Founded in 1500, this town originally allowed only Spanish

colonists to settle there. The town of Baní, on the southern coast, also pretends to a pure Spanish heritage, because its original inhabitants came exclusively from Spain's Canary Islands in the early 1800s.

But the vast majority of all Dominicans are mulatto, and they form the backbone of both rural and urban society. Mulattos dominate the military and have contributed more of the country's presidents than any other group. Even today, Trujillo is thought of as the archetypical mulatto of the middle class, who rose through society to power and prestige.

The Historical Creole

In many ways, Dominican society reflects a social system shared by many other Caribbean countries. Carribean islands all experienced the early extermination of native peoples, followed by a repopulation by white European landowners and black African slaves. In socioeconomic terms, Creole societies share a common plantation heritage, along with the subsequent social stratification that continues to divide the population. As in most Caribbean countries, in the Dominican Republic, the possession or nonpossession of various physical attributes determines a person's stratum, and consequently his/her access to power, wealth, and land. As a result, even at this point in Caribbean history, large segments of every island's population remain unintegrated and share no common ideology.

Original Creole culture is consonant with slavery. During the early days, there was a constant inflow of slaves into the Caribbean. For those slaves imported to work on Caribbean sugar plantations, life was even harsher than for slaves on American cotton plantations. Given the harder, more physical nature of sugar plantation work, Caribbean plantation owners saw no reason to purchase the less-hardy female slaves, who generally produced less work and died earlier than the males. With this sort of policy in effect, islands soon had few women and almost no black women. Eighteenth-century statistics show most islands with upwards of 75% male populations. At times, the power of imported women proved even stronger than the power of armies, as in the surge of the French in the 16th century toward Haiti. The French advanced their takeover of the western end of Hispaniola by sending women to the island to turn the buccaneers into farmers and family men. Likewise, the British advanced their colonization of Jamaica when Oliver Cromwell sent 1,000 Irish women to the island (involuntarily, I might add).

With this kind of male/female imbalance, what few dark women there were quickly became an acceptable alternative for white men. Throughout the history of the Caribbean, reports filter out about this activity, which caused concern in the courts of Europe. But there were simply not enough eligible women in the Caribbean for island residents to quibble about race. Then, especially in Spanish colonies, free blacks began to make up larger and larger portions of the population. Some were former slaves who had accumulated enough capital to buy their freedom; others had received their freedom in the wills of appreciative masters. Likewise, it was considered good form for a master to free the children of his slave mistress.

As blacks and whites came to share a culture, members of this growing mulatto presence began to live a more normal life, partly because there were more and more mulatto women to go around. White men took mulatto wives because they were readily available. Mulatto women themselves were usually open to white lovers, thinking that this would lighten their children and thus improve their lives. Black males also wanted mulatto women, to lighten the color of their own children.

Mulattos continued to achieve status in Caribbean society until about the late 18th century, when whites began to fear their emerging power and numbers. In many countries, including Jamaica and Haiti, whites passed strict racial laws placing limits on what mulattos could inherit and the amount of property or slaves they could own, and even banning mulattos from certain professions. The most absurd and ridiculous of these racial laws were adopted by the French colonies, especially Haiti, which attempted to categorize people by fractions of blood, down to a dozen subclassifications. But even British Jamaican law had its racial absurdities, defining class, privilege, and legal entitlement strictly by blood. The Dominican Republic never had strict racial laws on the French model, though its traditions remain distinctly Creole, giving credence to racial categorization in subtle and influential ways.

Throughout the Caribbean, the goal of many mulattos was to move their descendants upward through the racial social scale by making white offspring. This constant search by many mulatto women for white heirs sank many inheritance laws into a quagmire, because many children were born out of wedlock. Some colonies like Cuba and Suriname had administrative boards that decided who could marry whom and under what conditions, granting or refusing marriage to interracial couples in the hope that the race would lighten as it went along.

Perhaps the most infamous of all "race whiteners" was Rafael Trujillo, who was notorious for using pancake makeup. He was just a shade too dark for his own taste and in his later years would chase away photographers when his makeup began to crack under hot lights or midday heat.

Nevertheless, despite a number of typical Caribbean characteristics, the Dominican Republic differs from most of its island neighbors in several ways. For one thing, blacks do not enjoy a majority in the Dominican Republic—one of the few Caribbean countries in which this is true. The Dominican population is instead largely mulatto. While this fact has helped make Dominicana a unique Caribbean culture, it has also shaped racial attitudes in unfortunate ways.

The first thing that Trujillo did in racial terms was turn his attention to the Haitians. For years, Haitians had gone across the border to the Dominican Republic in order to cut cane on plantations. Many stayed on and intermarried with Dominicans. Haitians were darkening the Dominican people, or at least so Trujillo thought, based upon his purported experience as a guard on a sugar estate. In 1937, Trujillo sent his soldiers to the border regions to "trap a Congo," as he put it, instructing the soldiers to carry a sprig of parsley, or *perejil* in Spanish. Creole, the language of the Haitian peasant, has no Spanish "j," which is pronounced hard against the back of the throat, nor any specific "r," which in Creole is pronounced like "w." In that year alone, Dominican soldiers killed 20,000 peasants who could not pronounce the word for parsley.

Even today, some Dominicans, though surely not all, are slightly obsessed with Haiti and Haitians. The words "Haitiano" and "Negro" have become interchangeable. Many Dominicans, believing that Haitians threaten the national culture, avoid intermarriages and oppose Haitian immigration.

As late as 1983, President Balaguer published a book entitled *La Isla al Revés (The Island in Reverse),* in which he produces a paranoid picture of Haiti as bent on cultural conquest. In the book, he argues that Haiti wants a "pacifistic penetration of Dominican territory" and that Haitians, as blacks, are a threat to Dominican culture because blacks have a "characteristic fecundity." As if that weren't enough, Balaguer identifies Haitians as the carriers of many dangerous diseases, such as malaria and syphilis, and presents them as barbarians who are "morally deformed." The book, reprinted five times, never created a stir in the country or negatively affected Balaguer's standing whatsoever.

As a practical matter, Dominicans avoid calling themselves mulattos. If they have "white features" and reasonably "good hair," then they're white. In fact, "good hair" is one of the most prized natural attributes in the Dominican Republic. Sometimes, a person will be termed an *indio* if his hair is a little suspect. If the skin is very dark and the hair very wiry, the term is likely to be *Indio oscuro* (dark Indian). Dominican officials still use these labels sometimes, and there are places on Dominican passports where these denominations still appear. In Haiti, on the other hand, whites are so rare that the word *blan* means both white and foreign.

Another reason that the Dominican Republic is not typically Caribbean is Rafael Trujillo himself. Before Trujillo, the country was just another traditional, segmented Caribbean society; class lines had fixed boundaries. Then Trujillo came on the scene, bringing his mulatto heritage with him. During his long dictatorship he conducted, in effect, a controlled social experiment in which the political structure did not change but the underlying social and economic elements were shuffled about willy-nilly (all to serve Trujillo, of course). A mulatto middle class of businessmen, industrialists, and military officers was created, and both the church and the notion of the extended family were challenged. It was a cruel irony that while the society itself was mixing, political control was not. When Trujillo was finally assassinated, it left the Dominican Republic in turmoil—with a society and culture that was profoundly mulatto but a power structure that was entirely elitist. It was a formula for confusion.

Perhaps the most important way in which the Dominican Republic differs from its Caribbean neighbors is that Dominicans boast the purest Spanish traditions in the Western Hemisphere—far purer than those found in, say, Mexico. Almost all Dominicans are practicing Roman Catholics, and Dominican family structure and values further reflect Spanish culture. Consequently, no matter where you go in the Dominican Republic, save for those areas characterized by what I'll call "international tourist culture," the predominant feeling is of being in provincial Spain.

CLASS STRUCTURE

The Elites

Because there was so much turmoil and war during the Dominican Republic's early history, the development of the nation's aristocratic landowning class had to wait until almost the end of the 19th century, nearly 200 years later than in most other Latin American countries. Now, however, the primary social identity of many white elites is through kinship ties, which also is a pool from which business partners and political allies are selected.

In the major cities of Santo Domingo and Santiago, the upper class is composed of *la gente de primera* (first people) and *la gente de segunda* (second people). The first group is comprised of approximately 100 families that constitute the cream of the crop of the upper classes, referred to in slang as the *tutumpote* (totem pole), implying that they concern themselves with their ancestry. Families who achieved success around the turn of the century and came to prominence during the age of Trujillo compose the second group; these are called the *nuevos ricos* (nouveaux riches).

The geographic center for the elite is still the Cibao region, especially the city of Santiago, whose people consider themselves the pinnacle of Dominican society. These elites are focused on business and property, which, they consider, are more courtly pursuits than politics and the professions, which tend to be the interest of elites in Santo Domingo. The family is the bulwark of the elite class, which tends to center its social lives around family rather than social clubs or professional associations. The matriarch of

THE FIRST MESTIZO?

One of Columbus's principal officers on his second voyage to the New World was Miguel Díaz. During the troubled crossing, many officers and men became embroiled in quarrels and controversy, and the voyage ended badly. While Columbus was away from La Isabela, Díaz, who was out of favor with the admiral, left with some compatriots for the south of Hispaniola, where a Taíno tribe received them cordially. A female chief named Zacatecas fell in love with Díaz, who was as much interested in gold as anything else. In order to avoid losing her handsome officer, Zacatecas showed Díaz some gold deposits near the Haina River, which Díaz reported to Columbus in order to regain his favor.

The queen Zacatecas became a Christian and took the name Catalina. Díaz and Catalina had two children together—the first officially recorded offspring of a European-Indian marriage. In the Caribbean and Central America, this combination of people became known as mestizo.

the family still tends to manipulate marriage, so as to preserve a closed and exalted position. Most families try to point to an independently preserved tradition in which the acceptance of outsiders is rare. Sometimes members of the Lebanese or Syrian elites have married into old families, but it is less common for *nuevos ricos* to gain admittance into the inner circle of Santiago's elite.

Wealth is a kind of secondary factor to family status. Some family fortunes were made in rum and tobacco, while some were based on land ownership. The lifestyle of the *primera* is not necessarily ostentatious, though many maintain country homes in addition to their urban residences. Education plays a large part in retaining elite status, and families are very careful to send their girls to private Roman Catholic schools and their boys abroad, especially to Spain, whenever possible. The Church is a less important socializing factor, particularly since politics may come between an elite and his fellow parishioners.

Traditionally, the upper class has taken the lead in civilian government, especially in cabinet positions. The upper class can be found throughout the political spectrum, from left to right. Only during the Trujillo regime was the system of civilian elite leadership seriously undermined. Even today, the military and the elite are separated by a gulf in class, education, and temperament. The upper class in the Dominican Republic is by no means without social conscience. In fact, they often take a paternalistic attitude toward the lower classes. Unfortunately, this tends to increase the gulf. The upper class tends to concern itself with broad international issues, too, such as sugar prices, United States power and investment, trade, and tourism. As in any small group of hidebound traditionalists, gossip is chronic in the upper classes.

The Growing Middle Class
Throughout most of its history, the Dominican Republic simply didn't have a middle class to speak of. Dominicans were either rich or poor, and the society did not have the breadth of professional or business activity to develop a middle group of wage and salary earners. By the 1970s, however, during Balaguer's "miracle," a respectable middle class came into being, although nobody can say with any precision how many

people belong to it. A likely guess is that 30% of today's population belongs to this class, concentrated among Santo Domingo's salaried professionals and civil servants. This group of newly rich, modestly respectable persons—mostly mulattos of mixed shades of color—began to seek nontraditional avenues of economic activity, forming a classic bourgeoisie involved in professions, real estate, imports, and tourism. The sector tries to observe the traditional Hispanic values dictated and preserved by the elite. Color, family, and personal characteristics are very important among the middle class, and slight gradations of skin color can have lasting effects on business and personal relations.

The middle class is involved in a constant effort to move from blue collar to white collar to professional positions, while disdaining manual labor. Young middle-class students often want to be doctors, lawyers, and engineers rather than scientists or technicians, which they associate with manual labor. These days, however, with the expansion of science and technology (the Dominican Republic has cable TV and computer modems everywhere), technical professions are becoming more desirable.

The middle class acts as the vanguard of whatever impetus there is for social change. Because these middle-class people are somewhat insecure (neither poor nor exactly rich), they are not as bound to tradition as the elite and can demonstrate a willingness to change and adapt. They are very ambitious and upwardly mobile, tending to live beyond their means at times. They are also politically active, and not as bound to their families, inclining to join social clubs and political groups. Still, they like to think of themselves as part of la gente buena and, when they're on display, try to adopt the attitudes and fashions of the elite. On the other hand, the elites resent what they see as a penetration of their social sphere by the middle class. The groups are often forced into political and economic alliances out of necessity, though the social distance is rigidly maintained.

The Lower-Class Majority

A lot of this talk about elites and the emerging middle class is academic. Taking a drive or a bus to the fringe neighborhoods of Santo Domingo or, better yet, to many of the provincial towns

and villages will demonstrate rapidly the basic fact that for two-thirds of Dominicans, survival is everything. Composed mostly of blacks and mulattos, this majority of the Dominican population is engaged in a constant struggle for food, shelter, clothing, and some kind of minimal job with which to provide for one's family. Most members of this lower class are illiterate and unskilled; nearly a quarter are unemployed altogether. Back in 1978, a Dominican Planning Agency report concluded that 75% of the Dominican people had inadequate diets, and only 55% had access to potable water. In the countryside, 80% were illiterate and 50% unemployed. Things have likely improved, but they're still pretty dismal.

The fate of Dominican society was determined, initially, by the simple fact of slavery. At the beginning, there were two classes, one white and free, the other black and enslaved. After 500 years, and with the end of slavery, blacks were left to themselves to develop whatever culture and society they could inside a dominant culture that didn't provide them with any opportunites for social mobility, education, or political power. Now, many of the poor are outside the money economy altogether and live by bartering goods and services in exchange for provisions. Those in the lower class who are employed, no matter how small or insignificant the job and wage, are looked upon as fortunate and wield prestige. The lower class has not traditionally challenged the hegemony of the elite and generally follows hierarchical authority.

Once you get outside the main Dominican cities, it may come as a surprise at how full the countryside appears. Due to high birth rates, and a resultant high population density, competition for good farmland has long been fierce. Fertile acreage is now so scarce that many of the rural poor are fleeing the farms for the cities (where they're unlikely to be much better off than they were before).

Of those remaining in the countryside, you'll find two basic types—campesinos who own and work small plots of land for subsistence, and landless campesinos who find work as wage laborers. For every small landholder, you'll see perhaps 20 wage laborers roaming the countryside, looking for whatever work will get them from meal to meal. These peasants are hardly integrated into the larger consumer society at all. They produce very little, consume little, have no part in politics, and maintain a lifestyle similar to that of their ancestors.

The landed peasant generally builds a home of palm planking, with palm—or banana—thatch roofing. He may keep it patched with mud, old newspapers, or tin. On his tiny plot he'll raise cassava and beans. His village or neighborhood will huddle near a water source, with the houses connected by a series of dirt paths. The small rural neighborhoods are very close knit, often having been founded originally by one or two families. Thus, ancient kinship ties, called *compadrazgo* (godparentage), have developed between the families throughout the years. In this world, strangers are not much trusted, and quite often life revolves around the village marketplace, small church, and open-air bar. Society may depend upon evenings around a radio.

Men in this rural society may tend their tiny plots or engage in a hunt for migrant work during harvest time. Sometimes jobs are available in local construction. Approximately 85% of women contribute to family income in rural areas, and nearly 20% of rural households are headed by women. These women earn some income from cultivating garden plots, tending to goats, or selling lottery tickets and homemade sweets. They, too, work in the labor-intensive harvesting of cane, tobacco, and coffee, though they earn less than their male counterparts.

To many of the poor, it seems like a good idea to move to the city. Actually, however, the slums outside Santo Domingo are worse than anything in the countryside, and for most peasants who move to the city it is a lateral change, not an improvement. Many times, the newcomer to the city may get some help from more-established relatives, then work as a peddler or bottle collector. A small percentage may actually break into the money economy as stevedores or carpenters, but this is still a rarity. These *campunos,* rural-urban migrants, wind up living without running water, sewage systems, or electricity. During the 1980s, their numbers grew at an annual rate of 4.7%. There is so much moving around that about 25% of Dominicans no longer live in the province where they were born—an amazing statistic for a country that used to be very land tied.

Urban unemployment is very high, near 25%, and a large percentage of urban households in the slums are headed by women. In the cities, women are the more consistent wage earners.

Like their rural counterparts, the urban poor concentrate their social lives on small neighborhoods, where tight circles of neighbors and kin offer mutual assistance. Migrants maintain kinship ties with their families back in the country through a *cadena* (chain), which keeps money and aid flowing back and forth in both directions. Kin left behind care for family land or small businesses, and kin in the city offer their families employment or temporary housing. Today, the poor are still mostly outsiders. Almost all Dominican politicians claim to represent the poor, but their real concerns often serve to further undermine the poor's position in society. The dual favoritism-intimidation technique exploited so ruthlessly by Trujillo keeps the rural peasantry and urban poor in a submissive and fearful position.

Haitian Immigrants

The plight of the Haitian in the Dominican Republic is truly distressing. Since their own agricultural and land system collapsed in 1915, during the American occupation, many Haitians have come across the Dominican border, both legally and illegally. Rough estimates place the number of Haitians in the Dominican Republic between 200,000 and 500,000. Many of these Haitians work in cane fields or as migrant harvesters of other crops. The kind of work done by the Haitians, both men and women, is backbreaking. Twelve-hour days are the rule, and most are brought over the border in "Kongos," or work gangs, though some may even be kidnapped or lured by false promises and kept largely against their will.

Haitian workers live in *bateyes,* or caneworker settlements, which consist of nothing more than concrete barracks lacking proper sewage or electricity. The food is poor and the bosses are demanding and abusive. In 1983, the International Labor Office sent a mission which exposed the precise conditions: children sleeping in overcrowded bunkers, cooking facilities in poor conditions, and wages so low they created staggering poverty. Haitians earned less than 60% of the wages paid to Dominicans doing the same work over the same hours. The whole practice of recruiting Haitians to work the cane commenced under Trujillo, who signed a deal with the Duvalier government in Haiti, reportedly paying Duvalier huge sums for his connivance in the scheme. After Duvalier fell from power, many Haitians refused to participate in the worker-share program, in which *buscones* recruit workers, some children as young as eight years old.

Disturbances in the fields are not uncommon, and in 1985 several Haitians were killed for protesting delayed payment on a sugar plantation. During 1990, a law was passed in the Dominican Congress prohibiting persons under 14 years of age from serving as caneworkers and mandating improved living arrangements. During 1991, Balaguer rounded up 10,000 young Haitians and sent them home. With the coming of more liberal government to Haiti, relations between the two countries have deteriorated, especially when then-Haitian President Aristide began to attack Dominican abuses of his people. In a country in which racial prejudice is often subtle, discrimination against Haitians is open and notorious.

Dominican Emigrants

The hidden class of Dominicans are the emigrants. Some 8–15% of Dominicans live abroad. The city of New York alone plays home to more than half a million Dominicans. These *dominicanos ausentes* (absentee Dominicans) make New York City, where they are the largest minority group besides Puerto Ricans, the second-largest Dominican settlement in the world. Many Dominicans work and save for years just to get the chance to make the trip, and many finance it by hocking everything they have, including their houses. Many men make the journey alone, try to become successful, then send for their families (or return home with new prestige).

Other Dominicans flee to Puerto Rico, where they tend to blend in more easily with the dominant culture. In open boats known as *yolas,* they try to cross the very dangerous Mona Passage, which is known for its high winds, storms, and sharks. They often pay smugglers with boats as much as $500 to obtain a spot in 30-foot wooden death-traps that hold up to 50 people for the crossing. Once in Puerto Rico, Dominicans go about the process of picking up illegal birth certificates and other documents; some then head for the United States. Dominicans remit as much as $500 million back to their country each year, and these remittances are now the Dominican Republic's largest source of foreign exchange.

Most Dominican emigrants are relatively better educated and more skilled than their stay-at-home counterparts. Still, they aren't well assimilated into American culture once on the scene, and many return to the Dominican Republic. They are called "Dominican Yorks" or *cadenas,* after the gold chains popular with drug dealers. Sometimes their children are referred to as "Joes." It goes without saying that Dominican emigration is a mixed blessing for everybody concerned.

GENDER ROLES

Traditional roles for the individual in Dominican society were largely inherited from Spanish culture, which emphasized a male-oriented structure based on the values of individualism, paternalism, and male supremacy. In this regard, the Dominican Republic isn't much different from many of its counterparts in Latin America, though to some degree the modern effects of education and social diversity, especially in the two large cities of Santo Domingo and Santiago, are modifying the old gender roles and creating dissension among classes and individuals.

Men

For many young men and nearly all adult men, the role of dominant male results in a "machismo" attitude. In the first place, machismo probably entails a high degree of image, which is combed through with contradictions. For one thing, males in the Dominican Republic always strive to carry themselves in a strong and domineering way, while at the same time they may be totally self-conscious about how others perceive them. The image demands that they make comments to passing women and maintain strong male friendship groups. Sexual prowess—or the appearance thereof—is critical to the macho image; this often leads Dominican men into sexual relationships outside marriage and into fathering children by different

HAITIANS AND DOMINICANS

For a very large part of history, the people who share the island of Hispaniola have been divided by an animosity that beggars description. And one of the most brutal episodes of that animosity took place during 1937 when General Rafael Trujillo, the Dominican dictator, ordered the killing of thousands of Haitian immigrants and laborers in the border region. The killings, which took place along the Massacre River, were accomplished by Dominican soldiers using machetes and bayonets. Of course, when called to account, Trujillo blamed the victims. When he finally agreed to pay restitution to Haiti for the deaths, the negotiated amount equalled exactly US$29 for every dead Haitian.

The massacre masks a central theme in Dominican life, which is the barely disguised racism that blankets Haitian-Dominican relations. Trujillo especially sympathized with the Nazi race theories, and lightened his own skin with powder. He demonized black Haitians. Other Dominican strongmen like Balaguer resort to scapegoating of Haitians, and use code language to accuse populist leaders in the Dominican Republic of being Haitian. Race is a factor, even today, that keeps the Haitian-Dominican border not only undeveloped and nearly roadless, but tense with soldiers and guns. The theme of racism figures prominently in *Why the Cocks Fight* by Michele Wucker (New York, Hill and Wang), an excellent book that explores not only racism, but also migration, Carnaval, and magic realism, each of which resonates as a major factor in Hispaniolan history. For a fictional perspective read the highly regarded novel by Edwidge Danticat entitled *Farming the Bones,* the story of a young Haitian girl during the "Trujillismo."

placing personal integrity and trust far above legal rights or institutional responsibility. *Personalismo* leads individuals, especially males, into gross exaggerations of idealistic notions (chivalry, honor, personal identity) and downplays compromise and humility. This social attitude affects every level of Dominican life. In the simplest everyday meeting, politeness, cordiality, and pride dominate. These traits can make every encounter a small social drama as well. Likewise, Dominican history is filled with instances of haughty pride taking the place of common sense or group cooperation. The results are sometimes harmless, sometimes disastrous.

A good example of the disastrous is in the political arena. Here, *personalismo* virtually assures that political ideology and belief will be less important than individual personality. Thus, political parties tend to coalesce around magnetic human beings rather than a core set of values and interests. Most Dominican political rallies seem dominated by images of their leaders.

Related to *personalismo,* but different, is another individual ethic called the *patrón.* Under the early colonial plantation system, almost every personal encounter involved a face-to-face meeting with somebody to whom duties were owed or from whom obligations were expected. Whether it was masters and slaves or owners and overseers, the concept of the symbolic father now permeates Dominican society, with the *patrón* expected to be both demanding and fair, while the "child" is expected to return obedience and unquestioned loyalty. This relationship automatically attaches to anyone in a position of leadership—fathers, grandfathers, political leaders, or military generals.

Which leads us to males who are tied to the *caballero* style, which dictates that gentlemen be virile, forceful, competitive, humorous, and fatalistic. The caballero isn't (in theory, at least) supposed to do manual labor. He fancies himself an intellectual, even if his ideas are archaic, absurd, or both. This self-conception works pretty well if one belongs to an elite family, but it doesn't work so well for the uneducated or the lower classes. Usually, elites demonstrate their machismo and style through leadership, while machismo in the lower classes is a matter of physical

women. There is little shame in all this for Dominicans, at least so long as they take responsibility for their children. Machismo dictates that a Dominican man be the head of the family and take care of his kids, though Dominican women will tell you that in many cases it is women who actually do the job.

On a more abstract level, *personalismo* characterizes Dominican interpersonal relationships, stressing the uniqueness of each individual and prowess (baseball, gambling) or sexual conquest.

Women

In the traditional Spanish model, such defined and stylized male roles created a mirror image: the docile, protected, virtuous woman. Ideally, the woman derives her public status from that of her husband, rarely pursuing a career outside the home and leading instead a domestic life of self-sacrifice. In a strange way, however, the swaggering role model leaves plenty of room for women to compete in many affairs, whether it be managing the family, settling kinship disputes, or serving as family accountant. Nevertheless, beauty is important, and upper-class Dominican women spend hours on their appearance, in addition to their many "domestic duties" with charities, humanitarian concerns, and church involvement. Women are in charge of most of the family rituals, including births, deaths, parties, and worship.

Just as it is harder for lower-class males to maintain a macho image, it is very much harder for women to assume their idealized roles in lower-class life. In fact, most lower-class women head families and work outside the home day after day. In the cities, middle-class women pursue jobs in education, tourism, and business. Even President Balaguer expanded the participation of women in government by appointing women to serve as governors for every province in the country. As far as sex is concerned, the good old double standard (which seems to apply everywhere) is in full operation in the Dominican Republic. Almost all women in all classes are compelled to accept their husbands' macho transgressions with mistresses, while their own sexuality is harshly circumscribed. Female infidelity is the subject of violent scandal.

Inflation and the rising cost of living, outside influences like television and movies, and an enlargement of middle-class expectations in general are all leading women more and more into the wider world of Dominican business and politics. The old order—thankfully, perhaps—is cracking and wearing away; it's now common to see Dominican women, young and old, on the streets of Santo Domingo, and Dominican couples pursuing their relationships outside the old chaperone system. Many upper-class women

hold very prestigious positions indeed, especially in education and tourism. More and more middle-class women are becoming tour guides and owning their own small businesses such as art galleries, craft stores, and restaurants.

One sad fact of life in the Dominican Republic is prostitution. Because many lower-class mothers have been abandoned by their children's fathers, they suffer extreme economic hardship and often turn to prostitution to solve their problems. Some estimate that as many as 60,000 women work as prostitutes on the island, others preferring to work as far away as Amsterdam or on other Caribbean islands, where mulattos are popular.

All of these gender roles are introduced to Dominican children at an early age, and the children follow them all through their lives. Little boys, especially in the lower classes, get little supervision (you'll see them running around naked in the countryside with large groups of their male friends), and when they get older, they are expected to have as many extramarital and premarital affairs as possible. Little girls, however, are always taught about grooming and fashion. Mothers and daughters have an especially close relationship, while fathers are often distant, seen as authority figures rather than caregivers.

MARRIAGE AND CHILDREN

Legal, Christian marriages are the most accepted manner of consummating relationships in the Dominican Republic. The ideal marriage process involves a formal engagement period, followed by a religious wedding in church, then a huge fiesta for all the friends and relatives of the couple. There are two kinds of marriage: civil (celebrated according to the civil law) and religious (occuring under canonical law). Many upper-class families prefer to have both ceremonies, although this adds considerably to the expense involved.

However, as much as the Spanish ideal of marriage dominates the Dominican popular imagination, the reality is quite different for most of the lower classes and peasants. To them, the cost and pomp of a formal religious marriage is too much to bear, and their lives are too tenuous to count on such social amenities. Hence, common-law, or "free union," marriages are much more usual. They involve no formality, requiring just the consent of the persons involved. Perhaps 80% of young people nowadays involve themselves in free unions, the women quite often because they have no economic power with which to bargain for a mate. Sometimes young girls set up their first houses when they're 14 or 15, many while they are pregnant or already have children. These kinds of free unions are dissolved nearly half the time, with the women customarily receiving the house and a little child support—if the husband acknowledges the children. Couples who stay together and achieve some economic security will often marry later in a civil ceremony, which is not too expensive.

Poor couples who choose to marry inevitably do so under the civil law, partly because it is less expensive but mostly because the rules for divorce under such laws are quite lax. Quickie divorces are very common in the Dominican Republic, and sometimes government tourist brochures and pamphlets make much of this fact, hoping to lure dissatisfied foreigners to pursue their legal remedies on the island. On the other hand, religious marriages under Roman Catholic law are almost impossible to void.

The Extended Family

Whatever the method of cementing the male-female relationship, the family unit and the *compadrazgo* system form the backbone of all Dominican social life. These traditional Spanish values of solidarity and parental authority are hallowed in the upper classes of modern Dominicana and emulated by the middle classes, though perhaps less so by members of the lower class, whose African ancestors had their own family system greatly disrupted by years of slavery.

The average Dominican household encompasses three generations and is strictly patrilineal, with the oldest male in the group holding the most authority. He is responsible for the family, its fortunes, and its honor. Brothers have particularly strong ties that continue into adulthood, with sisters maintaining weaker ties among themselves and with their brothers, mainly because they are eventually expected to marry

into another family and thereafter give their allegiance to it. Still, don't underestimate the maternal role in the family; some Dominican mothers and grandmothers are quite strong, and fierce characters in their own right.

Compadrazgo

Compadrazgo literally means co-parentage. Though something like the system of godfathers and godmothers common in other countries, the business of godparenting carries much more social weight in the Dominican Republic. Often, poor farmers will seek out a *padrino*—commonly someone like an employer—who can be counted on to provide a child with financial assistance in hard times. At times, friendships are cemented by the ceremony, and from then on, the friendship is considered inviolate. When Trujillo was in power, he used to conduct mass baptisms of peasant children so that he could be considered the *padrino* of all of them. Even Balaguer practices this social craft, though not to the extent of Trujillo.

Within families, *compadres* are chosen a few months before the child is born. Economic factors mitigate in favor of certain godparents, as those chosen are expected to assist with the child's education, career, and finances. *Compadres* pay for the baptism ceremony and sometimes even medical care, marriage, and college tuition. The godson has the right to ask his godfather for loans under appropriate circumstances.

For lower-class Dominicans, the circumstances are quite different. The basic instability of informal marriages causes an instability in the family unit as well. Poverty often grinds away the authority of both parents and many times means that males are absent from the house altogether. In that case, mothers and grandmothers take over. The oldest woman may become the dominant figure of authority and take the male's place as breadwinner. If this kind of family persists over several generations, the "grandmother family" results, which becomes truly matrilineal. With a whole line of fathers absent, a grandmother may find herself in charge of a household of married and unmarried daughters and their children. In fact, Dominican cities and larger towns are full of such grandmother houses. Most times it works out pretty well, with the women performing all the vital functions of the family. In fact, the grandmother family is common throughout the Caribbean.

Dominican families tend to have a lot of kids. As you'd expect, the elite and upper-class families have fewer children than the poor—usually no more than four. Rural and lower classes generally never have *fewer* than four children. A family's inability to produce children is considered a serious problem, and males are considered of higher value than females. As modern life intrudes more and more on middle-class Dominicans, they are delaying having children in order to promote their upward mobility. Given the informality of many relationships, there is a lot of illegitimacy, though it is not given any particular social stigma.

The Dominican Republic is a fully modern country, with fast food, cable TV, and passions for popular culture. Even though these modern stresses have changed many attitudes about marriage, family, and children, the signs of strong family attachment are everywhere apparent. When you see a family strolling together in one of the many city parks or playing together in front of a humble house, you realize that in the Dominican Republic, family values is not an empty political slogan, but a vital way of life.

LANGUAGE

Dominicans in general, from the poorest campesino to the most educated elite, take a great joy in life and in the process of living. Perhaps language is this joy's most obvious manifestation.

The official language is, of course, Spanish, the mother tongue of all native Dominicans. Dominican Spanish is a pure, clear, almost classical Spanish, which experts say resembles the Castilian Spanish spoken in most of Spain—despite some differences in pronunciation due to the long-distance separation from the mother country. Dominicans also speak just about the quickest Spanish anywhere on earth, and it's a language laced with slang and innuendo, a rapid-fire lingo that's fun to hear but difficult to get hold of without practice.

Dialects and Influences

Because Spanish is such a dominant feature of the cultural landscape, it is remarkable that there

are almost no dialects on the Dominican side of the island. The only important regional dialect is Cibaeña, spoken in isolated pockets of the northern Cibao Valley, a dialect produced by the survival of archaic speech forms caused by the lack of communication with the outside world. Haitian Creole has had an effect on the Spanish of Dominicans who live along the border. And in all rural areas, the Spanish spoken hasn't the purity or grammatical form of classical Spanish.

Tremendous differences do exist between the speech of uneducated rural groups and their urban elite counterparts. Oratory and rhetoric are considered signs of breeding. I've seen more than one Dominican fix another with a stare and pour forth a calm Castilian cascade in order to convince the other of his purity, good breeding, and honor.

Other languages, particularly English and French, are gradually gaining currency in the Dominican Republic. Many of the Dominicans who have left the country have returned bilingual. The availability of more and more American and European television programs and films is having an impact as well. English has had an effect on everybody's speech, especially words relating to food and sports. Many middle-class Dominicans find that a knowledge of English increases their job opportunities and thus affects their upward mobility. Among educated Dominicans in the cities and in religious schools, studying English is very popular indeed. Educated Dominicans who know English and study foreign language tend to be very competent in French as well.

Yet while some educated Dominicans speak English and/or French, most working-class and rural Dominicans do not. When traveling in the Dominican Republic, plan ahead and come prepared with some basic Spanish for directions, accommodations, food, and emergencies. Even without good Spanish, however, travel in the Republic is more than possible. Dominicans are cheerful and ready to help when the need arises, and I've found that language is no barrier when push comes to shove.

Taíno Influences

Taíno influence is everywhere present in the speech of Dominicans, even though the Taínos themselves are long gone. The original Spanish conquerors used Taíno words, transcribed into their own tongue, to describe objects and places unfamiliar to them. In addition, many Taíno products caused a stir in Europe and entered the language in that way. English words including "hurricane," "canoe," "tobacco," "potato," and "cassava" derive from classical Spanish phonetic spellings of the words *huracán, canoa, tabaco, patata,* and *cazabe.* My favorite is *hamaca,* "hammock." Early Spaniards took over place names directly from their Taíno counterparts, like Cibao, which means "plain," or Baní, meaning "abundance of water." The city of Higüey in the southeast was named for the dominant Taíno regional chiefdom in the area.

Fucú

Dominicans' use of language is also influenced by African words and habits. One of the oldest elements in this cross-cultural pollination is the concept of *fucú,* or *fukú.* This word, and its related behavioral concept, was brought from Africa, though its precise derivation remains unknown. The *fucú* is an ill omen, something that is likely to bring bad luck, and it can also describe a person, thing, or event, connoting a sense of doom about the thing described. Certain words remain unmentionable (including Columbus's name), and the appearance of certain signs—like birds—is considered bad luck indeed. When a *fucú* is uttered or appears, some Dominicans will form a quick sign of the cross in the air with their index fingers and whisper *"¡Zafa!"* to try to negate it.

Slang

Like all language, Dominican Spanish is capable of delivering powerful emotional messages in the form of slang, expressions, and verbal play. Bartering, a primal form of Dominican exchange, is filled with wordplay and humor and is a most expressive form of street culture. *Dichos*—expressions used to state eternal truths or communicate shared values—are common as well. Many *dichos* relate to skin color and political power. "Money whitens" is a common saying, as is "Colonels are never black." Another *dicho* claims that "a rich black is a mulatto, and a rich mulatto is a white." Most of the time, these color-related *dichos* are used in a tone of lighthearted self-mockery.

Many Dominican expressions derive directly from Spanish culture, whether consciously or unconsciously. Dominicans might look around and say, "No Moors," meaning that the coast is clear. This expression relates not only to the Moorish occupation of Spain during the early Middle Ages but also to the Dominican Republic's own occupation by Haiti much later. Illiterate *campesinos* use the term *moor,* even though

BASIC DOMINICAN PRONUNCIATION

a—as in cart
b—as in boy
c—hard (as "k" in kind) except before "e" or "i", then soft (as "s" in sit)
ch—as in child
d—as in dog except at the end of a word, when it resembles th as in they
e—as "a" in day
f—as in off
g—as in go except before "e" or "i", then guttural (as ch in the Scottish word loch)
h—silent
i—ee as in meet
j—as "h" in hat, but with gutteral emphasis
l—as in ball
ll—as in yes

m—as in map
n—as in noon
ñ—as "ny" in canyon
o—as in note
p—as in purse
q—as "k" in kind
r—rolled, especially at the beginning of a word
rr—strongly rolled
s—as in sit
t—as in tilt
u—as "oo" in boot
x—as "h" in hat (see "j" above)
y—as "ee" in meet or, if at the beginning of a word, as "j" in jar
z—as "s" in sit

A FEW DOMINICANISMS

It takes a while to get used to Dominican slang, but learning it can be fun. Dropping a few Dominicanisms into a conversation can open doors, make friends, and protect you from the isolation travelers sometimes feel. It's also kind of fun to try to surprise people.

People get around towns in *guaguas,* which are public buses, or by *conchos,* public taxis. *Motoconchos* are motorcycles which will pick you up and scoot you wherever you want to go. If you need only a little bit of something, ask for *un chin,* (*un chinchin* for an even smaller amount). You probably know that *ahora* means "now," but did you know that *ahora mismo* means *"right* now"? *Ahorita* means "later."

Going to a party? It's a *bonche.* Don't confuse this with *boche,* which is a scolding or disagreement. When you get excited about something someone's said, just say, *"¡Bomba!"*—"Great" or "Wow."

Una bomba, on the other hand, is a gas station. Vendors on the street will chant, *"¡Marchanta!"*—basically, "Come and look at my stuff." Some of the stuff might include *chichiguas,* the colorful kites Dominicans love to fly. If you need a plastic bag in the supermarket, it's a *funda.* Need a straw for your drink? Ask for a *calimete.* Don't confuse anyone by using the word *bolsa,* which is pretty bad talk for a certain part of the male anatomy. You'll hear the expletive *coño,* which is about the strongest swear word there is--an almost unmentionable thing to say in countries like Cuba and Colombia.

Dominicans are very affectionate with babies and call them *chi-chi,* while small children are called *carajitos.* Adolescents who constantly misbehave are called *tigueritos, f*or obvious reasons. Finally, when you've had enough sun in the afternoon or a big lunch, you'll probably need, as the Dominicans do, a *pavita,* a nap or siesta.

---

most have never heard of the Moorish invasion of Spain. Moreover, many expressions carry rural connotations. "The skinniest dog has fleas" and "There is always a hair in the *sancocho* (stew)" demonstrate the pragmatic and fatalistic bent in rural thinking.

Riddles

For many, many years, Dominicans amused themselves, their friends, and their children with riddles. Since the advent of television, movies, and other leisure activities, many forms of riddles have disappeared and their popularity is sadly waning. However, in rural areas, people still spend many an afternoon or evening regaling one another with expansive, sometimes rhyming riddles. When campesinos gather, after they've exhausted the local gossip, they often start expounding their favorite riddles, playing at first, then commencing a kind of competitive but good-humored contest to see who can tell the most artistic, bombastic, or literary riddle. When a riddle is posed, the group analyzes the riddle, suggests answers, or gives up when it has to. When the riddler reveals the answer, the group once again criticizes and

analyzes the answer, or poses a new answer, or a new and different riddle with the same answer.

Most riddles have to do with everyday life and objects—avocados, honey, bees, garlic. Some riddles have obliquely sexual references and are for men only, with the offensive answers always kept from the ears of women.

EDUCATION

The Secretariat of State for Education and Welfare administers Dominican education. Everywhere you go in Santo Domingo and Santiago, you see young children going to and from school in their uniforms, and the universities are packed with young people seeking higher education. In fact, the most recent estimate of Dominican literacy put the level at 83%, up from 74% in 1986. Some of this can be accounted for by the fact that Dominican law requires each child to attend school for at least six years.

As you'd expect, money is a problem in the Dominican system. Dominican kids don't have much exposure to preschool activities and generally begin their educations at about seven years of age. Many rural schools can't provide the minimum required six grades. Children who are especially poor or who must work in the family fields still get little education.

Secondary

Secondary education is not required by Dominican law, so only about half of Dominican children go beyond elementary school. Secondary school begins at age 13, and many institutions are religious, engaging in essentially college-preparatory work. About 10% of secondary students attend vocational, polytechnic, or teacher-training schools in urban areas. Public education at the secondary level is infected with low academic standards and inadequate facilities. Students have to buy their own textbooks, and many eventually drop out. The elite and those middle-class families who can send their children to private schools and institutions.

Colleges and Universities

For the few who can afford it, higher education is quite good in the Dominican Republic. There are more than 26 institutions of higher learning in the country, and several renowned artistic conservatories. The only public university is the Universidad Autónomo de Santo Domingo (UASD) (Autonomous University of Santo Domingo), which can be traced directly back to the first Spanish university on the island, founded in 1538. For decades, the UASD was the center of student political action which focused on human rights and sovereignty issues. Today, students are more interested in budget problems and curriculum disputes, but politics is still important. Located in a shady, tree-lined Santo Domingo neighborhood, the university exudes an atmosphere of excitement, involvement, and learning.

The leading private universities are Catholic University Madre y Maestra, the oldest university in the country, located in Santiago, and Pedro Henríquez Ureña National University, in Santo Domingo. Private universities tend to enroll students from the upper classes, who are not as impassioned by political concerns.

Other Schools

The Escuela Nacional de Bellas Artes, in Santo Domingo, is the national art school. Altos de Chavón has an international school of design in La Romana. The Museum of Modern Art in Santo Domingo offers adult and children's painting classes.

LIVES AND CUSTOMS

Economic hardship is the determining factor in the lives of many, if not most, Dominicans today. To a large extent, most Dominicans manage to maintain an attitude of cheerfulness and adaptability in spite of all their difficulties, al-

---

DOMINICAN *FUCÚS*

The cooing of wild doves in the neighborhood means that someone is going to die in the near future. But when an owl screeches, it means that a member of the family is dead.

A group of hens suddenly cackling together signifies death, probably in a nearby home.

Oil spilled from a lamp announces misfortune for the one who spilled it.

A person may not sleep with his feet pointed toward the front of the house, for that signifies an early death.

A dream of excrement means that you will find some money or that someone will give you a lot of money.

When the palm of your right hand itches, it means that someone will give you money. When the left palm itches, it means that you will have to pay a forgotten debt or that you will soon lose money.

Opening an umbrella inside the house is immediate bad luck.

It is bad luck to sweep out a house after dark.

If your horse tires after going only a short distance, a ghost has been riding behind you. If you proceed, you will catch the illness which killed the ghost. Instead, stop and reverse the saddle, placing the pommel toward the tail of the horse.

though for much of their history Dominicans often felt fatalistic and resigned about their situation. Nevertheless, Dominicans are hardly ever alone in their struggle for improved housing, better jobs, and expanded horizons, because they so often share their difficulties within a web of relationships revolving around family and kinship groups. Every class of Dominican life depends heavily upon family ties to provide land, employment, child care, economic help, and political support.

In the Dominican Republic, men hold most of the important political and economic positions, but many still claim that the country is matriarchal because women take on such vital roles and carry such great responsibilities. Increasing numbers of Dominican women raise families alone. They are often able to obtain employment when men cannot, though they are paid less then men for the same work. In rural areas, children frequently provide support for the family by working fields and tending other children, and even in this case female children often take the lead.

The lives and customs of Dominicans took root in a unique triple heritage which combined the qualities of three ethnic groups. The Dominican heritage, rich in historical circumstances, is also contradictory in some ways: a blend not only of the old and new, but also of the prehistoric. Taíno, Spanish, and African influences pervade the island of Hispaniola, tumbling each other around in a vortex of countervailing influences.

Taíno Influences

Of course, the Taínos have been gone a long time. Nevertheless, most Dominican cities and towns rest upon old Taíno sites, and many central Dominican plazas spring directly from the Taíno *batayes*. The Taínos live on in legacies like food, place names, and language, as well as in some medicinal and health practices still prevalent in the countryside. More and more Dominicans are becoming aware of their country's Taíno past, and several fine museums offer a glimpse of Taíno culture.

Spanish Influences

It would be hard to overestimate the Spanish influence on Dominican life. Dominican culture, ethics, religion, and art all emanate from Spain, directly into the heart and soul of most Dominicans. According to tradition, the Spanish character is dignified though high-strung, volatile, and versed in self-denial and fatalism. Naturally, Roman Catholicism, which came to Hispaniola with Columbus, plays a huge part in developing Dominican culture, creating its mores, and solidifying its social life. Everything is influenced by the church, from nursery rhymes to folklore, educational methods, etiquette, and eating habits.

African Influences

Finally, African influence is indelible in the Dominican Republic. Most slaves on Hispaniola were brought from West Africa, which had a spectacular artistic and religious culture. Today, much of the Dominican agricultural practice springs from West African sources, as do native crafts, basket-weaving, tortoise sculpture, pottery, woodcarving, and painting. Folkways and superstitions, as well as the proliferation of cults and mystiques, spring directly from West African animistic beliefs, while some vague traces of Dominican voodoo still survive. Perhaps most important is the West African music, where dance rhythm and native song, accompanied by very specific percussion arrangements, all have their counterpart in African music. Sometimes all of these admixtures produce unique beliefs and customs. The prevalence of *botánicos* and herbalists selling concoctions from shops and carts along Santo Domingo streets is an African heritage.

Birth

For much of Dominican history, a peculiar set of beliefs dominated the birth, maturation, and death processes, especially for those in rural areas or among the lower classes. While most urban Dominicans see these customs withering away in modern times, many rural people still cling to their traditions when it comes to life and death.

For rural mothers it is customary to avoid eating fruit, especially bananas, during pregnancy, lest the baby be born with phlegm in the chest. In order to prevent the placenta from sticking to the back, or the uterus, she must likewise avoid eating anything crusty or burned from the walls of a cooking kettle. Similarly, the woman must avoid anyone walking behind her during the seventh month of pregnancy, lest the placenta stick to the womb. Dark country women are encouraged to drink fistulas of cassia plants dissolved in boiling milk in order that the child be born whiter.

When labor comes to a country woman, she will turn an image of Saint Raymond upside down and light a candle. When the baby comes, she may keep the candle burning for a while, then flip the saint right-side up. It is customary for the mother to be confined for exactly 40 days and to stuff cotton in her ears in order to prevent any diseases from invading her body. Almost from their first days, children sleep in hammocks. They don't get their first bed until they reach puberty, and then the bed is usually a cot.

For three days after the child's birth, the mother does not nurse it, but instead feeds it dried rose petals moistened with almond oil. She does not cut its fingernails until baptism, lest the child become a thief. The umbilical cord is kept as well and given to the child when it is seven years old. The child cuts it lengthwise with a knife, symbolically opening him to life.

The hard facts of both birth and death for most Dominicans are that health care is difficult to come by and poor nutrition common. Hospitals lack adequate management and equipment, and health care in rural areas is almost nonexistent. Infectious and parasitic disease is common in the countryside, and reliance on home remedies and folk medicine is pervasive as well. Nevertheless, life expectancy continues to improve in the Dominican Republic, from a 1980 average of 62.6 years to a 1992 average of 66 for males and 70 for females. Unfortunately, at the same time, infant mortality has nearly doubled, from 31.7 deaths per 1,000 live births in 1980 to 56 deaths per thousand in 1992. Children commonly die of enteritis (intestinal inflammation), diarrhea, and malnutrition.

Maturation

While birth may be somewhat dominated by African and rural beliefs, the maturation process for boys and girls is dominated by Spanish culture. Both boys and girls, when they get old enough, draw most of their playmates from a pool of cousins and siblings. Because Dominican culture places such importance on the production of a son, male children are often greatly indulged by their parents, receiving less discipline than girls. Female children are closely chaperoned and their lives are heavily circumscribed, while the boys, often the girls' brothers and male cousins, are expected to protect them and their reputations.

In poor families, this rigid structure isn't well maintained. Both boys and girls in rural areas often have to work right alongside their parents in the fields and have little time for games or playing. Wealthier families supervise their children's lives quite closely at times, engaging them in piano lessons or art classes after school. Baseball is big among the boys, and many join organized teams as soon as they're old enough—about seven years of age. It is a tradition in the upper classes to celebrate the *quinceañera* on a girl's 15th birthday. This big family party signifies the girl's achievement of womanhood. (This is now being replaced by a party held on the girl's 16th birthday signifying more of a coming out into society.)

Just a single night on the El Conde in Santo Domingo will teach you the social customs of Dominican young people. They love to go out at night in large groups and promenade up and down the avenues to see and be seen. These groups act as self-chaperoning units. Young women dress up with makeup, decorative jewelry, heavy mascara, miniskirts, and high heels. Boys and young men slick back their hair and use cologne by the bucket. Of course, flirting is a great game, though it rarely goes very far. While the urban promenade is common, in rural areas life is very much quieter—centered on family, village, and church.

Illness and Death

Not many people in the Dominican Republic die alone, and nobody dies in a nursing home. When anyone becomes seriously ill, close relatives and intimate friends commonly gather at the person's house, remaining there day after day until the situation is resolved. They relieve the patient's family of all burdens, including housework and cooking.

The process of dying is mediated; older women mourners may pray continually by the side of the patient, urging God to release the dying man from his painful life, until death finally does come. When death comes, all water vessels in the house are emptied, lest the ghost of the dead bathe in one of them. In rural homes, campesinos shut the front door for nine days, a period called *la novena,* during which any person wishing to enter has to use the back door, no matter how inconvenient. Mirrors are covered so that the ghost can't be seen. Driving through the countryside, you'll often see the result of funeral customs in small villages or remote hamlets. Outside the house of the dead, a large crowd of villagers, friends, and family members gathers in order to support the family inside. People tell stories about the deceased, laugh, eat, play dominoes, ask riddles, or play music and sing. Meanwhile, inside the house, intimate family members place the corpse in a casket, so its feet face the front door. Candles burn at each end of the casket. Mourners dress in black or gray, and there is a lot of wailing and crying, sometimes to the point of hysteria. When a young child dies, a special ceremony may be conducted involving hymns, accordions, and drums. Otherwise, at the end of *la novena,* a more elaborate ceremony is held, called the *velas de muerto* (vigil). In this ceremony, mourners construct a small altar to the deceased, burn candles, make offerings, and give a small glass of water to the person's ghost. Sometimes, families celebrate this ceremony at the first anniversary of the death as well. Bodies are interred in concrete tombs above ground.

CULTURE

When I think about "culture," I often think of it as something "out there" somewhere, something I have to go out and get. Dominican culture, on the other hand—and particularly the culture of Santo Domingo—will always be vibrantly and excitingly colorful for me, and something internal, not external.

Of course, like all societies, Dominican society has to function and earn its daily bread. Most Dominicans have to work hard to earn a living, have to keep their cars running and their children clothed. Once out in the Dominican countryside, it's easy to see that culture is something that needs leisure, and maybe urban life, to wholly vitalize itself. But even in the Dominican countryside, the blues and greens still vibrate. Music follows you everywhere in this country.

RELIGION

Dominicans overwhelmingly profess Roman Catholicism, and to witness the number of churches and convents, you'd think that religion was influential in the country. If you're in any of the cities or villages of the country during Christmas and Easter, you can witness an outflow of popular religious activity on the streets and in the sanctuaries. However, while 73% of Dominicans are, in fact, Roman Catholic, their personal religion tends to be based on formalized practices and rote memorization, rather than anything internalized or profound. Dominicans tend to approach their God exclusively through a personal intermediary such as a priest or folk spiritualist. Popular religious practices tend to mix elements of Catholicism and folklore.

Small evangelical sects are becoming more and more influential, or at least more vocal, and you'll frequently spot their proselytizers on Santo Domingo's busier intersections, handing out literature and soliciting funds. Other beliefs are represented in the country by small numbers of Jews, Mennonites, Muslims, Bahais, Mormons, and even a Buddhist sect from Japan. Nevertheless, the center of every small town or village is its Catholic church, and the Catholic clergy have had an indelible historical impact on the Dominican Republic.

Roman Catholicism

The Dominican Republic has one archdiocese, eight dioceses, and 250 parishes with around 500 clergy, most of whom belong to religious orders. The clergy represents about one priest for every 10,000 parishioners, the fourth-highest ratio in Latin America. Most of the Catholic hierarchy is very conservative and orthodox in outlook, while many village priests are given to more liberal views, assisting in village projects and community development and giving personal advice. However, the church has lost much of its influence, gradually weakening as the modern decades mount against it. Nowadays, the church is underfunded and understaffed, no longer able to offer many of the programs it once did, its educational institutions beginning to creak from old age and penury. Although the church has long tried to throw its weight against birth control and divorce, Dominican law permits extensive family planning and encourages easy divorce.

During the early colonial years, the Roman Catholic Church was the formal agent for transfer of Spanish culture to the island of Hispaniola, with the clergy considered the focal point of intellectual endeavor. At the center of Spanish intellectual debates were arguments about the nature of the Indians, and whether they were fully human and had souls. The clergy advocated hard for the Indians and protested, to no avail, their ill treatment at the hands of the colonizers and planters. In the first century of colonization, Dominican friars and other missionary orders were very active on the island, though not until 1564 did the Vatican establish the archdiocese of Santo Domingo, conferring upon its archbishop the title Primate of the West Indies. Thereafter, things went downhill rapidly for the church, paralleling the decline in economic importance of the island itself. The church managed to hang on by virtue of its private university, which was considered one of the centers of theological thought and practice in the Western Hemisphere.

During the Haitian occupation of the early 1800s, the church lost most of its authority and power under the heavy thumb of the occupying forces. The Haitians, viewing the church as a colonizing influence, took away much of its material worth, generating a controversy even over ownership of church lands. This legal controversy actually continued into the 20th century, when, with the coming of Trujillo to power, it was ended in the church's favor. Still, the church had come very close to losing its "legal personality" and all its lands, especially after the Dominican Supreme Court ruled that the church had no legal status and the Congress moved to liquidate its property. Only the intervention of Trujillo prevented a disaster for the church.

The Trujillo years were good ones for the church, right up to the very end, when things turned sour. Trujillo saw the church as a conservative force which could be used as an instrument of his own power, one of three sources of power alongside the military and the oligarchy. As the church grew in wealth and power during this period, Trujillo became known as the Benefactor of the Church, mainly because new churches were built, and a new large contingent of priests came to the country. The alliance between church and state was sealed in 1954, when a concordat established Roman Catholicism as the official state religion.

During the late 1950s, signs of discord between the church and state began to appear. The church tried to loosen Trujillo's hold on its administrative procedures, and a new archbishop named Octavio Beras, who had liberal leanings, replaced an octogenarian conservative. Then, in 1960, all hell broke loose when church officials protested the mass arrests of government opponents. In a resurgence of terror, Trujillo increased his campaign of imprisonment, this time including priests among those tortured and jailed. This whole incident must have come as a surprise for both parties; this was the church, after all, that had annulled Trujillo's second marriage and blessed his third.

For a short while after Trujillo's assassination, the church seemed to liberalize itself, speaking out for social, economic, and political reform. Pretty soon, however, the figure of Juan Bosch began to edge the church back into its regressive stance, with some clergy branding Bosch a communist. When Bosch was elected, the new constitution that came in with him made the church nervous, promoting divorce, common-law marriage, state inspection of religious schools, and protection for illegitimate children. All through the Bosch years of controversy, right through the "settlement" of 1965, when American troops came ashore, the church was ambivalent, a stance which probably cost it much influence.

All though Balaguer's "miracle" years, some church members involved themselves in social and economic protests, especially regarding the land policy that allowed Gulf and Western invasive control of the economy. Locally, the church still operates orphanages, old-age homes, and dispensaries, some of which provide much-needed services. Some priests serve as apologists for Balaguer, while others fight corruption by openly attacking it in their sermons.

The years since the death of Trujillo have seen a general decline in church influence, mainly because of benign neglect. Most Dominicans respect the advice of their priest concerning religious matters but assume he doesn't understand secular things. In many small villages and towns, however, priests remain not only the community's spiritual leaders, but its leaders in social and economic matters as well.

At this point, it is probably useful to distinguish between the power of the church and its good deeds. As its power in government wanes, and as it becomes less and less wealthy, the church seems to be doing more good deeds. The church manages clinics, pharmacies, convalescent homes, nursery schools, seminaries, and colleges, some of which provide the only social services available in their areas. Catholic Relief Services (CARITAS) handles refugee and relief problems and works with the rural poor. In the places where CARITAS does its work, the village priest is often the most educated person around.

Most Catholicism among the poor and in rural areas is a mixture of folk and Catholic beliefs. Rosaries are not uncommon. These religious processions are organized to pray for heavenly intercession to solve a problem, such as a lack of rain. A person carrying a rosary heads the procession, followed by an image of some saint or madonna, then persons singing and playing musical instruments. Also important in everyday belief is the *santos* cult, where images of saints are given extraordinary magical powers. Many families have shrines in their homes, usually to

St. Anthony and one of the virgins. The selection of particular saints is a personal matter and varies according to need, but every devotee is expected to perform the *promesa* (promise), a specific act of devotion, in return for which the saint grants wishes, prosperity, or good fortune. Of great importance to many Dominicans is the native Dominican patron, La Altagracia (the Virgin of the Highest Grace), the country's official patroness since 1922. Dominicans pray to her for miraculous cures and for intercession in their troubles.

Protestantism

Protestants in the Dominican Republic constitute a small but growing minority. Originally, Protestants came to the island in the 1820s from North America, though their numbers increased with an influx of West Indian laborers at the turn of the century. Evangelical Protestantism enjoyed a boom in the 1970s, and most proselytizing was done in the countryside. For the most part, Evangelical Protestantism is popular among the lower-middle–class families, who appreciate its emphasis on moral values like temperance, fidelity, and community. The evangelicals emphasize biblical fundamentalism, family rejuvenation, and economic self-dependency. Part of its allure is the egalitarian church service, so different from Catholic practice, wherein anyone is allowed to talk, sing, and testify.

Of late, there has been tension between Evangelicals and the Catholic hierarchy over the issue of privilege. Most Protestant converts are middle class or working class. Their religion emphasizes equal rights for women, a lay priesthood, and personal testimony, all of which tend to undermine priestly authority. Politically, Evangelicals are for land reform and democracy. Hence, they sometimes seem to threaten the older Catholic establishment.

Folk Beliefs

Folk religions, folk beliefs, and voodoo are still major influences in the Dominican Republic, although most of these are relegated to somewhat secret spheres or take place in rural or border areas not much visited by outsiders. With as many as one million people of Haitian descent living in the Dominican Republic, voodoo is still practiced, though the government and many citizens deride it as pagan and African. Actual worship, where it exists, takes place in *houmforts,* where sacrifices are made and believers are possessed by *lous,* or gods.

While most Dominicans deride voodoo, many of them practice a crude kind of spiritualism themselves. Many seek advice from *curanderos,* who are folk healers, and employ herbs, incantations, or roots in their cures. *Brujos* are more individualistic healers, authorized to drive out evil spirits infecting a soul. Some Dominicans believe in the power of the incantation, a prayer that each individual knows by heart and may whisper or recite in times of trouble or need. Some people carry copies of their incantations on engraved amulets around their necks. Even more specific are *ensalmos,* which are formulas against maladies. These *ensalmos* may be used against fainting spells, dizziness, and fevers.

LITERATURE

Most people, when they think of the "culture" of the Dominican Republic, will probably think about music and dance. Dominican music and dance translate from country to country with amazing ease. However, the Dominican Republic also has a relatively strong literary tradition, though it's not widely recognized outside the country. Part of the reason for its obscurity is that the literary arts stem from a deeply romantic European tradition unfamiliar to most Americans and already somewhat outmoded when modern European literature emerged at the turn of the century. Secondly, Dominican literature has tended to be dominated by writers from powerful families, many of whom combined their literary skills with political careers. The resulting nationalistic and polemic poems, fiction, and commentaries on exclusively colonial subjects have succeeded in keeping the rest of the world fairly uninterested in Dominican writing. Whereas the international fame of Dominican music and dance may be attributed to the African rhythms and moves that lose little in translation from culture to culture, the relative obscurity of Dominican literature may be caused by the language of the texts, which have remained largely untranslated from the Spanish.

Colonial Era

Early Dominican literature owes its principal debt to the churchmen who led the colony's spiritual and intellectual life. They were the original teachers, scholars, and patrons of music. Of course, one could argue that Columbus himself was Hispaniola's first writer—his log books are still fascinating to read. Later, the celebrated Dominican friar Bartolomé de Las Casas began his *Apologética Historia de los Indios* at a monastery in Puerto Plata and thus founded a style of nostalgic writing called *indigenísmo,* which came to be the dominant form of writing during the romantic period in the 19th century. Las Casas was one of the great men of the early colonial period, chronicling the brutality of the Spanish invasion, arguing for the souls of the Taínos and other Indians, protesting to the Spanish crown, to little practical avail. His work is searing reading even today. Most other early work takes the form of historical chronicles and journals of missionaries and explorers. Among the first of note are Gonzalo Fernández de Oviedo's *Historis Natural y General de Indias* and Cordoba's *Doctrina Cristina.*

The early adventurers, as opposed to the churchmen, brought with them an acquaintance with the heroic and romantic verse of Spain. One chronicler has said that during the early colonial period it was common for versifiers to circulate topical and satirical poems criticizing public officials. Poetry in general was an avocation of the upper classes and of church officials, and many of those poets enjoy a certain vogue today. Then, after its initial flowering of perhaps 200 years, Dominican literature fell on hard times at the coming of the Napoleonic wars and the subsequent Haitian invasion. During those days, Dominicans enjoyed no freedom of expression. Universities were closed, and the Church persecuted. Even the Spanish language itself was attacked by the Haitians, though Spanish traditions were kept alive by people like Juan Pablo Duarte. In addition to founding a rebel organization, Duarte and his group created an association devoted to preserving and promoting Dominican arts and culture. Thus, from the middle of the 19th century, one can date the emergence of a true Dominican literature, an indigenous form of writing not dominated by French or Spanish influences. Félix María del Monte, a poet, is often called the father of Dominican literature. He wrote patriotic texts and literary reviews, and created a genre of writing that emphasized local Dominican realism.

Post-Colonial Era

This new patriotic fervor in literature went hand in hand with the Dominicans' struggle against Spain in the early 1860s. At that point, it wasn't enough to merely fight for liberation; it was necessary to oppose Spain in the field of historical criticism as well and to further expose all the brutalities and errors of the original conquest. Hence, "Indianism" had a resurgence. It was at this time that the classic Dominican novel, *Enriquillo,* was written (published in 1882) by Manuel de Jesús Galván, a novel that emphasized the ideal of the noble savage. Robert Graves translated the novel into English in 1954 under the title *The Cross and the Sword. Enriquillo* is one of the masterpieces of Spanish-American literature. One leading contemporary of Galván was Salomé Ureña de Henriquez (1850–96), a teacher who wrote patriotic poetry in an intensely personal style.

Modernism

The changeover to modernism in Dominican literature took only about 10 years around the turn of the century. The leader of the modernist movement was Gastón Fernando Deligne (1861–1912), who wrote under the influence of such French symbolist poets as Valéry, declaring that "to write poetry is to turn ideas into images." This new movement in literature was devoted to an effort to cast off the formalities and restraints of all the old Hispanic traditions and to experiment with fresh materials and styles. Simplicity, elegance of movement, and introspection became prominent in modernism, although free verse did not appear in Dominican poetry until the 1920s. One new poetic style which came out of this casting about was called *postumismo,* which presented poetic images jostling about with each other in a current of change. Another group of writers, led by Domingo Moreno Jimines, sang the praises of simple peasant life.

As you'd expect, literary life slowed considerably under the fascist dictatorship of Trujillo. Many writers were forced underground or, like Manuel and Lupo Fernández Rueda, had to use symbols and metaphors to protest repression. In

GODFATHER DEATH

Once upon a time, the eighth child of a common laborer had not yet been baptized because the poor laborer could find no godfather for the boy. When Christ offered to be the boy's godfather, the laborer refused, choosing instead the devil, who told the laborer he would give the child magical healing powers. However, the devil warned the laborer that if the godson saw the devil standing at the foot of the bed of a patient, any effort to heal the patient would be futile.

Many years later, the king of the country fell mortally ill and offered the hand of his beautiful daughter to any physician who could cure him. When the healer who had been given special powers arrived, the king saw, to his surprise, the devil standing at the foot of the bed. The healer had fallen in love with the beautiful king's daughter and wanted her very much. Despite the devil's warning, the healer had four maids pick up the king's bed and turn it around, thus healing the king and winning the hand of the beautiful princess.

Before the wedding, however, the devil called the healer into a dark cave and showed him that the magic lantern of life had flickered out, a sign that the healer's life was over. Though the healer ran swiftly, before he could leave the cave, he was dead.

the 1940s, much foreign literature entered the country. This allowed for the emergence of "surprise poetry," which used images to shock its audience. Héctor Incháustegui Cabral led the *poesía de sorpresa* movement, and Antonio Fernández Spencer published collections of poetry that gained a wide international following. No mention of literary activity under Trujillo would be complete without mentioning Juan Bosch himself, a novelist, essayist, and short-story writer, who did most of his best work during the dangerous years of repression. He is best known for his two volumes of stories, *Cuentos Escritos en el Exilo* and *Más Cuentos Escritos en el Exilo,* as well as his history, *Crisis of Democracy of America in the Dominican Republic.* Bosch's stories of daily life among the Dominican peasants are engaging and highly regarded. Like many writers of the period, Bosch wrote in exile.

Contemporary

Dominican literature continues to thrive, not the least in the "Dom-York" groups living in New York. Contemporary poet and novelist Julia Álvarez wrote *How the García Girls Lost their Accents* (1991), describing an emigrant Dominican family in New York. Of the many other contemporary Dominican writers, Ivan García Guerra, Miguel Alfonseca, Jeannette Miller, and José Goudy Pratt are among the most influential.

Santo Domingo's neighborhoods, especially the colonial district and the middle-class neighborhoods of Gazcue and Naco, are filled with bookstores and newsstands. The selection of books and magazines is amazingly varied. Shelves are tightly packed with old and new volumes, and most bookstores are jammed with browsers and readers. All of this literary activity and interest is particularly amazing because books in the Dominican Republic are very expensive by anybody's standards and particularly so by a Dominican's. Still, the people come and often buy and enjoy, a testament to the cultural vibrancy of the country and its people.

GRAPHIC ART AND ARCHITECTURE

Graphic Art

Early Spanish conquerors quickly obliterated Taíno culture, and the settlers who followed failed to investigate or preserve records relating to the Taíno's lives. Thus, knowledge of pre-Columbian Taíno art and sculpture is very sketchy. It is, however, safe to say that the Taínos found rich possibilities in ceramic and sculptural arts. Many of their surviving works are based on totemic and ritualistic combinations. A great part of the surviving works are hardwood carvings or objects in terra-cotta and other ceramic material, mostly symbolic rather than naturalistic. These works demonstrate an abstract feel, along with a mastery of proportion and form. Also, the Taínos created more utilitarian works in the form of stools or low seats known as *duhos*. Made of dense black wood, ornamented sometimes with gold leaf, they were used by chiefs. Both the Museo del Hombre Dominicano, on the Plaza de la Cultura in Santo Domingo, and the anthropological museum at Altos de Chavón, near La Romana on the south coast, have wonderful, stimulating collections of Taíno art. Personal guides and helpful books in Spanish and English are available for tours.

Painting and sculpture developed very late in Dominican culture, especially in comparison with literature. Now, however, you'd think that just about everyone in the country wields a brush and palette. Santo Domingo in particular is a living, breathing open-air art gallery—and not just for tourists. Along with the beautiful Museum of Modern Art, at the Plaza de la Cultura, every Santo Domingo street corner seems to be occupied by Dominicans hawking cheap Haitian primitives, and every other fashionable corner in the prosperous neighborhoods has its own gallery with exhibits of modern art and paintings for sale. The Colonial District is especially important in painting, with numerous galleries and schools. Public and private buildings in Santo Domingo are often adorned with modern paintings, either on exhibit from the artist or as part of special collections. One summer evening in Santo Domingo, I watched a local artist create a huge mural on the street. I was not alone; hundreds watched, drank beer, and listened to merengue. It seemed an appropriate activity in a city so imbued with artistic spirit.

Nevertheless, Dominican painters have never quite developed a national style of their own. Much of contemporary painting and sculpture exhibits the same experimental trends and styles as European and North American work. Modern Dominican painting is a blend of African primitivism, color experimentation, and cubism. Numerous Dominican artists have achieved reputations in Europe and the United States, including Guillo Pérez, Gilberto Hernández Ortega, Ada Balcacer, and Adelardo Urdaneta. Much of their work is devoted to realistic Dominican scenes, peasant life, and landscape, though they do not share a common school of expression.

One thing is for sure about Dominican art: it is nothing like Haitian primitivism, which features bright colors, cubist style, and expressionist content. Some Dominican painters have a languid style, others devote themselves to abstract expressionism, and still others are religiously symbolic, but they all seem to steer clear of Haitian primitivism. Which is one reason why a lot of the stuff on sale to tourists throughout the Do-

*an example of
art deco architecture*

minican Republic isn't really authentic Dominican art. It's probably best to avoid buying cheap Haitian imitations, unless you want to decorate the kids' room. There's so much good Dominican work available, why not enjoy it?

If there *has* been a Dominican school of art during the 20th century, it is probably *costumbrismo,* which portrays common Dominican themes and customs. Abelardo Urdaneta was a precursor of *costumbrismo,* while Guillo Perez and Jorgi Morel have developed it. This particular school doesn't describe a style or philosophy so much as a subject matter—roosters crowing, sugarcane fields, oxen on rutted roads. More recently, the work of Candido Bido has taken on a cubist form, reflecting the influence of modern realism.

Architecture

While Santo Domingo may be the center of a flourishing painterly culture, the whole island is a complex and dazzling architectural spectacle. Perhaps nowhere else in the Caribbean are so many authentic styles on view. The seat of Spanish culture for 200 years before its economic decline began, Santo Domingo has maintained its importance as the architectural capital of the eastern Caribbean. Santiago, in the Cibao, rivals Santo Domingo in architectural complexity, though its history has seen a larger share of destruction from invasion and earthquakes.

The early builders of Santo Domingo worked with skill and daring. The forts, religious buildings, government structures, and houses of the nobles and governors are still impressive and appeared long before any similar structures were even dreamed of in Mexico or North America. The early architect and builder Rodrigo Gil de Liendo was responsible for the Church of Our Lady of Mercy and much of the old cathedral in Santo Domingo, structures which combine late Gothic and early Renaissance styles. Later builders developed a taste for medieval Gothic, classical Greek, and richly ornamented Spanish and Moorish styles. Almost every building in the colonial city of Santo Domingo shows some of these influences, and many are quite beautiful and fascinating in their own right. Taking a walk through much of Santo Domingo is like being back in the mid-16th century, up to and including the flourishing street life and artistically interwoven cultural activity.

Because of vast destruction from war and natural disaster, Santiago is a newer blend of styles, mostly Caribbean and Cuban Victorian. Much of the city retains a narrow-street, 19th-century look and feel. Because a lot of building was done during the 1920s and 1930s under the Trujillo regime, some of the urban architecture is reminiscent of art deco, with its emphasis on stucco, eyelid windows, and angular decoration. It's fascinating to see an art deco department store right next to a colonial facade, pink stucco abutting brown granite.

SALT AND PEPPER ARCHITECTURE

Much of modern construction in the Dominican Republic is in the "concrete box" style. Building these boxes is cheap and easy and contributes to the growth of the concrete industry—which is owned by important people in the government.

Fortunately, the Dominican Republic is full of another style of architecture which is truly Caribbean. Called "gingerbread" or "Victorian," these houses are practical and down to earth, made for a climate that includes heat, breeze, and hurricanes. These houses are bright with color, decorated intensely with wide verandas and spacious gardens. The roofs are peaked and low to protect the walls from rain and sun, with the verandas providing room to live outdoors on nice days. Wooden cut-out windows provide ventilation for interior rooms. Eaves and stairways are decorated with wooden cut-outs too.

Across the islands of the Caribbean, the combination of English, Dutch, Spanish, French, and African styles creates a unique style of its own, expressive of each island's character and needs. In the Dominican Republic, you'll find excellent examples of this style at Otra Banda, El Macao, Bayahibe, and Baní, among other small towns. Given the contrasting elements of the style, it is best called "salt and pepper" architecture.

Of particular interest in the Dominican Republic is a style of building which has come to be called Caribbean Victorian or Caribbean gingerbread. This style, more prominent on Antigua and in Haiti, is somewhat subdued in the Dominican Republic. In general, the gingerbread style involves a dazzling use of color, which seems to pulsate in the strong Caribbean sunshine. In its most elaborate form, the building usually consists of a facade and simple stairway lifting to the second floor, where there are clusters of balconies, open or closed, wooden, metal, or carved, or just made of planks. Sometimes the balcony is graced with simple or intricate fretwork in an organic or geometric motif.

The most important element of this Caribbean style of housebuilding is the peaked roof, usually constructed of thatch or wood shingles but today commonly composed of corrugated sheet metal or asbestos. Although most houses are uniform in shape, they vary wildly in detail. Contrasting colors tend to predominate; a white window frame may have yellow shutters, a blue door, a red frame, and a green handrail may crown a wooden or concrete block balustrade. Jalousie shutters may be multicolored. Sometimes, the style has a dormer window, characteristic of the French, or, in the style of the English, a bizarre array of porches. Every design emphasizes color—red, yellow, blue, green, and pink.

In the Dominican countryside, houses tend to be single story and porchless. They are nevertheless brightly painted, a treat to any eye. This style is everywhere, but you'll find particularly wonderful samples in the provinces of El Seibo and La Altagracia. The town of Otra Banda, just east of Higüey, is a fantasyland of great beauty and wonder. Santiago, in the Cibao, is noted also for its Victorian architecture, but it tends to be more stately and colonial, which is why many people think Santiago looks a lot like late-19th-century Cuba.

Folk Art

In recent years, folk art has seen a resurgence in the Dominican Republic. Part of this interest in craft is an expression of the modern Dominican search for roots, and part is the result of encouragement by governmental and international development agencies. Today, folk art is available for sale all over the island, and, as usual, represent a varying degree of value and quality. Many crafts are simple tourist curios, hardly worth the effort it takes to procure them. Some crafts, on the other hand, are truly magical works of art.

Campesinos in the Cibao region have preserved an already old tradition of making pottery for household use. Their decorative ceramics include dolls (especially spectacular in Santiago), nativity scenes, vases, lamps, ashtrays, and statuettes. Other popular crafts include palm weaving, woodcarving, and jewelry-making, most of these employing such local fibers as palm leaves. Shopping in any local market, you can find fine examples of mats and rugs, hammocks, straw hats, and baskets. Artisans utilize local supplies of amber and larimar to create truly beautiful, and quite expensive, jewelry. Unfortunately, tortoise shell and coral are also used.

The community of Salcedo is also known for its local crafts made from *higuero,* or calabash, a gourd from which the people carve fish, faces, and such musical instruments as Spanish maracas and the guiro, a merengue instrument. Local markets in every region of the Dominican Republic abound in unique products.

MUSIC AND DANCE

If I were a gambling man (and I am), I'd say it's about a 3-to-1 shot that when you step off an airplane at any of the Dominican Republic's international airports, a merengue band will be there to greet you. Not only that, but someone will hand you a plastic cup full of dark Dominican rum. In some ways, it's a perfect—and near-complete—introduction to the culture of the island.

As Dominican literature has defined itself over many years as the intellectual expression of the Dominican people, so music has defined itself as the people's emotional expression. The great thing about music is that it is composed in a language we can all understand.

Secular music had an important place in the daily lives of planters and the Dominican elite during the colonial era. Song and dance from Spain were imported directly, and forms like the bolero and fandango became important during the 18th century. Following a very old European tradition, itinerant musicians provided music on demand, using European stringed and wind instruments. Church music also followed the Spanish and European forms. As the centuries passed and time and distance from Spain increased, folk and popular music grew and developed a national character. Although some Taíno instruments seem to have survived the conquest, Taíno musical forms actually had little influence on the future course of Dominican folk music. What really powered music in the Dominican Republic were the African slaves, who brought ideas of certain dynamic rhythms and used several unique instruments, both of which contributed to turning Dominican music away from its Spanish roots.

Perhaps the earliest form of music and dance to emerge as a distinctive Dominican style was the sentimental serenade known as *barcarola criolla.* Some early dances, such as the *contradanza,* imported from Spain, evolved locally and became *tumba dominicana* or *contradanza criolla.* Eventually, the marriage of African rhythm to earlier European melodies produced the merengue, which in its pure form consists of a short introduction, followed by an eight-bar melody and a fast section of the same length. As both dance and music, the merengue is a national obsession, with music blasting everywhere at once, in taxis, self-service stores, restaurants, and bars. In the evenings, Santo Domingo's waterfront is like an open-air party, pulsating with music and street life. Late in July, Santo Domingo hosts an annual Merengue Festival, attended by thousands of Dominicans as well as tourists from Puerto Rico, Western Europe, America, and Canada. According to observers versed in musical forms, merengue is a fusion of the Spanish *paso doble* (two-step dance), and the African tom-tom. Whatever it is, it works.

Serious, or "longhair," music developed in the Dominican Republic in the middle of the 19th century, too. One leader in making Dominican music more distinctive was Juan Alfonseca, known as the father of the "national school," a composer of chamber orchestra music and liturgical songs. It is indicative that he also wrote merengues and many band pieces based on folk themes and tunes. Late in the 19th century, a modernist musical movement grew up that paralleled the trend in literature. Formed around the composer José de Jesús Ravelo, the musical movement tried to synthesize a link between indigenous themes and earlier romantic ones. Ravelo organized the first Dominican music school and composed oratorios, along with band music and piano works. Today, serious Dominican music owes its sense of direction to Juan García and Estéban Peña-Morell, both of whom used native song and dance for the foundation of their musical compositions. García even organized a new dance called *sambumbia* in order to more effectively fuse native and "serious" music.

At least one Dominican musical instrument is directly related to a Taíno instrument. The guiro, a hollow, notched, bottle-shaped gourd, is rubbed with a wire fork. It produces the shuffling sound that is a steady accompaniment to merengue music today. The *tambora* is a double-headed drum covered on one side with the skin of a male goat (doused with rum to increase its tautness). Supposedly, the other side of the drum is made from the skin of a female goat which has never given birth. Roving bands of minstrels, called *perico ripiao* or *prí prí,* often play these instruments and others including the *murumbula* (a thumb piano which is plucked), the *balsie* (accordion), and the *pandro* (tambourine). Naturally, modern guitars are used often by roving musicians, and in the rural areas flutes and homemade marimbas appear. Nowadays, merengue is often created with the help of modern synthesizers.

And while merengue may express the emotional exuberance of Dominicans, the *bachata,* a mournfully romantic ballad, often expresses their pathos. In fact, the bachata was once the most popular form of rural music, a kind of Dominican blues. The themes are often sad, although at times this popular folk music expresses satirical or sassy lyrics. Anthony Santos is one of the most popular *bachata* performers, and his "La Passola" is often cited as *bachata* at its best. *Perico ripao,* another popular folk music, is also often heard by tourists as they arrive at Santo Domingo's airport, and is often mistaken for merengue. Young Dominicans also enjoy reggae and salsa, and you'll find both featured prominently in concerts and in bars and dance halls.

Some older folkloric dances and songs are still hanging on, especially in rural regions. Along the south coast, the *mangulina* is celebrated on the patron saints' day festivals, as is the *jacana* in the north. These two dances are highly formalized ceremonials derived from Spanish forms. Vocal choruses such as the *salve* and *tornada* are directly inherited from Spain and, though they are not part of contemporary culture, are still performed at special events and shows. Likewise, the *sarandungza* is an African version of the rapid Spanish tap dance called the *zapateado.*

Several folkloric shows are produced in Santo Domingo, mostly for tourists. A number of national theaters and dance troupes perform in the capital regularly. There are a few restaurants in

Santo Domingo that feature waiters and waitresses who will burst into song and dance during the middle of an afternoon lunch or an evening dinner. Others, like the famous Mesón de la Cava, on the Parque Mirador in Santo Domingo, offer entire evenings devoted to Taíno and Dominican folk music and dance. And, of course, many feature strolling musicians who will play everything from Simon and Garfunkel to off-the-cuff merengue.

MERENGUE

Merengue! Imagine that you've just flown into Santo Domingo's International Airport, retrieved your bags, passed customs, and hopped that first taxi for downtown. Surprise! The cabby is playing merengue on his radio so loud, you can hardly hear yourself think. The highway into town runs along the blue Caribbean Sea, and in nearly every block, and at every intersection, bars and cafes have boomboxes out front, all blaring merengue. Kids on bicycles strap small radios onto their handlebars and keep them tuned to the loudest merengue station in town. Merengue, merengue, and more merengue! Never fear—you wouldn't be the first outsider to notice the omnipresence of music and dance in the Dominican Republic, nor to remark upon its seeming influence over the people and their attitude and behavior.

In fact, since the beginning of the 19th century, foreign travelers have admired the pronounced passion Dominicans seem to have for dancing and music. William Walton, a British soldier who came to Hispaniola as part of an 1809 expedition, observed many different dances, both urban and rural, which were featured as parts of the festive life of the country—the bolero, fandango, waltz, and Spanish country dance. Blacks and mulattos especially caught his attention, for they seemed to give these traditional dances an extra flair, a sexual air, and their musicians seemed to have added a spicy percussion to stately and romantic Spanish tunes.

During the brief period of Spanish annexation (1861–1865), the Spanish official Adriano Lopez Morillo noted in his memoirs, "It was already an old custom to dance in different houses on each of the holidays, in all the towns, just as with the country peasants who never missed a chance to have their *guateque.*" Later, the American judge Otto Schoenrich, who lived for several years in the Dominican Republic, pointed out in a travel book he wrote that nothing attracted all classes of Dominicans like dance and music. He remarked that every public holiday was an excuse to dance and that when there were no holidays, Dominicans danced anyway. In this way, merengue came to be the ultimate form of sociability on the island, expressing happiness and sorrow, love and death, politics and social strife. In merengue, one can be satirical, critical, ironic, sexual, or politically provocative. Having grown up in rural Hispaniola, merengue can take on the rough, pulsating beat of big cities as well.

The country's entire history—political, economic, psychosexual—is recorded somewhere in merengue (even technological events, as one old merengue reports: "Santiago has what it didn't use to have—an electric generator—and running water.").

For me, merengue is a great way to brush up on my Spanish. It is a good way to spend an hour over a couple glasses of rum and soda. As with many forms of Caribbean music, merengue depends upon participation. So in order to get it, you've got to get *with* it.

Tumba to Merengue

According to Dominican historian Emilio Demorizi, news of the merengue first appeared in local newspapers in 1854, written by an anonymous "Innocent" correspondent, which was a pseudonym commonly used by the Dominican poet Eugenio Perdomo. The article complained of the lasciviousness of the dance, its mischief, its chaos and confusion. The article read, "One dancer grabs the partner of the couple opposite to him. Meanwhile, the one remaining starts running from one side to the other, without the slightest idea of what he should do." And so forth. From this sample of journalistic outrage, it's clear many of the urban elite didn't quite know what merengue was supposed to be or do. In fact, coming from the rural regions of the country as it did, merengue tended to outrage intellectuals like writer Jesús Galván. The privileged, like Galván, saw merengue as perverse, with ridiculous movements. Many intellectuals in the middle of the 19th century called for the banishment of "this detestable dance of such poor taste."

When the merengue first appeared on the scene, the *tumba* was the favorite dance—considered, in fact, the national dance. One French travel writer, Paul Dhormovs, wrote of the *tumba* in 1859, "All the dancers form a double line, men on one side, women on the other. The orchestra gives a signal, they perform a four of conversion and face each other." He went on to describe a formalized dance of poses, awesome figures, and when each lady had danced with each gentleman, the dance was concluded.

THE MUSIC CHECKLIST

Dominican music is dominated by merengue, of course, but it also features traditional Caribbean jazz and folkloric music as well. The following checklist is only a sample, and you'll find a dazzling array of artists represented in every music store in the country. Most stores have CD players available so you can sample before you buy. I urge you to let your imagination and your ears find the sound you like.

Merengue
Keep in mind that there are around 20 different merengue styles. Most are regional. As you travel, you might try to find samples of regional sounds.

The Coco Band
Juan Luis Guerra
La Roca Banda
Milly, Jocelyn y Los Vecinos
Ramon Orlando
Los Hermanos Rosario
Juan Soriano
Wilfrido Vargas
Johnny Ventura
Fernandita Villaloma

Caribbean Jazz
Guillo Carias
Cesar Namnum/Grupo Maniel

Folkloric
Jose Fina
Fraruque Lieardo

Dhormovs concluded that in Paris, the dance itself would be considered immoral!

"The delicate lady embraces the gentleman, chest to chest!" This, according to many in Santo Domingo in 1859, characterized the sensuality and physical proximity of the new dance, and confirmed that the dance was given over to the devil. Apparently, the intellectual-led campaign against the merengue continued for 10 years, commencing about 1859 in Santiago, which caught the original anti-merengue fever from Santo Domingo. But the intellectuals didn't just object to the dance; they worried about the musical instruments used to create the rhythms as well. The elites detested all the "stringed instruments made in the country" and saved their wrath in particular for the accordion, which they thought was "insipid and detestable." According to an aristocrat called Espaillat, the merengue was part of a national failure of morals, which also included eating *sancocho* (Creole stew), watching cockfights, and leaving for tomorrow what can be done today.

What was actually the first merengue? Nobody knows, and it doesn't really matter. For years, during and after the Haitian invasion, and especially during the late 1840s, when the Haitians were finally kicked out the Dominican Republic, parties and dances in rural areas and small villages began to feature an array of stringed and percussion instruments, along with the accordion, and featured especially improvised lyrics, sometimes political, and sometimes lewd or bawdy. It is also true that Dominican soldiers in the struggle against the Haitians used to pass the time by playing improvised songs they'd learned in their countryside homes. With them, the merengue was used to record their victories in battle.

Similar dance forms were developing on Cuba and Puerto Rico at about the same time and were creating the same kind of moral outrages as well. In Cuba, the national dance was called the *upa,* and on Puerto Rico it was the *danza.* What all three dances shared was their sensual aspect, a reaction to formal modes of Spanish dance, and an eruption of national feeling.

The Ensemble

The original version of the merengue ensemble consisted of what is called Creole *bandurrias—* musicians playing strings. There could be from three to six strings in the ensemble, and all were charged with the duty of playing the melody for the dance. For the most part, the strings were traditional musical instruments from Spain, although they were fashioned from native materials.

The drum of the merengue ensemble came from Africa and was developed by Dominicans in the northwest of the country. Originally, the merengue drum was made from a hollowed tree trunk, with goat skin placed on both ends and tied with cord. Real ensembles tried to use billy goat skin on one end and nanny goat skin on the other to symbolize the bipolarity of the sexes. In real merengue, the drummer uses his left hand to pound on one end and to make a muted effect as background, while with his right hand he uses a stick to hammer out a sharp rhythm. Drummers can make a third distinct sound by simply tapping on the drum's rim with their sticks.

Because it is probably a native instrument, the guiro was the one that really pissed off the intellectuals. The original guiro was made of gourd, usually in the shape of a pear with an arched neck. On the neck, the musician carved grooves lengthwise. With a metal rod or with a stick to which nails had been added, the musician rasped up and down on the guiro, which produced a sharply percussive sound used to accompany the strings. After merengue really got going, around 1900, the gourd used to make the guiro became somewhat rare, and musicians began creating metal guiros. Materials such as tin were fashioned and called *guayo,* which produced much sharper and raspier sounds. The modern *guayo* consists of a cylindrical piece of metal with a cone shape at both ends and a rough surface which the player rubs with wire or wood to make a sound like nothing else, an unmistakable background to all merengue. Its relatives can be seen in groups playing Cuban and Puerto Rican music today and in all salsa ensembles as well.

Between 1874 and 1880, a real revolution took place in merengue. The diatonic accordion took the place of the traditional Spanish strings, and merengue as we know it today was off and running. The accordion had arrived in the Dominican Republic from Germany, as part of an active commercial exchange between the Cibao, served by the port of Puerto Plata, and Hamburg, where Dominicans sold their tobacco. For some reason, the accordion appealed to the musical sensibility of the rural people. Interestingly, about this same time in history, the accordion came to Argentina and was just as enthusiastically accepted there, leading to the tango, the national music of Argentina.

In the typical merengue band of the early 1900s, the accordion player sat in the center of the ensemble and formed an equilateral triangle with the drummer (the *bambotero*) on the right and the guiro player on the left. The accordion player traditionally rendered homage to the merengue dancer by nodding to his accordion and, according to tradition, used to stand at the end of every tune and say, "Now it's time to pay up!" In original merengue, the accordion speaks for lovers. An early merengue recites:

> *Listen, listen to me my darling,*
> *to what the accordion says*
> *from now until the morning*
> *from now until the morning*
> *my heart is yours . . .*

And then came a truly revolutionary development—the inclusion of the saxophone in the ensemble. According to an old story out of Santiago, one night a drummer became ill, and the sax was the only other musical instrument available. The audience liked the new sound so much that soon other musicians in the quarter made the saxophone a part of their ensembles as well. From Santiago, the saxophone as part of the ensemble spread throughout the island. After the introduction of the saxophone, the sky was the limit. With the coming of the 1920s, Dixieland emerged as a dominant musical form in North America. During that decade, bands emerged that included many different instruments, including whole orchestras that played merengue-type music. Pianos, strings, clarinets, and trumpets were added, especially in the social clubs of the elite, which had begun to accept the new music as part of their scene. According to history, an orchestra from Santiago first performed ballroom merengue at the Club de Comercio in Santo Domingo on December 31, 1920. The music was applauded enthusiastically. Traditional musicians accustomed to playing older,

slower styles like the *paseo* and *jaleo* began to incorporate merengue into their repertoires.

It seems that when American soldiers came to the Dominican Republic during the occupation of 1916–24, they couldn't adapt to the richly complex two-step style of the merengue, even though they liked the rhythms. They instead danced in a kind of jumpy fashion, which was called the *pambiche* by Dominicans trying to pronounce "Palm Beach." From then on, any slow merengue was called the *pambiche* and entered Dominican life, so to speak, through the back door.

Big Band Era

The Trujillo era was one of big bands, and with the arrival of radio broadcasting, movies, and the huge ballroom, merengue entered its heyday. Poets used merengue music as the source of their inspiration, and painters painted dancers and musicians above all topics. And, from his first electoral campaign in 1930, Trujillo used the merengue as a tool for political propaganda. His speeches were accompanied by a quartet that played themes allusive to his presidential campaign. Popular musicians participated in the campaign as well. Some of the most popular and prolific merengue composers and artists began their careers in the 1930s, like Nico Lora and Tono Abreu, who, along with Luis Alberti, gave merengue its modern features. One merengue by Isidoro Flores celebrates the victory of Trujillo:

> *Horacio has gone*
> *and now Trujillo is in*
> *we have hopes*
> *in our Chief (Caudillo).*
>
> *All will change*
> *in hot pursuit*
> *because now Trujillo*
> *is the President.*

With the emergence of musicians and composers like Alberti, the modernization—one should say the urbanization—of the merengue was complete. The accordion and guitar were replaced completely by the saxophone, clarinet, and trumpet, though the rhythm section was preserved with the drum and the guiro. Piano was added, as was a suave, urban singer, unlike the shrill rural singer of earlier years. In the years that followed, American jazz influenced merengue in many ways, especially in the interplay of the saxophones of the orchestra. So-called "Latin music" was all the craze in Europe and America, and Alberti's orchestra played dancing music during the evenings in the Patio Español of the Hotel Jaragua in Santo Domingo. Then the largest center of its kind in the country, the Patio Español was where the merengue and bolero reached their climax in the nasal voice of Pipi Franco, in the vocalization of Marcelino Placido, and in the grave and melodious phrases of Rafael Colon.

As the orchestras kept getting bigger and bigger, the music grew hotter and hotter. Of special note during the Trujillo era was the Super Orchestra San José, a musical group of the radio and television station La Voz Dominicana. This orchestra became a kind of cultural icon, an entire super-complex of activities supported by Trujillo's brother Petan. Its chief singer was Joseito Mateo, who came to be known as the "King of Merengue." Its style was distinctly American, and it played in one of the most luxurious ballrooms of the time, the nightclub of La Voz Dominicana. Through appearances on TV and in huge stage shows around the country, Mateo became phenomenally popular in the Dominican Republic. Even so, the advent of TV allowed many other stars of merengue to appear, and for rural, and slower, merengue to be presented as well. At this time, hundreds of merengue artists emerged, creating whole new synergies, styles, and compositions. At the same time, during the period 1927–58, recordings of merengue became more and more common and available on the world market. Even Leopoldo Stokowski stopped into Ciudad Trujillo in 1940 to perform and record some merengue. In 1955, Trujillo contacted the famous Xavier Cugat to perform and record merengue, hoping to carry the nation's image farther abroad (and thereby enhance Trujillo's own standing, of course).

Combos and Electricity

Trujillo and his family were big backers of orchestral merengue, not only giving it the political sanction to become huge in production values, but also providing continued forums in which orchestral music could be played for the elite and the emergent military middle class. After Trujillo's death, the big bands began inevitably to decline. These groups, about 20 in number, with singers and dancers, had reached an ultimate social level, and the new regimes were unable to afford that kind of musical commitment.

At the same time, a new model of musical organization, the combo, began to make waves, especially as first created by Cortijo and his combo in Puerto Rico. Combos reduced the number of musicians involved to about 10 or so, which made the music more affordable. The big ballrooms began to give way to smaller venues, called *boites,* which were more like nightclubs and cafes combined. American rock and roll came on the scene at the same time, and the combos began to use electric guitar, electric piano, and sound amplifiers. In the sixties, Johnny Ventura and his combo headed this new movement in merengue, which included new choreography for the singers and a hotter sound.

You might say that Johnny Ventura was the Elvis Presley and Bob Dylan of his country, because he headed both a hot new sound and a new liberality, questioning the traditional conservative values of Dominican society. Johnny Ventura claimed that merengue during Trujillo had been "totally committed to the tyranny" and that he had gone out and tried to change all that. When Trujillo was assassinated, people danced in the streets to Ventura tunes and a whole genre of merengue grew up around irreverant stances toward Trujillo and his family. A lot of this social protest still had to be expressed through double meanings and hidden metaphors. Many of Ventura's popular merengues are still available on tape and CD. They are a must for anyone interested in the evolution of modern merengue.

Opposed to the Ventura sound, but still dynamic, was the composer Félix del Rosario and his Magos del Ritmo, which appeared first in the Hotel Europa in Santo Domingo in 1964. Combining a dynamic chorus of saxophones (soprano, baritone, and tenor) with a clarinet, xylophone, flute, bass, and kettle drum, Rosario's merengue premiered a music that came to mean to 1960s Dominicana what Beatles music meant to Britain and the United States. Soon, Rosario's music was at the center of the social whirl of Santo Domingo, and the Hotel Europa became the backdrop for much intellectual and social butterflying.

In the 1970s, an even more accelerated merengue appeared, thanks to Wilfrido Vargas, who reinforced the style begun by Johnny Ventura. Now, all the electronic instruments came to the fore: piano, bass, and synthesized sound effects. One result of electrification was the ability of merengue to compete with other Latin rhythms such as salsa, reggae, and rock and roll. Now Antillean music could surge back into New York City.

As the years rolled by, many traditionalists will tell you, merengue lost its unique flavor. It has now blended into an international style, prompted partly by the internationalization of the record industry and partly by the need for new artists to compete with musical influences all over the world. Perhaps the most proficient artist in this international style is Fernandito Villalona, who has become something of a celebrity, especially among young girls.

New York City in its own time has given back a lot of merengue as well. Milly, Jocelyn y Los Vecinos embody the expression of the Dominicans overseas. The group, four brothers and sisters, projects the role of the family in the migration process, taking as their theme what it requires to be successful in America. Many of their songs are directly related to the lives of immigrants in New York and their haunted relationships to their native countries.

Modern merengue is a huge success and growing every day. Women are emerging as artists in their own right. Voices like Sandy Reyes, Ruby Peréz, and Miriam Cruz stand out in the new merengue. The record shops of the Dominican Republic are filled with merengue, and if you pass up the opportunity to take some home, you're really missing out.

As I've said, merengue tapes and CDs are available nearly everywhere in the Dominican Republic. If you're looking for merengue in North America or Europe, Karen Records of Miami, Florida, has a very large selection indeed. Its artists include 80% of all the merengue stars, including Guerra and Vargas. For more information, call Karen Records at 305/471-0073, or ask your local record store to stock or special order their CDs. You can write for a catalogue to Karen Records, 7062 N.W. 50 Street, Miami, Florida 33166.

HAZARD

CONTEMPORARY MERENGUE

Although merengue lyrics are often about love and relationships, just as often they deal with politics and social situations. By using irony and allusion, merengue comments on everyday Dominican life. The chorus of one contemporary song goes like this:

Buscando visa para un sueño

Buscando visa de cemento y cal y el asfalto

¿Quien me va a encontrar?

Buscando visa, la razón de ser

Buscando visa, para no volver

Buscando visa, la necesidad

Buscando visa, que rabia me da

Buscando visa, golpe de poder

Buscando visa, que mas puedo hacer

Buscando visa, para naufragar

Buscando visa, carne de la mar

Buscando visa, la razón de ser

Buscando visa, para no volver

<u>Translation:</u>

Looking for a visa to a dream

Looking for a visa of cement and lime and asphalt

Who is going to meet me?

Looking for a visa, the reason for being

Looking for a visa, to not return

Looking for a visa, the necessity

Looking for a visa, drives me crazy

Looking for a visa, to have strength

Looking for a visa, what else can I do?

Looking for a visa, to be shipwrecked

Looking for a visa, meat of the sea

Looking for a visa, the reason for being

Looking for a visa, to not return

—*Visa para un Sueño,* words and music by Juan Luis Guerra; used by permission of Karen Publishing Co.

BOB RACE

ON THE ROAD
OUTDOOR ACTIVITIES

Given the fact that most Dominicans pretty much have to struggle to make ends meet, recreation isn't something that most people have time for. Even so, they are a sports-minded people, and, in 1974, the 12th Central American and Caribbean Olympic Games were held in Santo Domingo. At that time, the Dominican government constructed some huge sports facilities, including a sports palace with seating for 10,000 spectators, an Olympic-size swimming pool, a bicycle track, and a shooting range. Located in a quiet neighborhood of Santo Domingo, this huge facility provides recreation for every citizen of the city and for visitors with special permission. Especially if you spend long periods in Santo Domingo, it is a wonderful place to go for swimming, bicycling, jogging, and games of pick-up basketball.

And although the average citizen of the Dominican Republic has little time for recreation, Dominicans still love to swim and ride horses. Of course, for the visitor with time on his hands, the country is a paradise.

SWIMMING

It's undeniable that many visitors come to the Dominican Republic for beaches and the swimming. All of the beaches in the country are public property, though you'll sometimes find access limited by resort rules, hotel buildings, and cabanas. I hate to be one to rate beaches, but everybody does it, so I'll give it a shot. Keep in mind the weather, including the mini-variations in rainy seasons from north to south. In general, southern beaches feature more placid water and less wind, while northern beaches feature stronger tides and more unpredictable weather.

Samaná Peninsula
Perhaps the best overall area for beaches is the Samaná Peninsula. Best in that area is the **Cayo de Levantado,** a small island fringed with palm-shaded white sand beaches and washed by beautiful turquoise water. You can reach this beach easily by ferry from the town of Samaná. About half an hour from Samaná town is **Las Galeras,** on Rincón Bay, which also has fabulous beaches and a number of isolated tourist hotels. North and west of Samaná town lies the well-known **Las Terrenas,** perhaps the peninsula's crown jewel when it comes to rustic resorts.

North Coast

Of course, the entire north coast to the east of Puerto Plata is known for its white sand beaches, making this area the center of resort development for the past decade or so. As you go around the Dominican Republic to the far east coast, you reach a 24-km stretch of palm-fringed, white sand Atlantic beach from approximately Macao to Punta Cana. You can rough it on these beaches and commute from nearby provincial towns, or you can stay at one of the resorts at Bávaro and Punta Cana, both of which provide luxury atmospheres for their guests.

South Coast

If you concentrate on the south coast for swimming you'll run into the problem of high cliffs, which are part of the island's limestone shelf. In the vicinity of Santo Domingo, you'll find the famous **Boca Chica** beach, widely popular with the international tourist crowd and with Santo Domingans who take their pleasure there regularly on Saturday and Sunday afternoons. The waters of Boca Chica are shallow and placid, and I found the swimming a little boring. Mostly, it's a holiday beach, crowded with swimmers, vendors, and sunbathers. Still, it's a place to go cool off when you're in Santo Domingo.

Beyond the airport, and along the south coast, are beaches at **Juan Dolio** and **Guayacanes.** These beaches and resorts are crowded on weekends and at the high season, but at other times draw a less pleasure-seeking crowd. The water is a little deeper than at Boca Chica and seems somehow much cleaner, too. **Bayahibe,** beyond Casa de Campo and its 7,000-acre resort, is the most beautiful beach on the south coast and one of the most idyllic beaches anywhere on the island. At the rate it's being developed, I don't know how much longer it will remain rustic, but you can still find peace and quiet there much of the year. It makes a stark contrast to the crowded conditions at Boca Chica and can be reached in a two-hour drive from

TOP 10 DOMINICAN SIGHTSEEING HIGHLIGHTS

1. Colonial Zone, Santo Domingo
Eminently walkable, the Western Hemisphere's first European city holds cultural and historical gems including the First Cathedral, Columbus Fortress, and House of the Governors, among many other sights.

2. Whale-watching, Samaná Bay
During January and February, thousands of Arctic humpback whales calve, feed, and rest in the sparkling waters of this beautiful bay.

3. The Silver Bank
Located in the Atlantic Ocean just north of Puerto Plata, this shallow coral and lagoon area is winter home to whales, turtles, and marine mammals.

4. Mt. Isabel de Torres, Puerto Plata
Just outside the historic port of Puerto Plata, a steep cable-car ride takes you to rainforest and a high-mountain view of much of the spectacular north coast of the Dominican Republic.

5. Pico Duarte
The highest peak in the Caribbean, this 10,000-foot

mountain can be hiked in three days. It's a unique adventure for travelers.

6. Los Haitises National Park
Definitely off the beaten track, this karst wonderland of sinkholes, mangroves, and cones is a must-see for nature lovers.

7. Bayahibe/Dominicus Beach
Idyllic blue water, superb diving and snorkeling, and excellent, inexpensive accommodations.

8. Sierra de Bahoruco Overlook
About as isolated as you can get in the Dominican Republic; a spectacular drive with an awesome view of stark mountain country.

9. Constanza/Jarabacoa
Small mountain towns with roses, strawberries, and waterfalls. A perfect climate.

10. Boca Chica
So gauche it's cool. People-watching at its best.

Santo Domingo.

Along the south coast west of Santo Domingo, you'll find only a few sandy beaches that are safe for easy swimming. Most of the coast is beset by rocky shelfs, steep drop-offs, uncertain tides, and undertows. At **Playa Monte Río,** south of Azua, you'll find a decent beach, ditto at **La Saladilla** and **Los Quemaditos,** south of Barahona. But the farther south of Barahona you go on the Pedernales Peninsula, the wilder and less hospitable the beaches get. You certainly shouldn't swim in any isolated spot down there. Besides, most of the water approaches are rock-and-pebble bound and lack roads and other facilities. This admonition includes **Playa San Rafael,** near Barahona, which some people use for swimming.

SCUBA DIVING

Scuba diving is in its infancy in the Dominican Republic, with few professional divers and dive schools available. But with coral reefs bordering on all three Dominican coasts and wrecks numbering about 400, the place is a paradise for both scuba diving and snorkeling. Because the sports (especially scuba diving) are basically unregulated, be prepared to bring your own equipment, in the interest of both safety and convenience.

La Caleta

Probably the best place for diving near Santo Domingo is at La Caleta, located about an hour from Santo Domingo along the Las Américas highway. As mentioned before, this spot has been declared an underwater national park and can be reached by a fast boat (for 15 divers) from Boca Chica beach in about 17 minutes at a cost of around RD$2,000. Also, the public park along the highway operates a fleet of leaky dinghies in need of improvement. Each of these wooden boats barely holds four divers and their equipment, and, if the swell is high, you'd best say a little prayer before you head out. The dinghies are all beached and you can see them from the highway. There is great pressure on the boat owners not to improve their boats—if an owner happens to buy a new boat, it often disappears overnight. Still, if you wish to chance

the small dinghy experience, you'll pay only about RD$200.

Despite the difficulty of getting to La Caleta, the reef and its wreck are pure paradise. The *Hickory* wreck is an iron ship in about 60 feet of water. Schools of fish hover around the hull, suspended in the current. Coral and shellfish have become part of the ship's outer and inner plates, and huge parrot fish have taken up residence in the hull. The visibility is about 60–70 feet and the light good, both of which make for excellent underwater photography. About a seven-minute swim from the *Hickory* is another wreck, at 100 feet. Visibility there is said to be about 80–90 feet. Coral is a carpet of color that has webbed itself over a large wooden sailing vessel, a wreck much more awesome than the iron-clad *Hickory*. Unfortunately, hurricanes and high winds will eventually break up this wooden vessel, so if you want to see it, go soon.

Catalina Island

Spectacular but suitable only for experienced divers is "the wall" off of Catalina Island. The island itself is located just off the provincial town of La Romana, about a two-hour drive from Santo Domingo. As with most wall dives, it is easy to go deeper than you intend, so care must be taken. The visibility is fair to good at 55–60 feet, and the coral formations are gigantic. You can see large fish like grouper here, which makes it a unique diving experience since most of the big species have been cleaned out of reefs by sport fishermen. There is also a shallower dive of about 25–30 feet off Catalina, and it features an abundance of sea fans and gorgonian gardens, fluorescent fish, and excellent visibility of about 90–100 feet with good light—great for photographs. You can take a boat to Catalina from the marina at La Romana, or join an excursion from Casa de Campo nearby. It's a popular spot, not hard to reach. With permission from the Naval Station at La Romana, you can stay the night, but the place is buggy and has no facilities.

Bayahibe

About a two-hour drive from Santo Domingo and just beyond La Romana is Bayahibe, a dive that has become known as the "feeding ground." Here large schools of fish feed on handouts from local divers. Waving a white glove will produce a

BOB RACE

flurry of activity. Although it's become popular to feed the fish, it isn't a wise thing to do, and in most countries it is prohibited for sound ecological reasons. For example, if you feed fish, their fear of predators lessens, and schools tend to react sluggishly when really threatened. Natural foraging also stirs up microorganisms, which then form part of the food chain. For these and many other reasons, please don't feed the fish anywhere you dive. If you go down to the "feeding ground," just enjoy—don't indulge.

Queen angelfish

Los Bajos

To the west of Santo Domingo, the isolated spot called Los Bajos in Bahía Ocoa (Ocoa Bay) has large fish populations. This spot is about a two-hour drive from Santo Domingo, and the bay itself has become a popular weekend resort for many people who live and work in the capital. The little town located there is called Palmar de Ocoa.

Samaná and Las Terrenas

The north coast has excellent diving around Samaná and Las Terrenas. It is here that you'll find the country's largest concentration of shipwrecks. In Samaná, you can contact Brigitte at 809/538-2480, the number for the **Tropical Lodge** diving shop, which rents equipment and runs excursions. This French-owned resort has been in Samaná for many years and keeps abreast of what's going on in the sport of diving. The staff can also direct you to reasonable snorkeling opportunities.

The **Tropical Dive Center** in Las Terrenas is a little more than two years old and situated on a beautiful beach. Owned and operated by Roland Fivat and Gerd-Peter Wiedmer (tel. 809/589-9410, fax 809/589-9412), the center provides English-language courses. Individual dives begin at RD$500 (including equipment) with 10-dive packages starting at RD$4,625 and rising to around RD$8,250. The usual price for a night dive is RD$560. The center holds a variety of classes, including one in underwater photography and underwater video filming. Next door to the dive shop is the **Hotel Tropic Banana,** which has comfortable, clean, but somewhat expensive rooms for RD$500–750. However, there are also several less-expensive hotels (RD$300–500) in the area. Another possibility in the Samaná area is located near the mouth of Samará Bay near Miches, where the wrecks of the 17th century Spanish galleons *Tolosa* and *Guadalupe* lie. Consult one of the Samaná dive shops for information and trips.

Puerto Plata and Sosúa

Forget the north coast around Puerto Plata and Sosúa; the reefs are damaged and the weather is bad most of the time. Still, you can go there to get your open-water certification.

SNORKELING

Anywhere you find a reef, you can snorkel. And this particularly applies to the east coast from Samaná Bay to Punta Cana. Along the north coast around Monte Cristi you can find good snorkeling in the extensive reef system and offshore islands. In fact, almost anywhere you can dive you can try your hand at snorkeling. Still, because snorkeling can be a little harder to find, it may be a good idea to join a tour at first. Along the east coast, **Punta Cana Beach Resort** runs expeditions, and the waters off **Club Med** are chock full of spiny urchins, tropical fish, and large quantities of brain coral. On the north coast, you can try **Caribbean Marine** in Puerto Plata (tel. 809/320-2249), **Aquasports** in Sosúa (tel. 809/571-3530), or especially **Gri-Gri Divers** in Río San Juan (tel. 809/589-2671).

Santo Domingans are getting deeper and deeper into diving and, as tourism grows, so, too, probably, will the capital's resources for the sport. Both **Gus Diving** and **Dominican Adventures** currently offer classes, equipment, and excursions from Santo Domingo. Both offer PADI (Professional Association of Dive Instruction) certification. PADI instructors can also be certified through the NAUI (National Association of Underwater Instruction), and a couple of other organizations. Gus Diving is a retail shop owned by Gustavo and Mechi Torreira, located at Plaza La Lira II, Roberto Pastoriza No. 356 (tel. 809/566-0818). Owned and operated by Michael McClellan, an Australian who has lived in the Dominican Republic for more than 10 years, Dominican Adventures is located at Calle Dr. César Dargam, No. 20 (tel. 809/541-7884). You can take courses at Dominican Adventures, usually lasting several days in length, with testing in pool sessions. You can generally get your certification for about RD$3,600, but call ahead for current prices. Bring your own equipment if you want to save some money.

From Santo Domingo, both Gus Diving and Dominican Adventures organize excursions to various diving sites. For about RD$800 you can go along with Dominican Adventures on a Saturday or Sunday trip to Catalina Island, which includes two dives and a snack (four-person minimum). Both shops organize groups on an on-call basis to La Caleta and Bayahibe for about RD$800. Dominican Adventures can take its customers to Saona Island for RD$1,100. Most of the time you have to pay your own transportation costs, although a boat journey to the site is generally included in the price of the tour.

Hazards

Diving and snorkeling are not inherently dangerous. However, a few cautionary words should suffice to get you thinking about the reef and some of its dangers. Avoid swimming or diving around population centers, as most Dominicans consider the ocean a sewage-disposal system. Many fantastic snorkeling and diving reefs line the northwest Dominican coast near Monte Cristi, reefs which haven't been exploited by tourists yet.

Never snorkel or dive alone, and avoid planning a snorkeling or diving expedition to the north coast during December–March, when winds and tides are strong. The same is true for the reefs along the east coast starting at Punta Cana. Weather and winds along the south coast are gentler, and the water shallower. Generally, diving and snorkeling are good all year.

As a general rule, you shouldn't snorkel when there is a heavy swell running or when waves are breaking on a reef. Crashing waves are very dangerous things and can drive a snorkeler into a reef, with disastrous consequences. Never snorkel where people are fishing, either with spears or lines. Avoid snorkeling at night, except on organized tours with qualified guides.

Finally, there are some (although not many) creatures that can give you a nasty wound on the reef. Fire coral, which looks like real coral, takes the shape of anything it encrusts but has tips that can produce a strong sting. Spotted scorpionfish are aptly named, and if you step on one of these creatures as it's hiding on a sandy bottom, it will spike your foot. Little bristle worms can break off their "arms" when you touch them, thus embedding a painful remnant in your skin. And, of course, the moray eel can cause a perilous bite. If any of these creatures gets you, get out of the water quickly and calmly, wash the affected area with soap and water, cleanse it with alcohol, and get to a doctor.

Etiquette

I don't much like snorkeling in groups. But sometimes it's unavoidable, and even preferable—especially in a country like the Dominican Republic, where many reefs are barely accessible or are dangerous at certain times of the month. All the major resort hotels organize reef tours, especially in and around La Romana and along the east coast at Punta Cana. Even if you feel more comfortable with a group, sometimes it is better to go off with one or two others, especially because large groups tend to frighten fish. Another idea is to take a group tour based out of a major resort hotel, explore the area, and then come back some other time. That way, you get the advantage of foreknowledge, which can be put to good use later, when you can explore quietly and at your own pace.

Visibility in a reef is best when the sun is high. Unfortunately, however, most reef fish feed early in the morning or as the sun sets. Whatever time you choose, being quiet, moving slowly, and leaving glinting jewelry behind in your room will improve your chances of seeing more species. Remember, mostly you're there to float, not to thrash around. Keep noise and sudden movement to an absolute minimum by keeping your fins just below water level. Before you go, study up on reef life, and take along a good picture guide to the animals and plants.

In fact, you may want to decide beforehand on an agenda. You might devote an afternoon or evening to observing predation on the reef. After all, coral polyps, starfish, and other tentacled feeders capture food from currents; invertebrates browse on algae; small fish eat tiny crustaceans; octopi eat mollusks; large fish eat small fish. Floating slowly, you can sometimes observe chains of such behavior.

Likewise, you might choose to observe color in the reef. Sharks and rays, for example, are monotone and blend into ocean water backgrounds. Flounders, groupers, octopuses, and others have developed the ability to change their body colors to fit in against different backgrounds. You might also try to observe the puzzling phenomenon of "poster coloration." Poster coloration applies to reef fish that are adorned in particularly bright hues and shades, with odd patterns on their bodies. Most of the time, such poster coloration isn't related to habitat, and it has thus puzzled scientists who have offered much speculation as to its cause and purposes.

Like most snorkelers, I began by seeing the reef as a whole—its colors, sheer wall drop-offs, coral gardens, the clouds of hovering fish, the occasional barracuda. It was almost like looking at a marvelous Picasso or Mondrian in a great museum. But the more you dive, the more refined your vision becomes and the more you can pick out each reef function, or at least speculate on them.

Luckily for Caribbean snorkelers, the voracious crown-of-thorns starfish is confined to Pacific reefs. Thus, the Caribbean reefs are likely to be delicately branched, as opposed to the denser, more squat Pacific kinds. Moreover, Caribbean reef fish tend to be different from their Pacific brothers and sisters. Divers might pursue fish identification with an eye to spotting many kinds of fish endemic to Caribbean waters.

It's okay, too, if you just want to float mindlessly. I do it all the time.

WHALE-WATCHING

Humpback whales migrate from cold arctic waters to the north coast of the Dominican Republic every year between mid-December and mid-March. These huge creatures make their long trek from areas around Newfoundland, Nova Scotia, Iceland, Maine, and Greenland to mate in warmer waters. They do not eat during their journey, nor do they eat during the time they spend in Dominican waters. They come to Dominicana strictly to breed. The pregnant females will carry for 11–12 months, then give birth to a calf that weighs nearly one ton and drinks 50 gallons of milk each day. The mature humpback is often 12 meters (50 feet) in length and can weigh 40 tons.

The humpbacks don't have humped backs. They arch their backs as they dive. They are also acrobatic and can be seen flying through the air in breach—part of the courting dance of the males. It is estimated that as many as 2,000–3,000 humpback whales spend the winter in Dominican waters, probably 80% of the entire north Atlantic population.

Since whale-watching began off the Dominican Republic in 1985 it has grown dramatically. Samaná is now the most popular whale-watching destination in the whole Caribbean, and all signs indicate continued growth. Only Puerto Rico has more absolute numbers of whale-watching tourists, but the gap is diminishing quickly.

In 1986 President Balaguer established the **Santuario de Ballenas Jorobadas del Banco de la Plata** (Silver Bank Humpback Whale Sanctuary). Many travelers now make the six- to eight-hour journey to the shallow silver bank off the north coast. Many more find that viewing whales in the Samaná Bay south of Santa Bárbara de Samaná is easier. The two-hour trips in Samaná Bay are a growth industry. The government estimates that 15,000 people watched whales in Samaná Bay in 1993, while only 200 made the journey to Silver Bank. Most Silver Bank visitors leave from Puerto Plata on the 80-km (50-mile) journey. Other ports of embarkation include Luperón and Grand Turk Island in the Turks and Caicos Islands. Wintering with the humpbacks on Silver Bank are spotted, spinner, and bottlenose dolphins and pilot, Brydes, and various other whales. Like the Samaná season, the Silver Bank season is January to March, with a peak in February.

Most of the tourists who now come to whale-watch are western Europeans. In the press of business, both at Silver Bank and on Samaná Bay, the plight of the whales and the danger they face may be increased by the pressure of tourism. Hence, all this attention is a double-edged sword.

Conservation

Right now a couple of reputable whale-watching tour organizers operate out of Samaná. Many other people just accept a ride at the dock from boats hired on the spot. Unfortunately, in the excitement of seeing a whale, many boats get too close, which is dangerous for both the tourist and the whale. Now, many whale-watchers and international ecological organizations are expressing concern regarding whale-watching, especially in Samaná Bay. Among those objecting are the Center for Marine Conservation (CMC) in the United States, the Worldwide Fund for Nature Conservancy in Germany, and the Centro para la Conservación y Ecodesarrollo de la Bahía de Samaná (CEBSE) in the Dominican Republic. These associations complain about the high number of boats which sometimes pursue a single whale or which speed through groups of the animals.

The Samaná Bay Boat Owners Association has formed some committees to work out the problems of whale-watching. The boat owners recognize that there are safety and ecology issues, including too many boats and tourists, inexperienced guides (often just young kids), a shortage of life jackets and radios, and reckless handling of boats. (Whale-watchers aren't the only violators; huge oceangoing vessels of the Dole Pineapple Company often speed through the bay to their port at Arroyo Barril, posing another danger to the whales.)

Tours

Each of the all-inclusive luxury hotels offers excursion visits to Samaná Bay. You can arrange one as part of your stay, but whether you arrange a tour through your hotel, use one of the independent tour guides in Samaná, or just go down to the dock and hire one of the many available boats (usually quite small), be sure to exercise some judgment and caution. First, consider safety: don't hire a boat from an inexperienced kid, and don't hire a boat that doesn't have proper safety equipment. If your boat goes too fast, gets too close, or does something crazy, complain and put a stop to it. Try not to participate in "hounding" tours, where dozens of boats pursue a single whale and her calf.

Whale Samaná is the oldest tour operator in the Samaná area, and you can contact them at any of the major hotels. **Whale Marine,** operated by Canadian Kim Beddell (Box 53-2, Samaná, tel. 809/538-2588, fax 809/538-2545), is an ecologically responsible tour operator in the bay. Bedell has a Victoria II 50-foot vessel, equipped with radio and life jackets and licensed to carry 60 passengers. She makes two trips each day, leaving Samaná at 9 A.M. and 1:30 P.M., carrying soft drinks, oranges, and crackers. She also distributes a booklet entitled *Whales of Samaná* and gives a short lecture onboard. Her rate is US$35 per person for a four-hour tour, and she has pledged to conduct herself according to the new Whale Watch Regulations.

If you are already in the Dominican Republic, then **Ecoturisa** or any of the competent tour agencies in Puerto Plata can help you arrange a trip to the Silver Bank. There are no pick-up adventures that I know of, and it would not be prudent to try to arrange a visit on a do-it-yourself basis. The water on the Silver Bank is shallow and reefy in some places, deep in others. The weather also changes quickly, and there have been many shipwrecks in the area. Do yourself a favor and contact a competent tour operator, then check with care the type of vessel, the crew, and the safety arrangements.

One good, safe, well-run outfit is **Bottom Time Adventures** (P.O. Box 11919, Ft. Lauderdale, Florida 33339, tel. 305/921-7798 or U.S. tel. 800/234-8464, fax 305/920-5578). Bottom Time runs tours to the Silver Bank about 11 times each season. Depending upon the departure date, the tour leaves from Puerto Plata or Grand Turk. If you depart from Puerto Plata, somebody from Bottom Time will meet you and get you aboard the vessel for a week-long stay on the bank. The vessel usually anchors in a place called the Nursery because of the large numbers of mother and calf whales. The female goes into estrus and is capable of conception three or four days afterwards, and in that period large numbers of males are drawn to the area. Bottom Time uses various smaller vessels to get closer to the whales, making staggered trips of less than two hours several times each day. During the evenings, the captain gives a slide show, and there are educational programs.

The typical tour leaves on Saturday and returns on Saturday, so you're a week on the water. This is probably the ultimate in whale adventures, and the people seem devoted to conservation and respect for the whale's environment. In 1996, the tour cost about US$1,800 for a complete week on the water, all meals included. Airfare to the port of embarkation is not included.

For a long time the Dominican Republic had little in the way of comprehensive "adventure" tour agencies. The relatively new **Iguana Mama** operating out of Cabarete on the north coast has remedied that situation in a big way. Run by American Tricia Thorndike de Suriel, who has married into Dominican life, Iguana Mama offers a wide array of outdoor adventures from biking to hiking up Pico Duarte, and includes mule rides, windsurfing, and scuba diving. Included in its most recent catalogue was an intriguing cross-country (literally) bike ride and a six-day mule trek up Pico Duarte. You can call them at 809/571-0908 or from the United States at 800/849-4720. Their fax is 809/571-0734. Their email address is info@iguanamama.com; they even have a website (www.iguanamama.com), where you can request a catalogue.

For more information on Silver Bank or Samaná whales, contact the **National Parks Office** in Santo Domingo (tel. 809/682-7628), the **Centro de Investigaciónes de Biología Marina** (CIBINA) at the University of Santo Domingo (tel. 809/668-8633), or the **Fundación Dominicana Pro-Investigación y Conservacion de los Recursos Marinos** (MAMMA) at Av. Anacaona #77, Apto. C-4, Santo Domingo. Kim Beddell in Samaná knows officials of MAMMA and can put you in contact with them and get you some official literature on whale conservation; she may be reached at tel. 809/538-2588, fax 809/538-2494.

WINDSURFING, PARASAILING, SURFING, SAILING

Windsurfing, parasailing, and surfing generally require the same kinds of conditions—namely, wind and waves. The best bet for windsurfing is the famous beaches at Cabarete, about 3.2km east of Sosúa, which is known as the windsurfing capital of the world. However, you can windsurf along the entire eastern Atlantic coast of the island because of strong seasonal winds. Playa Grande at Río San Juan, Sosúa on the north coast, and Macao on the east coast are noted for surfing, though conditions may vary and you can get both lucky and unlucky with waves.

The only outlet for parasailing activities on the whole island is through **Actividades Acuáticas,** a club that can be reached in both Santo Domingo (tel. 809/688-5838) and Puerto Plata (tel. 809/586-3988).

Sailing in the Dominican Republic tends to be the province of the rich and exclusive clubs and resorts. It's still possible to rent small sailboats at some hotels, but generally you have to bring your own yacht (you can usually rent slips and use services temporarily at several Dominican yacht clubs if you make arrangements in advance). The yacht club of Santo Domingo is called the **Club Naútico de Santo Domingo** and is located at Boca Chica (tel. 809/566-1682 or 809/685-4949). If you expect to use its facilities, you'd better know somebody or make arrangements through your own club. In places like Monte Cristi (tel. 809/579-2530), Playa Cofresí (tel. 809/535-6168), and San Pedro de Macorís (tel. 809/529-3383), clubs are less formal, though still quite exclusive. All the big resort hotels like Club Med and Punta Cana Beach Resort have their own small fleets, as does Casa de Campo near La Romana. Perhaps the easiest to deal with is the **Punta Cana Beach Resort,** which, like Club Naútico, has its own marina. Telephone them at 809/686-0084 or 809/684-0086.

SPORTFISHING

Sportfishing is very popular, and you can have some spectacular success with marlin, sailfish, dorado, bonito, tarpon, and snook if you're willing to put up with some hassles and expense. For the most part you're going to have to arrange for fishing through a hotel or one of the clubs such as Acuáticas or Naútico. Generally, the best spots are Cumayasa, La Romana, and Boca de Yuma east of Santo Domingo; Palmar de Ocoa and

Barahona to the west of Santo Domingo; and Samaná in the north. Going out for a day's fishing is great fun, and if you share the costs with three or four others, it can be quite reasonable. You can rent flatboats at La Romana and try your hand at snook and tarpon, though I can't vouch for its attractiveness as a sport.

The best fishing along the south coast is from June to October, along the north coast from August to October, though they say blue marlin can be caught all year long. You can find white marlin in east coast waters from Punta Espada to Punta Macao, the best times being March through June. Try white marlin at Cabeza de Toro, offshore near Punta Cana. One of the best bets for fishing all year round is the unsightly wahoo, whose mouthful of teeth will inspire you to be careful in landing. Regular fishermen report that the absolutely prime place for deep-sea fishing is in the Mona Passage, with its strong currents and relatively cold water, where you'll find bonito, skipjack, and albacore in spring. Boca de Yuma is at the mouth of the Río Yuma, and the town has an annual fishing tournament. In the far southwest, Cabo Rojo has good fishing, although it is very isolated and difficult to reach.

Although you can try freshwater fishing in the two man-made reservoirs if you wish, I wouldn't waste my time trying for a few bass. For the adventuresome, try finding a flatboat in any of the river mouths, coastal inlets, and estuaries in the many rivers east of Santo Domingo. It's a do-it-yourself adventure, but it might pan out, so to speak. For fishing and sailing information of all kinds, call or visit the people at **Andrés Boca Chica Club** (tel. 809/523-5579) or **DeMar Beach Club** (tel. 809/523-5579), neither of which is as exclusive as Club Naútico.

GOLF

For those who wish to take to the fairways and greens, the Dominican Republic is rapidly becoming something considerably more than just a resort-oriented place. In years past, there used to be one or two exclusive country clubs in the capital and at Santiago, and then the renowned courses at Casa de Campo, designed by famous course architect Pete Dye. Dominican tourist officials will proudly tell you that there are 17 golf courses in the country, although this figure is a little inflated—a few courses are nine-hole affairs and two others are private.

Near Santo Domingo

If you're up for golf the old-fashioned way—that is, with all the finery and smell of very old money and caddies to boot, you can try to play the ridiculously beautiful and superbly manicured **Santo Domingo Country Club.** This 18-hole course is strictly for the capital's elite, but you might be able to play if you know a member and can finagle an invitation. If cash isn't a problem, you can always pay the expensive fee and join. Ironically, the country club is located in one of the few tough neighborhoods in Santo Domingo, and the contrast between the two—the exclusive golf club and the barrio—is kind of jarring. Still, it's an exquisite layout, and very old fashioned, which is the sort of course design I particularly like.

About 20 minutes north of Santo Domingo on the Duarte Highway (40 minutes in traffic) lies the new **Cayacoa Country Club** (tel. 809/561-7288). This new club is semi-private, meaning that the public is welcome but there are special memberships sold to persons who wish to take advantage of the pool, tennis courts, and clubhouse facilities. If you're staying in Santo Domingo, this golf course, set in typical subtropical bush country, with bermuda fairways and greens, is quite attractive and welcoming. The management told me that US$35 would cover greens fees and include a taxi they'd send to your hotel and deliver you home. If you're staying in Santo Domingo for a longer period, monthly rates are available. Also reachable from Santo Domingo along Las Américas Highway, east of town, is the new **San Andrés Country Club,** which is also semi-private and welcomes casual players. When I visited the course the front nine had been opened and looked quite challenging, though the back nine were still under construction. Down the same road about 45 minutes east of Santo Domingo, in Juan Dolio, is the **Metro Country Club.** You can see it from the highway. Also in Juan Dolio is the **Cumayasa Golf Club.**

Casa de Campo

As golfers probably already know, the Cadillac of Dominican golf resorts is Casa de Campo, near

La Romana. Two hours east of Santo Domingo along the coast, this famous resort boasts two courses, both world-class. The first, Teeth of the Dog, has seven holes that play directly along the craggy and spectacular coastline and 11 more that are beautifully laid out and challenging. The other course on Casa de Campo's grounds is called The Links. It's not as spectacular as Teeth of the Dog, but it's probably tougher, all things considered.

It is expensive to stay at Casa de Campo, though you can lessen the cost by taking advantage of some of the many special packages offered by travel agents. Nearby Capella Resort sometimes offers special discount golf rates to guests. Pete Dye also designed the nearby **La Romana Golf Course,** but to play there you must be a member or the guest of a member, and there aren't any exceptions to this rule. You can play at La Romana if you're "introduced" by a member, but it's terribly expensive. You're better off playing with somebody.

In the Mountains

For golf in the mountains, you can play the course at **Falconbridge.** It is out of the way, so contact a local travel agent who can make arrangements. Also in the mountains, about two hours north of Santo Domingo and just off the Duarte Highway (past La Vega), is the **Jarabacoa Golf Club,** on the road leading to the lovely village of Jarabacoa. This is a private club, but you can sometimes make contact with a member, which then makes the course fees quite reasonable. The course has only nine holes but features mountain views and a cool climate.

The North

In the north, there are several golf complexes from which to choose. At **Playa Dorada,** you'll find a Robert Trent Jones course that caters to guests of this extensive complex of hotels. Farther east than Puerto Plata lies the **Gran Bahía** course in Samaná. Also in Puerto Plata, or nearby, are **Costambar, Playa Grande Golf Club,** and, down the road in Cabarete, the **Cabarete Golf Club.** At Las Galeras in Samaná is the **Loma de Chivo Golf Club.** Rounding out your selection is Santiago's exclusive **Las Aromas Golf Club** and the **Bonao Golf Club,** in Bonao.

East Coast

A Robert Trent Jones course at **Punta Cana** graces the east coast, and the 18 holes presently available are being expanded with a second course. On the east coast you'll also find a course at **Bávaro Beach.** Both of these courses are owned and operated by hotel resorts, so being a guest is part of the deal. However, golf packages are readily available and not that expensive. Check with your local travel agent. For information at the source, you can call the **Asociación Dominicana de Golf** at 809/563-7228, fax 809/567-3447.

TENNIS

Tennis courts are a standard feature at almost every resort and tourist hotel in the country. Tennis is probably one of the most popular participant sports in the city of Santo Domingo, which is filled with hotel courts, popular tennis clubs, and even public courts. In the *Santo Domingo News,* you can learn about amateur and professional matches, which are played throughout the year, some at private clubs and hotels, some at the Olympic Stadium. The most important professional competition is the Marlboro Cup, held at the Olympic Center in November. For players, the best facility is probably at **Casa de Campo,** which has 13 clay courts, some lighted for night play, and four all-weather Laykold courts near the main administration building. Casa de Campo has a resident pro and offers special tennis packages, daily clinics, ball machines, and programs for players at all levels. Some non-guests may use the facility if it's available, but you must make reservations. Don't count on walking onto Casa de Campo in the high season, however.

In Santo Domingo, you may as well be in tennis heaven. The **Caribbean Tennis Center,** Autopista 30 de Mayo, Km 10.5 (Malecón), tel. 809/537-7173, has 10 clay courts, floodlights, and a tennis school for kids. More exclusive is the **Santo Domingo Tennis Club** at Carretera Herrera Haina (tel. 809/533-2422), which offers tennis lessons. The identically named **Santo Domingo Tennis Club** is at Calle Euclides Morillo, with tennis courts and lessons, too. Call them at 809/562-6918. Other tennis clubs include **Casa de España,** Autopista 30 de May, Km 10 (Malecón), tel. 809/537-1802, and **Club Arroyo Hondo,** Calle J. Polanco, tel. 809/541-9911. The largest available public court setting is at the **Centro Olímpico,** Juan Pablo Duarte, Ave. 27 de Febrero, near Ortega y Gasset. All of the major resort hotels in Santo Domingo have excellent courts, including the **Embajador, Santo Domingo,** the **Sheraton,** and the **Dominican Fiesta,** most with pro shops and lessons. In addition, the Renaissance **Jaragua** has an 800-seat tennis stadium and a ranked pro. I watched some highly ranked amateurs from Latin America and the Caribbean play on the Jaragua courts, and the facility is beautiful. In the central neighborhoods of Santo Domingo, the hotel **Gran Lina** has courts as well.

All of the major resorts outside Santo Domingo have excellent tennis facilities. Of course, Playa Dorada, outside Puerto Plata, is a tennis destination of note, as are the major hotels at

Cofresí and Costambar. Also try the **Jack Tar Village, Club on the Green, Villas Doradas,** and **Montemar.** Note that the north coast is not a tennis hotbed for the simple reason that the strong, steady trade winds constantly pounding the coast can turn an ordinary tennis game into a study in advanced aerodynamics. All of the resorts on the Eastern Point have excellent courts as well, but, again, wind is a problem.

The south coast, on the other hand, is a tennis paradise. Except for Boca Chica, all the resorts are devoted primarily to tennis, especially Casa de Campo and the major hotels at Juan Dolio and Villas del Mar. Smaller hotels generally do not have tennis courts but can often arrange games at nearby establishments if you wish.

HORSES

When the Spanish came to Hispaniola, they brought with them their horses and their love of riding. That heritage persists today. Horse racing and breeding is alive and well in the Dominican Republic, and in the rural parts of the country you'll often see campesinos riding their jaunty horses around the cane fields. Certainly the best place to ride is Casa de Campo, which has an entire Equestrian Center with about 700 horses; you can arrange to take rides as long as eight hours on a horse specifically suited to your skill level and style. There is even a polo field that features matches and lessons. Other riding destinations are **Punta Cana Beach Resort,** where you can ride on the beach or past Arawak ruins; **Rancho Las Terrenas,** in Samaná (tel. 809/240-6060); and **Rancho Montaña,** in Cabarete (tel. 809/571-0787). The polo season in Casa de Campo runs from October through May, so bring your favorite steed and a mallet.

Horse racing is big at the new **Race Track V Centenario,** located on the Las Américas Highway, about halfway from downtown Santo Domingo to the airport. You can call them at 809/687-6060, or just look in the newspaper. The track is a great way to get the feel of the country, its people, food, music, and color. It's a very modern and comfortable facility.

horseback riding on the beach

CASINO GAMING

The Dominican Republic's casino scene is as exciting as any. The hot spot of casino gaming is Santo Domingo, with its rich diversity of major hotels in all areas of the city. Along the Malecón, every major hotel, including the Sheraton, Jaragua Renaissance, and the Hispaniola, sports a glittering and fashionable casino. Away from the beach, the El Embajador Hotel has its own beautiful casino.

Outside of Santo Domingo, casino gambling is less popular, probably because there is a greater focus on sun, swimming, and sports. Nevertheless, there is a popular casino in Puerto Plata, and one among the popular beach resorts on the Coconut Coast at the eastern point in La Altagracia.

But the gambler's haven in the Dominican Republic is Santo Domingo—not only for casino gambling, but also for horse racing. Casinos in the Dominican Republic offer all the standard games, from blackjack to high-class chemin de fer (very expensive). You won't see much poker being played, nor is craps very popular, but you'll always find at least one table in every house—if not necessarily a dealer. The games are played, generally, under stantard Las Vegas rules, and casinos commonly allow play to be made in American dollars or Dominican pesos. As you'd imagine, money is changed readily.

Keep in mind that Dominican casinos are much more formal than their counterparts in other Caribbean countries and very much more so than those in the United States. You are expected to dress, if not in suit and tie, then at least in dignified sports clothes. Casinos open at 4 P.M. and remain open until 4 A.M. (except on Friday and Saturday, when they stay open until 6 A.M.), so there is plenty of time to make your fortune. Since Santo Domingo's casinos play host to some of the most beautiful of Latin America's beautiful people, it can be a fascinating experience. Gambling is also available at all the major resort hotel casinos and at a few clubs in metropolitan areas. Good luck.

SPECTATOR SPORTS

It's amazing but true: soccer has almost no following among the sporting people of the Do-

minican Republic. Although popular team sports like volleyball and basketball are played in the country, and many urban Dominicans are addicted to watching NBA games on cable TV, the overwhelming national passion is baseball, introduced to the Dominican Republic during the American occupation early in the 20th century. Truly, baseball rules the Dominican sporting world. In addition to a team in Santo Domingo, almost every major provincial city fields a team, and every team is supported by fanatical and devoted fans throughout a wide area in the province. Many of the cities are poor and somewhat run-down, but the baseball stadium is always new and a source of great civic pride.

Baseball, politics, and dominoes—strolling the streets of any Dominican town, you'd swear that these are the governing themes. A typical scene has Dominican men hunched over a domino board, playing with intense concentration, banging down their "bones" with passionate force, pausing only to talk about the latest political uproar, while a baseball game roars from a nearby TV. You can see scenes like this in the **Lucky Seven Restaurant** in Santo Domingo, on the corner of Pasteur and Moya, where the management shows up to six games of baseball each day on satellite TV, and in Puerto Plata at **Willy's Sports Center,** where four TVs go simultaneously and legal bets are taken on every game.

If baseball rules the passions in the modern Dominican Republic, it is cockfighting that still holds sway as the traditional pastime of the countryside. In fact, until baseball swept the country, cockfighting was the national passion. Almost everywhere this "sport" is relegated to countryside and small village arenas, where men and boys take their favorite birds to be pitted in small circular arenas on Saturday afternoon.

Baseball

It wasn't until 1947 that the first non-white baseball player, Jackie Robinson, was signed into the American major leagues with the then-Brooklyn Dodgers. Nine years later, in 1956, the New York Giants signed the great "Ozzie" Virgil, and since that time, the Dominican Republic has become the largest single country of origin for foreign players in the United States. At any one time, there are usually about 50 Dominicans in the major leagues and around 500 in the minors, an astonishing figure for a country with a population only around seven million. In 1992 the Los Angeles Dodgers had six Dominicans on its 24-man squad and operated what many consider to be the best foreign training camp outside the United States, near Campo de Palmas at San Pedro de Macorís.

In 1951, the Dominican Republic's *Liga de Béisbol* was founded in Santo Domingo. Right now there are five teams in the league, including the Licey Tigers, Escojido Leones, Estrellas Orientales, Águilas del Cibao, and the Azucareros del Este, all watched closely by major league scouts and all considered stepping-stones for future talent into the major leagues. The Tigers and Leones are from Santo Domingo, while the Estrellas are from San Pedro de Macorís, a town many claim produces more American major leaguers than any other in the country. The Águilas play their home games in Santiago, and the Azucareros in La Romana.

In Santo Domingo, the baseball park is called **Quisqueya Stadium.** Anyone can go to a game, although for big matches getting a ticket can be kind of tricky because the sport is so popular. During the 1995 season, for example, players like Rafael Belliard, Andujar Cedeño, Mariano Duncan, José César Franco, Stan Javier, Tony Peña, Luis Polonia, José Rijo, and Sammy Sosa (among others) were scheduled to play in their home country. Despite the scarcity of tickets, making Santo Domingo home for a month in the winter and watching baseball can be an enormously rewarding experience.

Getting Tickets: First things first. These days ticket prices are going up because of inflation. It costs about 10 pesos to sit in the outfield bleachers, 50 pesos to sit in the main stands, 75 pesos to sit in the choicest reserved seats in the main stands, and 150 pesos to sit in the club house. Evening games begin at 7:30 P.M., afternoon and weekend games at 4 P.M. You can try calling 809/565-5565 for game information, but you'll be lucky to learn anything. The season is October through January, and if you go to see baseball, you'll see a league in operation that is second only to the American major leagues. And think about it—at 13 pesos to the dollar, the bleachers cost very little.

The real facts of life—as far as getting tick-

ets—are a little more complicated. Most tickets are sold out far in advance of the game, so if you want to go you're probably going to have to find a ticket on the black market. This isn't really so hard. You can just show up at the stadium before game time and buy a ticket from a scalper. At a recent game, a general admission ticket was going for about 400 pesos (still a bargain by American standards). If you're staying at a hotel in Santo Domingo, you can usually find a travel agent or knowledgeable taxi driver who has contacts and can get you a ticket.

When you get into a game, especially at Quisqueya Stadium, you'll have the time of your life, especially when the merengue bands break out in music before and after games and sometimes between innings. The bands sit on top of the dugouts, and everybody in the stands gets into the merengue mood. You can often see important major-league scouts in Section A-15 behind home plate. At one game there were 20 major-league scouts, along with Astros manager Terry Collins and then–general manager Bob Watson.

Quisqueya Stadium is located off Avenida Tiradentes just north of Avenida John F. Kennedy. There is a summer season for baseball that runs from April to September, and it is also fun, but for obvious reasons the best players are away in the United States. If you're in the Dominican Republic during these summer months, you can probably get a ticket more easily, though the competition will be less exciting.

Cockfighting

Cockfighting is something else again, a little bit underground because many Dominican authorities have tried, unofficially, to suppress interest in the sport because of its brutality. Still, cockfighting is popular in rural areas and small towns. Introduced by the Spanish, cockfighting often provokes criticism from foreign visitors who say that it is cruel to the birds. It probably is cruel, but I've gone to cockfights nonetheless because it is part of the national culture, and I wanted to see what a rural Saturday afternoon would be like. I enjoyed myself despite the spectacle of violence because there was music and authentic give-and-take. It's not something that I'd make a habit of doing, but seeing it once was interesting.

Popularized in ancient Rome, cockfighting

is a strictly amateur sport, one that takes place outside the normal sanction of any league or organization. The owners raise the birds on their own, take care of them, train them, feed them, and sometimes watch them die. At the appointed time, they place their birds in a circular ring usually about 20 feet in diameter, then let them fight. These birds begin fighting at between one and two years of age, and when they go into the ring they are equipped with metal or bone spurs, averaging about an inch and a half in length, which they use to hack and claw at their opponents. The birds are "set," or dropped opposite one another, and then they run and jump and try to spur one another, especially in the eyes and chest. Sometimes, one of the cocks will refuse to fight further, and the handler will put him breast-to-breast with the other bird. If the bird still refuses to fight, the judge rules that the *gallo* has quit, and the fight ends. Dominicans become passionate about their birds, and about the sport. The main point is to gamble on the outcome.

Cockfighting take place at the **Coliseo Gallístico de Santo Domingo,** on Luperón Avenue. Call 809/565-3844 for information. Suprisingly, cockfighting in Santo Domingo is something of a high-society sport, while in the countryside it is strictly for the peasants and workers. Going to a cockfight in the countryside is easy. Just find an arena on Saturday afternoon and walk inside. You won't get anywhere with the betting unless your Spanish is pretty good and you're familiar with slang.

THE FIGHTING COCK

Every town and village in the Dominican Republic has its *gallera,* or cockfight pit, a place that becomes a focus of activity every weekend. On Saturday and Sunday the *gallera* is filled with people who are passionate about their sport and come to watch locals pit their best cocks *(gallos)* against one another for sport and money. There is plenty of rum and music to accompany the action, and police make sure that good manners are observed at all times. Strolling bookies take bets by an established code of hand and facial signals.

Cocks are matched in weight and size, then thrown at each other to see if they'll fight. A referee makes sure that certain conventions of the sport are maintained, checking the spurs, combs, and legs of the cocks. The cocks, which are prized by their owners, are seldom killed, but at times a lot of blood is spilled. If a cock bleeds badly, his feet are placed in cold water, and the bleeding stops. In a couple of weeks, he's ready for another fight. Fights last about 20 minutes.

In every part of the Dominican Republic, you can see young men strolling the streets proudly, with their fighting cocks hung upside down from twine attached to their feet and looped around the owner's shoulder. In a country where few young men can own cars, the cock is a symbol of their machismo.

ARTS AND ENTERTAINMENT

FESTIVALS AND CELEBRATIONS

Everything having anything to do with Dominican celebrations is connected to music and religion. In fact, almost nowhere on earth are music and popular religion so closely connected. Perhaps that's because so much of Dominican culture is a syncretic mixture of Latin Catholicism and African music. Whatever the cause, one thing is for sure: Dominicans innately love celebrations, and musical and religious events form a natural fulcrum in their sometimes rather difficult workaday lives.

Fiestas Patronales

Every town on the island has its own *fiesta patronal,* or patron saint festival. While some tend to get lost in the rush of everyday life, as in Santo Domingo, the festival of the patron saint in provincial areas is quite a sight, with joyful processions, open-air musical events, prayers, services, and cultural events. The celebrations at Higüey and Samaná have become particularly famous for their color and pomp.

On the patron saint's day you might expect a somber atmosphere to predominate. True, a wooden image of the patron saint is customarily carried all over the town by four men or women, but the general mood is not exactly reflective: music, gambling, drinking, and dancing take place in the town plaza, while food stalls sell local crafts and foods.

Christmas Season

Dominicans celebrate Christmas with parties every weekend during December. Those living abroad flock back home, jamming airports. Some Dominicans have taken to erecting Christmas trees, but the traditional Dominican custom is to paint tree branches white or green, and then decorate them with works of straw or ceramic figures in the shapes of hats, baskets, angels, and saints. On Christmas Eve, the Dominican family partakes in a feast commensurate with its means, then attends midnight Mass if they are religious. Every Catholic church has its special *nacimiento,* or nativity scene. After church, Dominicans party until dawn. In the Cibao, children receive their gifts from the baby Jesus, while in Santo Domingo, Santa Claus prevails.

While most of this season is a private time spent with family, Dominicans, especially in Santo Domingo, celebrate *el año nuevo,* or New Year's Eve, with an especially loud merengue bang along the Malecón. Bands by the dozen play until Caribbean dawn. For a tourist, being involved in a Dominican New Year's Eve is a once-in-a-lifetime experience, almost as good as Carnaval.

The Christmas season ends on January 6, with the arrival of the Three Kings. This is a special day for children. Parents may lay out more gifts for the kids, and in some places there are processions featuring the kings themselves. During the entire season, groups of country musicians roam from house to house, singing. These musicians, known as trulls, sing their *aguinaldos,* Christmas carols. The month of December is a time for Dominicans who have moved to the city to go back to their hometowns.

Ga Ga

February is a great month to be in the Dominican Republic, mainly because of two festivals, Ga Ga and Carnaval. Of the two, Ga Ga is less well known, because it is a celebration which originated with Haitian sugarcane cutters and is predominately restricted to sugarcane villages. In Haiti, the celebration is known as *rara.* Ga Ga is a mystical celebration of religious inspiration. In the towns of Haina, Boca Chica, and Barahona (and in many small villages), the festival occurs around Ash Wednesday in February. In some places, Ga Ga is celebrated around March 28, as part of Holy Week.

Carnaval

As in other countries in the region, Carnaval is the high point of the Dominican year. Carnaval is a special time for Dominicans to go to parties, dance in the streets, and eat and drink heartily. While this might sound like a description of every other Dominican celebration, be assured, Carnaval is very much its own event. It's the biggest, most fun, most colorful, most enigmatic festival of the year.

Carnaval originated in medieval Europe as the final celebration of feasting before Lent, which commenced the 40 days of fasting and penitence that precede Good Friday and Easter. Because Independence Day in the Dominican Republic falls on February 27, Carnaval has become super-special to Dominicans. The Carnaval celebrations in the Dominican Republic resemble equivalent festivities in Rio de Janeiro and New Orleans. Participants dress in a colorful array of phantasmagoric masks and costumes, most of African origin. During Carnaval week, nearly 100,000 people participate in one way or another in Santo Domingo. Other large celebrations occur in Santiago and La Vega. Over time, each city in the country has developed its own unique costumes and events. Probably the most recognizable mask of the Carnaval originates in La Vega and Santo Domingo. The *diablo cojuelo* is a horned devil that lashes out at bystanders with an inflated cow bladder to purge the spectators of their sins. This folkloric devil is directly traceable to medieval legend. Other cities with trademark costumes include Monte Cristi (bulls), Santiago (pigs), Cabral (devils), Mao (goat), Cotui (butterflies), and the most original and interesting in San Pedro de Macorís (the *Gollois,* or good lawyer, a businessman bedecked with ribbons and feathers). Not only do the general figures differ in Carnaval masks from town to town, but individual decorative devices differ as well. In Santo Domingo, the devils sport multiple horns and exaggerated mouth configurations ranging from thick lips to duck bills and pirhanas' teeth. In Santiago, the masks are decorated with shells or jewels and have remarkably detailed horns. The devils from La Vega wear mocking or sarcastic smiles.

Of all the celebrations of Carnaval, those in Santiago and La Vega are most traditional, while those in Santo Domingo are the most enthusiastic. For my money, I'll take the Santiago parade, which has been going on since 1867. For those interested in the history and art of Carnaval, a visit to the Museo Folklórico de Tomás Morel (Museum of Folklore) in Santiago (tel. 809/582-6787) is highly recommend.

Easter
Dominicans don't celebrate Easter as enthusiastically as they once did, but for devoutly religious Dominicans, the Easter week, or *Semana Santa,* is highly ritualistic. In Santo Domingo, parishioners may take wooden images of Christ from the church and march them through the streets. In some places, a huge effigy of Judas is burned. In the southwestern town of Cabral between Good Friday and Easter Monday, costumed devils crack whips and prance around.

Other Holidays and Festivals
January also sees **Las Noches de Vela** (the Night of Prayer), another synthesis of African popular religion and Catholicism. Performed in San José de Ocoa, Monte Plata, Villa Altagracia, Pedernales, Paraiso, and Los Bavos de Haina around January 20, this night is celebrated in honor of the Virgin of Altagracia, the spiritual mother of the Dominican pueblos. Prayers are recited, and musicians perform hymns. The biggest event comes the next day in Higüey, where thousands of pilgrims come to the basilica of the Virgin. In July, there is a huge **Festival del Merengue,** usually in the third week, which is basically a week-long blowout with live music, contests, a motocross race, and various performances. A similar festival is held in October in Puerto Plata with bands, food, and contests. Also in October is *bambula,* a traditional African-derived festival of dance seen only in Samaná. It takes place on or about October 24.

ARTS AND CRAFTS

I know of no better place to buy art than Santo Domingo. If you're interested in painting, ceramic sculpture, and antiques, you'll find almost every neighborhood in Santo Domingo crowded with interesting, out-of-the-way little shops, galleries, and markets. Some I've chronicled elsewhere in this book; others you'll have fun ferreting out yourself.

Painting
Keep in mind that most of the "primitive" paintings you'll see lined up by the thousands (literally) on every street corner and against every wall all over the country are hardly worth a look and should only be purchased if you're self-con-

sciously interested in a souvenir. The true painting style of the Dominican Republic isn't "primitive" at all but extremely worldly, color conscious, and sophisticated and can be found in better galleries. My favorite Dominican painter is Ulloa, and I found a truly stunning abstract work by him in a Colonial District gallery for about US$900, which is a bargain. A few galleries in Santo Domingo sell genuine Haitian primitives, but you need to exercise caution and taste in making these purchases. A visit to the Museum of Modern Art on the Plaza de la Cultura in Santo Domingo is good preparation for an art-buying expedition to the rest of the city.

Jewelry

Other Dominican crafts include all kinds of jewelry made of amber and larimar, cow horn, bone, and semi-precious stones. Of course, amber is the most famous Dominican "stone" of them all, and you'll find an amazing variety of it in the stores and shops of the country.

Amber resembles a piece of clear soft stone, but in actuality is resin hardened from the sap of trees from as long as 48 million years ago. Some amber, as it dried and fossilized, trapped small animals and insects, twigs, foliage, and other organisms, and these pieces are the most fascinating and expensive gifts. The antibiotic property of the resin stopped the development of both bacteria and fungi, thus preserving every detail of any organism trapped inside. The ancient Egyptians knew some of the properties of amber and used it in their embalming. Dominican amber is found in the mountains north of Santiago at elevations of 700–1,500 meters and near Los Haitises, north of Bayaguana. A lot of amber is found in the Baltic as well, but it is somewhat opaque, while true Dominican amber is almost transparent, usually bronze, orange, or brown. The animals found in amber aren't very large, but small vertebrates occasionally show up, along with lots of dragonflies, praying mantises, scorpions, ticks, mites, and ants.

Many workshops on the island fashion amber into necklaces, pendants, rings, and miniatures set in silver. Workshops also handle larimar, which is turquoise in color but several times harder than turquoise. Larimar is pale and pretty and found in only one place in the world—near the coffee village of Las Filipinas, about 10km from Barahona in the southwest part of

AMBER AND LARIMAR

When you travel in the Dominican Republic, examples of handcrafted amber and larimar jewelry will be everywhere. In fact, larimar is found only in the Dominican Republic. The stone itself, which exists in colors varying in tone from deep sky blue to blue-green, is produced when copper and cobalt oxide combine during the geologic process. Deposits of larimar were first discovered in the Dominican Republic in 1974, and most Dominicans believed the semiprecious stone came from the sea. Actually, Dominican rivers wash the natural stone down from high mountain areas to deposit them in alluvial sources near the ocean. The stones are naturally polished by the action of the water as they tumble and drop. The first commercial supplier of the stone named it after his daughter, Lari, combined with *el mar*, the sea. The stone is mined in commercial quantities in open pits in and around the Sierra de Bahoruco.

Amber, on the other hand, is a stone in name only. It is actually the sap of prehistoric trees that has trapped various organic materials, such as insects, lizards, and flowers. Over millions of years, the sap petrifies, perfectly preserving its victims. In the past few years, scientists have discovered that they can investigate the DNA of animals trapped in amber, providing clues to biologic origins and destinies. For example, in 1989, scientists examined a piece of trapped mushroom and determined that it was more than 25 million years old, twice as old as mushrooms were thought to be.

Of course, most amber does not preserve trapped animals and insects. The stone itself is quite beautiful in its polished state, primarily brown or gold in color. Dominican amber, considered by many the most beautiful in the world, may also contain flashes of red, orange, green, blue, and purple. Traditionally, the Baltic was the source of most of the world's amber, but today, some geologists think that the Dominican reserves may be the world's largest.

the country. The output of the only larimar mine is limited and, believe it or not, reliant on weather. Despite its rarity, larimar is reasonably priced.

SHOPPING

If you're into shopping, the Dominican Republic is a place you can exercise the urge in an almost uncountable number of ways. As at any tourist destination, there are always a large number of souvenir shops that cater to travelers, and most take credit cards and traveler's checks. There are also duty-free shops at airports and a large duty-free zone in Santo Domingo, both of which feature interesting items at special prices. To my mind, the more interesting buys available in the Dominican Republic come from open-air markets, where a bewildering variety of goods is offered, for which you are welcome to bargain. Remember, bargaining is a Dominican tradition and isn't restricted to local trade.

You'll find three types of marketplaces in the Dominican Republic, and on any visit you should take the opportunity to experience all of them.

Open-Air Market

Probably the most interesting and authentic type of market is the traditional open-air market with row upon row of individual vendors in their stalls displaying wares spread out on blankets or on makeshift tables. The **Mercado Modelo** in Santo Domingo is a mega-amplified version of this traditional market. Only a few blocks from the Colonial District, the Mercado Modelo is located in a huge peeling plaster building that resembles an old art deco bus station. Crowded with stalls so closely set that you can hardly walk, it contains an astounding abundance of goods, including woodcarvings, ceramics, jewelry, musical instruments, leather products, mahogany rocking chairs, music cassettes and CDs, wicker, herbs, and T-shirts. Vendors along the outer edges of the market sell fresh vegetables, poultry, pork, and goat, and the array of fruit includes cassava, plantains, guava, bananas, and pineapple. Some of the vendors offer spectacular Dominican sweets (dulces) that are a treat to the palate.

It's at the Mercado Modelo that you might wish to become adept in the bargaining techniques of the Dominican retail trade. Dominicans love to haggle and even become disappointed if denied the opportunity to show off their abilities. To play the game, ask the price of an item with evident indifference. When quoted a price, express shock and disbelief and—if you're interested in buying—disappointment. The vendor will probably express disgust. He will begin to put the item back in its case, but then yawn or express dismay and quote you a lower price. You might give in, or put more pressure on if you wish, or even start to walk away. How far you wish to push the game is up to you, but you should always leave some room for the vendor to save his dignity. In the Mercado Modelo, many vendors will be vying for your business, so be prepared for an avalanche of attention. At other open-air markets, the pressure is not so great. But the Mercado Modelo is such a unique experience that you should wander in even if you have no intention to buy. Any taxi driver in Santo Domingo can get you there in a jiffy, and sometimes there are young men at the front entrance who will guide you through the turmoil for a couple of dollars and even translate for you.

Colmado

The second kind of market frequented by Dominicans is called the colmado. Colmados are small, multipurpose shops which you can find on almost every corner in every town in the Dominican Republic. In addition to being a kind of neighborhood gathering place for gossip and friendship, the colmado sells everything basic to Dominican life: rice, oil, sugar, salt, and rum. The colmado will also display specialty sweets, carbonated beverages, racks of fresh fruit, cigarettes (which you can buy one at a time if you're trying to quit), and some medicines.

The colmado is also a great place to get directions when you get lost.

Shopping Centers

Finally, the Dominican Republic is getting its share of modern shopping centers, where men and women of the middle and upper classes, especially in Santo Domingo, do a lot of their shopping for clothes and food. These supermarkets are as modern as anything in Europe and the United States, and just as cold and impersonal. Unless you're shopping for seriously high-fashion items (and the Dominican Republic has its share of high fashion), you're probably better off at a more traditional marketplace.

There are duty-free shops and duty-free zones, both of which offer the standard array of French perfumes, liquor, camera equipment, watches, and jewelry. If you've seen one of these shops anywhere, the Dominican Republic's shops are not much different. With regard to Dominican specialties like rum, coffee, and cigars, you'd probably be better off buying the item in town. In Santo Domingo, there are duty-free shops at the Centro de los Héroes, La Atarazana, and the Las Américas Airport, as well as at the Santo Domingo, Sheraton, and Embajador hotels in town.

Shop hours vary from place to place (and even day to day), but you can count on most markets and *colmados* to open at around 8 A.M. and stay open until about noon or 1 P.M., at which time the store will close for a couple of hours for siesta. Then the store will open again about 3 P.M. and stay open until early evening, say about 7 P.M. Saturday hours are a little shorter, and many stores are closed on Sundays, which tend to be quiet days for everybody. Many local *colmados* are open later, but never much after 10 P.M.

Dominican Specialties

Cigars are a favorite and are available at shops in almost every city, where many are handmade on the spot. Food is a favorite as well, and you

Juan Batista, a genial tour guide at León Jiménes cigar factory in Santiago de los Caballeros

can buy many kinds of sweets made from guava, oranges, coconut, or pineapple (which is particularly good). Buy it along any roadside and enjoy it with some roasted cashews.

Avoid buying black coral on principle, and don't buy tortoise shell—the turtles are endangered, and it'll be confiscated upon your return home anyway. Sometimes you can find authentic Carnaval masks—truly folk creations, quite colorful and surreal. The traditional faceless dolls produced in the Cibao and near Bonao are true folk-art specimens as well.

Avoid gold and hematite jewelry, as it is mass produced somewhere else—usually the United States. Leather products are a good buy, as are CDs and cassettes of original Caribbean jazz, merengue, *bachata,* salsa, and other musical forms. Thirty-six varieties of rum are sold in the Dominican Republic, and top-of-the-line rums are just as good as fine cognac, though much stronger.

Customs and Duties

American citizens returning to the United States can bring back up to US$400 worth of goods duty free, provided the stay overseas exceeds 48 hours and no part of the allowance has been used during the prior 30 days. You can include items shipped through the mails in this accounting. Above that, you'll have to pay a flat 10% duty on the next US$1,000 worth and varying duty for more than US$1,400 worth of goods. Families can declare their items jointly, so that a couple traveling with two children can bring into the United States US$3,200 duty free. You can send undeclared gifts back to friends duty free, and you can also bring back a fifth of liquor, as well as a carton of cigarettes. Plants potted in soil may not pass into the United States.

Canadian citizens may make an oral declaration four times a year to bring into the country C$100 worth of exemptions, which can include 200 cigarettes, 50 cigars, two pounds of tobacco, 40 ounces of alcohol, and 24 12-ounce cans of beer. In order to qualify for this exemption, you have to have been out of the country for 48 hours. Any Canadian out of the country for at least seven days may make a written declaration once a year and claim C$300 worth of goods as exempt. A Canadian out of the country for more than 48 hours may claim a special duty rate of 20% on goods in excess of the C$100 or C$300 they claim, though cigarettes and liquor are not included.

Each citizen of the U.K. over the age of 17 may bring into the respective countries one liter of alcohol or two of champagne, port, sherry, or vermouth, along with two liters of table wine, 200 cigarettes or 50 cigars or 250 grams of tobacco, 250cc of toilet water, 5 grams of perfume, and up to £28 worth of other goods.

German citizens may bring back 200 ciga- rettes, 50 cigars, 100 cigarillos or 250 grams of tobacco, two liters of alcoholic beverages not exceeding 44 proof or one liter of alcohol over 44 proof, two liters of wine, and up to DM 300 worth of other items.

You can take most personal items into the Dominican Republic, though you may have to declare sophisticated electronic equipment such as TVs, stereos, and certain cameras. You can't take a gun into the Dominican Republic, and you'll need a special permit for plants, meat products, live animals, certain drugs, and precious stones.

ACCOMMODATIONS

The Minister of Tourism claims that there are more than 28,000 hotel rooms in the Dominican Republic. It's probably true. The real question is what hotel room suits your personal style, your hopes, your expectations, and your budget. Because the Dominican Republic is very large by Caribbean standards, the traveler can easily plan a trip that includes accessible places outside the high pink walls of the international tourist enclosures. However, if it's a quick week in the sun at an exclusive resort you want, then the Dominican Republic has some of the most exclusive and beautifully maintained (and isolated) resorts in the world.

The best way to plan ahead for lodging is to read this book and sketch out a rough itinerary for yourself. Make a budget, and schedule some activities you really like—a couple of days at a resort, some time in the mountains, a long hike or two in a national park, and some whale-watching in Samaná. If an exclusive resort or tourist hotel is on your list, then you would do well to get your hands on a copy of the *República Dominicana Travel Guide,* a glossy 90-page look at resorts, hotel chains, restaurants, and bars. It is not particularly detailed, but it does have photographs of most resorts, along with phone and fax numbers. You can try to phone direct to the Travel Guide Office at 809/586-6930, or try the tourist information hotlines in your country (see "Information and Services"). You can also get the guide at the local tourist information service for your country. In New York, call 212/575-4966. In Miami, call 305/444-4592. Your own travel agent may have access to the guide and will certainly have many brochures on tourist facilities in the Dominican Republic. Of course, your trusty Moon Handbook is designed to give you all the information you need to choose a place to stay. The innocent traveler should be warned that sprinkled liberally on roadsides throughout the country are motels, sometimes called "turísticos", a misleading label for what are essentially places where couples go to have sex. Short-term rentals, these sex motels can look like ordinary motels. I've tried to leave them out of this book.

Electricity throughout the Dominican Republic is the U.S.-style 110v plug.

Resort Hotels

If you have only a week or so and money is not much of an object, you might wish to choose an exclusive resort hotel. The first, like the ritzy Casa de Campo on the south coast, and Plaza Dorado near Puerto Plata in the north, are actually walled, self-contained complexes. If you go to an exclusive resort you may as well expect to stay on the grounds for as long as your stay lasts. These resorts have it all in a sense—golf, tennis, snorkeling, polo, fancy restaurants serving a vast array of international foods, and bars. What they don't offer is an authentic Dominican experience. You might wish to combine your resort stay with a stay at Santo Domingo or at a small town in the mountains. These types of split trips can be easily arranged. To me, spending time behind walls in a soothing pink and beige environment where Michael Jackson videos play on cassettes isn't a particularly cultural experience. Still, there's something to be said for the no-worry approach of a package tour to an exclusive resort hotel, especially for weary snowbirds short on time.

Tourist Hotels

Tourist hotels are everywhere on the beaches and in major cities like Santo Domingo, La Romana, and Puerto Plata. If you want a little more freedom to roam and a little less structure, you can head to any beach—Juan Dolio, Punta Cana, Bávaro, Las Terrenas, and dozens of others (all chronicled in later chapters of this book)—and find a tourist hotel that offers major amenities like swimming, tennis, and snorkeling. Both exclusive resorts and tourist hotels often offer suites or *cabañas* and *casitas,* which are self-contained units with private entrances. All exclusive resorts and tourist hotels offer private baths, plenty of hot water, and air conditioning, and most have their own generators to counteract the many power failures.

Local Hotels

Other Dominican hotels can be anything from a bare-room commercial establishment in a provincial town to a comfortable inn in the mountains, or a recently refurbished colonial charmer constructed in the 16th century. Some have private baths and some do not, some have generators and some do not. Many Dominican towns are small enough so that you can walk from hotel to hotel until you find what you want at the right price. Remember that in the Dominican Republic, air conditioning is not necessarily vital for comfort. In a high-ceilinged room with a fan, you can be very comfortable, even on the warmest days.

Pensions and Bed-and-Breakfasts

Although not common, there are a few pensions and B&Bs. These are usually family owned, not advertised, and rather informal or out of the way. It's best to utilize these establishments as spur-of-the-moment choices.

Apart-Hotels

For longer stays, the apart-hotel, sometimes called apar-hotel or aparta-hotel, offers rooms or suites with kitchens or kitchenettes that come fully equipped with bedding and dishes. Santo Domingo is filled with apart-hotels, which can

make a six-week or six-month stay quite enjoyable. Forget about motels unless you have very special needs. Motels in the Dominican Republic (the establishments that line Las Américas highway outside of Santo Domingo) are strictly rented by the hour for sex.

Camping

Camping is not a convenient alternative on the island. Formal public and private campgrounds are extremely rare in the Dominican Republic, and it's unwise to plan on camping ad hoc, pulling off the road just anywhere to flop down in a tent. Dominicans might not appreciate you taking such liberties, and it could be dangerous.

A recent addition to the scene is a "camping" ground located about 45 minutes west of Santo Domingo called Casa de Europa (tel. 891/221-8850, ext. 241), offering security, bathrooms, a bar, disco, and shops. It is operated by Mr. Alberto. There are also a couple of places where determined individuals can actually camp in the great outdoors. You can park your tent at Parque La Confluencia outside the town of Jarabacoa, for instance. You might also camp in some of the national parks. If you plan to do so, bring plenty of food and water and make certain to work out logistics well in advance. For example, on a climb to Pico Duarte, you'll be camping out for at least two nights, probably in one of the primitive huts provided by the government for climbers. Make sure you're prepared to pack out your garbage (no trash disposal provided) and bury your own waste. Most Dominican parks offer absolutely no facilities. At some places, such as Parque Nacional Los Haitises, you need to obtain advance permission from the park office. Keep in mind, too, that mosquitoes in the karst and mangrove parks are terrible, especially in the early evening.

Ultimately, if you want to visit wilderness areas—and by all means, you should—you might want to establish yourself in a good, middle-budget hotel near the park or wild area, and spend long days outdoors. An evening shower will feel good, anyway.

Hostels

There are no youth hostels or university-based lodging for students. Vanning and caravanning have achieved no level of acceptance in the Dominican Republic, and there are no vans or recreational vehicles to be had on the island. Even if there were, there are no sites for hook-ups. The good news is that convenient, comfortable lodging is easy to come by and usually affordable and clean.

Rates and Taxes

Inexpensive hotels are located in the commercial and transient districts of every town. They cost US$6–20. Most hotels in the Dominican Republic are in the moderate range, US$30–80, and some offer cheaper rates in the off season or a special rate to business travelers called *la tarifa comercial*. Hotels in Santo Domingo, La Romana, and Puerto Plata rarely have off-season rates, as they are usually busy regardless of the season. In every town there are good, and sometimes wonderful restaurants offering fair prices, so it is a good idea to book your room without meals. In an exchange-rate economy that favors foreign currency, you can save money by eating out.

Exclusive resorts and tourist hotels are generally expensive, which means they charge more than US$100 per night for a double room without meals and drinks. For example, a room in the exclusive Casa de Campo complex runs about US$230 a day. (Keep in mind, though, that almost all resorts and tourist hotel rates drop 40–50% during the off season.)

You can quite often save a lot of money on hotel rates by booking in advance through a local Dominican tourist agent or guide. Most local hotels don't post their rates but have a kind of eyeball approach. In some towns, especially Santo Domingo, I've had an experienced tour guide book my room at a considerable savings.

Reservations are a must at tourist hotels and almost everywhere else during Christmas. During the rest of the year, you can have your pick.

Taxes and service charges are high. Most rooms have an added 5% government tax, 8% food and beverage tax, and 10% service charge, for a total of 23% in additional charges. Plan accordingly. Many inexpensive and budget hotels omit these taxes in whole or in part and usually charge by the room. Other hotels, and all tourist hotels, have double and single rates, with the single rate only slightly less expensive.

If you plan ahead, using the services of a Do-

ACCOMMODATIONS IN THE DOMINICAN REPUBLIC

Under US$30	Inexpensive
US$30–80	Moderate
US$80–100	Expensive
US$100+	Luxury

Be aware of two important factors when selecting and booking rooms. First, many prices are seasonal and drop in the off-season (between March and October). Thus, an expensive room in winter (the high season) can become less so in May. It is even possible to find off-season bargains in moderately priced rooms, especially at the lower end of the price scale. Most inexpensive rooms are always inexpensive and aren't particularly subject to seasonal rates.

Secondly, rates tend to vary depending upon how the room is booked. Many tourist agents can find you cheaper rates than those advertised or can negotiate cheaper rates for you, based upon the length of your stay. Some tourist agents are simply good at talking down hotel managers. Finally, it is sometimes possible to bargain with clerks and managers, especially at smaller hotels. If you speak Spanish, by all means ask politely if cheaper rates are available, and maintain a friendly attitude. You might find your lower-end moderate rate dropping to inexpensive.

It's always a good idea—especially if traveling on a restricted budget—to call ahead and verify rates. The prices listed herein are up-to-date as of press time, but may have fluctated depending on the season, economy, festivals, or whim of the owner.

minican tourist agency and guide, you can have a seamless holiday. But do-it-yourself is easy, too—it just takes a little flexibility. If you're on a low budget, traveling town to town, some hotels will subject you to TV and traffic noise, spiders, roaches, and early-rising roosters. If you choose these hotels, ask about the electricity *(la luz)* and inquire if there's a generator *(planta)*. In any case, pack candles and flashlights and drink bottled water. Most hotel owners are very hospitable, so try out your Spanish and be open to wild conversations.

FOOD AND DRINK

TRADITIONAL FARE

If you visited any home in the Dominican Republic on an average sunny day, you'd likely find lunch or dinner consisting of the traditional national dish called *la bandera nacional*. The dish is pretty simple, usually beans and rice, quite often served with savory chicken, beef, or goat, depending upon the means and locale of the family (beef in the Cibao, goat everywhere else).

When Columbus discovered Hispaniola, he found the native peoples cultivating corn, peppers, sweet potatoes, and peanuts. Their mainstay was cassava, which they called *yuca*. (Arawak is even often translated as "yuca eater.") The Caribs, on the other hand, included smoked meats on their list of foods much more often than did the Arawaks. Then, by the early 1500s, the Spanish began cultivating sugar and African slaves were imported to do all the hard work. Their presence introduced dishes like *mondongo*, which is an African-influenced stew of chopped tripe.

Everyday Eating

The everyday Dominican diet—the meals eaten by Dominicans in the countryside or in small towns—is a fairly simple combination of starches such as rice, tubers, and plantains. Because most Dominicans can rarely afford to eat meat, they derive most of their protein from red beans (a very good source when combined with their beloved rice). Poorer Dominicans use pigeon peas called *gandules* as a substitute for beans, which they then serve with rice as well. But whether a Dominican is rich or poor, food is very important as a ritual item in the cultural layout of the land, and Dominican people use food in most of their important celebrations and holidays. Mealtime is, in the Spanish tradition, an extended period of talk and sharing, a time to be convivial and happy.

These days, while *la bandera nacional* may be the standard dish, some other savory stews called *sancochos* combine all the island's flavors in one huge pot. The real *sancocho* has an almost infinite variety of combinations of ingredients, from goat, pork, and tripe to oxtails, chicken, rabbit, and pigeon peas. To make a good *sancocho*, you also mix in tubers like cassava and sweet potato, along with some plantains. In fact, the Dominican *sancocho* takes the place of other Latin American favorites like *puncheros* and *cocidos*. While it may be difficult to think of eating goat meat, goat is actually quite delectable, especially when flavored with familiar seasonings like onion, garlic, oregano, and lime.

One of the other staples of Dominican cuisine is the plantain. Plantains are eaten boiled and mashed, fried green or ripe, and as the main ingredient in *mangú*, often recommended for travelers experiencing upset stomach. In fact, *mangú* is the most common poor worker's breakfast, consisting of mashed green plantains fried with onions. In *mofongo*, mashed roasted plantain balls are spiced and served with *chicharrones* (little fried balls of pig skin), and in all restaurants and homes you can find traditional *plátanos maduros fritos* (twice-fried sliced ripe plantains) and *tostones* (fried green). For big, important meals, many poor campesinos eat plantains, which they boil with noodles and broth instead of rice and beans.

Especially delightful is the goat meat from Azua and Monte Cristi, which arrives at the pot already seasoned with wild oregano, which the goats are given with their normal feed. This goat makes a wonderfully savory stew, as the wild oregano permeates the meat. By tradition, all seaside towns specialize in crabs and oysters, usually prepared with a little lime juice and fried quickly.

Special Occasions

Almost any large gathering is a reason for celebrating with food for Dominicans, but the most common feast times are Christmas Eve, New Year's Eve, Easter, Carnaval (in February), and patron saints' days. Celebrations usually involve the standard staple dishes and *sancocho*, along with many specially prepared items not normally seen on Dominican tables.

The main dish at Christmas is *lechón asado*—roasted pig. The younger the pig, the better and more tender it is. *Lechón asado* is usually served with rice and green beans, or with rice, beans, and pigeon peas. In more prosperous Dominican households, the Christmas meal might also include turkey or chicken, cassava, spaghetti, and fresh green salad. A lot of rural Dominicans raise the Christmas birds themselves, and many raise the pig, too. A new and growing Christmas custom is to boil chestnuts and eat them. The typical Easter meal is based on fresh or cured codfish, served with potatoes.

Changes in Cooking

Unemployment has changed the nature of the traditional working-class Dominican kitchen over the years. Sadly, the high unemployment rate has forced many poorer Dominican women to seek jobs as domestic servants, most often as cooks in the kitchens of the upper classes. In fact, many upper- and middle-class families employ at least a laundress and cook. The kitchens in these homes are equipped with all the modern gear, stoves, refrigerators, and sometimes microwaves. In contrast, the food traditions of the countryside are suffering as more and more women are not at home during the day to prepare traditional fare, some of which requires long hours of work. Those women who do live and work at home in the countryside have to make do with very basic and primitive condi-

tions. Mothers cook meals in a clay oven called a *fogón,* which is heated over a wood fire. Because there is usually no running water, these women must walk to the nearest stream and haul water back to their houses. The result is rationing of water for cooking and cleaning, as well as drinking.

DOMINICAN MEALS

Most Dominican families eat their meals together, unless one or both of the parents cannot get away from work. It is common for the mother of the house to seat everyone at the table—especially in large or rural families—and oversee the distribution of portions. Children are generally indulged at mealtimes, with the mom taking care of setting the table and seeing to it that the kids get enough to eat. In some urban families, members must serve themselves from a buffet.

El Desayuno

El desayuno—breakfast—is the first meal of the day. The most common breakfast consists of plantains or some type of boiled tuber, especially in rural areas where campesinos need a dose of starch to start their grueling workday. In most cities, *el desayuno* may be only some bread and jam with coffee. In all my time in Santo Domingo, I saw only a few Dominicans do with

---

THE GROWTH OF A CUISINE

European exploration and colonization meant many things to many people, but one thing it certainly meant was a growth in the exchange of foods. Today's Caribbean cuisine is a combination of native and imported foods, blended in ways unique to the islands. Early Spanish colonists in the Dominican Republic incorporated numerous types of native fruits into their diet, and utilized the spices annatto and allspice. They took to the native cassava, sweet potato, hot pepper, beans, and fish. From America they brought the potato, tomato, peanut, papaya, cacao bean, and avocado. From Spain they imported carrots and such green vegetables as leeks, cabbages, asparagus, onions, and artichokes. The Spanish had been to Africa

and adopted many Portugese food discoveries as well, including watermelon, okra, banana, plantain, and millet. All of these they brought to Hispaniola. Later, when the South Pacific became more widely known, its foods were adopted as well—mango, taro, and breadfruit. And to spice them all, many varieties of flavorings were brought from Indonesia and India.

The actual diet now prevalent on Hispaniola, especially in the Dominican Republic, originated not with the elite but rather with the poor, who made colorful dishes replete with many types of exotic flavors, departing from Spanish tradition. These dishes were adopted by the elite, and became the national food.

anything more than bread, jam, and coffee with lots of sugar.

El Almuerzo

On the other hand, lunch, or *el almuerzo,* is a truly bombastic meal, usually consisting of huge quantities of beans and rice and often also including some type of meat, or perhaps *sancocho.* After lunch, Dominicans usually stretch out for their afternoon siesta, which lasts a couple of hours, before they're ready to face the world again. In small towns, and in many larger ones as well, business closes for several hours to accommodate the Dominican tradition of a large lunch and a short nap in the middle of the day. You'll see that government offices quite often post hours that show them open during the middle of the afternoon, but I defy you to find many civil servants on the job during that time.

Most Dominicans try to eat *el almuerzo* at home if possible, but increasing numbers of workers must take some type of lunch with them and don't have time for a siesta. More and more, the modern workaday world is gaining on the old Spanish traditions. And more and more businesses in Santo Domingo and Santiago are forgoing the siesta period altogether.

La Cena

The evening supper, *la cena,* is eaten late, after the family is gathered together from their days at work and school. Again, starch predominates, and Dominicans eat a supper of boiled roots, eggs, bread, spaghetti, mashed potatoes, or *mangú.* Evening is also the time for sweet desserts, some of which are also made from starchy staples like beans or plantains. Dominicans make candy from sweet potatoes and red beans, and they make especially delicious corn puddings. Dominican bakeries are chock full of lusciously sweet cakes and caramel flán, which is another Spanish sweet treat.

WHAT TO EAT

Meat Dishes

Among the meat dishes, other than *sancocho* and *lechón asado,* you can find other pork dishes which include *cuchifrito* (pork innards stew)

and *gandinga* (liver, heart, and kidneys, boiled with spices). These dishes can all be found in what's called *lechoneras,* but the specialty dishes are not for the faint of heart. *Carne mechada* is beef roast garnished with ham, onion, and spices, while *locrio de cerdo* (meat and rice) is another typical beef dish. Goat is very popular, and you should try it (you'll like it!). Young goat *(cabra)* is considered a special delicacy, along with goat fed on oregano. Dominicans make a delicious *fricasé* made of stewed chicken, rabbit, or goat, usually served with *tostones.* The simplest of all meat dishes is *arroz con pollo* (rice and chicken). The standard Dominican soup is the *sopa criolla dominicana,* which is a hodgepodge, served differently everywhere, and made of stew meat, pasta, onions, greens, and seasonings. *Cocido* is a soup made from meat, chickpeas, and various vegetables. *Pipián* is goat's offal made into a stew (imagine that!). Most restaurants are more than ready to broil a steak the way you might get it back home, but you'll probably find Dominican beef a bit stringy. Typical of street food or Dominican fast food is the ever-popular *chicharrón de pollo,* small pieces of fried chicken prepared with lime and

---

CHICHARRONES DE POLLO

1/2 cup lime juice
1/4 cup soy sauce
1/2 cup Dominican rum
1 2–3 pound chicken, cut into small pieces
1/2 cup vegetable oil
flour
salt and pepper to taste

Mix lime juice, soy sauce, and rum. Pour over chicken in a bowl. Cover and marinate chicken pieces for 2–3 hours in refrigerator. Heat oil in a large skillet. Dredge chicken pieces in flour, season with salt and pepper and fry on each side until golden brown. Serves four.

—Reprinted from *Américas,* a bimonthly magazine published in English and Spanish by the General Secretariat of the Organization of American States

oregano. This is not quite the same as *chicharrón,* which is pork cracklings.

Seafood

Since you're never very far from the sea in the Dominican Republic, you'd expect seafood to be a specialty in restaurants, and it is indeed. Don't bother ordering shrimp, which is imported, but almost everything else is caught right offshore. Available locally is wonderful *chillo* (red snapper), *mero* (sea bass), which is often freshly prepared and served with marvelous garnishes of all kinds, *pulpo* (octopus), and *lambi* (conch). Many of these are served with *mojo isleño,* an elaborate sauce of olives, onion, tomatoes, capers, vinegar, garlic, and pimento. Probably the most famous seafood dishes are *langosta* (local lobster), *cangrejos* (crabs), and *ostiones* (small oysters). You should try to order your seafood *sin sal* (without salt)—most Dominican chefs love to douse everything in salt. The north coast is especially rich in red snapper, sea bass, oyster, and octopus, and many dishes are made freshly with lime juice, coconut milk, and rum.

Vegetables

The vegetables *(verduras)* of the Dominican Republic come in all the standard varieties, with some unique additions. These include *chayote* and *calabaza* (West Indian squash), cassava, *yautia, batata* (sweet potato), and the *ñame* (African yam). Cassava is generally served boiled in stews since it can kill you if you eat it raw. *Catibias* are cassava fritters and meat.

Fruit

Another way to lunch or breakfast cheaply and healthily, or to enjoy a snack anytime, is to buy fruit. Vendors are everywhere, and their wares are cheap, so don't bargain. If you're able to buy a whole, sweet pineapple, peeled and cored, for about 30 cents, why be mean? Pineapples are native to Hispaniola. They were taken by Columbus back to Europe, introduced there, and spread throughout the world thereafter. The *piñas* you'll buy at roadside stands are much sweeter than exported varieties, because they are left on the vine to ripen. Mangos are common in the Dominican Republic as well, though they were only introduced to Hispaniola from Africa around 1740. The mango season is May and June. The traditional Dominican orange, called the *china* because it came to Dominicana from China, has a lot of seeds, but it is quite sweet and non-acidic, while the *naranja* is very sour. Vendors will peel a *chinola* for you so that you can pop pieces into your mouth. I find the chinola almost unbearably sweet, however. It's better in juices, cut with sparkling water. If you want a lime, you'll be ordering *limón. Zapotes* are a brown fruit, similar in shape to an avocado. *Mamey* (mammee apple), *guanábana* (custard apple), *caimito* (star apple), and *jobo* (hogplum) represent some of the more exotic fruits available. Naturally, you can obtain all kinds of bananas, in all shapes and sizes. You should also try the acerola, a wild West Indian cherry, which has half again as much vitamin C as orange juice.

CARNE GUISADA

2 tablespoons vegetable oil
2 pounds stew beef cut into small pieces
3 medium onions, finely chopped
6 cloves garlic, minced
3 stalks celery, finely chopped
2 green peppers, finely chopped
1 tablespoon oregano
2 tablespoons vinegar
5 tablespoons tomato paste
3 tablespoons cilantro, minced
black pepper and salt

Mix the oil with the beef, and brown meat in a covered skillet over medium heat. Mix onions, garlic, celery, green peppers, oregano, vinegar, and tomato paste together and add to the meat. Mix thoroughly, lower heat, and cover. Stir occasionally. After 30 minutes, add minced cilantro. Cook until thickened, about 45 minutes. Season to taste with black pepper and salt. Serve with rice and beans. Serves four.

—Reprinted from *Américas,* a bimonthly magazine published in English and Spanish by the General Secretariat of the Organization of American States

Sweets

Dominicans are pretty crazy for sweets, and on every street corner you'll likely find a *dulcería,* where huge collections of confections can be found, many made out of coconut, pineapple, and sweet potato. The traditional desserts are *arroz con dulce* (sweet rice pudding), which is delicious, and the delightful *majarete,* a corn pudding that will sear your teeth as it makes you happy. Flan is wonderful. You can spend a lifetime sampling flán in little cafes all over the country and never taste two the same. One called *quesillo de leche y piña* (a milk and pineapple flán) is a special treat; *cocoyuca* is cassava flán with coconut. Another dessert, *tres leches,* is made from the milk of goats and cows and who knows! Almost as traditional as *arroz con dulce* is *bizcocho* (sponge cake). *Cazuela* is a pumpkin and coconut pudding, while *tembleque* is plain coconut pudding. And you can always try *plata* (baked bananas).

Regional Specialties

The roadsides in Bonao are known especially for *puerco asado,* while the Cibao is known for its *longaniza* (mild pork sausage) and *morcilla* (heavy blood sausage). *Pan agua,* or water bread, may take the shape of a French-style baguette but is also available in smaller sizes at most local *colmados* and *panaderías.* Almost anywhere in the mountains, roadside stands offer roasted cashews. And, of course, I would be remiss for not mentioning the *chimichurri,* sort of the Dominican answer to the hamburger, and nearly as ubiquitous. The *chimichurri* is a sandwich like the Dagwood, piled high with everything the chef can find at hand and loaded with hot sauce and lots of lettuce. As with hamburgers, quality varies, but once you've found one that suits you, you're in like Flynn.

In and around the province of La Vega, you can find *gofio.* To make *gofio,* Dominicans crack corn and put it in a pot over a hot fire, grind and mash it, then sift in sugar. Try it sometime.

On the Go

Like many people, Dominicans often eat on the run. The variety of fresh and fried foods, along with sandwiches, available from cafes, cafeterias, and street vendors can be bewildering. A lot of times I'll just point to something that looks good

---

FATAL CIGUATERA

Fish poisoning is a dangerous illness which affects people who ingest certain kinds of seafood. The most common carriers of the poison are parrot fish (*papagayo*), barracuda, and pufferfish.

The poison shows up around 30 minutes after ingestion, and its symptoms include uncontrolled shivers, spastic movements of the lips and tongue, numbness, dizziness, loss of muscular control, and vomiting. It's a serious problem and can be fatal unless immediate medical attention is provided.

What to do? Vomit all you can to get the fish out of your system. Vitamin B complex helps, as do sweet potato and papaya juice. Get to the nearest hospital, clinic, or doctor.

---

under glass and pay a few pesos to try it. Quite often, it is delicious, and it's certainly never as bad as a fast-food hamburger back home. The most common kind of quickly prepared food, usually eaten for lunch, is the sandwich. A *cubano* contains ham, chicken, and cheese, along with a rich spicy sauce on a long crusty bread roll. The *cubano* can be fairly poor, or it can be a special culinary experience. Find them in local cafes, usually outdoor ones, and keep trying until you find a great one. A *medianoche* (midnight) contains pork, ham, and cheese. For a really quick and cheap meal you can try the almost ubiquitous *quipe* (sometimes *keepi,* with other variations, too) or *pastelito,* both of which are dough filled with meat, sometimes cheese, and sometimes coconut. You can order a quick *quipe* and a juice drink and find yourself ready to walk for miles again. About the only local Dominican cheese is the *queso de hoja,* which is very milky colored and milk flavored. Johnny-cakes, West Indian pancakes, are common streetside treats, too.

In villages everywhere, and in some *colmados* in larger cities, you can find the magnificent *arepa. Arepa* is corn bread, either plain or sweet, and it is the most marvelously heavy bread you'll ever eat. Order a portion and you'll get a slice, or you can order larger quantities to take home. I'll probably be shot by the Dominican food police for saying so, but I love to eat *arepa* with hot coffee for breakfast. Sometimes a dusty village will have a *colmado* and bakery, or sometimes you'll find a *colmado* at a deserted crossroads. If so, you're almost certain to find *arepa* there.

WHERE TO EAT

Though everyday Dominican meals can be rather basic, eating out in the larger cities or resort areas, especially Santo Domingo, is another story altogether. Dominican food is called *comida criolla* (literally, Creole food). The food is spicy but not particularly hot. Nor is it particularly haute, but it is unique and delicious in its own way. In general, Dominican cooking combines African, Indian, Spanish, and typical Caribbean styles. There are plenty of international restaurants as well—everything from Italian and Chinese to Mexican and Japanese—along with a few vegetarian and fine seafood restaurants.

Of course, now that international tourism has struck many areas of the island, you can also find international fast food, which consists of bad pizza, bad deli sandwiches, bad everything. Unless you're absolutely stuck in the middle of a fast-food jungle, you're much better off eating economical and healthy *comida criolla* and staying away from the multitudinous international junk food available around the resorts.

In restaurants, feel free to eat salads and have ice cubes in your drink. If you prefer, bottled water is always available. In rural areas, you should always drink bottled water or canned or bottled soft drinks.

BUYING GROCERIES

Except for the remotest regions of the far southwest and mountaínous provinces in the central parts of the country, the Dominican Republic has convenient and well-stocked stores and markets in which to buy food, sundries, and drugs.

Supermarkets

Major towns have *supermercados* that offer shelves stocked with all the provisions your heart could desire. While not large by some standards, most of the Dominican Republic's supermarkets offer staples, fruits and vegetables, liquors, juices, bread, sweets, and sundries. Prices for locally grown foodstuffs are very reasonable, but as in all island societies, imported goods and luxury items are expensive. There are no well-known market chains in the Dominican Republic, but the supermarkets are well marked. Hours vary. Most of Santo Domingo's supermarkets stay open until 9 P.M., while those in smaller towns close earlier.

Colmados

Everywhere you go in the Dominican Republic, you'll find *colmados*. Usually, there's one on every street corner in downtown areas, and every small town and village has several. *Colmados* are local gathering places for gossip and sell such staples as rice and fruits, some vegetables, candy, soft drinks, gum, cigarettes and cigars, and a small supply of pastries and bread. Their hours vary, since they're individually owned, but they're almost always open late. Listen for boom-box merengue and look for clutches of gossipers—you will have found the *colmado.*

Street Vendors

Street vendors and open-air markets are Dominican treats. Every town, big or small, has its fruit vendors, and you can always refresh yourself with juices and fruits for incredibly cheap prices. Vendors sell fresh coconut juice *(coco frío)*, gum, cigarettes, and sometimes sandwiches. The open-air markets are places where you can buy anything and everything, and where the majority of the working class does its shopping. Hence, they are good places to shop and simultaneously get to know the country.

DRINKS

It seems that everybody everywhere in the Dominican Republic drinks soda or soft drinks. Brands include Sprite, Pepsi, 7-UP, Coke, Country Club, Marinda, and Club Soda. Dominicans also favor Extracto de Malta, a malt extract. Far more interesting are the *jugos* and alcoholic drinks indigenous to the Dominican Republic.

Jugos

To cool off during the day, and for enjoyment at almost any other time, try some of the many delicious *jugos,* or juice drinks, for which the island is justly famous. Almost every fruit available becomes a fresh juice, especially the *chinola* (passion fruit), pineapple, and papaya *(lechosa).* At vendor stalls on the street, you can get shaved ice in cups covered with tamarind or guava syrup, a very cheap way to cool down on a warm day. (Some travelers worry about the ice, because it comes from tap water. Personally, I've never had any trouble, but this is no guarantee.) Everywhere you go, you'll see roadside vendors selling the famous *coco frío,* green drinking coconuts with their tops lopped off and a straw stuck inside. Most *cocos* go for about RD$5, which makes them cheap and healthy. For a not-so-healthy treat, go for *batidas,* thick homemade milkshakes, made with many kinds of fruit. My favorite is the *batida lechosa,* the papaya milkshake. Out of this world.

Alcohol

The Caribbean and rum are almost synonymous. Well-known brands like Bacardi and Captain Morgan helped put rum on the international map. Not as well known, but sought after by connoisseurs is the Barbancourt brand, from Haiti. But the Dominican Republic has its own famous brands as well. These are known as the "three Bs": Barceló, Bermudez, and Brugal. Other brands include Siboney and Macoris, and as you travel through the country you'll find that every province has its own favorite. Most Dominican rum is very smooth, but almost all of it is consumed on the island, leaving little for export. Brugal does have a distillery on St. Croix, but all the Dominican distilleries make enough profit not to need the export market.

It would be almost impossible to taste all the different blends and brands on the island. Which rum you choose to savor depends strictly upon your own personal preference and palate. Some people like their rum rough and ready, with a raw, scratchy taste. Others like the cool and heady aroma of dark rum, which can be as pleasant as fine cognac. Dominicans commonly use clear rum, called *blanco,* to mix daiquiris and other famous rum drinks. Clear rum, with a little lime rubbed around the edge of the glass, served with some cracked ice, is also a wonderful, and strong, drink. Most households tend to use the golden *(dorado)* blends. Rum called *añejo* and *gran añejo* are specially aged, somewhat dark, and usually much more expensive. They also go down like silk. Each distillery has its top-of-the-line rums.

The best Barcelo is the Imperial, which is light amber in color and very smooth on the throat. Bermudez's best is their Aniversario, a fine, dark rum, beside which many brandies pale. Other excellent premium rums include Macorix, which comes from a small distillery in San Pedro de Macorís, and the Bermudez Don Armando. These premium brands are good with ice or straight up.

Of course, rum is the distillate of sugarcane. The new alcohol is aged in wooden barrels stacked several high. The best rum receives flavor from the wood of the barrel. *Blanco* rums are the highest proof and the least aged in wood barrels. You can drink them with ice or mixed with fruit juice or some other soft drink. Order white rum as a *refresco.* Amber rum is aged at least a year in wood and is often referred to as *amarillo* (yellow). Amarillo has a lower proof, and you can drink it neat or with lime. *Añejo* rum spends several years in oak.

Outside of Puerto Plata you can visit the Brugal factory (on Avenida Luis Genebra). There really isn't much to the tour—the facility is devoted strictly to bottling and labeling. The payoff comes in the hospitality room afterward, where you can taste the rum and enjoy the best cold daiquiris in the world. If you're in a disco or club, you can order *un servicio,* which is a one-third–liter bottle of rum with a bucket of ice and *refrescos.* In rural areas, this costs just a couple of dollars, while the price can be steep in expensive clubs. Of course, you can do as I do: go to a *colmado,* order a small bottle of *añejo,* and drink it on a park bench. Cost: RD$22.

Mixing rum and fruit punch is popular in the Dominican Republic; you'll find drinks made with two or three different fruit juices, a dash of grenadine, ice cubes, lemon, and any kind of rum your taste fancies. Put it all through the blender and enjoy a 250-calorie dream. Probably the most famous rum drink is the *cuba libre,* which consists of rum, Coke, and a twist of lemon. Remember to always specify the brand of rum you desire. Keep in mind that alcohol in the tropics can dehydrate you badly, so it's best to drink rum after sundown, when the day is cooling off and your touring is done.

Rum is definitely one of the natural passions of the Dominican Republic, and you'll often see both city and country people passing a Sunday afternoon drinking rum and listening to music. In a country so fond of rum, it's surprising that you see so few dedicated drunks in the gutter. On the other hand, drunken driving is definitely a problem. You'll often see a truck driver tipping a bottle of beer as he drives, and many Dominicans cruise the streets on Sundays with plastic cups of dark rum in hand. The police don't bother these people unless they appear clearly out of control or have a wreck. By then, of course, it's too late.

Dominican beer is very rich and wonderful. All of the brews here would be considered premium beers back home. Presidente, Quisqueya, Bohemia, and Heineken are Dominicans' favorite brews.

Presidente is the most popular beer on the island, and its huge marketing efforts have given it a kind of stranglehold in many places. However, lesser brands are quite tasty, and should be tried whenever possible.

Coffee

Dominicans love their coffee. It is served as either *café espresso* or *café con leche* (steamed with milk). Most Dominicans drink small cups of espresso loaded with sugar, but you don't have to.

Regional Specialties

My favorite regional specialty can be found only in one factory in the town of El Seibo. Called *mabi seibano,* it can hardly be described, only experienced. *Mabi* is a bottled drink made from the bark of what's called the *Bejuco de Indio* vine. It has no alcohol, and tastes a little like sour root beer. I suppose that doesn't sound too good right now, but it tends to grow on you. Dominicans born in the province of El Seibo love the stuff and come long distances to get a case or two to take home with them. The factory where *mabi* is created stands on a street corner next to the Hotel Naranjo in El Seibo. I couldn't find a street name, so just cruise the town's main street until you see the hotel on top of a hill. The factory is on the north side of the road. You can go back into the factory and watch a couple of workmen feeding bark into a grist; then you can sample the finished product straight out of the tub.

From September through December, it is traditional to serve *guava velí* in the town of San Pedro de Macorís. *Guava velí* is a distilled drink that tastes something like hot dry schnapps and goes down like fire. An old saying had it that San Pedro was known for its *guava velí* and its music, though nowadays it's also known for its famous baseball players. If you're in San Pedro during the fall months or the early winter, try to sample this absolutely unique, fiery drink.

GETTING THERE

You can get to the Dominican Republic by air from anywhere in the world, usually cheaply and easily. The two major international airports are Santo Domingo's **Las Américas International Airport,** located about 25 minutes from the Colonial District along the coastal road called Los Américas Highway, and Puerto Plata's **Gregorio Luperón International Airport,** located between Puerto Plata and Sosúa, about a 15-minute taxi ride either way. There are six other airports in the country, though most are used for domestic and commercial traffic. However, American Airlines does provide American Eagle service to Punto Cana and La Romana and has now scheduled regular jet service from Miami to La Romana, mainly serving the huge Casa de Campo resort. The Samaná and Barahona airports are undergoing construction and renovation.

AIRPORTS

Santo Domingo
Las Américas is Santo Domingo's international airport (tel. 809/549-0226). When you first arrive, you'll think it's kind of dirty and crowded, but the airport works pretty well, and you can get through it easily with a little foreknowledge. First, try to buy your tourist card at the point of departure or on the incoming plane. Second, try to get to the baggage carousel quickly, and watch your luggage carefully. There are always a lot of porters around—some are helpful, some a little overly aggressive. If you want help, collect all your bags first, then hire a porter. Once you're out of customs, dozens of porters will besiege you, offering to carry your bags and find you a taxi. One trick is for a porter to carry each bag, until you've got five guys hauling your things. Don't let it happen if you don't want it to happen. Just be firm and polite.

There is no airport bus. A taxi to the Colonial District is about RD$250 (pesos), US$20. Duty free is open 8 A.M.–5 P.M.; the tourist information desk is open 8 A.M.–6 P.M. Although the change bank says it's only open 8 A.M.–6 P.M., I've been there at midnight and changed money.

Puerto Plata
The Gregorio Luperón airport (tel. 809/586-1992) is cleaner, less crowded, and easier to navigate. Like Las Américas, however, it offers no airport bus. All operating hours are the same here as at Las Américas.

Other Airports
Other important airports in the Dominican Republic include Santo Domingo's **Herrera** (tel. 809/547-3454); Samaná's **Arroyo Barril** (tel. 809/248-2766); Santiago's **Cibao** (tel. 809/587-6766); Barahona's **María Montes** (tel. 809/524-7000 or 809/524-4144) La Romana's **Punta Águila** (tel. 809/556-5565); and La Altagracia's **Punta Cana** (tel. 809/689-1548). Punta Cana and La Romana receive charter and American Eagle flights. Herrera and the Samaná and Santiago airports are domestic only.

AIRLINES

From North America
From North America, by far the largest scheduled carrier is **American Airlines** (U.S. tel. 800/433-7300). From New York, San Juan, or Miami, American offers about a dozen flights daily, some nonstop, some not. American also operates American Eagle flights from San Juan and Mayagüez daily to Santo Domingo, Puerto Plata, Punta Cana, and La Romana. **Continental Airlines** (tel. 800/525-0280) flies daily to Santo Domingo from Newark, New Jersey. To a large extent the Dominican Republic has sold itself on mass tourism, so package tours are not hard to find with airlines everywhere (American Airlines offers the best). If you're interested in an all-inclusive week or so, with airfare, transfers, and a room in a resort, check out the packages—they're almost always cheaper.

As of this writing, direct flights to the Dominican Republic originate in Boston, Dallas, Minneapolis, Detroit, Atlanta, Miami, Newark, New York—an impressive array of American cities. Canadians can fly direct from half a dozen cities, including Ottawa, Toronto, Montreal, Quebec, and Halifax. The dominant carrier by far is Amer-

DOMINICAN TRAVEL AGENCIES AND TOUR OPERATORS

Apolo Tours
Pablo Brugal
J.F.Kennedy 15, Puerto Plata
tel. 809/586-1802
fax 809/586-2671
email p.brugal@codetel.net.do

Borboletta
América Escovar Peñeyro
Max Henríquez Ureña 23, Santo Domingo
tel. 809/562-3403 or 809/566-9281
fax 809/567-2505 or 809/687-7012

Cafemba Tours
Separación 12, Puerto Plata
tel. 809/586-2177
fax 809/586-6313
email m.jimian@codetel.net.do

Daytours
Barnodys González
Catalina F. de Pou 8, Mirador Sur
Santo Domingo
tel. 809/473-6010 or 809/473-6596
fax 809/473-6268

Domitur
Roberto Salcedo
Nuñez de Cáceres 374
Santo Domingo
tel. 809/530-7313
fax 809/530-6500
email domitur@codetel.net.do

El Dorado Travel
Gustavo De Hostos
Av. Máximo Gómez/Juan Sánchez Ramírez
P.O. Box 22032, Santo Domingo
tel. 809/688-6661 or 809/688-6664
fax 809/686-6662

Emely Tours
Emilia de Rosario
San Fco. de Macorís 58
Santo Domingo
tel. 809/566-4545
fax 809/683-6499
email info@emely-tours.com

Go Caribic
Michelle Rosset
Av. Luis Ginebra
Plaza Turisol 55
Puerto Plata
tel. 809/586-4075
fax 809/586-4073
email go.caribic@codetel.net.do

Omni Tours
Tamara Simó
Roberto Pastoriza 204
Santo Domingo
tel. 809/565-6591
fax 809/567-4710
email omni.tours@codetel.net.do

Prieto Tours
Ramón Prieto
Av. Francia 125
Santo Domingo
tel. 809/685-0102
fax 809/685-0457
email prieto.tours@codetel.net.do

Tanya Tours
Fidelina Pimentel
Ml. Ma. Valencia 27, Los Prados
Santo Domingo
tel. 809/565-5691
fax 809/542-6224

Thomas Tours
Rosalinda Thomas
P. Henríquez Ureña 170
Santo Domingo
tel. 809/541-5868
fax 809/541-5667
email thomas.tour@codetel.net.do

Viajes Bohio
Boni Canto Rondón
Benito Monción 161
Santo Domingo
tel. 809/686-2992
fax 809/686-7227
email bohio.cxa@codetel.net.do

ican, which offers the most flights and usually the lowest prices among standard tourist fares.

To arrange for the cheapest flights from North America, one should always look for Apex fares, which always carry restrictions, usually a 21-day advance booking among others. Super Apex (Advance Purchase Excursion) fares exist, as do special discount and youth fares, though these are subject to unusual conditions and are sometimes hard to find. Shopping online is becoming more and more popular—a good bet for cost-conscious passengers.

Smaller airlines flying from Miami to Santo Domingo include **Carnival** (tel. 800/274-6140) and **Air Atlantic** (tel. 800/879-0000).

Charter packages are cheap and abundant, especially in the winter season when travel is heavy. **MLT Vacations** (tel. 888/267-8349) and **TransGlobal** (tel. 800/338-2160) are major American vacation charter companies, but there may be others from time to time. Any reputable tourist agency can also recommend packages, most of which offer cheap flights and all-inclusive resort stays at one of the major hotels. Most Canadian charter companies fly to Puerto Plata, which has become a winter mecca for snowbirds from Canada. Canadians can try **Royal Aviation** (tel. 514/739-7000). There are many, many others, most of which advertise regularly in Sunday supplements to major Canadian newspapers. Many Canadian travelers fly to America, then use American Airlines to Santo Domingo.

From Europe

From Europe, you'll generally need to fly through a gateway city like Miami or New York, though the connections are often very easy. Again, European travel agencies are chock full of package and charter flights. Many Europeans head for the north coast or Punta Cana, so prices have become amazingly competitive. **Iberia** does fly to Santo Domingo four times each week, and **Air France** flies twice a week from Paris. **Lufthansa** flies from Germany via New York, Miami, or San Juan. **KLM** and **Air Portugal** also fly via gateways.

From Central and South America

Getting to Santo Domingo from Central or South America isn't too tough with a connection or two. **COPA,** the Panamanian airline, flies through Puerto Rico. Try also **Viasa** and **ALM.**

Shopping for Tickets

These days, you can get a good deal if you shop around. Remember, always ask for the rock-bottom lowest fare the airline has available—specify a low fare, not just a discount fare. Be prepared to be flexible and ready to fly on weekdays. You might also check on special fares to a gateway city and then onward from there. One word of warning: it is terribly expensive to change discount tickets, so try to be sure of your schedule and stick to it. Also, although it might sound like fun to fly into Santo Domingo and out of Puerto Plata, or vice versa, it is actually a very expensive proposition, for reasons known only to airline computers. If you contact a travel agent, be sure to specify what you want, and don't hesitate to shop around from one agent to another. You'd be amazed at the differences you sometimes uncover. Allow no less than two hours for connections, especially when leaving the Dominican Republic, as flights are sometimes delayed.

Finally, cancellation insurance is always a possibility. This is sometimes offered by ticket agents and tour operators, ensuring that the cost of the ticket will be refunded if you cancel your trip. You should examine this type of insurance skeptically. Mostly, it isn't worth it, unless you have specific reasons for needing it.

If a package tour may appeal to your instincts, partly because it seems cheap, keep in mind that there may be charges you haven't counted on. The truth about package tours is that they are decisionless sweeps through a mass-tourist world. If you take one, you'll be sure to see nothing that doesn't look like home, with cable TV running in the near background and not a Dominican in sight—at least not a Dominican who isn't a waiter, bartender, or maid. To get at the real Dominican Republic, you have to get outside the gates and walls of the big resorts. It's worth it.

INTERNET RESOURCES

When shopping on the Internet for cheap airline tickets, it is best always to begin with the high-profile sites and work your way down. Sites like Travelocity.com and Expedia.com each list the major airline published fares for the route and date you choose. Access Travelocity at

LAST-MINUTE TRAVEL CLUBS

Discount Travel International
114 Forrest Ave.
Suite 203
Narberth, PA 19072
tel. 215/668-7184
fax 215/668-9182

FLY ASAP
P.O. Box 9808
Scottsdale, AZ 85252-3808
tel. 800/FLY-ASAP or 602/956-1987
fax 602/956-6414

Last-Minute Travel
1249 Boylston St.
Boston, MA 02215
tel. 800/LAST-MIN or 617/267-9800
fax 616/424-1943

Moment's Notice
425 Madison Ave.
New York, NY 10017
tel. 212/486-0500
fax 212/486-0783

Spur of the Moment Cruises
411 N. Harbor Blvd.

Suite 302
San Pedro, CA 90731
tel. 800/4-CRUISES or 310/521-1070 in California,
800/343-1991 elsewhere in the United States; 24-hour hotline 310/521-1060
fax 310/521-1061

Traveler's Advantage
3033 S. Parker Rd.
Suite 900
Aurora, CO 80014
tel. 800/548-1116 or 800/835-8747
fax 303/368-3985

Vacations to Go
1502 Augusta Dr.
Suite 415
Houston, TX 77057
tel. 713/974-2121 in Texas, 800/338-4962 elsewhere in the United States
fax 713/974-0445

Worldwide Discount Travel Club
1674 Meridian Ave.
Miami Beach, FL 33139
tel. 305/534-2082
fax 305/534-2070

---

www.travelocity.com/news/newfares.html for breaking deals, bookable online with a couple of clicks. Access Expedia at expedia.msn.com/daily/news. This daily bargain watch has deals, news, advice, and analysis. One intriguing concept is Priceline, at www.priceline.com, where you can decide what you want to pay for a flight, and see if an airline will accept your offer. In Europe, for example, a French site, www.degriftour.fr is a specialist in last-minute discounts from British, French, and other European discounters. This can yield amazing rates on air fares, hotel rooms, and other services.

Generally, one can always start with Travel.com at www.onetravel.com, which is a clearinghouse for money-saving hotel rates and cruise deals. An alert can be sent to you via email for up-to-date bulletins listing last-minute air fare deals. Tom Parsons has a site, www.bestfares.com, which blankets

the field of flights, hotels, car rentals, and other Internet specials. If you are flexible in your travel schedule, you might try Air-Tech, with a website at www.airtech.com, where savings go to those who are most flexible, with savings on a space-available basis within a two- or four-day window. Travelbids offers at least a six percent discount at www.travelbids.com, where you make the reservations yourself. In general, a "farefinder" service at Preview Travel, www.previewtravel.com, helps with both fares and car rental.

For specific airlines, try Lowestfare for TWA at www.lowestfare.com, where you can save twenty percent on TWA tickets and which lists some bargains on cruise and package vacations. American Airlines has a similar service where you can sign up for last-minute deals at www.aa.com. For specific travel agencies and tourism boards, try Tourism Offices Worldwide Directory at www.towd.com, which can make travel research more affordable. You can also drop a netnote to Internet Travel Network Fare Mail at www.itn.net, letting them know your destination and price ceiling, and they'll email you when something comes up that may match your needs.

And last but not least is Guidebookwriters.com, where a stable of approximately 75 guidebook writers from every well-known series on the market will answer your destination questions for about US$25 for 20 minutes. No guarantees, of course.

COURIERS

There must be someone out there who doesn't mind traveling light and all alone. That essentially is what couriers do, and they do it almost 40,000 times on international flights every year, according to an estimate by the Internal Association of Air Travel Couriers in Lake Worth, Florida. Even the Denver-based Air Courier Association reports steady demand for air couriers, and plenty of seats available, amounting to about 800 spots each week on flights worldwide. Couriers usually pay about half fare and the best deals often arise during the off season, or are those booked on the shortest notice. In exchange for reduced fares, couriers agree to allow a shipping company to use their space in compartments, expedite documents, and return at a specified time. They also agree to carry paperwork for the shipping company, to be handed over to company representatives after each flight.

Although it may sound fishy in some respects,

COURIER INFORMATION

Courier Companies
Courier Agency-Now Voyager
74 Varrick St.
Suite 307
New York, NY 10012
tel. 212/431-1616

Discount Travel International
169 W. 81st St.
New York, NY 10024
tel. 212/362-3636
fax 212/362-3236

Discount Travel International
801 Alton Rd.
Suite 1
Miami Beach, FL 33139
tel. 305/538-1616
fax 514/633-0735

F.B. On Board Courier Club
10225 Ryan Ave.
Suite 103
Dorval, Quebec H9P 1A2, Canada
tel. 514/633-0740
fax 514/633-0735

Halbart Express
147-05 176th St.

Jamaica, NY 11434
tel. 718/656-8279
fax 718/244-0559

Midnite Express
925 W. Hyde Park Blvd.
Inglewood, CA 90302
tel. 310/672-1100
fax 310/671-0107

Way to Go Travel
6679 Sunset Blvd.
Hollywood, CA 90028
tel. 213/466-1126
fax 213/466-8994

Publications
Insiders Guide to Air Courier Bargains
The Intrepid Traveler
P.O. Box 438
New York, NY 10034
tel. 212/569-1081 for information,
800/356-9315 for orders
fax 212/942-6687

Travel Unlimited
P.O. Box 1058
Allston, MA 02134-1058
no phone

there is little danger of becoming involved in shady narcotics deals and the like. United States Customs representatives report no case of this sort in many years, the trick being to deal only with reputable companies. It used to be that most couriers found their flights between business centers, with New York feeding Europe, Miami feeding Latin America, and Los Angeles feeding Asia. But business is booming, and the list of cities has increased dramatically.

Courier travelers must hold a U.S. passport, be at least 21 years of age, and be willing to present a clean-cut appearance. Some courier flights yield frequent flier miles and some do not. Most companies won't accept credit cards, so payment must be by check or money order. Couriers must sign on at least a couple of weeks beforehand, and be ready to travel on a moment's notice. For further information you can contact the International Association; call 561/582-8320 or check the web at www.courier.org, a site that sells memberships and offers a newsletter. Also, contact Air Courier Association in Denver; call 303/279-3600 or log on to www.aircourier.org. Each company charges a yearly fee for information and services.

OTHER OPTIONS

Discounts and Charters

From Europe, charters are a popular way to get to the Dominican Republic. Keep in mind that, as with all travel, the most expensive time to visit is during the peak season, which, in the case of the Dominican Republic, is winter. Cheapest travel is in the summer season. Fall and spring are called "shoulder seasons," and travel is less expensive then as well. Especially in the Dominican Republic, where seasonal weather varies little, consider traveling in the off-season.

If you're really—and I mean *really*—into traveling cheap, you might try contacting courier companies, last-minute travel clubs, and bucket shops (often called "consolidators"), all of which specialize in transportation discounts. It is also possible to check into something called generic air travel, offered by organizations specializing in standby service. One pioneer in generic travel is called **Airhitch** (2790 Broadway, Suite 100, New York, NY 10025, tel. 212/864-2000). Bartered travel is also a possibility—where a company has received travel services in exchange for services, and later sells the services. Try **Travel World Leisure Club** (225 W. 34th St., Suite 909, New York, NY 10122, tel. 800/444-TWLC or 212/239-4855).

If you have questions about these operations, and especially about safety, call the FAA Consumer Hotline (tel. 800/322-7873).

By Sea

Of course, if you've got time and plenty of cash, you can always charter a yacht. Try **The Moorings** (Suite 402, Clearwater, FL 34624, tel. 813/535-1446 or 800/535-7289), **Nicholson Yacht Charters** (432 Columbia St., Suite 21A, Cambridge, MA 02141, tel. 617/225-0555 or 800/662-6066), or **Sunsail** (3347 N.W. 55th St., Ft. Lauderdale, FL 33309, tel. 800/327-2276).

For those wishing to come to the Dominican Republic by yacht or private charter, there are several possible ports of entry and docking. Very popular along the north coast is Puerto Plata, which has a small harbor. Down the coast to the east is the town of Santa Bárbara de Samaná. Located on the "underbelly" of the Samaná Peninsula, Santa Bárbara de Samaná has an excellent anchorage, friendly port staff, and lovely, placid waters. In fact, the entire bay is quite popular with the yachting crowd, and every day in winter you can see hundreds of private vessels anchored on blue water, some coming especially to see the whales that gather in those waters during winter.

On the south coast, the most popular anchorage is Boca Chica, the site of the famous Santo Domingo Yacht Club. You'll need special permission in advance to anchor at the club (see "Sailing" in the Santo Domingo chapter). Elsewhere, docking is a matter of contacting the port authorities, going to customs, and sitting back for a relaxing vacation.

One or two cruise companies also call in at Santo Domingo and Puerto Plata. As a way to see the country, cruises aren't very good, since they usually only let their passengers off at a port for a quick afternoon of shopping.

GETTING AROUND

Depending upon the amount of travel you wish to do, the relative accessibility of your destination, and your budget, almost every kind of modern transportation is available to get you from place to place. Trying to hitchhike, hike, or motor scooter around the country is probably not a good idea, solely because many of the roads, highways, and tracks can get a little hairy. If hairy doesn't scare you, you can try biking, too.

All major Dominican towns are connected by highways, all smaller provincial towns by good paved roads. Large areas in the mountains and along the east coast are strictly dirt track, and thus very isolated and inaccessible. Most towns have bus and taxi service, and all the towns of the country are interconnected by a system of bus lines, some offering comfortable, high-quality service, some by van or minibus. Two internal airlines have begun semi-scheduled service between many Dominican towns, or you can always charter a plane (for which prices aren't at all unreasonable). Of course, you can rent many kinds of vehicles nearly everywhere, including some jeeps and motorcycles. Guided tours come in all sizes, shapes, and prices, some good, some bad.

BY AIR

Domestic Carriers

The saga of nationally owned and run Dominican air service has finally played itself out in bankruptcy. The national carrier APA International Airlines canceled its one-flight-a-day service from New York some years ago. At press time the major in-country carrier, **Air Santo Domingo** (tel. 809/683-8020), operates out of Santo Domningo's Las Américas International Airport. Air Santo Domingo serves most of the Dominican Republic's major tourist areas, including Puerto Plata, Punta Cana, and La Romana. Fares generally range US $50–90. Air Santo Domingo does not fly ultra-modern jets, operating a rather venerable set of turbo-props which are reliable and safe, but bumpy. For those made

nervous by this kind of flying, Dominican bus lines are terrific and cheap.

At this writing, a new company called **Caribair** (tel. 809/542-6688) operates daily flights to Barahona from Santo Domingo. Both Air Santo Domingo and Caribair now offer flights to Port-au-Prince in Haiti, and along with bus service, offer one way to get safely from Santo Domingo to Haiti's capital city.

In-country air service comes and goes, so be sure to check at the airport for the availability of domestic flights. No matter what the situation, however, Dominican bus service remains cheap and reliable.

Charter Planes

Chartering a small airplane to fly you from one town to another is fairly easy. The major air services offering charter flights from Santo Domingo's Herrera airport are **Turísticos** (tel. 809/566-1696 or 809/567-7406), **Transporte Aéreo** (tel. 809/566-2141), and **Uni Charter** (tel. 809/567-0481). **Prieto Tours** (tel. 809/685-0102) operates an air taxi service to and from Portillo. **Agencia Portillo** (tel. 809/565-0832) provides air taxi service to Puerto Plata and Punta Cana for about US$35. **Airborne Ambulance Service** (tel. 809/567-1101) provides emergency air ambulance and executive jets.

If you want to charter a plane to get from one place to the next, try to do it with several other people to reduce costs. However, the countryside of the Dominican Republic is lovely, and you'll miss it from the air.

BY CAR

It is an inescapable fact that a car is the best way to see the real Dominican Republic, to explore the mountains, tour the countryside, root out inns and government hotels, and enjoy the culture's special food, music, and hospitality.

Okay, so you want to drive in the Dominican Republic. You have to accept a couple of realities. Highways are crowded, hectic, and confusing. Traffic in large cities, especially Santo Domingo, is a killer on streets that are torn up and poorly marked.

Roads leading east and west out of Santo Domingo are in good shape with wide shoulders. Roads along the north coast, and in the Cibao between Santiago and La Vega, are also in good condition, as are the roads crossing the Septentrional north to south. However, the Autopista Duarte, the major highway connecting Santo Domingo and Santiago, and which looks so great on all the highway maps (a big red ribbon!), is undergoing a major construction and widening project at many points along its length. It can be nightmarish and dangerous. For more on the Autopista, with some survival tips, see "Driving Nitty-Gritty," below.

Rental Companies

Most of the major car rental companies operate in the Dominican Republic. Two of the bigger ones, **National** and **Honda,** have desks at Los Américas International Airport. National and Honda are also represented at half a dozen major cities around the country, while **Nelly** and **McDeal** are housed away from the airport. Agencies like **Hertz, Budget,** and **Dollar** can be contacted quite easily through their common international telephone reservation numbers. There are always locally owned Dominican agencies around as well, but these come and go.

Because telephone numbers change quite often, even in Santo Domingo, the best bet for anyone wanting to rent a vehicle on the spot is to read the official tourist magazine called *La Cotica.,* updated yearly. The car rental companies are well represented and their telephone numbers and addresses correct.

Sadly, renting a car isn't cheap, due to relatively high accident rates and lots of petty theft (banged-up cars are the rule rather than the exception in Santo Domingo, for example, and almost nobody bothers buying fancy hubcaps). Expect to pay at least US$50 per day, about US$250 per week, exclusive of insurance, which is itself somewhat expensive. Cars are usually rented on an unlimited mileage basis, and for the cheapest rates you need to reserve at least 14 days in advance.

You will need insurance, unless you're willing to stand the full cost of repairing or replacing any car damaged while you're at the wheel. Collision waivers usually run US$6–12 per day, and

you will still be liable for a hefty deductible—sometimes as much as US$700. Read both the rental contract and the insurance rider very carefully, and try to confirm the cost up front—hidden charges tend to pile up.

If you still want to drive, choose a car in good condition and equipped with seat belts and air conditioning. Inspect it carefully, noting any dents and scratches. You'll need a major credit card and a valid foreign driver's license or an international license, and you must be at least 25 years old to rent.

For getting around short term, you can rent mopeds and motorbikes in tourist hotel areas for about US$15 a day. Beware of the problem of theft, however. Scooter-swiping is a major pastime in places like Sosúa.

Driving Nitty-Gritty

The rules of the road, technically speaking, are the same as those in North America and Europe. Driving is on the right-hand side. Usual city speed limits are 40kph, while highway speeds are 80kph. Traffic lights operate sporadically due to malfunctions and power failures, but in big cities, police direct traffic. Speed bumps are always present around military posts and in provincial towns, ditches dug across the right-of-way serve the same purpose. A toll is charged part of the way east of Santo Domingo and on the Duarte Highway, so carry some small bills and change in pesos. An excellent map is essential, such as the topo map from the **Geographic Institute** (tel. 809/682-2680, Calle de las Damas, Santo Domingo).

Service stations *(bombas)* in the Dominican Republic usually close at 6 P.M., though some in larger cities are open until 10 P.M. There are a few new 24-hour stations here and there, but weekends, especially Sundays, can be gas dry, so keep your tank full. Gas costs about US$1.80 per gallon and may go up or down quickly depending upon supply and your foreign-exchange rate.

That's the nitty. Now for the gritty. The first gritty is that there are no traffic signs marking highways, no speed limit signs, and only a few safety markers. For example, the highway that commences in Santo Domingo and goes west to Baní, Azua, and the desert southwest disappears in each town along the way and may be hard to pick up again on the other side. Some

APPROXIMATE DRIVING DISTANCES IN THE DOMINICAN REPUBLIC

NOT TO SCALE

ATLANTIC OCEAN

CARIBBEAN SEA

HAITI

PUNTA CANA

35 mi/56 km

HIGUEY

LA ROMANA

26 mi/43 km

22 mi/37 km

EL SEIBO

32 mi/54 km

MICHES

26 mi/44 km

36 mi/63 km

SAN PEDRO DE MACORIS

53 mi/89 km

ISLA SAONA

SABANA DE LA MAR

SANTO DOMINGO

45 mi/75 km

44 mi/73 km

SAMANA

NAGUA

46 mi/77 km

SAN FRANCISCO DE MACORIS

SAN CRISTOBAL

18 mi/30 km

28 mi/47 km

78 mi/130 km

31mi/51 km

28 mi/44 km

LA VEGA

24 km

15 mi

22 mi/36 km

SAN JOSE DE OCOA

BANI

JARABACOA

27 mi/43 km

28 mi/47 km

PUERTO PLATA

36 mi/61 km

SANTIAGO DE LOS TREINTE CABALLEROS

39 mi/65 km

CONSTANZA

33 mi/55 km

AZUA

70 mi/117 km

48 mi/80 km

COMENDADOR

83 mi/137 km

54 mi/89 km

BARAHONA

32 mi/54 km

ENRIQUILLO

MONTE CRISTI

JIMANI

PEDERNALES

49 mi/82 km

ISLA BEATA

© AVALON TRAVEL PUBLISHING, INC.

roads are potholed, or may be gravel with narrow shoulders. When a highway disappears in a provincial town and you aren't sure how to pick it up on the other side, just ask. It may take 10 or 15 minutes, but you'll always get out.

The good part is that everywhere except Santo Domingo, Santiago, and on the Duarte Highway, traffic is very light. In the provinces, you can whiz down beautiful open roads surrounded by lovely fragrant fields and feel absolutely marvelous! You will need to take care for the occasional campesino on horseback or motorscooter, but otherwise, provincial driving is joyous indeed.

In city traffic, or on the Duarte Highway, it's a different story. Avoid driving at night or in the rain on the Duarte. From downtown Santo Domingo, just finding the Duarte can be a chore, so be sure to have an excellent city map, available from bookstores and service stations. Once you get on the Duarte, or anytime you're in traffic, remember that Dominican drivers go too fast, pass dangerously and unexpectedly, and use hand and horn signals only Martians can understand. My first rule for survival on the Duarte Highway is to find a big truck that is going a reasonable speed, then stay about 150 feet behind it, using it as a shield. Other drivers may pass you and go around the truck, but you'll be safe.

Hand Signals

There are two basic hand signals used in the Dominican Republic. Sometimes you'll see a forward passenger holding his arm straight out, palm up, sometimes waving the arm. Mostly it means "We're turning right," or "We want the right lane." If the driver holds his left arm straight out while the car is moving, he's usually going to stop or pull right or left. That's it—there's only one position, so you have to be ready and anticipate a quick move.

Horn Language

In the heavy traffic of cities like Santo Domingo and Santiago, Dominican drivers substitute the car horn for brakes. They use their horns from dawn to dusk, and each person develops an individual style. Most often, one short little beep simply means, "I'm here." Some Dominicans will give a short beep when a light turns green, just to say, "Let's get going." Really, the short beep just

means that the game has begun. Two short little beeps at an intersection (often blind and uncontrolled) translates as a rather nonchalant "I'm coming through now!" Two long, insistent beeps means not only "I'm coming through," but also something like "I'm coming through—you're in the way, so *get over!*" As part of the machismo phenomenon, Dominicans play a lot of chicken on the road, especially at intersections and when merging. Hesitation at an intersection is *always* interpreted by a Dominican as a signal that you are allowing him or her to go, so if you pause, stop—don't just hesitate and then proceed.

One very long honk of the horn means, "Danger!" Most of the time the danger has already passed, but watch out anyway. Persistent honking only means you've won the game and someone is angry. But you can relax: Dominican traffic anger is never actually threatening.

Headlight Language

Horn language is not all there is to Dominican driving; the blinking of lights has an important place as well. A driver who is blinking his lights on the open highway is usually warning you of a speed trap. More importantly, at night in traffic, any blinking from high to low beam and back means, "I'm coming through!" A driver who is behind you, blinking, is telling you he's going to pass— come what may. One long high beam is the signal of a guy saying he's on your side of the road.

Police

In the case of an accident, police will be called to the scene, and it can be quite confusing. If there are injuries, the police might hold witnesses, but this is very rare, and the time of detention is very short. If you're in a fender bender, be patient and ride out the storm.

I'm told that the police often flag down foreign drivers for violations of the safety code or minor speeding. It happened to me once, though the person driving was a very aggressive Dominican woman showing me around Baní. The driver stood up and demanded a ticket and a court appearance, and the cop went away. If you're stopped for a dubious infraction, either try a face-off (if your Spanish is good) or shell out a US$5 *regalo* (gift), which will be considered on-the-spot payment of a fine. It's a very small piece of graft that shouldn't trouble you unduly.

By the way, motorcyclists are required by law to wear helmets. It's a good idea, but I've never seen one here.

Two Final Tips

There are, of course, emergency vehicles with sirens. Unfortunately, Dominican drivers rarely pull over or yield to them, and if you do, you'll probably actually cause a tie-up. And finally, Dominican drivers often pull far to the right before turning left, even if they must cross several lanes to do so. Beware.

BY BUS

Getting around the Dominican Republic by bus is a snap. The absolute best inter-city bus service is the Metro Servicios Turísticos. Called **Metro,** this modern bus line has stations in every major city in the country. In Santo Domingo, Metro is located on Winston Churchill at the corner of Hatuey near 27 de Febrero. Call them at 809/566-7126 or 809/566-6590, and make reservations for daily bus service to Santiago, Nagua, San Francisco de Macorís, Castillo, La Vega, Moca, and Puerto Plata. Going across the country in air-conditioned comfort takes about four hours and costs around US$12—a bargain. Going north to south on the Duarte Highway, for my money, it's the only way.

Another bus company, called **Caribe Tours** (27 de Febrero at Leopoldo Navarro, tel. 809/687-3171), has scheduled service, too, though the operation is a little less organized. Caribe is cheaper than Metro, but it does not run east. Several other small companies operate, too. **Transporte Tanya** is another decent intercity service (tel. 809/565-5691). **Transporte del Cibao, Terrabús, Express Moto Saad,** and **Línea Sur** serve regional travelers. Only if you can't get there by Metro or Caribe should you contact a regional carrier. Metro and Caribe make fewer stops, and the equipment is newer.

If you feel you have the time, and want to save some money going from town to town, you can try the nation's system of **guaguas,** minibuses that run everywhere. These minibuses run only when they're full, and you're as likely to share seats with a chicken or a goat as anything else, but you'll get around. You will need Spanish in order to settle the fare and establish an itinerary.

BY TAXI AND *PÚBLICO*

Taxis

For those who have a little money to spend, getting around the Dominican Republic's cities by taxi is the way to go. Taxis really aren't that expensive, provided you establish the fare in advance. Most drivers are outgoing, sympathetic, and a little crazy in a good way. In Santo Domingo, a call to one of the many companies listed in the Yellow Pages can get you a cab 24 hours a day, and an English-speaking driver, too. If you have two or three in your group, taxis are really dirt-cheap transportation.

Taxis are quite a trip in the Dominican Republic. There are no meters in taxis, so it's important to set the rate at the outset. Sometimes you can talk down the price, sometimes not. For example, it's a standard US$20 from the Santo Domingo airport to the Colonial District. Services around the cities cost quite a bit less. Taxis also have different unions representing their drivers, so if you find yourself in the middle of a sidewalk argument between drivers, just stand back and await the outcome. They'll work it out. Taxi drivers are sometimes fast drivers. Don't be afraid to ask them to slow down—it's your life.

In Santo Domingo, some radio taxi companies are **Taxi Raffi** (tel. 809/685-2268 or 809/689-5468), **Apolo Taxi** (tel. 809/541-9595 or 809/531-3900), **Bravo Taxi** (tel. 809/686-1387), **Micro-Movil** (tel. 809/689-6141), **Terra Taxi** (tel. 809/541-2525), and **Tropi Taxi** (tel. 809/531-3991)—but there are dozens of others. Although there is no roving taxi system in Santo Domingo as there is in New York City, you'll find taxis at the airport, all around the tourist hotels, and in the Colonial District. At other places you may have to call, but someone can usually help you out. In smaller cities and towns you'll definitely have to call or make prior arrangements. In small towns, some taxi drivers can take you sight-seeing for a very reasonable price. Check with your hotel for someone who speaks your language.

Públicos

To the uninitiated, Santo Domingo's system of

public transportation can be very intimidating. Cars, vans, minibuses straight from the scrap heap, even motorcycles with sidecars and, in Samaná, rickshaws are all part of the *público* system. Whatever the type of vehicle, the *público* will be stuffed to the rafters, many people sitting in the back (called *la cocina*), where all the gossip is exchanged. Sometimes the side of the vehicle is marked with a route, sometimes not. But taking a *público* can be very cheap, usually around only five pesos (30 cents), even for the longest, most complicated route.

Here's what to do to get a ride: stand on any relatively major street corner and stick out your hand. Flick a finger parallel to the street you want to go down. Most *públicos* stick to main streets, then turn around and come back, but some make one or (at most) two turns (for example, one *público* route in Santo Domingo is west on Avenida Independencia, then north on Máximo Gómez). Jump on and ask the driver if he's going your way.

Even limited Spanish is enough to take the *público* anywhere you want to go. If you want to go straight ahead, just say (or ask), *"Derecho."* If you want to know if the vehicle goes as far as a specific street, just ask, *"Hasta la Kennedy* (or whatever street)?" A nod or shake of the head will give you your answer.

If you want to get out, you can take a number of tacks. You might have to scream over the blaring radio, but just shout, *"¡Déjame!"* (let me out!) or *"¡Dónde pueda!"* (wherever you can!). To stop at the next corner, yell, *"¡En la esquina!"* or *"¡Después de cruzar!"* If you get confused, hysterical screams will probably work, too.

Another more formal form of transportation is the *guagua,* which in Santo Domingo comes in the form of a large 25–40 passenger bus, usually crammed to the gills with people and their stuff. In Santo Domingo itself, *guaguas* often are identified with the legend OMSA on the side, and ply their trade down the east-west Ave. 27 Febrero. *Guaguas* also go east from Santo Domingo to the airport and Boca Chica.

To catch a *guagua,* stand along the road or highway and signal to any bus that comes along going your direction. If it's a *guagua* and not a Metro for example, it will stop. Get on, sit down, and tell the conductor your destination. Fares are incredibly cheap, less than US $2 from Santo Domingo to Boca Chica. The adventuresome can save tons of money by using inter-urban *guaguas* to get around.

Carros Públicos

Less formal than *públicos* (if that's possible), are the *carros públicos,* which are passenger vehicles, some very old and banged up. They usually are beyond help, with cracked or missing windows, no door handles, and holes in the floor. Getting a ride is very informal: just flag one down, see where it's going, and hop in or give it a pass. Likewise, local *guaguas* ply the public trade but are older and more dilapidated than those that work the intercity routes. *Guaguas* normally have a *cobrador,* a guy who hangs out the door or window and yells out the destination. He tells jokes and flirts with women and gives a running commentary on the social situation.

In Santo Domingo, a new "OMSA" bus system has been inaugurated along Av. Kennedy and 27 de Febrero. Modern Mercedes vehicles run regular routes for about three pesos, making east-west runs in Santo Domingo more convenient and modern.

BY TRAIN

If you're thinking of making a train journey around the Dominican Republic, think again. There is no passenger train service in the entire country. The longest stretch of track in the country was laid from the central towns of the Cibao Valley in the late 19th century and stretched to Santa Bárbara de Samaná. Used mainly for freight (although some officials did ride as passengers), this line has been abandoned for many years.

Today, a lone stretch of track near La Romana is used as a freight line for sugarcane. You can see it as you drive or bus to Casa de Campo.

TOURS

I run hot and cold on the virtues of taking a guided tour of the Dominican Republic. Touring Santo Domingo is easy enough to do on your own, and you can see plenty in and around a resort area without consulting a professional tour guide. For touring the countryside, however, and for special trips to national parks, wild areas, or long climbs in the Cordillera Central, some kind of help can be a good idea. Unless, of course, you're a very adventuresome and patient soul. To climb Pico Duarte, you absolutely need local guides.

Many of the larger Dominican travel agencies represent specific Dominican resorts. However, rooms in most resorts can be booked through almost any agent. Many tour companies (see below), provide specialized trips to locations throughout the Dominican Republic, often on air-conditioned buses with meals included. These can be convenient and even pleasant, and the guides will speak your language.

Tour Companies

Prieto Tours (Av. Francia No. 125, with a smaller branch at Arzobispo Merino No. 201) represents El Portillo Beach Resort in Samaná. **Turinter** (Leopoldo Navarro No. 4 in Gazcue, Santo Domingo) is another option. The **Metro Tours Office** (behind Plaza Central at the corner of Winston Churchill and Hatuey; tel. 809/544-4580) represents Metro Hotel at Juan Dolio. Metro Bus will hire out its modern coaches to large groups. **Viajes Barcelo** (Dr. Delgado No. 203; tel. 809/685-8411) represents Bavaro Beach Resort on the east coast. **Omni Tours** (Roberto Pastoriza No. 204; tel. 809/565-6591) represents Club Dominicus Beach Resort at Bayahibe. All the Dominican Tour Agencies have brochures, pamphlets, and English-speaking personnel. Check them out and maybe you'll find a day tour that suits you.

One of the best ways to get to know the whole of the Dominican Republic is though the series of tours offered by the **Museo Nacional de Historia y Geographía,** in Santo Domingo. The director of the museum, Vilma Benzo de Ferrer, created a scheme that started out as a way of raising funds for the maintenance of the museum, but the tours have been a big success. They're usually led by a noted Dominican scientist and highlight geographical and historical re-

RAILWAYS

Railways first came to the Dominican Republic at the end of the 19th century, most of them narrow-gauge plantation trains used for hauling sugarcane.

However, two lines were built to carry cargo and passengers. The English built one in 1886 running from La Vega to Sánchez on the north coast, a 100-km route that cost nearly $2 million. An old station still stands in Sánchez. Built by Germans, another line ran 68km from Santiago to Puerto Plata and passed through a tunnel in the mountains. The train had a saloon car and two cargo cars and took nearly eight hours to make the journey through the mountains. Trujillo admired the train and had it moved, lock, stock, and barrel, to his private sugar plantation in Haina. The United Fruit Company had its own railway network on Sosúa Bay, which it used to transport bananas to the docks. The south coast had several sugar and fruit trains, but none is in use today.

The largest railway in use is operated by Central Romana for hauling cane. Running nearly to El Seibo, it carries some passengers, too.

gions. Typically, several buses ferry about 165 people—all adults—to the sites, where participants can have lunch and listen to talks about historical and scientific subjects. In order to find out more, visit the museum, located at the Plaza de la Cultura, Calle Pedro Henriquez Ureña, or telephone 809/688-6952 or 809/686-6668. It is open from 9 A.M. to 4:30 P.M. When booking the tour, you'll be provided with an information sheet showing the route, a map, the towns you will pass through, and those where you'll stop. The tours are also announced in the large daily newspaper, *Listín Diario,* at least a week in advance.

For specialty tours of national parks and historic centers and specialty diving tours, contact **Ecoturisa,** Calle Santiago No. 203-B Gazcue, Santo Domingo (tel. 809/221-4104, fax 809/685-1544).

INFORMATION AND SERVICES

VISAS AND OFFICIALDOM

Departure Tickets

Every visitor entering the Dominican Republic as a tourist or pleasure traveler is required to have a departure ticket. I've never been asked to show my onward ticket, but it is legally required, so you should always carry one.

Tourist Cards

Travelers to the Dominican Republic are always required to show either a visa or a valid tourist card. Tourist cards are the cheaper, more convenient way to go. They may be purchased for US$10 from most airline ticket agents, or at the international airport of arrival or departure.

It's best to try to purchase the tourist card before arrival in Santo Domingo or Puerto Plata. Lines can be long once you're in the country and, while there might not be that much of a wait, you will likely be more interested in getting a cab to your hotel than waiting in line. When heading to the departure lounge in Miami, New York, or Western Europe, just inquire of the local agents about a tourist card. Somebody will know. Remember also that the tourist card must be paid for in American dollars, so it is always a good idea to carry enough $5 and $10 bills to cover the cost.

Tourist Visas

It's always possible to apply for a tourist visa at one of the Dominican consulates or at the embassy in Washington, D.C., but the time and trouble is generally not worth saving US$10. Go with the tourist card.

Passports

American and Canadian citizens may enter the Dominican Republic with either a passport or proof of citizenship. Although not required for entry, the passport is a respected and recognized form of identification and can prove beneficial in other ways as well, especially for banking, renting a car, replacing traveler's checks, and making reservations. Always travel with a passport if possible. With a passport, citizens of the United States, Germany, Great Britain, Greece, Italy, Spain, Switzerland, Denmark, Finland, Norway, Sweden, Israel, Costa Rica, and many other countries in the Caribbean and South America may stay in the Dominican Republic for 90 days.

Proof of Citizenship

If you don't have a passport, don't worry. Citizens of the United States, Canada, or many other countries may stay for 60 days with nothing more than a proof of citizenship—an official birth certificate, voter-registration card, or photo-ID driver's license. Of course, traveling without a passport has its risks, and you'll still need to buy a tourist card.

Alien Cards

Resident aliens living legally in the United States (including Puerto Rico) or Canada must show their alien cards, along with a valid tourist card. Legal residents of EEU countries must show their valid passports and resident cards. For most people traveling without a passport, entry to the Dominican Republic is good for a stay of 60 days.

Lost Documents and Information

It is a good idea to photocopy your birth certificate and passport, especially the key pages with passport number, photo, and expiration date. Keep the photocopies separate from your passport and money. Having a photocopy will make getting a replacement easier in case you lose your documents. If you should lose any of your documents, contact the consular representative of your country as soon as possible Photocopy your traveler's checks, airline tickets, and any itineraries you may have. Keep these separate from the originals, of course.

Should you need specialized information concerning visas and travel documents, contact the Visa Section-Consular Department of Chancery in Santo Domingo (tel. 809/535-6820, ext. 238). If all you need to do is extend your visa, just go to the Immigration Office in the Huacal Building in Santo Domingo or call the General Director of Immigration (tel. 809/685-2535 or 809/685-2505).

Traveling Minors

A person under 18 years of age traveling alone or accompanied by only one parent or legal guardian should be prepared to present written, notarized consent from the absent parent or guardian. This might sound a little legalistic, but be forewarned.

Departure Tax

A departure "tax" is collected from each person leaving the Dominican Republic, and this, too must be paid in American currency. The payment is made to the ticket agent at the gate of the departing flight, generally about 45 minutes before the flight is scheduled to leave.

Customs Regulations

I don't know of any limit on the number of pieces of luggage Dominican customs officials will allow into the country. Naturally, though, every airline strictly regulates the amount of luggage and carry-ons permitted to each passenger. A good rule of thumb is to travel light. In general, flights originating from tourist locales are given a pretty easy time in customs, and much of the time foreign travelers are waved through with friendly smiles. If for some reason you are asked to open your bags, cooperate and everything will probably run quite smoothly.

Visitors to the Dominican Republic are allowed to bring one liter of alcohol, 200 cigarettes, and gift articles with a value not to exceed US$100.

You should be aware that the Dominican Republic is not tolerant of drugs. It is against Dominican law to possess, consume, or traffic in many kinds of drugs, and the penalties are severe. Remember also that, regardless of your citizenship, when you are on Dominican territory, you are subject to Dominican law. Neither a consular nor an embassy official can help you once you're in jail. Keep in mind that for drug offenses there is generally no bail—and no right to trial by jury.

Embassies and Consulates

These government bureaus can sometimes be vital sources of assistance and advice to persons traveling in foreign countries. In addition, diplomatic and consular officials are intimately involved in visa and immigration matters, business and trade, legal disputes, and

---

EMBASSIES AND CONSULATES

Foreign Embassies and Consulates in the Dominican Republic

U.S. Embassy
1715 22nd St. NW
Washington, D.C. 20008
tel. 202/332-6280

U.S. Consulate
1 Times Square Plaza
11th Floor
New York, NY 10036
tel. 212/768-2480

Canada
2080 rue Crescent
Montreal, Quebec H36 2B8
tel. 514/499-1918

France
2, route Georges Beilles
75016 Paris
tel. 14-69-35-80

Germany
Bergstrasse #87
5300 Bonn, 2nd
tel. 00228-36-4956

Dominican Consulate Phone Numbers in the United States

California: 215/858-7365 or 415/982-5144
Florida: 305/373-4862
Illinois: 312/235-9708
Louisiana: 504/522-1843
Massachusetts: 617/482-8121
New York: 212/768-2480
Pennsylvania: 215/923-3006 or 412/363-2023
Washington, D.C.: 202/332-6280

---

medical and natural emergencies.

If you're an American citizen, the American Service section of any consulate can help you if you become seriously ill or involved in a dispute that can lead to legal action. The **U.S. Department of State** operates a travel advisory hotline (tel. 202/647-5225), or you can reach a duty

ORGANIZATIONS AND COMPANIES FOR SINGLE TRAVELERS

Gallivanting
515 E. 79th St.
Suite 20F
New York, NY 10021
tel. 800/933-9699 or 212/988-0617
fax 212/988-0144

Globus/Cosmos
5301 S. Federal Circle
Littleton, CO 80123
tel. 800/221-0090
fax 303/347-2080

Jane's International and Sophisticated Women Travelers
2603 Bath Ave.
Brooklyn, NY 11214
tel. 718/266-2045
fax 718/266-4062

Marion Smith Singles
611 Prescott Pl.
North Woodmere, NY 11581
tel. 516/791-4852
fax 516/791-4879

Partners-in-Travel
11660 Chenault St.
Suite 119
Los Angeles, CA 90049
tel. 310/476-4869

Singles in Motion
545 W. 236th St.
Riverdale, NY 10463
tel./fax 718/884-4464

officer weekdays from 8:15 A.M. to 10 P.M. EST at 202/647-4000. In Santo Domingo the **U.S. Embassy** is at Calle César Nicolás Pensón, esq. Calle Leopoldo Navarro (tel. 809/541-2171, fax 809/686-7437). The **U.S. Consulate** is at Calle César Nicolás Penson, esq. Máximo Gómez (tel. 809/221-5511, fax 809/686-7437). Most European and South American nations have either diplomatic or consular offices in Santo Domingo (see chart). Once again, these offices are not tourism bureaus but can help with other matters, especially lost passports and legal difficulties, along with registering births, marriages, and deaths, social security matters, passport renewal, and notary powers. But be warned: the embassy can't bail you out of *criminal* scrapes with the law.

Likewise, the Dominican Republic has diplomatic and consular services in most countries as well, which can sometimes be helpful with tourist-connected issues like visas, pets, and phone numbers.

SPECIAL INTERESTS

Single Travelers
For a long time, the travel industry has treated single people rather unfairly—or at least differently from travelers in groups or couples. There is a growing group of organizations and publications that cater to single travelers, some of them offering shared accommodations, some matching travel companions (let the buyer beware) and others providing information and discounts. A couple of publications include ***Traveling on Your Own,*** by Eleanor Berman (Random House, Order Dept., 400 Hahn Rd., Westminster, MD 21157; tel. 800/733-300, fax 800/659-2436), and ***Going Solo*** (Doefer Communications, P.O. Box 123, Apalachicola, Florida, tel./fax 904/653-8848). Organizations that help singles find traveling companions are designed to protect you from what's called the "single's supplement," that extra charge you find yourself paying when traveling alone. Some organizations that sell tours also provide information on prospective matches, including **Saga Holidays,** in Boston and at the 92nd Street Y in New York City. **Golden Companions,** in Pullman, Washington, limits its membership to people 45 years of age and older. The organization has 500 members who pay US$85 annually for a newsletter (six times a year). Members have numbers and communicate with each other about their travel plans. Write P.O. Box 5249, Reno, NV 89513 (tel. 702/324-2227).

Connecting is based in Vancouver, British Columbia, and its network and newsletter have 3,000 subscribers. Membership benefits include a directory of single-friendly accommodations and cross references to other publications, tour operators, and such. The newsletter also has tips about trips, items for those traveling by wheelchair, and a listing of events. Hospitality exchanges are offered to members who may wish to accommodate travelers in their homes. Write to Connecting at P.O. Box 29088, Delamont Postal Outlet, 1966 W. Broadway, Vancouver, British Columbia V6J 5C2, Canada (tel. 604/737-7791). Two other organizations are rather small but try to match traveling companions based upon a questionnaire. These are **Traveling Companions, Ltd.,** 131 Daniel Webster Highway, Apt. 502, Nashua, NH (tel. 603/891-2309), and **Vacation Partners,** 853 Sanders Road, Suite 272, Northbrook, IL 60062 (tel. 708/205-2008). Last, but not least, the oldie-but-goodie in the single-travel game is **Travel Companion Exchange,** for "single, divorced, and widowed travelers." For 13 years (making it ancient), this outfit has published a newsletter which contains tips on travel, articles by subscribers, listings of singles-friendly resorts, and listings of singles wanting partners. Write to Travel Companion Exchange, P.O. Box 833, Amityville, NY 11701 (U.S. tel. 800/392-1256 or U.S. tel. 516/454-0800).

Older Travelers

Older travelers now have a good chance to get special discounts, which allows them to see things and go places at affordable prices. Many tour operators and resorts offer special senior discounts, sometimes available to members of specific organizations. The most prominent seniors organization in the United States is the **American Association of Retired Persons,** 601 E St. NW, Washington, D.C. 20049 (tel. 202/434-2277). You might also contact the following organizations to see what they offer in the way of travel benefits to members: **National Council of Senior Citizens,** 1331 F St. NW, Washington, D.C. 20004 (tel. 202/347-8800, fax 202/624-9595); **Golden Companions,** P.O. Box 754, Pullman, WA 99163 (tel. 208/858-2183); and **Mature Outlook,** Customer Service Center, 6001 N. Clark St., Chicago, IL 60660 (tel. 800/336-6336).

Travel with Children

Since most intercity travel involves long, rough bus or car rides, it isn't all that easy for children to travel to various destinations in the country. However, while children may not enjoy those long, hot bus rides, I suppose seasoned adults don't enjoy them much, either. Bring the crayons and coloring books.

Once you get to your destination, however, your parental worries are over. After all, Dominicans absolutely dote on their own children. For the first 11 or 12 years of their lives, Dominican children are some of the most pampered and precious creatures on the face of the earth. Consequently, it's no surprise that most of the major resorts like Playa Dorada, Casa de Campo, and the resorts of the Eastern Point or Coconut Coast have complete plans for hosting children. Most feature children's programs, day care centers, and nurseries. Some resorts even offer specialized nurses, and a few have nanny service for very young children.

Keep in mind that in remote areas, food and water can be a problem. Moreover, stomach ailments and fevers can affect children more seriously than adults, and sometimes health care is hard to find. With that said, most children above age 10 or so will find adventuring in the Dominican Republic just as satisfying as any adult.

Travelers with Disabilities

There is no reason why travelers with disabilities should not go to the Dominican Republic. There are no special wheelchair ramps in the streets, but most avenues are open and people are helpful. Though many museums, forts, churches, and hotels are not yet fully accessible, most buildings are single story. By making arrangements well in advance, most disabled travelers will have a good time in the Dominican Republic. The first thing to do is contact a competent travel agent and explain your needs. Numerous organizations and publications also exist to serve the specially challenged traveler (see chart).

Gays and Lesbians

Dominican society is very traditional. Though the larger cities and tourist areas allow for slightly more relaxed cultural rules, most Dominicans view male-female roles in a rigid fashion. Certainly, gays and lesbians can travel freely and safely in the Dominican Republic, but public ex-

PACKAGE OPERATORS AND TIPS FOR OLDER TRAVELERS

PACKAGE TOUR OPERATORS

Elderhostel
75 Federal St.
Boston, MA 02110-1941
tel. 617/426-7788
fax 617/426-8351

Evergreen Travel Service
4114 198th St. SW
Suite 13
Lynnwood, WA 98036-6742
tel. 800/435-2288 or 206/776-1184
fax 206/775-0728

Gadabout Tours
700 E. Tahquitz Canyon Way
Palm Springs, CA 92262
tel. 800/952-5068 or 619/325-5556
fax 617/325-5127

Grand Circle Travel
347 Congress St.
Boston, MA 02210
tel. 800/221-2610 or 617/350-7500
fax 617/423-0445

Grandtravel
6900 Wisconsin Ave.
Suite 706
Chevy Chase, MD 20815
tel. 800/246-7651 or 301/986-0790
fax 301/913-0166

Interhostel
University of New Hampshire
Division of Continuing Education
6 Garrison Ave.
Durham, NH 03824
tel. 800/733-9753 or 603/862-1147
fax 603/862-1113

Mature Tours
c/o Solo Flights
63 High Noon Rd.
Weston, CT 06883
tel. 800/266-1566 or 203/226-9993

OmniTours
104 Wilmot Rd.
Deerfield, IL 60015
tel. 800/962-0060 or 708/374-0088
fax 708/374-9515

Saga International Holidays
222 Berkeley St.
Boston, MA 02116
tel. 800/343-0273 or 617/262-2262
fax 617/375-5950

PUBLICATIONS

Going Abroad: 101 Tips for Mature Travelers
Grand Circle Travel
347 Congress St.
Boston, MA 02210
tel. 800/221-2610 or 617/350-7500
fax 617/423-0445

The Mature Traveler
P.O. Box 50820
Reno, NV 89513-0820
tel. 702/786-7419

Take a Camel to Lunch and Other Adventures for Mature Travelers
Bristol Publishing Enterprises
P.O. Box 1737
San Leandro, CA 94577
tel. 510/895-4461 in California; 800/346-4889 elsewhere in the United States
fax 510/895-4459

Unbelievably Good Deals and Great Adventures That You Absolutely Can't Get Unless You're Over 50
Contemporary Books
1200 Stetson Ave.
Chicago, IL 60601
tel. 312/782-9181
fax 312/540-4687

pressions of affection will probably be viewed as inappropriate. No special resorts yet cater to gays and lesbians and, unless things change considerably, none probably will for years to come. Still, the country is hardly dangerous as long as a certain decorum is maintained.

Traveling with Pets

If you have to travel with a pet, you'll need to make special arrangements in advance. The Office of Animal Health in Santo Domingo requires that for cats you present a rabies vaccination certificate—indicating that an inoculation

ORGANIZATIONS FOR TRAVELERS WITH DISABILITIES

ACCENT on Living
P.O. Box 700
Bloomington, IL 61702
tel. 800/787-8444 or 309/378-2961
fax 309/378-4420

**Access: The Foundation for Accessibility
for the Disabled**
P.O. Box 356
Malverne, NY 11565
tel./fax 516/887-5798

American Foundation for the Blind
15 W. 16th St.
New York, NY 10011
tel. 800/232-5463 or 212/620-2147
fax 212/727-7418

Information Center for Individuals with Disabilities
Ft. Point Pl.
27-43 Wormwood St.,
Boston, MA 02210
tel. 800/462-5015 in Massachusetts; 617/727-5540
elsewhere in the United States; TDD 617/345-9743
fax 617/345-5318

Mobility International
228 Borough High St.
London SE1 IJX, England
tel. 71/378-1292.
U.S. office: MIUSA
P.O. Box 10767
Eugene, OR 97440
tel./TDD 503/343-1284
fax 503/343-6812

**Moss Rehabilitation Hospital
Travel Information Service**
telephone referrals only
tel. 215/456-9600
TDD 215/456-9602

National Rehabilitation Information Center
8455 Colesville Rd.
Suite 935
Silver Spring, MD 20910
tel. 301/588-9284
fax 301/587-1967

Paralyzed Veterans of America
PVA, PVA/ATTS Program
801 18th St. NW
Washington, D.C. 20006
tel. 202/872-1300 in Washington, D.C.; 800/424-
8200 elsewhere in the United States
fax 202/628-3306

Partners of the Americas
1424 K St. NW
Suite 700
Washington, D.C. 20005
tel. 800/322-7844 or 202/628-3300
fax 202/628-3306

Royal Association for Disability and Rehabilitation
12 City Forum
250 City Rd.
London EC1V 8AF, England
tel. 71/250-3222
fax 71/250-0212

**Society for the Advancement of Travel
for the Handicapped**
347 5th Ave.
Suite 610
New York, NY 10016
tel. 212/447-7284
fax 212/725-8253

Travel Industry and Disabled Exchange
5435 Donna Ave.
Tarzana, CA 91356
tel. 818/368-5648

has been given 30 days prior to the animal's arrival in the country—and a current certificate of health issued 15 days prior to arrival. For dogs, you must be prepared to submit a certificate of inoculation against rabies, distemper, lectropirosis, hepatitis, and parvovirus—all administered at least 30 days prior to arrival in the country, as well as a health certificate issued within 15 days prior to arrival. If these requirements are not met, the animal will be quarantined for 8–30 days, depending upon the country of origin. The National Cattle Office is in charge of arrangements for the admittance of other species.

You'll have to request the same health certificate upon departure also. The departure certificate is available from the Office of Animal Health (tel. 809/542-0132).

Public Worship

The Dominican Republic is an overwhelmingly Catholic country. Many of its churches are very beautiful indeed, especially the main cathedrals of Santo Domingo and Higüey. Protestant churches tend to be smaller and represented mainly by evangelical sects. Protestant worship predominates in Samaná town; church worship there is quite colorful.

Services in the Dominican Republic are almost always conducted in Spanish. There is simply not a large enough foreign contingent anywhere on the island to support a permanent assembly of speakers of English (or another language), except for the Haitian presence in the western hills and mountains and those in isolated *bateyes* or sugarcane settlements. For in-English worship in Santo Domingo, there is a Roman Catholic mass weekly at 10 A.M. Sunday at the Parroquia Santísima, 27 Febrero at Av. Abraham Lincoln (tel. 891/565-3476), as well as a nondenominational Protestant/Anglican service each Sunday at Epiphany Union church on Av. Independencia. Probably at 8:30 A.M., but please check.

If you desire to join or witness a worship service in the Dominican Republic, you can always sit quietly in a Catholic mass, especially in the Catedral de Primera in Santa Domingo, or in the cathedral in Higüey, and become a part of a serene spectacle that transcends particular beliefs.

There is no such thing as an inhospitable church in the Dominican Republic. Just remember that you should always abide by sumptuary observances. To be safe, women should cover their heads and wear conservative outfits to Mass. Men should wear black.

MAPS AND TOURIST INFORMATION

The best way to enjoy foreign travel is to be open to new experiences. Perhaps the second best way is to travel armed with information. Before you head off to the Dominican Republic, conduct a little private research. It will pay dividends in increased pleasure and added insight. Besides, the Dominican Republic is well supplied with information sources. These days it isn't difficult to put together a portfolio of maps, brochures, pamphlets, and guides from the comfort of your easy chair.

Maps

For anyone but the package tourist, a good map or set of maps is invaluable. The best overall is *Hildebrand's Travel Map to Hispaniola,* which provides a detailed guide to major roads and thoroughfares, a decent city map of Santo Domingo, and mileage charts and sites of historic and cultural interest. *Hildebrand's* is available in most good bookstores in the United States but especially in specialty travel shops such as **Map Link** (30 S. La Petra Lane, Unit 5, Santa Barbara, CA 93117; tel. 805/692-6777), **The Map Store** (1636 I St. Washington, D.C. 20006; tel. 202/628-2608), **Phileas Fogg's Books and Maps** (#87 Stanford Shopping Center, Palo Alto, CA 93404; tel. 800/533-FOGG), **The Complete Traveler Bookstore** (199 Madison Ave., New York, NY 100167; tel. 212/685-9007), and **Adventurous Traveler Bookstore** (245 S. Champlain St., Burlington, VT 05406; tel. 800/282-3963).

It's probably best not to wait until you arrive in the Dominican Republic to get a good map. Although there are many bookstores and tourist information offices in Santo Domingo and other major tourist areas, some of them offer only unhelpful, touristy brochure maps. A complicated but very complete topographic map is available from the Defense Mapping Agency; it's sold through many travel bookstores and can be ordered from Map Link as well. Ask for map TPC J-27D, Dominican Republic, Haiti, Puerto Rico. Topographic and other historical and local maps are available in Santo Domingo from the **Instituto Geográfico Universitario,** Calle de Las Damas, Colonial District (tel. 809/682-2680). Stop by the institute and see what they've got. Sometimes the Office of National Parks in Santo Domingo has maps of trails in the national parks,

but this is a hit-or-miss proposition. If you speak Spanish, call them and see what they've got on their shelves.

For those well versed in Spanish, the most fantastic and detailed maps can be found at the **Cartográfico Militar** located in Santo Domningo on the Malecón at Ave. Winston Churchill. Sales are made during the day, but no English is spoken. The scale is 1:50,000, many times more detailed

INFORMATION ABOUT THE DOMINICAN REPUBLIC

USA
Dominican Tourism Board
561 West Diversey Building
Suite 214
Chicago, IL 60614-1643
tel. 888/303-1336
fax 773/529-1338
email: domreptourism@msn.com

Dominican Tourism Board
136 E. 57th St.
Suite 803
New York, NY 10022 USA
tel. 212/588-1012 or 888/374-6361
fax 212/588-1015
email: dr.info@ix.netcom.com

Occidental Hoteles
2450 S.W. 137th Ave.
Suite 203
Miami, FL 33175
tel. 305/551-6010
fax 305/551-7667

Premier World Marketing, Inc.
2600 S.W. Third Ave.
Third Floor
Miami, FL 33129
tel. 800/877-3643
fax 305/858-4677
email: res@pwmonline.com

Dominican Tourism Board
2355 Salzedo Street
Suite 307
Coral Gables, FL 33134
tel. 305/444-4592 or 888/358-9594
fax 305/444-4845
email: domrep@herald.infi.net

CANADA
Dominican Tourism Board
2080 Rue Crescent
Montreal PQ, Quebec H3G 288
tel. 800/563-1611
fax 514/499-1393
email: republiquedominicaine@op.plus.net

Dominican Tourism Board
35 Church Street
Unit 53
Toronto, Ontario MSE-IT3
tel. 888/494-5050
fax 416/361-2130
email: dominicantourism@globalserve.net

SOUTH AMERICA
Dominican Tourist Board
Marcelo T. de Alvear 722(1058)
Buenos Aires, Argentina
tel. 114/315-3384
fax 114/302-2203
email: turismo.r.d.@cpsarg.com

Dominican Tourist Board
Trásversal 29 No. 120-59 (Santa Bárbara)
Santa Fé de Bogotá, Columbia
tel. 629-1459
fax. 520-7061
email: domreptu@multiphone.net.co
email: domreptu@columsat.net.co

EUROPE
Dominican Tourism Board
Hochstrase 17
D-60313 Frankfurt, Germany
tel. 69/9139-7878
fax 69/283-430
email: domtur@aol.com

than any of the best commercially available maps. But it is a challenge dealing with the "scene".

Tourist Offices

The official voice of the Dominican Republic in tourism matters is the Secretary of State for Tourism. The main government office in Santo Domingo is supplemented by tourist information bureaus located in the United States and Western Europe, though most European duties are handled by tour operators or consular officials operating as agents of the current Minister of Tourism. In the United States, the **Dominican Republic Tourist Information Center** is located at 1 Times Square Plaza, 11th Floor, New York, NY 10036 (tel. 212/768-2482, fax 212/768-2677). The ministry maintains offices or agents in Spain, Germany, and Italy, as well as a network of agents in

Dominican Tourism Board
Louise 271, 8ème étage
1050 Bruxelles, Belgium
tel. 322/646-1300
fax 322/649-3692
email: repdom.benelux.info@skynet.be

Dominican Tourism Board
Juan Hurtado de Mendoza 13
Apto. 305
28036 Madrid, Spain
tel. 91/350-9483 or 01/359-3923
fax: 91/350-6579
email: rep.dom@nauta.es

Occidental Hoteles
Jose Abascal 58
6to Piso
28003 Madrid, Spain
tel. 900/100-149 (toll free)
fax 91/399-0667

Grupo Piñero Cribe
Plaza Mediterráneo 5
07014 Paima de Mallorca, Spain
tel. 71/78-7000
fax. 71/73-1694

Dominican Tourism Board
11 Rue Boudreau
75009 Paris, France
tel. 1-43-12-9191
fax 1-44-94-0880
email: otrepdom@aol.com

Dominican Tourism Board
20 Hand Court
Hight Holborn WCI, England
tel. 171/242-7778

fax 171/405-4202
email: domrep.tourismboard@virgin.net

Dominican Tourism Board
25 Piazza Castello
20121 Milan, Italy
tel. 02/805-7781
fax 02/865-861
email: repdom@opimaint.it

CODETEL
Centro de Información Turistica
USA: 800/752-1151
England: 0-800-899805
Germany: 01/30-815561
Holland: 06/022-3107
Spain: 900-995087

TOURISM PROMOTION COUNCIL
Evelyn Paiewonsky
Av. Mexico 66
Santo Domingo, Dominican Republic
tel. 809/685-9054 or 809/685-5254
fax 809/685-6752
website: www.domrep.hotels.com.do

QUICK PHONE NUMBERS
USA: 888/358-9594 or 800/752-1151
Canada: 800/563-1611
England: 0-800/899-805
Germany: 0130-815561
Holland: 06-022-3107
Spain: 900-995087

New York and Miami authorized to provide official tourist information. In Canada, the Dominican Republic Tourist Office is at 29 Billair Street, Toronto, MFR 268, Canada (tel. 416/928-9188). There is no tourist office in the United Kingdom. The **Caribbean Tourism Organization** serves as a central clearinghouse for information about all of the islands, including Hispaniola. The CTO is located at 20 E. 46th Street, New York, NY 10017 (tel. 212/682-0435, fax 212/697-4258). Also in the United States, information about the Dominican Republic is available from **Kahn Travel Communications,** 4 Park Avenue, New York, NY 10016 (tel. 212/679-5055).

One important source of up-to-date information is a little booklet published by the Ministry of Tourism called *La Cotica,* readily available in Santo Domingo at the tourist information centers and at most bookstores. It is free, though you'll find some bookstores and vendors charging as much as US$3 for a copy. Your best bet, however, is to try to obtain a copy from the Dominican tourist information people before you go.

Besides the official government tourist bureaus managed by the Ministry of Tourism and its agents, there is a private group called the **Council for the Promotion of Tourism** (Consejo de Promoción Turística). In addition to its office in Santo Domingo, the council maintains a mailing address in the United States. Write to either Evelyn Paiewonsky or Marisol Ortiz at EPS # A-355, P.O. Box 02-5256, Miami, FL 33102. The council has a stock of pamphlets, maps, and brochures, as well as the latest issue of *La Cotica.* Write and ask nicely for what you want. Then, when you get to Santo Domingo, visit the council at Avenida Mexico 66, Santo Domingo (it's easy to find), or call them (tel. 809/685-9054, fax 809/685-6752). If you actually visit, you might stop by the office of the **National Association of Hotels and Restaurants** (Asonahores), located on the ground floor of the same building (tel. 809/687-4676, fax 809/687-4727). Although Asonahores is primarily a trade organization, it does have some promotional material, as well as a list of its members and telephone numbers. If you're just planning to wander from place to place, a list like that could come in handy.

Another way to gather information while still in your home country is to use the foreign services of the Dominican telephone company, commonly called **Codetel,** which maintains a kind of tourist hotline. The hotline number in the United States is 800/752-1151. Manned currently by Anna Bemendez, who is very helpful, Codetel offers answers to pressing questions, and you might be able to locate a copy of *La Cotica* by calling. Codetel maintains hotline information numbers for several European countries as well. The hotline phone of the **Ministry of Tourism** is 800/358-9594. With these hotlines, don't expect much more than quickie answers to basic questions.

In the Dominican Republic

In Santo Domingo, **The Dominican Tourist Information Center** is located at the corner of Avenidas Mexico and 30 de Marzo, Apartment 497 (tel. 809/221-4660, fax 809/682-3806). If you are absolutely bewildered, there are tourist information booths at Los Américas International Airport (tel. 809/542-0120) and La Unión Airport (tel. 809/586-0219) in Puerto Plata. These booths are operated by multilingual personnel who can help in a pinch, especially with airplane and taxi problems, though they're not really intended as full-service operations. Other government information centers are located in Puerto Plata on Avenida Hermanas Mirabal (tel. 809/586-3676) and in Santiago's city hall on Avenida Duarte (tel. 809/582-5885). All of these centers are closed on weekends and holidays. While in Puerto Rico, you can get tourist information from **Metro Tours,** Ortegón at the corner of Tabonuco, Caparra Hills, Guaynabo 00657 (tel. 809/781-8665, fax 809/793-7935). Should you be having such a good time in the Dominican Republic that you want to go to Haiti, you can generally do so on the road through the town of Jimaní, but you must have a passport. Citizens of the United States and Canada do not need a visa. Check with the Haitian consulate at 33 Avenida Juan Sánchez Ramires in Santo Domingo (tel. 809/686-6094).

For those desiring to dig a little deeper (sometimes literally) into local culture or to do certain volunteer work, several organizations devote themselves to various good works projects. **Oxfam International** has a Caribbean branch in Santo Domingo (Apdo. 20071, tel. 809/682-

7585, fax 809/689-1001). **Earthwatch** can be contacted at 800/776-0188. There is an American **Ecotourism Society,** which publishes a newsletter and other documents. For information, write P.O. Box 755, North Bennington, VT 05257. One British organization, **Tourism Concern,** promotes long-term social benefits in tourism. Write them at Froehel College, Roehampton Lane, London SW15, 5 PM, UK (tel. 081/878-9053).

Getting By on the Street

When you're beyond advice from books (or when you've ignored all the advice in books and are really hanging out there and you need to know something), go to the nearest local *colmado* and ask the clerk. If it's in the neighborhood, he'll know. If you're asking directions in the countryside and are told something is *allí mismo* (right over there), rest assured that it's probably quite a ways off.

Almost as good as store clerks are the Yellow Pages of the Codetel phone directory. The phone company takes great pride in its directories, which are always up-to-date and complete.

Don't rely on quickie tourist maps, which often leave out important streets. Many gas stations (like Texaco) have good maps, as does the **Cuesta** bookstore, located at the National shopping center in Santo Domingo, at the corner of 27 de Febrero and Ave. Abraham Lincoln. The shop **GAAR** (El Conde 502 and Arz. Nouel 355) specializes in maps of all sorts, especially technical nautical charts. If you must go to the American Embassy, try the Commercial Section and the American Chamber of Commerce.

One beautiful resource in Santo Domingo is the **Helen Kellogg Library,** at the Episcopal Union Church on Ave. Independencia (tel. 809/689-8949), which has a large selection of English-language books about the Dominican Republic. You can even become a member with check-out privileges if you plan a long stay.

For more technical matters, the **Dominican Central Bank,** on Pedro Henríquez Ureña, has

DOMINICAN REPUBLIC INFORMATION ON THE WEB

Here are a few websites that provide information and updates for tourism and travel to the Dominican Republic. Other sites involving airfare and accommodations are included elsewhere. You should be aware that some of these sites operate in Spanish only, while others are creaky at best. However, Dominican tourism officials are improving their services day by day.

General Dominican tourist information
www.dominican.com

All-inclusive resorts
dominicanresorts.com

Useful tourist information
www.hispaniola.com/DR

Current news and events
www.dominicanrepublicpage.com

adventure travel guides
www.iguana-mama.com

Cabarete
www.cabarete.com

North Coast information
medianet.nbnet.ca/index.html

New York consulate
www.consudom-ny.do/tourism.htm

Secretary of Tourism
www.dominicana.do

Dominican concerts, theater, exhibitions, and art
www.arte-latino.com/casadeteatro

Caribbean hotel information
www.nando.net/prof/caribe/caribe.com.html

Marine Mammal Sanctuary
www.business1.com/pcoptima/jorobada

Domnican Republic arts
www.aaart.com/domrep

a large library devoted to economics, but you'll need Spanish to take advantage of it. Other important book collections are at **The National Library,** at the Plaza de la Cultura in Santo Domingo (on César Nicolás Penson), and the **República Dominicana Library,** on Calle Dr. Delgado near the Palacio Nacional (National Palace).

CONDUCT AND COURTESY

Being aware of a few social customs and established practices makes a visit to any foreign country more pleasant. Here are a few tips on Dominican behavior.

Proper Dress

Unlike some other islands in the Caribbean, the entire island of Hispaniola is not geared to tourism—especially the rural parts of the Dominican Republic. In some places, locals frown on beachwear, so bare midriffs, bathing suits, short shorts, and other revealing fashions are best left at the hotel. Don't wear shorts when visiting churches and museums, government offices, or when going out to dinner in better restaurants. Some people also think a good way to prevent crimes of opportunity is to avoid looking too prosperous, so you might leave the Rolex and the gold chains at home.

Dealing with Street Vendors

The Dominican Republic, like any other poor country, has a lot of street vendors and hustlers, most of whom are simply trying to earn a living in a tough situation. Given a simple *"No, gracias,"* most vendors will take you at your word and move on. Sometimes beach hustlers offering guide services can be more insistent. In this case, keep moving and be firm. The hustler will likely lose interest in a short time. On the other hand, you might actually want a shoeshine or piece of gum from someone on the street, so be polite, ask the price, and accept the service.

Being firm and respectful is always a good way to deal with the people you meet in the Dominican Republic. Sometimes you'll find yourself face to face with an urban Dominican who is likely to make hand gestures and talk in a loud voice. Don't worry; it's a simple custom of the country, inherited from *el campo* tradition.

If you need to exercise your anger, that's acceptable also, but always be ready with a sense of humor and a smile at the end of the dispute. It should help smooth things over. Overall, I've found the Dominican Republic a safe place full of people with integrity and humor. Go with that attitude and be yourself.

WHAT TO TAKE

Clothes to Bring

First of all, travel with as little as possible. Breezing around the Dominican Republic is easy with a carry-on bag or two and, unless you plan to attend formal gatherings or conduct business, or unless you're aiming to stay a while in some of the wilder or more inaccessible areas (like national parks and mountains), washing clothes in a sink and traveling light is preferable to hauling around heavy luggage. In addition, traveling light saves time in airports and avoids some of the disappointment of lost or stolen luggage. Besides, the Dominican Republic is a modern country in every way, and whatever you might really need and don't have, you can purchase on the spot.

Perhaps the first thing to do is to choose your identity as a tourist, traveler, or adventurer. If you've decided to travel with a packaged tour and stay in a designated resort, then you should plan to travel light and dress casually by all means. One carry-on bag should be enough to take a couple of pairs of cotton pants or print dresses, underwear, socks, T-shirts, a sweater, two swimsuits, a robe, a beach towel, tennis shoes, hiking boots, flip-flops, and toiletries. Pack something long-sleeved for evening. Even if you plan to see the countryside and mountains, adding some simple raingear and a windbreaker will allow you to still travel with one or two carry-ons. Only if you're making plans for specialty adventuring—camping, mountain climbing, diving, or fishing—should you take extra clothing, equipment, and gear. If your plans call for you to be outside for long periods of time, include a crushable brimmed hat to keep off the sun.

Because temperatures vary only a few degrees between winter and summer, opt for lightweight cotton. Nylon and polyester are sticky and uncomfortable. If you know you're traveling to the Dominican Republic during the general rainy season (May–June and October–November), a light rain hat and a rain-resistant windbreaker are advisable, though showers tend to be brief and followed by clear skies and fresh air. It can rain steadily in the mountains and on windward slopes during summer or along the north coast, so you might want to pack a pair of rain pants, which are generally very lightweight and easy to pack. Shorts, tennis shoes, walking or hiking boots, khaki pants, skirts, dresses in natural fabrics, and maybe a light sweater round out the list of clothes to take. Even around the fanciest resorts, dress tends to be casual—at most a linen sports jacket and cotton trousers or a low-neck print dress and shawl.

In churches, men are expected to uncover their heads. Although women may wish to cover their heads as a sign of respect, it is no longer thought necessary to do so on every occasion. It is, however, possible to be very formal in the Dominican Republic, especially in connection with business or cultural events, in which case men should consider wearing a white suit (very chic). Women very rarely don formal evening wear. At really expensive restaurants in Santo Domingo (and nowhere else), men are expected to wear a tie.

A good idea when packing for the tropics is to lay out on a bed all the clothes you think you need. Then put half of them back in a drawer and pack what's left. Most airlines typically allow two or three checked pieces of luggage not exceeding 70 pounds each, and one or two carry-ons. Although carry-ons are usually defined as being less than 45 linear inches (height plus width plus length), and checked luggage as 62 linear inches, in practice a carry-on is whatever you can carry on and get to fit under a seat or in an overhead bin, while checked luggage is whatever you check.

We've all had the experience of sitting next to the person who's trying to carry on a steamer trunk filled with clothes and appliances. Find a modern, lightweight carry-on bag. Keep your money, passport, driver's license, airline tickets, and itineraries in a separate money belt, and carry it with you at all times—unless you can lock it safely in a hotel vault. Label all of your baggage, inside and out. Give somebody at home an idea of where you'll be at all times and when you're expected to return.

Toiletries

With a few exceptions, everything in the way of toiletries is available in the Dominican Republic. Certainly, you should begin your trip with

---

CODE OF ETHICS FOR TOURISTS

The **North American Center for Responsible Tourism** (P.O. Box 827, San Anselmo, CA 94979; tel. 415/258-6594 or 800/654-7975, fax 415/454-2493) suggests that travelers abide by the following Code of Ethics for Tourists.

• Travel with a spirit of humility and a genuine desire to meet and talk with local people.
• Be aware of the feelings of others. Act respectfully and avoid offensive behavior, particularly when taking photographs.
• Cultivate the habit of actively listening and observing rather than merely hearing and seeing. Avoid the temptation to "know all the answers."
• Realize that others may have concepts of time and attitudes which are different—not inferior—to those you inherited from your own culture.

• Instead of looking only for the exotic, discover the richness of another culture and way of life.
• Learn local customs and respect them.
• Remember that you are only one of many visitors. Do not expect special privileges.
• When bargaining with merchants, remember that the poorest one may give up a profit rather than his or her personal dignity. Don't take advantage of the desperately poor. Pay a fair price.
• Keep your promises to people you meet; if you can't, don't make them.
• Spend time each day reflecting on your experiences in order to deepen your understanding. Is your enrichment beneficial for all involved?
• Be aware of why you are traveling in the first place. If you truly want a "home away from home," why travel?

a small (emphasis on *small*) stock of anything you'll need to be comfortable as you travel, which might include a favorite deodorant, shampoo, toothpaste, floss, makeup, moisturizing cream, talcum, contraceptives, and a good supply of sunscreen (preferably with an SPF of about 8–15). Anyone who uses prescription medicines or ointments should bring them along—with a photocopy of the doctor-ordered prescription just in case. In all of the major towns and cities of the Dominican Republic, basic medicines, aspirin, talcum, and sunscreen are readily available, though somewhat expensive. Feminine hygiene supplies aren't commonly found outside major population centers, so bring a good supply. And regardless of your travel plans, bring a small bottle of something to ward off diarrhea. I've never had much trouble with insects in the Dominican Republic, but you might wish to bring a supply of mosquito repellent. Some say that Avon's Skin-So-Soft bath oil diluted with equal parts water serves as a good sand-flea repellent.

Special Equipment

Because power outages are common all over the Dominican Republic, pack a large flashlight and a small, spare penlight, along with extra batteries for those odd moments of darkness. If you plan to visit the Dominican Republic on a limited budget, taking buses and staying in the cheaper and harder-to-find hotels and pensions, then it might be wise to bring along a few extra items—rope for an improvised clothesline, toilet paper, a plastic cup, and a universal plug for the sink. Likewise, be sure to include a cotton sheet you can wash out, a towel, and washcloth.

Keep in mind that local buses, *guaguas,* and minivans are usually overcrowded, so traveling light assumes even more importance. When traveling on Dominican buses or *guaguas,* take some fruit and a candy bar, and perhaps a plastic canteen of water for those long, bumpy rides, unforeseen delays, and breakdowns. They happen, and there's nothing you can do about it.

I'd like to report that camping is all the rage in the Dominican Republic, but it isn't. Most ecotours and nature walks need to be planned well in advance, and most require the help of talented locals experienced in the kind of adventuring you plan to do. If your plan is to hike wild areas or climb one of the peaks in the Cordillera Central, then hiking boots, raingear, a day pack, a canteen, a broad-brimmed hat, long-sleeve shirts, khaki pants, wool socks, and mosquito repellent are musts. Jeans are worse than useless for either heat or rain, so leave them out. For lowland walking, khaki shorts and effective sun protection are key. Deep-sea fishermen will need to be especially mindful of sun protection—pack long-sleeve shirts, billed fishing hats, sunscreen, and special polarized glasses. Many catalogue outfitters and most fishing and camping retailers offer high-quality khaki and cotton shirts, pants, and shorts, as well as hats and rain gear.

Books

Although there are plenty of bookstores in Santo Domingo, I know from personal experience that books in languages other than Spanish are not only hard to find, but also tremendously expensive. If you think you'll want to read around the pool or on the beach, or that you might need something to tide you over between flights or on the bus, bring a stock of paperbacks with you.

FILM AND PHOTOGRAPHY

Film isn't prohibitively expensive in the Dominican Republic, but it's expensive enough that if you've got room in your carry-on for some spare rolls, by all means take them. Otherwise, film is readily available throughout the country. For slides, Kodachrome 64 is best; for prints, ASA 100 or 200 is best. Try ASA 1000 for underwater photography (use a polarizing filter to cut glare). Most people who take underwater photos prefer to avoid the harsh glare of mid-afternoon shoots. Taking shots on beaches can also produce glare, so keep the sun down with a shade. Make certain to keep your camera and film out of heat and sunshine, and pack some silica gel to prevent moisture and mildew from gumming up the works. Spare batteries can save you lost photos as well.

Since processing is also expensive in the Dominican Republic, wait until you get home to develop your pictures. If you carry exposed film of ASA 400 or greater, don't subject it to airport x-ray inspection; *hand-carry* it through.

One word of warning. In the Dominican countryside, you'll come across numerous army bases (you can't miss them—watch for green speed bumps and soldiers with automatic weapons everywhere); don't photograph these institutions. Also, try to avoid taking photographs across the Haitian border in the west. For some reason, the government is still sensitive to such intrusions.

WEIGHTS AND MEASURES

The official, legally sanctioned method of measurement is the metric system. However, there are some areas of commerce in which the imperial system still holds sway. For example, ounces and pounds are used instead of grams and kilograms in weighing some solids. Distances are always expressed metrically. Gasoline and motor oil are measured in American gallons, while cooking oil is retailed by the pound. Fabrics are measured by the yard. Rum, beer, and drinking water are sold in bottles of 0.756 liters.

In some small way, parts of an old Spanish system still have influence as well. While land surfaces in urban areas are measured by square meters, rural areas are measured by the "taven," which is equal to 624 square meters. There are other unconventional measurements as well. If you ask someone on a country road the distance to a certain place, he might say *allí mismo* (right over there)—which may mean just about anything but is usually at least eight kilometers. *Un chin* means "a little bit," *un chin-chin* an even littler bit, and *una numba* a whole lot!

The electric current is in American style 110–120 volts in 60 cycles with standard plugs with flat pins. The Dominican Electrical Corporation burns oil to produce their electricity, but because of mechanical and maintenance problems, there are failures. Clinics, hospitals, and many hotels have generators.

MONEY

The Dominican peso is the legal unit of tender in the Dominican Republic. In print, it is denominated RD$. Each peso is further divided into 100 centavos. Coins in circulation are the 1, 5, 10, 25, and 50 centavo pieces, as well as 1 peso, while in bills you'll find notes at 5, 10, 20, 50, 100, 1,000, and 5,000. I'm told there's a one-peso note, but I've never seen it. The bills vary in color, but most are thin and wrinkle easily, so you'd best keep careful track of each flavor; after a while, it isn't hard. The coins, on the other hand, can be somewhat bewildering. However, the smaller coins have such small value that all shops and retail stores, including most bars and food kiosks, round up or down to the nearest 10 centavos, so don't sweat the small stuff. Whenever I accumulate a bulging pocketful of small coins, I'd get my shoes shined or buy a pack of gum from one of the many vendors—who really appreciate the business. When traveling in rural areas, take plenty of small bills, as change for a bill larger than 100 pesos can be difficult to get.

Exchanging Money

The benchmark exchange rate between U.S. dollars and Dominican pesos is US$1=RD$13. Exchange rates fluctuate slightly up or down over time by about 5% here and there, but overall there have been no great rate crises to trouble travelers. Hence, only if you are dealing in relatively large sums of money should you trouble yourself about falling rates. I suppose it's always worthwhile to check the rate and, if it goes up, cash in a few extra dollars, francs, or marks.

Here are a few do's and don'ts about exchanging money. According to a 1991 Dominican banking law, only the major commercial banks and their branches are entitled to exchange foreign currency for Dominican pesos. The law also provides that all commercial transactions must be collected in or paid for with pesos. Under the law, many tourist hotels are authorized to change money and cash traveler's checks as well. But **black market** transactions—changing money in the street—are illegal. Under the same law, leaving the Dominican Republic with more than US$10,000 in cash or traveler's checks is not allowed. If you break these laws, you can be fined or imprisoned or both. In Santo Domingo and tourist areas you will be approached in the street to change money. Don't do it. Go to a commercial bank. They're all very pleasant and well run, and gaining a dozen pesos isn't worth the risk of a confrontation with police. Besides,

I've heard that some street traders work in conjunction with people who claim to be cops. You can be set up, big time.

Because of the problem of counterfeit money, most commercial banks are very wary and will examine your bills. Take newly made bills in moderate denominations if you're coming from the United States. Old American "hundreds" were the counterfeiters' choice, so take new "big twenties." When signing travelers checks, take care to duplicate your signature carefully. I've had Dominican bankers hesitate when looking at my hastily scrawled signature which doesn't quite match the one on the check. The **Scotia Bank** on Isabel La Católica just north of Calle Conde is often quick, with no hassles.

Commercial banks are open Monday–Friday 8:30 A.M.–3:30 P.M. Airport branches often are open later to accommodate incoming flights. When traveling to the Dominican Republic, you should absolutely avoid carrying the American $100 bill. Rightly, everyone in the Caribbean is suspicious of the bill because there has been a worldwide flood of counterfeits lately. Even if the new US$100 bill becomes common, carry only US$10s and $20s and lots of traveler's checks. And, when traveling to smaller towns and provincial areas, be sure to have a good supply of RD$50 and RD$100 notes.

You can get cash on major credit cards through commercial banks, but you will be charged a 5% commission. Avoid this method of getting cash unless you're really stuck. In a pinch you can get away with paying U.S. dollars to cabbies for longer rides, and some commercial establishments also accept dollars (despite the law)—but usually not Canadian or European notes. For example, if you get to Santo Domingo's airport late at night, an American $20 bill will get you a cab ride downtown, and the porters will gladly take US$1 bills as tips. In any foreign-exchange transaction, examine the rate and commission charge carefully. The *International Herald Tribune,* available at hotels and bookstores, carries the latest commercial rates. There are some ATMs at major downtown banks in Santo Domingo, but try not to need one. Change only the money you need when you need it, as most banks can't change pesos back to foreign currency. Forget cashing personal checks, unless you have an American Express card and want to go to the main Express Office in Santo Domingo. Why bother?

Changing Back

One final but very important word about your exchange transactions: when you change money, you will be presented with an official receipt recounting the transaction amount, the bank, and the date. At the airport when you leave, you can present your receipts, and then you will be entitled to change back your spare pesos into foreign currency—up to 30% of the total you've changed, minus a 2–3% surcharge. So hold on to all your exchange receipts.

Transfers

In an emergency, money can be sent to you via **American Express Money Gram** (U.S. tel. 800/926-9400) or **Western Union Financial Services** (U.S. tel. 800/325-4176). As a last resort, see your diplomatic representative. Good luck with that route, though.

Credit Cards

The major cards are accepted by many commercial establishments like hotels and gift shops. If you must pay by credit card, be sure there is no special commission, and check to be sure the ultimate price is denominated in pesos, not dollars. Credit cards are of no use at most service stations and outside tourist areas.

Tipping

At restaurants, the bill *(la cuenta)* includes an 8% government tax and a 10% government-imposed gratuity shared by the kitchen staff and others not in direct contact with the guest. Don't feel bad if you want to settle for that. But if you like the waiter, then add another 5%. Porters and chambermaids are very poorly paid and will appreciate your tip for their services.

COMMUNICATIONS AND MEDIA

POSTAL SERVICES

Every town and city has post offices, generally open 7 A.M.–3:30 P.M., though hours vary, especially in Santo Domingo. When mailing letters and postcards from town, don't use the postal boxes you see on some corners. Postal service in the Dominican Republic is unreliable at best—especially when you're mailing cards and letters to people who live in the Republic. Mailing things out is better, but to have any luck you need to go to the post office yourself, see to it that the stamp you've purchased is affixed properly, and then shove it in the slot with your own two hands. That way, you've got about a 75% chance of your mail being delivered. My favorite post office in Santo Domingo is located on the east side of the Plaza de Colón. It is small, friendly, and never crowded, and conveniently located in the Colonial District. Use it.

For each 10 grams, or fraction thereof, the cost to mail a card or letter is RD$1 to North America, Venezuela, Central America, and the Caribbean; 50 centavos elsewhere in the Americas; 70 centavos to Spain; and RD$1.50 to Africa, Australia, and Asia. There is, in most offices, a window marked *entrega especial* (special delivery), which costs an extra RD$2. You might try it. There are also special courier services listed in the Dominican Yellow Pages for interurban delivery, and Federal Express and UPS handle major deliveries in Santo Domingo.

Sending mail *into* the Dominican Republic is much more risky. If you really need to correspond with someone inside the country, try to do it by fax or phone.

TELEPHONES

Since 1930, Dominican telephone service has been handled by a company called Compaña Dominicana de Teléfonos, known commonly by its shorter name, **Codetel.** Codetel is an amazingly efficient operation, and you can call anyplace inside the country or in the world for relatively cheap rates, from offices that are clean and efficiently run. Almost all Codetel employees working front desks speak English. As you might guess, Codetel is not government run but is rather a subsidiary of GTE. Codetel gives direct service to 120 cities worldwide and has more than 500,000 phones in service. Recently, a couple of services have sprung up to compete with Codetel: **Tri Com** and **All-America Cables and Radio,** the latter of which offers cheaper long-distance and internal fax service. There are some pay phones scattered through the cities, and you can call for 25 centavos. By dialing the operator, you can find a bilingual operator, and there is a bilingual Spanish/English business phone book available from Codetel. Emergency is 911, and local information is 411. You can generally call collect from any hotel phone, but if you wish to pay for the call yourself, you'll have to go to Codetel. Don't worry, though—Codetel offices are usually conveniently located in the main downtown areas and stay open late.

Using Codetel is easy. Just go into the office and tell the clerk where you want to call. He'll direct you to a private booth where you'll dial "1" and your number. You'll get an overseas operator, and after a few short questions, you'll be connected to your party. If you call collect, that's the end. If you're paying, the clerk will hand you a bill and give you a receipt after you make payment.

If you're calling the Dominican Republic, the **area code** is 809. Calling in is easy and cheap. Remember that the Dominican Republic is one hour ahead of Eastern Standard Time, so when it's 1 P.M. in New York, it's 2 P.M. in Santo Domingo.

Fax

Fax service is common in the Dominican Republic. Most hotels have fax machines, and it's a good way to communicate with hotels, tourist agencies, airlines, and travel guides. The only glitch with fax is that frequent power failures can screw up your message. Many Codetel offices offer fax service along with their phones.

MEDIA

The Dominican constitution ensures a free press, and these days the press seems to have achieved in actual fact what it used to have only on paper. The newsstands on the streets are packed with lively and colorful morning and afternoon papers, and discussions of political and economic issues seem relatively open.

Newspapers

Papers come and go, but right now there are eight newspapers in Santo Domingo—five in the morning and three in the afternoon. Some of these have national circulations. Among the most important morning newspapers are *El Listín Diario, Hoy, El Siglo,* and *El Caribe. El Nacional, La Noticia,* and *Última Hora* are published in the afternoon. The newspaper of Santiago is called *La Información,* while Juan Bosch's Dominican Liberation Party publishes *Vanguardia del Pueblo.*

You won't have any trouble finding something to read in English, either, as many bookstores and some newsstands handle the *New York Times, Miami Herald, International Herald Tribune,* and *The Wall Street Journal.* If you're staying for any length of time in Santo Domingo, you can arrange for home delivery, too. For *El Listin Diario,* call 809/682-8407; for *El Caribe,* call 809/566-8161. For those wanting a fresh *New York Times,* you can surely pick one up at Recuerdos Dominicanos on Avenue Isabel la Católica on Parque de Colón in the old city in Santo Domingo. The owners of Recuerdos live on Calle Caonabo No. 34, one block south of Avenue César Nicolás Penson near La Plaza de la Cultura, and you can call them at 809/682-6165 if you really need a *Times* fix.

There used to be one English language newspaper in Santo Domingo. Called the *Santo Domingo News,* it has sadly closed its doors. Once containing soft stories, wire-service reprints, and lots of news about cultural events, music, and film, it is certainly missed. Maybe one day it will make a comeback.

Magazines

Common at hotel desks is a publication called *Touring,* which is strictly oriented to tourists and printed in English, Italian, and German. Something called *Bohio,* a free quarterly magazine devoted to tourists, is also available, as is *La Cotica,* which is quite good.

TV and Radio

You can get all the TV and radio you want in the Dominican Republic. There are 10 television stations operating out of the country, and almost all tourist areas have cable TV, with NBC, CNN, and 18 other cable channels, all operating 24 hours a day. Dominicans love *telenovelas,* which are the equivalent of soap operas. The radio is full of music and the loudest ads and commercials in the world. With 179 AM and FM stations, you can get plenty of contemporary adult music and lots of merengue.

HEALTH AND SAFETY

By all rights, the island of Hispaniola should be one of the healthiest environments on earth. And for the Taínos, who called the island *bohio,* it was an almost entirely disease-free place, with no endemic illnesses of epidemic proportions. Even Columbus referred to Hispaniola many times as "salubrious." Today, Hispaniola has come through a disease-filled era and is now a *relatively* healthy place. If you take a few minimal precautions and exercise common sense, you'll have no problems. Likewise, crime is hardly a problem on the island, at least on the Dominican side. Unlike North America, violent crime hasn't gotten a toehold, and even the major cities seem restful and safe.

CARIBBEAN DISEASE HISTORY

These days, hundreds of thousands of tourists visit the Dominican Republic every year and come away thinking of the island as a place where they've achieved a certain amount of physical health and a great deal of spiritual peace. It's restful, easy, open, and genuinely invigorating. However, for hundreds of years, Europeans believed that the islands of the Caribbean were among the unhealthiest places on earth, a veritable "whiteman's graveyard." For 400 years, in fact, the Caribbean's semi-tropical climate *was* an ideal environment for microbes. A peculiar circumstance of history and geography created this situation.

In the first place, the Caribbean, because of winds and currents, is a kind of natural highway for both men and parasites traveling between Europe, Africa, and America. Many of the port cities of the islands became entrepots for diseases native to three continents but which did not originate in the Caribbean itself. This mixing of diseases and people became dangerous because of the way the human immune system operates.

Humans and microbes coexist, for better or worse. Over time, the human immune system adjusts, providing a population with the ability to weather attacks of a given disease. Only by suffering through a disease can the human organism become completely immune, but over many years certain immunities can develop naturally. Humans may develop a mild case of something like chicken pox in childhood and be immune forever after. Prior to the 15th century, when few humans traveled from continent to continent, this kind of physical and genetic immunity kept populations safe from all but the disastrous pandemic diseases such as the plague.

In the Caribbean there were no endemic diseases—no smallpox, measles, typhus, yellow fever, malaria, or tuberculosis. Europeans and Africans, however, have roughly the same tolerance for diseases endemic on both continents—roughly the same list as above. Africans were more likely than Europeans to suffer from diseases like yaws, leprosy, and intestinal worms, but they were at least partially immune to yellow fever and *falciparum* malaria—then found only in Africa. After the Taínos had been exterminated on Hispaniola, only the Europeans and Africans were left to mix, and the combination, in terms of disease profiles, was deadly.

Malaria and Yellow Fever

In the first place, Europeans had no immunity to yellow fever and malaria, two diseases spread and carried by mosquitoes. Both diseases travel from one victim to another through the insect, but not directly from human to human. Malaria,

over the years, killed many more people than yellow fever, but its action was hit or miss, taking children, women, and the elderly, often slowly and in widely scattered geographical areas. Yellow fever, on the other hand, pounced on whole cities, devastating populations all at once. In a packed city, yellow fever could take as much as half the population in a few months of epidemic, then be gone, sometimes for years.

One of the world's oldest and most widespread diseases, malaria is transmitted to humans through the bite of the *Anopheles* mosquito, widespread throughout Africa and America. As the mosquito feeds on human blood, malaria parasites rapidly enter the human bloodstream, then the liver, and multiply. They break back into the bloodstream and feed on the victim's red blood cells. Though West Africans enjoyed a relative immunity to the disease, at least 25% of whites afflicted with malaria died before the arrival of quinine in the 1840s. Once bitten, victims, even if they survived, remained infested with the parasite. Since the *Anopheles* mosquito prefers to breed in standing water and swamps, the relatively dry islands of the Caribbean—Barbados, Saint Kitts, and Anguilla—were free of malaria, while humid islands such as Cuba, Jamaica, and Hispaniola were infested.

Yellow fever is also carried by a mosquito, but a different mosquito, *Aedes aeypti*. This mosquito carries a virus (not a protozoan), which is passed in the same way as malaria. The yellow fever mosquito, however, is eccentric, in that it can't fly very far and favors breeding in water kept in open containers with solid sides—such as cisterns or water casks. Consequently, the mosquito needs a closely packed human population, and the disease can be stopped by quarantine and flight from the area. Unlike victims of malaria, a yellow fever survivor cannot support the virus again and thus has a lifetime immunity. That's the reason why yellow fever would only visit a city every so many years: it needed enough time for a new, non-immune population to come into being. Thus, the arrival of new boatloads of slaves often signaled the onset of a new bout of yellow fever, as did the arrival of boatloads of soldiers during war. Yellow fever is a terrible disease, causing high fever, debilitation, vomiting, and coma. Between malaria and yellow fever, the historical death rate for Europeans in the Caribbean was extremely high.

Doctors were slow to recognize the cause of both diseases. However, by the late 1880s, the species carrying yellow fever was identified, and an eradication program for the islands was formulated. In 1898, the life cycle of the *Plasmodium* parasite (malaria) was also identified. Filtered pipes, sewage systems, steel ships, and pesticides helped to eradicate malaria and yellow fever from the islands. By the First World War, the diseases were all but gone, and the islands once again became a healthy place.

BEFORE YOU GO

You'll be perfectly safe during your visit to the Dominican Republic if you exercise a few precautions. First of all, prior to departure, please visit a local hospital where the staff is knowledgeable about tropical islands and where health bulletins are issued which can guide a doctor or nurse into prescribing inoculations and medications tailored to your destination. (The Moon Handbook *Staying Healthy in Asia, Africa, and Latin America* is full of pertinent health information.) Second, if you have a permanent medical condition, consider wearing a medic-alert identification tag, available from **Medic Alert,** P.O. Box 1009, Turlock, California 95381 (tel. 800/432-5378). The medic-alert tag provides doctors anywhere with a 24-hour hotline where they can find out about your illness in case you're unable to talk about it yourself. Malaria in particular calls for some measure of caution. Before you go, check with a tropical specialist for the latest information and advice.

Water
It is not safe to drink tap water in the Dominican Republic. And it is probably best to avoid brushing your teeth in tap water as well. This does not hold true for every place on the island, but you can avoid nasty surprises by drinking bottled water, which is available everywhere and is not particularly expensive.

Vaccinations
Most of us are immunized against **diphtheria, tetanus, and polio** at an early age. Review your

medical records to make sure you were. Even if you have been immunized, sometimes you'll need a booster shot. Diphtheria is a bacterial infection spread by secretions from the nose and throat or skin lesions of infected persons. The symptoms are sore throat, high fever, lethargy, and sometimes skin infections. A bacteria also causes tetanus. Infection occurs through contact with contaminated surfaces. Some clinics also suggest polio boosters for travelers to the Caribbean.

Hepatitis A is present in the Dominican Republic, so inoculations are a good idea. However, the inoculations aren't effective in every case, so it's always a good idea to practice regular hygiene when you're on the island. Wash your hands before and after eating, and try to keep clean at all times. Wash your pocketknife if you're peeling fruit. Avoid drinking tap water in the Dominican Republic—instead, enjoy *coco frío* (fresh coconut juice), bottled water, or carbonated beverages.

Hepatitis B is also present in the Dominican Republic. Vaccination for this is expensive and requires a series of three inoculations over six months, but if you want to play it safe, it's well worth it to protect yourself against this serious disease. Be sure to give yourself enough time before your trip to complete the series.

First-Aid Kits
Everybody traveling should pack a small first-aid kit. There are plenty of well-stocked pharmacies in most towns, but you never know. Pack your regular prescription medicines, of course, and bring along the written prescription from your doctor in case of legal hassles. Pack malaria pills and anti-diarrhea medicine, adhesive bandages, disinfectant, pain relievers, suntan lotion, condoms, extra glasses, and antibiotic ointment.

Information
For up-to-date information on current health conditions on the island of Hispaniola and in the Dominican Republic, call the Centers for Disease Control's **International Traveler's Hotline** at 404/332-4559 in the United States. In an emergency, contact your hotel's house physician or go to a local clinic. Referrals for doctors are also available at consulates and embassies.

COMMON HEALTH PROBLEMS AND DISEASES

Traveler's Diarrhea

This probably comes as no surprise, but diarrhea is the traveler's greatest enemy. I've traveled extensively in the Dominican Republic and never suffered once, but then I've got a cast-iron stomach.

If something doesn't agree with you, and you find yourself battling diarrhea, take several steps. Soothe your stomach with Immodium, and by eating soft foods in small amounts. Also, go for carbonated beverages, weak tea, and the like, but avoid milk. To remedy severe dehydration, there are commercial preparations (such as Gastrolyte), or you can make a solution of two or three teaspoons of salt and one teaspoon of sugar in a liter of water to help reestablish the body's fluid balance. Imodium and similar preparations are quite effective. If something more serious develops, or if the diarrhea persists with high fever and lassitude, then you'd best get to a doctor. Remember to always eat fresh foods and drink bottled water. Sometimes when the power fails, refrigeration units go out and food spoils. Watch out for questionable food in restaurants and even in your room's mini-fridge, especially after prolonged blackouts.

Sunburn

Sunburn can also sneak up on you in the Dominican Republic. Wear sunglasses and a wide-brimmed hat and use plenty of sunscreen. Limit yourself when first going to the beach. If you happen to overexpose yourself, stay out of the sun until you recover. If you get fever or chills, a headache, or nausea and dizziness, see a doctor.

Insect Bites

All of this brings us to insects, especially the mosquito. To minimize bites, religiously use a repellent with a high concentration of chemical commonly referred to as **DEET.** Ask a pharmacist; he'll know what you're talking about. Wear long-sleeved shirts and heavy clothing wherever possible, especially when tramping through wet areas. Indoors, use an insect spray containing permethrin (the brand name is Permanone) on clothing, under beds, and in closets and dark corners. Most insect sprays don't work on gnats (also called no-see-ums), but Avon's Skin-So-Soft and similar products might. Take an antibiotic ointment and avoid scratching an infected area. Remember that insects are most active during sundown and twilight. Avoid brightly colored clothing, wear socks and shoes when hiking, and dose yourself with repellent.

Ocean Stings

When you're swimming at the coral reefs, be careful not to step on sea urchins or fire coral. The scorpion fish lives on the ocean bottom near reefs, and stepping on one of its spines can cause pain and swelling. Immerse the affected area in hot water for 60 minutes. The stings of both Portuguese men-of-war and jellyfish are also painful and sometimes dangerous. If you're stung, leave the water immediately and remove any tentacles, then treat the wound with alcohol and meat tenderizer for 5–10 minutes.

Malaria

The only place you're at risk of malaria is along the Haitian border in the far western Dominican Republic. If you plan to visit this area, you should probably get a prescription for anti-malarial tablets, and follow the instructions for their use. The symptoms of malaria include high fever, chills, lethargy, and severe headaches. I've seen this disease operate on friends in Africa, and it can knock you out for a week (and that's if you're lucky). The incubation period can be up to eight weeks.

AIDS

It would be irresponsible not to mention AIDS, which is known as *SIDA* in Spanish. As in many areas of the world, this disease continues to be a significant health concern. Because the Dominican Republic is in close proximity to Haiti, and because the disease can be spread by heterosexual as well as homosexual contact, you should be vigilant in protecting yourself. When tourists engage in sex without adequate protection, or if they use intravenous drugs or undergo a blood

BOB RACE

transfusion, they've been put at risk. Travelers who might engage in sex with locals should carry condoms. Most locals don't worry about AIDS and don't come prepared.

Bilharzia

Another potential hazard is something called bilharzia (schistosomiasis), which is a parasite that can be contracted when wading in shallow water where certain snails are present. Although not . widespread, it has been reported in parts of the eastern province of El Seibo.

Dengue

A new infectious disease called dengue hemorrhagic fever has appeared in the Americas. On November 15, 1995, the Pan American Health Organization noted that dengue had reached epidemic proportions. Spread by mosquitoes, there is no known treatment or vaccine. The only prevention is to avoid being bitten by a transmitting mosquito. Dengue is spread by our friend the *Aedes* mosquito, which does most of its feeding during the day, often near human dwellings. It is most prevalent during and after the rainy season.

Ciguatera

I've eaten plenty of fish in the Dominican Republic, but it's always wise to be informed about the dangers of a toxin known as ciguatera. Not all fish are susceptible. You can acquire the toxin from eating fish that have eaten smaller toxic fish, which themselves eat a single-celled marine plant called *Gambierdiscus toxicus,* which grow on coral reefs. It's found mostly during the spring and summer months, especially after storms. There is no specific treatment, though vomiting is often induced to rid the stomach of the toxin. Reef-feeding fish like red snapper *(chillo),* grouper or sea bass *(mero),* barracuda, mackerel *(cabala),* and kingfish carry the toxin, or can. Deep-sea fish like shark *(tiburón),* marlin, salmon, and tuna don't feed on reefs. You're safe with shellfish and lobster as well.

DOCTORS AND EMERGENCY CARE

You can find good or decent clinics in major cities, but it would be best to prepare yourself not

to get sick. In rural areas, clinics and hospitals are rare, and health care in the countryside is in some places nonexistent.

If you encounter a real medical emergency or need firefighters, police officers, or an ambulance, find a telephone and dial **911.** For an ambulance, you can also phone Red Cross ambulance services in Santo Domingo at 809/689-4288. Private ambulance service in Santo Domingo is available from **Rojas** (tel. 809/546-4060) or **Servicio de Ambulancias 24 Horas** (tel. 809/530-8221). If you need specialized medical equipment or care, just tell the person you call—and stay on the line if possible, in case there is a need to reconfirm your situation or location. Sometimes calling a taxi can be a faster and cheaper way to get to a hospital or clinic. In Santo Domingo, I'm told that the best emergency medical service is found at **Clinica Abreu,** Calle Beller No. 42 (corner of Independencia). You can call them at 809/688-4411. The **UCE Medical Center**'s emergency room at the corner of Máximo Gómez and Pedro Henríquez Ureña (tel. 809/688-9511) is also reputed to be good.

MEDICINE

Many pharmacies in Santo Domingo are open 24 hours a day and will even make deliveries. Most accept major international credit cards. You can find a pharmacy in almost every neighborhood in every city and town, and you can always check the Yellow Pages, which are very complete.

You will find that many drugs are available in Dominican pharmacies without prescription, including antibiotics. It's tempting to practice medicine on yourself and bypass a doctor, but self-diagnosis can be very dangerous. Some medicines available in the Dominican Republic have been banned elsewhere, so if you're medicating yourself, ask for name brands like Tylenol, or specify known drugs like acetaminophen, rather than just asking for something to cure a headache.

INSURANCE

Before you travel, check your insurance coverage. Health insurance is the most important kind of coverage you can get. If you get sick in the Dominican Republic, you can usually find someone to treat you adequately, but the cost is very high. You should have a comprehensive policy of health insurance that covers hospitalization. It should have a repatriation clause, in case care is not available where you are and you need to get home. Carry proof of your health insurance with you at all times.

CRIME

The Dominican Republic is just not a dangerous country. There aren't any guns and no gangs. Although there is some drug smuggling, it's limited in scope, and you're not likely to come into contact with it anywhere you go. I guess this is a way of saying that the island is not a violent place—not that there isn't any crime.

Crime Tips

As in many poor countries where people live close to poverty, in the Dominican Republic, certain of your possessions may look like lifesaving items to a poor kid. Jewelry, electronic equipment, video cameras, suitcases, and wallets can all become targets of opportunity for sneak thieves, snatchers, or pickpockets. Here and there, a car will lose hubcaps. Your best bet is not to be ostentatious or foolish. Distribute your money in different pockets, or wear a belt that has a place for your passport, traveler's checks, and cash. Don't wear expensive jewelry or flash a lot of bills around and act like a big shot. Drive a simple car. In many places, kids will offer to watch your car for a few pesos. Cultivate their friendship and let them handle the job. Many hotels have safes; use them. Serious con men may pester you, trying to make monetary exchanges or offering guide services or prostitutes. This doesn't happen very often, but if it does, ditch these characters quickly.

Away from Santo Domingo and the tourist enclaves, the peace and freedom you'll experience are almost absolute.

TO HAITI

As these words are written the Haitian border remains a monument to historical mistrust, eco-

logical disaster, and economic ruin. The historical mistrust is long lasting, the result of centuries of racial antagonism and outright warfare, especially during the time of the French Revolution, and more recently during the reign of the Duvaliers over a corrupt government in Port-au-Prince. Everywhere in this mountaínous and remote region, the signs of ecological disaster are apparent. Although there are spots hereabouts where one can glimpse remnants of rain forest, or be dazzled by long views over rugged terrain, for the most part the Haitian border is devegetated in the worst sense, rutted by erosion runoff, devastated. In part, it is this air of danger and ruination that interests many people in the border.

In truth, the nearly 190 km border that curves back and forth in no rational fashion is a poor and remote part of both Haiti and the Dominican Republic, an area of small townships or villages in which most of the cross-border traffic goes only east. Here, Haitians often cross to attend small markets that cater to their needs, then recross before dark, all with the permission of Dominican authorities. The government of the Dominican Republic has set up many army stations to monitor illegal immigration, but the border remains quite porous, a witness to the many poor Haitians who work in cane fields around San Francisco de Macorís, or live in hovels outside Santo Domingo. And thus the border is also a monument to economic ruin.

The Carretera Internacional

One should be wary of the misnamed "International Highway" (the Carretera Internacional) and not expect to use it as a secure passageway between north and south along the border. At almost no place along this so-called highway are passenger cars allowed to pass into Haiti. In some areas the road is barely suitable for 4WD vehicles of any kind. Haitian residents long accustomed to horrendous roads advise that in many areas the road is actually only an animal track, and that even the Haitian 4WD pickup truck, famous for its tenacity over bad roads, can't negotiate sections. For example, around the village of Costanza via Bohechio, the roads are impassable.

Readers have advised that motorcycles can negotiate the track, presuming one thinks it is worth it. And that becomes the ultimate question—is it worth it?

For a few years now, Haiti has experienced relative political stability despite a demonstrable lack of economic growth. There is, even now, some movement on the tourism front. A growing number of curious travelers in the Dominican Republic travel by bus across the border at **Dajabon** to visit Haiti's premier tourist attraction, the Citadelle and Sans Souci Palace, and in general the city of Cap Haitien. One can cross by private car at **Dajabon** in the north, and at **Jimaní** in the south, after obtaining the proper authorization permits at immigration offices at the border.

The only other town of any size on the Haitian border, **Elias Pina**, has no Customs or Immigration office, and cars cannot cross legally. Readers have reported paying bribes to cross to the Haitian town of Belladere for the day, and then paying again to recross. I strongly advise against this action, which runs counter to the law and common sense and could land you in prison.

Dajabon

The most pleasing place to cross into Haiti is Dajabon, a large town with the largest Haitian market on the border. In fact, on Monday and Friday, hundreds of Haitians pass over the so-called "Friendship Bridge" to participate in selling and buying. Haitians sell individual clothing items or swap them for grain and produce.

Crossing the border is a time-consuming and expensive mess. For starters, Dominican officials charge US$10 to cross, and Haitian officials then extract US$10 in gourds, which can be obtained from money changers near the border. Other informal payments may be required to speed up the process, or to a motorcycle driver to take you to the nearby Haitian town of Ouanaminthe. When you reenter, Dominican officials will take another US$10. The border is open 8 A.M.–6 P.M., and staying on the Haitian side isn't much of an option.

Jimaní

Dusty, dirty, and concrete, Jimaní is quite unappealing as a place to spend any time. It does have a large Haitian market, and at many times of day one can gaze on the Haitian border across a strip of uninhabited brush and witness *guaguas* steaming down from the heights that are Haiti. The *guaguas* are filled with Haitians on their way across the border, sometimes to Santo Domingo to shop and look for work, sometimes on buying excursions. They are colorful and noisy, but hanging out at a bar near the border is a test of temperament, what with beggars, kids, motorcycles, and diesel fumes.

Crossing at Jimaní is virtually pointless, as there are no major towns or villages of consequence on the Haitian side, just a large saltwater lake, once connected to Lake Enriquillo. Most people who cross at Jimaní do so on the bus from Santo Domingo and are on their way to Port-au-Prince. When crossing, expect to pay the same charges mentioned at Dajabon.

And it is safe to say that going to Haiti is less dangerous and more comfortable on a bus from Santo Domingo, or on one of Air Santo Domingo's flights to Port-au-Prince.

BOB RACE

SANTO DOMINGO
INTRODUCTION

You'd think a bustling city of two million would be an urban nightmare, difficult, dirty, and hard to get around in. But Santo Domingo, with its seaside parks, shady plazas, dignified and intelligent people, and powerful cultural allure, has to be one of the most pleasant surprises in the western hemisphere. Oh sure, sometimes the traffic seems a bit daft, with smoke-belching cars and buses locked in what seems like a life-and-death struggle, and services like electricity interrupted for an hour at a time. But the traffic has more of busy gamesmanship to it than mortal combat, and the citizenry takes the power outages in stride. What's left is a city with powerful historical resonance, unique architectural color, and genuinely human proportion. In fact, it's the human proportion that makes Santo Domingo so attractive.

Santo Domingo is the first city of the so-called New World. It is a huge but walkable city—especially the mile-and-a-half square Colonial District, which unfolds with endless and pleasurable surprise. The rest of the city, the older, upper-middle-class residential neighborhood of Gazcue, the hustling shopping and commercial neighborhood of Naco, and the cultural center around the Plaza de la Cultura are but a few

short, and cheap, minutes away from the Colonial District by taxi. Only the outer fringes of Arroyo Hondo and the Las Américas Airport seem anything like distant, and even these distances seem to melt into an endless panorama of life, motion, and color.

If you think I think Santo Domingo is terrific, then you're absolutely right.

Santo Domingo is a city combustibly drenched in history. It used to be that sailors and adventurers arrived in Santo Domingo (later known as Ciudad Trujillo) and walked down a gangplank only a few steps from where Columbus chained his own ships. Looking right and left along the Ozama River, sailors were met by the sight of darkened walls surrounding the great home and palace of Diego Columbus, Christopher's son and the former governor of the province of Santo Domingo. Across the way stood the silhouette of the hemisphere's first Roman Catholic church. From this spot one could see, crosswise, the ancient street called Calle de las Damas, the first residential and imperial street in the New World, intersected by El Conde, a road with its own monumental history. El Conde, traveling due west, intersected with the park now known as Parque Independencia at the western end of the

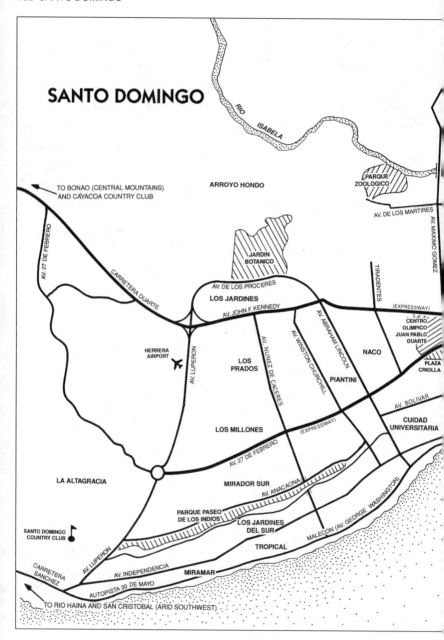

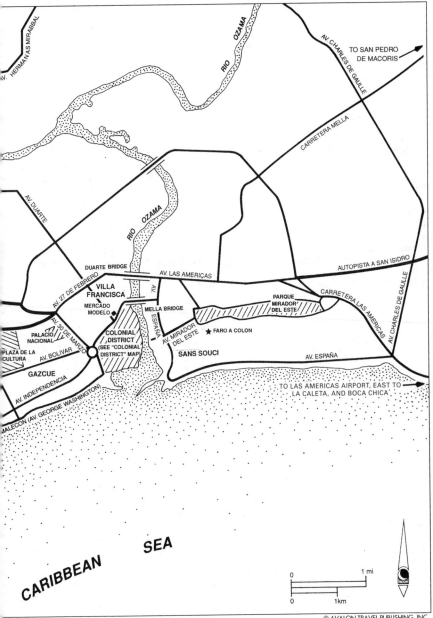

AV. HERMAN AS MIRABBAL

RIO OZAMA

AV. CHARLES DE GAULLE

TO SAN PEDRO
DE MACORIS

CARRETERA MELLA

RIO OZAMA

AV. DUARTE

AUTOPISTA A SAN ISIDRO

DUARTE BRIDGE

AV. LAS AMERICAS

AV. 27 DE FEBRERO

VILLA
FRANCISCA

CARRETERA LAS AMERICAS

AV.
ESPAÑA

MERCADO
MODELO

MELLA BRIDGE

PARQUE
MIRADOR
DEL ESTE

AV. 30 DE MARZO

PALACIO
NACIONAL

COLONIAL
DISTRICT
(SEE "COLONIAL
DISTRICT" MAP)

AV. MIRADOR
DEL ESTE

★ FARO A COLON

AV. CHARLES DE GAULLE

PLAZA DE LA
CULTURA

AV. BOLIVAR

GAZCUE

SANS SOUCI

AV. ESPAÑA

AV. INDEPENDENCIA

TO LAS AMERICAS AIRPORT, EAST TO
LA CALETA, AND BOCA CHICA

MALECON (AV. GEORGE WASHINGTON)

CARIBBEAN SEA

0   1 mi

0   1km

© AVALON TRAVEL PUBLISHING, INC.

street, once the barren outer edge of the much-threatened city of Santo Domingo, mauled by the specter of European wars and besieged by English pirates. During the city's struggles against pirates, Bernardo de Meneses Bracamonte y Zapata, the Count of Peñalva, so distinguished himself in battle that an arch in the city wall was named Puerta el Conde (The Count's Bulwark and Gate), while the thoroughfare became Calle Conde (Count's Street).

Today, Calle Conde is both ancient and modern, which pretty much sums up Santo Domingo itself. Here you can see *chiriperos* (pushcart vendors), modern office towers, businessmen on cellphones in their Mercedes sedans, ancient Spanish ruins, strolling musicians, and New York baseball on cable TV. A *cinturón de miseria* (belt of misery) girds the city's northern and western sides. It's visible from the posh hillsides of Arroyo Hondo, where the rich live in air-conditioned comfort.

Santo Domingo has a larger and faster-growing population than any capital in the Caribbean. It contains more museums, theaters, parks, and plazas than any city between Rio and Miami. Like any great city, it demands to be explored, not just visited.

LAND

The city of Santo Domingo lies on a flat coastal plain that is about 60km wide. In fact, much of the eastern part of the Dominican Republic is located on a limestone structure known as the coastal plain of Santo Domingo, a band of flat subhumid agriculture country commencing just west of Santo Domingo, near the mouth of the river called Río Ocoa, and stretching east all the way to the Atlantic Ocean. Santo Domingo itself is cut by two rivers, the Río La Isabela and the Río Ozama. Although predominately flat, the land on which Santo Domingo stands rises slightly south to north, until in the far northern outskirts of the modern city, a series of buttes and river terraces seems to enclose the city from an arid area to the north. Santo Domingo is thus an old marine terrace made of limestone, and you can see evidence of karst formations in the caves that dot the coast.

Two small ranges of hills to the northwest and

northeast poke their heads up, remnants of the great Cordillera Central. While these ranges in no sense dominate the skyline of Santo Domingo, they do provide some local color and affect weather patterns.

CLIMATE

The climate of the coastal plain of Santo Domingo is subhumid, meaning that it enjoys abundant seasonal rain. While the city of Santo Domingo is located perilously near the Tropic of Cancer, its climate is milder that you would expect. Temperatures during the day are quite reasonable until about noon, when the sun, standing straight overhead, tends to become somewhat hot. By two or three in the afternoon, however, the temperatures moderate considerably. Being near the sea, Santo Domingo's climate is influenced by morning and evening breezes, which further temper the tropical heat. Evenings are always mild, almost perfect. Just after the sun sets, you'd think you were in paradise.

Santo Domingo has two pronounced rainy seasons: one in the fall and one in early summer. Rain almost always arrives in brief squalls and thunder showers, usually no longer than 20 or 30 minutes in duration. A brilliant sun dries the streets afterwards. Things can get humid in Santo Domingo, especially during and immediately following a squall. Only during late summer and fall, at the height of the hurricane season, is Santo Domingo in danger of prolonged storms. Naturally, hurricanes are very dangerous events, and you'll want to keep an eye on them if you're in Santo Domingo during hurricane season.

HISTORY

Early Years

According to legend, the founding of Santo Domingo came about as a result of the perfidious search for gold and riches. It is said that an early Spanish conquistador named Miguel Díaz, who was at La Isabela on the north coast with Bartholomew Columbus, fought with and wounded another settler. When Díaz fled south to avoid being penalized for his breach of the peace, he

DOMINICAN SUNSETS AND THE GREEN FLASH

Few things are more colorful than a sunset in the Caribbean, and especially along the Malecón in Santo Domingo. About an hour before sunset, the sky turns a vivid set of pastel hues. The clouds, usually bulky cumulus balls over the ocean, illuminate as if from within. At the same time, waiters begin the work of cleaning and setting up tables at outside cafes and bars, and the first few tired workers, and curious visitors, begin to arrive for an evening daiquiri. As the sun sinks, the sky erupts in a dozen different colors, the air softens, and a warm breeze arises. Who could resist this kind of ambience?

Sunset is also the time to look for the green flash. The green flash? It's a very narrow band of bright green color that strips across the horizon just as the sun sinks from view.

A long time ago, people thought that the green flash was some kind of optical illusion. But now we know there is a fairly simple physical explanation. If you think of the way white light is bent when passing through a glass prism, producing red, orange, yellow, green, blue, and purple strips, then you're on your way to understanding the green flash. Something similar happens when the sun sets, only it's the atmosphere that bends, or refracts, sunlight.

When the sun is high in the sky, its rays are jumbled, crossing over one another so that the spectrum can't be seen. However, when the sun sinks toward the horizon, the atmosphere causes these colors to disappear one at a time. The progression is something like this: red disappears first, then oranges and yellows are absorbed (usually by water vapor and ozone, or oxygen). Some light scatters, especially blue and violet. After all these are eliminated, that leaves green, a bright pure green, which appears momentarily, right on the horizon.

You can't always see the flash, however. There's a lot of luck and fortitude involved. To get the best chance at the green flash, you'll need a clear view of the horizon, such as that from Santo Domingo's Ozama Fort at the mouth of Ozama River, or from a west-facing mountaintop. You'll also need a day with relatively clean air free of dust, haze, and high winds. And you may need some binoculars (don't look directly at the sun), to widen the width of the bands.

Seeing the green flash takes practice, so don't get discouraged. The green flash is capricious, even fickle, but well worth the effort.

---

met a Taíno Indian maiden named Catalina, who revealed to Díaz the location of certain gold mines on the banks of the Haina River, not far from present-day Santo Domingo. In order to free himself from Bartholomew's wrath, Díaz traded his secret information to Columbus's brother in return for a pardon. This information, true or not, prompted the struggling Spanish garrison to move south from La Isabela to search for gold.

Thus, in 1496, Bartholomew Columbus founded a small settlement called Nueva Isabela on the east bank of the Río Ozama, a settlement that was soon destroyed by a violent hurricane. However, before the hurricane struck, in 1502, Bartholomew changed the name of the new town to Santo Domingo. Some say Columbus picked the name because the city was founded on Sunday (*domingo* in Spanish), but others assert that the name honors his father Domenico, whose patron saint was Saint Domingue, or Santo Domingo. Just after the hurricane of 1502, the new governor of the colony, Nicolás de Ovando, chose to rebuild on the west bank of the river, adopting a grid pattern and commencing construction of several major buildings. In 1508, under Ovando, the settlement received its royal charter from Spain, thus becoming, officially, the first city in the New World. The final, full name of the city became Santo Domingo de Guzmán, from the founder of the Dominican religious order, Dominic de Guzmán (1170–1221).

The original settlement of Nueva Isabella was constructed of wood. Considerations of weather and defense prompted Ovando to begin building in stone and to lay his streets at right angles, in order to provide for easier defense against both internal and external enemies. The original city wall planned by Ovando extended only along the seafront because he considered a land attack unlikely. By the middle of the 16th century, the wall, replete

THE ILLUSTRIOUS DRAKE

January 10, 1586, dawned a sunny Sunday morning in Santo Domingo. On this beautiful morning, Sir Francis Drake, an English privateer, anchored his fleet of 23 ships out of sight down the coast from the city. He marched his 1,200 men nearly 10km, to a point just behind the city walls. Naturally, the governor of Santo Domingo expected any attack on his city to come from the sea and so had left the city's back walls relatively underbuilt. The English soldiers poured inside, and the city fell easily.

Drake had simple wants and even simpler demands. In the first place, he ordered a ransom of 250,000 ducats—a sum the city could not possibly raise. Drake ordered many of the buildings in the center of the city burned, its churches sacked, and some officials hanged. Then he left the city, with only about one-tenth of his ransom demand in hand.

But Drake wasn't through. He sailed to Cartagena, on the South American mainland, and extorted what he could from that underdefended city. He even went to St. Augustine, in Florida, but the city was new and had little wealth of interest to a privateer—or pirate.

BOB RACE

with seven gates, entirely enclosed the old city. This all served as a model for many of the New World cities that followed.

From 1509 to 1524, Diego Columbus, the explorer's oldest son, ruled as governor, at a time when Santo Domingo was essentially the seat of colonial government for the entire western hemisphere. At this time, the city was truly the capital of the Indies, and the principal trade and transshipment port for Spanish expansion into Mexico and Peru. The first church in the New World was built in Santo Domingo during this time, and the city became a center of religious practice and learning. It was about the time of Diego's departure that the Spanish began to discover the truly astounding amount of gold and silver in Peru and Mexico, and Santo Domingo was gradually eased out of its lustrous position as the center of the colonial empire. More and more, Mexico City, Bogotá, and Lima came to the fore. For many years, Santo Domingo remained a small, somewhat backward town.

Hurricanes and Pirates

The city has also had bad luck with hurricanes and pirates. After the original hurricane of 1502 came devastating storms in 1673, 1684, 1842, 1946, and the terrible hurricane David of 1979. In the early years, pirates proved an even more persistent nemesis. The savagery came to a peak in 1586, when Sir Francis Drake raided the city and left it in ruins. Because of these external threats, Santo Domingo remained confined within its original walls for 350 years, all the way to the independence movement and civil wars in the early 1840s. Only after independence from Haiti in 1844 were a few new neighborhoods built beyond these walls, inhabited by immigrants from the overpopulated Canary Islands.

Modern Era

By the time Trujillo came to power, in 1930, Santo Domingo retained a slightly backwater, provincial air, despite its position as the Dominican Republic's capital and primary seaport. Trujillo, however, owned most of the land to the west of the city, and he began an aggressive and systematic building program, designed to turn Santo Domingo into a showplace of fascist might while lining the pockets of the party in power—meaning Trujillo himself, his cronies, and his family. He ordered the building of the Palacio Nacional (National Palace), the Palacio de Bellas Artes (Palace of Fine Arts), and the Malecón, along with several other important governmental and cultural centers.

As the bureaucracy grew, so did the city. Around 1930, the population of Santo Domingo was probably about 200,000. Although population continued to increase steadily during the Trujillo era, only after his death did the explosion commence. By 1962, the city of Santo Domingo had appropriated all the land west of the old city walls, and the new neighborhoods— Naco, Piantini, Los Prados, and Los Millones— were built and settled by people migrating from the countryside. By the 1970s, more than a million people lived in Santo Domingo, and in the last 15 years, its population has doubled again.

Today, Santo Domingo is larger than 400 square km in area. The country's financial, industrial, and commercial center, it leads the way in petrochemicals, metallurgy, textiles, and plastics. It is the center for education and the arts. And despite its frenetic growth and seemingly endless motion, the city is studded with distinct neighborhoods, each possessing its own character and allure.

SIGHTS

ORIENTATION

If you arrive in Santo Domingo by air, you'll probably come into the international airport called Las Américas. Located about 23km from the main part of the Colonial District, it is a good place to buy your tourist card (if you haven't already bought it) and change some money. Just after passing through immigration and picking up your baggage, you'll have to make a decision about how to get into the city. The most logical way is by taxi, which you can pick up right outside the baggage-claim area. You shouldn't need to pay more than RD$250 (about US$20) for as many people and as much luggage as you can cram into the vehicle. Consequently, if you can find someone willing to share a cab with you, do it. If you want to try the *público,* you can sometimes pick up one on the upper level, or you can walk to your right and out of the airport grounds, cross Las Américas Highway, and wait for a bus into town. Don't try this late at night or on Sunday or your wait could turn into a vigil. Internal flights from Santiago, Barahona, and La Romana arrive at Herrera Airport, in the far western part of the city. The streets thereabouts are very complicated, and a taxi downtown would be the best idea unless you know your way around and speak good Spanish.

General Layout

Plan to walk around Santo Domingo, unless you're going long distances, say from the Colonial District to the Jardín Botánico Nacional Dr. Rafael M. Moscoso (National Botanical Gardens), when you'll need a taxi or bus. The city is unbelievably pleasant, the weather hospitable, and the opportunities for diversion endless. Also, the original grid pattern of the Colonial District makes it a snap to explore, and the rest of the city can be divided into a number of districts, each crisscrossed by easily recognizable major streets.

Coming from Las Américas Airport on the Las Américas Highway, you'll cross the Ozama River at the Duarte bridge. Once over the bridge, take almost any left turn and you'll find yourself in the Colonial District, bounded on the east by the Ozama River, on the west by the Parque Independencia, and on the south by the famous Malecón, the seaside boulevard, officially named Avenida George Washington. The Colonial District itself is bisected east to west by El Conde. Nobody can be disoriented in the Colonial District, and after half a day, you can become very familiar with its hidden treasures.

The rest of the city is traversed by major roads running roughly east and west. Many of the major luxury hotels of the city are located on the waterfront Malecón, with sea views and casinos. Just behind the Malecón, and running parallel with it is the Avenida Independencia, which

Ozama River,
Santo Domingo

angles south and west out of Parque Independencia. Jutting out of the northwest corner of the park is the Avenida Bolívar, another major east-west artery. Avenida John F. Kennedy (which becomes the Duarte Highway) and Avenida 27 de Febrero are other major east-west streets.

When sightseeing in Santo Domingo, one should be warned that all opening and closing days and hours are subject to change at short notice. Churches and convents, for example, may open their doors one day, close them the next. The whole Dominican Republic is in the throes of widespread changes in telephone numbers as well. A number good today may be gone tomorrow. Major north-south (roughly) streets include (in order from east to west) Avenida Duarte, Avenida Máximo Gómez, Avenida Abraham Lincoln, and Avenida Winston Churchill. Way out west, Avenida Luperón is the major road. Across the Ozama River from the Colonial District is the Columbus Lighthouse and the Parque Mirador del Este. Almost everything going east travels via the Las Américas Highway.

Once you get to know the Colonial District, you can venture out through Parque Independencia for short walks and shopping in the pleasant neighborhoods of Gazcue and Villa Francisca. Pretty soon you'll find that getting around is easy. When you get tired, you can always stop at a cafe for a papaya milkshake or a cool rum and soda. If you drive, try to avoid rush hours, which can be hectic and confusing. It won't be long before you venture into the Naco and along the Plaza de la Cultura. By that time, you'll be an old hand, able to negotiate the city with ease.

The best place to establish your bearings in Santo Domingo is in the Colonial District. Keep in mind that the Colonial District is not just a museum of stone and artifact, but a living and breathing home for thousands and thousands of working Dominicans who give life to the old place by endowing it with many cafes, bars, art museums, libraries, music stores, and theaters. You can easily guide yourself around the Colonial District to gain an appreciation of its 16th-century Spanish architecture, or you can hire one of the many competent, inexpensive guides available at hotels and tourist bureaus.

THE COLONIAL DISTRICT

The Colonial District in Santo Domingo is a constant delight. Not only is the district historical to the nth degree, but it is filled with colorful events and remarkable people.

Both the Avenida 27 de Febrero and Av. Kennedy have recently undergone major renovations. Tunnels have been added, and a kind of "parkway" thoroughfare aspect given to both, reducing, for the time being, the length of time to cross the city east-west from an hour to less than half that. In addition, a new metropolitan

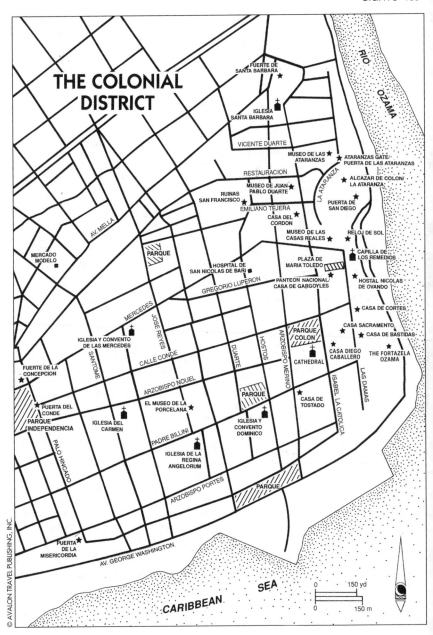

THE COLONIAL DISTRICT

FUERTE DE SANTA BARBARA ★

IGLESIA SANTA BARBARA

VICENTE DUARTE

MUSEO DE LAS ATARANZAS ★

ATARANZAS GATE/ PUERTA DE LAS ATARANZAS

RESTAURACION

ALCAZAR DE COLON/ LA ATARANZA

MUSEO DE JUAN PABLO DUARTE ★

RUINAS SAN FRANCISCO

PUERTA DE SAN DIEGO

EMILIANO TEJERA

CASA DEL CORDON ★

MUSEO DE LAS CASAS REALES ★

RELOJ DE SOL ★

CAPILLA DE LOS REMEDIOS

MERCADO MODELO ■

PARQUE

HOSPITAL DE SAN NICOLAS DE BARI ■

PLAZA DE MARIA TOLEDO

HOSTAL NICOLAS DE OVANDO

GREGORIO LUPERON

PANTEON NACIONAL/ CASA DE GARGOYLES

CASA DE CORTES ★

MERCEDES

JOSE REYES

CASA SACRAMENTO ★

CASA DE BASTIDAS ★

IGLESIA Y CONVENTO DE LAS MERCEDES

SANTOME

CALLE CONDE

DUARTE

HOSTOS

ARZOBISPO MERINO

PARQUE/ COLON

CATHEDRAL

CASA DIEGO CABALLERO ★

THE FORTAZELA OZAMA ★

FUERTE DE LA CONCEPCION ★

ARZOBISPO NOUEL

PUERTA DEL CONDE ★

EL MUSEO DE LA PORCELANA ★

PARQUE

PARQUE INDEPENDENCIA

PALO HINCADO

IGLESIA DEL CARMEN

PADRE BILLINI

IGLESIA Y CONVENTO DOMINICO

CASA DE TOSTADO

ISABEL LA CATOLICA

LAS DAMAS

IGLESIA DE LA REGINA ANGELORUM

ARZOBISPO PORTES

PARQUE

PUERTA DE LA MISERICORDIA ★

AV. GEORGE WASHINGTON

RIO OZAMA

LA ATARANZA

AV. MELLA

© AVALON TRAVEL PUBLISHING, INC.

SEA

CARIBBEAN

0   150 yd
0   150 m

MOON

bus run by the government plies both streets. Called OMSA bus (a new Mercedes), the service costs just 3 pesos. Plans are underway to expand OMSA service to other areas of the city at the expenses of the *guaguas*.

Parque Colón

Perhaps the best starting point for an orientation to the historic Colonial District of Santo Domingo is the leafy and very pleasant Parque Colón (Columbus Park), located at the corner of Calle Arzobispo Meriño (*arzobispo* means archbishop) and Calle Conde. If you find yourself on Calle Conde, which runs east and west, bisecting the Colonial District, just walk east toward the river and soon you'll see a bronze statue of Christopher Columbus. On the north side of the park is an excellent cafeteria and bar in which to have a drink, and directly facing the statue, a locally owned cigar store features hand-rolled Dominican smokes. At times the park can fill up with tourists, shoeshine boys, hawkers, vendors, and guides, but it has never seemed particularly unpleasant to me. The hawkers and vendors have an amazing sense of when to go away. Besides, for a few pesos you can enjoy a shoeshine while sipping rum from a plastic cup. Often you'll also get to hear a folk guitarist playing out in front of the police station near the park, serenading not only the tourists but the inmates as well.

The original city plans called for a green area set in the center of town, surrounded by public and religious buildings to include a cathedral, the governor's palace for the king's representatives, the city hall, and the court of justice. Wars, pestilence, and poverty intervened, and only a cathedral and city hall were built.

Catedral Basílica Menor de Santa María, Primada de América

Facing Parque Colón on the south, this beautiful cathedral is the oldest church in the Americas and was built on the orders of Real Miguel de Pasamonte. Its buildings, walkways, gardens, and quarters take up most of a city block. Diego Columbus set the first stone of the cathedral in 1514, but the real construction didn't get under way until around 1520 because the original Spanish architect left Santo Domingo to build another cathedral in Mexico. The financing of the building was left in the hands of the Bastidas, a wealthy church family, and the building was finally completed in 1544 by Rodrigo de Bastida's son, who was a bishop of the church and financed the construction out of his own pocket. The bell tower, which was to dominate the old city, has never been completed. Because construction of the cathedral was so slow and involved so many architects, the structure itself features gothic and Spanish Renaissance facades with baroque ornamentation. If you look closely, you can see a gothic vault, a Renaissance facade, and Romanesque arches. From the outside, the cathedral looks rather imposing with its heavy gray stone and squat appearance.

As you walk around the cathedral you'll notice the Gate of Pardons (north, facing Parque Colón). The main portal is called St. Peter's Gate. It has an impressive double arch, with a unique frieze combining gargoyles and other mythical figures. The niches on each side of this main door supposedly once contained figures of St. Peter, St. Paul, and four other apostles; all were taken away by Sir Francis Drake. The inside of the cathedral is quite restful, even elegantly dramatic, with a number of small chapels, life-size wooden animals, an abstract Jesus in the manger, and stained-glass windows crafted by Rincón Mora, a Dominican artist. The beautiful mahogany altar dates from 1684; after being allowed to deteriorate over many years, it's being restored and cleaned. As the story goes, for years the remains of Columbus himself were housed in this cathedral, kept in a white marble and bronze memorial built by the dictator Ulises Heureaux in 1898. Later, they were transferred to the Columbus Lighthouse *(Faro a Colón)*. A long history of anthropological and historical wrangling has failed to settle where the actual remains of the Admiral came to rest, but it's nice to think they're in Santo Domingo. There is no charge to visit the cathedral, but you must not wear shorts. Generally, the cathedral is open from 9 A.M. to 4 P.M.

South of the Cathedral

On the south side of the cathedral is a tiny

Fortaleza Ozama

street called Calle Arturo Pellerano Alfau, which crosses Arzobispo Nouel and may have been the first pedestrian path in Santo Domingo. As you pass along the Alfau, just across Calle Isabel La Católica you'll see the **Casa Diego Caballero** and **Casa Sacramento.** The first of these houses was constructed in 1523. The second was home to many important colonial figures, including Alonso de Fuenmayor, responsible for the completion of the city walls and the construction of many buildings in the middle of the 16th century. The facade of the Casa Diego Caballero is distinguished by two square towers. The inside has galleries composed of solid stone arches. On the west side of Parque Colón is what remains of the original city hall, built in the 16th century and now part of the Banco de Trabajadores (Worker's Bank), with a huge tower known as El Vivaque. This building also contains a jail and police station. On the east side of Parque Colón is the Palacio de Borgella, which dates from the 19th century and was once the seat of executive power, now housing administrative offices and a small and convenient post office.

Heading east from the cathedral, either down Calle Conde or between Casa Diego Caballero and Casa Sacramento, will bring you to one of the most truly dramatic and historic thoroughfares in the western hemisphere. Not originally designed for common pedestrian traffic, the **Calle de las Damas** was a regal and imperial promenade and is today lined with carefully restored colonial buildings of great significance.

The Fortaleza Ozama

Very near the river in the far southeastern corner of the Colonial District is the **Fortaleza Santo Domingo** (Fortress of Santo Domingo), site of the **Torre del Homenaje** (Tower of Homage) and the **Fortaleza Ozama** (Ozama Fortress), open Tuesday–Sunday 8 A.M.–7 P.M., admission about RD$6. These dual forts and the somber tower sit on a bluff overlooking the conjunction of the Ozama River and the Caribbean Sea and were built by Governor Nicolás de Ovando in 1503, making this the oldest military building complex in the Americas. It was on these grounds, in the warden's lodge, that Diego Columbus lived when he first arrived in Santo Domingo with his wife, and it was here that Trujillo housed some of his many political prisoners. The tower is a wonderful place from which to watch a Caribbean sunset at about six o'clock in the evening. The land, too, is restful and imparts an eerie sense of antiquity. On the grounds stands a statue of Gonzalo Fernández de Oviedo, famous military historian of the New World. When you buy tickets to the fortress, several young men will approach you as guides. They generally provide congenial and competent service and seem to take great pride in both their own work and the historical context of their city.

Around the corner from the fortress, facing the Caribbean Sea on George Washington Avenue, stands a large black statue of **Antonio Montesino,** one of the earliest of 16th-century defenders of the Taíno Indians. From Santo Domingo, he appealed to the Spanish government for justice to the Indians. This is another good spot to do both sunrise and sunset.

Calle de las Damas

In front of the fortress complex runs the beautiful Calle de las Damas. Built in 1502, it's the oldest street in the hemisphere. This street runs north and south for about half a mile and is one of the most pleasant and historic walks in the Colonial District. This street became the "walk of the ladies" because Diego Columbus's wife, María de Toledo (a niece of King Ferdinand), established the habit of walking down this street to Mass accompanied by the noble wives. Just to the north of the fortress is the **Casa de Bastidas,** with an 18th-century plaque on the right wall and an 18th-century stone sculpture of Santa Bárbara on the roof above the gate. This large home and the enclosed courtyard inside was the residence of Rodrigo de Bastidas, conquistador, explorer, and governor of Santa María (now Colombia). Open 8 A.M.–6 P.M. every day, the spacious courtyard is graced by Romanesque arches and houses and several beautifully appointed art galleries. A gift shop operates just inside the entrance. At times, concerts and parties are held in the courtyard, some open to the public.

Proceeding along Calle de las Damas to the north, at the corner of El Conde you'll find the former house of the explorer/conqueror of Mexico, Hernán Cortés. Built in gothic style by Governor Ovando in 1503, the **Casa de Cortés** currently houses the French Cultural Alliance, which runs a small gift shop and quite often displays modern art from the Dominican Republic. On the same side of the street as the Casa de Cortés are several art and gift shops where you can buy tasteful cards and souvenirs. Perhaps the most impressive historical structure on the Calle de las Damas is the **Hostal Nicolás de Ovando,** an early 16th-century mansion built by Governor Ovando, once split into two houses for Ovando himself and the Davila family. Now, however, the residence is an excellent hotel.

You are welcome to go inside and have a look around. Most unusual is the gothic portal, a rare architectural feature. Although nobody knows for sure where Columbus himself lived when he governed Santo Domingo from fall 1498 to 1500, it is certain he was a guest in the Nicolás de Ovando house.

Panteón Nacional and Casa de Gargoyles

Nearly across the street from the Hostal Nicolás de Ovando is the Panteón Nacional (National Pantheon). Originally the Convento de San Ignacio de Loyola, a Jesuit convent, the pantheon was later a tobacco warehouse, then a theater. Now, heroes and public figures are buried there. Built in 1747, the convent was restored as the pantheon in 1955 by Trujillo, who made elaborate but unfulfilled plans to have himself interred there (he wound up in Père Lachaise Cemetery in Paris). Look up and you'll see an impressive copper chandelier hanging from the ceiling. It was donated by Spanish dictator Francisco Franco. Just around the corner from the pantheon is the weird **Casa de Gargoyles,** which now houses the Dominican Development Foundation. Here you can see the gargoyles that were once part of the structure of the cathedral. Next door to the house of gargoyles is the **Casa de los Jesuitas** (House of the Jesuits). Made of brick and stone, it is one of the oldest buildings in the city. Governor Ovando originally ordered its construction. In 1701, it was given to Jesuits, who used it as a college. It became a full-fledged university in 1747. Twenty years later, in 1767, the Jesuits were expelled from the Dominican Republic, and the building was given to the Crown. Across the street stands the lovely **Capilla de los Remedios** (Chapel of Our Lady of Remedies). The earliest residents of the colony attended Mass in its stark and simple interior before construction of the cathedral was completed. The chapel is sometimes open to visitors. Make an inquiry. Small musical groups occasionally perform in the chapel, whose acoustics are perfect for quartets and trios.

Museo de las Casas Reales

Just across the way from the Capilla de los Remedios is the **Museo de las Casas Reales** (Museum of the Royal Houses), one of the finest small museums in the whole Caribbean. Located on the

Alcázar de Colón

corner of Calle de las Mercedes, the museum charges a small entry fee of about RD$20 and is open Tues.–Sat. 9 A.M.–5 P.M. and Sunday 10 A.M.–1:30 P.M. (closed Monday). The building is the restored 16th-century palace of the Spanish Governor's Royal Court and is a delightfully cool and spacious place to spend a few hours viewing an excellent collection of artifacts from the colonial period, including maps of sea voyages, paintings, restored court rooms, carriages, and treasure from sunken ships. The museum also houses a fantastic collection of weapons from many countries, originally assembled by Trujillo. One of Trujillo's offices was once here as well. One of the more interesting features of the museum is its apothecary shop and collection of dolls and handblown glass. The museum was inaugurated in 1976 by President Balaguer, in company with King Juan Carlos I and Queen Sofía of Spain. As you walk north, away from the museum, you'll see the **Reloj de Sol** (Sundial), built in 1753, positioned in order that the judges seated in the court across the way could always tell the time.

Alcázar de Colón and La Atarazana

Standing at the sundial, you're almost on the **Plaza de María Toledo** (named for King Ferdinand's niece), which overlooks both the two-story rectangular Alcázar de Colón (Castle of Columbus) and La Atarazana, first commercial center of the New World. The Alcázar is sometimes closed on Tuesday but is open every other weekday 9 A.M.–5 P.M., Saturday 9 A.M.–4 P.M., and Sunday 9 A.M.–1 P.M. For a modest admission charge of RD$12, you'll see a magnificent restoration of what was once a crumbling relic, originally built 1510–1514 by order of Diego Columbus. Inside is the Viceregal Museum featuring an armored knight on a wooden horse, antique pottery, furniture, musical instruments, and tapestries. Of course, not many of the relics and antiques date from the early colonial period—most are imports from later Spanish centuries—but the Alcázar nevertheless provides the visitor with an authentic look and feel. From the second story, you can get a good view of the Ozama River, the Columbus Lighthouse, and the whole colonial environment. You can almost imagine it as the residence of Diego, who was called back to Spain in 1523, in part because of his self-indulgence. His descendants continued to occupy the building as a residence until the early 18th century. The grounds of the Alcázar are beautifully maintained, leading down in back to the **Puerta de San Diego** (Gate of St. James), which was, for many years, the original gate of the old city. Here you can see a section of the old wall, originally built in 1571 to protect the city from attack along the river.

Directly across from the Alcázar is La Atarazana, eight 16th-century warehouses on brick foundations. Today these architecturally unique buildings function as shops, restaurants, and bars: Drake's Café, Montesinos, Nancy's, Rita's Café, and the Museo de Jamon. La Ataranza is a good place to pull up a chair under an umbrella and enjoy a cold drink.

If you proceed north and walk down a flight of steps from the Alcázar, you'll find yourself across from the 17th-century **Atarazanas Gate** and directly in front of the **Museo de las Atarazanas**, sometimes called the Museo Maritimo (Shipyard Museum). This museum attempts to tell the story of many of the most famous shipwrecks along the Dominican coast and the efforts to recover treasure from them. In particular, the museum houses recovered treasure from the wrecks *Guadeloupe* and *Conde de Tolosa* (wrecked off Samaná in 1724), known as the "quicksilver galleons" because they were carrying mercury with which to refine silver and gold. The museum is filled with enchanting finds including clay pipes, brandy bottles, fused coins, pottery shards, Ming Dynasty porcelain, and contraband cargo like an eight-day clock made in London. The museum is closed on Wednesday but otherwise open Mon.–Sat. 9 A.M.–5 P.M. and Sunday 9 A.M.–1 P.M. Near the museum are some shady areas, restaurants, and a public parking area where parking is sometimes available (though it's crowded).

Casa del Cordón

Just around the corner from La Atarazana and near the Palacio de Comunicaciones (an ugly green building and television tower you can't fail to see) is the **Casa del Cordón** (House of Cord), located on Calle Isabel la Católica at the corner of Calle Tejera. Although the House of Cord is quite plain, it is historically significant as, allegedly, the oldest stone building in the Americas. Above the entrance is the sash or cord, a symbol for the Franciscan order. Now the building is occupied by a commercial bank, which will allow you to visit during normal business hours. Before moving into his official residence, Diego Columbus lived here with his wife, and here were born two of his children. This is also the place where the women of Santo Domingo lined up to surrender their jewelry to Sir Francis Drake in 1586 during his sack of the city. Business hours are 8:30 A.M.–4:30 P.M., and tours are free.

Museo de Juan Pablo Duarte

One block north of the Casa del Cordón is the Museo de Juan Pablo Duarte. Duarte, the hero of the fight for independence, was born here on January 26, 1813 (open Mon.–Fri. 9 A.M.–noon and 2 P.M.–5 P.M. and Sat.–Sun. 9 A.M.–noon, admission RD$12). The museum has a representative sampling of belongings and mementos but is otherwise architecturally uninspiring. It's worth a short visit. If you continue to walk uphill (north), you will come to the **Iglesia Santa Bárbara** (Santa Barbara Church and Fort), at the corner of Calle Isabel la Católica and Avenida Mella, one of the large shopping and commercial streets bordering the Colonial District. The church was constructed in 1562 and combines numerous architectural styles, including gothic and baroque. Take a peek inside if you can.

Museo Mundo de Ámbar

There is a new museum/store called the Museo Mundo de Ámbar. Located on Arz. Merino 452 at the corner of Restoracion, this museum is small but excellent and admission is only RD$15. Located in the museum is a small workshop and one can sometimes catch an artisan at work over stones. The store is a bit pricey, but the amber is top quality. The owner is named Sr. Jorge Cridad, a real amber buff who knows everything about the subject and is glad to share his knowledge.

Ruinas San Francisco

If you walk back downhill and look up and to the right, you'll see the ruins of the monastery called San Francisco on Calle Hostos. The Ruinas San Francisco are just that—ruins. This old monastery was built during the 16th century and destroyed by an earthquake in 1673. Dating from 1508, the grounds originally contained three connected buildings, including the chapel of María de Toledo (Diego's wife). Over the centuries the monastery was sacked by Drake, destroyed by a 1751 hurricane, and used as an insane asylum after 1881. You can see the chains used to secure the "patients." During the Spanish Civil War, artists took refuge within its walls, and, as legend has it, the remains of Bartholemew Columbus are buried here. The ruins are open every day, generally about 10 A.M.–5 P.M., with no admission charge. Although there isn't much to the ruins except ancient crumbling walls and some inner chambers, it still exudes an echo of the past, and the grounds are a nice place to rest in the shade. Set on a hill surrounded by an authentic Santo Domingan neighborhood, there's something very relaxing about the environment. Just up from the ruins is the **Ermita San Antón** (at Calle Hostos at the corner of Calle Restauración), built in 1586.

Hospital de San Nicolás de Bari
Headed downhill on Calle Hostos you'll walk along a high sidewalk with an iron railing. This area, with its modest homes and shops, is very pleasant and, looking down, you'll see the impressive ruins of the Hospital de San Nicolás de Bari, built by order of Governor Ovando in 1503–1508 to care for the poor and needy of the new city. Totally complete by 1552, the hospital was one of the best constructed buildings in the city and survived almost intact until 1911, when its walls were idiotically condemned as a danger to pedestrians, and demolished. Even though the buildings are gone, see if you can make out the cross-shaped outline of the ruins. The chapel of the hospital has been incorporated into the church next door, Our Lady of Altagracia. (Two well-known pubs, **Raffles** and the **Village,** are located nearby and provide the hip and others with live music on weekends.)

Iglesia y Convento de los Dominicos
Another important spot on Calle Hostos, across El Conde and at the corner of Paseo Padre Billini, is the Iglesia y Convento de los Dominicos (Dominican Church and Convent), built in many stages beginning in 1510. As you'd expect, the church was destroyed by an earthquake at the end of the 16th century, then reconstructed with a chapel in 1649. People around Santo Domingo considered the building the most elegant of its time, and for a while it housed the original Universidad de Santo Tomás de Aquino. Inside, the altarpiece was a gift from the grandson of Ferdinand and Isabela, known simultaneously as both Spain's Emperor Charles I and Charles V, Emperor of the Holy Roman Empire. Take a peek at the rosary chapel and its representation of 12 astrological figures on a map of the stars. From the outside, the building appears in formidable brick and squared stone, decorated with 16th-century Spanish tiles. It is mostly a gothic building, but there is a touch of Renaissance about it, too, with rose motifs around the windows and decorative vines. Next door to the church is the 18th-century **Capilla de la 3a Orden** (Chapel of the Third Order), where Eugenio María de Hostos founded the Escuela Normal, a teacher-training school. Both of these are open Tues.–Sun. 9 A.M.–6 P.M. And, if you're wild about churches and convents, just down

Ruinas San Francisco

Padre Billini at the corner of Calle José Reyes is the **Iglesia de la Regina Angelorum** (Church of the Queen of the Angels), where the remains of Father Billini are interred. The first female poets in the New World, Leonor de Ovando and Elvira de Mendoza, lived here. Now it's inhabited by nuns, from whom you can get permission to enter. Open Mon.–Sat. 9 A.M.–6 P.M.

Casa de Tostado and the Museum of the Dominican Family

If you backtrack down Calle Padre Billini, at the corner of Calle Arzobispo Meriño you'll come to the most genteel of colonial residences, known as the Casa de Tostado. This early–16th-century house was built in late gothic style and now houses the quaint Museum of the Dominican Family, which is worth a look. Francisco Tostado, the original owner, was the first Hispaniola-born person to become a university professor (at Universidad de Santo Tomás de Aquino) but had the misfortune to be killed by Drake's men in 1586. The museum inside has a good collection of 19th- and 20th-century Victorian wicker and mahogany furniture and a courtyard where you can wander and rest. Climb a wooden staircase to the second-story terrace and get a good view of the city. Admission to the house and museum is RD$20; it's open every day except Wednesday and Sunday. If you're in the Casa de Tostado, you can exit onto Calle Arzobispo Meriño and head just behind the cathedral. There, you'll find the picturesque alley known as **Callejón de las Curas** (Alley of the Priests), where the cathedral's clergy live. The residences are closed to the public, but it is a nice walk amid historic buildings.

El Museo de la Porcelana

Going the other way from the Dominican Church and Convent, you'll find yourself in Calle José Reyes, which for the most part is typical of Colonial District residential streets, narrow and busy. Between Padre Billini and Arzobispo Nouel, you'll see the tiny (from the front) Museo de la Porcelana (open Tues.–Sun. 10 A.M.–6 P.M.; admission RD$10). The building that houses the museum was built at the turn of the century by the wealthy Vicini family, reportedly on the model of the Alhambra Palace in Spain. The porcelain

collection is lovely, and the inner courtyard is a respite from the busy street outside.

Iglesia del Carmen

A short walk up Calle Arzobispo Nouel from Calle José Reyes will take you to the Iglesia del Carmen and its **Capilla de San Andrés,** an 18th-century church and chapel containing an interesting wooden sculpture of the Nazarene. In this church, it is said, conspirators planned a revolt against Haitian occupying forces in 1844. The chapel and church are open and closed willy-nilly, but if they are closed, you can often gain entrance from the Padre Billini Hospital next door.

Iglesia y Convento de Las Mercedes and Other Churches

By heading up Calle José Reyes, you'll eventually cross El Conde (which you should use as your bearing point anyway) and reach the corner of Calle de Las Mercedes, where you'll find Iglesia y Convento de Las Mercedes, a huge structure built during the first half of the 16th century in homage to the Virgin Mary. The church was finally completed in 1555 just in time to—you guessed it—be sacked by our friend Sir Francis Drake, who apparently had no great love for Catholics. The architect of the original structure was Rodrigo de Liendo, and the grouping of the buildings is both harmonious and attractive—even the massive stone tower. The retable of ornately carved wood is one of the most beautiful in the city. Only the cloister escaped damage in Drake's attack and is in original condition. The other churches in the area, **Iglesia San Miguel** and **San Lázaro,** both on Calle Restauración, are of late vintage and are rather forebodingly dark and uninteresting.

Parque Independencia

Now that you've become familiar with El Conde, you can walk its length toward the west and find the Parque Independencia area. Santo Domingo was fortified in the mid–16th century by walls running along the Ozama River to the Malecón, then up present-day Calle Palo Hincado to a point just beyond Calle Restauración, and then east back to the Ozama River, all of which became the boundary of the original Colonial District. After darting through the heavy traffic on the Calle Palo Hincado (good luck!), you'll see directly ahead of you the **Puerta El Conde** (Gate of the Count), named for the Count of Peñalva, the Captain General who repelled the English in 1655. The park, a bit dusty from the heavy trucks rumbling by it all day, contains the **Altar de la Patria** (Altar of the Nation), built in 1976 and containing the remains of several national revolutionary heroes, including Duarte, Sánchez, and Mella. Just past the gate, and set into the walkway, is a nautical star that points to 32 directions on the highway and is supposedly kilometer one, from which all distances are measured in the country. At the northern edge of the park are the ruins of the **Fuerte de la Concepción,** which marks the far northwestern part of the old Colonial District. Nearby, on the corner of Palo Hincado and Calle Arzibispo Portes, is the **Puerta de la Misericordia** (Gate of Mercy), which provided protection to the masses in times of natural disaster. If you look over the corner of El Conde and Avenida Arzibispo Meriño, you'll see a building which was originally the town hall (now a bank) and still houses murals painted by Spanish artist Vela Zanetti, exiled in Santo Domingo during the Spanish Civil War.

MERCADO MODELO

Don't even think about driving a car to the Mercado Modelo. For some reason, the area around the market is jammed with traffic during almost all hours of the day. Even experienced taxi drivers find it a frustrating place and avoid it like the plague. Besides, the market is just an easy uphill walk from the Colonial District. If you're coming from some other part of town, get off at El Conde and you'll find your way to the market without any trouble. A third option is to have the taxi driver drop you off on Avenida Mella, a few blocks from the market before the street really narrows, and walk down. Any way you choose to get there, the Mercado Modelo is a surreal experience.

The market, located only a few blocks from Santo Domingo's "Little Haiti," is housed in an old two-story building on Avenida Mella near Santome. It's one of the liveliest open-air trading areas in the city. To get inside, go up a wide staircase and through a large arch, picking your way past the dozens of vendors who will already be seeking your business. Try not to wear gaudy valuables—pickpockets and con artists cruise the crowds. Once inside the market you'll find yourself surrounded by a maze of market stalls, counters, stands, and roving ambassadors of sales, many of whom can speak enough English to make for a confusing and enjoyable bargaining session. There is a lot of schlock and a lot of junk for sale at the Mercado Modelo, but some authentic pieces of folk art as well.

Many items are hand-crafted, like woodcarvings, ceramics (try to find the faceless dolls of Neiba), larimar and amber jewelry, Carnaval masks, musical instruments, wicker, cigars, sandals and shoes, mahogany rocking chairs, and lots of cassettes of merengue music, T-shirts, and the ubiquitous "Haitian" primitive painting. Of great interest are the herbalists, who sell home remedies, love potions, and snake oil. On the second floor and outside round the fringes you'll find vendors selling locally raised meat and fresh produce and fruit, mainly to local Dominicans.

If you've a scent for the bizarre, then try wandering "Little Haiti." Beginning outside the market itself, you can probably spot a cadre of Haitian *guaguas,* multicolored buses that deliver loads of Haitians into Santo Domingo to do some cross-border trading. It's an activity the Dominican government formally discourages but informally encourages (because it brings in foreign capital). If you're willing to roam around the area, you can find some bargains in straw mats and woodcarvings outside the confines of the market walls. It's worth taking a look at the vegetable and meat markets, then deciding if you like outdoor trading better than the local supermarket back home. Any way you cut it, the whole area is a unique cultural experience.

OTHER NEIGHBORHOODS

Santo Domingo is a city of real neighborhoods, each of which seems to have an individual flair or character, good and bad. Just west of the Parque Independencia (follow Avenida Bolívar west, or jog north to catch Avenida César Nicolás Penson going west as well), you'll find the lovely old neighborhood of Gazcue. This particular neighborhood was very elite during the 1930s and 1940s. Today, it's a little long in the tooth, but that gives it flavor. Filled with small antique stores, *colmados,* expensive homes, mahogany-shaded streets, and art galleries, Gazcue is a place to be savored on foot. The houses incorporate many styles, including Tudor, Victorian, Spanish, and what can only be called Late Fascist.

A few other Santo Domingo neighborhoods are also well worth walking tours. The old **Autonomous University** (Ciudad Universitaria) is located in San Gerónimo, just south of the Plaza de la Cultura. Although run-down and neglected by the government, it has a lively intellectual life and is also the site of the Dominican-American Cultural Institute. Farther west is the entire Parque Mirador del Sur, and Miramar, Tropical, and Los Jardínes del Sur, all residential middle-class neighborhoods where many types of Dominicans live, work, and play. Across the river, the Mirador del Este is located in lovely seafront neighborhoods as well.

MUSEUMS NEAR THE PLAZA DE LA CULTURA

Palacio Nacional

If you follow Avenida Bolívar west and turn right on Calle Dr. Delgado, you'll see the huge Palacio Nacional, the seat of government. Designed by Italian architect Guido D'Alessandro, the palace is built of roseate marble in a neoclassical design and has a dome measuring 34 meters in height, 18 meters in diameter. Inaugurated in 1947, the rooms are furnished with old mahogany and gold-inlaid mirrors, elaborate crystal, and antique furniture. Inside, one room is called the Room of the Caryatids, after the 44 sculpted, draped women that line it. With good enough cause, you might be able to jerry-build a guided tour by calling 809/586-4771, ext. 340 or 360. If you get in, dress up. Supposedly the building is open for special tours on Monday, Wednesday, and Friday. The grounds are beautifully landscaped (18,000 square meters), though they're closed to visitors. The whole complex occupies more than a square block along Avenida México and was built by Trujillo, of course.

Plaza de la Cultura and Palacio de Bellas Artes

Just west of the Palacio Nacional is the Plaza de la Cultura, a huge park area once owned by Trujillo. The Plaza de la Cultura houses four large museums and the National Theater. Its western boundary is Avenida Máximo Gómez; the U.S. embassy is on the other side. If you're going north on Máximo Gómez, you'll pass the Palacio de Bellas Artes, a huge reddish building where various exhibits and performances are presented on an irregular basis. To attend a performance at the Palacio de Bellas Artes, you'll need to check the newspapers and be in town at the right time. Two blocks north, you'll pass the residence of former president Balaguer, noticeable for the prominence of armored vehicles, jeeps, and armed troops outside.

Museo del Hombre Dominicano

The absolute best of the bunch, when it comes to museums, is the Museo del Hombre Dominicano (Museum of Dominican Man) (open Tues.–Sun. 9 A.M.–5 P.M., admission RD$14, tel. 809/687-3622), which houses anthropological displays about the indigenous Taínos, African slaves, and Spanish conquerors. In sum, the museum is devoted to the historical and social development of the Dominican people, and almost all the displays have excellently maintained collections. The first floor of the museum houses an excellent bookstore, with many monographs and books in Spanish and a few in English and other languages. Also on the first floor are Taíno monoliths. The third floor is full of Taíno artifacts including grinding stones, axes, pottery shards, jewelry, and religious artifacts, including the stone head of Mictantechuti, god of the dead. Every exhibit is accompanied by a legend in Spanish, which provides the scientific and historical background of the display. Unless you read Spanish, you'll need some help with the explanations. Luckily, an enthusiastic and thorough English-speaking guide is always available on the first floor where you buy your ticket. For a US$3 or $4 tip, the guide will take you through the entire museum piece by piece, making the experience thoroughly enjoyable. On the fourth floor are the displays of Spanish and African artifacts, including many old photographs of the island, a voodoo altar, Carnaval mask collection, and a model of a *casa de un campesino.* While you're on the third floor, check out the Taíno *duhos,* thrones used by caciques when they inhaled hallucinogenic materials during religious ceremonies. The second floor is devoted to colonization events, of which the history of slavery is given special attention. A renovation has been under way, causing certain rooms on some floors to be closed. Hopefully, the work will be over soon.

Galeria de Arte Moderno

The Galeria de Arte Moderno (Gallery of Modern Art) (open Tues.–Sun. 10 A.M.–5 P.M., tel. 809/685-2153, admission RD$20) is located in an ultramodern building on Pedro Henriquez Ureña. The museum can seem rather ill lit, but in general the displays, the arrangements, and the artists represented are quite excellent, including Dominican masters like Albert Ulloa, and a collection of artists from Spain and Latin America. The fourth floor features moving exhibits, as does the basement. On the ground floor, just around the corner from the entrance, is a nice little bookstore where you can purchase exhibit catalogues and many works about Dominican, Haitian, and Latin American art, most in Spanish. Upstairs, the art museum also has a library, where you are free to browse and study. There's no admission charge on Tuesday, so if you're in the neighborhood, drop by. Pay special attention to the work of José Vela Zanetti, a Spanish artist whose murals grace the United Nations building in New York. The murals he did for the art museum trace the "life of the country Dominican" and, though somewhat dark, are marvels. To those who think that Dominican art is somehow primitive, this museum will be a revelation.

Museo Nacional de Historia y Geografía

Very near the art museum, on César Nicolás Penson, stands the Museo Nacional de Historia y Geografía (Museum of Geography and History), which contains a comprehensive collection of Trujillo memorabilia, photos, and personal items and is one of the few places in town where the name of the dictator is openly mentioned. Like some of the other museums of the plaza, the Museo Nacional de Historia y Geografía is open Tues.–Sun. 10 A.M.–5 P.M. and has a nominal admission charge of RD$14 (tel. 809/686-6668). The museum is divided into three large rooms, each covering a different period of Dominican history: 1822–61, 1861–1916, and 1916–61. The first room concentrates on the Haitian-Dominican battles of the 19th century and contains ship models, weapons, and depictions of both the Haitian occupation and the 1844 liberation. The next room features memorabilia relating to dictator Ulises Heureaux, with period uniforms, portraits, and money. The final room is where you'll find the story of the American occupation and the Trujillo dictatorship—probably the most interestingly presented of all the rooms. If you get a kick out of seeing such items as a dictator's wallet, shoes, razor, combs, death mask, and briefcase, this is the place for you. On the other hand, you might feel this museum is a little musty and bleak.

Museo Nacional de Historia Natural

Directly on the Plaza is the Museo Nacional de Historia Natural (Natural History Museum), which is worth a look, though some of the exhibits are a bit anachronistic. Open Tues.–Sun. 10 A.M.–5 P.M. (tel. 809/689-0106), the museum charges a nominal admission fee, and you are free to browse the first-floor bookstore, which has some materials on natural history (though nothing that rivals the bookstore in the Museo del Hombre Dominicano, which you should visit if you're serious about natural history and anthropology). The exhibits, which include a model of Lake Enriquillo and Spanish-labeled exhibits on geology, space, and zoology with dioramas and stuffed animals, seem somewhat stiff, and you'll soon want to be out in the wilds looking around for yourself. However, do pay attention to the excellent amber collection and the exhibits chronicling the evolution of life on the Greater Antilles.

Teatro Nacional

While you're in the area of the Plaza de la Cultura, cruise by the Teatro Nacional (National Theater), on Avenida Máximo Gómez (tel. 809/682-7255). It's the home of the Dominican national symphony (since 1941) and the scene of frequent operas and stage productions, as well as individual concerts and musical performances in its 1,600-seat theater. Out in front of the theater are statues of three masters of Spanish literature: Calderón de la Barca, Tirso de Molina, and Lope de Vega. During the high season—fall and winter—you can often attend a concert or local ballet performance for RD$50–150. You'll find notices of scheduled performers posted outside the hall or in the local newspapers. The ticket office is open every day from around 9:30 A.M. to noon and 3:30–6:30 P.M. Many Dominican and Caribbean artists appear in concert at this theater, and there can be no better cultural experience than seeing the best of local art. Dominicans consider going to the Teatro Nacional a formal event, so you should always dress up to attend.

Biblioteca Nacional and Museo Numismático

If you're determined to become acculturated, visit the Biblioteca Nacional (National Library), on César Nicolás Pensón. Open Mon.–Fri. 9 A.M.–11 P.M. (tel. 809/688-4086), the library is packed with musty Spanish-language volumes that would have given even Jorge Luis Borges a monumental headache. Just as esoteric as the Biblioteca Nacional, but loads of fun, is the Museo Numismático, located on Pedro Henríquez Ureña at Leopoldo Navarro (headquarters of the Central Bank). This museum has a rather complete (and spectacular) collection of Caribbean stamps and coins, if that's your bag. It is open Tues.–Sat. 9 A.M.–5 P.M.

The place to go on the Plaza de la Cultura for excellent *comida criolla* (the *plato típico* is great) is the **Maniqui** restaurant. You can't miss its cool blue neon sign.

PARKS OF SANTO DOMINGO

Jardín Botánico Nacional Dr. Rafael M. Moscoso

The most beautiful and serene natural place in the city of Santo Domingo, and a must-visit for nature lovers, is the Jardín Botánico Nacional Dr. Rafael M. Moscoso, located in the far northwestern part of the city. This particular location, squeezed between the old neighborhood of Arroyo Hondo and Los Jardínes, has a little elevation and seems to catch a cool breeze every afternoon, thus making it a pleasant place to plan a picnic or quiet walk through the 2.5 million square meters of gardens, shaded walks, pools, fountains, and forests. There are so many wonderful things about the gardens that it's hard to know where to begin. Perhaps the greatest surprise is the meticulous care with which the garden itself is tended and the serenity the park in-

spires in the visitor. While you might find yourself somewhat pressed by the hubbub of Santo Domingo's two million residents, it's possible to forget you're even in a metropolitan area when you visit the gardens. On most weekdays, the gardens themselves are not very crowded, allowing you even more peace and quiet than usual.

The botanical garden itself was created by public law in 1976, another of Balaguer's miracles. It was named after the botanist who, in 1943, wrote the first catalogue of Hispaniola's flora. The park's emblem is a *guanito* leaf, from a beautiful endemic palm.

The park, located on a hill above the city, was hard hit by Hurricane George. Many trees were downed, facilities wrecked. It is making a slow comeback.

Officially, the park is located on Avenida República de Colombia and is open Tues.–Sun. 9 A.M.–6 P.M. (tel. 809/567-6211 or 809/567-6213). Unofficially, if you're driving a car, go up Abraham Lincoln until you get to a tricky and confusing roundabout, bear right on John F. Kennedy, which eventually becomes Avenida De Los Próceres. From there you can see the garden's hilly confines, at which point you'll hit Avenida República de Colombia and the entrance of the gardens on the right. Of course, if you have no heart for driving, a taxi driver can take you there from anywhere in the city for about US$5. By bus, it's Route 6 on Winston Churchill. During the week there aren't many taxis in the area, but the ticket booth will gladly telephone one to take you back to your hotel. Admission for adults is only RD$10 (RD$5 for children). Once inside you can look downhill and see the bookstore and train station where you can catch a miniature train (RD$10) for a 30-minute guided tour (in Spanish) around the grounds. It's a good way to get oriented. Of course, the romantically inclined can hire a horse-drawn carriage for RD$150, which will take a maximum of four people on an hour-long drive. Included on the grounds are an herbarium and small ecological museum, which cost RD$10 to enter.

On the grounds of the Jardín Botánico Nacional are nine permanent collections, which include bromeliads, ferns, exotic plants, palms, the forest reserve, fancy flowers, cacti and suc-

SANTO DOMINGO'S ORCHIDS

If orchids tickle your fancy, Santo Domingo is the place to experience them. There are hundreds of varieties, in colors ranging from purest white to every shade of violet, red, yellow, green, and even blue. Tiny, insect-like flowers adorn some plants, while others sport huge ruffled blossoms.

In the United States, a flowering orchid plant could set you back US$100. In Santo Domingo you can acquire one for under RD$100. If you are confident in your gardening and nurturing abilities, a non-flowering common species may cost between RD$175 and RD$500. You can pay as much as you like for an orchid, if you decide to become a connoisseur.

These prices are cheap when you consider that the blossoms on a plant in bloom may last for months, whereas cut flowers have a duration of only days.

The Jardín Botánico in Arroyo Hondo has an orchid garden which is open to the public. Once a year, they have an orchid competition and sale, at which many beautiful plants are available for reasonable prices. Check with the Jardín for dates and times.

Orquideario Arroyo Hondo (tel. 809/565-1930 or 809/567-1351) has extensive greenhouses. It is difficult to find, on Calle J.A. Polanco Billini in Arroyo Hondo. Drive northwest on Camino Chiquito from the extension of Av. Lope de Vega. You will see a pharmacy on the right and a landscaping store called Walpa on the left (where a few orchids are also available). Turn left and watch the houses to the right-hand side of the road. The sign is not very obvious. Beautiful cut-flower arrangements are also available from these shops.

For more information on orchids, contact the Sociedad Dominicana de Orquideología (the Dominican Orchideology Society). It is a nonprofit organization dedicated to encouraging the study and cultivation of orchids, promoting research on and the conservation of native species, and providing a forum for the exchange of information. Their meetings are held the second Wednesday of each month in the Museo Nacional de Historia Natural in the Plaza de la Cultura.

culents, herbs, and endemic plants. In addition to the permanent exhibits, the gardens also host several special events, including spring shows, Earth Day, Tree Day, Environmental Day, and some spectacular orchid exhibits. Check the local newspapers for events. Probably the most colorful exhibit is the orchid hill, which features most of the flowering orchids you are likely to see on your trip to the Dominican Republic. Equally impressive is the forest reserve—really nothing more than a huge hillside that has not been disturbed by the city, leaving it lush and green and spectacular. There is a little snack bar where you can get a cold drink and a sandwich.

Parque Zoológico Nacional
While you're in the northwestern part of Santo Domingo, you can visit the Parque Zoológico Nacional (National Zoo), located on Paseo de los Reyes Católicos. Zoos are, in my opinion, iffy propositions. When the animals are poorly cared for and the grounds dirty, visiting a zoo is worse than anything I know. Fortunately, however, the zoo in Santo Domingo seems to take pride in caring for the animals and the grounds, and the areas of captivity are quite beautiful. The zoo covers about 371 acres (1.5 million square meters) and is designed to maximize open country for animals to move around in. Many of the natural environments have an African feel, and there are plenty of aviaries, ponds, and grasslands. The aviary features the palmchat and Hispaniolan parrot (native species), while the serpent and reptile house features the native hutia and solenodon, which you'll never see in the wild. Pink flamingos, native to the area, seem to come and go in complete freedom. From all I've heard and seen, the Santo Domingo Parque Zoológico Nacional is one of the best and largest zoos in Latin America.

If you're at the Jardín Botánico Nacional, just turn north on Avenida Jardín Botánico when you leave the gate and take the second right on Avenida de los Caciques. It becomes Paseo de los Reyes Católicos. Surrounding the zoo is one of the poorest neighborhoods in the city, so be prepared for a jolt of reality. The zoo is open

Tues.–Sat. 9 A.M.–5 P.M. (tel. 809/562-3149). Admission runs only RD$6 for adults, less for children. An enjoyable 15-minute train ride (good for orientation) costs RD$5. The zoo also has a souvenir shop, snack bar, and rest areas.

Parque Mirador del Sur– Paseo de los Indios

In the seaside neighborhood of Mirador del Sur stretches the long and narrow park called Parque Mirador del Sur–Paseo de los Indios, located between Avenida Anacaona and Avenida Mirador del Sur. You can't miss the park because it runs parallel to Winston Churchill and the Malecón and is situated on a high limestone terrace overlooking the beautiful Caribbean Sea. It's a great place to observe the citizens of Santo Domingo as they jog, walk, rollerskate, fly kites, picnic, and watch sunsets. You can rent a boat on the park's small man-made lake, and there are bicycle trails if you're so inclined. A remarkable variety of Hispaniola's native trees and shrubs have been planted all through the park, and the western section is dominated by fascinating cacti and aloe. Various sculptures adorn the natural wonders as well, including the *Fountain of Poetry,* by Spanish artist Juan de Avalo.

Sometimes at three o'clock in the afternoon, or thereabouts, several neighborhoods in the area of the park become infested with police and *guardias* riding in armored vehicles. That's when you might catch a glimpse of Balaguer taking a walk in the Parque Mirador del Sur, a practice on which he insists (at press time, anyway) even in his 90s.

For more commonsensical fun, you might visit the Cueva del Paseo de los Indios, the largest of several caves at the park's ocean edge, formed as wave action undermines the weak limestone cliffs. One of the caves has been transformed into an underground restaurant called Mesón de la Cava, another into a popular disco and nightclub called Guacara Taina, which also features folkloric dances on selected nights. This disco and nightclub, located 33 meters underground, is huge, accommodating 2,000 couples. Sinkholes like these sometimes house bats as well as disco dancers. During the day, food stands and roving vendors ensure that you're always within a stone's throw of *coco frío* or an empanada.

Faro a Colón (Columbus Memorial Lighthouse)

Three bridges go east and west across the Río Ozama, the main one being El Puente, or the Duarte Bridge. Of course, anywhere in the Colonial District you can see the famous (or infamous) Faro a Colón, which seems to loom up from the terraces above the river. At night, when there is a clear sky and the electricity is working, a bright white cross is projected into the black sky. The white cross can be seen for 60 miles around the city of Santo Domingo and is created by 149 Xenon Skytrack lasers. Inside the huge cruciform building are six museums, exhibition halls, and a library, all dedicated to Columbus.

The germ of the idea for the Columbus Lighthouse probably originated in the middle of the 19th century, when Dominican historian Antonio Delmonte y Tejada called for the construction of a colossal statue of Columbus. The idea kicked around until 1923, when the Fifth International American Conference in Santiago de Chile resolved that a lighthouse should be built in Santo Domingo. In 1929, the Pan American Union organized an architectural contest to find a designer for the monument. A total of 1,926 architects from 48 countries sent 445 designs. Ultimately, the winning design was by an unknown British architecture student, Joseph Gleave, who, at age 23, had designed absolutely nothing before in his life. Unfortunately, the project had no funding at the time, and it seemed that every move made in connection with raising funds met with failure. Ground was finally broken under the Trujillo regime in 1939, but the outbreak of World War II interrupted all work.

After the war, nuclear energy had become a worldwide topic, with particular emphasis placed on its "peaceful" use by Western countries, particularly the United States. In typical bombastic fashion, Trujillo hatched a plan to make the lighthouse project an illustration of atomic energy's useful purposes—without, of course, actually using nuclear energy at all. Thus, in 1948, some sticks of dynamite were placed in what the public and press were told was a nuclear excavation site. A blind archbishop was brought by to publically bless this bold new venture in nuclear energy, and Trujillo saw to it that a professor from Puerto Rico was nearby, probing with a Geiger counter to give the appearance of some sort of nuclear connection to the event. Unfortunately, nearby vibrations set off the dynamite unexpectedly, and the farcical celebration of nuclear energy went up in a puff of smoke. Finally, after 20 years of waiting, the architect Gleave returned to England, where he died before the lighthouse opened in 1992, for the quincentennial of the Admiral's arrival.

The real work of building the lighthouse began under Balaguer, who wished for something spectacular to serve as a beacon for tourism and investment in the Dominican Republic. Nobody knows for sure how much the lighthouse cost to construct, but estimates vary between 70 and 250 million dollars, a staggering sum for a poor country. As inauguration day came closer and closer, the elaborate ceremonies planned began to collapse. Of the notables invited for October 12, 1992, only Carlos Menem of Argentina attended the dedication. Even the Pope disassociated himself from the festivities, though he did conduct a Mass from behind the lighthouse the day before the inauguration. When Balaguer's sister suffered a fatal heart attack after visiting the lighthouse, Balaguer canceled his appearance at the dedication. Most importantly, arising from all the hoopla was the feeling that Balaguer had betrayed the Dominican people. Many of those who lived along the roads to and from the site were ejected from their homes during the inauguration, their shanty huts hidden behind a 10-foot wall specially constructed for the occasion. Scattered violence erupted, and a few shootings connected with political protests took place as well. Even today, Dominicans have mixed feelings about the lighthouse.

Perhaps the lighthouse's main attraction is the fact that a huge, elaborate marble and bronze tomb of Columbus lies just inside the main entrance. Of course, it is debatable whether the navigator's remains are actually in the tomb, because another church in Seville, Spain, makes the same claim. Down the hallways on either side you'll see huge mahogany doors with brass handles, and behind these are museums and libraries, mainly commemorating the life and exploits of Columbus, though one museum details underwater archaeology and another 15th-century ceramics. A visit to the lighthouse is definitely worthwhile, though the building itself is rather ungainly. You might want to scout the area in combination with another excursion to sights across the river, such as a day at the race track, aquarium, or beach.

THE CURSE OF COLUMBUS

Columbus is a strange kind of national hero for Dominicans. For centuries, it has been considered bad luck to speak his name, so Dominicans usually referred to Columbus as The Discoverer or The Admiral. Should a Dominican mention his name, he has committed a *fucú*, inviting bad luck and misfortune. Dominicans even use "¡Colón!" (the Spanish name for Columbus) as an expletive, the same way English speakers might say, "Shit!"

During the celebrations leading up to the quincentenary, government-sponsored propaganda tried to drown out the superstition surrounding Columbus's name. However, it achieved only limited success. Dominicans prayed that they would not be cursed, and some government officials secretly refused to attend the inauguration of the famous lighthouse of Columbus.

In fact, Dominicans claim a *fucú* has already cursed some events connected with the Columbus Lighthouse itself. For example, in 1937, Trujillo sent three planes on a European tour to raise money for the building of the lighthouse. Named the *Niña,* the *Pinta,* and the *Santa María*—after Columbus's ships, of course—the three planes encountered fog and bad weather in Europe, and two of them crashed. At a ceremony in 1946 honoring the 450th anniversary of the founding of Santo Domingo, an earthquake shook the city when the urn containing Columbus's ashes was opened. During the 1940s, a celebrated politician was pricked by a Columbus medal he had just been awarded and soon died of infection.

The next time you say the name "Columbus," just snap your fingers, make the sign of the cross, and exclaim *"¡zafa!"* Maybe you'll remedy your mistake.

Parque Mirador del Este and Parque Tres Ojos

The Faro a Colón is located in what's officially called the Parque Mirador del Este, and you can't miss this green space because it's on the main road to the Santo Domingo airport. It is located in a quiet residential area, and is nice for long walks, jogs, and quiet evenings of sunset watching. What you can't miss in this park is the Parque Tres Ojos (National Park of the Three Eyes), which is toward the eastern side of the park itself. This best-known of Santo Domingo's natural attractions consists of three main *cenotes,* or large limestone sinkholes, carved by the wave action against the limestone terrace that borders the Caribbean. This park is open every day from 8 A.M. to 5 P.M., and there's a small admission fee of RD$15.

If you can forge your way through a hailstorm of vendors and hawkers you'll find the three sinks, each of which has a different water environment. One sink holds fresh water, another salt water, and the third sulfur water. Once you're through the vendors you can take stairs down to the center of the sinks, and walk around and even take a small boat through an underground passage to an outside sinkhole. (The trip is an extra RD$5.) The sinks are cool and refreshing, lined with stalagmites and stalactites, and rimmed with natural vegetation. The best time to go is early in the morning when the tourists haven't started arriving and the day is still mild. Surrounding the sink area is a path along which you can wander for a glimpse of a fourth sinkhole, which looks like a volcano crater.

Acuario Nacional

While you're across the river you should not fail to see the impressive Acuario Nacional (National Aquarium), another of the Balaguer administration's controversial and expensive additions to the tourist front of Santo Domingo (open Tues.–Sun. 9:30 A.M.–6 P.M., admission RD$20). The aquarium is located south of Parque Mirador between Calle Cuarta and Avenida 28 de Enero (tel. 809/592-1509) on Avenida España in the Sans Souci district. In addition to a large collection of tropical fish, the aquarium has an underwater walkway where you can be cruised by a big shark. Impressive, too, is the turtle-breeding project, where you can see endangered slider turtles. The aquarium is on the ocean, surrounded by a large tree-studded park, and is a pleasant place to rest and have a bite to eat. Recently the aquarium scientists rescued a small motherless manatee; you might inquire about its whereabouts.

Parque Nacional Submarino La Caleta

Farther east, about 22 km from Santo Domingo, is the Parque Nacional Submarino La Caleta (La Caleta Submarine National Park), which combines a world-class scuba-diving area and an onshore ethnological and archaeological park containing Taíno artifacts. At its deepest, La Caleta is 180 meters deep, with an irregular topography and three well-defined terraces extending parallel to the coast. The depth of the levels varies between 10 and 50 meters, and there are a number of reefs where multicolored fish find refuge.

The main attraction is the *Hickory,* a submerged boat purposely sunk in 1984. Get to La Caleta by taking the airport highway and forking to the right along the shore. The onshore portion of the park contains six Taíno graves in a thatched-roof museum and a small beach from which scuba divers leave for the submarine portion of the park.

Admission is free, though you'll pay your dues to hawkers and vendors. Many artists set up easels here, and you'll have the opportunity to buy paintings (usually cheap primitives). Divers should outfit themselves prior to arrival at La Caleta, though numerous Dominicans are available to take you to reef locations in small fishing boats.

Malecón

Strolling down the Malecón at sunset is highly recommended as a soul soother. On almost any evening at about six o'clock, you can see huge cumulus clouds building up over the Caribbean. Sometimes the colors and smells are fabulous as waiters get ready for the outdoor diners who arrive throughout the evening. Just walking and sitting on a bench is guaranteed to end a day pleasantly, especially if you dose yourself with white rum as you go. At the far eastern end of the Malecón you'll see a statue of Fray Antón de Montecrios, a gift from

Mexico in October 1982. Montecrios boldly stood up for the Taínos during the initial phase of Spanish conquest. There are two obelisks farther west, one commemorating—believe it or not—the payment of the national debt to the United States in the 1930s, the second celebrating the renaming of the city to Ciudad Trujillo during the height of the dictator's rule. People in Santo Domingo call the structure the *Obelisco Macho,* for obvious reasons. On one side of the street is the Parque Eugenio María de Hostos, of 1940 design, now a little tumbledown and dirty. Mostly the Malecón is for strolling and evening dining outdoors, though you can stop in at one of the stupendous luxury hotels that line Avenida George Washington (as the Malecón is officially named) to gamble or dance.

Museo de Trujillo
Elsewhere in the city is a small Trujillo museum, the Museo de Trujillo, at Store 7 in Plaza Criolla, which houses memorabilia of the dictator. More interesting by far is the **Museo Prehispánico,** at Avenida San Martin 279, near the intersection of Máximo Gómez and 27 de Febrero, which houses pre-Columbian artifacts and is open Mon.–Sat. 8 A.M.–noon. If you're headed out the Duarte Highway, you'll probably pass the Centro de Los Heroes on a traffic circle which was the setting for the 1955–1956 Fair of Peace and Fraternity, a monstrosity of a gathering on which Trujillo is alleged to have spent nearly $40 million. This old collection of buildings now houses government offices. Whatever you do, don't go out of your way to see this Plaza: it's hot, dirty, crowded most of the time, and not particularly inspiring.

Western Outskirts
Persons with adventure in their hearts might choose to attempt a visit to two obscure sights on the western edges of Santo Domingo. The first adventure is a visit to **Casa Palave,** a 17th-century country house that sits on top of a small hill overlooking a town of the same name. The Palave house has been partially restored, but there are no guides or signs on the premises. You're free, however, to wander from room to room. The original house had two stories, but

the roof and second story are missing, though the walls are completely intact. To get there, go to Parque Independencia and take Avenida 27 de Febrero for about 14km, then turn left on the road to Manoguayabo and go straight until you pass the National Police Operations Center. After crossing a bridge, turn right after another kilometer on a dirt road that may bear signs for Anetilla Aramilla and Repuestos Julisa. Down this road three km you'll find the Palave house.

Even harder to find is **Casa Engombe,** a 16th-century gothic manor house and sugar plantation. As with Casa Palave, the second story of the house is missing, and almost no restoration has been done, though the walls and sills of the windows remain. With foliage overgrowing the house and grounds, one can almost imagine what it was like while the house was in use as the center of a huge sugar plantation on the Haina River. After being owned by several Spanish officials, the property eventually came to be owned by Héctor Trujillo, the

face tree

dictator's brother. In 1962, the land passed to the government and then to the Autonomous University of Santo Domingo. To get there, start from Parque Independencia and turn right off the traffic circle just beyond the government building called INESPRE. At the next roundabout, turn right at the third road between Codetel on the right and Industria de Pintura on the left. This road ends in a T, where

you should bear right at a small *colmado* and go two km until you see a sign for USAD. The grounds constitute an agricultural research station, and there is usually university personnel who will be glad to see you. If you don't spot anyone around, go straight down the dirt track for 1.5km and turn right until you reach the ruins. It is an undeveloped place, and there is no admission charge.

ACCOMMODATIONS

Santo Domingo is not just a tourist town. It is, in fact, an active, bustling, busy city of two million people, a major port, industrial zone, business center, and cultural entrepôt for a huge area of the Caribbean. What this means for visitors is that there are literally hundreds and hundreds of hotels from which to choose, in all sizes, shapes, and locations. No matter where you decide to stay in the city, whether along the Malecón at a luxury hotel, or in a commercial hotel in the Naco near the Plaza de la Cultura, or even in the Colonial District itself, this oldest continuously inhabited European city in the Americas will make you feel at home almost instantly.

Santo Domingo hotels cater to tourists from all over the world and also host businesspeople, conventions, and locals on holiday. This means two things for the traveler. In the first place it means that prices at hotels aren't as subject to seasonal change as hotels that rely strictly on the tourist trade. Second, it means that you can *always* find a room, sometimes without worrying about a reservation, except during Christmas, Easter, and the very high tourist months of January and February. Even then, reservations aren't *much* of a problem.

For purposes of pricing hotel rooms in the Dominican Republic, consider under US$30 inexpensive, US$30–80 moderate, US$80-100 expensive, and US$100+ luxury.

Be aware of two important factors when selecting and booking rooms. First, many prices are seasonal and drop in the off-season (between March and October). Thus, an expensive room in winter (the high season) can become moderate in May. It is even possible to find off-season bargains in moderately priced rooms, especially at the lower end of the price

scale. Most inexpensive rooms are always inexpensive and aren't particularly subject to seasonal rates.

Secondly, rates tend to vary depending upon how the room is booked. Many tourist agents can find you cheaper rates than those advertised or can negotiate cheaper rates for you, based upon the length of your stay. Some tourist agents are simply good at talking down hotel managers. Finally, it is sometimes possible to bargain with clerks and managers, especially at smaller hotels. If you speak Spanish, by all means ask politely if cheaper rates are available, and maintain a friendly attitude. You might find your lower-end moderate rate dropping to inexpensive.

It's always a good idea—especially if traveling on a restricted budget—to call ahead and verify rates. The prices listed herein are up-to-date as of press time but may have fluctuated depending on the season, economy, festivals, or whim of the owner.

Most hotels in Santo Domingo fall into the moderate or expensive range, but you'll find inexpensive and dirt-cheap accommodations scattered about the city as well. I've listed some such places in this book. To dig out the remaining cheapies, either ask around (you'll need some Spanish) or consult the daily *Listín Diario.*

Perhaps the most important choice you have to make about hotels in Santo Domingo is not how much you want to pay, but in what part of town you wish to stay. I'm assuming here that nobody would voluntarily want to stay in a grimy industrial district miles from the central part of the city, but if that's your choice, pick up the Codetel Yellow Pages and a map of the city and go for it. Instead, I've focused on Santo Domingo's traditional lodging choices: the Colonial District, the Malecón, and the neighborhoods of Gazcue and Naco.

Since Santo Domingo is so spread out, wandering around town and hoping to find a place to stay is not a good idea unless you're committed to staying in one certain area and arrive there early in the day to begin your hunt. It's better to reserve something beforehand; you can always move on if you're unhappy. Wherever you stay, remember to add about 23% room tax to your price calculations.

Apart-Hotels

Unless you have special dietary needs that make it necessary for you to have access to a kitchen, it doesn't make sense to rent an apart-hotel if you'll only be staying in Santo Domingo for a few days. You'll be paying extra for things you don't need, like towels, sheets, utensils, and laundry service. However, if you'll be in Santo Domingo for a month or more, then apart-hotels—with their long-term rates and kitchen facilities—might be the way to go. If you stay for several months, you can usually negotiate an even better rate.

GAYLORD DOLD

Calle Hostos, Colonial District, Santo Domingo

More Alternatives

If staying east across the river sounds like your cup of tea, avoid the motels on the Las Américas Highway—they're mainly sex stations. Nice, though, is the **Hotel Acuarium,** (Calle 11 esq. 2, Av. España, tel. 809/593-4484), which has 54 rooms, a pool, bar, and restaurant. It's also near a golf course and Boca Chica beach. Rates are US$50, more during high season.

Some people prefer to stay in Boca Chica itself when they're in the Santo Domingo area. Full of tourist hotels, Boca Chica is about 30 minutes from downtown Santo Domingo and served by excellent public transportation.

THE COLONIAL DISTRICT

My favorite area in Santo Domingo is the Colonial District. It's the heart of what's most important about Santo Domingo to me—history and culture. Many of the district's buildings date from the 16th and 17th centuries. The streets are narrow, and there are many interesting cafes, bars, and restaurants. The narrow streets also tend to choke down traffic when evening comes, making the district much quieter than other parts of Santo Domingo, which tend to buzz and buzz long into the night. Several lovely art galleries make their homes in the Colonial District too.

The district's confined nature does, however, limit your selection of hotels a bit. You will find no modern luxury hotels here, for example, no hotels that look like something out of a tourist brochure, and no hotels that classify as expensive. But there are wonderful hotels here indeed, as well as a sprinkling of inexpensive places.

Inexpensive

If you're looking for inexpensive accommodations with access to the Colonial District, you'll have to choose a basic hotel on the fringes of the area. As inexpensive as you'll get in the Colonial District are two pensións on El Conde: **Pensión Dominicana** (El Conde 454, tel. 809/689-0722) and **Pensión Gilette** (El Conde 505, tel. 809/685-7815). At Avenida Mella 609, just uphill from the district, is the **Hotel La Fama** (tel. 809/689-1275), where you can rub shoulders with Haitian traders and pay cheap rates.**The Benita** is a very basic hotel with bath or without, located on Benita Gonzalez very near the market. Cost is US$5–10. The **Radiante,** on Avenida Duarte between Mella and Benita Gonzalez, runs about US$10 with bath. As you begin to scout around the Mercado Modelo area you'll see dozens of cheap hotels, most of which are little more than flop houses or places where prostitutes take their johns. They have loud music and cockroaches —at no extra cost. If you can stand it all, you can go cheap. All of the ultra-inexpensive hotels with good access to the Colonial District are located on or near Avenida Duarte or Calle Benito González in the Villa Francisca neighborhood near the market. This part of Santo Domingo could be called downtown. It's noisy, crowded, and hot, but it *is* cheap. Try the **Luna del Norte** for clean rooms and friendly service at about US$20 (Benita González 89, tel. 809/687-0124). Close to the sea is the **Montesino** (Jose Gabriel García III, tel. 809/688-3346), which is near the Malecón and overlooks the Montesino statue across the way. Its few basic rooms with shared bath and fans go for about US$20. It isn't bad for longer stays when you can negotiate a price and use the kitchen. Just up the street from the Hotel Comercial on El Conde is the inexpensive **Hotel Aida** (El Conde 474, tel. 809/685-7692, fax 221-9393), at the corner of Espaillat, which has a dozen or so rooms available for around US$25—less if you don't desire air-conditioning. Given its location above a record store and on El Conde, you'll have to put up with some noise to get the good price.

The **Hotel Independencia** (Estrelleta 267 near Arzobispo Nouel and Parque Independencia, tel. 809/686-1663) offers recently renovated rooms and a roof terrace, art exhibits, and moderate (US$30) rates. Being near Parque Independencia makes this hotel both convenient and noisy, but it's also within easy walking distance of the heart of the Colonial District and the Malecón and its gambling and dining.

Moderate

Moving into the moderate range, the strictly functional **Hotel Comercial** (Calle El Conde 201, corner of Hostos, tel. 809/682-2814, fax 809/221-8207), has 75 basic but clean rooms with air-

conditioning and baths. Prices average around US$30–40 for a double, with the quietest rooms located higher up in the building. It offers a cafeteria, but you'll do better to choose another restaurant in the area. The Commercial is kind of antiseptic, and even though El Conde is a wonderful street, it is also a very noisy street being near Parque Independencia.

Considerably more downtown and consequently not quite as convenient for the Colonial District is the **Royal Hotel** at Avenida Duarte and Teniente Amado García (tel. 809/686-5852, fax 809/686-6536), which has 64 rooms with bath and phone for US$30–40, most with air-conditioning. The Royal is in a bustling working-class neighborhood that is very real.

The **Hostal Nicolás Nader** (tel. 809/687-6674, fax 809/688-0757) is, in my opinion, the best value in the whole Colonial District. At the corner of Luperón and Duarte, it stands about two blocks north of El Conde in the heart of the Colonial District. This extremely pleasant and winningly friendly hotel is located in a 16th-century colonial building that has been completely refurbished and transformed into an art gallery, which means that you are surrounded on all sides by lovely paintings from all over the Caribbean and Latin America. Organized around a central skylight plaza filled with tropical plants and palms are about 20 rooms, each with private bath, high ceilings, and air-conditioning. Rooms are priced around US$40 d. The staff is extraordinarily friendly and will fix you breakfast in the morning and serve you coffee when you're pooped out in the afternoon. There's a small bar where you can get a drink and watch Dominican cable TV if you wish, though you'll probably be happier sitting in the open air admiring paintings and mixing with the clientele, who tend to be a delightful combination of touring Dominicans, Puerto Ricans, and other foreigners. The Nader is spotlessly clean, so the occasional green lizard scooting up the lovely pink limestone inner wall seems welcome. A *colmado* across the street will sell you an evening bottle of rum, and a fruit vendor sets up out front for pineapples and bananas.

Another possible choice in the moderate range is **Hotel David's** (Arz. Nouel 308, tel. 809/685-9121, fax 809/688-8056), on a quiet street. The rooms on the second floor are basic, with TV and refrigerator, and are priced at around US$40.

One block from the Nader is the equally classy **Hotel Palacio** (106 Calle Duarte, near Salomé Ureña, tel. 809/682-4730, fax 809/687-5535). This colonial building once served as residence to relatives of Buenaventura Baez, five-time Dominican president in the mid-19th century. Now a two-story hotel located in the middle of the block, the Palacio has 10 rooms for about US$50. Small and intimate, it has no restaurant but does offer quiet and a certain German-owned efficiency and elegance. Rooms have baths, and the hotel has a generator for blackouts.

Best for overall elegance and historical resonance, the **Hotel Palacio Nicolás de Ovando** (Calle de las Damas 55, tel. 809/221-4542, fax 809/688-5170) is right in the center of an area called La Atarazana, near shops, parks, museums, and the Ozama River. In an old building built by Governor Ovando in 1502–09, the structure has a tower overlooking the river and 45 rooms which vary in size and ambience. Rooms average about US$70, and all have bath and air-conditioning with a generator for power outages. It's a classy address and very quiet for Santo Domingo, with a restaurant called the Extramadura open every day for breakfast, lunch, and dinner. This is not a resort hotel in any sense (no hotel in the Colonial District is), and there is no pool or casino. But there are public rooms with tapestries, bronze mirrors, and heavy Spanish furnishings, and an excellent staff.

Francés, at the corner of Mercedes and Arz Meriño, is a newly refurbished 16th-century house with a good restaurant, a courtyard, and rooms decorated with period furniture (tel. 809/684-9200). Rates are US$75, slightly more during the high season.

Apart-Hotels

Most of Santo Domingo's apart-hotels are located around Naco and Gazcue—areas that are supposed to be, in some sense, residential. With that said, the big exception is the aforementioned **Hotel Palacio Nicolás de Ovando,** in the heart of the Colonial District at Calle de las Damas 55. Each of the seven regular rooms has a kitchenette and minibar, so you could conceivably set up here for a long time, though it would be expensive. The hotel features a pleasant inner courtyard, tourist guide service, and fax. Another place for apartments in the Colonial District is **La Arecada** (Calle Arz. Meriño 360, tel. 809/686-7456), where you'll find spartan accommodations for around US$15 per night, with discounts for longer stays.

THE MALECÓN

"The Malecón" is what the Dominicans call Avenida George Washington and refers to the fact that it is a seaside boulevard. Santo Domingo is known for its expensive tourist hotels, which line the Caribbean Sea and generally offer luxury accommodation, first-class food, casino action, swimming pools, and, quite often, evening entertainment and dancing. Tourists come here from Puerto Rico and all over Latin America to holiday and shop, so you can meet a lively variety of people, including hookers, who sometimes crowd the street on Saturday nights.

Best of all, staying on the Malecón doesn't mean you give up anything about Santo Domingo, because the Colonial District is only a few blocks away and easily walkable. Many of Santo Domingo's top-of-the-line restaurants operate on the Malecón or are connected with Malecón hotels, so for fine dining, the Malecón is a logical choice as well. And though traffic tends to be hectic on Avenida George Washington at rush hours and especially frenetic during Christmas and Easter, things quiet down at night.

While the Malecón is the place to go for Caribbean luxury, ocean views, superb service, and sports like tennis and swimming, that's not to say there aren't a few inexpensive and moderate hotels in the Malecón area. There are, though they tend to be on side streets, away from the ocean. Here's a selected list of Malecón-area lodgings, starting from least expensive:

Inexpensive

Palmeras del Caribe (Cambronal 1, corner of Malecón, tel. 809/689-3872) has small but decently attractive rooms with black-and-white TVs and a friendly staff. Rates are around US$25. Also in the $25 range is the **Ocean Inn** (Av. Independence 654, tel. 809/689-9148), which has large, clean rooms that you may find rather stark.

Jaragua Renaissance
Resort and Casino,
Malecón,
Santo Domingo

There are restaurants nearby and you can walk to the Malecón and the Colonial District easily. Another choice is the newly opened **Hotel Restaurant la Casona Dorada** (Av. Independencia 255, tel. 809/221-3535, fax 809/682-1832), which is small but rather elegant in its own way.

Moderate

One block from the Malecón at Avenida Máximo Gómez 16 is the **Hotel Continental,** which looks rather plain and offers 100 rooms, some suites, a bar, international restaurant, cocktail lounge, disco, and pool. Only a few rooms have an ocean view. Around the same price range is the **Sea View** (Av. Cambronal at Malecón, tel. 809/688-3979), which stands behind a green and white facade and has clean apartments with kitchens and no style at all. It costs around US$40 a night, but for longer-term stays it can work.

A modest tourist hotel at the top end of the moderate price range is the **Hotel El Napolitano** (Av. George Washington 51, tel. 809/687-1131, fax 809/687-6814), which features 72 comfortable rooms with bath, television, air-conditioning, and sea view. Rooms run about US$60 s or d and include free parking. Breakfast is US$6 extra. This is a "basic" tourist hotel catering to Dominicans on holiday, which means there can be a lot of action around the disco and second-floor pool. There's a terrace that stays busy, too. Don't mind the decor, which is a little worn.

Expensive

The **Melía Santo Domingo,** at Av. George Washington 365 (tel. 809/221-6666, fax 809/687-8150), boasts 260 luxury rooms with cable TV and a good view if you're above the third floor. You'll find a gym, a sauna, a spa, tennis courts, and three restaurants, along with a casino and disco. Rates are US$75–100 off season and US$90–120 s, US$100–130 d in winter. Breakfast costs US$8 extra, and there is 24-hour room service. A first-class value.

Three smaller hotels on the Malecón are very nice, and a good value in the expensive range. **La Casona Corada** (Independencia 256, tel. 809/221-3535) is away from the bustle of the main road and has the usual amenities including restaurant and bar, laundry, and pool. The **Wellington** (Independencia 304, tel. 809/682-4525) is a smaller hotel where the service is friendly and the rooms are spacious and clean. At Llúberes 8, the **Maison Gatreaux** is near the Colonial District with large rooms. It charges extra for cable TV.

Luxury

This **Hotel Santo Domingo** is an interesting luxury hotel set slightly back off the Malecón, in leafy seclusion from the hustle of George Washington. Owned and operated by Premier Resorts and Hotels, it is located on Avenida Independencia at Abraham Lincoln. The Hotel Santo Domingo (tel. 809/221-1511 or U.S. tel.

800/877-3643, fax 809/535-4050/4052) is a stylish stucco creation designed by William Cox, with rooms (220 of them) by Oscar de la Renta. It seems to attract Latin American notables, as well as the cream of Dominican society. The hotel's two three-story structures are covered by lattice, and rooms face either the sea or an inner garden. You can dine at the El Alcázar or the gourmet El Cafetal or have lunch at the poolside Las Brisas. The piano bar Las Palmas is supposed to be charmingly hip. Use of all the facilities is included, as are three lighted tennis courts. Rates run US$115–130 all year, more for an "Excel Club" suite.

On the other side of the Jaragua from the Sheraton, at Av. George Washington 218, is the luxurious, yet understated **V Centenario Continental** (tel. 809/221-1889, fax 809/221-2020), on the corner of Pasteur. Somehow all 230 rooms and 30 suites in this spacious hotel face the sea. Facilities include restaurants, pool, spa, tennis, squash, disco, casino, and piano bar. The slot machines in the lobby are a bit much, but this is a friendly place, if getting a bit rundown.

If you go strictly by price, the top of the line is the **Jaragua Renaissance Resort and Casino,** (tel. 809/221-2222, fax 809/686-528, U.S. tel. 800/228-9898, Canada tel. 800/272-6232) located right next door to the Sheraton on 14 acres of lushly manicured grounds at 367 Av. George Washington. Judging by all the facilities available, this hotel is the top of the line too, with 355 rooms with marble bathrooms, huge makeup mirrors, 24-hour room service, two separate towers of rooms and suites, and an exclusive "Garden Estate." There are four lighted tennis courts, a spa, a pool with 12 private cabanas and what's called the largest (20,000 square feet) casino in the Caribbean. Believe it or not, the resort boasts five restaurants, including the Manhattan Grill, Figaro, and a Las Vegas–style showroom called La Fiesta. Rates range US$190–230 in winter, US$115–145 off season. Suites run around US$610 winter, less off season.

IN THE NEIGHBORHOODS

Finally, many people prefer to stay in the neighborhood hotels of Gazcue and Naco, which offer proximity to the contemporary cultural activities in the Plaza de la Cultura as well as shopping at high-fashion boutiques and elegant art galleries. The atmosphere actually reminds me a little of modern-day Spain. Though a 20-minute taxi ride from the Colonial District, and really too far from the sea to walk, the neighborhoods are authentic Dominican places, away from the standard tourist grind, and some offer service and comfort equal to the best of the Malecón's tourist hotels. In addition, the hotels of Gazcue and Naco are more a part of the modern city, a place where Dominicans and Latin Americans living modern lives tend to stay. Consequently, these hotels are good spots to meet people who aren't just other tourists.

Of course, Gazcue and Naco feature some inexpensive hotels as well. Before locating in one of these, check it out first to make sure you like the location, the available transportation, and the feel. It's possible, for instance, that a few of the hotels in Gazcue might leave you feeling a bit isolated. Still, staying in the neighborhoods can be very satisfying. It gives you a feel for the pulse of Santo Domingo.

Inexpensive

There are some inexpensive-to-moderate places to stay in Gazcue. One of the cheapest—and most basic—is the **Alameda** in Calle Cervantes opposite the Hotel Cervantes (tel. 809/685-5121, US$30). Also inexpensive are **La Mansión** (Calle Danae 26, tel. 809/686-5562) and **Hotel La Residence** (Calle Danae 64, tel. 809/412-7298), which have modest rooms in the US$20–30 range.

Moderate

In the moderate range is the **Hotel El Señorial** (Calle Pte. Vinci Burgos 58, tel. 809/687-4367, fax 809/687-0600), which has air-conditioned rooms and a pleasant dining room. The place seems to be social and relaxed and is near the obelisk in the Malecón.

The **Hotel Cumbre** is a good example of a hotel that might cause you to feel either charmed or isolated. Located in a neighborhood near the Presidential Palace, the Hotel Cumbre is definitely off the beaten track. The rooms are modest, the furniture tired, but the restaurant serves honest Dominican fare (Dr. Delgado 206, tel. 809/689-0863). Another example of this kind of place is the new **Hotel Casa Vapor** (Av. Francia 40 at Dr. Delgado, tel. 809/221-8888, fax 809/686-6216), built to look like a ship and offering nice rooms, a disco, and a restaurant.

Also modestly priced is the **Hotel San Gerónimo and Casino** (Av. Independencia 1076, tel. 809/535-1000), a 72-room facility with pool, cafeteria, and restaurant, all more for locals on holiday. The rooms are basic, and some have kitchenettes.

Smaller, and in the upper-modest range of prices is the **Hotel Commodoro** (Av. Bolivar 193, tel. 809/541-2277), which offers small, clean rooms, a disco, and TV.

An efficient but not spectacular hotel nearby is the family- and business-oriented **Hotel Cervantes** (tel. 809/688-2261, fax 809/686-5754). Its 179 rooms have air-conditioning and TV, and there is a basic 24-hour restaurant. It is moderately priced at around US$40–50 year-round, and it does feature the Bronco Steak House if beef is your thing. There is a pool, and it's possible to walk to the Malecón from here, though it's a healthy, but interesting, hike. This hotel is a good choice for budget-conscious shoppers.

Also on Avenida Sarasota is the **Hotel Delta** (Av. Sarasota 53, tel. 809/535-0800, fax 809/535-5635), which has 75 rooms with air-conditioning and TV, a restaurant, and a solarium. It offers moderate prices in a small tourist-hotel atmosphere, but can be fun because of the pink Antilles architecture and modern decor. Rooms are about US$65 and it is rather far from the city center, but leafy and quiet. Still in the far west is the luxury hotel (or trying to be) **Dominican Fiesta Hotel and Casino** (tel. 809/562-8222, fax 809/562-8738), which, with 316 rooms and prices in the US$80 range, is competitive, though transportation is a problem. The hotel offers everything from tennis to swimming to dancing.

Expensive

The heavyweight hotel in Gazcue is the **Gran Hotel Lina** (tel. 809/563-5000, fax 809/686-5521), which rises 15 floors above the busy surrounding neighborhood jammed with great art galleries, boutiques and shops, restaurants, and businesses. The Lina has played host to American presidents and many celebrities, and lies at the heart of the "real" Santo Domingo; one of the best bakeries in town is right next door. The

hotel has a business-posh atmosphere, tennis courts, pool, shopping arcade, and one of the best and most exclusively expensive restaurants in the Caribbean. Rates are US$73–92 s, $100–112 d in winter, off-season about US$15 less.

Located in the northern reaches of Gazcue, the **Hotel Bella Vista** (tel. 809/508-1800, fax. 809/535-2988) is new. At the corner of 27 Febrero and Rómalo Betancourt (technically in Bella Vista), this small, residential-style hotel has 32 clean, pretty, and comfortable rooms with all the extras like cable TV, whirlpool baths, and air-conditioning. It caters to business people and could be a nice place to meet real Dominicans in a relaxed setting. Rates are US$80 for a double.

Luxury

At least one hotel farther west deserves special attention. **El Embajador Hotel Casino** (Av. Sarasota 65, tel. 809/221-2131 or 800/457-0067, fax 809/532-4494, 280 rooms, 20 suites) was built during the Trujillo years; the dictator had a luxury penthouse where he entertained the ladies, and his son and cronies played polo on the grounds of the old racetrack nearby. The rooms are decorated in French style and cost US$135–160, US$210 for a suite. There are all the usual facilities including eight tennis courts and a swimming pool, as well as a fine Chinese restaurant called the Jade Garden and the deluxe Embassy Club for gourmet dining. Some people consider this hotel the most beautiful in town, even though it's been surrounded by high vines. It certainly has the most spectacular surrounding gardens.

Apart-Hotels

Remember that you should have long-term needs before you take up residence in an apart-hotel. Most of the time that means you'll be in Santo Domingo for a month or more, either on extended holiday or to work or study. (If you can stay for several months, you can usually negotiate a better rate.) That's part of the reason why most apart-hotels are located in and around Naco and Gazcue—they are supposed to be, in some sense, residential.

Apart-hotels dominate the Naco scene. Many locals use them as condos due to the local housing shortage, and if you're going to stay in the Naco, which is pretty far west—away from the sea and the Colonial District—you should have a very good reason. The center of life is the **Plaza Naco Hotel** at the Plaza Naco Mall (Av. Pte. Gonzalez at Av. Tiradentes, tel. 809/541-6226, fax 809/541-7251). With 220 suites, priced at US$90–100 d or US$125–150 for a larger suite (US$15 less in off season), the Naco caters mainly to business travelers who have dealings in the area, which is the financial, insurance, and corporate center of the city. Of course it has a good restaurant, deli, market, and convention facilities. It's a busy place not generally frequented by tourists. Nearby is the **Hotel and Casino Naco** (Av. Tiradentes 22, tel. 809/562-3100), which caters to Caribbean tourists and businesspeople and has three bars, gardens, and a cafeteria.

More traditional apart-hotels are located in the Naco and are cheaper in the long run. The **Apart-Hotel Aladino** (Heriberto Peter 34, tel. 809/567-0144, fax 809/567-0677, US$615/

month) has rooms with air-conditioning or fans. The slightly more expensive **Apart-Hotel Drake** (Augustin Lara 29 near Plaza Naco, tel. 809/567-4227) and **Apart-Hotel Naco** (Av. Tiradentes, tel. 809/541-6226) are also near the Plaza Naco. Going east, you can choose the **Aparta-Hotel Turez** (Av. 27th de Febrero at Av. Winston Churchill, tel. 809/562-5271), which has both studios and one-bedrooms with kitchenettes and also offers a pool and snack bar. The one-bedroom units are in the US$800/month range.

In Gazcue the upscale place is the **Apart-Hotel Plaza Florida** (Av. Bolivar 203, tel. 809/541-3957), which has 32 full-kitchen apartments, a pool (at the nearby Commodoro), fans, phones, and air-conditioning if desired. The rooms run about US$850/month, but ask for long-term discounts. At the same intersection as the Turez is the **Plaza Central** (tel. 809/565-6905), which caters to business travelers and offers "suites," secretary services, and fax.

FOOD

Santo Domingo is a food-lover's paradise. The city boasts a bewildering array of restaurants, many of them serving food equal in quality to fine restaurants anywhere in the world. And, of course, you can find yourself paying world-class prices, too, though even the best restaurants in the city come nowhere near to matching the prices in places like New York, London, or Paris. Dining out at the best restaurants in Santo Domingo is more like splurging in, say, Atlanta or Denver, which means you can get out the door for about US$60, unless you choose to drink wine and liquors.

While most of the prestigious and expensive restaurants are located in elegant hotels on the Malecón or at exclusive addresses in the neighborhoods, there are many excellent restaurants scattered throughout the city where you can enjoy first-rate meals for about US$25 for two, and that includes a nice white rum and lime to start, dessert, a cup of coffee, and maybe a glass of beer with your fish. At the other end of the scale are hundreds of cafes, cafeterias, bars, and shops where you can have

a good soup and sandwich, some flán, and a milkshake for just a couple of dollars. And, of course, it's always possible to make up your own lunch and breakfast by purchasing bread and cheese in a supermarket and fruit from a vendor. In short, breakfast and lunch should be quite delightful and cost you very little.

The types of cuisine to choose from in Santo Domingo are the same types you'd choose in any large city in the world. You can get Japanese, Mexican, Spanish, French, Italian, international, Creole, seafood, and American fast food, including terrible plastic pizza. About the only thing I haven't yet found is Indian food, but there's probably an Indian restaurant in Santo Domingo somewhere. But it would be a shame to come to Santo Domingo and not eat *comida criolla* and seafood before you eat anything else.

THE COLONIAL DISTRICT

Inexpensive

The pizza at **Pizza Capri** near La Bahía is much

better than at the road stands on El Conde, where I've found the slices dry and brittle. You're better off going into cafeterias and ordering the Cubano or Medianoche sandwiches and a glass of beer. **De Nosotros** in Calle Hostos specializes in *empanadas* that are ready in a few minutes and can be taken to go. Also on the El Conde is the **Palace Cafe,** a modern restaurant where you can get Cuban sandwiches as well. If you're walking up El Conde toward the gate and you get to Calle José Reyes, look around the corner to your left and you'll see (yes) **Mr. Burger,** which has about four or five stools at an "American-style" counter and serves both passable hamburgers and breakfast. Nearby is **El Sartén,** a quickie restaurant where you can have a sit-down meal and not lose an arm and a leg (Calle Hostos 153). Across from the Alcázar, all of the little cafes and pubs offer drinks, quick sandwiches, and fresh soups. You can sit and have a bite to eat at **Café Montesinos, Drake's Pub,** the **Museo de Jamon,** or **Rita's Café.** Take your pick—they're all comfortable and fun.

The oddest name in all of Santo Domingo goes to **Cafetería Dumbo** on Arzobispo Nouel behind Parque Independencia. The **Village Pub** (Calle Hostos 350), in the Colonial District opposite the ruins of Hospital Bari, is a great place to stop for snacks and a drink. Or try **La Taberna,** at Padre Billini and Calle de las Casas, where classical music is the theme.

A **Wendy's** lurks at Av. 27 de Febrero at Abraham Lincoln, tel. 809/547-1772. If you get the urge, lie down and it will pass.

Moderate

Although there are no restaurants in the Colonial District that classify as truly expensive or luxurious, there are many excellent places to eat. Keeping in mind that the many establishments of the Malecón are only a stone's throw (or a short taxi ride) away, it is perfectly possible to spend many days in the old part of the city and find a new restaurant every day. The Parque Colón is an excellent place to get your bearings. Right on the square across from the Columbus statue is the **Café Restaurante El Conde,** an open-air place that serves good coffee, flán, and specialty sandwiches and is just fine for lunch or a late snack on the way home from sightseeing. Just west of there, down El Conde and toward

the Calle de las Damas are several fine restaurants, including **El Advocat, La Cocina,** and **Ché Bandoneón,** where you won't need a reservation and can dine outside or in on excellent Creole, seafood, and international cuisine. And just the other way is **Café Mundo Europa** (El Conde 154), which serves a decent Creole menu, and where you can stop for a quick sandwich and beer during the hustle of the day.

There are a number of quite nice restaurants scattered on the back streets of the Colonial District, some of them almost unnoticeable in the clutter. The restaurant known as **América** (Calle Santome 201, tel. 809/682-7194) serves what it calls Spanish food but is in reality an excellent seafood restaurant, quiet and tucked away. Serving "English-style" food is the **Café Coco** at Calle Sánchez 153, near El Conde. This should not be confused with **Loco's Restaurant** at Padre Bellini #53 (tel. 809/687-9624), which, run by two Brits, serves good and reasonably priced English food. Going north from the Parque Colón, and located on Calle Atarazana across from the popular Alcázar (and therefore quite convenient as a break from sightseeing and shopping) is the expensive but nice **Fonda Atarazana** (Calle Atarazana 5, tel. 809/689-2900), a patio restaurant that serves regional specialties including curried baby goat in sherry sauce, octopus, and lobster thermidor. In the evenings, musicians may perform as well. Also near the Alcázar is the **Mesón de la Atarazana,** offering outdoor dining and Creole dishes.

Il Buco (Arzobispo Meriño 162A, tel. 809/685-0884) is one of the most popular restaurants in the Colonial District and serves excellent seafood, homemade pasta, and Creole dishes. Less expensive is **El Bodegón,** on Padre Billini at the corner of Arz. Meriño (tel. 809/682-6864), a small place that serves Spanish dishes and specializes in soups and other delicacies.

One of the most distinctive places in the whole Colonial District is the **Mesón Bari,** at Calle Hostos 308, just around the corner from the Hostal Nader and the Hotel Palacio. Featuring good seafood combinations and steaks on a fixed menu, this very dignified Dominican bar and restaurant hosts much of the artistic and intellectual life of the district, especially on weekend afternoons when the place is absolutely jammed. The dignified mien doesn't mean that the music doesn't get loud, especially on Friday evenings. Near the Alcázar is the fabulously decorated **Café Concierto Bachata Rosa** (named after a song by Juan Guerra and the band 440), founded by a group of Dominican designers, artists, and collectors. Located near the Alcázar on the Plaza de Expana, the club and restaurant is filled with gold records, hats, shirts, and photos, all souvenirs of the founders' careers. The place stays open late and tries to rock. Just down the steps from the Alcázar and across from La Atarazana Museum is the **Salón de Té**, which features Chinese food and is okay but nothing too special. Don't forget Hotel Palacio Nicolás de Ovando's **Extremadura** (Calle de las Damas 52), which features traditional Spanish-style cuisine.

In the past few years the whole colonial Zone scene has gone a bit more upscale with new restaurants coming and going at a dizzying pace. Of course, restaurants everywhere come and go, but among the best of the brand new eating establishments is **La Bríciola** (Arz Meriño 152, tel. 688-5055), which is housed in a former colonial mansion. Great for seafood and pasta. **Tu Casona** (Tejera 101 at Meriño) is a self-styled Argentinian steak house that also features rabbit. **Paté Palo** is super-new, and located on the popular Columbus square at Ataranze 15. The grilled dorado is supposed to be its specialty, and the people watching at the Plaza España is terrific. Slightly less formal is the **Plaza Toledo** (Isabela Católica at Luperón), an outdoor courtyard restaurant that serves pasta, especially seafood linguini, and nice desserts. Almost invisible in an office building is **La Taberna** (Mercedes 155), which serves Dominican breakfasts and lunch during the week.

Seafood

If you're staying in the Colonial District (or elsewhere, of course) and are in the mood to take a stroll downhill toward the Malecón and the Montesino statue, then you can find several excellent places for seafood. On the old town side of the Malecón are the **Restaurant del Mar** and the **Restaurant la Llave del Mar.** Across Avenida George Washington and right on the sea is **Manresa,** which is particularly nice in the evenings with the clouds building up over the Caribbean through strands of colored lights. The **Llave** has

an astounding decor, including a stuffed crocodile, sea turtles, and birds on the ceiling, and is worth a look for this alone. One of the best, and perhaps the most unassuming, of seafood restaurants in all of Santo Domingo is the **Jardín de Bagatelle** (Avenida George Washington 39, tel. 809/682-1625), with **La Bahía** down the road serving good seafood as well. La Bahía is known for its conch, lobster, and shrimp done Creole style, while Jardín de Bagatelle does its seafood (and other dishes) French style and also has folkloric shows from time to time.

Pica-Pollo (Fried Chicken)

One of the national dishes of the Dominican Republic is *pica-pollo,* or fried chicken. At its best, it is wonderful, crisp, and luscious. At its worst, it is terrible, chewy, and greasy. In Santo Domingo, for examples of the former, try **Frank Chicken** (L. Navarro 15, tel. 809/682-5070), **Pollo Nando** (Carratera Duarte Km 101, tel. 809/560-7646), **Restaurante Pica Pollo** (Padre Billini 401, tel. 809/686-2420), **Chicharrones y Pollos** (Mirabel, tel. 809/569-0046), **El Provocon II** (Duarte 47, tel. 809/564-8135), and **Pica Pollo El Sason** (Aguiar 396; tel. 809/561-4252). This is, of course, a partial list. There are plenty of other good spots in the capital, so feel free to experiment.

ON OR NEAR THE MALECÓN

Moderate

The **Crucero del Mar** is located at the east end of the Malecón near the Colonial District, featuring local seafood dishes that are quite delicious, including grouper stuffed with shrimp and lobster covered with hot sauce. The Crucero is away from the crowds that tend to gather near the larger hotels to the west. The Crucero's waiters stand outside and act as hawkers. Once inside, pay close attention to your waiter (Av. George Washington 27, tel. 809/682-1368); otherwise, he'll guide you rather ostentatiously through the menu. Another excellent choice is **Malecón 7** (its address, as well), a roofed but open-air dining spot next to the sea. Good seafood soup, Creole shrimp with rice, and plenty of good drinks for about US$20.

If you're looking for crowds, especially late-night crowds, then you can try **La Canasta** in the Melia Santo Domingo (Av. George Washington 365), which is set back a bit from the Malecón and is between the hotel's casino and disco. This is a good place to sample real Dominican dishes with a mostly Dominican crowd. Try the goat meat braised with rum sauce or the real *sancocho*. Just for a rest you can also try **The Deli** in the Jaragua Renaissance Resort and Casino. Naturally you'll find corned beef and pastrami sandwiches, though the deli also offers a few Dominican specialties. The Deli is patronized mostly by hotel guests and overlooks the hotel garden and falls. It offers a break from late-night gambling.

Just behind the Jaragua at Av. Independencia 407 is the Spanish restaurant **La Mezquita** (tel. 809/687-7090), which is informal and moderately expensive but serves very good rice-and-seafood dishes with an excellent selection of wines. Also in the vicinity of the Jaragua hotel is the **Restaurante Tonde de Tasis,** which serves a mix of Dominican, Spanish, and French cuisines. On Av. Independencia 54 is **Cantábrico,** which is within walking distance of the Malecón, and popular for paella and seafood among an executive-type crowd. Also within walking distance from there are **Don Pepe** (corner of Calle Pasteur and Calle Santiago) and **El Toledo** (corner of Calle Pasteur and Casimiro de Moya), both of which serve Spanish food at moderate prices. Sort of in between neighborhoods at Parque Independencia near El Conde gate is **Paco's Café** for basic local food like beans, rice, and stews.

Expensive

All of the expensive tourist hotels on the Malecón maintain one or more gourmet restaurants on the premises, and they are all very good. The other really elegant restaurants in Santo Domingo are in the neighborhoods of Gazcue and Naco. If you wish to try out these elegant dining experiences without incurring the nighttime cost, check and see if they're running a lunchtime buffet. Sometimes you can chow down for about US$10, eating the same food cafeteria style that would set you back far more during the evening. Most of the restaurants listed below are formal affairs—reservations are necessary for dinner, and men will need to wear jackets.

Of all the elegant restaurants, the best known, or perhaps just most advertised, is **Vesuvio** (Av. George Washington 521, tel. 809/221-3333), which is owned by the Bonarelli family, and which serves justly famous Neapolitan food like homemade soups, crayfish specialties, bass, oysters, and veal that comes from their own herd. Desserts and pizza are specialties as well, though you may wish to try the pizza in **Pizzeria Vesuvio** (next to Vesuvio, tel. 809/685-7608), which is informal and inexpensive. Across town in the neighborhoods is **Vesuvio II** (Av. Tiradentes 17, tel. 809/562-6060), which offers the same menu as its older brother, though in a somewhat quieter milieu. Located in the Jaragua Renaissance Hotel, the **Manhattan Grill** (tel. 809/221-2222) serves traditional steak-house food, along with clam chowder, gumbo, and lamb. All of the meat is supposed to be imported from the United States, which makes one wonder why you'd travel to the Caribbean to try American steak. But if that's your preference, this grill is the best. Also located in the Jaragua Renaissance is the **Latino,** which features Dominican and South American fare but also has tapas (hors d'oeuvres). Here you can get thick bean soup and "goat in rum." Latino is relatively small as restaurants go, much smaller than its sister Italian restaurant, also in the Jaragua Renaissance, the **Figaro,** which probably rivals Vesuvio as the premier Italian place in Santo Domingo. The atmosphere is strictly trattoria style, and the food leans towards cured ham, fresh mozzarella, and specialty lobster. Both the Latino and Figaro are dinner only. Sorry—no lunch buffets.

Near the Malecón in the Santo Domingo Hotel is the moorish spectacle called **El Alcázar,** a tent-like environ designed by Oscar de la Renta that sparkles with tiny mirrors (tel. 809/221-1511). For lunch the Alcázar offers a shifting international buffet, while in the evening continental cuisine comes on line. If fizz is your thing, there is a champagne bruch on Sundays. If Chinese is good for you, then the **Jardín de Jade** inside the Hotel Embajador on Avenida Sarasota serves quite elaborate meals, specializing in Sichuan and featuring sweet corn soup, lemon duck, and Peking duck. Also interesting is **La Parilla** on the Malecón about three blocks east of the intersection with Av. Abraham Lincoln. The grilled rabbit and parilla are good and substantial.

Of course, there are a loads of restaurants just east of the Obelisko Macho (the Lake Washington Monument). They come and they go like restaurants everywhere, but they are all fine for people watching.

Of special note is a restaurant called **Fogarate** (Geo. Washington 517), which some claim serves the most authentic and best, purely Dominican food in the city. The *asopao* is reknown. It isn't cheap, but you'll see Dominicans enjoying themselves. Also, note the **Palacia de Jade** (Heredia 6, tel. 686-3226) for very expensive, but great, Mongolian dishes like Peking duck.

OUT IN THE NEIGHBORHOODS

Inexpensive

Perhaps the oddest restaurant in town is the vegetarian **Ananda** (Casimiro de Moya 7, tel. 809/682-4465), located in Gazcue, where an Indian-connected yoga group serves generous portions of excellent vegetarian food in mystical ambience. You can get lunch or dinner, and order a fixed menu of three items, or mix and match your own.

A bit out of the way and hard to find is **Iberia** (Miguel Angel Monclus 165, tel. 809/530-7200). This restaurant is in a private house; there is no sign, no printed menu, but excellent home cooking. To reach Iberia, drive west on 27 de Febrero and go left (south) at a traffic light on Calle Privada just past Nuñez de Cácares. If it's German food you crave, you can find it at **Aubergine** at Plaza México on Av. México.

There is family-style service at **Boga-Boga,** located at Apart-Hotel Plaza Florida's lobby, where seafood is good and tapas are served at 5 P.M. In Gazcue, **Paco's Bananas** (Calle Danae 64, tel. 809/682-3535) boasts "modern" atmosphere and Creole food. Advertising the "most tasty breakfast in town" (which would be quite a feat) is the **Buen Provecho** (Gustavo Mejía Ricart 59, tel. 809/562-4848). Way out in Naco, the Buen Provecho is actually a good place to get the standard eggs, grapefruit, and toast, if that's what you're dreaming of, far from home.

Moderate

Very unusual and quite delightful is **El Conuco,** on Calle Casimiro de Moya, behind the entrance to the Jaragua in the Gazcue neighborhood. At El Conuco the waiters and waitresses wear traditional Dominican dress; the place is clean, quiet, and seems buried in tropic verdure. If you go for lunch, it is more than likely that the serving staff will perform traditional dances for you after they're through with the afternoon service, so stick around. The specialty of the house is *sancocho* made with seven meats, and *cocido,* which is cow's foot and garbanzo beans. The hot dishes are guaranteed to *revive muertos,* if you get the picture. Occasionally tour buses bring loads of tourists in for lunch, but they sit up front and don't bother anybody very much. Sit in back.

Way out in the Mirador del Sur is the **Mesón de la Cava,** which has to be seen to be believed. Located in a cave, you can sit under stalagmites and stalactites and eat good Dominican food, listen to merengue, and watch folk-dancing (Av. Mirador del Sur 1, tel. 809/533-2818). You should probably make reservations if you're coming from a long ways away. Back in Gazcue, a really traditional Dominican restaurant, and an experience not to be missed, is the **Aurora,** on Avenida Hermanos Deligne. Aurora also serves hot *sancocho* and *cocido,* along with many other traditional dishes like *ñame* and *mofongo.* For a real *mofongo* experience, you can try **Palacio de Mofongo** (Av. Independencia, tel. 809/688-8121) or the rather more distant **Casa de Mofongo** (Av. 27 de Febrero). If you're that far out anyway, or perhaps jogging in the Olympic Stadium area, you can find good value at the **Juan Carlos** (Av. Mejía Ricart). One find in Gazcue is **Restaurant Pappalapasta** (Calle Dr. Baez 23, tel. 809/682-4397), for quick pasta and spaghetti dishes. Probably the best variety of Chinese-style seafood is at **Chino de Mariscos** (Av. Sarasota 38A, near the Embajador), which is rather expensive but worth it if you've got the fever for Chinese. Cheaper Chinese can be had at **La Gran Muralla** (Av. 27 de Febrero), which has inexpensive and good buffets. You can find decent Chinese all over town. And don't forget when you're out in the Plaza de la Cultura to stop in at the **Maniqui** for lunch, dinner, or even a drink. Located near the College of Fine Arts, it is run by Rafaela Camaiño who serves delightful Creole dishes and good rum.

As Dominican society undergoes a gradual

move in favor of middle-class families, the neighborhoods of Naco and Gazcue are seeing some new restaurants that cater to those with higher incomes. Some of these new restaurants are both elegant and good. There is also a case of creeping multi-culturalism. For example, **A. Arirang** (27 de Febrero 346, tel. 809/565-5611) features Korean food, and nicely prepared at that. **David Crockett** (Ricart 34, tel. 809/547-2999) is a classic American-style steak house that serves porterhouse, prime rib and the like, in huge portions. Also new is **Samurai** (Av. Lincoln 902, tel. 809/541-0944), a truly authentic sushi bar, an absolute rarity in Santo Domingo, and first rate. Not to be left out is Middle Eastern food. **Scheherezade** (Pastoriza 226, tel. 809/227-2323) serves traditional lamb and couscous in a mock mosque. Occasional belly dancing is the entertainment! And at **Tacos del Sol** (Av. Lincoln and 27 de Febrero), those hungry for stand-up outdoor Mexican food are in for a real treat.

Expensive

Some of the most interesting restaurants in Santo Domingo are little places out in the neighborhoods, some of which are well known, some of which are not. No matter where you wish to go, though, taxis are cheap and readily available, so don't hesitate to take a chance and leave your hotel—you can have truly amazing and authentic meals.

Out in the neighborhoods, probably the best-known fancy restaurant is the **Lina Restaurant** in the Gran Hotel Lina on Avenida Máxima Gómez (tel. 809/686-5000). The original Lina was Lina Aguado, who came from Spain to be Trujillo's personal chef, then later opened a small restaurant for herself. The chefs at the Lina have learned her tricks and now serve a mighty repertoire of Spanish and international dishes. Try the seafood casserole and flambé sea bass. The best independent restaurant is probably **Reina de España,** located on Avenida Cervantes 103 (tel. 809/685-2588). This classy restaurant is near the Sheraton Santo Domingo and serves Creole, Spanish, and international food, including suckling pig, roast quail, and big lobsters any way you wish. For shellfish you might try the **Restaurant Jai-Alai,** located just behind the Melía on Independencia W (tel. 809/685-2409). Owned by a Basque, it serves such things as oysters in red sauce, Peruvian ceviche, garlic soup, and rabbit. The specialty fare is Peruvian and Dominican food, and you can try a glass of Peruvian Firewater called *pisco*. In the evening strolling guitarists serenade and there is an occasional sing-along. Continental and Caribbean food is served at the first-rate **Cafe St. Michel** (Lope de Vega 24, tel. 809/562-4141), which features a shifting menu and a *menu de degustación* on weekends, allowing you to try a number of different foods. Excellent French food is served at **La Fromagerie** (Plaza Criolla, tel. 809/567-8606). The specialty here is fondue, and the atmosphere is modern. Look for this restaurant at the corner of Máximo Gómez and Av. 27 de Febrero in front of the Olympic park. Finally, inside the Hotel Comodoro on Avenida Bolivar 193 is **Le Gourmet,** which also features Dominican and international specialties.

Some people think that the best seafood is Santo Domingo is at **Sully's** on Charles Sumner #19 (tel. 809/566-6405) where the seafood caldereta is out of this world. This particular dish is expensive for Santo Domingo, but not expensive by any other standard. The service is excellent, attentive and generous. Another good choice for an independent restaurant is **la Tescana,** located just north of the traffic circle created by Av. J.F. Kennedy and Av. Abraham Lincoln. Excellent house made pastas, fine desserts and good wine. Some people compare it favorably to Vesuvio. For a Spanish-style place try **Rio Miño** in the shopping mall just west of the old Embajador Hotel near Av. Sarasota.

PUERTO TURÍSTICO SANS SOUCI

Now that cruise ships have begun to call at

BOB RACE

Santo Domingo more and more, an area called Puerto Turístico Sans Souci has been developed just across the narrow neck of river and sea from the Colonial District. Set in a parklike open space, away from buildings and not far from the Dominican Naval Academy, the **Restaurant Bucanero** is a lovely new place for excellent seafood and grilled meat. If you go over, go by taxi during the early part of the evening when you can watch the sunset (it's spectacular), have a drink, and then stay for dinner. I'm afraid the restaurant is used mainly by cruise passengers, but it certainly deserves to succeed. You'll sit in front of long panels of glass overlooking the harbor and the Colonial District, where the evening colors are a blend of pink, turquoise, and maroon.

STREET VENDORS, BAKERIES, AND MARKETS

Street Vendors

Almost anything you buy from a street vendor is going to be cheap, and sometimes quite satisfying, too. Try to find a place that sells *chimichurri* (spiced sausage) or empanadas. Avoid cardboard pizza, but there are many fast-food places that make a pretty decent Cuban sandwich for half the price you'd pay at a hotel cafe. You can get good cheap food at cafeterias located all over town, especially in the Parque Independencia area, and around Avenida Mella.

Bakeries

Just as there are cafeterias and small cafes all over Santo Domingo, so there are bakeries that specialize in pastry, cake, candy, and sweets. **Casita Dulce** (Lea de Castro 205 in the Colonial District) is typical and good. Across the street, **Delicatesa** sells pastries and bread.

Markets

If you're into the apart-hotel lifestyle, or if you just want to buy some inexpensive items to bring back to your room, there are *colmados* and supermarkets all over the place. In the Colonial District, a good supermarket is **Casa Velásquez** at Gran Luperón and Arzobispo Meriño, which also has an excellent liquor store attached. In the neighborhoods, you can't fail to find a good place to buy food.

If you're shopping with a healthy bent, try out **Restaurant Bethel** (Calle Luperón 9, corner Arzobispo Meriño), which sells whole wheat bread and very sweet peanut butter. Also in the Colonial District is **Vita Naturaleza** (Calle Mercedes 255), which sells health food.

Finally, be sure you don't miss out on one of the great joys of the city; drop into a tiny candy shop and buy yourself a few pieces of coconut candy.

ENTERTAINMENT AND EVENTS

Santo Domingo is a city in which a resourceful foreigner can live happily for an extended period. Savvy Santo Domingans check the local newspapers to find out the latest cultural events, the times of films (which can be a trick), and out-of-the-way programs of music, theater, and art.

Although many of the provincial towns of the Dominican Republic tend to shut down early, Santo Domingo is a late-night place. There are hundreds of bars and nightclubs if dancing, drinking, and music are your thing. At times, just being on the street is a party in itself—especially near Christmas, when the Malecón is particularly lively, and during the Merengue Festival in July. However, almost any weekend night on the Malecón represents a concert in motion, and Carnaval is nonstop carnality. If you check the local newspapers, you'll also catch special concerts, theater performances, and music revues. No matter where you are in Santo Domingo, you are never far from art. Architecture and sculpture dominate the spaces in the Colonial District, while painting is predominant in the neighborhood galleries of Naco and Gazcue. From popular culture to high swank, Santo Domingo has it all. It is simply one of the swingingest cities around.

CONCERTS, THEATERS, AND ART EXHIBITS

If you pay attention to the local newspapers, you'll also never be far from a theatrical performance, classical music, modern popular concert, or dance recital. The poshest performances with the biggest names, and the center of the National Symphony, is the **Teatro Nacional** on Avenida Máximo Gómez, which offers many musical and theatrical events in season, along with chamber music and recitals in the smaller Sala Ravelo. Drop by, study the coming attractions, and visit the ticket office or telephone for information (809/682-7255). The surprisingly imposing building located at the corner of Avenida Independencia and Máximo Gómez is called the **Palacio de Bellas Artes**, which hosts special

events, though it is not a regularly scheduled venue. Seeing something in its ornate halls and venues is a treat.

Especially appealing, and set in the Colonial District, is the **Casa de Teatro** (tel. 809/689-3430), in the middle of the block at Calle Arzobispo Meriño 110. This drama workshop and experimental theater was founded in 1975. It also puts on poetry readings, art exhibits, and dance, and has a coffee bar where you can go to meet artsy-craftsy types and discuss theory. Drop by and see if they've got anything scheduled by looking at the posters on the walls and front door, or check local newspapers. Also in the Colonial District is **Casa de Francia** (corner of El Conde and Calle de las Damas, tel. 809/685-0840), the French cultural center which provides a place for extemporaneous music, special theatrical productions, and parties. If you're walking by and something seems to be happening, stick your head in and find out what it is. **Centro Cultural Hispánico** (Arz. Meriño, corner of Arz. Portes, tel. 809/686-8212) hosts a wide variety of events. Also in the Colonial District is the **Casa del Cordón** (Isabel la Católica, corner of Mercedes), which often has exhibits of paintings and photography.

Similar to the Casa de Teatro is the **Teatro Nuevo** in Barrio Don Bosco, which offers experimental and special theatrical performances, though you'll have to pay attention to local papers for notices. Teatro Nuevo is on San Juan Bosco (tel. 809/682-5132). Somewhat far afield is **Kovos Café Teatro** (Dr. Pineyro 153), near the university, which is a kind of center for blues and folk music—and jazz on Thursday nights at 10 P.M. This intellectual hangout also puts on modern dance from time to time.

Many events on the Plaza de la Cultura have a certain social cachet. The Museum of History and Geography has a theater, and the Museo del Hombre Dominicano hosts a well-attended crafts sale each December. And don't forget the **Casa de Bastidas** on Calle de las Damas, which sponsors art openings and many chamber music recitals.

Normally a huge, pulsating discotheque, the **Guácara Taíno** in the Parque Mirador del Sur suspends its normal craziness and noise to present folkloric dance Thurs.–Fri. at 10:30 P.M. These performances are especially colorful and should not be missed if you've a free evening. Sometimes the **Instituto Cultural Dominicano Americano** (Av. Abraham Lincoln 21, near the university), puts on performances, readings, and musical recitals, most primarily directed at the university community. Check the paper for offerings.

CINEMAS

Much of the film in Santo Domingo is American trash, which is to say, the finest films Hollywood has to offer, dubbed into Spanish, or subtitled. You can see Arnold or Bruce chopping his way through dozens of dead bodies and burning cars at almost any time.

The big cinemas in Santo Domingo are modern multiplexes, similar to those in the United States, only a little rougher and noisier. At all films, get there in plenty of time, because they tend to start early or late, depending on some whim of the gods.

With seven screens, the **Cinema Centro Dominicano** stands on the Malecón near Máximo Gómez (tel. 809/688-8767), while **Cineplex Naco** is on Fantino Falco, behind the shopping area. In the middle is **Cinema Lumière,** located on Av. Independencia, west of Winston Churchill. For a mall-style, teenage cinema that will make you think you're in Westwood, you can go to **Manzana de Oro,** inside the shopping center Plaza Central at the corner of Winston Churchill and 27 de Febrero. Very visible on 27 de Febrero between Abraham Lincoln and Winston Churchill is **Palacio del Cine.**

For a real experience (though not of the movies), you can attempt to go to **Triple** (with four screens, of course) on the Malecón, just east of the V Centenario Hotel, which features sticky floors and deafening noise.

As time passes, a few new venues in film have appeared in town. For example, **Broadway Cinema** (Plaza Central, 27 de Febrero and Churchill) sometimes offers alternatives to the Hollywood blockbuster. The **Casa Francia** (Vicioso 103 and Las Damas) has started a French film series Wednesday through Friday. How long it will last is anybody's guess. **Casa Italia** (Calle Hosbos and Luperón) has done the same with Italian film.

The Best

Some Dominicans say that **Issfapol** (tel. 809/541-3255) is the best movie house in Santo Domingo, which is unusual because it is located in the rather poor El Millon neighborhood. To get there, go north on Núñez de Cáceres from 27 de Febrero and turn right before the Supermercado Nacional. It's located between Guarocuya and Centro Olímpico. It's clean and has a good snack bar.

Cine Cultural Universitario

For something of an adventure in itself, try going to Cine Cultural Universitario, located on the campus of the Autonomous University. Try to enter from Alma Mater (the extension of Tiradentes). Once you get on campus, ask for directions to the cinema. You have to get a parking pass, and traffic can be a mess, but maybe it's worth the effort if you're tired of Arnold and Bruce.

CLUBS, BARS, AND PUBS

The hotels also feature quieter piano-type bars, some of which can be very enjoyable, especially when they offer original Latin jazz, one of my favorite types of music. Especially soothing is **Las Palmas,** in the Hotel Santo Domingo (Av. Independencia, tel. 809/221-1151). Decorated by Oscar de la Renta (like the hotel itself), the bar has a vaulted ceiling, painted walls, and a terrace open to the sea. The piano music tends toward lush and romantic, but on occasion, jazz, samba, bossa nova, and salsa music is played live. Drinks aren't cheap (at more than US$5), so sip slowly and enjoy the view and the music. The view is not quite so inviting, but the **Fontana Bar** in the El Embajador Hotel (Av. Sarasota 65, tel. 809/221-2131) presents live music, and the drinks are cheaper. The evening usually starts with a trio, followed later by Dominican folk, samba, and merengue. It's all very hip and cool.

Supposedly, Grace Slick, lead singer for Jefferson Airplane, once said, "Our eternal goal in life is to get louder." She wouldn't like the Fontana Bar much. However, it's an ideal spot to perch for those of us whose eternal goal is to get quieter and quieter.

The Colonial District

The Colonial District is home to a nice array of clubs and pubs, at least one of which is sure to have something to suit your tastes and moods. For example, right across from the Alcázar on the square is **Drake's Pub, Café Montesino, Nancy's Snack Bar, Rita's Café,** the **Candray Bar,** and the well-known **Bar Mesón Museo de Jamón,** which has flamenco dancing to recorded music on weekend evenings. The famous Dominican merengue musician and writer Juan Luis Guerra owns **Bachata Rosa** on the Ataranza as well. All of these small bars are located in a tight semicircle and you can cruise them, having a drink and a snack at each, or find one that will suit your mood. Besides, it is always pleasant on the square, and the view of the Alcázar is quite beautiful, especially on moonlit evenings. Just down the street in the Calle de las Damas, inside the Hotel Palacio Nicolás de Ovando, is the **Nuevo Mundo,** which features a traditionally colonial atmosphere for quiet drinks and soft music. For the Kerouac crowd, and for sober jazz in a living-room ambience, try **Chez Duke** (Arz. Portes 99, corner of Arz. Meriño near the cathedral), which has different groups every week. Go by and check out the billboard plastered on the front wall for information. The **Crazy Pub** in the Colonial District features karaoke, if that's your bag. The opposite ambience is at **La Taberna** (Padre Bilini at Calle de las Damas), where you can listen to classical music with your drink. Two pubs are located on Calle Hostos opposite the ruined hospital. Both **Village Pub** and **Raffles** are pleasant and unassuming. The **Clásico Delicatessen** becomes a bar at night (Palo Hincado 101 at Arz. Portes). The **Maubo Café** is located at 151 El Conde and has terrific atmosphere.

Another great bar is the **El Japada Restaurant and Bar,** located in the Padre Bellini, right next door to **Alcoholics Anonymous** (tel. 809/687-4943). Next door to that is another bar, called **La Bahía.** For spiritual relief of another kind, you're welcome to visit **Centro Espiritual**

Internacional Swaminarayan at 104 Luperón. Passing by you can smell incense and hear chanting. Everybody welcome.

The Neighborhoods

Sometimes smaller is better, sometimes bigger is. For a selection of both, the neighborhoods are quite good. For example, **Ortolio** (tel. 809/686-4282) is a small pub bar located on Santiago near the Palacio de Bellas Artes, frequented by university types and intellectuals. Also popular with students, and often frequented by visiting Spaniards, is **No Lo Sé** on Av. Bolivar, near Máximo Gómez. One block east of the Melía on Independencia is the **Mento Bar,** which is popular and often very crowded. It's a good place to mingle with real people. On the lowest floor of the Plaza Naco Hotel is **Bottom's Bar,** which features quiet live entertainment and good drinks way out in the neighborhoods. On Robert Pastoriza is the **Iguana Café.** As the name indicates, this bar-cafe features an "exotic" ambience and seafood, though probably no reptiles are on the menu. Right in the middle of the action at Av. Máximo Gómez and Av. Abraham Lincoln is the **Atlantico Café,** which claims to serve Tex-Mex dishes and has innovative music. It's a trendy spot with three bars from which to choose, and a noise-level between loud and quiet. More subdued is the **Marrakesh Café Bar** in the lobby of the Santo Domingo Hotel, a place designed to be quiet and which serves specialty coffees, pastries, and cocktails. Very loud and quite dizzy is the **Café Capri** (Av. Tiradentes, tel. 809/566-3679), where you can join in the game and contests or just sit back and enjoy the vast array of giant screens and speakers blasting images and sound your way. In the early evening a great place for Spanish tapas and a quiet drink is the **Mesón Las Tapas** (Av. Roberto Pastoriza, tel. 809/549-7264), well worth an early cab ride for inspiring delicacies from Spain.

Sports Bars

The sporting crowd is not neglected in Santo Domingo either, with the main watering hole for serious baseball fanatics being the **Lucky Seven** (Calle Pasteur 16), which is not only a pretty good steak and seafood restaurant, but also a sports bar with televisions blaring games at all hours via cable. Football (soccer, that is) is the passion at **Sports Center Bar and Restaurant** (Av. 30 de Marzo 31, tel. 809/688-3125), where big screens howl out the best games available on TV. In the Colonial District, sports fanatics hang out at **Restaurante Banca Para Apuestas Deportivas** (El Conde 159), which has international sports events of all types on tube.

MORE NIGHTLIFE

Casinos

Naturally, all the major hotels have their casinos, and most of them operate according to Las Vegas rules, with a few exceptions. The dealers and waiters generally are bilingual in English and Spanish, so you can lose your money in both pesos and dollars—take your pick. Probably the poshest casino is the **Omni** in the Jaragua, but all are pretty much the same if you're sitting at a table staring at cards, looking for faces and aces. For something a little different, you might catch the **Maunaloa Night Club and Casino** in Centro de los Héroes, which is an authentic Dominican experience.

Dance Spots

Grace Slick's spirit is certainly alive and well in Santo Domingo; if your goal in life is to get louder and louder, then you might try some of the big discos and hotel nightclubs, both of which are represented in great number along the Malecón and out in the neighborhoods.

With folkloric shows on Thursday and Friday, the **Guácara Taína** (Calle Mirador in Parque del Mirador, tel. 809/530-2666) rocks with merengue and salsa every night until late. The admission to this underground acoustical dreamworld is rather stiff (US$10), but the noise is contagious and the crowds sometimes number as many as 2,000. As long as we're on the subject of caves, the aforementioned **Mesón de la Cava** (Avenida Mirador del Sur, tel. 809/533-2818) is a lively nightclub with music for dancing and good food. The waiters sometimes become the whole show. Fifty feet underground, this nightclub stays pretty cool all the time, so to speak. For loud and popular (as well as sweaty), you can't beat **La Belle Blu** (Av. George Washington, tel. 809/689-2911), which stays open until dawn and charges US$5 to grunt and grind around a huge dance floor to

live or sometimes recorded music. As always, you need to exercise some caution on the Malecón if you emerge in the wee hours. **Shehara** is nearby and is almost as sweaty—you can locate both discos by finding the famous restaurant Vesuvio. Two discos located on Av. Independencia, **Jet Set** and **Opus,** tend to serve a slightly older clientele than the hotel discos, but they're just as loud.

In the hotels you'll find plenty of action as well. Perhaps the most popular hotel disco is the **Neon Discotheque,** located in the Hispaniola Hotel on Av. Independencia (tel. 809/221-1151), where there is lively Latin jazz with guest stars each week, and in between, heavy-duty merengue under flashing lights that would set John Travolta's pants on fire. The admission is about US$4, and drinks average about that much, which is pretty standard in all the hotel and boulevard discos in town. The Neon doesn't stay open until dawn, just until 4 A.M., serving its youngish, sometimes university crowd. Also popular is the **Omni Disco** in the Sheraton Santo Domingo Hotel (Av. George Washington 361, tel. 809/221-6666), which caters to an older and more sophisticated crowd, and is only open until 2 A.M. Admission is about US$5. At the Jaragua Renaissance Resort (Av. George Washington 367, tel. 809/221-2222), the **Merengue Bar** presents a mixture of live bands, including jazz and vocalists early and loud merengue late, all in a colorful and somewhat swank atmosphere adjacent to the hotel's casino. Drinks are quite expensive in the Merengue, averaging more than US$4. Fairly unusual is **Gasolina** (Roberto Pastoriza, corner of Av. Abraham Lincoln), built to resemble a 1950s gas station with half a car embedded in the wall on the first floor.

Other discos of note in Santo Domingo are **Axel's Club,** located near the La Belle Blu on George Washington, and so tends to be hectic; the **Vertigo** on Av. Independencia; and out in the neighborhoods, the **Euro Club Disco** in the Plaza Naco Hotel. **String Fellows** is located on Pasteur 23. All of these discos charge a modest admission fee, have relatively expensive drinks, and stay open until early morning, though not until dawn. If you're at the Teatro Nacional, you might go across the street to the **Columbus Club 60,** which features merengue, rock and roll, and some ballads. Fairly far east on Av.

George Washington is the **Babilon Disco,** which is large and luxurious, almost astounding. The **Kuora Disco** features *"sensurrom"* sound, and the **Exquisito** rocks and rolls on Av. Tiradentes.

For the truly incurable romantic of soul, or for somebody just looking for a different experience, don't fail to check out **El Rincón Habanero** in the Villa Consuelo neighborhood (Sánchez Valverde at Baltazar de los Reyes), where blue-collar workers enjoy Cuban *son* music of the 1940s and 1950s, or the equally sentimental **Secreto Musical Bar,** one block away on Pimentel, which headquarters the **Club Nacional de Soneros** (the Son Musical Club). In Villa Mella on the city's north side, **La Vieja Habana** also plays Cuban music from the old days. It's good stuff.

By now you've probably got the picture: music is readily available in this town, almost anywhere, anytime.

Best Happy Hours
One way to beat the high cost of drinks in the hotels is to enjoy happy hours, which are ubiquitous in Santo Domingo. Almost all hotels offer the happy hour 6–8 P.M., and although there is rarely live music, you can usually hear a piano and enjoy snacks. For example, the bar **La Cascadas** in the Hotel Jaragua is usually open until 11 P.M., but offers its happy hour 6–8 P.M. Open slightly later for happy hour is the **Hispaniola Bar** at the Hispaniola Hotel, where you might hang out and catch a set of Sonny Ovalles and his orchestra playing merengue and dance tunes as your buzz settles in. Probably the best happy hour of all is at the **Café del Sol,** located on the 12th-floor terrace of the Plaza Hotel Naco, with a different show from Thursday through Saturday starting with Cuban music on Thursday. The good thing about the happy hour here is that it stretches 8–10 P.M. The **Las Palmas Bar** at the Hotel Santo Domingo also has happy hour when drinks are two for one and you can nosh on snacks. At the Sheraton Santo Domingo the **El Yarey Piano Bar** has a happy hour 6–8 P.M. and even live music with the Sheraton orchestra. Other evenings at El Yarey see Cuban music on Monday, Dominican folk music on Thursday, and traditional Spanish groups on Friday, though sometimes on Friday there is a comedian, which can be hard to negotiate unless your Spanish is good. If your buzz is good enough, you can go upstairs to the **Omni Disco** on Thursday and enjoy a fashion show. In fact, a number of discos and clubs in Santo Domingo feature fashion shows which are generally advertised in the hotel magazine *Touring.*

Other good happy hours are at the **Lobby Bar** of the V Centenario Intercontinental Hotel and the **Embassy Casino Bar** at the Hotel Embajador, both running 6–8 P.M.

Walking the Malecón
For really cheap entertainment, just wander up and down the Malecón, where, especially at Christmas time and during Carnaval, the *perico ripeao,* groups of street musicians, stroll up and down the waterfront serenading everybody in sight. Rum is drunk, and people occasionally dance. On a balmy tropical night, nothing could be finer.

"Adult" Entertainment
At **La Petit Chateau** (Av. 30 de Mayo, tel. 809/537-7262), they advertise sumptuous buffets during the day, dancing and "live shows" during the night. The live shows are a combo of striptease, transvestites, and female impersonators. To get there go west on the Malecón until you think you're leaving the city. Somewhat more hard-core shows are featured at **Instrumental Night Club,** on the Las Américas Highway on the way to the airport, or at **Exodus** (Av. George Washington 511). **Manolo Piano Bar** (Mauricio Baez 209, tel. 809/562-6678) advertises company "if you're alone," whatever that means.

SPORTS AND RECREATION

For my money, Santo Domingo is one of the most beautifully livable big cities, and that's taking into account the horrible traffic. If you've an idea about staying in the city for more than a few weeks, perhaps to study Spanish at one of the fine language institutes or to attend classes or teach at the Dominican-American Institute, or perhaps to locate a job (not as hard as you might think), then you'll need to know some of the sporting keys to staying active. It isn't hard if you know where to look.

WATER SPORTS

Ocean Swimming

In the vicinity of Santo Domingo, there is the ever-popular **Boca Chica** beach, which by now is widely popular with the world tourist crowd, and with Santo Domingans who take their pleasure there regularly on Saturday and Sunday afternoons. The waters of Boca Chica are shallow and placid, and I find the swimming a little boring. Mostly, Boca Chica is a holiday beach, crowded with swimmers, vendors, and sunbathers. Still, it's a place to go cool off when you're in Santo Domingo. Beyond the airport, and along the south coast, are beaches at **Juan Dolio** and **Guayacanes.**

Scuba Diving

Probably the best place for diving near Santo Domingo is at **La Caleta,** located about an hour from the city along the Las Américas Highway. This spot has been declared an underwater national park and can be reached by a fast boat from Boca Chica beach in about 17 minutes at a cost of around RD$2,000 for 15 divers. Also, from the public park along the highway is a fleet of leaky dinghies in need of improvement. The wooden boats barely hold four divers and their equipment, and, if the swell is high, you'd best say a little prayer before you head out. The dinghies are all beached and you can see them from the highway. If you wish to chance the small dinghy experience, you'll pay only about RD$200.

Despite the difficulty of getting to La Caleta, the reef and its wreck is pure paradise. The *Hickory* wreck is an iron ship in about 60 feet of water. Schools of fish hover around the hull, suspended in the current. Coral and shellfish have become part of the ship's outer and inner plates, and huge parrot fish have taken up residence in the hull. Visibility is about 60–70 feet, and the light is good, both of which make for excellent underwater photography. About a seven-minute swim from the *Hickory* is another wreck, at 100 feet. Visibility there is about 80–90 feet. A colorful carpet of coral has webbed itself over a large wooden sailing vessel, a wreck much more awesome than the iron-clad *Hickory.* Unfortunately, hurricanes and high winds will eventually break up this wooden vessel, so if you want to see this artificial reef, you'd best go soon.

Santo Domingans are getting more and more into diving, and as tourism grows, so probably too will the resources for the sport in the capital. Both **Gus Diving** and **Dominican Adventures** currently offer classes, equipment, and excursions from the capital. Both offer PADI (Professional Association of Dive Instruction) certification. PADI instructors can also be certified through the NAUI (National Association of Underwater Instruction) and a couple of other organizations. Gus Diving is a retail shop owned by Gustavo and Mechi Torreira, located at Plaza La Lira II, Roberto Pastoriza No. 356 (tel. 809/566-0818). Dominican Adventures is owned and operated by Michael McClellan, an Australian who has been in the Dominican Republic for more than 10 years. It is located at Calle Dr. César Dargam, No. 20, and you can reach them at 809/541-7884. You can take courses at Dominican Adventures, usually lasting several days in length, with theories tested at pool sessions. You can generally get your certification for about RD$3,600, but telephone for current prices. Bring your own equipment and it's cheaper.

From Santo Domingo both Gus Diving and Dominican Adventures organize excursions to various diving sites. For about RD$800 you can go along with Dominican Adventures on a Saturday or Sunday trip to Catalina Island, which includes two dives and a snack (four-person minimum). Both shops organize groups on an on-call basis to La Caleta and Bayahibe for about RD$800. Dominican Adventures can take its customers to Saona Island for RD$1,100. Most of the time you have to pay your own transportation costs, although a boat journey to the site is generally included in the price of the tour.

Parasailing and Sailing

The only outlet for parasailing activities in Santo Domingo is through **Actividades Acuáticas** (tel. 809/688-5838). For sailing, Santo Domingo's yacht club, the **Club Naútico de Santo Domingo** is located at Boca Chica (tel. 809/566-1682 or 809/685-4949). If you expect to use its facilities, you'd better know somebody, or make arrangements through your own club.

Sportfishing

Sportfishing is very popular, and you can have some spectacular success with marlin, sailfish, dorado, bonito, tarpon, and snook if you're willing to put up with some hassles and expense. For the most part you're going to have to arrange for fishing through a hotel or one of the clubs like Acuáticas or Naútico. Generally, the best spots are Cumayasa, La Romana, and Boca de Yuma east of Santo Domingo; Palmar de Ocoa and Barahona to the west of Santo Domingo; and Samaná in the north. Going out for a day's fishing is great fun, and if you share the costs with three or four others, it can be quite reasonable.

The best fishing along the south coast is from June to October, and along the north coast from August to October, though they say blue marlin can be caught all year long. One of the best bets for fishing all year round is the unsightly wahoo, whose mouthful of teeth encourages you to be careful when you're landing it. For the adventuresome, try finding a flat boat in any of the river mouths and coastal inlets and estuaries in the many rivers that are east of Santo Domingo. It's a do-it-yourself adventure but might pan out, so to speak. For fishing and sailing information of all kinds, talk to or visit the people at **Andrés Boca Chica Club** (tel. 809/523-5579) or **DeMar Beach Club** (tel. 809/523-5579), both of which are not as exclusive as Club Naútico.

LAND SPORTS

Sports Clubs

There are a couple of sports clubs worth looking into for long-term residents. The **Club Deportivo Naco,** Calle Salvador Sturla, Ensanche Naco (tel. 809/565-6606), offers swimming, tennis, bingo, table tennis, basketball, and volleyball. Swimming and tennis lessons are available for members. **Club Naútico** in Boca Chica is a worthwhile membership for long-term residents. The Club has sailing, water-skiing, yachting, windsurfing, freshwater swimming in the pool, a private beach, and restaurant. You can drydock boats as well. The cheapest way to get sporting entertainment in Santo Domingo is to try out the **Centro Olímpico Juan Pablo Duarte** (tel. 809/565-5700). Located in a busy traffic area of central Santo Domingo, the Olímpico is the large sports complex built for the 1974 Central American and Caribbean Olympic Games held in Santo Domingo. It is a public facility and supposedly only legal residents may use it. However, you can probably get permission if you're living in Santo Domingo. The facilities include an Olympic-size swimming pool, a separate pool of spring boards and platforms for diving, a gymnasium, volleyball courts, and public tennis courts. You can jog in the areas around the center as well. If you're living in Santo Domingo, call the administration and plead, or get to know someone who knows his or her way around and follow the leader.

If you're Dutch, you might try the **Hola Holland** (The Dutch Club of Santo Domingo), which was formed in 1981 to bring Dutch residents on the island together. Various social activities are conducted year-round. For information, contact Peter Groendijk (tel. 809/682-3171) or Wim Brouwer (tel. 809/567-9155).

Jogging and Walking

If you're a long-term resident in Santo Domingo, you'll probably get into jogging or walking sooner or later, as the city is perfect for this activity. The city's many parks are ideal, and many people choose the **Parque Mirador del Sur** along the Avenida de la Salud (Avenida Mirador del Sur), a long stretch of paths and gardens running east from Av. Luperón almost to Av. Winston

Churchill. Joggers and walkers gather at 6 A.M. and 6 P.M.—sunrise and sunset. It's very beautiful along the park at that time, if you can make it up. Others may prefer the more urban Malecón, for its view of the Caribbean and the uninterrupted stretch of sidewalk. Many Dominicans walk or jog around the Centro Olímpico and in the Jardín Botánico in Arroyo Hondo. Both are good, but some people have gotten mugged around the Centro.

Health Clubs
There are many modern health clubs in Santo Domingo, some expensive, some not. Almost all offer day rates, as well as long-term memberships. Most memberships have initial fees, so you'll want to become a long-term member if you're staying in town for more than a year. The prices listed for some of these clubs are day memberships, but they can fluctuate, and long-term prices are much cheaper. The **Fitness Studio** at Boy Scout No. 8 (near the corner of 27 de Febrero and Abraham Lincoln) offers free weights, weight machines, a swimming pool, aerobics, personal trainers, medical checkups, and follow-ups (RD$50, tel. 809/567-5030). **Body Health,** at Av. 27 de Febrero near Ortega y Gasset (tel. 809/565-5156), has Nautilus machines, aerobics, racquetball, volleyball, track, a juice bar, a steam room, a sauna, and massage (day membership RD$100). **The Body Shop** at Hotel Plaza (tel. 809/541-6226) has the standard exercise machines, along with a nursery and whirlpool. You can also try the **Caribbean Health Club,** Av. Abraham Lincoln, No. 301 (tel. 809/535-6226), which also has karate lessons, or **Gimnasio Ketty,** for women only, at David Ben Gurion No. 3 (tel. 809/562-1757). You can get a day membership at Ketty for RD$40, which entitles you to an aerobics session. **Your Place** (corner of Núñez de Cáceres and Rómulo Betancourt, tel. 809/530-7695, RD$30) and **Gimnasio Zeus** (Av. Lope de Vega No. 82, tel. 809/562-5528, RD$40) also offer good value for the facilities.

Golf
If you know a member and can finagle an invitation, you can try to play the ridiculously beautiful and superbly manicured **Santo Domingo Country Club.** This 18-hole course is strictly for the elite of the capital and their guests. If cash isn't a problem, you can always pay the expensive fee and join. It's an exquisite layout.

About 20 minutes north of Santo Domingo on the Duarte Highway (40 minutes in traffic) is the new **Cayacoa Country Club** (tel. 809/561-7288). This new club is semi-private, which means that the public is welcome but special memberships are sold to persons who wish to take advantage of the pool, tennis courts, and clubhouse facilities. If you're staying in Santo Domingo, this golf course, set in typical subtropical bush country, with Bermuda fairways and greens, is quite attractive and welcoming. The management told me that for US$35, they'd send a taxi to your hotel door and deliver you home, all greens fees included. If you're staying in Santo Domingo for a longer period, monthly rates are available. Also reachable from Santo Domingo along Las Américas Highway east of town is the new **San Andrés Country Club,** which is semi-private and welcomes casual players. When I visited the course the front nine had been opened—and looked quite challenging—but the back nine were still under construction. Down the same road about 45 minutes east of Santo Domingo in Juan Dolio is the **Metro Country Club.** You can see it from the highway. Also in Juan Dolio is the **Cumayasa Golf Club.**

Tennis
In Santo Domingo, you may as well be in tennis heaven. Really cool is the **Caribbean Tennis Center,** Autopista 30 de Mayo, Km 10.5 (Malecón), tel. 809/537-7173, which has 10 clay courts, flood lights, and a tennis school for kids. More exclusive is the **Santo Domingo Tennis Club** at Carretera Herrera Haina (tel. 809/533-2422), which offers tennis lessons. The identically named **Santo Domingo Tennis Club** is at Calle Euclides Morillo, with tennis courts and lessons, too. Call them at 809/562-6918. Other tennis clubs include **Casa de España,** Autopista 30 de May, Km 10 (Malecón), tel. 809/537-1802, and **Club Arroyo Hondo,** Calle J. Polanco, tel. 809/541-9911. The largest available public court setting is at the **Centro Olímpico Juan Pablo Duarte,** Ave. 27 de Febrero, near Ortega y Gasset.

All of the major resort hotels in Santo

Domingo have excellent courts, including the **Embajador, Santo Domingo,** and **Sheraton** hotels, along with the **Dominican Fiesta,** most offering pro shops and lessons. In addition, the Renaissance **Jaragua** has an 800-seat tennis stadium and a ranked pro. I watched some highly ranked amateurs from Latin America and the Caribbean play on the Jaragua courts, and the facility is beautiful. In the central neighborhoods of Santo Domingo, the **Hotel Gran Lina** has courts as well.

Racquetball and Squash

If you're into racquetball or squash, you can play at **Body Health** (see "Health Clubs," above) and the **Sol Poniente Athletic Club,** Av. Sol Poniente (tel. 809/541-0424).

Bowling

Call me crazy, but bowling appeals to me somehow. You can bowl in Santo Domingo at **Bolerama Naco** on Av. Tiradentes in Centro Commercial Naco (tel. 809/566-3818), or at the new and plush **Sebelen Bowling Center,** located on the corner of Abraham Lincoln and Roberto Pastoriza. There are 24 lanes (huge for the country), each with electronic scoring system and a private television monitor. This complex has a bar and cafeteria as well.

Team Sports

Basketball, softball, and touch football games are almost always going on at the Centro Olímpico. You can play volleyball, too, if you're able to catch someone to talk to at the **Asociación de Voliból** (tel. 809/544-2355).

Martial Arts

If you're into martial arts and miss smashing boards while you're away from home, you can get back into the discipline at **Institute Shoon Rhee de Tae Kwon Do,** Av. Independencia No. 78 (tel. 809/689-0065) or **Judo Matsunaga Dojo** (tel. 809/565-5817; ask for Michiko Matsunaga).

Tai Chi

Somebody is always doing tai chi at the Parque Mirador in the mornings. Check at **Club Mirador del Sur,** or call Laura or Dr. Amiro Perez Mera at 809/565-4601.

SPECTATOR SPORTS

Baseball

Santo Domingo's baseball park is **Quisqueya Stadium.** Anyone can to go a game, although for big games getting a ticket can be kind of tricky, simply because the sport is so popular. During the 1995 season, for example, players like Rafael Belliard, Andujar Cedeño, Mariano Duncan, José César Franco, Stan Javier, Tony Peña, Luis Polonia, José Rijo, and Sammy Sosa (among others) were scheduled to play in their home country. Despite the scarcity of tickets, making Santo Domingo home for a month in the winter and watching baseball can be an enormously rewarding experience. For tips on getting tickets, see "Baseball" under "Spectator Sports" in the On the Road chapter.

Horse Racing

Horse racing is big at the new **Race Track V Centenario,** located on the Las Américas Highway, about halfway from downtown Santo Domingo to the airport. They can be called at 809/687-6060, but just look in the newspaper. The track is a great way to get the feel of the country, its people, food, music and color. It's a very modern and comfortable facility as well.

Greyhound Racing

Also interesting are the greyhound races at **Canodromo El Coco** (tel. 809/567-4461), a track located about 15 minutes north of Santo Domingo on the Duarte Highway. Races are held Wednesday–Saturday in the evenings, and Sunday afternoon.

Cockfighting

Though strictly for peasants and workers in the countryside, cockfighting in Santo Domingo is something of a high-society sport. Fights take place at the **Coliseo Gallístico de Santo Domingo,** on Luperón Avenue. Telephone 809/565-3844 for information.

Tennis

If you consult the daily sports pages, you can learn about amateur and professional matches played throughout the year, some at private clubs and hotels, some at the Olympic Stadium.

*V Centenario
Race Track*

The most important professional competition is the Marlboro Cup, held at the Olympic Center in November.

Wrestling
Wrestling matches are occasionally held at **Estadio Eugenio María de Hostos.**

SHOPPING

The best way to go shopping in Santo Domingo is to walk and keep your eyes open for something that catches your fancy. Some tremendous bargains, and extraordinarily odd purchases can be made in the most unlikely places. In the last ten years, Santo Domingo has exploded in terms of new shops and services, all of which makes for a bustling commercial hive of activity. Also, keep in mind that the name of a store or shop may not be fully indicative of the things sold inside. Consider, for example, **Tokio Motors,** which sounds like it sells cars but in fact sells new and used electrical appliances. Hardware stores *(ferreterías)* may sell bicycles or Oriental rugs. **Farmaplex,** a huge drugstore, sells luxury products, snacks, videos, and many other oddball items. If you need to purchase specific items and don't know exactly where to go, you should always begin your search with the Yellow Pages *(Páginas Amarillas).*

Shopping Hours
Shopping hours are generally from about 8:30 A.M. to around 7 P.M., minus a midday hour or two for siesta. Sometimes you'll find a shop locked in the morning and in the evening, but open during lunch. More and more people are working what's called the *horario corrido,* which means straight through without a break. Too bad, really. Saturday is generally not a good day to shop, as you'll find many shops closed, but if you shop, try doing it before one o'clock in the afternoon. Sunday, as you'd expect, most things are closed.

Mercado Modelo
Located in a huge peeling plaster building that resembles an old art deco bus station, the Mercado Modelo in Santo Domingo is a mega-amplified version of the traditional market. Only a few blocks from the Colonial District, it's so crowded with stalls that you can hardly walk. It also contains an astounding abundance of goods, including woodcarvings, ceramics, jewelry, musical instruments, leather goods, mahogany rocking chairs, cassettes and CDs, wicker, herbs, and T-shirts. Vendors along the outer edges of the market sell fresh vegetables and poultry, pork, and goat, and the array of fruit includes cassava,

plantains, guava, bananas, and pineapple. Some of the vendors offer spectacular Dominican sweets *(dulces)* that are a treat to the palate. Any taxi driver in Santo Domingo can get you there in a jiffy, and sometimes you'll find young men at the front entrance who, for a couple of dollars, will guide you through the turmoil and even translate for you.

Specialty Shops

There are thousands of little shops in Santo Domingo; nobody could possibly catalogue them all. Keep in mind that the downtown area, meaning that zone from Calle 27 de Febrero to Avenida Mella between Calle 30 de Marzo and Vincente Noble, is where you go to find bargains, where you go to visit the Mercado Modelo, and where you go to visit Haitian shops selling wicker, art, and knickknacks. Wandering in the Avenida Duarte area is very different from wandering in Gazcue and Naco, which tend to be much more upscale, featuring art, fashion, and design. The Colonial District has art galleries and antique stores, with its share of gift shops. In the heart of the Colonial District, the **Calle El Conde** hosts a variety of stores, many of which are patronized by Dominicans in the evenings and on holidays. In the neighborhoods, new shopping centers seem to be going up like mushrooms in the forest, as the Dominican Republic joins the rest of us in the rush to out-consumerize each other. The **Plaza Central** is the largest shopping mall in the city, located on the corner of Winston Churchill and 27 de Febrero. The center of high fashion may be the **Plaza Naco** (Av. Tiradentes, corner of Fantino Falco), while the newest mall of them all is the **Unicentro Plaza** (corner of Abraham Lincoln and 27 de Febrero). Maybe the best shopping center is the **Plaza Criolla** (Av. 27 de Febrero at Anacaona). For a shopping mall it is tastefully designed; the shops are posh and not franchised or mass produced.

Antique Shops

There are many hideaway junk stores in the capital. Some have real treasures. To get your

SHOPPING MALLS IN SANTO DOMINGO

There are small shopping areas on most of the major streets, including 27 de Febrero, Bolívar, Sarasota, Winston Churchill, Gustavo Mejía Richart, Roberto Pastoriza, Abraham Lincoln, Tiradentes, and so on.

Larger shopping malls include Plaza Central, at 27 de Febrero and Winston Churchill, where a wide variety of stores sell shoes, clothing, jewelry, furnishings, and electric appliances. There is an eating area with a number of small restaurants, a video games arcade, and a cinema. Teenagers hang out there on weekends.

At Plaza and Centro Comercial Naco, on Av. Tiradentes, north of Gustavo Mejía Ricart, you will find a wide variety of shops in two separate shopping areas. Park on the east side of the street, in front of Asturias supermarket, or in the parking garage behind the plaza. (As you are going north on Tiradentes, turn left on Fantino Falco, just before the plaza, and enter the garage to the right, after Plaza Lama. The exit is to the other side.) The parking attendants at the lot in front of Plaza Naco will sell you a ticket even if the lot is full; it is easier to avoid them.

Shops are still being filled at Unicentro Plaza, on the corner of Abraham Lincoln and 27 de Febrero, which includes clothing, shoe, book, and gift shops. Casa Virginia, selling women's clothing and gift items in two separate shops, is a tradition among Dominicans.

The Colonial District's El Conde is not a shopping mall, but it has a wide variety of shops. It is particularly good for shoes, but you can find practically anything.

Plaza Lama and La Sirena, located at Av. Duarte, sell everything from shoes to refrigerators and shampoo at some of the lowest prices in town. Plaza Lama recently opened up an appliance store at Plaza Central and a children's store at Plaza Naco; La Sirena is expected to build a new branch on Winston Churchill Avenue, off Gustavo Mejía Ricart.

Two large hardware stores have several branches, with Ferretería Americana in a new mall at Av. J.F. Kennedy. Ferretería Haché has expanded its main branch on the same avenue.

hunt started, try **Ancestros** (R. Pastoriza 463, tel. 809/563-3072), **Centro de Antigüedades** (C.N. Penson 19, tel. 809/687-7758), **Circa Antiques** (Caonabo 18, tel. 809/689-0101), **Siglo XVII Antigüedades** (Sarasota 79, tel. 809/534-5268), and **Tarjetas Nader** (Av. W. Churchill, tel. 809/563-3078).

Flea Markets

Sometimes wandering in flea markets is a kick, and there are good ones at **Mercado de las Pulgas** and the **Centro de los Héroes.** On Sunday, walk down to the Atarzana parking lot below the Alcázar and check out the flea market where you can sometimes find decent antiques.

Tariff Considerations

Wherever you shop, remember that the Dominican Republic's high tariffs mean that most foreign-produced goods are quite expensive by international standards. Also keep in mind that Hispaniola is an island and must import most of its basic necessities and most of its luxuries. Therefore, things like foreign-made clothes, shoes, cosmetics, foodstuffs, wine, and machine goods are very expensive. On the other hand, anything made locally in the Dominican Republic is very cheap. These items include hand-tailored suits and dresses, furniture, art, crafts, jewelry (amber or larimar), fruit, coffee, cigars, merengue, CDs, and rum. If you're thinking about souvenirs to take home, make your picks from these items.

Duty-Free Shops

There are duty-free shops at the Centro de los Héroes, La Atarazana, and at the Las Américas Airport, as well as at the Santo Domingo, Sheraton, and Embajador hotels in town, which offer the standard array of French perfume, liquor, camera equipment, watches, and jewelry. If you've seen a duty-free shop anywhere, these shops are not much different. With regard to Dominican specialties like rum, coffee, and cigars, you'd probably be better off buying the item in town.

ART

Serious art may be the best buy you can make for the money. That is not to say that serious art is cheap, because it isn't. However, you can find wonderful painting, sculpture, carvings, and antiques, which, while expensive by Dominican standards, are relatively cheap in the art world. Of course, some paintings are sold for many thousands of dollars and become precious collectors' items. In this case, you should have a good idea of what you're buying and why. On the other hand, some galleries offer good bargains on paintings by well-known Dominican artists. One of your first moves should be to investigate the **Museum of Modern Art** in the Plaza de la Cultura at Máximo Gómez and Cézar Nicolás Pensón. The Museum has a bookstore and pamphlets available to help you navigate the history of Dominican art. At that point you can examine the galleries and see what moves you. There is a small store in the museum that offers local artists' works for affordable prices, and charges only a small sales commission.

The main areas for examining and purchasing art in Santo Domingo are the **Colonial District** and the **Naco-Gazcue** neighborhood. Of course, one place to start looking at art in an informal setting is the aforementioned **Hostal Nader** (Calle Duarte, corner of Luperón), where the walls of the hotel—and the rooms—are lined with paintings, and there is a small store and gallery. The same family has a formal art gallery in the Colonial District. You can find **Galería de Arte Nader** at La Atarazana 9, near the Alcázar. The works are expensive but of high quality. One of my favorite galleries in the old city is **María del Carmen** (Arz. Meriño 207, tel. 809/686-7409), where the friendly staff of two will conduct you on a guided tour of the labyrinthine gallery whose walls are packed with interesting work.

One gallery also excites interest because it is run by a Haitian artist named Cedon Fritzner. Called **Los Primitivos** (Calle Duarte 154, tel. 809/688-2628), it is one place in Santo Domingo where you can get real Haitian art, though you must exercise some caution in what you're buying, as always. Perhaps the most interesting works there are Haitian hammered-tin wall hangings, which are colorfully painted representations of *guaguas,* Victorian houses, and street scenes. For surreal paintings, lamps, and very unusual works of sculpture, visit **Marialejos** (Arz. Nouel 53, tel. 809/687-1858). Many of the works there are by Peruvian artisans.

An absolute must visit for those interested in antiques, furniture, and modern sculpture is the **Makana Gallery Shop** located near the ruins of the San Francisco Convent, high on a hill overlooking the Colonial District (Calle Hostos 313, tel. 809/221-8700, fax 809/221-8820). The Makana represents about 30 local artists who sculpt, build furniture, paint, and create unusual gifts of jewelry, laminated maps, and vases. You can find almost everything from photography to engravings or silkscreen. Just walking around the place is like going to a superb new museum. Also in the Colonial District is the **De Soto Galería** (Calle Hostos, corner of Luperón), which features paintings and antiques. Near the Alcázar, too, is **Galería Rosa María** (La Atarazana 7), while **Galería de Arte Sebelén** is at Calle Hostos 209. There are a couple of decent galleries on El Conde as well: the **Affant** (El Conde 513) and a branch of **San Ramón** in the same building. Most of the stuff on El Conde looks a little suspect, but maybe your cheesy is not my cheesy. Near the Colonial District, but more downtown, is **Cándido Bidó** (Av. Mella 9-B).

In the Neighborhoods

Art in the neighborhoods is slightly more upscale, at least the surroundings in which it's presented. If the Galería de Arte Nader in La Atarazana is in one of the oldest buildings in Santo Domingo, the supercharged **Galería George Nadar** (Rafael Sánchez, corner Federico Geraldino, tel. 809/544-0878) is very modern indeed. One of the leading galleries in Santo Domingo is the justly famous **Nouveau Centro de Arte** (Av. Independencia 354, tel. 809/689-6869), which has a wide choice of Latin American art but features primarily Ceballos, Avilés, Perdomo, Varela, Recto Capellán, Pineda, and Ramirez. They also specialize in emerging Latin American artists, who have their own permanent display. Of equal importance to the art world of Santo Domingo is **Arawak** (Pasteur 104, tel. 809/685-1661), which usually features exhibitions of Dominican and Haitian art and at least one important artist from South America. Keep in mind that most of the neighborhood galleries feature some serious Haitian primitive art, so that's where you should go if you're looking for Haitian work. Other important galleries in the neighborhoods are **El Greco** (Av. Tiradentes

16, tel. 809/562-5921), **La Galería** (Gustavo Mejía Ricart 93, tel. 809/563-7677), or **Deniels** (Av. Independencia 1201, tel. 809/565-6755). One way to get good information is to drop in on the Hostal Nader on Duarte in the Colonial District, and get the curator to give you some of his art catalogues and folders on Dominican and Latin art. One of the most knowledgeable people in the city is Mildred Canahuate, who runs the Arawak Gallery. You can also get good background, and see impressive art, at **Galería Paiewonsky** (Calle Espaillat 260), which features ultra-modern art.

Individual Artists' Galleries

Keep in mind that many individual artists such as Guillo Pérez (F. Prats Ramirez 302 in Evaristo Morales) and Cándido Bidó (on Calle Dr. Baez 5 in Gazcue) have their own galleries. My own personal favorite among Dominican artists is Ulloa, who maintains a gallery in Calle Duarte 302. Art purchased in Santo Domingo can be shipped home cheaply, and the gallery can make the arrangements for you. Most galleries can also arrange framing or tell you where you can get it done.

CRAFTS

Typical Dominican crafts include ceramics, porcelain dolls, mahogany carvings, furniture, and jewelry made of amber, larimar, or coral. Some so-called "Dominican" crafts are imports from Haiti. Make certain you know where a craft is made before purchasing. The aforementioned Mercado Modelo on Av. Mella near the Plaza de Independencia has a large collection of stalls selling crafts, music, and paintings. In a more tranquil atmosphere you can try bargaining for T-shirts, jewelry, and craft items at Plaza Criolla (Av. 27 de Febrero, just west of Máximo Gómez), which is more expensive than the Modelo but might be more to your liking.

Colonial District

The Colonial District is crammed with gift shops selling a wide array of things from tourist gimcrack to authentic carvings. A representative place is the **El Conde Gift Shop** (Calle El Conde 153, tel. 809/682-5909), which has the famous

Dominican rocking chairs that can be purchased for reassembly at home. The gift shop in the **Casa de Bastidas,** located on Calle de las Damas near the Fort, offers genuine artisan crafts. **Ambasa,** on the corner of Calle Hostos and Restauración, sells jewelry made from genuine amber, as well as other significant craftworks. You can go inside and view the artisans at work in the shop adjacent to the retail space. One of the most fascinating stores is **Musical Padilla** (Arz. Nouel 151-1), which sells musical instruments—mostly handmade guitars that are hanging in view. Go in and play one for yourself.

The Atarazana

The Atarazana area around the Alcázar is loaded with art and gift shops, with **Atarazana** (La Atarazana 21) being representative. In all these shops you'll find amber and larimar jewelry, carvings, Haitian paintings, hammered tin, and dolls.

The world of amber is well represented in the Atarazana as well. Located just around the corner from the Alcázar is **Ámbar Tres** (La Atarazana 3, tel. 809/688-0474), which offers not only jewelry with amber and larimar, but also coral carvings, paintings, and some mahogany work as well. Open every day, it closes Sunday at noon. Also nearby is **Ámbar Maldo** (Atarazana 1, tel. 809/688-0639), which in addition to necklaces and other amber work has pottery and masks. You should always be on the lookout for Carnaval masks, which are among the most distinctive Dominican handcrafts. If you find an original, take it home. Also in the Colonial District is the **Amber Factory** (Restauración 110, corner Calle Hostos, tel. 809/686-5700), which also specializes in leather purses.

The Neighborhoods

All of the neighborhoods along Av. Independencia, throughout Gazcue, just behind the Malecón, and, of course, the Naco, are cluttered with small, out-of-the-way shops. Take a long walk in any of these lovely, shady places and you're sure to find a unique spot to satisfy your curiosity. A typical example of such a shop is **Tu Espacio** (Av. Cervantes 102, tel. 809/686-6006), which has a cluttered look but is actually very special. Filled with reproductions of Taíno art, European antiques, bamboo furniture, and

plenty of esoteric odds and ends, it is sure to inspire a sense of excitement. The shop called **Artessa** (Calle Roberto Pastoriza) carries Haitian and Latin American crafts and has the same feel as Tu Espacio.

Both Haitian and Dominican crafts, as well as hand-painted birds, are the specialty at **Nuebo** (Calle Fantino Falco 36), while **Habitat** at Plaza Lincoln (near Av. Abraham Lincoln at 27 de Febrero) sells its own designs. The shops **Mary** and **Alfonso** are at Plaza Naco. If you go to the Sheraton and find the back door and parking lot, directly opposite is the personal workshop of **María del Carmen Ossaye** (Calle Cervantes 52), who fashions purses, guitars, and furniture. **De Piel** (Calle Santiago 405) is a workshop and warehouse that sells very high-priced leather goods, which often show up in boutiques like **La Maleta** on Av. 27 de Febrero near Av. Abraham Lincoln.

JEWELRY

Although amber and larimar are the most native of all the types of semiprecious and precious stones available in the Dominican Republic, the country is also well known for its distinctive styles in jewelry. If all that glitters is your special thing, you can start at **Brador,** next door to the Amber Factory in the Colonial District. Its specialty is rings, and you'll find hundreds from which to choose. On El Conde, in the Colonial District, the well-known jeweler **Casa Tonos** (El Conde 259, tel. 809/221-4820) is a large and busy place with knowledgeable salespeople who can tell you about watches, calculators, and sunglasses, as well as gold jewelry and earrings. Next door is **Capriles** (El Conde 225, tel. 809/689-4654), a quiet and air-conditioned shop where you can browse through gold chains, bracelets, medallions, and rings, as well as coral and larimar. Another spot on the colonial zone for locally made jewelry is **Macaluso's Jewelry Café** (32 Duarte St., corner of San Felipe, tel. 809/586-3433), which, as the name suggests, offers food and drink along with shopping. If you wander down to the Plaza Central on Av. 27 de Febrero and just east of Av. Winston Churchill, you'll find four popular jewelry shops, including Casa Tonos' main showroom and the nearby **Joyería Charlie,** which has a good reputation in the business. **Casa Virginia,** in Centro Comercial Nacional (Corner of Abraham Lincoln and 27 de Febrero), represents Cartier in the Dominican Republic and specializes in European lines. Torre Alessandra, on Av. Abraham Lincoln (tel. 809/642-6509), is the home of **Joyería Michelle,** the only store in Santo Domingo affiliated with the Jewelers of America. Michelle has stores in the Hotel Jaragua and Plaza Central as well. They are geared to elegance and price and specialize in diamonds.

One-of-a-kind items of ceramic jewelry are available from Carlos Despradel and Eduardo Fiallo, whose designs are available at many shops. One such shop is the **Nouveau Gallery,** next to the Sheraton on Av. Independencia, or the **Plaza Shop,** behind the Menor Catedral in the Colonial District.

FURNITURE

Furniture made in the Dominican Republic comes in wrought iron, wicker and rattan, and mahogany.

Wrought Iron

While it may seem impossible to purchase wrought iron to take home, if you stick to small things like lamps or end tables, you'll be surprised at what you can find light and distinctive enough to be alluring. Even candle holders and napkin rings can be suitable in wrought iron. For wrought iron, **Ingrid Fernández** (Plaza Fernández, Av. Winston Churchill 1552, tel. 809/544-2390) can't be beat. Fernández, an architect by profession, has been designing furniture and accessories for several years and has a workshop behind the offices, so you can see the pieces under construction. **Fierro Arte Hierro** (Av. 27 de Febrero 321, tel. 809/566-5230) is a small house covered in greenish blue wrought iron leaves, which ought to get your attention. The pieces are specially designed, quite expensive, and very hot on the Dominican designer scene. Three streets north of Av. 27 de Febrero is **Forjarte Plaza Palmeras** (Av. Winston Churchill, tel. 809/565-1525), which houses five different design shops. While much of the iron is too large for transport, you can find smaller things like plant stands and chairs.

Wicker and Rattan

Wicker and rattan pieces are probably the easiest to ship and the cheapest to purchase of all furniture items. A wide selection of inexpensive but attractive boxes, accessories, and hand-painted cushions is at **Ambiente Decoraciones** (Av. Independencia at Dr. Delgado), while more expensive items of furniture can be found at **Hipopótamo** (Calle Maz Enrique Ureña 31), **Bonsai** (Calle Fantino Falco near Plaza Naco), or **La Nueva Dimensión** (Calle Gustavo Majia Ricart 79, Plaza Naco). At a small store near the U.S. embassy called **Delgados** (Av. Maximo Gómez 58), there is plenty of nice wicker and rattan furniture as well. **Rattan Industrial,** in the Alma Rosa at Calle Costa Rica 136, is a large exporter of rattan and wicker furniture of all types and sizes.

Mahogany

Although mahogany and soft-wood furnishings would be difficult to package and export, many shops that produce large pieces also carry small accessories, antiques, carvings, and jewelry. The Cadillac of these shops is **Patricia Reid** (Av. Máximo Gómez at the corner of Malecón, tel. 809/686-0858). Reid is an exclusive designer who specializes in heavy stone tables. Her other shop is in the Colonial District at Arz. Nouel and is filled with beautiful armoires, tables, chairs, lounges, silk rugs, and antiques. For mahogany rocking chairs that are top of the line, try **Sabina** in the Colonial District (Arz. Nouel 204-1). They will package for export. For smaller pieces and unique bric-a-brac, check out **Circa Antiques** (Calle Caonabo 18, corner Pedro Lluberes, tel. 809/689-0202) and the small boutique called **Palladium** on Plaza Fernández. Beautiful and unusual art is the specialty at **Abu Naba** on Plaza Palmeras (tel. 809/563-3078). Although it is highly unlikely you'll actually be exporting any huge pieces, you should check out **Muebles Von** (Plaza Palmeras, Av. Winston Churchill, tel. 809/566-1433), which has a large selection of mahogany and pine furniture from which you might begin comparisons. And, of course, for the really big show, the largest furniture store in all of the Dominican Republic is **González Muebles** (27 de Febrero 336, tel. 809/562-2372), where there are five floors of furniture, including one whole level devoted to unusual imports.

CLOTHES

Santo Domingo's modern shopping centers, where middle- and upper-class Santo Domingans do a lot of their shopping for clothes and food, are as modern as anything in Europe and the United States, and just as cold and impersonal. Unless you're shopping for seriously high-fashion items, you're probably better off at a more traditional marketplace.

Small tailor shops for men are scattered here and there throughout the downtown area and the neighborhoods. You might consult the Yellow Pages to find one near where you're staying, and then drop by and check out what they can do. For menswear (and remember, it must be Dominican made to be worth buying here), try **La Coruña** near Av. 27 de Febrero and Av. Winston Churchill, which is fairly expensive. **Solo Para Hombre** (Av. Betancourt 1560) and **Sunny** (Calle Roberto Pastoriza 152) offer contemporary men's clothes at affordable prices.

For women, start at any of the recognized fashion centers from the Plaza Naco to the Plaza Nacional and the Centro Comercial Naco, each of which houses many women's clothing stores, some quite high fashion. For example, at Plaza Naco there is **Abraxas, Marian Cristina Boutique, Cachet Boutique,** and others. Nearby is **Mimosa** (Calle Fantino Falcon 59). You'll find high-quality swimwear, shorts, and T-shirts at **Patapoof** at Plaza Criolla. A favorite is **Natacha** (Calle Sánchez y Sánchez, corner of Av. Lope de Vega), where they sell nightgowns and lingerie.

VARIOUS CONSUMABLES

Coffee
You can buy excellent coffee, most of it freshly ground, in any supermarket in Santo Domingo.

There are many varieties to choose from. No matter where you buy it, the coffee should average about US$2 per pound. There is an excellent place to buy coffee next to the Mercado Modelo, on the left as you go up the stairs, or you can buy inside the market, or at many of the stores on Av. Mella nearby. There is an excellent coffee shop located on El Conde, about three blocks from Calle de las Damas.

If you get stuck with some Dominican pesos at the airport on the way home, you can buy coffee very cheap.

Cigars
A wonderful cigar store is located just across from the cathedral and the Parque Colón, where you can buy hand-rolled cigars and watch others being made before your very eyes. These cigars are expensive by Dominican standards, but cheap by most others.

Rum
Like coffee, there is no need to buy rum anywhere but from a supermarket or *colmado*. You won't save a thing buying from a duty-free shop, and you may even find yourself missing out on regional specialties. If you're going to take home rum, buy only the top-of-the-line dark aged rums like *añejo,* which are marginally more expensive in the Dominican Republic but compare favorably with excellent cognacs and are tremendous bargains.

ENGLISH-LANGUAGE BOOKS

New Books
Santo Domingo is packed with bookstores, but most do not feature English-language books. My favorite hangout in the Colonial District is **Linea Studebaker,** on Arz. Nouel, just down the street from the main entrance to the cathedral. Here you can get your fix of major newspapers and

guides. **Casa Cuello** (El Conde 201) has some interesting stuff tucked away under dust. Just dust, not dust jackets. Keep in mind that most major hotels on the Malecón carry international magazines and newspapers. **Bookies,** located on the second floor of the Plaza Central shopping mall at 27 de Febrero and Winston Churchill, sells English-language books. Perhaps the largest selection of U.S. magazines and newspapers is at **Tienda Geyda** in the Centro Comercial Naco (tel. 809/566-4577). For general wandering around convenience, try the ubiquitous **Yellow Tempo Kiosks,** where you'll find *U.S.A. Today* and the *Herald Tribune.*

Used Books
The first Saturday morning of the month, the **Helen Kellogg Library,** located behind Epiphany Union Church at Av. Independencia (tel. 809/689-2070), holds a used-book sale. Near Hostos on El Conde, a gentleman holds sway over a huge pile of used books. It's a mess, but in the mess are some English-language books. Dig in and be prepared to bargain.

Library
Finally, longer-term residents should consider becoming members of the **Helen Kellogg Library,** where they can enjoy check-out privileges on a wide array of English and American books. Hours are Sunday 9–11 A.M., Tuesday 2:30–5 P.M., Wednesday mornings and afternoons, and Saturday 9–11 A.M.

SERVICES

Telephones
With about 15 Codetel offices located in Santo Domingo, telephoning shouldn't be a problem. The most convenient Codetel is at #20 Calle El Conde, right in the heart of the Colonial District.

Post Offices
You'll find Santiago's main post office on Héroes de Luperón/Rafael Damirón at the Centro de los Héroes (tel. 809/534-6218, fax 809/534-6318). Also convenient are the Hotel El Embajador (tel. 809/221-2131), Ciudad Nueva (tel. 809/685-6920), and Sans Souci (tel. 809/593-1306) branches.

Language Classes
Unfortunately, Spanish for foreigners is not a big business in Santo Domingo. There is, however, a growing number of small language schools that offer courses of interest. First and foremost in the business is **Instituto Cultural Dominico-Americano,** located at Av. Abraham Lincoln 21 (tel. 809/533-4191). The institute is near the university and was founded in 1947. At present, it has about 10,000 students and 150 teachers. The students are mostly Dominican, study either in the language school or the technical school, and are taught by teachers from all over the world. As a nonprofit institution, the Instituto holds classes for pre-schoolers

and elementary and secondary school students, and has two choirs and some musical education as well. There is a small bookstore on the bottom floor where you can find textbooks.

The courses in Spanish for foreigners at the Instituto are conducted for one hour each day, five days each week, and are offered in two-month cycles depending on demand. The classes are always in the morning.

As for other schools, one of the newer language schools for foreigners is called **Hispaniola Caribe de Linguas,** founded in 1992. Visit them on the Web at www.hispaniola.org.

Universidad APEC (Máximo Gómez 72, tel. 809/686-0021) has a language school that offers classes in Spanish for foreigners as well. These courses are based on the trimester system and are given two hours each day, five days a week. New enrollees take a placement exam.

Entrena (Calle R.F. Bonelly 26, tel. 809/541-4283) offers personalized Spanish lessons structured in four-week programs. What's special about this program is its intensive four-week course in which the student lives with a Dominican family and takes seven hours a day of language instruction. There are other programs as well, offering both three-hour and one-hour courses. Call two weeks in advance to set up your program. A new private business called **Instituto Internacional de Español para Ex-**

tranjeros (IIEE) has set up shop to teach company members and small groups Spanish for business purposes and also offers cultural immersion (Calle Jose A. Polanco Billini, corner of Arroyo Hondo, A, tel. 809/565-0086, fax 809/566-0682).

Probably the newest language institute in Santo Domingo is **Lengua y Cultura** (Wenceslao Alvarez 201, tel. 809/682-8986, fax 809/682-8645) in Gazcue, offering four levels of classes on two hourly schedules (10-hour and six-hour). The business of teaching Spanish certainly seems to be growing in the city.

Other foreign languages are taught in Santo Domingo as well, especially French, German, and Japanese. Call the embassy in question to find out details.

SANTO DOMINGO MEDICAL SERVICES

Centro Clínico Las Mercedes: 232 San Martin, tel. 809/565-5779

Centro de Obstetricia y Ginecología: Independencia, tel. 809/221-7100

Centro de Otorrinolaringología: 27 de Febrero, tel. 809/685-0151

Centro de Pediatría: 504 Independencia, tel. 809/685-1111

Centro Médico UCE*: Pedro Henríquez Ureña, tel. 809/221-0171

Clínica Abel González: 101 Independencia, tel. 809/682-6001

Clínica Abreu*: 42 Beller St., tel. 809/688-4411

Clínica Dr. Yunen: 652 Bolivar, tel. 809/689-9840

Clínica Gómez Patiño: 701 Independencia, tel. 809/685-9131

Corazones Unidos*: 21 Fantino Falco, tel. 809/567-4421

*also provides emergency services

BOB RACE

THE ARID SOUTHWEST
INTRODUCTION

Land

The vast arid regions to the west and southwest of Santo Domingo will be familiar to those who have traveled in the American Southwest, or perhaps the dry coastal regions of Chile. Without the deep-hued roses and purples of the New Mexican sage country, the southwest of the Dominican Republic is nonetheless beautiful in its own way and can be very alluring to those who crave sparsely populated country, long vistas, and places off the beaten path. The region itself is shaped like India, with its pointed end facing due south toward Venezuela, a shape which ends at Cabo Beata and is dotted by large lagoons, then cut off from Isla Beata by a channel of the same name. The towns here, even the major ones, are relatively small and not much visited by outsiders, and whatever agriculture survives does so by virtue of irrigation and in spite of a salty soil that exists because so much of the area was once under the sea.

The southwest is divided administratively into six provinces. Due west of Santo Domingo is San Cristóbal and its major city of the same name. Located about 30km west of Santo Domingo, San Cristóbal is perhaps the most tourist-oriented city in the region. Farther west is

Baní, the capital city of the province of Peravia, called the "city of poets," while another 60km west is Azua de Compostela, capital of the province of Azua. When tourists do head southwest, they are usually bound for Barahona province, and the city of Barahona itself, which is located on a pretty bay, and is just now developing tourist hotels and an international airport.

Rounding out the picture of the arid southwest are the provinces of Pedernales, Bahoruco, and San Juan, which are dry, mountaínous, and rugged. Keep in mind that this region is also the home of three national parks, a scientific reserve, and a huge saltwater lake that is below sea level.

As you move west, away from the hustle of Santo Domingo, sugarcane fields give way to sparse vegetation that includes scrub and cactus, along with the huge aloe that comes to dominate the countryside. In the upland valleys of the Neiba and the Bahoruco, however, coffee, grapes, and bananas are all grown on both large and small plots, and where there is some rain, the mountains are stupendously green. Most of the beaches in the region are too rocky and wild to be of use to swimmers and can be dangerous because of heavy tides. There are, however,

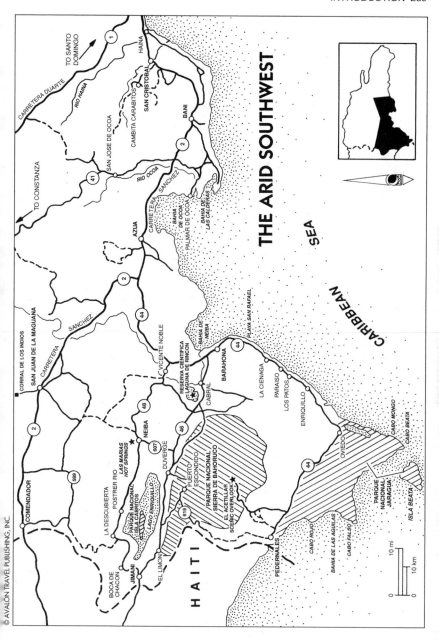

THE ARID SOUTHWEST

© AVALON TRAVEL PUBLISHING, INC.

some untouched beaches composed of good gray sand, where the rough rocky cliffs give way to open spaces.

The main highway of Santo Domingo, going west, is called the Carretera Sánchez, which extends to San Cristóbal and Baní, and beyond all the way to Barahona and Pedernales, running through waving sugarcane fields and, later, desert-like country. The good beaches here are located near Las Salinas, Azua, and Barahona, while other beaches are accessible on dirt roads by car along the way. As you go west on the Sánchez, which is a very good paved road and not much traveled, you'll emerge into country of organ pipe cactus, mesquite, and irrigated vegetable farms, and you'll notice the air becoming drier and drier as the mountains rise up on either side around you. Just beyond Azua, at Cruce de Ocoa, a paved road heads for the Cordillera Central and San José de Ocoa, a nice foothills town that is the gateway for a rough dirt track which goes uphill toward Constanza.

Climate

Traveling west from Santo Domingo, all the way to the Pedernales along the Haitian border, the climate becomes drier and drier, hotter and hotter. Mountains in the north, including the massive Cordillera Central, wring almost all of the rain out of the tradewinds and clouds. Due to its location in the mountains' rain shadow, the region around Barahona and low-lying Lake Enriquillo (below sea level) can see temperatures in excess of 40°C (104°F). However, the low humidity makes things tolerable, if a bit dusty. Naturally, in the Sierra de Bahoruco and Sierra de Neiba, altitude moderates the heat, and the coastal areas are cooled somewhat by ocean breezes. Still, months can pass without rain in this region, and what agriculture exists does so purely because of well-water irrigation. Cactus and succulents are the main flora.

When rain falls it generally arrives in one of two ways—the occasional brief squall from cumulus buildup, coming in the late afternoon, or, in hurricane season (September through November), tropical storms can skirt the southwest coast and produce heavy rainfall. Full-blown hurricane strikes, however, rarely hit this coast.

Getting There

Expeditions to the arid southwest could be of two or three kinds. By excellent road it is possible to leave Santo Domingo and traverse the main highway all the way to the valley of the Neiba, go around Lago Enriquillo, and return back to Barahona and Santo Domingo in one long, hot, and dusty day. Making the same trip, one could stay in Barahona and descend into the Pedernales to investigate this lovely and haunted coast all the way to Enriquillo, Oviedo, and the road to Pedernales, stopping on the way to climb into the isolated Sierra de Bahoruco. For intrepid adventurers, who don't mind plenty of inconvenience in return for a splendid experience, expeditions into the mountains themselves can be arranged through the facilities of Ecoturisa, or could even be arranged solo, though the going is tough and dangerous. Whatever route you choose, the country is colorful, untraveled, and altogether delightful.

WEST FROM SANTO DOMINGO

The best way to leave Santo Domingo for the southwest is very early in the morning, before traffic thickens and makes the Malecón a living nightmare. It is Avenida George Washington that becomes the Carretera Sánchez and leads you all the way to Barahona on good paved roads. Going west out of Santo Domingo, near the small (and undistinguished) little place called Ciudad Ganadera, where the road leaves the shore, there is a monument commemorating the assassination of Trujillo on May 30, 1961. This white concrete monument was erected in 1981. Keep in mind while driving to Barahona that, though traffic is normally fairly light, crazy truck drivers rumble along the road at all hours, and for a good bit of the way to San Cristóbal, you'll be passing through toll booths that require small change. After San Cristóbal, however, the toll booths disappear, and it's clear sailing all the way. You'll find plenty of gas in the major towns, though you should keep your tank filled, just in case. Past Barahona in the Pedernales, you should always beware of the lack of facilities like water and gas, and take care to protect yourself against mosquitoes, heat, and fatigue.

Another annoyance, beyond the heat, is the fact that the good paved road called the Carretera Sánchez seems to disappear into a welter of cross-streets and alleys in every major town, especially San Cristóbal, Baní, Azua, and Barahona. At one point you're cruising along an open road enjoying the clean air, the high gray and green mountains, and the roadside attractions like honey and grape stalls, and then all of a sudden you're lost in a maze of narrow lanes. Never fear and persevere. The good road always appears again on the other side of town, and the locals are friendly and willing to help put you on the right track. Besides, cruising around a friendly Dominican town for 10 minutes can't be so bad as all that.

Haina

If you wish to visit Santo Domingo's main port and the largest sugarcane mill in the country (and, they claim, the world), turn south from Sánchez Highway, which is, at this point, well marked. Like most ports, the town is fairly drab, but there is a country club with a swimming pool and a place to stay at the teacher's vacation center for budget accommodation. On the water, the **Club Naútico Haina** (tel. 809/532-3561) is outside of town on the Carretera Sánchez at Km 131.5, where you can sail and sport if you've made previous arrangements.

The few sights include the **Capilla de San Gregorio Magno,** a ruined 16th-century chapel. To the south lie the ruins of the 16th-century **Ingenio de Diego Caballero** and **Hacienda María.** Coming to a bridge over the Río Nigua (which around here is terribly dirty), you'll see the ruins of **Ingenio Boca de Nigua,** a sugar mill built in the 18th century when sugar was truly king.

For a decent place to have a bite to eat in Haina, try the **Delimer Restaurant-Cafeteria** (Américo Lugo 23, tel. 809/542-2414).

SAN CRISTÓBAL

INTRODUCTION

Christopher Columbus ordered that a fortress be built on the banks of the Haina River, and somewhat later a town was founded on the right bank of the Río Nigua. Here the first Constitution of the Dominican Republic was signed on November 6, 1844. In 1934, the region was elevated to the rank of Province, and in 1939, by law No. 93, the title of Meritorious City was conferred upon San Cristóbal in recognition of the fact that the constitution was signed here, and because of the fact that dictator Leonidas Trujillo Molina, known as the Generalíssimo, was born here.

Nobody uses the term Meritorious City anymore, and in fact San Cristóbal is a bit of a rough industrial area. The highway back to Santo Domingo is choked with traffic at most hours of the day and night. Roughly 30km from Santo Domingo, the city has about 140,000 inhabitants, and it is growing as the suburbs of Santo Domingo creep west and San Cristóbal creeps east. Gold dominated the early history of the city, which had been discovered in the local rivers, but the gold soon gave way to sugar, and then to insouciance. Most of San Cristóbal isn't much to look at, although some lovely spots have a distinctive provincial architectural appearance, and a few nearby beaches are good.

If you're lucky enough to be around June 6–10, you'll witness the spectacular patron feast day, when locals dance the *carabiné,* a typical folk dance of the southwest. If you're on your way to the southwest, you can easily slip into San Cristóbal and investigate everything in a morning's time. It's hardly the kind of town you'd want to spend a lot of time seeing.

SIGHTS AND RECREATION

Iglesia de San Cristóbal

Facing the town's central park is the main church of the city, the Iglesia de San Cristóbal, which also houses Trujillo's formal tomb. Trujillo himself may be elsewhere—probably far below—and his actual bones rest in France.

petroglyphs near
San Cristóbal

Still, the inside of the church is nice. While visiting the church, stop by the local market just down the street, where you might find an interesting bargain or two.

Casa de Caoba

The Casa de Caoba (Mahogany House) is Trujillo's country house, and seeing it is more or less a do-it-yourself experience. To get there, or to the La Toma baths, turn right on Avenida Constitution just past the town square and go 2.7km through the Río Nigua Valley. At an intersection you'll see a sign to La Toma baths, and in less than a kilometer you'll also see a sign for Casa de Caoba on the left. The road goes uphill, and you might have to walk, but it is a very pleasant tropical walk through almond trees hung with Spanish moss. A caretaker stays on the grounds, and the house itself is supposedly under restoration, though no one knows when it will be complete.

La Toma

On the same road you'll find the La Toma baths—a series of shallow pools, swimming pools, and streams fed by an underground spring, which are popular with Dominicans on holiday and out to cool off. The pools are open Mon.–Fri. 9 A.M.–6 P.M. and Sat.–Sun. 7 A.M.–8 P.M. The pools are shaded, and there is a restaurant and snack bar for food and drink. Admission is RD$20 for adults.

Castillo del Cerro

Outside the city on a hill is the Castillo del Cerro (Hill Castle), a six-story house that once belonged to Trujillo and now houses a museum devoted to his career and achievements.

Beaches

The best beaches near San Cristóbal are at **Najayo, Nigua,** and **Palenque,** all south of town off the main highway, and all marked.

More Sights

While you're in San Cristóbal you can see the **Iglesia de Piedras Vivas,** a church, and the **Santa María** caves. Just seven km north and west of the city are some nice caves that contain Taíno petroglyphs. Called **El Pomier,** the caves are near an inactive limestone quarry. The whole area is now called the **Reserva Antropológica Cuevas de El Pomier.** Farther northwest is the nice and cool town of **Cambita Carabitos,** which overlooks San Cristóbal.

PRACTICALITIES

Accommodations

When you enter San Cristóbal on the highway from Santo Domingo to the east, the road crosses the Río Nigua and immediately faces a roundabout. On the far side is **Hotel Las Terrazas,** which is government owned and best avoided, though you can stay there really cheaply if you need to. Other inexpensive hotels in San Cristóbal include **Hotel San Cristóbal** (Av. Libertad 32, tel. 809/528-3555), **Hotel Constitución** (Av. Constitucion 118, tel. 809/528-3309), and several on Av. María Trinidad Sánchez, including **Hotel Formosa** (tel. 809/528-3229), **Hotel El Caminante** (tel. 809/528-3167), and **Hotel Wing Kit** (tel. 809/528-3229).

The main hotels are all in town, except for the Constitución, which is on the road to La Toma. The truth is that San Cristóbal isn't a great town for hotels; unless you absolutely must stay or are having great fun, perhaps you should push on in your journey.

Food

The main part of San Cristóbal holds a few restaurants and cafeterías—they're basic at best. Try **Cafetería Dulcería Airos, Restaurant Formosa,** and **Cafetería Pica Pollo la Terraza,** all on main street María Trinidad Sánchez. Order *pasteles en hojas,* the local specialty, made of bananas and minced meat.

Information

The main **Codetel** office is located in San Cristóbal at Palo Hincado 14 (tel. 809/528-4196). If you're driving and need to wend your way through town, find the first roundabout; then go two blocks to the main square and find the crowded local market. On the right you'll see an army base (you can't miss the green walls and imposing facade); straight ahead you'll be on the road to Baní and Barahona westward.

Getting There and Getting Around

If you need to take public transit to get to San Cristóbal, you can catch an express or regular bus from Santo Domingo at the edge of the Parque Independencia. The bus terminal in San Cristóbal is on the main road, and straight ahead are the Casa de Caoba and La Toma baths.

If you're driving, you'll be able to visit the sights of San Cristóbal, several of which are north of town on a decent road, and several of which are west of town on the main highway. If you're on foot once you get into town, you catch both the *públicos* and motor-taxis behind the market down the street from the main plaza in the center of town. If you're coming from Santo Domingo by bus, you'll be let off at the main plaza. The market is a short walk away, where you'll find local transport.

BANÍ TO PEDERNALES

The provinces of Peravia and Azua are both fairly productive agricultural areas that grow coffee, sugarcane, bananas, and, now, surprisingly, grapes. This particular section of the southwestern Dominican Republic has seen a certain prosperity due to irrigation and sugarcane, and the cities and villages are quiet and tranquilly beautiful, if not spectacular. The farther west you drive, the more you'll find the traffic thinning out, the air becoming drier, and the vegetation turning to scrub, mesquite, and cactus.

Baní, the next town west of San Cristóbal, is about 70km from Santo Domingo, about 30km west of San Cristóbal. The section of highway between Baní and Barahona is about 100km long and crosses desolate but striking countryside that is sparsely inhabited. When you're on the road from Baní, you'll soon leave the palm trees and irrigated fields behind and steadily progress into long stretches of semi-desert, some sand dunes, and terrain that steepens between ranges of hills and mountains in the far distance. The only villages between cities consist of thatched huts or concrete shacks, and there are few services. As you go west, though, you can see the gradually looming Sierra de Neiba on the northwest horizon, strikingly blue in the often hazy distance.

BANÍ

The capital of the province of Peravia, Baní is known in the Dominican Republic as the city of poets. It is named after Chieftain Baní, Caonabo's right-hand man, who is said to have possessed admirable intelligence. In the Taíno language, *baní* means "abundance of water," though in fact Baní in modern times seems little more than a dusty provincial town without much to attract the permanent resident. These days, the town is noted mainly as being the birthplace of Máximo Gómez, who led the 19th-century struggle for Cuban independence from Spain. Its inhabitants, who number roughly 106,000, are mainly merchants or agricultural workers.

Sights and Events

The highway leads directly into downtown Baní, and you'll find a number of shops for food or drink in the area around Calle Padre Billini and Calle Mella. The local church, **Iglesia Nuestra Señora de Regla,** hosts the *fiestas patronales* every year on November 21, and the town is noted locally and regionally for its super-sweet mangos, which are pink in color. June is the month for mangos.

Sights in Baní include **Generalíssimo Máximo Gómez's House** and the local **Municipal Museum,** a large gray and white building on the western side of the town square closed on Sunday but open during the day otherwise. The museum doubles as City Hall and is called Palacio del Ayuntamiento, though it isn't really too palatial.

Accommodations and Food

Inexpensive are the **Hotel Brisas del Sur** and the **Hotel Alba** (tel. 809/522-3590), both on Calle Bellini and Calle Mella, near the central park in a quiet part of the city. The Alba in particular is simple but satisfactory. In town, moderate hotels include **Hotel Caribaní** (Calle Sánchez 12, tel. 809/522-4400), **Hotel Las BBB** (Carretera Sánchez Km 1.5, tel. 809/522-4422), and also on the highway **Hotel Sylvia** (tel. 809/522-4674) and **Hotel La Posada** (tel. 809/522-4541). The new **Los Almedros** (tel. 809/571-3530) at Baní beach has 78 rooms, a restaurant, pool, whirlpool, water sports, and cable TV in some rooms.

For eating, try the **Restaurant Heladería Capri** at Calle Duarte 20, though there are a number of small cafes in the central part of the city, including **Pizzeria Mi Estancia** (Calle Mella 33), which serves pizza and basic fast food. The most popular spot in town, located near the market in the western part of the city, is **Pollo Rey** in Celle Bellini, which serves breaded chicken.

Information

When you get tired, you can rest in the **Parque Duarte,** which is quite pleasant. **Codetel** is at Padre Billini 3.

SIDE TRIPS FROM BANÍ

Baní Beach

The local beach, called simply Baní Beach, isn't too good for swimming or diving but does have the new **Los Almedros** hotel. Actually, three beaches are reachable south of Baní, including the above-mentioned **Palenque, Baní,** and the preferable **Las Salinas** beach.

Las Salinas

To reach Las Salinas, take the road south from Baní, and go to Las Calderas naval base (you'll probably have to ask directions for Las Calderas in town). The road turns to gravel and dirt down toward the dunes of Bahía de Calderas, but soon you'll see the bay, which is shallow and lined by mangroves, and good for windsurfing and fishing, though there are no waves. The salt pans give way to a gray sand beach and a little bar with no facilities. In the village is a hotel called the **Las Salinas High Wind Center.** The town itself is only a small cluster of modest Dominican houses. But the High Wind Center (Puerto Hermosa 7, tel. 809/310-8141) is a small resort where wealthy Dominicans do their surfing. It has a bar, disco, pool, and good seafood patio restaurant.

Palmar de Ocoa

For another side trip, try Palmar de Ocoa, north of Las Salinas beach, where there is a gray sand beach, and Dominicans host a big fishing tournament every year. There are many summer homes built by Dominicans who come down from the city, a new village built of concrete blocks, and not much else. But the view is excellent and the water good for fishing if you can find someone to take you out. Much luck.

San José de Ocoa

One of the best bets for a wonderful side trip is San José de Ocoa, a town in the foothills of the vast Cordillera Central small enough (67,000) to be easily negotiable by foreign visitors. In fact, few foreign visitors make it to San José, so it provides a glimpse of true provincial Dominican life and is quite a bit cooler than the surrounding desert-like countryside below it. There are some good views from San José as well. To get there, stay on the main Sánchez Highway west from Baní until you've gone about 18km, where you'll find the clearly marked turnoff on your right (north). The road is paved, quite good, and goes uphill for about 28km (17 miles). Note that there is a road that goes even farther north into the mountains from San José toward the town of Constanza, but you should only attempt to negotiate this drive in a solid 4WD vehicle with high clearance and in good weather.

The best hotel in San José de Ocoa is **Rancho Francisco,** run by Fernando Issa. Located near the Ocoa River, it has 15 inexpensive cabins and a swimming pool fed by the river for use by the guests. You can telephone Rancho Francisco at 809/558-2291. Look for it on the right side of the main road into town, just before you get there. Also available is the inexpensive **Hotel Elias** (Las Carreras, tel. 809/588-2627). In town are a couple of other pensions. Both **Sagrato de Jesús** (tel. 809/558-2432) and **Pensíon San Francisco** (tel. 809/558-2741) are basic cold-water establishments with cable TV but no fancy restaurants. One local restaurant called **Baco** is near the *parque central* and serves decent goat stews, rice, and chicken. Another is **Marién,** which has good fried chicken. There are a lot of serious-looking bars south of town.

The climate in San José de Ocoa is absolutely ideal, with low humidity and perfect temperatures. However, it is quite remote and there are no official tourist spots to visit. Like most of the towns between Santo Domingo and Barahona, including San Cristóbal, Baní, Azua, and Barahona, nightlife is fairly sparse, especially when compared to the big city or the tourist spots along the north coast.

AZUA

Officially this town is called Azua de Compostela, and after San Cristóbal it is the largest city between Santo Domingo and Barahona. Located about 120km west of Santo Domingo, Azua was founded originally in 1504 by the infamous Diego Velásquez, who later subdued Cuba for Spain and who was granted a coat of arms by King Ferdinand in 1508. Azua was once home to Hernán Cortés, the conqueror of Mexico. Origi-

nally, Azua was a large port before it was destroyed by an earthquake and flood in 1751, and moved to its present site, north of the huge Bahía de Ocoa. Several times during its history, Azua has been burned to the ground by one conquering or marauding army or another, usually French or Haitian passersby, such as Jean-Jacques Dessalines, the Haitian general who torched the place in 1805. Along with its surrounding region, Azua became a province of the newly established nation in 1845.

Azua is located in an agricultural area and is known for its sugarcane, rice, coffee, and fruit—especially grapes and apples—as well as watermelons and cantaloupes. The local economy is boosted by mining and lumbering. Even so, the town itself isn't much to look at, a rather drab and dusty home to around 9,000 hardworking people. Much more interesting are several sights outside of town, including the old colonial ruins and the area around Bahía de Ocoa.

Sights and Recreation
The main reason to go to Azua is to visit the coves and beaches of the **Corbanito,** an area along the bay with about six miles of nice beaches. Getting to the bay entails following the road south out of Azua toward **Monte Río**—the main, but by no means the most enticing, beach in the area. Ask for directions if you feel lost. The little dirt road will lead you to Monte Río, the city beach for Azua. You should probably continue west until you find **Playa Chiquita** (Little Beach) on an open inlet about a mile and a half in length, with gray sand, tranquil water, and no waves. Even better is **Playa Blanca,** which also has some undeveloped hot springs. A reef rings the bay, so diving is possible here. Ask around. All around the Corbanito area you'll see behind you the fringes of the Sierra de Bahoruco, which emerges from the sea and cuts across the southwest corner of the country.

Accommodations and Food
Hotels in Azua are inexpensive, should you decide to stay in town. The really budget places are clustered around the Calle Colón, but beware. On the main road into town try the **Hotel Restaurant San Ramón** (Sánchez at Km 1.5, tel. 809/521-3529). Also inexpensive is the **Hotel Brisas del Mar** (Calle de Leones, tel. 809/521-

3813), **Hotel Altagracia** (Calle Duarte 59, tel. 809/521-3286), and **Hotel El Familiar** (Calle Emillo Prudhomme, tel. 809/521-3556). None are special.

For food, there are **Restaurant Patio Español el Jardín** (Calle Duarte 49) and **Restaurant El Gran Segovia** (Federico del Sánchez 31), both of which serve basic meals.

Information and Transportation

In Azua, the **Codetel** office is at Av. 19 de Marzo 118, while the **Metro Bus Terminal** is at Parque 19 de Marzo. The Azua–Santo Domingo route takes about two hours by *público*, and the service is also good to Barahona, which takes under two hours. If you need help, go into City Hall and look around for somebody to assist you.

AZUA TO BARAHONA

The road from Azua to Barahona is excellent, paved, and mostly free of traffic. Although the countryside is extremely dry and, some would say, desolate, it has an intriguing beauty all its own, as anyone who loves desert country will tell you. As you progress westward, the beautiful Sierra de Neiba start heaving themselves up in front of you, the road gradually becomes steeper and windier, and on the left as you leave the sea, the dry Sierra Martín García heft themselves between the highway and the sea. About 15km outside of Azua, the roadway splits, with the right (northerly) offshoot heading for the Haitian border crossing at Comendador. Straight ahead, the Sánchez Highway heads for Barahona, and ultimately Pedernales on the Haitian border, through the desolate Pedernales peninsula. Officially, the highway to San Juan is called Route 2, but don't bother looking for highway signs or markers way out here. The cutoff is pretty obvious.

Another 42km along the Sánchez Highway (officially called Route 44), you'll come to several cross-highways heading toward Vicente Noble, Neiba, Postrer Río, Descubierta, Jimaní, Duverge, and Cabral, which describes Route 48 and its circular tour of the Lago Enriquillo area.

For another 20km past these complicated crossroads, the Sánchez Highway cuts through a region of *carata* palm, poor cousin to the straight *palma regis* of the Cibao. This region is sparsely inhabited, and the few villages that appear will rarely have any facilities. You will cross the widening mouth of the Río Yaque del Sur.

BARAHONA

History

Barahona is three hours by car, and four hours by bus from Santo Domingo. The city is not very old by Dominican standards, having been founded in 1802 by Haitian General Toussaint L'Ouverture. It is, however, the largest city by far on the Pedernales peninsula, and the center of mining and agriculture for a very large region of the southwest. For adventurers, fishermen, and birdwatchers, Barahona is the jumping-off place for the Sierra de Bahoruco, Parque Nacional Jaragua, and Isla Beata, famous for its birds.

During the 1930s, when Trujillo was getting his juggernaut into full gear, the dictator seized thousands of acres of land around the town in order to establish sugarcane fields owned and operated by him and his cronies.

Today, sugarcane farming is still central to the local economy. The water off the coast is rich in fish and crustaceans, as a result of the shallow coastal trough that runs parallel to the coast. South of Barahona, many fishing villages dot the coast. The people of Barahona have lately been the victims of economic circumstance. When the sugar mill closed, many lost jobs and the economy nosedived. Municipal facilities began to decay. Evidence of this turndown is everywhere to be seen, from potholed roads to trash on the beaches to bums and panhandlers on every corner. The Malecón, which should be beautiful, is lined with liquor shacks and fairly seedy discos. The great plan to open a large all-inclusive resort (Bahoruco Beach Club) fell through a few years back, and now even tourism has suffered.

Even so, visitors who can afford the Riviera Beach Hotel (see below) will find the town pleasant, its surroundings magnificent and interesting by turns.

With slightly more than 80,000 inhabitants, Barahona is just now getting used to being a tourist destination and offers a couple of quite adequate tourist hotels. Like many Dominican towns, Barahona is laid out around a central plaza and park. There really aren't any major tourist sights, and the small public beach here is unsatisfactory because of poor water quality and stinging jellyfish. However, several beaches south of Barahona are quite good, and the drive south on the Sánchez Highway provides some of the most spectacular scenery in the whole country.

Accommodations

There's **Hotel las Magnolias** near the bus station (Calle Anacaona 13, corner of Cacique, tel. 809/524-2244), where you can get a decent room with air-conditioning for under US$20. Other inexpensive hotels in town include **Hotel Brasil** (Calle Padre Bilini 31, tel. 809/524-3661) and **Hotel Bohemia** (Calle Sánchez 72, tel. 809/524-2109). In the same neighborhood is **Hotel Victoria** (Padre Billini 15-A), which has air-conditioning. The budget hotels, which have fans but no air-conditioning and can be noisy at times, are **Hotel Barahona** (Calle Jaime Mota 5, tel. 809/524-3442); the **Micheluz** (Av. 30 de Mayo 28, tel. 809/524-2358), with cold water and shared bath; and the **Mencia,** across the street, which is your basic traveler's room with fan. In between price-wise are the **Hotel Palace** (Calle Uruguay 18, tel. 809/524-2500) and the **Hotel Cacique** down the street at Calle Uruguay 2, tel. 809/524-4620.

For a simple and inexpensive tourist hotel, try the **Hotel Guayocuya** (Av. Enriquillo at Playa Saladilla, tel. 809/524-2211), which has 22 rooms, a restaurant that serves reasonably good meals, and potable water. Some rooms have balconies that look out over the water, but you should avoid lower floors, which tend to rock with disco later on. Sometimes you'll get a room with no screens, so you should be prepared to protect yourself against mosquitoes. The Guayocuya is on the western edge of town, and you can swim on the public beach if you feel adventuresome. A similar value and similar facility is the **Hotel Caribe** (Av. Enriquillo, across from Guayocuya, tel. 809/524-4111, fax 809/524-5115), which has 23 rooms and offers clean but unspectacular accommodation with bath.

The largest tourist hotel in Barahona, and one with modest luxury (it is said that members of the old ruling juntas kept rooms there for their various mistresses), is the **Riviera Beach Hotel** (Av. Enriquillo 6, tel. 809/524-5111, fax 809/524-5798), which offers 108 rooms with phone and satellite TV, a pool, tennis courts, and two restaurants. Located just outside town on the Malecón, it's still within walking distance and is run by a chain. Try to get a room with a balcony, facing the ocean. Prices start about US$75 d, about twice what you'd pay for hotels like the Caribe and Guayocuya, but worth it if you're in the mood for a nice tourist hotel.

There is a good hotel south of Barahona, along the spectacular highway that fronts the sea. **Swiss Hotel** (10km south of Barahona, tel. 809/545-1496, US$35 d) has a garden with a view of the sea. Rooms are spacious and clean, the restaurant okay but overpriced. Farther down the highway, a new **Bahoruco Beach Club and Resort** (17km south of Barahona, tel. 809/685-5184), a three-armed resort featuring 90 hotel rooms, 84 apart-hotels, and 34 apartments, along with whirlpool, pool, restaurant, bar, TV, horseback riding, tennis, and water sports, was planned. At this writing, the hotel still hasn't gotten off the ground, thus leaving Barahona without a full-scale, exclusive resort—the kind of thing residents have dreamed about for years. Economic difficulties, transportation (especially air service), and politics are the usual suspects.

There are no expensive luxury hotels in Barahona, which is not to say that there are no *nice* hotels. The inexpensive and budget hotels are all located away from the beach, uphill, toward the center of the town. The moderately priced hotels, and those near the decent restaurants, are all located on or near the Malecón, which in Barahona is called Avenida Enriquillo. It can be confusing coming into town from the Sánchez Highway, as the traffic in town tends to be willy-nilly, but if you just keep heading downhill, and keep your eyes open for a glimpse of the blue bay below, you'll eventually come to the Malecón, which is a bit scruffy, but shaded with palms and breezy to boot.

Food

There are several good eating places in Barahona. The most popular spot along the Malecón is **La Rocca,** next door to the Hotel Caribe, an open-air place with a covered roof where you can get basic seafood and *comida criolla* along with a sea breeze. Also along the Malecón is the **Brisas del Mar** for Chinese food, or the **Restaurant Costa Sur** and **Restaurant Brisas del Caribe,** both serving basic meals. As mentioned before, the Riviera has its own restaurants, and in downtown Barahona, there are several small cafeterias and cafes where you get budget food.

Next door to the Melo coffee factory at the eastern end of town is **Melós Café,** a good place for breakfast and nightly dinner specials. Fast food vendors and small pizza joints abound near the park, as do the aforementioned discos and bars along the Malecón.

Information and Events
Codetel is located at Nuestra Sra. del Rosario 36. The official *fiestas patronales* (in honor of Nuestra Señora del Rosario) is held on October 4, which features the *carabiné* dance. You can get tourist information at City Hall on Calle 30 de Mayo.

THE BARAHONA-PEDERNALES ROAD

In 1991, the Dominican government completed a beautiful paved road that runs from Barahona south along the coast through the small towns of Paraíso, Enriquillo, and Oviedo, turning inland across acrid scrub forest country all the way to Pedernales. Some say the drive from Barahona down to Oviedo is the most spectacular in the whole country. For the first 50km you'll be driving with the mountains on one side, high cliffs, sand beaches, and rocky outcroppings on the other, with many stretches of magnificent coconut palms interspersed with fishing huts. At times, the forest comes right down to the sea, and there are reefs offshore, which makes this whole area among the best for snorkeling and diving in the whole country, though it is very little known or used.

Playa San Rafael
Between Barahona and Enriquillo (where the road turns slightly inland away from the ocean), you'll be able to take your pick from many undeveloped but wonderful beaches. The first along the road is Playa San Rafael, where you'll see a small sign for the turnoff on a dirt road that passes by several fishing huts. A freshwater stream feeds a pool by the shore and makes a nice contrast with the warm ocean water and hot sun. The beach itself is pebbly, but not unpleasant, though it is crowded on weekends with holidaymakers from Barahona. You can camp on Playa San Rafael, which has a little restaurant.

La Ciénaga, Río Caña, and El Quemaíto
As you progress farther south along the highway, there are several other beaches just off the road, including La Ciénaga, Río Caña and El Quemaíto. Some have very high waves, and undertows can be dangerous in the area, so beware. For example, at Playa San Rafael, many people use the freshwater swimming hole in lieu of the ocean, as the waves tend to get scary.

Paraíso
The area around the town of Paraíso is beautifully forested, with fruit stands, high cliffs, and stunning views. The new **Hotel Paraíso** (US$20 d, no phones, TV) has large, clean rooms. Try to see the nearby **Limón Lagoon,** usually frequented by flamingos.

Playa los Patos
A beautiful beach near the end of the line (that is, just past Paraíso) is Playa los Patos, with smooth white pebbles and waves suitable for swimming and surfing. The beach is utterly undeveloped, and the only people who come here regularly are villagers. At los Patos (the Ducks), another river empties into the sea. This far south you'll frequently find freshwater lagoons behind the highway, and domestic animals roaming the beaches.

Enriquillo to Pedernales
Once you've become accustomed to the beautiful terrain around Paraíso, the road to Pedernales beyond Enriquillo will seem somewhat dull. And so it is. From Oviedo to Pedernales there is only thorny scrub in a karst landscape.

If you must, you can stay the night in Enriquillo at the **Hotel Dajtra** on the main highway, but its rooms are very basic. The cactus, the occasional soldier, and the karst all make this stretch of road look like Haiti. It's a long, hot 50km from Oviedo to Pedernales, so you'll need to take a vehicle in good condition and fully gassed, with plenty of water and food just in case of breakdown. The villages of Los Tres Charcos and Manuel Golla are on the road, but they have no services or hotels.

Some 32km down the road from Los Tres Chacos is the south turnoff for **Cabo Rojo** in Parque Nacional Jaragua, where the Alcoa Company once mined bauxite, and where some limestone is still taken out. The entire Parque Nacional Jaragua area is accessible with permission, a local guide, and a sturdy 4WD vehicle. Less than half a mile from this turnoff, you'll see a marked turn right (or north) for Al Acetillar Nature Reserve, and drivers with heavy-duty 4WD and plenty of supplies can take the trail up the mountainside to a beautiful scenic overlook, and continue on to Puerto Escondido on the other side. But this is one tough journey and should only be attempted with a very good vehicle and permission from the National Parks Office in Santo Domingo. It's quite beautiful, though, and makes a great adventure.

Pedernales

Pedernales is a dusty fishing village straddling the Haitian border on the Pedernales River. There are a few shops and hotels. Inexpensive hotels include **Hotel Noruga** (Calle Libertad, tel. 809/524-0152) and **Pension Familiar Hungria** (Calle Libertad, tel. 809/524-0144). A newly established place is **Hotel Caribe Sur** (Av. Libertad, tel./fax 809/549-5366), which has 29 decent and inexpensive rooms. Food can be had in Pedernales from a couple of very basic cafes.

The Haitian Border

Crossing the border into Haiti from Pedernales is impossible without permission from the Dominican government. Should you wish to cross, you should try to do so at Jimaní or Dajabon, and only after you've complied with all visa requirements.

On the northwest edge of Pedernades begins the so-called International Highway, which straddles the Haitian border, straight through the Bahoruco Mountains. At this time it is hazardous because of smuggling and tension. Avoid the road.

PARQUES NACIONALES JARAGUA AND SIERRA DE BAHORUCO

PARQUE NACIONAL JARAGUA

The remote Parque Nacional Jaragua covers the entire Pedernales Peninsula south of the Sánchez Highway from the towns of Oviedo to Pedernales and includes the amazing sum of 520 square miles, or 1,350 square km. Included in this total are the remote, barren offshore islands of Isla Beata and Alto Velo. Named after a famous Taíno chieftain, the park is distinguished by its hot climate, its dogtooth limestone geologic formations, and its series of distant capes, including Cabo Rojo, Cabo Falso, and Cabo Beata, as well as lagoons and saltwater lakes. Much of the park is accessible only by boat or long, exhausting hike.

Natural History

The peninsula now known as Parque Nacional Jaragua came into being about 50 million years ago during the Oligocene, when land emerged from the sea. The offshore islands and the huge lagoon of saltwater known as Lago Oviedo (south of the town of Oviedo) were created much more recently, about one million years ago. The soil is limestone, of marine origin, with many fractures filled with ferrous oxide. That's what gives this country its reddish appearance from a distance. The offshore currents around the peninsula aren't strong, but there is a submerged current that depends largely upon specifics of topography. The average yearly temperature is 27°C (81°F), and the average annual rainfall is 500–700mm (20–28 inches).

Botanists officially call the peninsula a thorn forest. The dominant species of plant in the park is the cactus and the aloe. Other plants include the copey, the Hispaniolan mahogany, catalpa, senna tree, wild frangipani, senna tree, and, near the beaches, the seagrape, red and button mangrove, and rare patches of white mangrove.

The park contains about 130 species of animals, most of which are aquatic birds. You can see the country's largest concentration of flamingos at the Oviedo lagoon, but other species readily seen are the great egret, little blue heron, sooty tern, American frigate bird, little green heron, white-crowned pigeon, black-crowned tanager, and green-tailed warbler.

Land animals include the endemic ricard iguana, rhinoceros iguana, and four marine turtles—hawksbill, leatherback, loggerhead, and green. It is said that the hutia and solenodon inhabit the park, but you're unlikely to run into them. Bats are common.

If you are able to make special preparations to visit Isla Beata off the southern coast of the peninsula, you'll be rewarded with a bird-watcher's paradise: flamingos, thrashers, willets, green-tailed warblers, burrowing owls, and Ridgeway's hawks, as well as egrets, terns, herons, roseate spoonbills, and frigate birds.

This part of the peninsula was an old Taíno haunt and contains several caves. If you're able to reach Guanal, La Cueva de la Posa, and Cueva Mongó, you'll be able to see ancient pictographs and petroglyphs. Perhaps the easiest cave to access is **Cueva de Abajo,** on the southern edge of Bahía de Las Águilas. The very remote **Plaza Larga** is on the south side of Cabo Falso, a nice place accessible by the coastal trail.

Practicalities

An excursion into the Parque Nacional Jaragua isn't something to approach lightly. On anything but short drives into the interior, you should be well prepared in advance for lack of services, hot weather, scarcity of good maps, and rough terrain.

Always try to obtain advance permission to enter the park from the National Parks Office in Santo Domingo. According to official regulations, visitors to the park must be accompanied by a guide, so as to maintain the integrity of the flora and fauna. Except for the very hardy, it might be best to organize an extensive tour by using one of the many guide services in Santo Domingo or elsewhere.

The Parque Nacional Jaragua office is in El Cajuil on the main road just east of Oviedo. There is a south turnoff from the Pedernales Highway to Cabo Rojo, which provides some access to the fine beach at **Bahía de las Águilas,** one of the most beautiful in the country. Outlying ranger stations exist at Trujille, Fondo de Paradise, and Bahía de las Águilas, and those

with 4WD vehicles and plenty of water and gas can proceed on the Sánchez Highway to the small village of Los Tres Charcos and turn left at the weathered park sign. Down the road nine km is Fondo de Paradise, where you'll find a trailhead for a four-hour hike to the fishing village of Trujillo. There are some rustic places to stay overnight there. Other trails in the park exist but aren't marked or much used. Keep in mind that walking among the thorny shrubs and cacti and across limestone is very tough. The coast itself is a limestone shelf—quite spectacular but hard to access except by boat or difficult hike. For the adventuresome, well-prepared traveler, Jaragua is a wonderful challenge.

PARQUE NACIONAL SIERRA DE BAHORUCO

The Parque Nacional Bahoruco is bordered on the south by the Sánchez Highway (leading to Pedernales) and on the north by the good paved highway on the southern edge of Lago Enriquillo, which connects Jimaní and Cabral. It is a rugged and spectacular mountain range that rises as high as 2,367 meters (7,766 feet) at El Aguacate near the Haitian border (a town reachable by a decent road from Duverge). The park covers 800 square meters, or 309 square miles. Because of its relative height, the mountains catch some sparse rainfall, and pines grow in relative abundance.

Natural History

The Sierra de Bahoruco was where the famous chieftain of the Taíno, Enriquillo, made

Mahogany branch and leaves

his last stand against the Spanish in 1532, leading ultimately to his recognition by the Crown and his receipt of a fiefdom encompassing the area, including the lake which bears his name.

The Sierra de Bahoruco were formed approximately 50 million years ago in the middle Eocene. The mountains themselves are made of crystallized upthrust limestone. Botanists probably would call the mountains a mixed-forest zone, containing large areas of pine forest, and many broad-leafed plants. Because of extremes in relief, and because some slopes are north facing and others are south facing, there are moderate ranges of both temperatures and precipitation. The average rainfall is 1,000–2,500mm, while the average temperature is between 15° and 20°C.

The most common trees are Creolean pine, West Indies laurel cherry, Hispaniolan mahogany, myrtle, Ekman juniper, West Indian sumac, and trumpet tree. You'll also see wild cane, copey tree, silver palm, and auquey plant, depending on whether you're in the *bosque seco* (dry forest) or humid subtropical forest. Of special interest in the mountains are the many varieties of orchid, which amount to perhaps 166 species (more than half the total in the country), and about 10% of which are endemic to the mountains.

Of the animal species that live in or pass through the mountains, most are birds. These include the Antillean siskin, La Selle's thrush, narrow-billed tody, white-winged warbler, Hispaniolan trogon, white-crowned and red-necked pigeon, doves, Hispaniolan parakeets, Hispaniolan lizard cuckoo, and the ubiquitous palm crow. If you're lucky, you might also see the Vervain hummingbird, the peewee, and the solitaire. You might also catch a glimpse of the white-necked crow, extinct everywhere in the West Indies except Hispaniola. In all, bird-watchers have cataloged 49 species of birds in the park: 28 resident, two migratory, and 19 endemic.

Practicalities

Though rugged and remote, the Sierra de Bahoruco is a lovely region to visit. To reach the main park entrance, drive to Duverge on the good paved road leading along the southern edge of Lago Enriquillo. You can reach this road by either a northern tour of the lake accessible by a cutoff from the Sánchez Highway through Vicente Noble, or by taking the road to Cabral, which turns right (west) just north of Barahona. Either way, the road is easygoing, well-maintained, and lightly traveled, with gas and services available in several towns surrounding the lake. At Duverge is a dirt road on the southwest edge of the town (ask if you can't find it), which takes you into the mountains toward Puerto Escondido, only 11km distant. The first right in the village of Puerto Escondido takes you to the National Park Office.

To drive through the heart of the park, take the road on the left, which leads to Loma de los Pinos and eventually to the scenic overlook at El Acetillar. If you wish (or if the roads are good enough), you can go over the top back down to Las Mercedes and eventually the Sánchez Highway just outside of Pedernales. The other road reaches Loma del Torro (at 2,367 meters, the mountains' highest peak), the area along the Haitian border, and the miliary post at El Aguacate, a distance of some 19km. From El Aguacate there is an unmarked trail up to the top of the Bahoruco. It's best not to travel down the road south of La Altagracia along the Haitian border.

Both roads require high-clearance 4WD vehicles, and you should be well equipped with gas, water, and food, just in case. Tours to this area can be arranged in Santo Domingo, though it's a trip you can do if you're of the adventuresome sort. Check with the park office for any trail guides, though I doubt you'll find anything available.

LAGO ENRIQUILLO AND PARQUE NACIONAL ISLA CABRITOS

The best way to see Lake Enriquillo and Parque Nacional Isla Cabritos is to take the scenic loop on a good highway that begins at Vicente Noble, circles the lake, and ends at Cabral. Making this trip is possible in a single day by car from Santo Domingo, though you'd have to start very early in the morning and be prepared for hard traveling and an early evening return to Santo Domingo. If you wish to make the trip by boat from the mainland over to Isla Cabritos, the best time is early in the morning, when many of the animals are foraging for food and thus visible, and when the temperature is relatively cooler. Later in the day it's stupefyingly hot, and the animals seek shelter. Therefore, it might be best to headquarter in Barahona and explore the whole southwest over several days.

LAGO ENRIQUILLO/ISLA CABRITOS

Lake Enriquillo and Isla Cabritos are hot, hazy, and beautifully situated between the startlingly abrupt mountain ranges of the Sierra de Neiba on the north and the Sierra de Bahoruco on the south. The lake itself is 265 square km (102 square miles) of terrifically salty water—perhaps three times saltier than the sea—which at its lowest point is nearly 40 meters (131 feet) below sea level. Isla Cabritos is nearly in the center of the lake. It's nearly flat and encompasses an area about 12km in length and two km in width. There are two smaller islands nearby, Barbarita and La Islita, but these are not currently visited. Most of the soil of the island is crushed coral, and given its location, the temperatures are almost always stiflingly hot, averaging about 35°C during the day (95°F).

There are many reasons to visit Lago Enriquillo. Situated between high mountains, it is a wonderfully scenic spot, reminiscent in some ways of Mexico. But most people go to Lago Enriquillo and make the crossing to Isla Cabritos for the crocodiles, flamingos, turtles, and huge iguanas.

History

The lake of course derives its name from Enriquillo, the famous Taíno leader who rebelled against Spanish rule. Enriquillo's father was killed by conquistadors. He was raised by friars in a monastery in Santo Domingo, becoming educated and cultured in the European fashion. He was, however, required to work as a slave on a plantation until he fled in the 1520s to the re-

---

CHIEF ENRIQUILLO

The Taíno chieftan Enriquillo is one of the great heroes of early Hispanic conquest history. As the son of a great chief, Enriquillo was taken by friars and given a Christian education, then later married a Christianized Taíno woman. Although he owed feudal duties to a Spanish landowner, he led a peaceful and productive life and was a leader to the abused Taínos who still lived on the island. When the original Spanish landowner died, the son who inherited the property treated the natives cruelly and began to abuse Enriquillo's wife.

Enriquillo pursued protests through legal and church channels, but to no avail. Gathering some of his people together, he moved to the mountaínous southwest of present-day Dominican Republic and fought against numerous Spanish attacks. He and his small group were the last free Taínos and remained so for many years. Finally, around 1530, the Spanish Emperor Charles V sent an envoy to Enriquillo in order to sue for peace, and to present a treaty. The treaty was delivered on Cabrito Island, in what is today known as Lake Enriquillo. The treaty guaranteed him and his people a reservation where they could live in peace and granted to Enriquillo the honorary title of Don.

This was considered a great victory for the Taínos, and Enriquillo expressed his gratitude to the emperor in a letter. The chief died soon thereafter, and his remains are buried at the chapel of Azua Vieja.

mote Sierra de Bahoruco and organized a re-sistance movement. Enriquillo and his followers followed the practice of disarming their pursuers and releasing them unharmed, which eventual-ly led to his recognition by the Spanish crown.

Land, Flora, and Fauna

The sunken lake is what remains of a channel that once connected the Bay of Neiba with the Bay of Port-au-Prince. Land emerged as the Río Yaque del Sur deposited sediments at the mouth of the bay, eventually cutting off the lake from the sea, leaving it salty and hot. This ulti-mate formation took place perhaps one million years ago. Isla Cabritos ranges from 40 meters below sea level to about four meters below sea level, and its soils are flat coral beaches without reefs. The underlying soil is limestone. Temper-atures can rise to 50°C, and there is only an av-erage of 642 meters of rainfall a year.

The flora of the island is almost all either cac-tus—mainly the cayuco, cholla, or common lignum vitae—or catalpa and palo de viento. The animals are either birds or reptiles, with the most important of the latter being the endemic American crocodile. The lake has one of the largest crocodile popula-tions in the world, but you need to be there in the morning or evening to see them; during the heat of the day, they hide out under lily pads. Both the rhinoceros iguana and ricord iguana make their home on the island, and you'll also run into scor-pions and spiders. Flamingos lead the list of the is-land's birds, but there are also great blue herons, ibis, burrowing owls, roseate spoonbills, Hispan-iolan parrots, nighthawks, village weavers (intro-duced from Africa), and numerous wading birds.

Practicalities

The National Park Office for Isla Cabritos is lo-cated only about 1.6km past Las Caritas, that in turn is only a few kilometers east of La Des-cubierta. There is a parking lot and a park of-fice and usually at least one friendly park em-ployee to show you the ropes. The park service tries to keep two motorboats available to take visitors over to Isla Cabritos (a one-hour jour-ney), but there is a rowboat for emergencies (two hours). There is also a sulfur bath that the park ranger can show you.

To take the loop highway back from Lago En-riquillo, just continue on the highway to La Des-cubierta, then Jimaní, and finally turn back coun-terclockwise on the southern side of the lake and continue past the statue of Enriquillo at the Mella junction.

You should try to make advance arrange-ments to visit Isla Cabritos. The easy way is to take a tour and have the arrangements made for you. For do-it-yourselfers, first try the Eco-turisa Office in Santo Domingo (Parque Eugenio María de Hostos, Malecón, near Vicini Burgos, tel. 809/221-4104, fax 809/689-3703), to buy a permit, which is usually RD$50 for foreigners. Try also the National Parks Office in Santo Domingo (Av. Independencia). Another possi-bility is to show up at a park office in La Descu-bierta and see what happens.

The motorboats are operated by park per-sonnel who accompany visitors to the island. The official tariff is RD$500, but you could be charged anywhere from US$20 to US$85, and you'll need at least three people for a group. You can make arrangements to go to the island seven days a week. The ranger will escort you to the island and show you a small museum, then squire a hike on the southern shore where you can scout for crocodiles.

Be aware that buying permits can be a tricky business. You should carefully negotiate the price of a permit, the boat rental, and any other fees well in advance.

AROUND THE LAKE

The Loop Highway

From Azua take the Sánchez Highway going west. In 57km, you'll come to the village of Fondo Negro, and shortly thereafter the turnoff for the village of Vi-cente Noble, which is on the road to Neiba and Lago Enriquillo. Finding this road can be a bit con-fusing—it is not marked. The best idea is to simply ask a local for the road to Vicente Noble. The road swings off the Sánchez Highway and turns north for a few kilometers. You may think you're going the wrong way, but persevere. By taking this road, you'll pass through Neiba, Postrer Río, Descu-bierta, then round the west end of the lake and head on to Jimaní, Duverge, and Cabral, returning to the Sánchez Highway just north of Barahona. Of course, you can take the loop around the lake commencing from Cabral, which would make sense, especially if you're headquartered in Barahona. And besides, the road to Cabral, past Laguna de Rincón, is easier to pick up.

If you don't have a car, you can take a tour from Santo Domingo offered by one of many tour agencies (such as Ecoturisa). For the adventuresome, catch a *guagua* from Av. Duarte and Av. 27 de Febrero in Santo Domingo to Neiba, then make a connection for La Descubierta. You can also take a nice Riviera del Caribe bus to Jimaní. You will have to be prepared for long hours of travel, though.

Driving the loop highway, which is officially called Route 48 in the north and Route 46 in the south (don't expect a single highway sign), you'll first pass through the banana town of **Galván,** which is much too hot and flat to be enticing. Later down the road, however, the mountains of the Sierra de Neiba begin to rise up to the north, and the towns become more pleasant and colorful.

Neiba

Neiba is known for its grapes. You'll find young girls and women selling grapes from roadside stands. Stop and buy some. They are not terribly sweet, and the juice is raw, but they are very cheap. There are actually a couple of places to stay in Neiba. The **Pensión** (Calle Las Marías at San Bartholome) is a basic bed-and-breakfast place offering clean rooms for about US$10. **Hotel Comedor Babei** is on the main square, and **Hotel Comedor Dania** is on a side street off the main highway going out of town. All have shared bath, no air-conditioning. The **Codetel** is on Calle Cambronal at Calle Felipe Gonzalez.

La Descubierta

La Descubierta, on the northwest edge of Lago Enriquillo, is probably the nicest town on the loop, especially because of the oak forest and *balneario* called **Las Barias,** which is cool, shady, and popular with locals on hot days. You can picnic and walk in the shade, though the place tends to be somewhat littered. Straight ahead in La Descubierta, you'll see the *balneario* and parking places. Just beyond La Descubierta you'll cross paths with the *balneario* **Bocas del Chacón.**

You'll find the sulfur hot springs called **Las Marías** on the northern portion of the loop highway between Galván and Neiba. Other unnamed pools in the area are in various stages of devel-

opment. These hot and cold springs arise in the Sierra de Neiba, trickle down the hillsides, and are collected in limestone sinks along the road.

Las Caritas

On the highway, just a few kilometers before entering La Descubierta, you'll see a sign on the highway for Las Caritas (The Faces), a set of Taíno petroglyphs carved on the side of a rock cliff about a five-minute climb above the highway. Although there is no parking space, a sign plainly marks the spot, and you should be able to pull over to the side of the road in safety and climb up the rocks for a close look. It can be a hot ascent, but you'll get a good view of Lago Enriquillo. The petroglyphs are not protected, and some have been defaced.

Jimaní

Jimaní is a border town at the eastern edge of Lago Enriquillo. It is a rough-and-tumble place, typical of any border town, and if you must stay there, you'll only find basic budget hotels like the **Hotel Jimaní, Hotel Quisqueya,** and **Hotel Mellitzos.** The town is dirty, noisy, and hot, though it has a *balneario*. Visitors wishing to cross over into Haiti, perhaps to visit the Laguna del Fundo (a saltwater lagoon, complete with crocodiles), had best be prepared with the proper visas and permits, obtained in advance from Santo Domingo. You can go right up to the border, however, past the Jimaní Army Base, and cast a gaze into Haiti. You'll see Haitian *guaguas,* gaily painted, coming into the country, filled with Haitians going to Santo Domingo to trade. Don't photograph the army barracks or any soldier. It isn't worth the hassle.

Back towards Cabral

After Jimaní, the loop highway turns back east toward Cabral, going through the towns of El Limón, Duverge, and Cabral. Outside of El Limón is **La Zurza,** another sulfur *balneario*.

CABRAL/RESERVA CIENTÍFICA NATURAL LAGUNA DE RINCÓN

About 20km down the loop highway from the town of Duverge on the south side of Lake Enriquillo is the town of **Cabral.** Although the town isn't much to look at, it is set near the beautiful

Laguna de Rincón (sometimes referred to as Laguna de Cabral), which is the country's largest freshwater lagoon and second-largest inland lake after Lake Enriquillo.

Polo Magnético

If you wish, you can test out something called the *polo magnético,* an optical illusion fun site that Dominicans (and plenty of others) swear violates the law of gravity. If you wish to visit the *polo magnético* just for fun, take a good paved road south out of Cabral for 15km until you see the large sign on the right side of the road. Park your car between the lines on the highway and watch it roll uphill. (Someone should stay behind the wheel, of course.) Even if you're not impressed by optical illusions like this, the drive into the fringes of the Sierra de Bahoruco is spectacular, green, and vibrant, with a good view of the lagoon in the background. The road goes on over the mountains to Paraíso, if you wish to head back to the coast that way.

Laguna de Rincón

The Laguna de Rincón is easy to visit. Just drive north through the town of Cabral. The road leads you past the central park and straight to the lagoon. You can hike around the lake and observe the many species of birds, though you should be on the lookout for the freshwater slider turtle, which is an endangered species.

The bird species on the lagoon include the masked duck, ruddy duck, flamingo, Louisiana heron, glossy ibis, blue-winged teal, sora crake, and northern jacana. The lake itself is 47 square km, and the temperatures are not nearly so hot as near Lake Enriquillo. With two mountain ranges as backdrops, it is an ideal place to stop for a rest. You can pick up soft drinks and snacks in Cabral.

NORTH OF LAGO ENRIQUILLO

San Juan de la Maguana

For visitors wishing to leave the beaten track, or for those adventurers who are starting their ascent of Pico Duarte from the Sabaneta Dam, the town of San Juan de la Maguana is a reasonable destination. To reach San Juan, drive to Azua and continue for 16km west until the plainly visible road forks north (Route 2, but don't ex-

pect a sign). A further 70km will take you to San Juan, an agricultural and ranching town of 140,000 people on the southern edges of the Cordillera Central. The town takes its name from a combination of San Juan El Bautista (St. John the Baptist) and the Maguana Indians, which represented one of the original large Taíno tribes that inhabited Hispaniola before Columbus.

The countryside is quite arid because of the significant rain shadow produced by the northern Cordillera Central. The only real tourist sight in the area is the **Corral de los Indios,** north of San Juan. The Corral is a large flat circle approximately 300 meters in diameter, with stones arranged along the perimeter. It is presumed that the Corral was a meeting place of the Taínos and may have been used for ball games and rituals. To get there, drive into town on the main road; find Av. Anacaona, and turn right. On the left you'll see a statute of John the Baptist. Five km later you'll approach the Corral, marked by a government sign.

This same road leads you farther north another 19km to Juan de Herrera on a very rough road to the dam, where there is a trailhead for Pico Duarte. Check with the locals for how to hire mules and guides.

Lodging: A distinctive arch stands in the center of town. Just right of the arch is the **Hotel Maguana** (tel. 809/577-2244), which has 24 somewhat rundown rooms and a pool sometimes open for swimming. Its inexpensive rooms are probably the best available for many miles. Across from the Maguana is the budget **Hotel Tamarindo** (tel. 809/557-2256), which is dirty and rough. The new **Hotel Areito** (Av. Mella, corner Capotillo, tel. 809/557-5322) has 32 rooms and seems worth an inexpensive try. The brand new hotel **O'Angel** is relatively expensive (RD$575 double), but the rooms are spotless and you'll find air-conditioning, television, hot water, and two beds.

Heading west from San Juan, the scenery becomes gradually more and more beautiful as you climb toward the Haitian border.

Comendador

The town of Comendador on the Haitian border is a sleepy place, except for the activity of police, soldiers, and smugglers. Roads north from Comendador going along the border are rugged and dangerous—not recommended.

BOB RACE

CORDILLERA CENTRAL: THE CENTRAL MOUNTAINS
INTRODUCTION

The Cordillera Central is one of the most unique features of the Dominican Republic, one Dominicans cherish but few foreigners know about. If you told a stranger on a sun-splashed beach near Puerto Plata that he could take a four-hour drive to a place where he'd need a jacket and boots, nighttime temperatures were quite likely to dip below freezing, and he could see a snow-covered peak—an area covered by scented pines, dotted with waterfalls, and criss-crossed by streams—he'd probably laugh.

Most geologists believe that the central mountains of Hispaniola were formed about 60 million years ago during a period of intense volcanic activity and plate shifting. The rocks hereabouts are all igneous, diorite, slate, and marble. This accounts for the vista in all directions of magnificent rock outcroppings and sharply angled cliffs, and even some jagged peaks, which are volcanic remains.

During the early history of the Dominican Republic, colonial authorities left the Cordillera Central alone because they were involved in plantation economics in the lowlands. The mountains early on became the home of a congeries of outcast groups, including slaves on the run from their owners, marginalized peasants from the Cibao, and people moved from their land by the consolidation of large land-holdings by second and third generation Spaniards.

These earliest settlers formed themselves into traditional villages called *conucos,* tilling the land in slash-and-burn methods and moving from place to place when the land wore out. As during the 1950s, the government established two large national parks in the region and began to move villagers to the outer boundaries. Now, only a few traditional villages remain, though there is still a large population present on the edges of the national parks. Today, wood-cutting, illegal commercial timbering, and poaching what remains of the animal life remain continuing but diminishing problems. With the advent of ecotourism and a certain degree of conservation and consciousness, both the government and people are beginning to stop erosion and pollution.

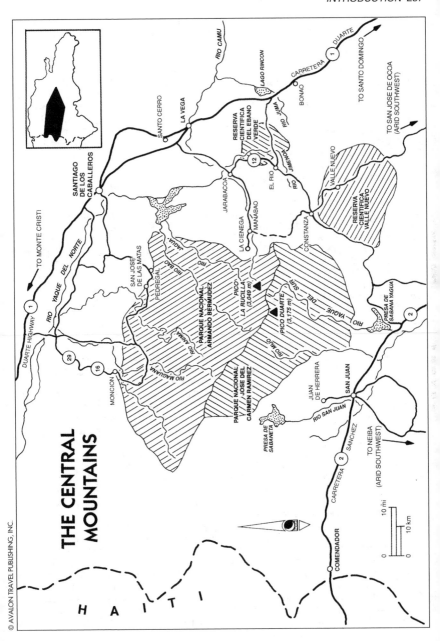

THE CENTRAL MOUNTAINS

© AVALON TRAVEL PUBLISHING, INC.

LAND

The fact is that the Cordillera Central of the Dominican Republic boast of two mountains in excess of 3,050m (10,000 feet) in height, by far the highest in the Caribbean. Pico Duarte stands 3,175m (10,417 feet), and its sister, Pico La Pelona 3,168m (10,393 feet). Pico La Rucilla, at 3,049m, is just a shade over 10,000 feet. Two others, Pico de Yaque del Norte (2,995m, or 9,826 feet) and Pico del Gallo (2,650m, or 8,694 feet), are under 10,000 feet but still spectacular by Caribbean standards. The central mountain range gives rise to 14 rivers (and many tributaries of these main watercourses), including the two giants of the country, the Río Yaque del Sur and the Río Yaque del Norte. By island standards, the area encompassed by the mountain system is huge, approximately 500,000 acres square, with much of that area (380,000 square acres) taken up by two national parks that are as beautiful as they are remote. Some of the region is stupendously rugged, hardly inhabited, and isolated by lack of roads. Some of the region has been deforested and mined and is subject to soil erosion and continued logging and clearing. And some of the region is composed of lush valleys where lucky residents are able to grow temperate crops like potatoes, strawberries, apples, garden vegetables, and flowers.

Climate

Much of the northern and southern foothills are very dry, shaded by rain shadows, especially in the far south. At the higher elevations, however, coffee is cultivated and pine trees give the visitor a sensation of being in another world. The climate throughout, except at the highest altitudes in the winter, is temperate, verging on ideal for most of the year. In December and January, temperatures can fall to 0°C (32°F) in the Valle Nuevo near Constanza, and to well below freezing in the highest peak areas. However, in valley towns of Constanza and Jarabacoa, the temperatures remain between 5° and 12°C all year round, allowing for the growing of crops. A city like San José de las Matas, on the northern foothills of the Cordillera Central in the state of Santiago, has a climate on the order of 1920s Southern California, before smog and sulfur dioxide poisoned the air—perfect at all times, with a background of bougainvillea and frangipani.

Birds

The humid forests of the Cordillera Central are home to numerous bird species, including the Hispaniolan parrot called the *cotorra,* an especially endangered species now protected by Dominican law. Birds common to the forests surrounding Jarabacoa include the La Selle's thrush, rufous-throated solitaire, Greater Antillean elaenia, and Greater Antillean peewee.

GETTING THERE

There are any number of ways to see the Cordillera Central. For those unfortunate souls on a short string, you can always rent a car in Santo Domingo or Puerto Plata and try to make a circuit of the two main towns, Constanza and Jarabacoa, in a single day. Much more pleasant is to plan to stay overnight closer to the mountains, in a city like La Vega or Bonao, from which you can easily strike into the mountains and spend some time. For viewing the mountains from afar (there is, alas, no roadway into the national parks), San José de las Matas is ideal with its perfect climate and lovely, government-sponsored hotel where it is possible to swim and visit the new pine reserve near the hotel grounds.

Of course, it's even better to visit the mountains for *several* days, or even a week. Hotels in Constanza and Jarabacoa offer perfectly comfortable rooms and tasty food, and the weather and views up there can be superb. For those desiring to make the long climb up Pico Duarte along spectacular trails, the gateways are Jarabacoa or San Juan de la Maguana, though the entry to the Pico Duarte region from Jarabacoa is somewhat smoother and shorter.

By Public Transport

The area covered by the Cordillera Central is large, encompassing the provinces of Azua (in part), San Juan (in part), La Vega, Santiago, and Santiago Rodríguez (in part). Getting to La Vega by **Metro** bus is a snap, with departures twice a day. Check with Metro or the local newspapers for exact times of departure during your stay. From La Vega, *públicos* leave for Santiago and Jarabacoa from the bus station at the center of town. **Moto Saad** (tel. 809/573-2103) has runs to Santo Domingo from its depot at Calle Colón 37. Getting to Constanza from Jarabacoa isn't too tough. A *guagua* leaves every so often from a small stand opposite the Shell service station; the fare runs about US$3. You'll have to check on exact departures, but nothing leaves after about 3 P.M.

Alternatively, one can take a Metro to Bonao, then a *guagua* across a good road, as well as through the new Reserva Científica del Ebano Verde, and on to Constanza, accomplishing the trip in one day. The road from San José de Ocoa over the mountains to Constanza is too rough to be regularly plied by any public transportation whatsoever. In fact, the road from San José de Ocoa to Constanza is too rough for anything but the highest-clearance 4WD vehicles. Public transport by Metro from Puerto Plata to Santiago, and then on to La Vega or Bonao, is very convenient.

By Car

The best way to see the mountains is to drive yourself into them. You can do this in one day, and even in just a few hours, depending upon the route. The long, spectacular, and difficult way is to take the cutoff from Piedra Blanca on the road toward Rancho Arriba and San José de Ocoa. This road is a difficult gravel drive all the way, particularly so in the Valle Nuevo area, and should only be attempted in a suitable 4WD vehicle. To reach Constanza by normal vehicle, take the Carretera Duarte (Duarte Highway), which you get in Santo Domingo by following Av. John F. Kennedy west past the Centro de los Heroes. After passing through a toll booth, take the highway for another 66km (41 miles), which puts you north of Bonao, where you'll see a sign marking the highway to the west for Constanza. The road up into the mountains is paved and well maintained, and you'll be afforded a stupendous view of the Cibao Valley. You will pass through coffee plantations, fields of commercial flowers, and finally pine forests. At El Río, approximately 31km along the way, there is a rough dirt turnoff for Jarabacoa. In all, the journey to Constanza from the Duarte Highway is about 49km long. If your goal is to go back to Jarabacoa, then you can take the El Río turnoff on your way back, which will entitle you to bump and grind over 22km of rough dirt track, going very slowly. To make the circuit in a street vehicle, some people like to go back to the Duarte Highway from Constanza, and proceed north past La Vega and take the well-marked Jarabacoa turnoff, which puts you on a good, paved road into the mountains and finally to Jarabacoa.

There are almost literally no paved roads into the national parks or near the high peaks areas. One can drive to San José de las Matas on a good paved road from Santiago, and from San José on to Monción, though the road is unpaved and lacks brilliant scenery. Another unpaved road leads north from Bohechío but is not recommended due to its difficulty and isolation. Finally, north of San Juan is the road to the Sabaneta Dam and the southern Pico Duarte trailhead, good but gravel, and ending at the foot of the tall peaks.

ALONG THE DUARTE HIGHWAY

The Duarte Highway links Monte Cristi in the far northwest with Santo Domingo on the south coast. It also passes through Bonao and La Vega, which are towns in valleys below the Cordillera Central. Officially, La Vega is part of the Cibao, a pretty and historical town without much for the foreign traveler to see. The same, or less, can be said for Bonao, which has little history and has in recent times grown from a village to a modest commercial town based on mining and the constantly increasing traffic on the Duarte Highway. Both can be used as jumping-off points for visits to the high mountains, though La Vega is far preferable in terms of beauty and good weather. Neither, though, has excellent hotels or services.

BONAO

The commercial town of Bonao lies about halfway between Santo Domingo and Santiago on the main Duarte Highway. Because the Duarte Highway is undergoing major construction, traffic is always *interesting* along its route, but it is probably no worse than driving bumper to bumper on the Santa Monica Freeway any time of day or night. You can reach Bonao in about two hours from Santo Domingo, so unless you're pressed for time, you should pass through to La Vega.

Accommodations

Hotels do exist in Bonao, and you'll see a couple of them on the Duarte Highway just outside of town. The **Hotel Bonao Inn** (tel. 809/525-2727) is at Km 85, and the **Hotel Viejo Madrid** (tel. 809/525-3558) is right next door. By all reports these two accommodations are short-term "sex" hotels and not recommended for tourists. In town there are some hotels and restaurants near the city center, including the **Hotel Plaza Nouel** (tel. 809/525-3518, Calle Duarte 153). There are several other hotels around the market. All of these hotels are in the inexpensive range. Just north of town in the Jacaranda Plaza is the **Hotel Jacerada,** perhaps the best in town at US$35 a night.

Food

One restaurant to try is the **Restaurant Típico Bonao** on the Duarte Highway at Km 83. The Duarte Highway is also well supplied with what most of us would call truck stops, where you can pull in and get hot coffee, fresh rolls, pastries, and empanadas, as well as heavier fare like stews and sandwiches. The Restaurant **Típico Bonao** has opened a new **Típico II**

A typical roadside fruit vendor's stand

north of Bonao on the new bypass. The restaurants **Melanfo's** and **Disco Terraza Wendy** are in town and both have good food. The restaurant at the **Hotel Plaza Nouel** is very ordinary, with slow service. If you are on the "old" highway, try the roadside restaurant **Duesto de Chivo.** Its goat *guisado* with black beans and rice is great.

Information and Services
Codetel in Bonao is at Av. 27 de Febrero 69. If you feel you need to stop on the Duarte, look for what the locals call *plazas turisticas* or *posadas,* and when turning off the highway, be particularly careful of drivers behind, who may decide to pass you on the right.

LA VEGA

La Vega stands in the heartland of the Cibao, the fertile plain that cuts the island in half, two-thirds of the way northward. A busy city of about 200,000 people, La Vega serves the agricultural interests of the nearby hills and countryside, where rice, cattle, tobacco, coffee, and fruit are raised.

History
The history of La Vega is the history of Spanish obsession with gold. In the late 15th century, Columbus built a fort to protect the gold mining operations and provide security for local Spanish interests against the Taíno Indians. Colonists in the area soon began raising sugarcane for export, and constructed the New World's first mint. Columbus's son Diego spent time in old La Vega, as did the famous monk Bartolomé de las Cassas. All of this came to an abrupt end in 1562, when an earthquake destroyed the town. Although it was rebuilt the next year at a site south of its original location, La Vega never recovered its place in society. Even today, it fights with Santiago for supremacy in the Cibao, but will probably never win.

Sights
La Vega is a relatively quiet provincial town. The long, shaded lane leading into town from the Duarte Highway derives its optimistic tenor from the beautiful *amapola* trees bending over the street. The homes on either side of this

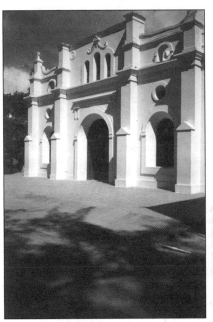

Santo Cerro

avenue are quite attractive. In fact, during winter, from late December through February, the amapola trees bloom all over the valley, turning everything into a pink wonderland. It's quite stunning to the eye, especially from a viewpoint somewhere up a mountain road.

By the time you negotiate this nice shady lane and get to the city square, La Vega has transformed itself into what many provincial centers are by nature: a noisy, crowded town. However, near the city square you'll find the **Casa Amarilla,** a large yellow emporium of goods, crafts, food, and knickknacks. Famous all over the Cibao for both its authenticity and the sheer volume of goods for sale, the Casa Amarilla is a distinct and distinctly Dominican experience. The **La Vega Cathedral** is something of a modern concrete monstrosity, though the interior is spacious and light.

Accommodations
While La Vega is well worth a visit during the Carnaval festivities (see "Events," below), the

paucity of decent hotel rooms is somewhat of a hindrance. There are a number of commercial hotels around the central park, but most are hot, dirty, and noisy. The **América, Astral** and **San Pedro** are somewhat seedy and barely passable. Chicken shacks and pizza joints, along with rather somber discos, abound in La Vega. Take your pick.

Events

Probably the best reason to come to La Vega, other than as a gateway to the mountains, is for **Carnaval.** Every Sunday afternoon in February, the colorful *diablos cojuelos* assemble in the streets and chase each other, sometimes castigating the spectators to allure them into misdeeds and sins. The old devil costumes of La Vega are famous throughout the Caribbean and are among the oldest and most authentic of the many Carnaval disguises. They alone are worth the trek north. Of course, as with any Carnaval celebration, there is food and music aplenty. Keep in mind that during February the *amapola* trees are blooming as well. The *fiestas patronales* celebrating Nuestra Señora de Antiqua are held in La Vega on August 15.

Service

You'll find the local **Codetel** office on the square.

SANTO CERRO

Santo Cerro is a must-see if you're in the La Vega region. Located only about five km northeast of La Vega, and high on a hilltop overlooking the beautiful Cibao Valley, Santo Cerro means literally "holy hill."

History

Santo Cerro was the site of a tragic battle between Spaniards led by Columbus and Taínos led by the famous cacique Guarionex. According to Dominican legend, at one point in the battle, Columbus placed a cross on the hill, and a group of hostile Taínos attempted to pull it down. As they attacked the cross, however, the Virgen de las Mercedes (Virgin of Mercy, Virgin Mary) appeared above one of its arms and frightened the Indians away with her radiance, thus winning the battle for the Spaniards.

Historians confirm that on March 25, 1495, Columbus planted a cross on the hill during a battle. After that, they assert, the Spaniards' huge mastiffs and horses won the battle, allowing the gold-hungry conquistadors to drive the Indians out of their beloved valley and into Spanish mines.

Iglesia Las Mercedes

On the hill, the white Iglesia Las Mercedes (Church of Our Lady of Mercy) offers beautiful views of the Cibao Valley. Open most days, the church was built in 1880. Inside is the spot where legend says Columbus planted the first cross. Supposedly a piece of the cross has been preserved, but it's not on display. You can see the hole, however; it's called **Santo Hoyo de la Cruz.** If possible, try to make a small donation towards the parish's upkeep. Shops nearby sell religious mementos, and there is a tiny museum you can enter on the side of the church. If you're lucky enough to be in Santo Cerro on March 25, you'll see a huge religious procession up the hill by thousands of Catholic faithful. However, the winter months provide a breathtaking view as well, especially if the weather is mild and the amapola trees are in bloom.

La Vega Vieja

While you're in Santo Cerro, take time to visit what remains of La Vega Vieja, the original townsite and fort built by Columbus. If you're on the Moca road going north, continue by the turnoff for Santo Cerro another two km until you can see the turnoff for the ruins of the old **Franciscan Monastery.** The monastery itself was established in 1512, making La Vega the first archbishopric on Hispaniola. There isn't much to see, just some unearthed foundations reached by a footbridge. Nevertheless, the sight has a kind of mystery about it, and if you're lucky, the locals might show you the skeletons they've found.

Continuing only another kilometer up the Moca road you'll see the ruins of **Fortaleza de la Concepción** on the left. This fort and small church are all that's left of the original townsite, established by Columbus and destroyed by an earthquake in 1562. The fort was attacked by Taínos in 1498, but withstood this considerable onslaught to grow into the largest town in Hispaniola during 1505–10, spurred mainly by the discovery of gold. The gold soon ran out, and the town was finally destroyed.

The excavations of La Vega Vieja are extensive and ongoing. There are many walls, passageways, and rooms, as well as a small museum containing a variety of Spanish and Taíno artifacts. From La Vega Vieja you can go to Jarabacoa in the mountains either by continuing straight ahead to the L in the road and going toward the highway, or by backtracking to La Vega.

Accommodations

All of the hotels in La Vega are inexpensive, or bordering on it. Unfortunately, they aren't particularly enticing either. Several hotels operate out on the highway, including **Hotel América** at the south end of town (tel. 809/573-2902) and **Hotel Guariano** (tel. 809/573-2632) on the north. The latter is on the Río Camú and offers air-conditioning and neverending noise and music. Downtown holds the **Hotel San Pedro** (Calle de Cáceres 33, tel. 809/573-2884), **Hotel Astral** (Calle de Cáceres 18, tel. 809/573-3535), and down the street the **Hotel Santa Clara** (Calle de Cáceres 91, tel 809/573-2878). All of these basic commercial hotels offer very simple accomodations for about US$12. Check out the noise levels before you decide. Downtown, Avenida Rivas has some inexpensive commercial hotels as well. **Hotel Bello** (tel. 809/573-5282) and **Hotel Cafetería Genao** (tel. 809/573-4878) are right next door to one another. There are several hotels in the Calle Restauración area, the best being **Hotel**

Restaurant Quinto Patio (Calle Restauración 48, tel. 809/573-6842), where the US$15 rooms seem quieter and better kept than most.

Food and Dancing

Quinto Patio has a decent restaurant for *comida criolla*. The other restaurants in the downtown area are your basic rice-and-beans type of places, nothing special, but nothing terrible either. Both the **Restaurant Maturijere** and **El Coche** are on the Duarte Highway, while the **Restaurant Malecón** is on Av. Imbert. **La Casona** is on Calle José Gómez 127, while **Restaurant La Cocina** is at Calle Mella 29. If you're desperate for something to do at night, a disco on the Duarte Highway called **Astromundo** offers loud music and sweat.

Service

Codetel is at the corner of Juan Rodriguez and Duverge.

Getting There

Getting to Santo Cerro from La Vega is easy and convenient. Continue on the Duarte Highway just a few kilometers past La Vega. On the right will be a fork in the road that turns north toward the town of Moca. Take the Moca road north five km. You'll see the hill in front of you and a well-marked road that leads up it. Follow that road for about 1.5km, past 17 religious statues. The white church will loom before you, and the small town of Santo Cerro will magically appear. Turn left and park outside the church.

WEST OF THE DUARTE HIGHWAY

Just a few kilometers north of La Vega is the good paved road for Jarabacoa. It's well marked on the highway, though turnoffs can be hectic in the breakneck truck race known as Dominican traffic. Once you leave the Duarte, however, it is a very pleasant drive on a pine-lined road.

JARABACOA

Jarabacoa is a pleasant modern town with an ideal climate and beautiful surroundings. At an altitude of 500 meters, it is warm in the day and cool to cold at night all year round, which makes its climate ideal for both human beings and plants. The houses in town are quite attractive in general, and the weather draws numerous wealthy Dominicans here during the summer to escape the heat and dampness of the coasts. The great thing about Jarabacoa is that it is a resort town without that resort-town look and feel, so often cheesy and inauthentic. Downtown Jarabacoa is cozy, with a lovely central park and a rather elegantly eccentric church.

The town of Jarabacoa, situated right next to the river, has a simple set of streets in a north-south grid. As in most Dominican towns, the central park is also the center of social life, and on the square is the town bank and a small, poorly staffed and barely adequate tourist office that will perhaps be handing out a scruffy town map. A map, however, is hardly needed in this compact, easily negotiated small town.

One of the main reasons tourists and travelers come to Jarabacoa, besides the change in climate from the heat of the lowlands, is the possibility of rafting and canyoning. In the past few years, several tour operations have surfaced, the largest being **Máxima Aventura** (Rancho Baiguate, tel. 809/574-6890). Other tour guides include **Get Wet** (Calle del Carmen, tel. 809/586-1170, fax 809/586-1655) and **Franz Aventuras** (Rancho Jarabacoa, tel. 809/574-2669). Each of these operators offers kayaking and tubing, some hiking, and both long and short trips. The Rancho Baiguate group can get you tours of a cassava factory and a coffee factory and can

handle paragliding, trekking, canyoning, and horseback riding on request. Most of the basic rafting trips down the Río Yaque del Norte are in the range of US$50–60.

The basic river tour involves an early breakfast, a load-onto truck for travel toward the river, and an easy paddle trip downstream. The Río Yaque is a mild white-water experience and can be disappointing to some because of the overused banks and lack of spectacular scenery. Tin cans and garbage can be a problem on the river too.

Rancho Jarabacoa, located two kilometers north of town (tel. 809/574-4811, fax 809/574-4815), offers an all-day mountain horseback ride for RD$200. This may be the nicest and most economical outdoor trip in the area. Rappelling and canyoning are new to the area, but both Maxima and Get Wet offer the experience for about US$60.

Sights and Recreation

The town of Jarabacoa sits on the confluence of the rivers Jimenoa and Yaque del Norte. **Parque La Confluencia** is located about three km outside of town and down a pleasant road lined by relatively expensive homes. You can drive right to the river's edge, where you'll find a small restaurant, horses to rent, and a swimming hole. Though somewhat dangerous because of currents, this particular *balneario* is quite popular with both locals and tourists and tends to be crowded, especially on weekends, holidays, and in the summer. It is possible to camp in the park, and there are trails in the vicinity for hiking. Given the number of vendors, it's surprising there isn't more trash than there already is. Another *balneario* is called **La Poza** and is just a short walk from Jarabacoa. Like La Confluencia, it is somewhat marred by crowds, trash, and signs painted on rocks, but the swimming is okay.

Many people come to Jarabacoa to see the waterfalls. Of the three in the general region, probably the most famous is **El Salto**—sometimes called **El Salto de Jimenoa**—which is directly on the river north of Jarabacoa on the road to Buena Vista. To reach the falls, take the road north. Keep driving north toward Buena Vista until you see a sign for the falls and follow the road. Parking is a little tricky. There is a restaurant with parking a short ways from the river. There is a RD$10 charge to enter, money probably used to maintain the cable bridges. Don't go on a holiday, or weekend in summer, as the area is impossibly crowded. Also, during certain rainy periods, the pool can be dangerous for swimming—so exercise caution.

Much closer to town, and therefore much more frequented, are the falls called **Salto de Baiguate.** Though it's only about a half-hour walk to an entrance marked by a sign, the walk to the falls will probably take about an hour, and you're likely to encounter tourists on horseback. The El Salto de Jimenoa are referred to as the upper falls because they are located upstream on the Jimenoa. The third local waterfall, known as the lower falls, is actually on the Río Yaque del Norte, just a few kilometers outside of Jarabacoa on the road to Monabao. A suspension bridge in the area will tell you that you're close to the trail.

Finding all three of the waterfalls can be somewhat confusing. If you want to be doubly sure, you can locate El Salto de Baiguate by going to the Pinar Dorado Hotel, only a few kilometers from Salto de Baiguate. Folks there can give you ample directions. In fact, the Salto de Baiguate is almost an adjunct attraction to the Pinar Dorado Hotel.

Perhaps Jarabacoa's greatest attraction is its proximity to the high mountains of the national park areas, and in particular, to Pico Duarte trails. Be warned: to a large extent, access to the back country is limited to 4WD vehicle or horse. You *can* make it in a car to the Pico Duarte trailhead at La Cienega, but only very slowly. South of Jarabacoa, the road is passable for a number of kilometers, certainly enough to allow you access to the hotels south of town, as well as to sights for bathing and horseback riding.

Birds
Birds common to the forests surrounding Jarabacoa include the La Selle's thrush, rufous-throated solitaire, Greater Antillean elaenia, and Greater Antillean peewee.

Sports
If you enjoy formalized sports, you'll find tennis courts at some of the area's better hotels, and a nine-hole golf course outside of town. The golf course is technically private, but you might be able to scratch your way in if you hang around long enough and know golf etiquette.

Accommodations
When you approach Jarabacoa, a town of about 50,000 people, you'll pass many hotel complexes. Just 5km east of town is **Rancho Baiguate,** a large 72-square-kilometer property bordered by two local rivers. There are 17 guest rooms on the grounds, each with private bath and hot water, screened windows, and sports fields. The price is US$30–50 or US$55–80 single, depending on meal options. It seems a happy place, ultra-quiet at night. On the road to La Vega is the old fashioned but quite nice **Hotel de la Montaña** (tel. 809/682-8181), which has 27 rooms that are large and have good views of the mountains. This charming hotel was once the *grande dame* of the region but is on its last legs. The restaurant is gone and only about 25 rooms remain habitable. There is no telephone or generator. For about US$20, one can give it a try and imagine good times past.

Some downtown hotels offer value as well, and in them you can meet everyday Dominicans who are on their own special vacations. Try the **Hotel Hogar** (tel. 809/574-2739, US$12). Also downtown are the **Dormitorio** and **Hotel El Carmel** nearby, both very basic and budget-oriented.

Going north from Jarabacoa, towards the Parque La Confluencia, is **Anacaona Villas** (tel. 809/574-2686), which has concrete bungalows you can rent with fans and kitchens by the week for about US$120. Slightly farther down the same road are the units of **Jarabacoa River Resort,** which has three-room cabins with kitchens and TVs (tel. 809/574-2772), or you can rent one room when available. The cabins are about US$50 per night, rooms somewhat less of course.

On the south side of town, going out toward Constanza on the El Río road is the **Pinar Dorado** (Constanza Km 1, 809/574-2820, with 77 rooms), which is very popular with German and other European tourists. Rooms have double beds and fans, the service is quite friendly, and you can walk to a waterfall. Horses can be rented as well, and there is a small pool and restaurant. It's located near town; guests have a good choice of local restaurants as well. The Pinar Dorado has a Santo Domingo contact as well. Contact Señor Reyes (Av. Bolivar 810, tel. 809/687-7012) for reservations. For those going to Pico Duarte, there is a rustic hotel in Manabao on the road to La Cienega. Called the **Patria Muñoz**, it is extra cheap and very basic.

The town's best hotels stand next to each other just east of town. The **Altocerro** (tel. 809/696-0202) is small, has a few private cabins, and offers limited camping. Rooms average US$25. More expensive, and slightly nicer, is **Cabañas de la Montaña** (tel. 809/561-1131), which offers large villas some with kitchens. The hotel offers day hikes.

Food

Food is not hard to come by in Jarabacoa, of course, though there isn't anything you'd call world class in town. Simple and inexpensive *comida criolla* can be had in numerous *comedores* and cafeterias around the main downtown area and all the main hotels, including **Montaña, Pinar Dorado,** and the **Hogar.** These hotels charge very modest prices for food, except for breakfast. You can also buy fresh fruit from vendors, and bread from several bakeries. Perhaps the nicest atmosphere for sit-down eating can be found at the **Restaurant Brasilia** (Calle Colón 26) and the **Restaurant Sandy. Restaurant Don Luis** is on the square next to Parque Duarte. The most pleasant cafeteria may be **Cafetería Angel** on Avenida Independencia. For a splurge of international cuisine you can try the restaurant at the **Alpes Dominicanos Hotel,** and Italian food at **De Paolo Restaurant.** The town has a pizzeria or two as well.

Information

The Jarabacoa **Codetel** is on Avenida Independencia, and there is a tourist office near the main highway entrance to town from La Vega.

Getting There

Try to avoid taking the other approach to Jarabacoa, which is from the south on the road through El Río. The road from El Río is enough to make a tank commander weep. Caribe Tours offers bus service to Jarabacoa from Santo Domingo, or you can take Metro to La Vega and a *público* from La Vega.

CONSTANZA

Constanza's 50,000 residents live in one of the prettiest places in the whole Dominican Republic. For one thing, the town stands at an altitude of 1,212 meters (4,000 feet), which makes its climate brisk and healthful at all times, even a little frosty in the so-called Dominican winter. The town is an agricultural community, hardly touched by tourism, though it looks as though that might change in the future. For now, Constanza's relative isolation assures its anonymity. In terms of economics, Constanza is a mix of affluent and poor, revealing the social side of the Dominican Republic nobody likes to mention.

The surrounding countryside is, however, amazingly lovely, green with forest, replete with bubbling streams, waterfalls, and fresh, clean air. Located in a valley, the town provides dramatic views for those who hike to a high escarpment on the southern rim.

One tantalizing feature is Constanza's large Japanese community. During the 1950s, Trujillo allowed the immigration of 50 Japanese farm families whose task it was to develop the temperate agricultural prospects of the farmland in the Constanza valley. This they did by starting an industry of vegetable and fruit growing that now provides the country with much of its temperate-zone food. Farmers in Constanza grow strawberries, lettuce, apples, and potatoes, among many other vegetables, and have a fresh flower concession as well. These days the Japanese families keep a low profile, suitable probably to their social instincts. There is a Japanese community building in Constanza, and you'll see Japanese tourists on occasion. Otherwise, the Japanese families prefer to cultivate and prosper in private.

Strangely enough, the one Cuban effort to overthrow the Dominican government began when a C-46 transport plane landed in the valley carrying 56 Castro-trained Dominican rebels. The rebels were quickly rounded up and killed, ending the revolt. In the 1970s, residents began to report UFO sightings and continued to do so in the 1990s. Perhaps the UFOs are swooping in to inspect the large, camouflage-painted military base in the area. Keep in mind that Constanza has few facilities for tourists and that the hotels are rather ordinary. The scenery, fresh air, isolation and quiet, and hiking trails are everything.

Sights

Sad to say, but one of the interesting sights in Constanza is a government-owned and run hotel called **Nueva Suiza,** built by Trujillo and set on a towering cliffside mountain about the town. It is a huge hotel (some call it the Swiss Chalet) on the south side of town on the road to San José de Ocoa and set in woods about extensive fields of irrigated crops. Like one or two other government hotels (I can think of one in the eastern town of Seiba, in particular), the old lady has been allowed to tumble down, through neglect and simple economics. Getting to the old hotel is easy, because you can see it from town, though you should wait until it is renovated before actually booking a room (this is the kind of wait that could wind up being like something out of Gabriel García Márquez, I'm afraid). However, there are some hiking trails that spike out from the hotel, and while you're in the process of assessing the old lady's current features, you could hike the wooded mountains behind her. Respectfully, of course.

Aguas Blancas (White Water) falls represents a much more significant hiking effort, though well worth it. The falls themselves are located on the Río Grande River in a valley south of Constanza about 9.6km (6 miles) on a dirt road that heads toward the Valle Nuevo area. The road climbs as it leaves Constanza, heading into pine forest, though there are some areas of pure montane forest remaining in patches. Looking to the west, one can see the falls on a crest of hill, with a lovely cascade that drops in two stages down a steep mountain. At a place called El Convento (really just the name of a hill), a road leads up to the base of the falls. It is narrow and demanding, and unless you feel the particular need to risk it, just walk the mile uphill to the falls where there is a pool for bathing, though the water is ice cold. The quail-dove, the Hispaniolan trogon, and the sharp-shinned

hawk are all native species, so keep an eye out for them.

Reserva Científica Valle Nuevo

Continuing on another three km south of Aguas Blancas brings you to Reserva Científica Valle Nuevo (Valle Nuevo Scientific Reserve), a huge area of mostly natural forest that is one of the most isolated and undisturbed places in the Dominican Republic. The program of establishing scientific reserves was begun by the Dominican Republic in 1983, partly in recognition of a need to preserve some delicate tropical (both montane and oceanic) environments. To reach Valle Nuevo, it is necessary to drive south of Constanza on dirt road, keeping in mind that rain, and therefore muddy and rough conditions, are possible at almost any time of the year as the altitude increases on your way to the reserve. The road climbs past Aguas Blancas, finally reaching an altitude of almost 2,134m (7,000 feet). In all, the reserve is approximately 39km (24 miles) in extent, beginning just south of Constanza and extending nearly to the provincial boundary at Peravia in the upper Río Ocoa valley—where you'll see farms!

In the main part of the reserve, you'll see species like holly and lyonia, which grow nowhere else in the Caribbean. Some species are interesting because they usually grow in the northern United States and southern Canada. Speculation has it that passing birds dropped the seeds and conditions proved hospitable. Keeping to the main road through the reserve is difficult but not impossible. Many side roads, used for logging activities, do slice off and head uphill. Conditions on these roads are not favorable, especially in wet weather.

Terrestrial species in the forest are long gone. Birds, however, still make the forest home, including the Antillean euphoria, Ridgeway's hawk, black-crowned tanager, narrow-billed tody, and Hispaniolan woodpecker.

The farther south you go in the reserve, the denser the pines grow, though later there are expanses of pine savannah. Here, bird species like the Greater Antillean elania, peewee, palm crow, and siskin can be spotted. At its height, the road through the reserve reaches an altitude of 2,438m (8,000 feet), where there are rocky mountaintops. Descending, the road passes through some more montane remnants, then reaches the Ocoa River valley for the run to San José de Ocoa.

If you're adventurous, you can try the whole trip from Constanza to San José, though you'll need a vehicle in good condition, preferably 4WD. Take plenty of emergency provisions, some gasoline, water, food, and extra blankets. You never know, you might have to walk out. There is a military post near the entrance to the reserve in case of emergency.

As one descends into the Ocoa River valley, the country becomes much drier and covered by mesquite, acacia, and mahogany. Keep in mind that you should budget all day for the trip from Constanza to San José. From Santo Domingo to San José is about two hours, an easy drive. It's all uphill from there, as they say.

Accommodations

The hotels in Constanza are all relatively inexpensive, and you'll find most a good buy with basic rooms, fans, and not too much noise to handle. The main street of Constanza is Calle Luperón, where you'll find **Hotel Margarita** and **Casa de Huéspedes,** your basic downtown commercial hotels. Each has reasonably comfortable rooms for about US$12. **Hotel Lorenzo** (Calle 16 de Agosto) is a good buy at about US$10 with shared bath, slightly higher with private bath. Surprisingly, the Hotel Lorenzo also features one of the best eateries in Constanza, serving good steak Creole and chicken, with a bar for drinks. The **Hotel Restaurant Mi Cabaña** (Calle Espinosa 60, tel. 809/539-2472) is a large establishment with 60 rooms, some with private baths. Those with shared bath are about US$10 s or d, private bath somewhat higher. The **Brisas del Valle** is a simple hotel (Calle Gratereaux 76, tel. 809/539-2356) where rooms start at less than US$10. Even cheaper is **Hotel Restaurant Sobeyda** (16 de Agosto 22, tel. 809/539-2498).

Food

For the best food in town, head to **Lorenzo's,** which has cold drinks, decent steaks, and televisions blaring sports. As in any provincial Dominican town, the main street and the central plaza area are lined by *comedores, colmados,* cafes, and cafeterias. At any of these you can get a decent sandwich or *comida criolla.* Near the

plaza you'll see **Anacaona** bakery. There is a market located on **Avenida Gratereux** where you can find good fruits and vegetables, and many kinds of food shops are in the same vicinity. For a wide selection of pizza and baked goods, go to **Restaurant Pizzería y Heladería Rey** (Calle S. Ureña 22). Aside from Lorenzo's, there is no standout eatery in Constanza, but a short walk will reveal a whole world of small restaurants, bars, and cafes where decent food can be had for a small price.

Entertainment and Events

Constanza isn't much on nightlife, though there are a disco and·a few bars in town. The *fiestas patronales* of Nuestra Señora de las Mercedes is observed on September 24.

Getting There

From Santo Domingo try the **Línea Cobra** for runs to Constanza. From Bonao, catch *públicos* at the central bus station. If you wind up in La Vega, the best public transport bet is to go down to Bonao and catch the *públicos* over to Constanza.

By car, the easiest route is to take the main (paved) road off the Duarte Highway about 10km north of Bonao. It is a plainly marked exit, and then you'll get on a winding and sometimes muddy road that requires about an hour if you're lucky. However, this particular road, which passes the El Río cutoff, is one of the most beautiful drives in the country manageable by regular passenger vehicle. If you're in Jarabacoa, going to Constanza, the road to San José de Ocoa passes through town. It is quite rough and can be muddy, but a regular passenger vehicle should be able to negotiate it with care. Before setting out from Jarabacoa on this road, check with somebody in town, or at the hotel, for current conditions. Many drivers who wish to visit both Jarabacoa and Constanza do so by returning to the Duarte Highway—say, from Jarabacoa—then going south to the main Bonao road to Constanza. Under certain weather conditions this may actually save time. With a 4WD vehicle, you can easily go from Jarabacoa.

The hour drive from Bonao over to Constanza takes you up to a ridge from where you can view, behind you, the Lago Rincón on the Río Juma, one of the few man-made lakes in the country.

Hotel la Mansión

Once you're in Constanza, you'll find the **Línea Cobra** offices at Calle Sánchez 37 (tel. 809/539-2415) for the trip to Santo Domingo.

SAN JOSÉ DE LAS MATAS

You can easily reach the lovely mountain town of San José de las Matas by *público* from Santiago. Located in the foothills of the Cordillera Central, the town has no access to the interior sections of the mountains and national park, but it was once well worth a visit for the moderately expensive **Hotel La Mansión** (tel. 809/581-0395), which has 276 rooms, including villas with air-conditioning and phone, costing US$68–80 per night. You can hardly miss seeing the hotel from town, as it sits high on a hill in beautifully maintained surroundings rich with flowers and pines. Behind the hotel is a newly opened "tourist park," which is actually 12 square km of pine reserve that winds up into the hills behind the hotel. The hotel has a pool and spa, and an excellent restaurant. There is a separate sauna and massage cabana. The hotel arranges horseback riding, excursions, and walks. There isn't much to do in San José, but it is the perfect place to relax and enjoy the excellent weather, lovely views, and an unhurried atmosphere.

The Mansión was expected to close in 2001, however. The government, which probably loses money operating the place, had shut off funds.

When I visited the hotel, it was nearly empty, and a lone waiter hovered over me, offering delicious coffee and carrot cake. Definitely check with a tour operator or local officials ahead of time to see if the hotel is open. Perhaps, with luck, this fine hotel will be salvaged.

The town of San José has about 70,000 residents, though it seems much smaller because it is spread out nicely in the mountain valley. The town also has a European look and feel, probably because it was settled early in the history of the country and has not suffered as much destruction from war as cities like La Vega.

Recreation

There are a few *balnearios* in the area for bathing, and one of the best cockfight pits in the country is nearby, if that's your thing. While the drive to Monción looks tempting on the map, it is actually rather dry and dusty and unremarkable. San José is near the jumping-off point for long and arduous treks to Pico Duarte. Called the Mata Grande trail, these hikes are considerably longer than others by a matter of several days. The *balnearios* at Anima, Las Ventanas, and Agues Calientes are 5–6 km from town. Your hotel can help find them for you.

Accommodations

Most hotels in San José are very inexpensive. Try the **Las Samanes** (Av. Santiago 16, tel. 809/578-8316) or the budget **Hotel Restaurant Oasis** (Av. 30 de Marzo 51, tel. 809/578-8298).

Upon entering town you'll see signs for the **Hotel La Mansión** and the **Parque Turístico,** the hotel getting its name from the fact that Tru-

jillo maintained a mansion in town for his own personal use. This hotel—if open— is one of the greatest bargains in the country. Even though it technically belongs to the government, the hotel is managed and operated by a private corporation, Occidental Hotels.

PARQUES NACIONALES ARMANDO BERMÚDEZ AND JOSÉ DEL CARMEN RAMÍREZ

The Parque Nacional Armando Bermúdez was created in 1956 and is the northern section of the Cordillera Central. Two years later the Dominican government created Parque Nacional José del Carmen Ramírez, so that now almost all of the Cordillera Central are part of protected areas. Armando Bermúdez itself contains 766 square km (296 square miles) and together the two parks contain the four highest peaks in the Greater Antilles: Pico Duarte, Pico Yaque, La Pelona, and La Rucilla. The two parks are divided by a stream called Río La Compartición. Both areas are utterly isolated and almost completely without roads, though you will find a few trails and old logging tracks. Through Parque Nacional José Del Carmen Ramírez run the important Yaque del Sur, San Juan, and Mijo Rivers, all of which are of major importance to villages in the San Juan Valley in southwestern parts of the country.

NATURAL HISTORY

The areas encompassed by the national parks began to form 60 million years ago during the Cretaceous period. Almost all of the geologic formations in the mountains are igneous, diorites, volcanic limestone, slate, and marble. The Cordillera Central give rise to some 14 rivers, including the major Río Yaque del Norte, all of which serve to sustain, in some form or another, the agricultural needs of the country. Without these mountains and the rivers formed in them, life in the Dominican Republic would be very much harsher. Large hydroelectric dams surround the mountains at Taveras, Sabaneta, Sabana Yegu, and Bao. Despite the isolation and

extremes of temperature and precipitation, some people do manage to scrape a meager living out of the country. In fact, illegal squatting and logging are both becoming more of a problem as population pressures mount.

Temperatures and Precipitation
At Armando Bermúdez, temperatures during most of the year average between 12° and 21°C, though in winter at higher elevations temperatures sometimes drop as low as -8°C at dawn. The lowest temperatures have been recorded at the high mountain valleys of Bao and Macutico. Rainfall has extremes, depending upon the elevation and orientation of the slope, the north-facing slopes receiving far more rainfall than the south-facing ones. Precipitation averages between 1,000 and 4,000 mm per year. At José Del Carmen Ramírez, the average temperature is between 12° and 18°C, though in some areas like the Valle de Tetero, the temperature may dip to -5°C. In many parts of the park, yearly rainfall averages 2,500mm per year.

FLORA AND FAUNA

Going up into the Cordillera Central presents a remarkable opportunity to see at least half a dozen different zones of flora and fauna. These zones are segregated according to elevation, with the lowest, in areas around 1,000m, being mostly palm. In general you'd have to classify most of the Cordillera Central as subtropical humid forest or rain forest. In areas up to 1,200m in elevation, West Indian cedar, mountain wild olive, and petitia predominate, while close to streams you'll see growths of West Indian walnut and wild cane in fields. At the next level, from about 1,200 to 1,500 m, grow myrtle laurel cherry, copey, pasture fiddlewood, and sierra palm, while 200m higher in elevation grow the West Indian sumac, palo de viento, wild brazilleto, cyrilla, wild avocado, tree ferns, and a few pines. At the highest elevations, the mountains are covered by the justly famous creolean pine.

The most conspicuous fauna are the birds, terrestrial species having been hunted out long ago. Of special interest are the Hispaniolan parrot, Hispaniolan woodpecker, white-necked crow, palm chat (the Dominican national bird, some say), Hispaniolan trogon, ruddy quail dove, and mourning dove. At José Del Carmen Ramírez, you might also encounter the rufous-throated solitaire, loggerhead flycatcher, red-necked pigeon, and black swift. Terrestrial species in the parks include mainly reptiles and amphibians. The government has introduced the wild boar to Armando Bermúdez, and some say the hutia is still present. If so, these animals inhabit only the wildest parts of the park.

PICO DUARTE PRACTICALITIES

Amazingly, Pico Duarte, the highest mountain in the Caribbean, was not climbed until 1944, and then only as part of national celebration of the one hundredth anniversary of the nation's independence.

Everyone who plans to hike the trails to Pico Duarte should visit the National Parks Office in Santo Domingo in order to obtain the necessary permits. The closest and easiest trail to reach is the trailhead at **La Ciénega,** upriver from Jarabacoa. Technically speaking, the road from Jarabacoa to the trailhead is called the Manabao Road, and you can reach it by taking the main road through Jarabacoa and, at the fork, turning right on a route some locals call El Carmen. Some buses go to the town of Manabao, and at least one bus goes all the way to la Ciénega, but you'll need to check on schedules at one of the gasoline stations near the Manabao road in Jarabacoa. The road from Jarabacoa to Manabao, I'm happy to report, has been recently hard topped and is similar to any two-lane road in a rugged part of the American Rockies. After Manabao, the road is im-

proved gravel and can probably be negotiated in a regular passenger vehicle in good weather conditions. The scenery is very beautiful, and gas can be purchased at Manabao at one of several small roadside stalls.

You'll need a guide and mules to make the trip, and these can be had in the small village of La Ciénega, at the end of the line. The proprietress of a small hotel called **Patria Muñoz** in Manaboa can help visitors with guides. The road to Manabao is 21km (13 miles); it is 30km (19 miles) to La Ciénega. From La Ciénega it is 23km to the top of Pico Duarte.

If you are unable to arrange for park permits in Santo Domingo, it should be possible to get them at the entrance to the park, which is just down a dirt path on the outskirts of La Ciénega. At the present time, permits cost RD$20 for residents, RD$50 for foreign visitors.

According to regulations, visitors must be accompanied by at least one park guide. Mules are available for hire, and you might be told they are necessary. In my opinion, they're not absolutely necessary, but they *are* a welcome addition. There must be one guide for every five mules.

Within the park, along the route of the climb, you'll find seven cabins for visitor use. The cabins have kitchens with wood-burning stoves. Tent camping is certainly permitted in the park and some water is available from streams. Most hikers tend to believe the water is okay to drink without purification, but it is best to take along water purification tablets.

There is a small *colmado* in La Ciénega, and after arranging for guides and mules you'll need to buy food—usually rice, beans, and canned meat—for the guides to cook. Pack warm clothes, hiking boots, sleeping gear, canteens, flashlights, matches, and a medical kit.

If you're still thinking about going without a guide and mules, be advised that the hike is very strenuous, and because of numerous side trails, it is quite possible to get lost. As late as January 1988, someone tried to go up alone, and never came back. Don't try it.

Since the mountain's heaviest rainfall comes in May through November, most climbers ascend the peak between December and March, during the driest, albeit the coldest, months.

Whichever way you choose to enter and exit

these parks, you'll find fresh rivers and forests full of ferns, orchids, bromeliads, and bamboo. From Pico Duarte you can see the Caribbean Sea, Lake Enriquillo, the Cibao Valley, and smaller mountain ranges. It is a fantastic experience only enjoyed by a few hundred people every year.

LA CIÉNEGA TRAIL

Having located a guide and muleteer in La Ciénega, you're ready to go into Parque Nacional Bermúdez. The trail from La Ciénega to Pico Duarte and back (46km) requires about three days, though it might stretch out to four depending upon the weather and your own physical condition. At first, the trail follows the Los Tablones River, which forms one boundary of the park. It's an old road still used by locals, and so it is quite different from the rest of the trail. Along this first four-km section is tropical broadleaf forest interspersed with wild cane. At Los Tablones you'll find a cabin where you can spend the night.

The second part of the trail climbs from Los Tablones to La Cotorra. It's a very steep rise, from a broadleaf forest that includes almond trees and sierra palms (the wild boar's principal food sources) to a pine forest. The tall trees are filled with epiphytes; the forest floor is rich with ferns. You'll come across a rest area at La Cotorra where you might see a Hispaniolan parrot or two. The spot also features a stunning view of the La Ciénega valley.

Next the trail follows the ridge line for about two km before reaching a rest area at La Laguna, then climbs steeply again and reaches a side trail which leads to Valle Tetero, a high mountain valley with natural grass meadows. If you have an extra day to spend hiking, this particular valley is certainly worth seeing. Not only does it provide a spectacular sight, but it serves as one of the most important watersheds for the Yaque del Sur River system. On this trail, too, is a large boulder which has Taíno Indian petroglyphs. There is also a cabin where you can spend the night. Again, remember that the side trip will probably increase the length of your excursion by a day.

The rest of the trail passes by landmarks

known as La Cruce, then Aguita Fría, then onto La Compartición, at which you can begin the ascent of Pico Duarte. This 14-km hike takes a stiff upper lip; it's a steep and steady climb. The Aguita Fría trail passes a large bog that is the source of two rivers, the Yaque del Norte and Yaque del Sur, then drops slightly upon entry to La Compartición, where you'll see open pine.

The final ascent is usually begun before dawn. You'll commence with a steady climb through a pine forest following a ridge, then pass through an open meadow at Vallecito del Lilis, where you'll get a good view of both Pico Duarte and La Pelona. For the final part of the climb, you'll pass between large boulders until you reach the summit. There, you'll be rewarded with spectacular views in all directions. You can see the Caribbean Sea, Lake Enriquillo, the Cibao Valley, and smaller mountain ranges.

Probably the most sensible way to approach the hike from La Ciénega and back is to go to Valle Tetero on day one, the summit on day two from La Compartición, back to La Compartición on day three, then back to La Ciénega. It is possible to shave a day off this schedule if you feel like pushing yourself. Plan to spend about US$240 for a party of four on a three-day trip with mules. Settle fees well in advance to avoid problems and hard feelings.

MORE TRAILS

The Mata Grande Trail

The Mata Grande Trail officially commences at the National Park Station in Mata Grande, near the small town of Pedregal, which is near San José de las Matas on the northern rim of Parque Nacional Bermúdez. For those who wish to climb Pico Duarte from the northern approach, take the road from Santiago to Janico, which you can pick up by crossing the Río Yaque del Norte and taking a road parallel to the river. It is a little confusing in this part of Santiago, what with construction and heavy traffic, so if you get confused, ask for directions. Once you get the Janico road, though, you'll be rewarded with a lovely drive on good pavement.

Approximately two kilometers through Pedregal is a village called San José. If you're interested in hiking into Parque Nacional

Bermúdez from Mata Grande, turn left (north) from San José. Take the paved road for 10km, where the road becomes dirt and gravel for another 14km. At the end of the road is a national park ranger office where you can get permits and arrange for guides and mules.

The first section of the Mata Grande trail follows an abandoned road from which you can see Santiago and the whole Cibao Loma de Loro. You'll find two more cabins at El Rodeo and Los Corrales, where the trail crosses the La Guacára River. The third section of the Mata Grande trail ascends and descends in and through the Bao River system, an area of broadleaf forest rich with ferns and epiphytes. The Valle de Bao is the jumping-off point for the ascent to Pico Duarte, a distance of about 12km. The total distance from the Mata Grande ranger station to Pico Duarte is about 45km. The trip takes about six days, or two days longer than the trip from La Ciénega to Pico Duarte and back.

The Sabaneta Trail
Reach the Sabaneta Trail by going first to San Juan de la Maguana and taking the road north from town toward the Corral de los Indios. From the corral continue north another 19km (12 miles) through Juan de Herrera along a very rough road. You'll see a dam, and the locals thereabouts know where to locate guides and mules. Come armed with permits if possible, as the park office is not always manned.

Planning Ahead
Keep in mind that, with proper logistical support—meaning two cars and a driver—you can hike into the national park from La Ciénega and exit through Mata Grande (or even Sabaneta if desired). However, you should be absolutely sure that you're ready for a week of hard climbing and hiking, and that you'll have transportation when you come out on the other side.

Arrangements for any of your hikes can be made by travel agents in Santo Domingo. One person specializing in outfitting Pico Duarte hikers is **Oskar Nausch** in Santo Domingo (Av. Federica Ureña, tel. 809/687-7212). At La Ciénega you can ask for **Juan Canela,** though all the guides are licensed by the national park system and are competent. Ecoturisa has a good staff to help you with tours to the wild areas of the Dominican Republic. All of the guide services in Jarabacoa can arrange ascents on all the trails.

BOB RACE

THE CIBAO VALLEY

INTRODUCTION

Take a look at any map of the Dominican Republic, and you'll see that the Duarte Highway-Highway 1 nearly splits the country in half, running roughly north and south. For much of its route, approximately north of La Vega, the highway charts a course down the middle of one of the most fertile valleys anywhere on earth, land so rich that it is said to be three feet deep with topsoil for most of its length. This central region of the Dominican Republic, set between the huge and isolated Cordillera Central to the south, and the steep and purple Cordillera Septentrional on the north, is called the Cibao.

Sometimes while traveling in the Cibao, it's easy to forget you're in the Caribbean. Many streets in Santiago, for example, have the look and feel of Cuba in the 19th century. The countryside is fenced and well managed, and many of the towns and villages are quite prosperous, with brightly painted houses and public buildings, shady central plazas, and busy streets. For tourists, most of the Cibao isn't terribly interesting, lacking facilities, beaches, and recreation. Though many could enjoy a trip from the valley up into the Septentrional Mountains or to San José de las Matas, on the way into Pico Duarte turf, the Cibao itself is probably too civi-

lized and overpopulated to be of terrible interest to adventurers. Still, the valley is very pleasant to travel through, with good, if confusing, roads, decent hotels, and fine food.

Land

The triangular area by lines from La Vega to San Francisco de Macorís to Moca and to Santiago de los Caballeros makes up the heart of the Cibao. As you pass eastward toward Cotuí, the land flattens and the horizons widen into the cane fields of the eastern provinces; going west up the Cibao, the land grows progressively drier, and what is rich agricultural country turns gradually into dusty cattle land. By Monte Cristi, the valley has petered out into arid cactus, aloe, and grassland.

It was the Cibao about which Christopher Columbus wrote back to Spain so ecstatically, though at first he believed gold lay in the slopes of its mountains. Nevertheless, from the first, colonists set to work cultivating the valley, dividing it into huge landholdings and raising cattle, cane, tobacco, and coffee. These days, agriculturalists have added bananas and rice to the mix, along with fruit orchards and some temperate vegetables as well. The Cibao valley is also becoming important in manufacturing. Santiago is responsible for some of the best cigars in the world.

The Cibao valley comprises the provinces of Santiago, Monsignor Nouel, Duarte, Espillat, Sánchez Ramirez, and Salcedo. In the region of Bonao, La Vega, Santo Cerro, and Moca, you find the heart of coffee and tobacco country. Here the weather is nearly always perfect—warm and dry in winter, warm and wet in summer, with an ever-present profusion of green and an abundance of flowers, especially in winter when the trees are in flaming bloom.

From Moca to Santiago the valley of the Cibao cuts through lush savannahs (from the Spanish word *sábana,* meaning "sheet"). The whole bottom of the valley is dotted with royal palms, though beyond Santiago the land becomes rapidly more and more arid, despite the fact that it is still technically a savannah. In fact, the name of the small provincial town Sabaneta gives witness to the presence of grasslands. The city of Santiago is old, nearly as old as Santo Domingo, and could very easily have become the original capital of Hispaniola, though it did not.

History

Many of the original cities of the Cibao were established as forts to protect what Columbus and his followers hoped would be huge gold diggings. Some of those towns are now among the most important in the country. The Cibao is densely populated, much more so than any other part of the country, and the force of its natural character has been forged by Cuban refugee *independentistas* who settled in the region during the Cuban troubles of the late 19th century. These Cuban refugees, who were mainly tobacco growers, traders, and ranchers, intermarried with local families and created what became a dynamic tobacco-exporting set of clans. Many natives of the Cibao think very strongly in regional terms, emphasizing their European and Cuban heritage, the high Castilian Spanish they speak, and their importance to national political life. Some natives even call their valley the Republic of the Cibao.

Moca and La Vega are towns steeped in tragic memories. Moca seemed always to be in the direct path of Haitian invasions, and it was where the dictator Ulises Heureaux met with an assassin's bullet. In Moca, the Haitian generals Christophe and Dessalines slaughtered thousands of hostages on their retreats, until the city absorbed so much punishment so gallantly that Dominicans took to calling it *Moca heróica.*

SANTIAGO DE LOS TREINTA CABALLEROS

For many years, Santiago of the Thirty Gentlemen was the largest and most important city in the country. Now, with a population of nearly 500,000, it has been relegated to second place economically, though many of its inhabitants would still claim a first socially. The city lies in the heart of the lush Cibao, and the local economy runs on both rum and tobacco, though Santiago also serves as an entrepôt for nearby agricultural and ranching transactions. Santiago has what many consider to be the best Carnaval in the country—meaning the most ancient and authentic, though perhaps not the most frenzied (that honor surely belongs to Santo Domingo).

Above all, the country is verdant. Bursting into the Cibao from either north or south—that is, from Santo Domingo or Puerto Plata—-he city seems to drift lazily, like a dream. From the city center, you see in the distance the sharp inclines of the Septentrional range, usually with clouds piling up on its northern slopes. As you near the buildings downtown, however, it's clear that Santiago is big in every way. The traffic seems dizzying, especially since the highways and many office buildings are undergoing so much construction (and consequent destruction). Yet even as this "development" takes its toll on many of Santiago's stately neighborhoods, the city enjoys a reputation for having a slower and more sophisticated pace than Santo Domingo. Older sections of the city still feature venerable mansions inhabited by the aristocratic families of the city. On the suburban outskirts, however, the new developments look very much like those in Southern California, or anywhere else for that matter: white cubes of condos sprouting satellite dishes, circled by German cars.

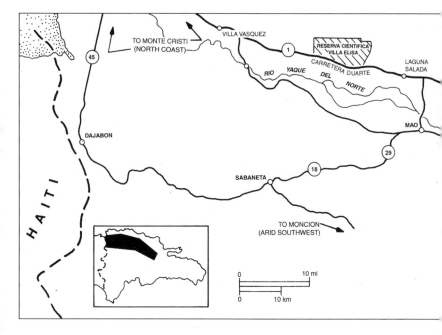

HISTORY

Founding

A number of stories circulate concerning the founding of Santiago, though there is one core legend that most of the city's people will claim. As the story goes, somewhere around 1494 Columbus ordered a fort built on the banks of the Río Yague del Norte to protect burgeoning goldfields. Some say that Bartholomew Columbus built the fort and is the official founder of the city, while others say that Christopher Columbus himself built the fort some years later,

Downtown Santiago is busy, dirty, noisy, and exciting, with Calle del Sol one of the main stopping streets in the whole country. The eastern part of the city is more modern and green, quieter, less enticing in some respects. In the western fringes of the city, where the Río Yaque del Norte runs northwest, the city is poor and rough, though filled with interesting sights, sounds, and, of course, smells.

in 1498 or 1499. Given the Indian troubles and the general disappointment with gold prospects, the original fort and settlement disappeared, and a few years later, Governor Frey Nicólas de Ovando granted land to a new group of settlers whose patron saint was St. James (El Orden de Santiago), and to others migrating down from Isabela on the north coast of Hispaniola. Historians are divided on whether the "thirty gentlemen" in the name of the city refers to gentlemen who arrived originally with Columbus or with the new group of settlers. Whatever the truth, the name of Santiago de los Treinta Caballeros held on, even after the city was destroyed by the devastating 1562 earthquake, which also ravaged La Vega.

Rebirth and Prosperity

After the earthquake, the city was rebuilt a few miles from its old location and became known as Villa de Santiago, though everybody continued to refer to it by its more distinguished, and longer, name. Because of its strategic position on the Río Yaque del Norte, and smack in the center of the

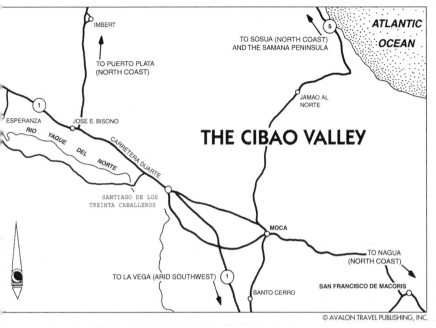

THE CIBAO VALLEY

© AVALON TRAVEL PUBLISHING, INC.

Cibao valley where armies could march and trade could pass, Santiago was destined to become vital in Dominican history, particularly in the struggle with Haiti and the battle for independence.

During the age of piracy, Santiago did not escape the notice of brigands either. In 1660, for example, the French pirate Fernando de la Flor sacked Santiago on one of his periodic raids of the Cibao. Given the difficulties of piracy, European war, and disease, the city had a population of only 500 in 1737, not counting slaves. It was with the beginning of the 19th century that Santiago began to take off, largely because of the export of tobacco. During the early 1800s, the population had risen to about 27,000, and the city was as strong, large, and prosperous as any in the country.

As Cuban refugees settled the Cibao, Santiago became the center of a vast and fertile region known for tobacco (and excellent cigars), rum distilling, coffee and sugar processing, livestock, mining, and logging. Many believe that merengue has its origins in the country music played by Cuban refugees.

Today

Today Santiago is a kind of alter ego to Santo Domingo, retaining a great deal of traditional culture, a slower pace, and a haughtier attitude than the colossus to the south. The picture is changing rapidly, however. The Duarte Highway, currently a nightmare of construction in the area of the city, will surely open to uncongested through traffic in the near future, and one can't help but wonder how long it will be before an international airport makes its appearance. Yet even though modernity has reared its head in Santiago, the side streets, particularly around the Parque Duarte, seem haunted reminders of another century.

SIGHTS

Orientation

Orienting yourself in Santiago isn't too difficult once you've negotiated the ubiquitous traffic construction. From anywhere near the Duarte Highway, you should be able to see

SANTIAGO DE LOS
TREINTA CABALLEROS

© AVALON TRAVEL PUBLISHING, INC.

CIGARS

The American embargo against Fidel Castro's government in Cuba forced many Cuban planters and manufacturers to relocate. Many of them chose the Dominican Republic. Dominican tobacco was always of high quality, but now the Cibao valley—and especially the city of Santiago—is not only the source of some of the world's choicest tobaccos, but the center of the world's cigar industry as well. Some famous brand names include Davidoff, Churchill, Dunhill, Avo, Partagas, and Carbonell. While Santiago is the center of the cigar industry, small cigar shops can be found in other towns and cities as well, principally Santo Domingo.

Cigars are made individually by craftsmen, who roll as many as 300 a day. The Dominican Republic exports nearly 60 million cigars annually, at an average wholesale price of US$2.50 each. The main markets for Dominican cigars are the United States and western Europe.

the huge monument, officially called El Monumento a los Héroes de la Restauración de la República (Monument to the Heroes of the Restoration of the Republic). Orienting yourself between the huge Monument and Parque Duarte will allow you to wander all of the downtown area. Directly to the east of the monument is the broad Avenida Sadhalá, which cuts directly north and south across the eastern part of the city. To the south of the monument is the Calle del Sol, the main shopping street of the city, and where some of its best hotels and restaurants are located. The Calle del Sol runs smack into the Parque Duarte, at the corner of 30 de Marzo, and is the heart of Old Santiago. Restauración is the other main "downtown" street and runs just north of, and parallel to, Calle del Sol. The main neighborhoods of Santiago are called Parte Alta and El Centro, and unless you have a particular interest in seeing the suburbs, this is where most of your time will be spent. The Río Yaque del Norte defines the city's eastern boundaries. You leave the El Centro neighborhood on the south by means of the Trujillo-built Hermanos Patiño bridge.

Parque Duarte

The place to start in Santiago is this gentle and pleasant park, located in the heart of old Santiago at the corner of Calle del Sol and 30 de Marzo. The park is surrounded by historic buildings and the cathedral and is busy with shoeshine boys, hawkers, and vendors. Despite the business, the park is still an oasis in the midst of the city, and all of the streets surrounding the park, especially toward the west and south, are representative of the Cuban influence on architecture and lifestyle in the old city. The park contains a lovely pavilion for shade and public music, and from the park you can take a carriage ride around the city for about US$10. Combine a rest in the park with a stroll up and down Calle del Sol for shopping, and you've seen some of the best that Santiago has to offer in both shopping and relaxation.

Catedral de Santiago Apóstol

On the south side of the park is the 19th-century (1868–95) Catedral de Santiago Apóstol (Cathedral of St. James the Apostle), which combines gothic and neoclassical styles with a modern exterior. Nevertheless, the cathedral is cool and impressive inside and houses the tomb of the tyrant Ulises Heureaux. The church also serves as resting place for some heroes of the Restoration, when the Dominican Republic became independent a second time (from Spain) in 1865. The stained-glass windows are by the artist Rincón Mora. Behind the cathedral on the south side is a lovely row of small private town homes in the Cuban style, painted in strong basic tones and delicate pastels. Entirely representative of earlier Cuban times, these small dwellings are used by individuals to sell religious items, or just as abodes. If you happen to be there near sunset, colors seem to explode out of the street and bathe the entire area in an unearthly glow.

Edificio del Centro de Recreo

To the north of the park are two old colonial buildings built in Mudéjar style. You'll probably see one or two men smoking cigars on the porch of the Edificio del Centro de Recreo (Recreational Center), and if you're polite you'll be able to tiptoe up to the windows and peek inside. What you'll see is the most exclusive billiard club in Santiago, an almost perfectly preserved aspect of bygone days in the Cibao. Of course, you can't go in, but the peek is well worth the effort.

Palacio Consistorial

Next door is the Palacio Consistorial, the 19th-century town hall that now is a public building and houses a small Santiago town museum. The museum has been in stages of restoration and readiness for some time. Check and see how things stand.

Museo del Tabaco

On another side of the park square, across from the cathedral on the east side, is the Museo del Tabaco (Museum of Tobacco) at Calle 30 de Marzo and 16 de Agosto, where cigar-making is demonstrated. Tobacco is extremely important to Santiago, and the Cibao is where the drug nicotine was first introduced to Europeans.

Centro de la Cultura

Just a hundred meters up the Calle del Sol from the Parque Duarte is the Centro de la Cultura (Cultural Center), another 19th-century building

Monument of the Heroes, Santiago

where the local town council displays works of Dominican artists and sometimes schedules special events. Check the billboards outside for specifics.

Museo de Artes Folklóricos Tomás Morel

For my money, the most fascinating, bizarre, and interesting sight in all of Santiago is the Museo de Artes Folklóricos Tomás Morel (Calle Gen. Lopez, tel. 809/582-6787). This small, but exquisitely exhaustive museum was created by Tomás Morel, a famous Dominican folklorist, collector, and writer. Morel began collecting masks, musical instruments, posters, dolls, and bric-a-brac characteristic of life in the Cibao valley of old, and particularly of regional styles of Carnaval as celebrated in numerous old communities of the Dominican Republic like La Vega, Monte Cristi, and Moca. Morel's collection dates to the turn of the century, at a time when some of the Carnaval and merengue traditions were still quite young by historical standards. The museum itself was founded in 1962 and is now run completely and lovingly by Morel's son, who is always on the premises to give tours and talk about art, poetry, folklore, and music. Admission to the museum is free, but please give the guy a substantial donation; it's obvious the premises could use some work. Morel the younger maintains a visitors book, which makes for fascinating reading in and of itself. The walls of the museum are covered with old and authentic masks, works of art as odd and surreal as they are beautiful. While the Carnaval collection in Santo Domingo's Museo del Hombre Dominicano is impressive, the Morel collection is stranger, more idiosyncratic and frightening. The museum is only a 10-minute walk downhill from the Parque Duarte. Don't miss it.

Monumento a los Héroes de la Restauración

Towering above the city at its eastern edge is the Monumento a los Héroes de la Restauración, built by the Trujillo government during the 1940s, ostensibly as a monument to the dictator himself, the ultimate in self-referential fascism. Now however, the monument commemorates heroes of the restoration of the Dominican Republic to independent government in 1865. The monument is 67 meters high, and, if the elevators are working, from its top you'll enjoy a splendid view of the city and the Cibao valley. The interior is devoted to a small museum and has murals by the Spanish artist Vela Zanetti. The monument has been undergoing extensive restoration for quite some time, so it is difficult to tell when it will be open for the public, or what the admission charge will be when it is open.

Tours

Special tours of the **León Jiménes Industria de Tabaco,** a large cigar-making and exporting company, can be arranged just by showing up at the front gate on Avenida 27 de Febrero, or by calling Juan Batista (tel. 809/241-1111). The tours of this famous cigar plant include a look at the actual cigar rollers in action, and free glasses of beer and cigars at the end. You can purchase cigars on the premises. You can also visit **La Aurora Tabacalero** (Av. 27 de Febrero, tel. 809/582-1131), as well as the **Brugal Distillery** (Av. 27 de Febrero 130, tel. 809/575-1427). The Jimenes tour is particularly friendly and enlightening. The old colonial ruins are at **Jacaqua,** and you can take a taxi there for just a few dollars, though there is only a concrete block and a flagpole for your trouble. When coming into town you'll pass the **Universidad Católica Madre y Maestra** on the Duarte Highway at Km 1.5.

ACCOMMODATIONS

Inexpensive

There are squads of low-budget hotels in Santiago, most of them hovels in and around the Plaza Valecio in downtown Santiago. You'll also find a cluster of cheap, cheap, cheap hotels on Calle Cucurullo, four blocks north of the park.

For spartan accommodations you can try **El Gallo de Oro,** facing the Plaza Valerio, or the **Santiago Plaza** on Calle Colón near the plaza, both of which offer rooms in the US$10 range that are a little grim, but clean. Slightly higher in price is the **Hotel Colonial** (Restauración at 30 de Marzo, tel. 809/583-3422), which offers rooms with TV and balcony for about US$15, as do the **Hotel Monte Rey** (tel. 809/582-4558) and **Hotel Dorado** (tel. 809/582-7563), both nearby on

Calle Cucurullo.

Another inexpensive lodging option is the **Hotel Mercedes** (Av. 30 de Marzo at Máximo Gómez, tel. 809/583-1171), built in ornate style during the 1920s, Santiago's heyday. It features a winding marble staircase and quaint balconies off of each of the rooms, which have a fan, hot water, and a gentle run-down feel. Rooms with fans are US$20, those with air-conditioning twice that. Beware, no matter how much the feel of the Mercedes gets to you, the noise is considerable until about 11 P.M.

Moderate

North on Av. Estrella Sadhalá, near the airport, is the **Hotel Don Diego** (tel. 809/575-4186), with 40 comfortable rooms priced around US$40 for single, slightly more for double. The Hotel Don Diego features a pool, tennis court, disco, and a Chinese/international restaurant. Right across the same street is the **Hotel Ámbar,** which has 36 rooms with air-conditioning, TV, bar, and restaurant for about US$30. Keep in mind that the Avenida Estrella Sadhalá is strictly a commercial street, busy during the day with traffic and vendors hawking everything imaginable, and little to see in the way of sights.

Closer to town, just near the Monumento a los Héroes de la Restauración, is the **Hotel Matun** (Av. Las Carreras, tel. 809/581-3107), an older hotel with 50 generally well-kept rooms, cable TV, pool, disco, and casino. At around US$35, it's a pretty good value. From the hotel to Calle del Sol, downtown is about a 15-minute walk.

At the upper end of the scale, yet still modest in price, is the **Hotel Santiago Camino Real,** located on the Calle del Sol on the corner of Mella, which puts it right in the middle of town, convenient to Parque Duarte, shopping, and the monument (tel. 809/581-7000 or 809/583-4361, fax 809/582-4566). Starting at around US$45 per night for a single, slightly more for a double, you'll find the rooms a little run down but pleasant, with working air-conditioning, cable TV, good service, and comfortable beds. Just off the lobby is a place to get quick eats and cool drinks, and the plush piano bar that opens during the evenings for drinks seems popular with Santiago's yuppies. On the upper floor of the hotel is the **Olympus Restaurant,** where you can get some of the best food in town, along with a view of the city that sparkles whenever the electricity is working. The hotel's 72 rooms are mostly quiet, although you should specify one away from Calle del Sol if you prefer total quiet.

For quality similar to the Camino Real's, at a slightly higher price, try the newer **Hotel Gran Almirante** (Av. Estrella Sadhalá, tel. 809/580-1992, fax 809/241-1492), which also has a restaurant. The Gran Almirante is in an area called Los Jardines, and its rooms start at US$60; it is preferred by business visitors and is quite good.

Outside Town
Those with transportation might wish to stay on the outskirts of town for the green environs and quiet atmosphere. Two such spots are the **Hotel Cabanas** La Posada (Aut. Duarte Km 4.5, tel. 809/583-3291) and the **Cabanas Palmar** half a kilometer away (tel. 809/583-7247), both of which feature air-conditioning, TV, and private baths and kitchenettes.

FOOD

Inexpensive
Up and down the Calle del Sol is a series of cheap restaurants that provide basic beans and rice, though the area around the Monumento a los Héroes de la Restauración is thriving with good restaurants, outside terraces, and the occasional lively evening of singing and dancing.

Moderate
Like Santo Domingo, Santiago has plenty of small, good restaurants serving basic *comida criolla,* along with many stands serving *chimi,* empanadas, and *arepa,* any of which will make a good meal on the run with soft drinks or coffee. Downtown near the park, many restaurants offer basic meals for US$5 or less. Right *on* the park is the **Las Antillas,** which has meals for under US$4, while at the Calle Restauración and Duarte is the **Restaurant Panchito,** specializing in inexpensive sandwiches and ice cream, along with okay pizza. Also on Restauración is **Restaurant Yaque** for basic *comida criolla.* You can get good *comida criolla* at **Restitamia** (Av. Juan Pablo Duarte 28, tel.

809/582-2518) for a very modest price as well.

For moderately priced, but quite good, Chinese food, try the **Restaurant Pez Dorado** (Calle del Sol 43, tel. 809/582-2518), which specializes in seafood dishes but also serves some international cuisine, or the **Monumental** (Calle Beller 1, tel. 809/583-1894), which is near the monument. Outdoors behind the monument is La Pista, which serves regional food on a terrace. If you want to have good Cuban food, as well as regional dishes, try the **Don Miguel** on the Duarte Highway opposite the Catholic University. On the upper part of Calle del Sol, near the monument, is the **Elysée Bistro,** offering good French food.

Expensive
Most of the medium-priced hotels have good restaurants, with the best—if most expensive—in town at Hotel Camino Real, described above. However, the restaurants at El Gran Almirante and Hotel Don Diego are also good. The Olympus, at Hotel Santiago Camino Real, serves wonderful desserts—try the coconut pudding or flán especially.

El Café at Av. Texas and the corner of Calle 5 in the Jardines Metropolitanos caters to the politicos and socialites of Santiago. Rather ritzy, it's where you can glimpse Santiago's answer to Santo Domingo's glitterati approach.

Italian
The Cibao valley has a goodly portion of Italian immigrants who came to the valley because of its agricultural characteristics. Perhaps one of their legacies is Santiago's renowned Italian food. Restaurant **Osteria** on Avenida 27 de Febrero is for formal sit-down Italian dining, and while not cheap, the food is excellent. **Restaurant Roma** on Juan Pablo Duarte also serves Italian, though less expensively and formally so. Even though the Roma is moderately priced, it serves good pasta and meat and has a surprisingly good wine list. Also for Italian try **El Sol** on the upper Calle Máximo Gómez and Benito Manción, which serves cheap breakfast late, just when you might need it. For decent pizza and good atmosphere, there is **Pizzería Roma** (Av. Juan Duarte 72, tel. 809/582-8603).

Out of Town
If you're staying in Santiago, don't overlook the small town of San José de las Matas, espe-

cially for the restaurant in the **Hotel Mansión,** which serves wonderful food in a truly inspiring mountain setting. Check to see if the hotel is open. San José is not so far away that you could not drive there for lunch or dinner, and return to Santiago. For another trip outside Santiago for lunch or dinner, you might try to get to **Camp David Ranch** (tel. 809/583-5230), which is on the Carretera Luperón at Km 5, off an unmarked roadway and up into the Septentrional Mountains on a paved road. Before setting off to find this place, consider taking a taxi from Santiago, which will cost about US$12, but might save you from becoming terminally lost. The restaurant at Camp David Ranch is so-so, but the views are terrific. Also on the mountainside are several cafes where you can get a drink along with the view. Besides the view at Camp David, there is a small collection of old cars from the Trujillo era, just for flavor.

NIGHTLIFE AND ENTERTAINMENT

Discos and Bars
Disco is alive and well in Santiago, as it is in most places in the Dominican Republic. For something a bit different, try driving out to San José de las Matas for a quieter evening in the Hotel Mansión and its bar, and a walk around the grounds. However, if you're in the mood for noise and motion, the Hotel Matun has **La Nuit,** one of the noisiest and movingest discos anywhere around, equipped with solid laser. The **Hotel Camino Real's** popular nightspot often has live music and is frequented by the young and the restless. Go inside the lobby of the hotel and you'll see the stairs leading down to this glitzy basement bar. Out on the Duarte Highway is the **La Mansión** (not to be confused with the hotel in San José). Other modern disco-type nightclubs are **La Antorcha** (Av. 27 de Febrero 58) and **Las Vegas,** on the Autopista Navarete, Km 9. There are smaller bars and cafes around the Parque Duarte and the Monumento where you can stop in for a drink and sandwiches. Also on the outskirts of town is the **Disco Riverside** (Carretera Janico, Km 2.5) for live entertainment most nights.

Perhaps one of the most unique bars in all of Santiago is called **Casa Bader.** Located on Calle 16 de Agestos, it is a Santiago institution. The place is filled with ice chests containing beer, and patrons lean against or sit on them. People say Casa Bader has the coldest beer in the country as well as the best *quipes.* Locals create a fantastic atmosphere, shooting the breeze and boasting of exploits, though it might be rough for some.

Baseball and Cockfighting
Santiago fields a baseball team, and if you have the time, you should go to a game during the season. The games, played in winter, are quite popular, so go out to the stadium located north of town (you can see it anywhere from the Duarte Highway as you enter the city). Finding a way to get tickets on the black market is possible, usually through somebody at your hotel, while you can always go to the game and buy tickets from scalpers. The other main sport in Santiago is cockfighting, which takes place at the **Gallera Municipal.** Check the local papers for times.

SHOPPING

For shopping, wander up and down the Calle del Sol. For general goods, there is the **Mercado Central** on Calle 6 Septiembre or the **Mercado Modelo** on Calle de Sol at the corner of España. The general area is known for pottery, and you'll find shops and stands lining the Duarte Highway on both sides of town.

Aside from the specialized pottery shops, Santiago is best known for its music and its Carnaval celebration. Santiago has its own form of merengue, and many consider it the home of regional Dominican music. Although merengue CDs and tapes aren't cheap by any means, many stores along and around the Calle del Sol offer recordings of authentic, older musical styles found nowhere else on the island.

Santiago's Carnaval celebration is also considered one of the most authentic on the island. Some stores feature replicas of Carnaval masks, along with unusual musical instruments.

SERVICES AND INFORMATION

There is a tourist office in the old **Ayuntamiento** (town hall) on Avenida Juan Pablo Duarte, though there isn't much available, and only Spanish is spoken. The **post office** is centrally located on Calle del Sol near the Mercado Modelo on España. **Codetel** (tel. 809/582-8918) is on Estrella Sadhalá at the juncture of Duarte, rather distant from downtown.

GETTING THERE AND GETTING AROUND

Public Transportation

Without a private car, the best way to get to Santiago is by **Metro Bus** from Santo Domingo or Puerto Plata. The Metro from Santo Domingo runs seven times a day and is extremely clean, cheap, and efficient. Of course, there is regular bus service up and down the Duarte Highway from every town along the way. Once you've arrived in Santiago, it is very easy to get downtown by foot. Walking anywhere for sightseeing, shopping, and accommodation is easy. You can always fly into Santiago's airport on a domestic flight and take a taxi to the main hotel and shopping area downtown.

There is an extensive bus, *público,* and *carro* system that is as complicated as possible—the systems are marked with letters to indicate the routes. Many buses and *públicos* congregate on the northeast corner of the Parque Duarte.

Sometimes the Metro buses up and down the Duarte Highway are full, in which case you can take **Caribe Tours,** which has a terminal at Avenida Sadhalá and Calle 10. *Guaguas* are available to Moca, Mao, Sabaneta, and San José de las Matas. To Moca, catch the *guagua* from Autopista Duarte near the roundabout on Avenida Sadhalá. To San José, leave from Puente Hermanos Patiño, down the river not far from the city center. The Metro terminal is on Duarte,

just a block toward the town center from the highway roundabout on Maimón. If you're leaving Santiago, and don't mind (or wish) local stops, try the **Terra Bus** (Calle Restauración and J.P. Duarte, tel. 809/587-3000), which also serves Santo Domingo. **Transporte de Cibao** serves Dabajón near the Haitian border.

Driving

Driving into Santiago from the north isn't too confusing, as the Duarte Highway is not under construction. The highway becomes Avenida Sadhalá. You can take Avenida Juan Pablo Duarte downtown, or continue on and take the highway at the roundabout. Coming in from the south and Santo Domingo, there is a lot of highway construction as you enter town. Just continue on until you see the huge 66-meter-high structure on top of a small hill. You'll find downtown behind it to the west.

Car Rental

Car rental is expensive, but readily available. There are booths at the airport, or you can try **Budget** (Av. 27 de Febrero, tel. 809/575-2158), **Honda** (Av. Estrella Sadhalá at Av. Bartolomé Colón), **Nelly** (Av. Duarte 106, tel. 809/583-6695), or **Rentauto** (Av. Bartolomé Colón 4, tel. 809/582-3139). Don't rent a car unless you have some special need or itinerary. Santiago is so easy to walk, it isn't necessary.

Blackouts

One word of caution as you move about Santiago: at night, blackouts are common. When they occur, the stoplights stop working, and everything turns grim. You can't really prepare for these times, other than packing a flashlight and penlight, so just be aware that things can get a little hectic after dark.

CIBAO VALLEY TOWNS

The towns that anchor the Cibao valley are Monte Cristi in the far northwest and San Francisco de Macorís in the southeast, where the Septentrional Mountains finally become gently rolling hills in sugarcane country. From Santiago, the Duarte Highway follows the lower slope of the mountains through the towns of Bisonó, Laguna Salada, and Villa Vásquez, provincial ranching and farming towns with little to hold either tourist or traveler. In the same direction, the road to Mao, Sabaneta, and finally Dajabon on the Haitian border branches off the Duarte Highway at Esperanza. Going west on this road, you'll find that the land becomes very dry and dusty. It's hot during the winter, very hot during the summer, and there is much evidence of deforestation and overgrazing by cattle and goats. Dajabon is a very drab little place, a typical border town, but it does give a glimpse of "the other side," namely the Haitian desert.

In the other direction from Santiago, the towns of the eastern Cibao are set in very lush and green country indeed. Moca, home of the famous faceless dolls, is a pleasant market town that is the turnoff for the beautiful road north across the Septentrional Mountains, a sensational way to reach the Atlantic coast. Past Moca, the roads become a rather confused maze, with few markers, but it is possible, and delightful, to pick one's way to the Samaná peninsula.

THE EASTERN CIBAO

Moca

Moca is set east of Santiago, in the middle of coffee and cocoa country, and makes for a good day trip from Santiago, or a nice stop on the way through to the road north and the Atlantic coast. The quiet and shady town center houses a statue of Ramón Cáceres, who killed the tyrant Ulises Heureaux on July 25, 1899, thus ending one terrible chapter in Dominican history (and ushering in another). Buildings surrounding the town center exhibit the best of peaceful nineteenth-century Caribbean architecture in lovely pastel colors.

The town of Moca is dominated by its church tower, which you can climb if you wish. Be sure to make a donation to the cathedral's poor fund while you're enjoying the view of the town, the valley, and the mountains. Inside the main cathedral, **Iglesia Corazón de Jesús,** you'll find a huge and ornate organ worth seeing, though the rest of Moca has little in the way of interest for the traveler. Mostly, people go to Moca for the faceless dolls, which the area's craftspersons have made since the mid-19th-century, and which have become a local cottage industry. South of town on the main road leading to the Duarte Highway is **El Higuero,** the center of the industry. You can't fail to see the vendors and their shops and stands where these dolls are sold at bargain prices. However, to get the bargain prices you'll have to bargain. These dolls make a unique and fitting gift from the Dominican Republic.

The mountains around Moca are also worth exploring. True, they're very rugged, but a drive up into them by the adventurous will reveal well-sculptured coffee plantations and cacao farms. The roads are not marked, so you'd best bring along some Spanish and a sense of adventure.

Lodging: Unfortunately, the hotel situation in Moca is rather skimpy, and you must be careful to avoid places that charge hourly rates. Perhaps the best bet for accommodations is the **Hotel L'Niza** (Carretera Santiago, tel. 809/578-2248), located on the highway toward Santiago. It charges inexpensive rates for basic rooms. Downtown, **Hotel Panorama** (Av. Independencia 27, tel. 809/578-2252) and **Hotel La Casona** (Calle Imbert 77, tel. 809/578-3465) seem like reasonably comfortable commercial hotels, also in the inexpensive category.

Information and Services: There is a **tourist office** in the *ayuntamiento* (town hall) on Avenida Independencia, corner of Antonio de la Maza. **Codetel** in Moca is on Calle Nuestra Señora del Rosario, corner of Calle Duvergé.

Getting There: You can reach Moca easily by marked paved road from the Duarte Highway in either direction, or by Metro bus out of Puerto Plata and Santo Domingo. From other local towns like Santiago, check with Caribe or Transporte de Cibao. *Guaguas* run regularly in the valley.

Gallera near Moca

San Francisco de Macorís

Set in fertile farmland to the east of Moca, San Francisco de Macorís is one of the most densely populated cities in the Dominican Republic. Its population of almost 180,000 has relied heavily in the past on agriculture, mostly the growing and shipping of rice and the trading of cattle for its economic prosperity. In the last decade, however, it has gained infamy because of its alleged links to the Colombian drug trade. Rumors have it that some of its citizens are becoming middlemen to the notorious cartels, others foot soldiers for the Colombians on the streets of New York. Whatever the case, there are some fabulously wealthy individuals in San Francisco, and you have to wonder how they came by the cash to build their mansions.

San Francisco de Macorís has little for the tourist or traveler. Its central park is pleasant. Located on Avenida Castillo, it is flanked by two churches and a university building. In the vicinity are many small restaurants, banks, cafes, and gas stations. Perhaps the main claim to fame for San Francisco is its position on the main road from the Duarte Highway, to Nagua on the Atlantic coast, and then to the beautiful Samaná peninsula.

If you're in the mood to stay in San Francisco, the best hotels are the **Hotel Macorís** (Av. Restauración, tel. 809/588-2350), the **Nuevo Central** (Calle San Francisco, tel. 809/588-2350), and the **Olímpico** (Av. Libertad, tel. 809/588-

3584), each of which is a basic commercial hotel, with rooms in the inexpensive range.

Codetel in San Francisco is at Calle 27 de Febrero 54. The banks, Codetel, cafes, and restaurants are all within a few block area in the central zone.

THE MOCA ROAD NORTH

An impressively scenic, deliciously paved road connects Moca in the Cibao with the little coastal town of Sabaneta de Yásica on the Atlantic coast between Sosúa and Gaspar Hernández. Coming from the north coast it is easily located and well marked as the turnoff for **Jamao al Norte.** The road from Sabaneta winds through lush coastal grassland, then winds its way up through steadily more verdant mountain country, until at the crest one is on top of the Septentrional Mountains with a view of the entire Cibao valley. Coming from Moca, the road is not very well marked, and thus a bit harder to find, but negotiates the same terrific mountain and coastal country in reverse. If your desire is to go to the coast, this route is worth taking to avoid the grind of the Duarte Highway and its spike toward Puerto Plata. This road could also serve as an alternative to the highway between San Francisco and Nagua as a gateway to the Samaná peninsula. It is lower but avoids the repetitive agricultural panorama of the eastern Cibao.

Coming from Santo Domingo on the Duarte Highway, take the turnoff to Santo Cerro and continue north 11km (seven miles) to the town of Moca. In Moca, drive by the central park and the large cathedral (La Iglesia del Corazón de Jesús) on the left and continue on Avenida Angelo Morales (the main street) until reaching Duarte, a main street perpendicular to Morales. Take a right here, then a left on José Rodriguez. A marked road on the left leads to Santiago; straight ahead is San Francisco. Take the Santiago road. Then, when you come to it, turn right at the sign marked for **Jamao.** It sounds pretty complicated, and it is. If you have any doubts, stop and ask a local for the road to Jamao.

At the summit, on the Cibao side, about halfway along the length of the highway, you'll find two restaurants and a collection of fruit vendors. The restaurant **El Molino,** at the summit, has wonderful views of the valley, a terrace, and good food, featuring chicken crepes. Up the hill is the restaurant **El Cumbre** (The Summit), which offers a wide selection of *comida criolla* and excellent views as well.

Going north, the road ends along the coast. Turn left for Sosúa, right for Río San Juan and the Samaná peninsula. The little town of **Jamao** has no services but is in a lovely stream valley and has a decent cockfight arena.

THE WESTERN CIBAO

To the northwest of Santiago the Duarte Highway runs along the Río Yaque del Norte, all the way to Monte Cristi on the coast. The towns of Laguna Salada and Villa Vásquez are no more than agricultural truck stops, though they do have gas stations and small cafes for travelers.

Monte Cristi and its national park, wetlands, and offshore islands are worthwhile as destinations, but for the most part the northwest Duarte Highway is pretty flat and desolate country, having been overgrazed for years.

Mao

South of the highway, situated on the banks of the Río Yaque del Norte, stands the quiet provincial town of Mao, on the road to Sabaneta and Dajabon. This highway is the main route to Haiti, and ends at the border town of Dajabon, which has little to interest travelers beyond a noted *balneario* at **Loma de Cabrera,** worth a visit if you are nearby—perhaps trying to cross to Haiti.

Mao has a few inexpensive hotels. Try the **Cahoba** (tel. 809/572-3357), **Hotel Céntrico** (tel. 809/572-2122), and **Hotel San Pedro** (tel. 809/572-3134), all with rooms US$15–20 and near the central square downtown. A few cafes are clustered around the square as well, and the old buildings on the plaza are colorfully painted. Other than its peace and relative agricultural prosperity, Mao is simply what it is: a quiet, provincial place.

Towards the Atlantic Coast

For those heading to the Atlantic coast at either Luperón or Puerto Plata, an alternative route crosses the Septentrional Mountains, though less spectacularly than the Moca road north. Take the Duarte Highway out of Santiago to the northwest and look for the small village of Navarette, just a few kilometers before the town of José Bisonó. The road, which goes to Imbert, should be marked, but beware and ask if you don't see it. Once across the mountains at **Imbert**—a town with a cheese factory, a Codetel office, and little else—the road forks: northwest to Luperón, northeast to Puerto Plata.

BOB RACE

THE EAST COAST

INTRODUCTION

The contrast between, say, Santo Domingo, or the Cordillera Central, and the Dominican Republic's eastern region could not be greater. For one thing, the eastern region was settled much later than the rest of the Dominicana. Consequently, except for the self-consciously touristy areas, the whole region—including the provinces of San Pedro de Macorís, Hato Mayor, El Seibo, La Romana, and La Altagracia—has a bucolic feel. It is a place where Dominican life is largely led according to its own provincial terms, where cattle raising, sugarcane, and family life predominate. Throughout the interior, where the landscape takes the shape of gently waving sugarcane before a background of pale purple mountains, you are just as likely to see a campesino riding a horse as an automobile cruising the highway. In fact, most of the roads throughout the east, though quite excellent, are sparsely traveled, making for an enjoyable day's outing in the car.

But make no mistake about it, the east is also a tourist hangout of monumental proportions. From Santo Domingo in the south, to Sabana de la Mar on the northeast, there are probably fifty white sand beaches that are easily accessible, many of them with excellent snorkel, scuba,

and windsailing possibilities. The Dominican Government claims to have 11,500 hotel rooms in the eastern region, and you can bet that most of them are clustered along the coastline. It's the eastern region that is home to resorts on the Costa Caribe like Casa de Campo and on the Costa del Coco, with complexes like Punta Cana and Bávaro Beach, world-class luxury resorts if anything ever deserved the name. And while both eastern coasts cater predominately to package tourists, there are plenty of tourist hotels where you can unpack your bags for a leisurely stay and be assured of individuality and freedom.

Among the most famous beaches along the Caribbean coast are **Boca Chica, Juan Dolio, Guayacanes,** and **Villas del Mar,** though the more remote beaches of **Bayahibe** and **Dominicus** are becoming increasingly popular. Of course, you'll find numerous coves and small beaches away from the highway where you can escape for a pleasant, and isolated, afternoon. And while the Caribbean coast tends to be reef protected with calm water, the Coconut Coast is subject to the moods of the Atlantic Ocean with its currents, tides, and waves. Thus the beaches at Playa Juanillo, Punta Cana, Playa Cabeza

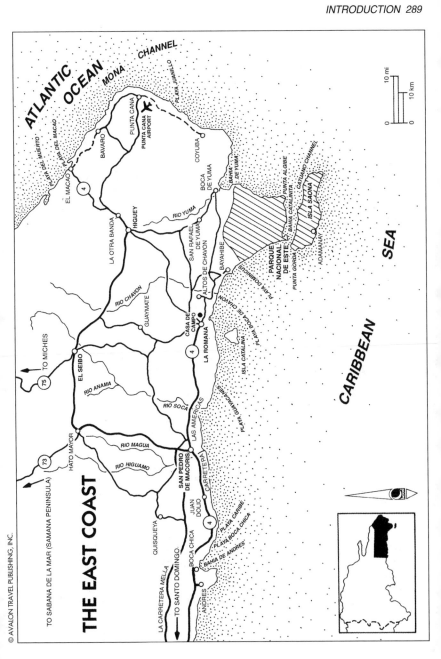

THE EAST COAST

© AVALON TRAVEL PUBLISHING, INC.

de Toro, and Playa del Muerto (beware!) have a rougher kind of beauty and challenge.

The eastern region challenges travelers and adventurers as well. Stretching over 112 miles in length, the eastern coastal plain contains two of the most remote and tempting of the Dominican Republic's national parks, as well as a stretch of isolated mangrove swamp and lagoon situated on Samaná Bay. Because the coastal plain is primarily limestone, karst formations can become quite elaborate (as in Parque Nacional Los Haitises). The wickedly futuristic caves and sinkholes of Los Haitises seem like a landscape you'd encounter on the moon, if the moon were lush and green. Like other Dominican national parks, the parks of the east are not well serviced. Depending on your point of view, this either makes them romantic or inconvenient. Perhaps both.

Nevertheless, when you cross the Mella or Duarte Bridge in Santo Domingo (or fly into the regional airports in La Romana and Punta Cana) going east, you can be assured of balmy temperatures, palms bent by ocean breezes, and a leisurely pace.

Climate

The entire eastern region has a beneficent climate of relatively low rainfall, persistent breezes, and pure blue skies tempered only by the occasional cloudburst. If you travel to the east, either to visit the richly traditional interior, or to stay at one of the many tourist resorts on the south or east coasts, you'll be assured of wonderful weather and a friendly reception.

GETTING THERE

One of the great beauties of the Caribbean coast is the fact that it is connected to Santo Domingo by a smoothly paved and well-marked highway. Thus, it is possible to make Santo Domingo a home base and still take one- or two-day trips to swimming, snorkeling, and fishing spots along the Caribbean coast. There are a couple of good golf courses within striking distance of Santo Domingo to the east. And for anyone who wishes to take a morning or afternoon to explore an underwater reef, La Caleta is the perfect destination, a national park built

around a pair of sunken ships that are home to thousands of tropical fish. (For descriptions of these destinations, turn to the Santo Domingo chapter.) Of course, the resorts of Boca Chica and Juan Dolio are justly famous for their beaches and hotels.

By Car

Heading east from Santo Domingo by car is about as easy as driving gets in the Dominican Republic. The major through-street of 27 de Febrero going west eventually merges into the Duarte bridge which crosses the Ozama River. The Las Américas Highway, which leads to the airport, continues east all along the coast, connecting Santo Domingo with the Caribbean towns of San Pedro de Macorís, La Romana, and San Rafael de Yuma. If you're leaving Santo Domingo by car, and crossing the Ozama River, try to do so early in the morning before rush hour (at least by 7 A.M.), or in midafternoon, before the madness of the evening traffic commences. If you're staying in the Colonial District in Santo Domingo, it is also possible to cross the Mella Bridge by following Avenida Mella across the river, skirting the Columbus Lighthouse, then taking the roundabout just beyond the Parque Mirador where you'll connect with the Las Américas Highway. There is some highway construction in this area, but it can be a good shortcut, especially when traffic is heavy on the Duarte Bridge, or there has been an accident.

Whether you cross the Ozama Bridge and connect directly with the Las Américas Highway going east, or cross the Mella Bridge and make your connection with Las Américas past the Columbus Lighthouse, the smooth, well-maintained highway meanders along the coast nearly all the way to Bayahibe before turning inland to San Rafael. In order to reach the Atlantic coast and Punta Cana, however, you'll need to turn inland to Hato Mayor and Higüey on roads that are lovely, bordered by lush fields of cane and dotted by palms and ceiba trees. Driving the northeast coast from Punta Cana to Sabana de la Mar is more of a chore on rough, potholed roads and dirt tracks. The overland route from Hato Mayor to Sabana de la Mar is better, though if you're in Samaná town, it is perhaps better to take a ferry from Samaná across to Sabana de la

Mar, just for an afternoon look-see.

As always, there is only one proviso that applies to driving Las Américas Highway. Every few miles, until you're well outside Santo Domingo, you'll pass a pile of wrecked cars along the road. These are the cars of Dominican drivers who took the big gamble and lost, usually passing without sufficient room, failing to slow down during rainstorms, or taking one sip too many out of the rum bottle. So if you're driving the Las Américas Highway, be very careful, drive slowly, and practice super-defensive driving. Try to drive during the day; avoid evenings, rainstorms, and rush hours. Once you're outside the Santo Domingo zone, past the airport, the driving smoothes out, and you can truly enjoy the ocean view. Inland driving on the highways connecting Higüey with Hato Mayor is relaxing in the extreme.

By Public Transport

Buses run from Santo Domingo to San Pedro de Macorís, La Romana, and Higüey on a regular schedule; you can catch them in Santo Domingo on the Calle Duarte. Regular services between coastal towns run along the Las Américas Highway. You'll also see *guaguas* and *públicos* cruising regularly along the highway. Just stand on one side and wave your arm like crazy. It is particularly easy and cheap to catch *guaguas* in Santo Domingo heading for Boca Chica, a very popular weekend destination for Santo Dominicans. Regular passenger service connects Higüey with the inland towns of El Seibo and Hato Mayor, and *guaguas* are a regular sight on the island highways, usually chock full of campesinos and their bags and animals. The same rules apply to catching rural *guaguas* as to catching urban ones.

By Plane

The closest international airport to the Caribbean coast is, of course, Las Américas in Santo Domingo. Located some 20km outside Santo Domingo, the airport itself is just 22km west of Boca Chica, and the gateway to all the beaches of the shore. American Airlines serves the new La Romana International Airport and is geared to passengers disembarking for the huge Casa de Campo resort. The Punta Cana Airport in Higüey caters to package tourists heading for the eastern point resorts, with American Eagle again the biggest carrier. It is possible to make arrangements to fly along the Caribbean coast out of the domestic airport in Santo Domingo, though with the highway in such good condition, and the views so beautiful, why bother?

BOCA CHICA

The famous Boca Chica beach (and the town of the same name) is only five minutes beyond the Las Américas Airport along the highway of the same name. If you're on public transportation from Santo Domingo, you'll see the signs for Boca on your right, or just follow the hordes of people leaving the bus—the ones in bathing trunks, and carrying suntan oil, baskets of food, and boom boxes. If you're driving, Boca Chica is easily accessible from Las Américas Highway. Just look for the signs and turn right toward the beach on Juan Bautista Vicini or Avenida Caracoles. The main drag in town is Calle Duarte. San Rafael runs next to the beach, and Abraham Nuñez is a small, jammed roadway that is almost on top of swimmers.

Boca Chica began its storied existence as a simple port town in the 1930s, and gradually came into ultra-vogue during the 1960s, when it was a small and exclusive resort. By the 1970s Boca Chica had lost its cachet to Puerto Plata on the north coast, but it is reviving now and on its way to achieving a kind of renown as an international tourist melting pot.

SIGHTS

Depending upon your point of view, Boca Chica is either a human zoo or a pleasure fantasyland. The bay itself (actually more of a shallow lagoon) is generally not more than 1.5m deep and is guarded on its outer limit by a well-worn reef that minimizes wave action and tidal pull. There are several kilometers of rockless, white sand bottom, making the water warm and perfect for simple swimming and wading, especially for kids and others who like to splash about.

Lagoon Islands
There are two small islands in the lagoon. One, **La Matica,** can be reached by wading at low tide. The second and larger island, **Los Piños,** is too far from land to walk to. You can rent a boat for the trip, but the only suitable beach on the island is private. If you go out to the reef, don't expect much. It's been trashed. Still, it isn't unpleasant to try your hand at snorkeling or even scuba, if you don't mind murky warm water and crowds.

Nearby Beaches
It's always possible to make Boca Chica a kind of hub for visits to nearby beaches including those at Juan Dolio, Guayacanes, and Villas del Mar, as well as the ever-popular Embassy beach.

People-Watching
People are the main attraction at Boca Chica. Depending upon the day of the month, the day of the week, the time of the day, and the hour, you'll see just about every example of humanity possible, from wealthy Dominicans (many of whom have built homes here) to prostitutes, drunken tourists, hawkers, vendors, and tramps.

SPORTS AND RECREATION

Excellent fishing, diving, snorkeling, and windsurfing make Boca Chica a good choice for sporting folk.

Fishing and Boat Charters
As you'd expect, with water sports popular at all times, the major resort hotels organize many deep-sea fishing trips for the area swordfish or inshore species. The best trips from hotels are organized by the **Hamaca** and **Don Juan** resorts, though if you wander down to the **Demar Marina** in the town of Andrés (tel. 809/523-4365), you can find many charter boats available for rent. Depending upon the number of persons in the boat, and the amount of time you spend on the water, the cost of deep-sea fishing is variable. For a half-day charter for four people, expect to pay at least US$75, though for that you'll usually get lunch and drinks along with bait and tackle. Expect to tip the captain and one or two crew members. The hotel charters are generally all inclusive. When you manage a do-it-yourself charter at the Demar Marina, you should be careful to negotiate the price in advance. If you've seen *To Have and Have Not* with Bogie and Bacall, you'll know what a hassle it is to leave loose ends about price.

Diving and Snorkeling
Though deep-sea fishing tends to be expensive, you can outfit yourself for diving and snorkeling relatively cheaply. The big-boy of the snorkeling and diving business in Boca Chica is **Treasure Divers** (Don Juan Beach Resort, tel. 809/523-5320), which rents and services scuba equipment, snorkel masks, and organizes night dives, video dives, cave dives, and visits to wrecks. The personnel of Treasure Divers are well trained and can even organize "safaris" to view tropical species in all their splendor. For do-it-yourselfers the **Demar Marina** rents snorkel equipment for about US$7 an hour, as does the **Don Juan** hotel. Unless you're experienced and know your way around the reefs of Boca Chica, it isn't advised to try diving on your own.

Sporting Clubs
Several of the luxury resorts have tennis courts, some with lights. Five kilometers down the road to the west of Boca Chica is the newly opened **San Andres Golf Club,** just to the north of Las Américas Highway. You can't miss the golf course because it sports a huge sign and a driving range near the highway. Although it has only nine holes at present (another nine are under construction), the layout is formidable and charming, cut through tropical brushland, with plenty of bunkers in play. You can horseback ride

BOB RACE

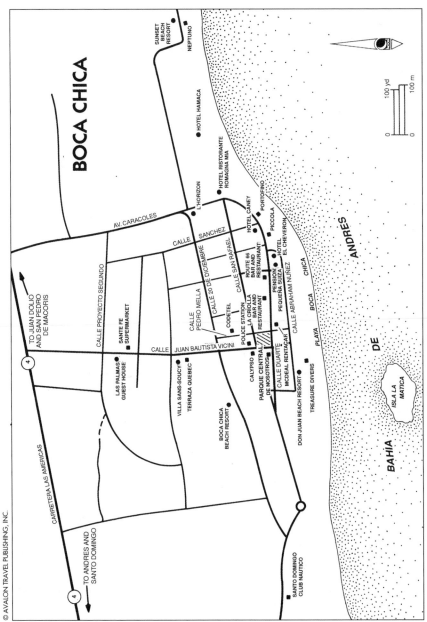

BOCA CHICA

© AVALON TRAVEL PUBLISHING, INC.

at the club, too. The **Santo Domingo Club Naúti-co** is at the west end of the beach, but it is rather exclusive. Plan ahead if you think you want to patronize this club. (See the On the Road chapter for more on the Santo Domingo Club Naútico.)

Windsurfing and Sailing
Boca Chica isn't the greatest windsurfing and sailing territory in the world, partly because the lagoon is so sheltered. Nonetheless, windsurf boards are available for rent from the Don Juan hotel, as are small sailboats. Cost of windsurf boards is about US$15 per day.

More Recreation
For a truly campy experience, try the go-cart track that's been built near the Las Américas Highway at the entrance to the city. If gambling is your sport, the Hamaca has a casino.

The newly formed **Crazy Horse Ranch** at 20 de Diciembre 1 (tel. 809/523-4199) operates horseback riding on the beach for about US$20. Of course, one can enjoy baseball games at the field on Calle Del Sur.

ACCOMMODATIONS

For the most part, Boca Chica is not cheap. However, in a town devoted body and soul to tourism, you can certainly find something to suit both your taste and your budget, ranging from reasonably priced guest houses and small hotels in the US$25–40 range to luxury resorts where a room goes for more than US$100 in the high season. Remember that in winter Boca Chica tends to crowd up with tourists from many countries, so reservations are advised. During the off season, however, it isn't risky to arrive and wander the streets until something strikes your fancy.

Inexpensive Downtown Hotels
It is true that Boca Chica's downtown has been swamped by tourist development, but you can still find inexpensive commercial hotels, including **Hotel Caney** (Calle Duarte, tel. 809/523-4314), **Hotel El Cheveron** (Calle Duarte, tel. 809/523-4333—its few rooms have a/c), and **Hotel Ristorante Romagna Mia** (Calle Duarte 60, tel. 809/523-4647), all of which offer rooms in the US$20–30 range, though you might be able to

get a better price with a little negotiation. The **Hotel Don Paco** (Calle Duarte 6, tel. 809/523-4816) is centrally located and cheap. Keep in mind that most of these commercial hotels are going to be slightly noisy at times, especially on weekends.

Among the smaller pensións and guest houses, **Neptune's Club Boca Chica** (restaurant-bar–guest house) is intriguing because of its secluded location at the far eastern end of the lagoon. Located just off the beach where Av. 20 de Deciembre and San Rafael converge, this German-owned guest house caters to foreign tourists, and serves fresh fish in its restaurant. Telephone them at 809/523-4703.

Moderate Downtown Hotels
More small hotels with a personal, pensión-like atmosphere include **L'Horizon Hotel and Restaurant** (tel. 809/523-4375) and **Pensión Pequeña Suiza** (Calle Duarte 56, tel. 809/523-4619), which offer modest rooms in residential settings in the US$30 range.

With a small-family atmosphere, the **Casitas del Sol** (Primera at 2 de Junio, tel. 809/523-4386) has a nice pool, restaurant, and bar; rooms are priced at about US$40. In the same category is **Las Palmas Guest House** on Calle T.B. Vinci, across from the Santa Fe Supermarket.

On Las Américas Highway
There are several inexpensive or moderately priced hotels and cabañas on the Las Américas Highway. If you prefer to stay near the airport, with access to both Santo Domingo and Boca Chica, you can try the **Tropicana Night Club Hotel-Villas** (Av. Las Américas Km 8, tel. 809/596-8885), which has a kind of kinky look but does boast 50 rooms with air-conditioning, a nightclub, bar, pool, and whirlpool, and 12 suites with, yes, marble floors. You can get barbecue in the restaurant if that suits your mood. Farther out on the highway is the **Hotel Brescia** (Las Américas Km 32, tel./fax 809/523-5857), which has 20 cabañas, located not far from the turnoff for Boca Chica. Both highway hotels are in the US$35 range.

Small Hotels, Pensions, and Guest Houses
One of the nicest things about Boca Chica is its excellent range of modestly priced small hotels,

pensions, and guest houses. In this regard, Boca Chica is rather like the less-explored town of Bayahibe, and many of the towns along the north coast like Cabarete, Río San Juan, and Sosúa. The **Villa Sans-Soucy** (Calle J.B. Vinci 48, tel. 809/523-4461 and 809/523-4327, fax 809/523-4138 or 800/463-0097) has clean and attractive rooms opening to a courtyard with a pool, which makes for a quieter-than-average atmosphere. It features a restaurant and bar as well. The rooms run around US$50–60—a good bargain. Down the street is the **Auberge La Fontaina de Soleil** (Calle J.B. Vinci 11, tel. 809/523-4679), which has large and comfortable rooms, a garden with a pool, and breakfast served on the terrace out back. Rooms at the Auberge run about US$40 with breakfast. Similar in style and atmosphere, but perhaps more family oriented, is the **Mesón Isabela** (Calle Duarte 3, tel. 809/523-4224, fax 809/523-4634), located just outside the busiest part of Boca Chica and run by a Dominican from Canada who sees to it that the lush garden and lovely pool are well maintained and attractive. Golf packages can be arranged through the staff, and guests have access to a private beach. The rooms are in the US$40–55 range, depending upon seasons, and you can't fail to enjoy the aesthetic of the building itself.

Expensive Hotels

For a slightly smaller version of the luxury resort hotel, try the **Hotel Don Juan** (often referred to as the Don Juan Beach Resort), located right on the beach on Calle Abraham Nuñez, giving its 124 rooms a good view of the ocean. The Don Juan Resort (tel. 809/687-9157 in Santo Domingo, 809/523-4511, fax 809/688-5271) offers air-conditioning, TV, a pool, a restaurant, and tennis at a cost of US$75 and up, depending upon whether you want the standard room, a junior suite, or a luxury apartment. The Don Juan has a U.S. number too: 212/432-1370, fax 212/488-9580. The toll-free number for the Don Juan is 800/922-4272.

Slightly smaller, and in the upper-moderate price range is the **Sunset Beach Resort** (Calle Duarte, tel. in Santo Domingo 809/523-4511, 809/523-4580, fax 809/530-7824), whose 70 rooms are very nice, with air-conditioning, TV, and facilities like a pool, solarium, and restaurant. The Sunset does not have immediate access to the beach, but it faces the sea, and its rooms are comfortable. Some have kitchenettes and are priced in the US$65 range. The **La Helle Resort** (tel. 809/523-5320, fax 809/523-5077) is very new, but worth looking into. The moderately priced **Terraza Caribe** has pleasant rooms, a pool, and shade. Call them at 809/523-4488 or fax 809/523-4444. A good value, the Terraza is located on #7 Calle Sánchez.

Luxury Hotels

The granddaddy of the luxury beach resorts at Boca Chica is the **Hotel Hamaca** (Calle Duarte at the east end of town, tel. 809/523-4611, U.S. tel. 800/472-3985, in the DR 800/955-0792, fax 809/523-5183). Built over the main road in Boca Chica, you can't miss this pink structure. It isn't too inviting from the outside, but has a cool insouciance inside, with an excellent beach and a bar on the water. Its 111 rooms are tasteful and calm, and go for about US$115. The hotel has a good restaurant featuring Dominican food.

The largest and most expensive luxury beach resort in Boca Chica is the **Boca Chica Beach Resort** (Calle J.B. Vinci at 20 de Deciembre, tel. 809/523-4521, fax 809/523-4438). The Boca Chica Beach Resort is a huge complex which features 209 apartments, a large lobby, gardens, and excellent staff, with a per-night charge of US$120–150, depending upon the number of persons and the season. You can call the Boca Chica Beach Resort from the United States at 800/828-8895. Both of these luxury hotels, of course, feature air-conditioning, TV, pool, and tennis. The Boca Chica can arrange trips to the islands of the lagoon, and will pack food for day trips of snorkeling and diving.

FOOD AND ENTERTAINMENT

The whole Boca Chica experience is about, I suppose, pleasure. As a result, Boca Chica swarms with many kinds of eateries, from the simple fruit vendors who wander the beaches selling fresh pineapple and banana to elaborate fish and shellfish restaurants in the hotels and resorts. In between are many, many (and I do mean many) bars and restaurants that offer a monumental assortment of international specialties (including your own local dish prepared

Dominican-style), or the sinfully delicious grilled fish and empanadas available from local food stalls.

Boca Chica is a place where people (usually beet red and glassy eyed) tend to overdo the rum and beer; dozens of outdoor bars cater to an all-day party crowd. This is to say, you can get what you want in Boca Chica, for just about any price you want to pay.

At the Hotels

Each of the luxury resort hotels has a restaurant that serves good regional dishes, and selected international specialties, along with fresh seafood. The large buffet of the **Hamaca Hotel** is a good value, though the smaller **Las Chorales** restaurant serves excellent *comida criolla* and international dishes in a more intimate atmosphere. The Las Chorales is, however, relatively expensive. The **La Caleta** in the Don Juan hotel is also an excellent, though somewhat expensive, restaurant serving several types of international cuisine, including German, French, and Dominican, reflecting the international clientele. The restaurant in the **Villa Sans-Soucy** is less expensive and serves Quebecois food and good breakfasts. As you'd expect, the **Terraza Quebec** (Calle J.B. Vinci 45) serves Canadians their favorite cuisine but also offers international food including good lobster. For anyone craving fondue, the best is **L'Horizon,** which has a French ambience.

Seafood

Seafood is always a tasty treat in Boca Chica. Insist on fresh fish when you order. The **Neptuno,** at the far eastern end of the beach, across from the Sunset Beach Resort, has one of the best seafood menus in Boca Chica and features everything from locally caught fish to paella. You can dine on a terrace overlooking the ocean. (Call them at 809/523-4703.) Seafood is also the specialty at **Buxeda,** while you'll find inexpensive Chinese at **Bambu** (San Rafael 10-A, tel. 809/523-4828).

Italian

Portofino, on Calle Duarte, offers a grab-bag menu, though Italian is the specialty. Decent Italian food is also available at **Piccola** (Calle Duarte 36, tel. 809/523-4620). Neither Portofino nor Piccola is expensive at all. For seafood with an Italian lilt, try the **Calypso** (Calle J.B. Vinci), which is moderately priced, but offers wonderful shrimp and scampi.

Creole

Despite the existence of a numbing horde of outdoor bars and restaurants, some of them offer excellent value, especially on Creole food. An example is **La Criolla Bar and Restaurant** on Calle Duarte. Probably the best places to try good, cheap Dominican food from vendors and food stalls are the open-air tables of **De Nosotros** on Calle J.B. Vinci on the central park, and at the **Santa Fe Supermarket** (Supermercado), where you can buy freshly prepared johnnycakes and empanadas, along with wonderful *dulces.*

Indonesian

Next door to La Criolla Bar and Restaurant on Calle Duarte is the famous **Route 66 Bar and Restaurant,** which swings into the late hours and serves, of all things, Indonesian food (tel. 809/523-5744).

Nightlife

Nightlife isn't hard to come by in Boca Chica, though the selection of bars and discos tend to merge into insensibility through a haze of loud merengue and rum. Discos include **Golden Beach** and **Disco Elegancia Cumbre** and the ever-popular **Masiel Disco** (Calle Duarte 34). The major luxury resorts all have nightclubs with discos or piano bars, and the standard happy-hour entertainment.

Shopping

Shopping opportunity consists of many gift shops specializing in coral or amber trinkets, and these shops are spread out evenly through the town.

INFORMATION AND SERVICES

If you happen to take an **express bus** from Santo Domingo (along the Calle Duarte), you'll be deposited at the main square in central Boca Chica. Express buses leave for the city from the same square. In order to go east down the coast, you'll have to walk to Las Américas Highway (only a few short blocks) and flag down a *guagua* going east (or to the right).

Communications and Tourist Information
Codetel in Boca Chica is located on Calle J.B. Vicini, between San Rafael and 20 de Deciembre, near the police station. There is a **Western Union** office on Calle Duarte 65. So far as I know, there is no tourist information office in Boca Chica, but you hardly need such a thing; the entire beach area, including the small town of **Andrés,** up the beach to the west a couple of kilometers, is easily walkable. You'll know your way around Boca Chica 15 minutes after you arrive.

Parking
A word of warning about Boca Chica: don't drive a car into the place on weekends—it's just too hard to park. On weekdays, drive down to the beach and look for one of many sandy areas that will always be "protected" by Dominican teenagers. Drop RD$20 into some kid's hand

and he'll stand by your car. Don't think of it as extortion either, because the kid is likely providing a real and necessary service. Lately, Boca Chica has experienced some trouble with prostitutes and pickpockets. In my experience, it isn't anything that can't be handled with common sense, and it shouldn't mar the experience for anyone.

Car Rental
Car rental is available from **McDeal Rentacar** on Calle Duarte near Pedro Mella (tel. 809/523-4414) or from **Alpha 3000** (tel. 809/523-6059) on Calle Primera. Scooters and motorbikes can be rented as well, but it's a dangerous proposition being a waterbug in a town of ball-peen hammers. Nevertheless, **Guest House No. 14** on Calle Juan Bautista Vinci or **Alpha 3000** will rent you one for about US$25 per day. The **Hotel Hamaca** rents bicycles for much less, a cheap way to save your own life.

JUAN DOLIO/VILLAS DEL MAR

Between Boca Chica and the major sugar town of San Pedro de Macorís, about 40km east of Santo Domingo, is a long stretch of beach, interrupted only by occasional cliffs. Unlike Boca Chica, which was an authentic port town of the 1930s, the 10–12 km of resort began its life as a tourist development in 1987, and, like Topsy, simply grew willy-nilly. If you're driving by car from Santo Domingo along the Las Américas Highway, you can't fail to miss the start of the resort area, signalled by the mushrooming signs for hotels, guest houses, and resorts. There is a lot of construction going on in Juan Dolio, and there are some new golf courses in the area, but you can't really look for the town of Juan Dolio or Villas del Mar because, if there is going to be a town at all, it's in its infancy. This is an area that came into being because of the tourist boom, and what social area there is belongs to a single block of Juan Dolio itself.

Getting Oriented
The best way to get oriented to the Juan Dolio experience is to know the names of the beaches in order, marching west to east: Playa Caribe, Playa Guayacanes, Playa Juan Dolio, and Playa Villas del Mar. These beaches, collectively, are

usually called the *playas del este,* and, while not spectacular, they are good for swimming and sunning. Many of the hotels are all-inclusive resorts that cater to those desiring to stay in one place for a long time, coming in on a package deal or as snowbirds. The Playa del Este region is popular with Canadians and Europeans. Almost all the hotels, even the smaller ones, have tennis courts and can arrange for horseback riding, golf packages, snorkeling and diving tours, and excursions to nearby tourist sights.

The big, expensive hotels tend to cluster near the beach. Smaller, less expensive hotels tend to cluster nearer Las Américas Highway, which leaves their guests with a 10-minute walk to the water. A number of Santo Dominigans have built villas and condominiums in the area. If you'll be staying in the area for a while, long-term rentals of private property can save you a good deal of money. Contact **Villas del Mar Realty** (tel. 809/526-1411, fax 809/526-2804) to inquire about apartments and condos for daily, weekly, and monthly stays.

You can get to Juan Dolio on the public buses leaving from Santo Domingo (heading toward San Pedro de Macorís) at the Parque Independencia, though getting off a bus at Juan Dolio could condemn you to a rough afternoon of walking and inquiring. Most people arrive by car, with reservations in hand. In the off-season, though, that isn't a real necessity.

Sports and Recreation

All of the resort hotels along the *playas del este* come well stocked with sports and recreational opportunities. If playing tennis is not your bag, then golf packages can be arranged at the newly built courses. Certainly, the existence of reefs offshore presents snorkelers and divers with ample opportunity to exercise their craft. The people at Treasure Divers in Juan Dolio can fill you in on snorkeling and diving opportunities at Juan Dolio. In the Juan Dolio area are **Jerry's Dive Center** and **Neptuno Dive Center** (near Punta Garza), both competent outfitters that conduct classes and offer diving certification. Most of the major resorts operate water sports concessions, horseback riding, and most have beaches and pools for swimming. You can call Jerry's Dive Center at 809/526-1242, or Neptuno at 809/526-1473, fax 809/526-1441.

ACCOMMODATIONS

Inexpensive

Unfortunately, there aren't many inexpensive accommodations at the *playas del este*. For so-called "budget" pension-style accommodation, there is the **Damar Guest House** (tel. 809/526-3310, fax 809/526-2512). Located on the frontage road by the ocean, this popular spot

LEO DE WYS

offers a number of basic rooms, each with cooking facilities for about US$30. Close by is **Pensión Don Pedro** (tel. 809/526-2147). Quieter and calmer than Damar, this guest house is slightly cheaper and less hip, but the rooms are okay and there is a good dining room.

Moderate

In the moderate range, and a good value, are the **Sol y Mar** (tel. 809/529-8605), the **Hotel Ramada** (tel. 809/526-3310), and the quiet and centrally located **Fior di Loto** (tel. 809/526-1146, fax 809/526-1664). On the Playa Guayacanes at Las Américas Highway #21 is the **Auberge Sueño Tropical** (tel. 809/526-2304), which has 25 rooms (double, triple, or quadruple), kitchens, one suite, a bar, restaurant, pool, and whirlpool, all only 10 minutes down the highway from Boca Chica. You can take a long-term rental at the Auberge and save money.

Some other accommodations at the *playas del este* offer the flexibility of bungalows and kitchenette living for larger groups, or those who wish to cook for themselves. For example, the **Punta Garza Bungalows** (tel. 809/526-3411) have a number of independently standing two-story apartments and some cabanas with kitchenettes, all with air-conditioning and TV (some with fans), and the **Los Coquitos Beach Resort** (tel. 809/457-3211) has 80 apartments, some with two bedrooms, with air-conditioning and color TV. On-site at Los Coquitos are a restaurant, pool, and water sports arrangements. Other apart-hotel type arrangements can be found at **Apart-hotel Marena** in Juan Dolio (tel. 809/526-2121, fax 809/526-1213), and the **Sotbe House Aparta Hotel** (Calle Central 66, tel. 809/526-3007), each of which is in the moderate price range, depending upon the type of accommodation desired.

Expensive

A number of resort hotels fall in this category but still offer many amenities. Among the best is the 167-room **Embassy Beach Resort** at the Playa Caribe (tel. 809/526-1246, fax 809/535-5292), along the highway, but with tennis courts and pool, easily accessible beaches for water sports, and a decent restaurant. The Embassy is well away from any clusters of hotels or commercial buildings and has a nice terrace with a view of the ocean. Nearby is **Coco Village** (tel. 809/524-1065, fax 809/526-1309) with villas in the US$70 range for doubles, higher in winter. A freshwater pool is featured.

Also in the expensive resort category is **Talanguera Country and Beach Resort** (tel. 809/541-1166, fax 809/541-1292), an all-inclusive resort of 260 rooms priced at about US$80–100 per night, with accompanying restaurants, disco, game room, sauna, and whirlpool, as well as all water sports, horseback riding, archery, and even rifle shooting.

The baby sister of the Caribbean Village group (see Luxury Resorts, below) is the **Tropics** (tel. 809/526-2009, fax 809/526-1430), a slightly smaller, 78-room establishment that is not all-inclusive, but does offer attractive grounds, pool, tennis, and water sports, with rooms priced US$70–100 per night double.

Luxury Resorts

Pricey luxury resorts are the sine qua non of the *playas del este.* The top of the line, in terms of elegance, service, and price are the Caribbean Village resorts, of which the beachfront **Coral Costa Linda** (tel. 809/526-2161, fax 809/526-3601) is the choicest, with its 162 carefully decorated rooms, countless amenities, and gardens full of flowers. It's all-inclusive for about US$200 d. It would be useless to say what the Caribbean Village Costa Linda has, because it has everything.

Its sister resort, the **Caribbean Village Decameron,** is a self-contained world, a spread-out complex of 355 rooms surrounding a central pool, with exercise rooms, casino, bars, and restaurants (tel. 809/526-2009, fax 809/526-1430), rooms all-inclusive for about US$170, though prices vary according to the room you choose. The Decameron has a kids' playground, disco, complete tennis facility, and can outfit you in any water sport you desire. In fact, all of the Caribbean Village resorts offer water sports.

The very quiet and elegant **Villas Jubey Talanquera** (tel. 809/541-8431, toll free 800/922-4272 in the DR) has a waterfall in its garden. At about US$150 per night, it is slightly more subdued than some of the others, though at 258 rooms, is still very large. The relatively new

Capella Beach Renaissance Resort at Juan Dolio (tel. 809/526-1080, fax 809/526-1088) has 283 luxury rooms, priced at around US$150 double, though it's not all-inclusive.

The **Metro Hotel and Golf,** while expensive, has 236 rooms with all the pleasurable extras you could want, including a pool, tennis courts, and beachfront balconies on many rooms, all for about US$120. Call them at 809/526-1808 (which is sometimes turned to fax) or 809/526-1811. The Metro can be a good choice if you're interested in the reef that runs along the shoreline in front of the hotel. Naturally, water sports are attractive, and so are the marina, two restaurants, and whirlpool. Call toll free from the United States at 800/322-4872. The Metro is managed by the group that manages the Embajador in Santo Domingo and the Villa Dorada in Puerto Plata. Visible from the main highway is the **Tamarindo Sun Resort** (tel. 809/526-1410), and farther east, the **Villas del Mar** (tel. 809/529-3735), with 30 attractive rooms and beach access.

In the same price category, but nearer the ocean, is the **Hotel Playa Real** (tel. 809/526-1114 or 809/526-1117, fax 809/526-1013), which has 56 rooms, all with air-conditioning and TV, a seaside coffee shop, restaurant, and disco. Slightly less expensive is the **Ramada Guest House** at Juan Dolio (tel. 809/526-2512, fax 809/526-2065) which also has a pool, whirlpool, and bar.

MORE PRACTICALITIES

Food and Drink

All the resorts and hotels at the *playas del este* have restaurants and bars, most of them quite good. More and more, the road along the beach is being built up with small restaurants. Perhaps the most concentrated restaurant area of them all is the **Plaza la Llave,** near the Metro Hotel, with a wide selection of international restaurants appealing to Italian, German, and Dominican tastes. Scattered along the beach are the **Oasis BBQ, JR's,** and the popular **Quisqueya.** Even now, the sprawl of Boca Chica is reaching the *playas del este,* and on weekends you'll find plenty of sun-worshipers from Santo Domingo mingling with international tourists, and a complement of street vendors and food stalls. **El Sueño,** in Juan Dolio, is probably the best place for Italian food. A good independent restaurant near Playa Real, **Allen's,** specializes in seafood. To eat inexpensively, try food stalls and quiet restaurants along the beach, or cook for yourself. A number of inexpensive local restaurants have sprouted up along Las Américas as well. You'll find many little bars along the beach for a quiet drink.

Information and Services

The **Codetel** office is located at the Centro Comercial Plaza Quisqueya. Good tours can be organized by **Venus** (tel. 809/526-1197, fax 809/526-1340). Hotels like the **Talanquera** have agencies that can conduct you far afield. Several car rental agencies have small offices in the area, including **National** (tel. 809/529-8656), **Budget** (tel. 809/526-1907), **General** (tel. 809/529-8371), and **Honda** (tel. 809/529-8221). But ask yourself, do you really need a car?

SAN PEDRO DE MACORÍS

INTRODUCTION

The next stops on the Las Américas Highway, along the Caribbean coast, are two sugar mill towns, San Pedro de Macorís and La Romana. In these parts, the highway juts inland and leaves the ocean views behind, coursing through sugarcane country and past well-tended fields, small villages, and across some broad rivers like the Río Soco, Río Higuamo, and the wide, brown Río Chavón. It is a bit of a shock to be traveling the paved, straight, and clearly discernable Las Américas Highway, and then to be suddenly thrust into remarkably congested towns such as these. The highways in town aren't marked, and it can get a little confusing. For the most part though, your instincts will surely guide you in the right direction (east!), and when the going gets tough, ask.

In actuality, neither San Pedro de Macorís nor La Romana have a great deal to offer the casual visitor. Both are sugar towns, both have histories extending back only into the late 19th century, and neither town is directly dependent upon tourism, though La Romana is, of course, home to Casa de Campo, the luxurious resort spread across hundreds of acres of beachfront south and east of the city. Both towns are hardworking provincial capitals. Each has a cathedral near the main square. Each is connected to Santo Domingo by regular bus service leaving from near the Parque Independencia, and connected to the interior provinces of El Seibo and Higüey by *guagua*. Only La Romana has an airport.

The population of San Pedro de Macorís, 64km (40 miles) east of Santo Domingo, is past 90,000 and growing. It is a relatively poor city, even though it was once a rich town built by sugar, sugar mills, and high sugar prices in the late 19th and early 20th centuries. Perhaps because of the town's close connection to sugar, which makes the population intimately familiar with economic exploitation and quasi-colonialism, it has always been politically to the left of center, and therefore out of favor with the institutional parties of Balaguer, and before that, of Trujillo. San Pedro de Macorís was certainly one of the centers of resistance to the American occupation.

History

The history of San Pedro de Macorís really begins in the 1820s, when the eastern region of the Republic was not highly populated and a series of terrible wars raged between Dominicans and Haitians. Many Dominicans, fleeing the destruction, settled in and around the Río Seco. During the middle of the 19th century, these Dominicans were joined by Cubans fleeing their own revolutionary disruptions, at a time when sugar-growing and processing was establishing itself as a major industry in the east. In 1867, a port facility was completed, and the town grew rapidly as a center of the sugar-processing industry. In its heyday, San Pedro was quite a place, bustling with activity, and home to many wealthy sugar entrepreneurs and speculators who built spectacular residences in the surrounding areas. As the town thrived, it began to be settled by a wave of

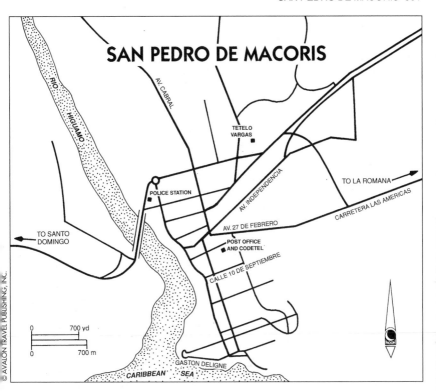

SAN PEDRO DE MACORIS

RÍO HIGUAMO

AV. CABRAL

TETELO VARGAS

POLICE STATION

AV. INDEPENDENCIA

TO LA ROMANA

CARRETERA LAS AMERICAS

AV. 27 DE FEBRERO

TO SANTO DOMINGO

POST OFFICE AND CODETEL

CALLE 10 DE SEPTIEMBRE

0   700 yd
0   700 m

GASTON DELIGNE

CARIBBEAN SEA

© AVALON TRAVEL PUBLISHING, INC.

German, Arab, Spanish, French, and Italian immigrants who added spice to an already boiling cauldron of ethnic peoples.

San Pedro became a province, with San Pedro de Macorís its capital, on June 23, 1882. Two years later, the first telephone conversation on the island took place in San Pedro between the tyrant Heureaux and General Gregorio Billini. In the 1920s, as sugar prices advanced toward the all-time high of US$.22 a pound, San Pedro became a prosperous city. The newly rich built in various styles, from neoclassical to Victorian. A seaplane, the Pan-American Clipper from New York, routinely landed on the waters of the Río Higuamo to discharge a cargo of millionaires. At the same time, workers were imported from the Leeward and Windward Islands of the Caribbean. These *Cocolos* brought with them the gingerbread style of ar-

chitecture, a culture closer to African religion and music than it was to Dominican-Spanish culture, and a love of spectacle, color, dance, music, and costume.

Today, the *Cocolos'* traditions are preserved in many different musical dance styles, including the *danza salvaje* (savage dance). In the Carnaval celebrations, the *Cocolos* become *guloyas,* who dance arm in arm, costumed in every imaginable way, carrying mirrors of African-influenced musical instruments. During festivals and dances, the *guloyas* are traditionally showered with small-denomination coins and passed bottles of rum, as they dance furiously to the sound of drums. You can witness this tradition in its finest form each June 29 during San Pedro's **All Saints Festival,** which celebrates Saints Peter and Paul. During **Carnaval** in February, the parades are spectacular, rivaled only by those in Santiago and La Vega.

By the way, it was explained to me that the early immigrants were always having trouble with customs officials and police officers. These people, mostly poor workers in the fields (precursors to today's Haitians), were constantly in need of a good lawyer. Hence, they came to refer to certain characters as *guloyas*. It sounds like the gospel truth to me.

Today, Macorís like to call themselves "Serie 23." In the 1930s, Trujillo, like all Great Dictators, forced his subjects to carry an identification card. Since the region was notoriously anti-Trujillo, and since all of Macorís's cards bore the series number 23, the people soon began to register their protest to this new imposition by calling themselves "Serie 23." Even today, the people of San Pedro are known for their politics and their baseball. And while the town these days is a little dirty and disorganized, it is palpably, dynamically real. What hurt too was the devastation of Hurricane Georges.

SIGHTS AND RECREATION

There are only a couple of sights in the town. As you arrive in the outskirts of San Pedro de Macorís, you should be able to look down and to the right (if you're heading east) and see the Río Higuamo, a bridge across the river, the port, and the large **Iglesia San Pedro** (Church of St. Peter) in the distance. Continue into town and follow the signs for *puerto,* which takes you downhill and toward the sea. Don't mistake the highway through town for downtown San Pedro; the older part of town is near the church and the **Malecón.** The church itself was built in 1913 in a neoclassical style, and while lovely, is not particularly exciting to historical sensibilities. Near the church you'll discover a pleasant **town square,** and a few blocks from the church, the Malecón. In the same general area as the park are a number of shops, restaurants, and some larger, older, Victorian homes. Keep in mind that the park is located at the corner of Avenida Independencia and Calle Gran Cabral. A few blocks east of the central park are the mansions of professional

ballplayers George Bell, Alfredo Griffin, Joaquín Andujar, and Juan Samuel. Look for Avenida Tío in Barrio Enriquillo.

Beaches

Beaches include **Playa Cumeyesa** and **Playa El Soco,** both only so-so, though nearby San Pedro on the coast is the **Cueva de las Marevillas** (Cave of the Marvels) with Taíno petroglyphs. Sportsmen might head to the Village of Cumayasa on the Río Seco, and try to arrange a river-fishing expedition.

ACCOMMODATIONS

The hotels in San Pedro de Macorís tend to be basic commercial hotels, most of them rather noisy and somewhat rough and tumble. They are, however, very inexpensive, averaging about US$10 per night, most with only fans. These include **Hotel Datni** (Calle Toconal 6, tel. 809/529-4020), **Hotel Altagracia** (Av. Libertad 132, tel. 809/588-6470), **Hotel Nuevo Central** (Calle San Francisco 49, tel. 809/588-2304), **Hotel Buffant** (Calle 10 de Septiembre, tel. 809/526-6983), **Hotel del Jaya** (Calle San Francisco 40, tel. 809/588-2705), **Hotel Macorís** (Calle Restauración 44, tel. 809/588-2530), **Hotel Brisa del Caribe** (Calle Rojas, tel. 809/526-8956), and **Hotel Independencia** on Avenida Independencia in the downtown area.

The only decent hotel in town is the **Howard Johnson Hotel Macorix** (tel. 809/529-2100, fax 809/529-9239), which is also the place for live music on weekends and good food. Doubles are about US$50 and the service is wonderful.

FOOD

As in any provincial Dominican town, the place is littered with cafeterias, bars and cafes dishing up cheap *comida criolla*. Most areas have street vendors and food stalls as well. The **Hotel Macorix** has a good restaurant that serves *comida criolla* at very modest prices. The most attractive restaurants in town are on the Malecón, especially the modestly priced **La Roca** near the medical school specializing in Italian food. Another good option is the **Restaurant Club Náutico El Puerto** on the Malecón, specializing in seafood. Also on the Malecón and specializing in Italian is **Portofino**. Smaller, cheaper restaurants abound, including the **Restaurant Independencia** (Av. Independencia 148), **Restaurant Don Luis** and **Restaurant Osteria** on Avenida 27 de Febrero, and **Restaurant Arias** on Calle España 9.

EVENTS AND ENTERTAINMENT

Baseball

The main event in town is baseball. Macorís are crazy for the game, and more Dominican players in the American major leagues come from San Pedro than from any other place on the island. Kids in San Pedro grow up playing the game,

DOMINICANS AND AMERICAN BASEBALL

Perhaps baseball is still America's game, but nearly a quarter of players on major league rosters are Latin Americans, many of them standouts. If history is any guide, the numbers of Latin players in America's major leagues will increase. After all, there are 3,000 Little League teams in 32 Latin American and Caribbean countries. No country has sent more players to the majors than the Dominican Republic, and many of those come from the town of San Pedro de Macorís.

Dominican baseball got going in the 1950s. Between 1955 and 1980, 49 Dominicans played in the majors, and as the 1980s got going the number of Dominicans going north to play swelled into the hundreds.

Among the early players, the brothers Jesus, Felipe, and Matty Alou each had very successful careers with a variety of teams. Probably the most famous Dominican player of them all, and a man still tremendously popular in the Dominican Republic, is the great San Francisco Giants pitcher, Juan Marichal—the first Dominican elected to the Baseball Hall of Fame.

These early successes led to the signing of many more players, including Juan Samuel (Phillies and Mets), Jose Rijo (Reds), Tony Peña (Red Sox), Pedro Guerrero (Dodgers and Cardinals), and Tony Fernández (Toronto Blue Jays), as well as American League MVP George Bell (Toronto Bluejays).

American prospects—and established major leaguers, too—now play regularly in the winter leagues in towns like Santo Domingo and San Pedro. Manny Mota, pinch-hitting star of the Dodgers has said, "If you ask any Dominican what he is proudest of, he will read you a list of ballplayers. This country doesn't have much, but we know we are best in the world at one thing."

But there are some downsides to the virtually un-

limited enthusiasm for the sport. In a relatively poor country like the Dominican Republic, baseball is seen as a way out of poverty. Wealth like that of Pedro Martínez of the Boston Red Sox, whose US$75 million six-year contract is well known on the streets of Santo Domingo, and Sammy Sosa's new $5 million home there inspire many Dominican youngsters to take up baseball with a passion unknown to America's kids, whose opportunities for success are much greater.

Moreover, there are some irregularities in the recruiting and signing process. Some American major league teams stand accused of signing Dominican players at too young an age. For example, the Los Angeles Dodgers were penalized in February 2000 for signing young Adrian Beltre before he turned 16 years of age, an act specifically prohibited by League rules. And the Beltre case is not isolated. The Florida Marlins, the Tampa Bay Devil Rays, and the Atlanta Braves, who signed both Wilson Betemit and Winston Abreu, may have done the same thing. Related to these early signings of under-age Dominicans are the dual practices of "hiding" players until they turn 16, and offering contacts to players who don't have the capacity to understand what they're signing.

Another downside comes from the nature of baseball's allure to young Dominicans. Many think that they can emulate the great success of Sammy Sosa, and skip an education. If they fail, they have missed school, cannot read or write, and have poor prospects in a country in which prospects are poor to begin with. But with American cable television pouring images into the Dominican Republic—images of Sosa rounding third and heading for home—one can hardly blame a kid from the slums of San Pedro de Macorís for dreaming.

and you can see them on street corners and in vacant lots. The main baseball season in San Pedro is from October to January, and the games are played at **Tetelo Vargas,** home of the Estrellas Orientales (Eastern Stars). The baseball stadium can't be missed; it's the largest, nicest, and most expensive edifice in the city, just off the main highway on the road to Hato Mayor. If you pass through San Pedro, make sure to attend a game if the team is in town. Buy tickets at the stadium, usually available through scalpers at the gate.

Discos, Bars, Dancing
For pure entertainment, you'll find several discos along the Malecón, and the standard complement of bars. For an extraordinary treat, try the nightclub called **Camayasa,** which features faux voodoo and *gugá* (African) dances and ceremonies.

The famous baseball star Sammy Sosa has built the **Plaza 30/30** shopping center at Independencia 97, away from the waterfront. In it is the super-crowded and noisy **Sammy Club** and the **Hit Bar.** The first is a disco-merengue scene, while the second is a sports bar.

SERVICES

Directly across from the church on the town square is the **bus station,** where all the local traffic makes a stop, and nearby is the main **post office.** In the same general area are a number of banks. There are two **Codetel** offices on Avenida Independencia, in case you need to make a call. For rental cars, see the chart "Car Rental Agencies on the East Coast."

LA ROMANA

INTRODUCTION

La Romana is just 38km (24 miles) east of San Pedro de Macorís, in all about 112km from Santo Domingo, an easy day's journey by car and back from the capital. Although La Romana is slightly smaller than San Pedro de Macorís in population, it is still the main administrative, agricultural, and processing center for the entire southeastern Dominican area. Given its proximity to nice beaches and the huge Casa de Campo and Altos de Chavón complexes, the town is influenced by tourism. Sugar is, however, still king in La Romana, as evidenced by the huge sugar mills and stately sugar estates near the oceanfront and port.

History
La Romana was originally founded on the Dulce River by Juan Esquivel in 1502. It shares pretty much the same history as San Pedro de Macorís—Dominicans and Cuban immigrants moving to La Romana to flee the mid-eighteenth-century wars, then an influx of Italian and German immigrants in the late 18th century, all influenced by the rise of sugarcane farming and cattle ranching. As was the case with San Pedro,

La Romana remained a sleepy backwater until its economic heyday in the mid-20th century as sugar prices rose to new heights and, for a while, stayed there. From the time the huge sugar mill was built at La Romana in 1917 until Gulf and Western began its forays into tourism, sugar, and bribery during the 1960s, La Romana was a sugar town all the way. In fact, the name La Romana means "scales," after the Roman weights used to weigh sugar for market.

Everything changed for La Romana with the coming of the huge conglomerate Gulf and Western during the 1960s. This company had not only tourism on its mind when it turned the old Hotel La Romana on the outskirts of the city into the 7,000-acre Casa de Campo, but also sugar, cement, cattle, manufacturing, and marketing. By the time Gulf and Western got through, it had invested nearly $200 million in the country and was involved in political corruption up to its neck. The company destroyed independent labor unions, employed thuggish administrators left over from the Batista regime in Cuba, and involved itself in local political bribery and intimidation, much to the chagrin of the Dominican people. The company even poured $20 million into La Romana itself, to make it the "Showcase of the East" and impress the many wealthy visi-

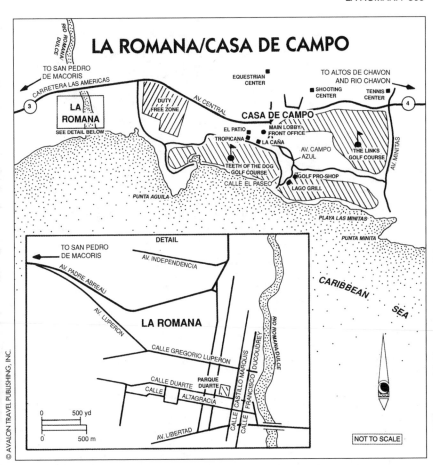

LA ROMANA/CASA DE CAMPO

Detail: LA ROMANA

tors of its tourist complex on the city's outskirts.

The 1970s proved somewhat disastrous as sugar prices fell, and the country as a whole suffered political turmoil. Gulf and Western is long gone, and its investments turned to dust. The Casa de Campo complex is under independent management and runs as smoothly as oiled clockwork. Like San Pedro, La Romana has a huge duty-free zone. Look at the labels in some of your clothes, and you may find them manufactured or assembled at La Romana. Today, the La Romana sugar company is by far the largest employer in town, with perhaps 15,000 local citizens currently working there—though times have once again become hard for the sugar industry.

Orientation

La Romana is a pleasant town, not as rough as San Pedro, perhaps because of the tourist money from Casa de Campo. Two of the main streets leading down the hill toward town are Avenida Libertad and Calle Santa Rosa. On higher ground away from the highway to the north is the more residential section of town, with old wooden houses and shady streets, while

oxen-powered
transportation
in La Romana

south toward the water are the commercial and retail sections of La Romana, leading ultimately to the La Romana sugar mill and the sugar estates on the water. The bridge over the Dulce River leads ultimately to the Casa de Campo complex, though the road to the complex is well marked.

Once you find your way to Parque Duarte, the central park of La Romana, a shady comfortable place, you are very close to the main sights, information, services, restaurants, and hotels of the city. From the central park, it is only a few blocks to the shady complex of old houses that make up the sugar estates and the La Romana mill itself. Otherwise, all roads lead to Casa de Campo.

SPORTS AND RECREATION

Sport and recreation is, of course, dominated by the huge Casa de Campo complex, which offers every sport and recreation you can imagine. However, the local beaches of **Playa Boca de Chavón** and **Playa las Minitas** are available for public swimming.

Fishing

About six km to the east of town flows the wide, brown Río Chavon. The Las Américas Highway crosses the river on a lovely bridge, and down below you can see the boats of fishermen. To me, it looks like an excellent river for sport fishing, though there is nothing really organized in the region specializing in freshwater fishing except at Casa de Campo. You might try your luck organizing your own trip (if you know Spanish) by contacting a fisherman along the river. One tour operator in La Romana—**Tropical Tours** (tel. 809/556-2636)—organizes excursions up the Río Chavon, an alluring deep chocolate river lined by coconut palms.

Diving

Just off the coast of La Romana is Isla Catalina, a long, low island with wonderful diving, snorkeling, and swimming. Coming along the Las Américas Highway on the coast west of La Romana, you can see the island way out in the Caribbean Sea, glistening under a hot sun. The island is, perhaps, the main dive location in the whole southeastern section of the island. The island has a wall formation on its north side which begins at 12m (40 ft.) and makes for wonderful reef diving. Unless you are part of an organized expedition, you'll need to reach the island from the marina at La Romana. Keep in mind that the island has no facilities and no water to drink, so you must outfit yourself completely if you're on your own. Perhaps the best way to go to Catalina is with an organized tour from any of the dive shops along the Caribbean coast, or organized by a tour operator. The island is hot and buggy, so go prepared.

ACCOMMODATIONS

For those not staying at Casa de Campo, accommodations in La Romana are usually in the US$10–15 range; only a few hotels charge as much as US$20. If you're coming into town from the west by car, you'll see the relatively uninteresting group of cabins called **Cabañas Tío Tom,** with 72 air-conditioned rooms, a pool, restaurant, and disco. The rooms are spacious and clean, priced at about US$35 double. You can call ahead at 809/556-6212, or fax at 556-6201. Also on the highway, but closer to La Romana, is **Hotel Adamay** (tel. 809/556-6102), which has basic rooms for US$20. On the main road, almost to town, are the **Hotel Frano** (Pd. Abreu 9, tel. 809/550-4744) and the **Hotel Bolivar** (Pd. Abreu 61, tel. 809/550-2626), both at around US$15. Among the commercial and inexpensive hotels are **Hotel Condado** (Altagracia 55, tel. 809/556-3010), the **Hotel Persia** (Calle Luperón 45, tel. 809/550-0816), and the **Hotel Rendy** (Calle Ferry 178, tel. 809/556-3540). For longer stays, on the eastern edge of the town is the **Libra Apart-Hotel** (Calle Gil 11, tel. 809/556-3787).

Expensive

There are a couple of resorts in the vicinity of Casa de Campo. Near a private beach is the **Dominicus Beach Village,** east of town, with 58 stone and wood *bohio*-style rooms, hammocks with raised-platform beds, and a private beach for swimming. Because it is complicated getting there, you'll need to get directions in town—or call at 809/533-4897. Half an hour outside town is the **Apart-Hotel Casa de Campo** (tel. 809/566-7464), with a swimming pool, bar, and restaurant.

FOOD

The central park, Parque Duarte, is the place to start looking for restaurants. **Las Américas** (Calle Castillo Marquís, tel. 809/556-4582) is a very popular local restaurant with great seafood and Creole dishes. It is decorated with local art and cooled by ceiling fans. The drinks, es-

pecially margaritas, are super. Make reservations. It is closed Sundays and does accept credit cards. The **Shish Kebab** (Calle Castillo Marquís 32, tel. 809/556-2737) is a great Lebanese restaurant (with Dominican touches) for *kebbeh,* milk shakes, and Dominican *pasteles en hajas.* Reservations aren't required and they take credit cards. If you're at Casa de Campo, try escaping to sample this food! One excellent restaurant right on the edge of the park is **Don Quijote's** for moderately priced Dominican and Spanish dishes. **El Huerto** serves *comida criolla* and is located on José Rodriquez and Moya (tel. 809/573-4348). Just to the west of the Dulce River is **La Casita** (Calle Docoudry 57, tel. 809/556-5509), for excellent and modestly priced Italian food. La Romana has many cafes and cafeterias on both sides of the highway, and a market on the main road as well.

SERVICES AND INFORMATION

You'll find **Codetel** on Parque Duarte, as well as the competing **Tricom** on Calle Duarte. You can change money at **Banco Nacional** on Parque Duarte or at **Banco Popular** on Calle Duarte. The car rental agencies are mostly clustered near or on the main highway, Las Américas. See the chart "Car Rental Agencies on the East Coast."

GETTING THERE

Getting there is easy. Buses leave from Santo Domingo's Parque Independencia bound for the southeast and will deliver you right to La Romana's central square. Driving the Las Américas Highway is also quite easy. Continue through San Pedro and keep straight on the highway. La Romana itself is a bit spread out on both sides of the highway. If you're driving from the west (Santo Domingo, for example), you'll have the choice of heading toward Guaymate (north), Bayahibe (east), and Higüey (northeast). As you enter La Romana, you'll see a big stadium and a roundabout, the center road (bearing right) for the town center and Casa de Campo, and another old highway heading through the countryside for Higüey. Another fork leads to Guaymate. It's a confusing place for drivers. If you are in fact heading for Higüey, it's best to continue through La Romana until you see a plainly marked turnoff for Higüey about 5km through town. This is a brand new road—take it.

Other travelers, mostly package tourists bound for Casa de Campo, arrive at La Romana International Airport (see below).

CASA DE CAMPO

INTRODUCTION

Casa de Campo is probably the Dominican Republic's most exclusive and upscale resort. At 7,000 acres, it is certainly the largest resort in the country, and as of February 2001, it grew larger and easier to reach by air.

First, the old La Romana airport with its short runway and small terminal have been replaced by a new and larger airport nearby, La Romana International Airport. This new airport accomodates the largest jets, as well as a growing number of commuter lines with ease. These days, American Airlines flies each day to the new airport from Miami, and American Eagle flies daily from San Juan, Puerto Rico. In addition, there are numerous charter flights arriving from Britain, Canada, Belgium, Italy, and the United States. La Romana International Airport has a modern terminal constructed of steel, glass, and coral, and at 80,000 square feet, is designed in the "sugar mill" style in line with La Romana's history as a sugar town.

Casa de Campo is updating itself as well, adding a 200-slip yacht marina and a third golf course, the first nine holes of which are scheduled to open in late 2001. All this activity is a sign that tourism on the southeast coast of the Dominican Republic is growing by leaps and bounds.

Casa de Campo is not for everybody. It is a self-contained resort—an entertainment, sports, and dining establishment that is both expensive and exclusive. If you're the kind of person who hopes his every need will be catered to and to whom a vacation means freedom from the exhausting details of everyday life, then Casa de Campo is for you. There is no question but what Casa de Campo is one of the most, if not *the* most, luxurious and beautiful resorts in the entire Caribbean.

Background

Casa de Campo means "house in the country." This particular house in the country, however, occupies nearly 7,000 acres of land near the sea and was designed by Miami architect William Cox and decorated with flair by Oscar de la Renta. The feel is red-tile-and-tropical-flower chic. Those guests arriving by plane are shepherded by a hostess, and the resort makes every effort to give a personal touch to what might otherwise become a rather impersonal stay.

Many of the luxury villas have maid and butler service, there are baby-sitters attached to the family villas, and you can touch a button and get a guide for just about everything except tying your shoes.

SPORTS AND RECREATION

Golf and tennis are probably the main attractions at Casa de Campo, though you can engage in just about any activity you can dream up, including horseback riding, polo, skeet and trap shooting, deep-sea and river fishing, snorkeling and scuba diving, and, of course, swimming and exercise.

Golf

The golf courses are Pete Dye's world-famous **Teeth of the Dog** and **The Links.** Both courses are challenging and beautiful, and as a guest you can buy into golf packages or purchase special guest memberships allowing you three-day privileges (or 14-day privileges, if you prefer). Golf lessons are available. People crazy about golf often take the "Golf Inclusive" package, which allows almost unlimited access to everything connected with the courses.

Tennis

Tennis players are confronted by the huge La Terraza Tennis Center, which features play beginning at 6 A.M. on 13 courts. Of course, lessons are available, and 10 of the courts are lighted for night play. Many people come to Casa de Campo on tennis packages as well.

Horseback Riding and Polo

Horseback riding and polo are popular activities too. Casa de Campo has an equestrian center complete with Dude Ranch, Jumping Ring, Polo Fields, and Rodeo, and the resort offers guided trail rides, riding lessons, jumping shows, and polo lessons, along with the occasional winter polo match featuring some of the best players in the Dominican Republic. The trail rides consist of one- or two-hour jaunts around the complex and into the nearby hills. They cost RD$230–410.

Shooting

The shooting complex at Casa de Campo in-cludes a shooting range, a clays course, and a pigeon range. There are 150 stations and one 110-foot tower projecting clays up to 45 yards into the sky. A team of instructors offers basic shooting instructions, and you can receive advanced instructions if you make reservations. You can get anything from a simple round of skeet to a round of sporting clays and pigeons for RD$305–2,130.

Water Sports

Water sports include trips to **Las Minitas** beach, a small private white sand area exclusively reserved for Casa de Campo visitors. Sports include windsurfing, sailing, Hobie Cats, snorkeling, and pedal craft. Of course you can swim if you wish. There are 14 swimming pools at the resort, and lap pools and special children's pools near the main area.

Boat Charters and Excursions

The resort offers a private marina for charter vessels. You can go deep-sea fishing, river fishing (on the Río Chavón), and sailing. The main catch for deep-sea fishermen is the marlin, while on the Chavón, river snook are a hardy and challenging catch. The deep-sea trips are taken on two 31-foot Bertrams boats, which hold up to eight people (four can fish at one time). Half- and full-day charters are available, averaging RD$3,600-5,100 plus tips. In addition to marlin, you can land kingfish, sailfish, barracuda, and wahoo. Snorkeling tours of Catalina Island leave from the marina as well. Trips run RD$350 and are subject to a 10% service charge.

In addition to all the sports, Casa de Campo runs an excursion service. As a guest, you can sign on for sight-seeing trips to Santo Domingo, swimming excursions to Catalina Island, and river excursions on something that resembles a 19th-century riverboat. At times the resort can arrange trips to Bayahibe for swimming, and to Isla Saona (Saona Island), a very isolated island off the southeast mainland coast.

ACCOMMODATIONS

There are two basic kinds of accommodations at Casa de Campo: casitas and villa homes.

Casitas

Casitas are large hotel rooms arranged in one- and two-story groupings, mostly near the main buildings and grounds, some of which have views of the golf course, the gardens, and the ocean. The casitas have two double or one king-sized bed, air-conditioning, cable TV with remote control, alarm, refrigerator, bar, direct-dial telephone, walk-in closet, room safe, coffee maker, dressing area, and bath. They also have balconies.

Villa Homes

These are strategically located throughout Casa de Campo to correspond to a theme (golf, tennis, etc.), and feature the "comfort of a country home," according to Casa de Campo officials. In fact, each villa offers a living room, dining room, fully equipped kitchen, and screened terrace. Each bedroom has a separate air-conditioning system and a private bath.

Rates

The rates at Casa de Campo vary considerably, according to what casita or villa you choose, how many people occupy it, what kind of sports and recreation plan is involved, the number of meals included, and taxes, tips, services, and the occasional cart ride or privately organized tour. Hence, it is difficult to be precise—which is the reason you should order the *Individual Rates and Packages* brochure right off the bat. In general terms, suffice it to say that the casita rates can go from a per-night low of US$125 to US$225. Villa rates range from US$260 to US$830. Casa de Campo also offers a special "Excel Club Villa," which is larger (three or four bedrooms) and includes special services like maid and butler service, airport transfer, breakfast, and concierge services for US$534–1,308. Be fully aware that these rates are per person and are subject to local taxes. Perhaps the way to go is to take a stab at the "inclusive packages" available for casitas and villas, which include meals, certain events, sports, and use of gyms and facilities. Naturally, Casa de Campo offers a variety of sports vacations, including popular golf and tennis packages.

FOOD AND DRINK

Since Casa de Campo is all about pleasure, eating and drinking assume major importance. Each of the resort's three large restaurants caters to basic Caribbean-American tastes. **The Tropicana,** the complex's most basic restaurant, operates near the main administrative offices, featuring a breezy, exotic atmosphere. The menu has a wide range of Caribbean seafood specialties, Dominican dishes, and American stuff like steaks and surf and turf. During high season the restaurant often puts out a seafood bar. Prices range from US$8–20 for main courses.

Above one golf course fairway and the sea is the **Lago Grill,** open for breakfast and lunch. The main function of the Lago Grill is to offer an informal alternative to breakfast and lunch. Hence, they've got an omelette bar, juice bar, and salad bar. Lunch features burgers, sandwiches, conch chowder, and *sanchoco*, most for about US$5–14. Sometimes during the high season the Lago Grill serves dinner, usually a revolving set of steaks and seafood. The Grill is the site of live music during the late nights.

For less formal dining at lunch and dinner, Casa de Campo offers the **El Patio,** which serves Dominican dishes, pasta, fish specials, and big desserts for lunch and dinner. The resort tries to feature one "adventure" each month, something like chocolate or Asian or Cajun. El Patio is essentially a coffee shop shielded by lattices of potted plants and banks of waving bougainvillea, but you can still get black bean soup and ceviche if you wish. Main courses go for about US$9–15.

Bars: The **Cocomar Bar** at Las Minitas beach is open every day for beach drinks, and the **19th Hole Bar** near the golf course serves sandwiches and cold drinks. The **La Caña Bar** is a thatched-roof open-air drinking establishment featuring merengue, folk music, and the occasional ballet. People like to congregate at La Caña for the "sunset drink" routine. Artists begin to play at about 11 P.M. every night. Of course, if you're pooped, you can order room service and forget it.

INFORMATION AND SERVICES

Every travel agent in the world knows about Casa de Campo, and can provide brochures on request. In fact, if your travel agent *doesn't* know Casa de Campo, you should reach over and summarily tear off his or her badges and epaulets. However, for those who wish to receive information direct from the horse's mouth, the official address for Casa de Campo is P.O. Box 140, La Romana, Dominican Republic (tel. 809/523-3333, fax 809/523-8548 or 809/523-8394). The official representative of Casa de Campo in the United States is Premier World Marketing, 2600 S.W. Third Avenue, Third Floor, Miami, Florida 33129. You can call toll free from the United States at 800/877-3643, or call 305/856-5405. The toll free number for Casa de Campo in the United States, Canada, Puerto Rico, and the Virgin Islands is 800/877-3643. If you call either Casa de Campo or its representatives, ask for a basic brochure and specify a packet called *Individual Rates and Packages,* so that you can make an intelligent choice of vacation plans. While you're at it, you might also request a map of the grounds, which will give you an idea of your geographic situation should you choose to vacation at Casa de Campo.

Childcare

Recently, the resort has developed a "Kidz'n Casa" program of baby-sitting, and activities for children during the day. Certain packages offer this service as well.

Car Rentals

For car rentals, see the chart "Car Rental Agencies on the East Coast."

ALTOS DE CHAVÓN

INTRODUCTION

About 15 minutes from Casa de Campo, on a plainly marked road northeast of the tourist resort, you'll find an oddball sort of place, but one which is strangely compelling. Called Altos de Chavón, it is the brainchild of Charles Bluhdorn, who in 1976 was the chairman of Gulf and Western, then the owner and manager of Casa de Campo. Originally conceived as a kind of instant tourist at-traction to complement the resort complex, today Altos de Chavón is a worthwhile artistic site in its own right, despite its construction in mock 16th-century Italian style, its artificially aged stone edifices, and its boutiques and galleries, which could be something out of suburban Los Angeles In truth, Altos de Chavón, set on a hilltop over-looking the Río Chavón, surrounded on all sides by lush tropical countryside and housing one of the finest museums of Taíno art and artifacts in the country (not to mention its museums, work-

Rio Chavón

shops, and galleries of fine Dominican art, sculpture, silkscreening, and photography), is an impressive, unique artistic accomplishment.

In its coral block and terra-cotta brick buildings, this $40 million Roberto Copa creation houses the studios of artists and crafters, along with three distinct art galleries and a world-renowned school of design. On a good day, the shady environs of Altos de Chavón are quite pleasant, and the view from the hill down to the brown river is fantastic. This is one place you can really see for miles and miles in several directions.

SIGHTS

School of Design

For me, the heart of Altos de Chavón is its artists. Its School of Design, associated with the Parsons School of Design in New York and Paris, was founded in 1982 and offers students degrees in the areas of communication, fashion, environmental study, product design, fine arts, and illustration. If you go in summer, or during the Christmas season, many students and artists will be away on vacation, though there will still be plenty of artisans manning open-air stalls and selling crafts. During much of the year, however, the winding streets are jammed with artisans and craftsmen offering unique gifts for sale. Many of these craftsmen are official Altos de Chavón *talleres* people—men and women who produce ceramics, silkscreens, woven fibers, clay pottery, and folk art. All of these products are sold at **La Tienda,** the foundation village store.

Church of St. Stanislaus

The Church of St. Stanislaus was blessed by the pope on his visit to the Dominican Republic. This church is located on the main plaza and surrounded by a fountain with four stone lions and a colonnade of obelisks.

Museo Arqueológico Regional

Outside of Santo Domingo's Museo del Hombre Dominicano, the most important archaeological and ethnological museum is the Museo Arqueológico Regional at Altos de Chavón. Well worth a visit, this museum is wonderfully and beautifully organized and allows the visitor to wander in comfort through showcase displays of representative artifacts in domestic and ceremonial use during several periods of Taíno history. The displays of artifacts, well illustrated (though the explanations are in Spanish) and very thorough, offer a glimpse into every aspect of Taíno life, agriculture, ceremony, and religion. There is a small admission fee of RD$20. The creators of Altos de Chavón also constructed a 4,000-seat amphitheater which is occasionally the scene of artistic presentations, though mostly it's empty except for wandering minstrels. You

the exterior of
Casa del Rio,
Altos de Chavón

LEO DE WYS

might get lucky and visit while one of the concerts or jazz festivals is taking place.

ENTERTAINMENT

For entertainment, Altos de Chavón has **Genesis Disco,** one of the most glittery and expensive dance halls you'll ever want to see. Its multicolored dance floor seems hallucinatory, its music, loud and varied. Genesis operates 9 P.M.–2 A.M., and in winter is only open Friday and Saturday. The place caters mostly to Casa de Campo residents, though some outsiders find their way inside. Outsiders pay US$16 admission. Drinks go for US$10. Before venturing up, it's best to inquire at Casa de Campo.

PRACTICALITIES

Food
The **Café del Sol** (tel. 809/523-3333, ext. 2346) is the least expensive place to dine, offering pizza and ice cream in an indoor-outdoor setting, for prices ranging about US$4–10. Of course, you can get salads and bar drinks and snacks as well. **La Piazetta** (tel. 809/523-3333, ext. 2339) offers elegant Italian food. Main courses range in price

US$11–26; reservations required. For simpler, Mexican fare, try the **El Sombero,** which is still expensive, but not as ritzy.

The top-of-the-line restaurant is the **Casa del Río** (tel. 809/523-3333, ext. 2345, reservations recommended). Many guests of Casa de Campo come over for the truly gourmet dining. This place is crawling with style, from the bougainvillea climbing the walls to the wine racks and piano music. Main courses like duck and lobster go for US$18–26.

Shopping
At least three formal shops offer designer crafts, perfume, sculpture, jewelry, and "style." On the grounds you'll find **Bugambilia, Everett Designs,** and **Oscar de la Renta Boutique.** These shops are open daily from 9 A.M.–9 P.M., except the Oscar de la Renta shop, which closes nightly at 6 P.M., and all day Sunday.

Accommodations
A small place called **La Posada** on the grounds once operated as an inn, but now apparently is reserved for employees only. Nevertheless, you might check with Casa de Campo to see if any of the rooms or suites are available if you have a burning desire to bed down at Altos de Chavón.

BAYAHIBE AND PARQUE NACIONAL DE ESTE

It is almost a shame to write about Bayahibe and its isolated, pure, and tranquil coastal environment; it waits to be exploited into a booming development. The village itself has everything travelers have always dreamed about: long slices of white beach backed by lush tropical vegetation, bays, inlets, and lagoons protected by coral reefs, small hotels, and inexpensive open-air restaurants offering good service and quiet times.

These days you can have your choice. You can stay right in Bayahibe village at one of several small hotels that are not too expensive (though the price climbs yearly), or you can stay along Dominicus beach at a stylish resort. Plans have long been in place to turn the Bayahibe vicinity

into something resembling Planet Hollywood. In many ways, the fate of Bayahibe illustrates the moral dilemma of modern travel in a nutshell.

BAYAHIBE

History
Bayahibe has been a fishing village through much of its history. Many of its modest wooden houses in the best Caribbean architectural style line the shore and cluster just inland to form a unique social circle, now being gradually consumed by tourist development. Still, the bay and lagoon are lovely, with cool blue water, tranquil winds, and white sand. It's really like a

postcard of itself. The coral reef offshore has many varieties of tropical fish, and the diving and snorkeling possibilities are endless. It's at Bayahibe where you can find fishermen to take you over to **Isla Saona** (part of the Parque Nacional de Este), a trip that takes a couple of hours at best.

Accommodations

A simple wooden tourist hotel, **Hotel Bayahibe** (tel. 809/707-3684) is right "downtown" and has signs in English on its side announcing the availability and price of rooms. There isn't really any use in phoning ahead; just show up and see if you can get one of the 10 rooms priced at about US$20–25, with fan and generator for those power interruptions. Very similar and right next door, is **Cabañas Trip Town** (tel 809/707-3640), 15 cabins with fans and private bath, but no generator for the air-conditioner when electricity fails, as it does. Still, the owner is friendly and helpful. Just away from the water is **Cabañas Nina** on the Calle Segunda (tel. 809/224-5431). These spots are similar and similarly priced at about US$20, slightly higher with breakfast. The nearby **Hotel Cabaña Milysade** offers rooms and cabins priced at US$20 per night as well. Off the beach no more than a hundred yards are several motel-type establishments that offer simple rooms with fans for about US$12–15. Keep in mind that these hotels and guest cabins have no hot water.

The newest all-inclusive at Bayahibe is the expensive, exclusive, and tony **Casa del Mar** (tel. 800/472-3985 or 809/221-8880), which is reached by paved road at a turnoff just before the main turn to Bayahibe. It is all here, of course—tennis, archery, pool, massage, scuba, 536 rooms of fun. Rooms are US $160–200 for a single or double, higher for one of the 32 suites.

Development has really heated up about 5 kilometers down the coast at **Club Dominicus Beach** (tel. 809/686-5658) an Italian-run complex facing the long white stretches of sand. Its 480 rooms have all the amenities, and there is, of course, a restaurant, a pool, a tennis court, horseback riding, and entertainment. All-inclusive packages cost in the range of US$175. This vast complex sits on nearly 3,000 acres of land and is staffed by young Italians who make life interesting. You can fax the resort at 809/687-8583. Be sure

to get brochures for accurate prices from a travel agent. For Club Dominicus Beach, you might try looking into non-inclusive packages as well, making room rates more like US$75–85 per night.

Food

Of course, the big resorts have their own restaurants. In Bayahibe you'll find two restaurants near the beach. The **Bahía,** which serves great seafood and good cold beer in an open-air setting, and the **Bayahibe,** with modest prices, fine *comida criolla,* seafood, and excellent lunch sandwiches. Quite different is **Cafetería Julissa,** which is known for its fresh juices and can fix you up with a delicious and inexpensive breakfast while you watch day begin on the beach. For lunch they make ham and cheese sandwiches, among others. Also pleasant are the **Barco** and **Café de Luna.** There are several other food stall restaurants, and restaurants in guest cabins serving basic meals. All of these offer good value, perfect for budget travelers.

Sports and Recreation

It isn't hard to find something to do in Bayahibe. Lying on the beach is a particular favorite. Watching Dominican children play baseball on the beach is another. If you want more action, don your snorkel gear and visit the outlying reefs for snorkeling in nearly perfect water. The diving here is great as well, with a "wall" and clouds of tropical fish. Although you can arrange trips to Isla Saona, be forewarned that the island is befogged by mosquitoes and is hot, though there are two trails across and around it for bird-watchers, as well as a couple of delightful beaches. You can try your hand at deep-sea fishing off the coast. The big resorts can arrange an expedition for you, or you can negotiate with a local if you've brought your own gear. Everything, up to this point, is very informal.

Hang around long enough, and you might get to play in a beach volleyball game with the kids.

Getting There

Buses run from La Romana to Bayahibe. Buses also run from Higüey. If you are without a car, the bus to Bayahibe is as close as you're going to get to the entrance of the Parque Nacional de Este. Still, the best way to get to Bayahibe is by car, taking the main road through La Romana. Bayahibe is only about 15km (nine miles) from La Romana, though the last few kilometers are over a smooth red-dirt road. Just a few kilometers outside La Romana you'll see a plainly marked fork in the road. The turn slightly left takes you to Higüey; the right fork takes you down the highway toward Bayahibe and Dominicus beach. About 10km (six miles) after you hit the red-dirt road, you'll see a rusted, pock-marked sign for Bayahibe. Bear right for Bayahibe, left for Dominicus and the Parque Nacional de Este (west entrance).

PARQUE NACIONAL DE ESTE

Background
The Parque Nacional de Este comprises most of the southeastern peninsula of the mainland Dominican Republic, and the offshore Isla Saona. The park has a total area of 103,520 acres, 77,203 on the mainland and 26,316 on Isla Saona. The Parque Nacional de Este was established on September 16, 1975, which makes it one of the newest parks in the Dominican system.

The park's area is noted for its geological and cultural features, including limestone cliffs, subterranean tunnels, pictographs, ceremonial squares, ritual sites, and Indian burial grounds. It was, in fact, the original home of Chief Cotubanamá's group of Taínos. Keep in mind that most of the park is dry, hot and dusty, and its few sandy beaches are only accessible by boat. The average yearly temperature is about 80°F, and the mainland receives about 47 inches of rainfall per year, though precipitation on Saona is considerably less. From west to east, that is from Bayahibe to Boca de Yuma, the park stretches about 25km in length, while Isla Saona is about 22km long (14 miles) and 5–6 km wide (3–4 miles). There are no towns or villages on the mainland portion of the park. Isla Saona has two tiny fishing villages: Punta Gorda on the west coast and Adamanay on the southwest coast, each connected to the other by a dirt track. Adamanay is the docking location for the Dominican Coast Guard, and for any boat coming from the mainland.

Land
The park's mainland portion consists of limestone and coral terraces rising from cliffs along the coastline. The peninsula itself rose from the sea only about 125,000 years ago, making it relatively young in geologic terms. The territory is generally flat and formed of rocks of marine origin. You'll find almost no arable soil in the park, and in many places small salt water wells rise, while in other places sinkholes fill with rain water. No rivers or brooks flow in the area, mainly because the subsoil is so highly porous. The terrain is generally flat, though there is a series of hilly terraces. Of course, near the beach, the cliffs are quite spectacularly high, rugged, and dotted with limestone caves caused by wave action. These remote and spectacular areas can only be visited by boat. Although there are no springs or rivers in the park, there are a few saltwater lagoons close to the coast, and some springs near the beaches of the Catuano Channel, which separates the mainland from Isla Saona. On the south coast lies the bioluminescent Catalanita Bay.

Flora
The predominant flora of the mainland is subtropical humid forest near the coast, and layers of tropical deciduous and seasonally dry forest as you recede from the coast. The predominant plants of the area are the zamia, copey, gumbolimbo, Hispaniolan mahogany, wild olive, sea grape, coconut palm, and holywood.

Fauna
People know the park for its bird species, and Isla Saona is nearly perfect as a breeding ground, given its low salty marshes and lagoons. Of the 112 known bird species, eight are endemic to the area, while another 11 are endemic only to the Caribbean. Chief among the bird species are the endemic Hispaniolan lizard-cuckoo, wood stork, black-crowned tanager, limpkins, Antillean village weaver, red-legged thrush, palmchat, black-cowled oriole, and the endangered white-crowned pigeon. Also important are the Hispaniolan parrot, barn owl, stygian owl, plain pigeon, herring gull, American frigate bird, brown pelican, and on the island of Saona, the flamingo. All of these species can be found on Isla Saona in great numbers, along

with the American oystercatcher, which inhabits the area of Punta Algibe on the mainland in front of Saona, and the Antillean piculet found in dry coastal areas. Probably the flying insect with the greatest impact in the area is the mosquito. They're everywhere.

Aside from bird life, the main animal presence is in the sea. Endangered marine mammals like the manatee and bottlenose dolphin are seen along the coast and in the mangrove areas. There are a number of amphibians and reptiles, lizards and snakes, but they are rarely seen. There are two species of sea turtle found off the coast, and on the mainland one occasionally runs across a huge Rhinoceros iguana.

It isn't likely, but the Parque Nacional de Este is one of the few places you *might* encounter those elusive endemic mammals of the Dominican Republic, the solenodon and the hutia. The most ancient and peculiar of endemic mammals of the Antilles, the solenodon is the only surviving insectivorous animal in the region. It has a small body with a longish snout (good for sniffing up ants, etc.). As a night creature, the solenodon lives in small caves and dry tree trunks. Supposedly a separate species of solenodon dwells on the island of Cuba, but both solenodons are highly endangered. The hutia is an endemic rodent represented by two subspecies on the Dominican island. The hutia looks much like a gerbil and lives in caves and dry tree trunks, and it is also a night feeder. Since it's unlikely you'll be out tramping around in the national park at night, you won't likely run across either of these two elusive animals.

Cultural Sites

Culturally, the mainland park has many ceremonial sites. You'll find a number of pictographs and petrographs in the eastern sector of Guaraguao.

Trails

The **Sendero de la Cueva del Puente** (Bridge Cave Path) leads inland from the park's western entrance to an underground cave formed from the interaction of limestone soils and rain cycles. It's about a two-hour hike. Nine yellow signs in the path and seven signs in the cave mark the way. For the most part, the path is relatively

flat and easy to access, and since there's only one trail, the track in is also the track out. Most of the flora consists of coastal humid forest and transitional humid forest, a mix of tropical and deciduous forests.

The first part of the Bridge Cave Path goes along the coast where one can see coral, mollusks, sea urchins, starfish, crabs, shorebirds, and occasional butterflies. Thereafter, the path leaves the coast and traverses the transitional humid forest with trees and bush growing in height on the terraces. As you go inland, you get into more and more karstic formations and the birdlife becomes more prevalent. At the end of the path is Bridge Cave, which one enters in a small depression. Inside the cave are several signposts (in Spanish) indicating the numerous formations. It takes guts to go into this cave, but the paths are not particularly dangerous, unless you try to leave them to explore. Remember, inside Bridge Cave, do not leave the path!

The **Eastern Coastal Path** begins at the reception area south of Boca de Yuma. The walk takes approximately five hours. Plan to stop for rests, with lunch on the beach. Along the way, the path passes coastal humid forest, mangrove swamps, and cliffs. The Coastal Path crosses country altered by the addition of coconut palms, though the farther into the country you get, the more these intruders are replaced by humid pine forest. Some of the humid forest grows on sand, causing it to have high tops and spread-out branches, while some grows on rock, making for a much shorter, dryer forest. On sunny days (which is most of the time), you can catch glimpses of the ocean bottom through utterly blue-green water. The two stretches of the Eastern Path run from Guaraguao to Palmillas, and from Palmillas to Calderas' Bay on the beach. You can take a swim at Calderas' Bay and take a look at the well-developed mangroves along the coast as well. When the water in Calderas' Bay is rough, it becomes bioluminescent, due to the presence of microscopic unicellular seaweeds that radiate light.

Isla Saona

It's possible to make advance arrangements in either Bayahibe or Boca de Yuma (at the marina) for boats to cruise the coast of the national park, and to cross to Isla Saona. Isla Saona was part

*a quiet cove
near Bayahibe*

of Chief Coubamaná's bailiwick, and is where the great Taíno chieftain died. Columbus sighted the island on his second voyage, and during the late 16th and early 17th centuries, the island was used by pirates, corsairs, and privateers who wanted firewood and rest. The island is drier than the rest of the park, with an average annual rainfall of only 39 inches.

To get to the island, you must boat across the Catuano Channel. Swimming is allowed on the island at **Punta Catuano** and **Mano Juan,** where you can buy cold drinks. There are plans to make lunches available at these spots, but you'd best pack food just in case. The island contains several lagoons lined by mangroves, the most important being **Canto de la Laya. Punta Caleta** has 632 acres of mangrove, while there are 1,378 total acres of mangrove on Saona itself.

Getting to and from Isla Saona takes some advance planning, some fortitude, and some time to burn, but the adventure is worth it. Be sure to take plenty of repellent, sunscreen, a broad-brimmed hat, flashlight, drinking water, camera, binoculars, and good hiking boots with socks.

Getting There and Getting Around

The Parque Nacional de Este is one of those wild and remote places that pays dividends only for those willing to go the extra mile in terms of discomfort. For one thing, neither of the park's entrances can be reached by public transportation. The closest you can get by bus to the western en-

trance is Bayahibe, and even then the entrance and ranger station is down a hot, red-dirt road about 10km. The eastern entrance is located about 10km south of the town of Boca de Yuma. *Guagua* and motoconcho will take you to Boca de Yuma from Higüey and La Romana, but it's a long dusty walk to the eastern entrance and ranger station from there. All in all, it is best to have some kind of personal transportation to either entrance, especially because the hikes in the Parque Nacional de Este are themselves very hot and tiring, and because you'll need to carry your own water, food, and emergency supplies. Several tour agencies in Santo Domingo serve the national park.

If you go into the park on its western end, you'll take the marked turnoff to the left just before the road to Bayahibe. At the park's entrance you'll see a ranger cabin, though you won't usually find any literature on the park there. The ranger can serve as a guide, but be prepared with permits from the National Parks Department. The west entrance leads to the inland trail that ends at a cave famous for its bats. The eastern entrance has a ranger cabin and leads to a trail along the coast.

Perhaps a better way to see some of the park is by boat, rented in Bayahibe. They are called *lanzas,* or launches. However, make certain you have a Spanish speaker who can talk to the owner.

Otherwise, you'll end up on a crowded small

boat going to a beach for lunch. Negotiate a launch and a "nature ride" and you should be okay.

Most of the area of the national park is not marked by trails. Most of the coastline is inaccessible except by boat. It is possible to rent boats at Bayahibe or Boca de Yuma (which has a good marina) for the trip to Isla Saona. Several trails crisscross Isla Saona, but there are no services.

THE COCONUT COAST AND VICINITY

INTRODUCTION

The Costa de Coco is almost, but not quite, completely reserved for package tourists who come for the big hotel resorts, the long stretches of white sand beach, the water sports, and the all-inclusive atmosphere. The eastern point of land jutting out into the Atlantic Ocean is a near-continuous beach. The beaches touch the dangerous **Canal de la Mona** (The Mona Channel) which separates the Dominican Republic from Puerto Rico, and which is the passage to freedom for many Dominicans who flee their country seeking better jobs and improved lives for their families.

As the name indicates, the scenery on the eastern point is dominated by the majestic coconut palm. Winds tend to blow hard in the region, bringing relief from the heat and the energy necessary to push windsurfing boards. The winds, deep water, and strong tides also make this coast bumpier and relatively more dangerous than the north and south coasts. There are few reefs along this coast, and many of the huge hotel complexes have privatized their stretches of beach, though there are still some isolated stretches accessible to individuals on adventure holidays. The population of the coast is limited to tiny hamlets. Except for the ones running between the large hotel complexes and the small Punta Cana airport, the roads are dirt track. Camping is possible, but I wouldn't want to vouch for its safety or desirability.

Of course, the extreme east of the Dominican Republic is much more than simply white sands and holiday travelers sitting around bars under thatched-roof canopies. The approaches to the eastern beaches, across the lovely provinces of El Seibo and La Altagracia, or through the town of La Romana, offer a real glimpse of laid-back countryside dominated by sugarcane, small villages, and in the background, the lovely Cordillera Oriental, which appears rather like a delicate etching against the northern horizon, seen through a waving green gauze. And of course, for those who don't approach the national park and the lagoons through Samaná, the eastern point is the gateway to great adventure.

Getting There

Most package tourists to the big hotel complexes will arrive at Punta Cana's small airport. **American Eagle** (U.S. tel. 800/433-7300) generally flies one or two 36-passenger airplanes each day from San Juan, Puerto Rico. Coming from Europe, the connections are easy to make in San Juan. The flights from San Juan are only 50 minutes in length, and the last flight of the day leaves late enough for almost all visitors from the United States or Europe to make connections. You might check with American Eagle about its plans to fly from Santo Domingo to Punta Cana Airport. Another fly-in alternative is to take the American Eagle to La Romana, or the daily jet from Miami to La Romana, and then take the 90-minute drive across Higüey to the eastern point beaches.

Getting to the far eastern coast isn't easy by public transportation. Riding the buses, you'll first have to get yourself to Higüey from Santo Domingo. To get to Puna Cana, take a camioneta from Higüey. As a last resort, try some of the domestic or charter flights from Santo Domingo's Herrera Airport, which fly into Punta Cana but tend to be somewhat expensive.

If you are not a package tourist, if you have made do-it-yourself reservations at either a luxury hotel or tourist hotel, or if you are an extreme individualist and want to stay at a non-affiliated hotel to save money, then driving through the eastern interior is a good alternative. An excellent, beautiful, and nearly deserted road connects the towns of Hato Mayor, El Seibo, and Higüey, a road that you can find by going north from San Pedro de Macorís. A second lovely highway runs to Higüey from just beyond La Romana. Both roads wind through gorgeous scenery of coconut and ceiba trees, waving cane fields, grazing cattle, and campesinos riding horses. If Santiago and La Vega are the traditional urban places in the Dominican Republic, then the countryside of El Seibo and Higüey is the traditional rural place.

BOCA DE YUMA AND VICINITY

On the northeast side of Parque Nacional de Este, the town of Boca de Yuma stands at the mouth of the Río Yuma, in the armpit of the Bahía de Yuma. Many people come to Boca de Yuma to do some deep-sea fishing, which is said to be fabulous for blue marlin. In fact, this small village hosts a major international fishing tournament every June. Boca de Yuma is also the place to hire a boat to take you down the coast toward Isla Saona, and to cruise the national park offshore to some of its otherwise inaccessible coves and beaches. In the area is **Cueva de Berna,** a limestone wave-carved cave along the coast, with Taíno petroglyphs. North from Boca de Yuma, the paved road is very good, and you'll pass through San Rafael de Yuma, a dry and undistinguished town. If you take this road, you should look for the residence of Ponce de León, about one kilometer north of San Rafael de Yuma on the road to Higüey, which is in the process of being restored.

The Ponce de León Residence
Juan Ponce de León built his residence during 1505–06, while he was officially in charge of Higüey and a very important man in the early administration of colonial Spain. This particular house is still located in a totally rural setting, far away from any other structures, and gives one a good idea what Dominican colonial life was like at the beginning of the country's existence. Ponce de León himself went on to adventures of conquest and plunder in Puerto Rico, and then later to adventures of discovery in Florida. After passing through San Rafael de Yuma

going north, look after about one kilometer for an unmarked dirt road on the right. The house is solidly built and contains original furniture, armor, and artifacts. There is a small entrance fee of RD$20, and the knowledgeable guide, who speaks Spanish, will conduct a tour. The grounds around the house are extensive.

Getting There
If you're driving overland on the Higüey road (officially called the Mella Highway), you'll find Boca de Yuma some 14km beyond the turnoff for Bayahibe and Dominicus beach, beyond La Romana. The main reason to take this road is to find the eastern entrance to the Parque Nacional de Este.

THE HIGÜEY ROAD

The Higüey road is officially called the Mella Highway. In its infancy, the Mella Highway is a clutch of urban industrial and market streets in far northwest Santo Domingo, where traffic is a true nightmare. It would almost literally take infrared satellite photography and a host of topographical civil engineers to find the highway through the maze of Santo Domingo streets, though some locals I traveled with apparently had no trouble. The Mella Highway itself parallels the Las Américas Highway going east from Santo Domingo toward San Pedro de Macorís, so the best thing for an untutored and unguided driver to do going toward Punta Cana is to take Las Américas to San Pedro de Macorís, then turn north at the first roundabout for Hato Mayor, a modest cattle-agricultural town.

The other alternatives for drivers are to drive the Las Américas Highway all the way to San Rafael del Yuma, then go north, or to take the Higüey cutoff just after La Romana. The Higüey cutoff just after La Romana is probably the best alternative; it's a newly paved road going through gently rolling hills. Besides, if you drive all the way to San Rafael del Yuma, you'll miss most of the El Seibo and Higüey countryside.

Hato Mayor and El Seibo
Hato Mayor and El Seibo are both provincial farming and ranching communities, with nothing in particular to recommend them to tourists or travelers, except that they are, in fact, unremarkable and therefore typical. The road that

*Basílica de Nuestra Señora de la Merced,
Our Lady of Mercy, Higüey City*

connects Hato Mayor to Higüey runs through cane country, across numerous lovely, slow-moving rivers like the Río Cibao, Soco, and Chavón, and splits the hardworking heart of the eastern Dominican Republic. Although there are numerous commercial hotels in both Hato Mayor and El Seibo, these towns are quiet and lack tourist attractions. Even so, passing through them reminds one of the real country behind the airline posters and car-rental promotional brochures, and it is a reality that is both calm and pleasingly normal. El Seibo is the site of a formerly grand government-owned hotel, but the hotel has fallen on hard times and at present is not a recommended destination.

HIGÜEY

Some 40km northeast of La Romana is Higüey, also the capital of the huge province of La Alta-gracia, famous in the Dominican Republic for its oranges. The town itself has a long history, distinguishing it from the rest of the eastern provinces and towns, having been founded in 1494 by conquistador Juan de Esquivel. Residents of Higüey consider themselves at the cradle of early Spanish civilization in the New World and are justly proud of their history and their churches. Their towns were favored by Frey Nicolás de Ovando, who ordered a program of building and centralization in 1502. The town was governed by the famous Ponce de León from 1502–08.

Higüey is not an unpleasant town at all. It's known strictly for its huge cathedral, the **Basílica de Nuestra Señora de la Merced,** and for the pilgrims the cathedral draws from all over the Dominican Republic for blessings and absolutions. Regardless of whether you come from the south and San Rafael, or from La Romana, you can't fail to spot the huge cathedral from anywhere in town—it has the tallest carillon in the Americas. Higüey, a town of about 100,000, isn't hard to get around in, so keep your nose pointed to the basilica and you'll get there eventually.

The site of the church is allegedly the site of a miracle, this time as well (as in the case of Santo Cerro) at the expense of the poor Taíno Indians. Apparently Columbus and his men had been surprised by the Taínos and were fighting for their lives when the Virgin Mary appeared on the cross, allowing the Spaniards to repel the attack. In 1922, La Altagracia (the Virgin of the Highest Grace) became the patron saint of the country, and ever since, pilgrims have been coming to the site on January 21 and August 16. It is said that the first pilgrimage was made as early as 1669, following a promise made to the Virgin by colonists fighting a French attack. No matter when you go to the church, you'll see the afflicted and the thankful on its steps, praying, making offerings, and contemplating the mercies of the Virgin.

The modern church was built in 1952 by French architects Pierre Dupré and Dovnoyer de Segonzac. Done all in concrete, the basilica is in the shape of two folded prayerful hands, both 200 feet high. To some extent, the style resembles that of Gaudí, whose basilica dominates the skyline of Barcelona, though there is none of the surrealist baroque in Higüey's church. Whatever you think of the style, it is worth a visit, especially since beyond the cathedral, Higüey is rather drab.

Accommodations and Service
Accommodations and services in Higüey are restricted. Almost all the hotels in Higüey average under US$20 per night, and most are also located on the Calle Colón or nearby. Typical of these are the **Hotel Colón** (Calle Colón 46, tel. 809/554-4283), **Hotel Brisas del Estate** (Calle Mella, tel. 809/554-2312), **Hotel Genisis** (Calle Colón 51, tel. 809/554-2971), and the ultra-low budget hotels **Hotel Presidente** (Calle Hermanos Trejos 136, tel. 809/554-5990) and **Hotel San Juan Plaza** (Altagracia 40, tel. 809/554-3518).

When picking a hotel, watch carefully for restaurants, cafes, or discos nearby that might increase the noise levels, especially if your stay includes a weekend night. The **Hotel Topacio** (corner Duarte and Cambronal, tel. 809/554-5892) is reputed to be the top-of-the-line hotel in town, with clean rooms going for about US$30, and a downstairs restaurant that serves as one of the meeting places for Higüey's elite. **Codetel** is located on Avenida Bertillio.

Food
Everybody says the best restaurant in town is the **Gran Gourmet,** for *comida criolla* and steaks.

Located on General Santana just off Avenida Hermanos Trejo, it is about two blocks from the basilica. Other inexpensive restaurants are **Restaurant La Fama** (Arz. Nouel 2) and **Restaurante El Español Original** (Carretera Mella at Km 1).

NORTH OF HIGÜEY

La Otra Banda
When you are in the area of Higüey, it would be a shame not to drive north toward Playa Macao (ask directions in town) on the good highway for a short visit to the village of **La Otra Banda.** La Otra Banda is only a few kilometers from Higüey, located in sugarcane and cattle country of rolling hills and well-tended fields, but it is a splendidly maintained example of near-total gingerbread construction. The houses are phantasmagorias of pastel color. For some reason, the town is known for its butchers and fresh meat, and you'll see villagers displaying their food items, including fresh sausages, in front of their shops.

Playa del Muerto and Playa Macao
Continue on from La Otra Banda to the beaches at Playa del Muerto (reached over rough dirt track) and Playa Macao, where you'll find a good tourist hotel.

THE EASTERN POINT

Since the coastal road peters out beyond Coyuba, you don't have the option of continuing on to the eastern point that way. If you fly to the eastern point, you'll be doing so with a reservation for one of the luxury hotels on the beach, and you'll be met at Punta Cana Airport by a representative of your hotel with a van to carry you and your belongings. Enough said. If you happen to be driving to your luxury resort hotel on the eastern point, be sure to time your arrival before nightfall, as many of the hotels have extensive security arrangements, with gates that lock for the evening at a certain hour. Besides, the coast is hard to negotiate after dark.

If you drive, proceed north from Higüey on

the road to La Otra Banda, then past La Otra Banda a few kilometers until you reach a clearly marked right turn for the Bávaro and Punta Cana beaches. The sparsely populated countryside on this stretch is quite lovely and green. Be sure to stop at any local *coco frío* stand and try the wonderfully cool coconut juice for about RD$15 a nut, well worth the price. On some of the road on the Higüey Highway, and past La Otra Banda, you'll see characteristic Caribbean gingerbread houses covered with bougainvillea, where you can purchase *coco frío* and sit with the local matron, usually an older woman, in the shade of tall coconut trees.

On the far eastern point, there is a fairly good

road along the coast between Juanillo and El Macao. North of El Macao, the land tends to become swampy, and the road degenerates quickly, though the road inland to Miches is better. For those heading to Miches or Sabana de la Mar, it is better to pass through El Seibo.

In the unlikely event that you arrive at the eastern point by public transport, you can take camionetas from Higüey.

RESORTS

The resort experience is pretty much the same wherever you go, so pick what seems best suited to your choices. As you can see, there are a lot of rooms, styles, and price schemes from which to choose. The best thing to do is to get a bundle of brochures and spread them out all over the living room floor. Have fun.

Bávaro Beach Resort Complex

The official name of this huge complex run by Barcelo Hotels is the Bávaro Beach Resort Hotels Golf and Casino. As it now stands (it grows now and then), the complex consists of the **Bávaro Beach Hotel,** the **Bávaro Garden,** the **Bávaro Casino,** the **Bávaro Golf Apartments,** and the relatively new **Bávaro Palace.** Although the idea of the resort was to have several kinds of hotels that cater to the different tastes of guests, the names are clearly clues to their focus. The Bávaro Beach and the Bávaro Garden focus on water sports, the Bávaro Casino is near gambling, and the Golf Apartments are located on the 18-hole golf course.

For information, write Apdo. Postal 1, Punta Cana, Higüey, Dominican Republic. Again, travel agents the world over know these hotels, and they can give you brochures with price lists and activities. For general information call 809/876-6612, 800/876-6612 in the United States, fax 809/686-5859. In Santo Domingo, the general number for information on the complex can be had at the Hotel Lina, telephone 809/686-5797.

Within the complex lie an astounding 1,425 rooms in various configurations. The whole construction is arranged in the shape of a horseshoe, containing four low-rise sections, most parallel to the beach. The Bávaro Beach Hotel (tel. 809/686-5797) has 600 rooms in five four-story buildings served by elevators. The Bávaro Garden has 401 rooms in two 40-story buildings with elevators. The Bávaro Casino features 234 rooms with 64 junior suites, while the Bávaro Golf offers 126 one- or two-bedroom apartments. All of the rooms are air-conditioned, with two double beds or one double bed and a single bed, full bathroom, safety deposit box, telephone, and cash mini-bar. The apartments have equipped kitchenettes. Rates, including a modified American plan, range from US$145 per day single, US$178 double. In the off-season, they run US$100 single, US$130 double, with extra charges for suites, inclusive plans, and packages. If you get a modified American plan, you can have breakfast and dinner. The resort has a shuttle service and offers numerous opportunities for sporting activities, including some good diving and snorkeling, tennis, sailing, and golf. The complex has four swimming pools, daily aerobics, deep-sea fishing, horseback riding, an onsite bank, and a medical center. The brand-new **Bávaro Palace** offers 594 units located in six three-story buildings; all rooms are air conditioned and have a living area, two double beds or one king-sized bed, a full bathroom, cable TV, mini cash bar, and a balcony. It would be hopeless to try to list all the activities of the complex, but suffice it to say that if you want it, you can get it at the Complex, for a price. The Bavaro Palace adds three restaurants and numerous snack bars and bars to what had previously been 15 restaurants.

Melía Bávaro

The Spanish hotel chain Melía owns this resort hotel located on miles of beautiful beach surrounded by mangrove clusters. The Spanish architect Álvaro Sanz designed the hotel and grounds, and it is something of a sanctuary for birdlife. It is certainly a glitzy place with 750 suites, gardens, forested grounds, an aviary, four lighted tennis courts, seven restaurants, 10 bars, and nightly musical performances.

For information, write Playa El Cortecito, Punta Cana, Higüey, Dominican Republic, call 809/221-2311, toll free 800/336-3542, fax 809/686-5427, or consult any travel agent. Rates average US$94–202, depending upon the plan chosen, with extra for the modified American plan. Summer rates are about 25% less all around.

The Melía Bávaro is one of those places that takes fantasy one step beyond. Its beach is at least a mile long and all but 100 of its units are located in two-story bungalows very near the water. The architect created some freshwater lagoons, and an international restaurant called **El Licey** is on a pier over the artificial lagoon, while another restaurant featuring seafood is actually on an island in the middle of a swimming pool. One of the bars is a disco, floating on top of a lake. There is a swim-up bar in one of the pools. Naturally, there is also every sport you can imagine.

Keep in mind that the all-inclusive, single-place resort vacation isn't for everyone. Also keep in mind that some hotels like the Bávaro Complex don't accept credit cards. For these resorts you need to pay a travel agent the full amount in advance, and then calculate what you'll be needing once you get to the Dominican Republic. After that, it's all cash.

Other Bávaro Area Resorts

Two other all-inclusive options round out the large resort selections. The **Hodelpa Bávaro** has 336 rooms, a couple of restaurants, two pools, a gym and sauna, tennis courts, and even a theater and dance club. This hotel rents skates, motorbikes, and bicycles. Rates are reasonable at around US $80. Telephone them at 809/683-1000, fax 809/683-2303. Slightly larger is the **Hotel Carabela Bávaro Beach Resort** (tel. 809/221-2728, fax 809/221-2631); both of these resorts offer similar amenities, and both share the same lovely beach. Farther north is the Hotel Fiesta.

Also relatively new is the **Club Hotel Carabela Beach Resort** (tel. 809/221-2728, fax 809/221-2631), with 275 rooms, an inclusive plan, and all the amenities. Also new to the Bávaro area is the **Iberostar Bávaro Resort** (tel. 809/221-6500, fax 809/688-6186), a 750-room luxury resort. An old favorite is the **Fiesta Bávaro Beach Resort** (tel. 809/221-8149, fax 809/221-8150), a 900-room luxury resort.

Playa de Macao/Arena Gorda

Farther up the coast are the less-developed sections called Playa de Macao and Playa Arena Gorda, both of which can be reached by driving north of Higüey and following the signs for El Macao just north of La Otra Banda. In this area of white sand beach there are two sister hotels. The **Hotel Río Taíno** (tel. 809/221-7515, fax 809/685-9537) is a German-run luxury tourist hotel with 360 rooms and all the amenities, while the 374-room **Hotel Río Naiboa** (tel. 809/221-2290, fax 809/685-9537) is equally luxurious. The rooms are spacious and beautiful, have phone, satellite TV, air-conditioning, and terraces.

The entire stretch of coast from Playa Cabeza de Toro to Playa de Macao to El Macao, can be driven on dirt track and is basically white sand beach, though the currents are very strong on this part of the beach. Except for a few cabanas, it is undeveloped. In Macao, there is the **Hacienda Bárbara** (tel. 809/685-2594), a large inn featuring tennis and its own beach. To reach Hacienda Barbara from the United States, call 516/944-8060. **Coco's Cabañas** near El Macao are low budget and somewhat rough. This part of the beach gets a little wild, with vicious undertows and lots of stingrays.

Punta Cana Beach Resort

The Punta Cana Beach Resort is just seven km (four miles) east of the small Punta Cana Airport, and directly on one of the smoothest, most beautifully white beaches in the Dominican Republic. For information on this resort, as with all the luxury resorts of the eastern point, contact any travel agent in the world, the Dominican Tourist Information offices, or most of American Airlines' worldwide ticket bureaus. For information direct, call 809/221-2311, fax 809/686-5427. Punta Cana Beach Resort has an office in Santo Domingo at Av. Abraham Lincoln 960, and you can call in Santo Domingo at 809/541-2714, fax 809/541-2286. The number for the resort desk is 809/688-0080 or 800/972-2139, fax 809/687-8745. Prices and packages tend to vary, but you'll not pay less than US$250 per night, all-inclusive. As with any all-inclusive package, be sure to read the brochures carefully, and pay strict attention to taxes, surcharges and tips.

The people at Punta Cana Beach Resort like to tell you it is located on 105 acres and surrounded by 2,000 coconut trees. There are 340 carefully decorated rooms, and the resort has all the amenities, including air-conditioning, direct-dial telephone, safety deposit boxes, color cable TV, refrigerators, and hair dryers. The resort, like all of them on the eastern point, is totally self-contained with both buffet and à la carte restaurants, shows, orchestra dancing, a children's program, 24-hour medical staff, a gift shop, a boutique, and a local rent-a-car.

The big deal at all the resorts is sports, including water-skiing, sailing, pedal boats, water bikes, volleyball, snorkeling, windsurfing, kayaking, ping-pong, and tennis. You can take merengue lessons, learn to scuba dive, and go horseback riding as well. Naturally, there are swimming pools, spas, and a vast, strollable beach that runs, literally, for miles in either direction, north or south. Rooms come in separate villas or in double townhouses.

Whatever you want in the way of sports—fishing, diving, snorkeling, tennis, riding—the resort will provide it. The resulting experience may not be totally spontaneous, but it *is* immediate.

Club Mediterranée

Who doesn't know Club Med, that all-inclusive love feast? For the one at the eastern point, you'll find a number of ways to make reservations. Write Apdo. Postal 106, Province La Altagracia, Dominican Republic (tel. 809/687-2767, 212/750-1670 in New York, 800/CLUB-MED anywhere in the United States, fax 809/687-2896; tel. in Santo Domingo 809/687-2767, 809/686-5500, 809/567-5228, or 809/567-5229). As with all of the eastern point resorts, a travel agent anywhere in the world can get specific information about Club Med. Charter flights from Canada and Europe depart often, bound for Punta Cana Airport, and many of them contain passengers headed for Club Med. Although Club Med is apparently a unique experience, it is one I've never tried.

No matter what the experience, you'll pay approximately US$1,450 per person per week double, in midsummer US$700 per week per person double. These rates can vary depending upon the exact time of the year. Children are admitted at reduced rates, though you must check the brochures and price lists carefully.

This particular Club Med faces a white, sandy, reef-guarded beach, making it one of the best for diving and snorkeling on the whole Coconut Coast. There are 334 deluxe rooms with twin beds in three clusters of three-story townhouses. Some of the rooms face the sea; others face the pool and coconut trees of the inner courtyard. Be aware that at Club Med nobody gets a single room. If you come alone, you'll be paired with another single. There is also an annual membership fee of US$50 per adult and US$20 per child, along with a one-time initiation fee of US$30.

The heart of this Club Med is a bar, dance floor, and theater complex located at the center of the townhouses, facing the sea. You'll find the usual activities: nightly dancing, shows, and optional excursions. There are 10 tennis courts and a whole complement of water activities.

BOB RACE

THE NORTH COAST

INTRODUCTION

These days, Dominican tourist officials call their north coast the Amber Coast. Though it is true that vast amber deposits are found in the coastal mountains, this new appellation is mainly a way of adding a patina of luxuriousness to what's already one of the world's most popular destinations. Indeed, the past 20 years has seen a steady growth in activity along the north coast, the building of many luxury tourist resorts, repaving and patching of roads, improved airline services, and the incessant homogenization of cultural productions like food, entertainment, and sport. In fact, some parts of the north coast threaten to become one long international pleasure fair featuring sun-worshipers from all over the world.

The northern coast of the Dominican Republic from Puerto Plata to the town of Nagua is a windy 150-km stretch of beach, cliff, palm forest, and grassland. Highway 5, which connects all the towns from Puerto Plata to the Samaná Bay, like its counterpart on the south coast, is a beautiful and easily driveable stretch of road, one of the nicest in the country for the casual driver and tourist. The coastline takes in the provinces of Puerto Plata, Espaillat, and María Trinidad Sánchez and is backed by the Septentrional Mountains, which decline slowly and recede into the background as one goes east. There are many famous beaches along the way: Playa Sosúa, Playa Cabarete, Punta Goleta, Playa La Ermita, Playa Río San Juan, Playa Grande, Playa El Caletón, Playa El Bretón, Playa Diamante, and Playa Poza de Bojolo. At Sabaneta along the highway between Sosúa and Gaspar Hernández is the spectacular turnoff for the over-mountain road to Jamao al Norte and Moca. Highway 5 is ultimately the gateway to the beautiful Samaná Peninsula, where there are more sublime beaches, wild national park areas, and incredible marine environments.

Land and Climate

As tourist officials might say, the thing that makes the Amber Coast so alluring is its lovely climate and its recreational possibilities. The Dominican Republic's northern Atlantic coast stretches nearly 300km from the Haitian border to the beginning of the Samaná peninsula. Probably half of that length is made up of delicate white sand beach. Some parts of the coast are bounded by elegant reef systems, particularly in the western sections less frequented by tourists. The water is shallow toward the

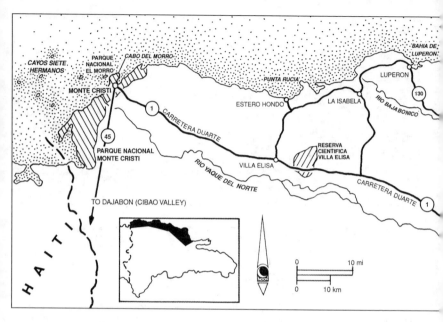

coast and deeper than average farther out to sea, which makes for good swimming and excellent fishing. Winds can be high, particularly in the late winter season, thus increasing the likelihood of good windsurfing and sailing weather. At all times of the year, the steady breeze moderates the warm temperatures.

History

On Columbus's first exploratory sail-by of the island in 1492, it was the north coast that attracted the Admiral's attention. Near the border of Haiti he founded an early settlement called La Navidad, but returning on his second voyage, he found that the settlement had vanished. Thereafter, he founded a second settlement called La Isabela. It wasn't long before all of the early Spanish conquistadors turned their attention to the Cibao valley and its legends of gold, then to the south coast, which faced the new conquests in South America and Mexico. Only at Puerto Plata did the Spaniards find something worth having: a good port.

For 300 years, the north coast was a dirty colonial backwater, nothing more. Puerto Plata

was the only city of any size, and it was essentially a banana port, exporting fruit to North America and Europe. More and more, however, the port business was going to the emergent Santo Domingo, until finally, there was almost nothing left for Puerto Plata to do. Of course, sugarcane brought some wealth to the area, as did the growing of tropical fruits and vegetables, but the area was very isolated from the rest of the country, separated from the fertile Cibao by the steep Cordillera Septentrional and the economic dominance of the valley by Santiago and La Vega. In fact, it was not until 1922 that a road linked Santiago and Santo Domingo with Puerto Plata, much less the rest of the north coast. In an early travelogue written in the 1940s, one writer said, "Puerto Plata is a friendly place of about seventeen thousand. Its size is of no particular importance." The writer went on to remark that Puerto Plata was relatively less receptive to tourists because so few were seen, much fewer in fact than in Santo Domingo.

My, how things have changed. Blink your eyes,

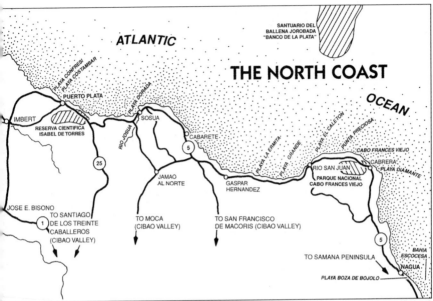

THE NORTH COAST

© AVALON TRAVEL PUBLISHING, INC.

and you'd think there was nothing *but* tourists in Puerto Plata. However, it is still possible to see vestiges of the old north coast—the coast of bananas, sugarcane, rum, and wild ocean waves. As in so much of the Dominican Republic, the eye of the beholder is everything here.

Getting There

One thing that makes the north coast so accessible is La Unión International Airport (it's formal name is Aeropuerto International Luperón), just about 20 minutes by taxi to the east of Puerto Plata, smack in the middle of

---

THE WRECK OF THE *CONCEPCIÓN*

In late October 1641, a huge hurricane battered Hispaniola's north coast. That year the lead ship of the silver fleet was a huge galleon called *Concepción,* which was badly mauled by the storm. It drifted into the Silver Banks 60 nautical miles north of Puerto Plata and hit a reef. The huge ship sank with all her silver, a treasure of freshly minted coins. After the storm passed, the Spanish on Hispaniola attempted to recover the treasure but were unsuccessful due to dangerous reef-bound waters and weather.

Forty-five years later, a New Englander named William Phipps, backed by London investors, sailed to the Silver Banks intending to raise the treasure.

Phipps organized his investigation by trading in Puerto Plata and Santiago for hides, wood, meat, and tobacco, and he hired pearl divers. Surprisingly, he was successful in raising 69,000 pounds of silver and 25 pounds of gold—worth about 225,000 English pounds, a hefty sum in 1698. The English government took a 10% cut and knighted Phipps, who later became governor of Massachusetts colony.

In 1979 the Dominican government allowed American Burt Webber to dive for more *Concepción* treasure, and he recovered tons of silver overlooked by Phipps. The treasure was split 50–50 between the Dominican government and Webber.

the tourist action. Also, the main road linking all the coastal towns from Playa Cofresí all the way to the Samaná peninsula is excellent, beautiful, and uncrowded. Finally, the north coast is now linked to Santo Domingo (235km away) and Santiago by the generally good Duarte Highway, with its turnoff to Puerto Plata north of Santiago. Even the cross-mountain roads at Imbert, the Moca-Jamao al Norte route, and the San Francisco-Nagua road are all excellent; the Moca-Jamao road is particularly scenic.

PUERTO PLATA AND VICINITY

In places like Punta Cana, Juan Dolio, and Guayacanes—all major tourist destinations in the Dominican Republic—there is, in the words of Gertrude Stein, "no there there." First there is a white beach, then there is a hotel, and then there is a pizza and hot dog stand. Finally, something like a town emerges, though it resembles a Frankenstein of international design. Puerto Plata, on the other hand, is a real place, a very historic town, with its own distinct personality, despite the fact that everywhere you look this personality is under assault by the forces of international tourism, cable TV, homogenized food, and the English language.

Puerto Plata itself is no longer a provincial town of 17,000 residents and of "no particular importance." It has grown to a major center with a population of about 200,000, many of these newcomers during the 1990s. Many inhabitants are involved in one way or another in tourism and its supporting service industries, though a significant percentage of citizens still works in sugar, sugar processing, and rum trades. The original architecture of Puerto Plata was pure Victorian gingerbread, and houses survive today with typical balconies, ornamental terraces and windows, bright colors, gardens, and courtyards. These days, those original houses are under considerable pressure from economic forces, and even as we speak, some are being demolished to make way for modern cement block buildings to house the latest franchise food delivery system.

As an economic center, Puerto Plata hangs on to something like 12% of the shipping or export trade in the country and handles about 2% of imports. Santo Domingo dominates the rest. The country surrounding Puerto Plata is well known for its production of sugar, coffee, cacao, tobacco, rum, and dairy products.

HISTORY

Puerto Plata could easily have been the first town in the New World. Columbus, coasting the region, spotted the fine port, but storms forced him to land near the Haitian border where he quickly—and disastrously—founded La Isabela, a colony of 39 sailors. His original report about sighting the small bay included his vision of the mountains, which, he thought, shone like silver when covered in mist. Even today, the high mountains behind Puerto Plata can suddenly cloud over and become silver, all in a matter of a few minutes. Puerto Plata became a town in 1502, when Nicolás de Ovando, on Columbus's orders, established a settlement to take advantage of the small bay which provided the only cover for ships on the whole north coast of Hispaniola.

For a few brief years, during the heyday of the Spanish empire in the New World, Puerto Plata lived up to its name by being one of the jumping-off points for galleons heading back to Spain. This period lasted only three decades, and by the early 17th century, the whole coast became infested with pirates of many nationalities, leading the Spanish authorities to actually destroy the town in order to save it. It was in Puerto Plata during the early 16th century that the famous priest Las Casas began his epic history, *Apologética Historia de los Indios,* considered to be the most eloquent defense of the Taínos, and other native peoples, ever written.

Reestablished as a "free port" in 1750, Puerto Plata shared much of the history of Dominican unhappiness: war with Haiti, economic decay, and political confusion. When Cubans began pouring into the Dominican Republic and began establishing sugar plantations and farms, the fortunes of Puerto Plata took a turn for the bet-

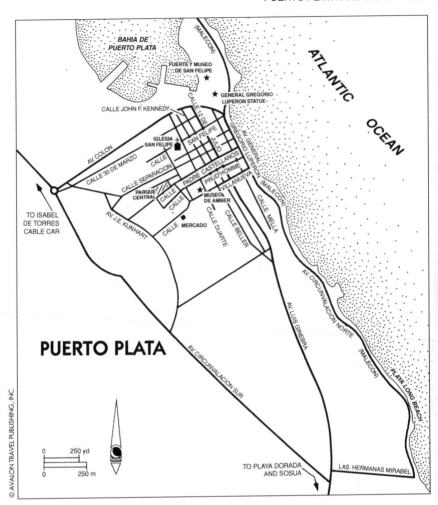

PUERTO PLATA

ter. During the period 1820–1920, the economic outlook for the north coast stabilized, some trading developed, and many of the architectural gems known as Caribbean gingerbread were built.

Tourism Boomtown

During the early 1970s, the Dominican government under Balaguer established a government agency known as Infratur—part of the

Central Bank—to begin developing a tourism village known as Playa Dorada, only three kilometers east of Puerto Plata. Playa Dorada, with its long sandy beach, succeeded beyond anyone's wildest dreams, and Puerto Plata (and, indeed, the whole north coast east of Luperón) grew wildly.

As the area grows, Puerto Plata inevitably is losing some of its style. Even the beaches surrounding Puerto Plata—Costambar, Cofresí,

Long Beach, Sosúa, and Cabarete—are heading toward a great leveling into one luxury resort. Nevertheless, there are small hotels, real downtowns, and local restaurants with charm and individuality. You can choose to stay in the heart of Puerto Plata and seek out the smaller town that feels much like an older Antillean city. There are many villages up and down the coast in either direction from Puerto Plata where island flavor still exists; but with a host of cruise ships arriving in the old port and the abundance of major luxury resorts, it is difficult to escape the press of tourism and its common problems, crowding, homogenization, petty theft, and bustle.

Nevertheless, as you wander around Puerto Plata, try to imagine the old girl as she was only a century ago, and recall what she has contributed to Dominican history. Columbus reached the bay of Puerto Plata on January 11, 1493. The sugarcane brought by Columbus was first planted on Hispaniola at Puerto Plata. Puerto Plata has also contributed to the Dominican Republic the famous general of the Restoration, Gregorio Luperón, and the poet and educator Emilio Prud'Homme, author of the lyrics to the Dominican National Anthem. Even today, *El Porvenir,* a newspaper edited in Puerto Plata since 1873, is considered the most venerable in the nation.

SIGHTS

Beaches

Beaches are the single greatest attraction in and around Puerto Plata. In the stretch of coast in and around Puerto Plata, you'll find nearly 11km of white beach. The main public beach for Puerto Plata is **Long Beach,** located just to the east of Puerto Plata, along the Malecón. **Playa de Long Beach** is the public, urban beach for Puerto Plata, and as such is rather tatty, crowded on weekends, and unlovely, despite the almond trees and coconut palms that crowd the sand. On weekends, Long Beach is nutty, and petty theft isn't uncommon, so watch your things. On the other hand, it is an authentic Dominican place, and when the wind blows, waves pile up around the offshore rocks in a spectacular display. Unfortunately, so does garbage.

To the west of Puerto Plata are several more isolated beaches, including **Punta Rucia,** which has a large vacation resort, and other reachable and secluded beaches like **Playa Goya** and **La Encenada.** You'll probably need help and directions to reach these secluded spots.

Both **Cofresí** and **Costambar** beaches are located west of Puerto Plata and are now dominated by luxury resorts. Supposedly, all beaches in the Republic are owned by the public, but it is difficult to make your way to these beaches, though you may try if you wish. Cofresí is about a kilometer long and backed by coconut palms, with a splendid view of the coast. Costambar is slightly less developed, shaded by almond trees. The beaches in and around Puerto Plata are fronted by coral reefs, so you can dive and snorkel when the tides are good.

In the vicinity of Puerto Plata lies **Playa Dorada,** the famous luxury resort beach on an inlet protected by a coral reef. The beach has an amazing 24km (15 miles) of white sand. Up and down the coast are other beaches like **Cabarete, Boca de Cangrejo, Cano Grande, Bergantin, Playa de Copello,** and **Playa Mariposa.** To the west of Puerto Plata is a favorite, the shaded **Guarapitao Beach.** If you think you're having trouble locating some of these more unknown beaches for an outing, you'll surely come across a local "tour guide" on the street to help you. However, beware of entanglements with these young guys; don't get too involved to notice what is really going down.

Downtown

Historic Puerto Plata is actually rather compact, an enjoyable afternoon of walking, sightseeing, and shopping. The hub of life in old Puerto Plata is the central park, sometimes called **Parque Luperón,** sometimes called Parque Central. It is bounded by Calle John Kennedy, Separación, and Calle Beller. It is in this vicinity that you'll see the most Victorian gingerbread, survivors of the current wave of tourism and commercial development. Take a good, hard look, because these elegant dames may be gone soon. You'll find many gift and souvenir shops in the area, and numerous cafes and cafeterias for a quick bite to eat and something cool to drink. Public structures also line the central park, including the modish art-deco church, **Iglesia de San Felipe,** which is worth peeking into, though it has lit-

Fuerte San Felipe

tle historical resonance. Nearby is the **Club Comercio** and the **Sociedad Fe en el Porvenir** (Society to Preserve the Faith). Considered a sight, the **Mercado** located south of the central park just off Villanueva isn't much, but it is a lively place to find fruits, vegetables, clothes, and oddball things for sale.

El Museo de Ámbar

Perhaps the most self-conscious tourist sight in the whole city is the widely advertised El Museo de Ámbar (Amber Museum), which you will see as you meander north of the market at the corner of Calle Prud'Homme and Calle Duarte. Located on the second floor of a Victorian mansion, the museum is open 9 A.M.–5 P.M. every day except Sunday (tel. 809/586-2848), and it's a big draw. It boasts a roof area for viewing, a cafe in the back, and a shop downstairs. Here you'll also find collections of fossilized resin from a type of pine long since exterminated by logging in the area. Some of the transparent pieces contain trapped centipedes and crickets, leaves, and other objects. Unfortunately, the museum is often jammed with tourists, and the surroundings can get loaded near their buses. If you're staying in town, try to time your visit to avoid the hordes. Admission is RD$30.

Fuerte San Felipe

If you're on foot, the Malecón heading west leads straight to the Fuerte San Felipe (San Felipe Fort), located on a small peninsula on the Bahía de Puerto Plata, the bay Columbus once had such high hopes for. The fort is, in fact, the only vestige of Puerto Plata's colonial past. For an admission fee of RD$10, you'll be able to look in on a small historical museum, and the tiny cell in which the hero of the Independence movement, Juan Pablo Duarte, was briefly confined. You'll certainly find a number of "independent guides" hanging around the entrance to the fort who, for a small fee, will give you a tour. They aren't particularly necessary, as the museum isn't extensive, or very exciting for that matter, but they seem earnest and need the work.

By 1541, when the construction on the fort was commenced, Puerto Plata was being threatened by the earliest pirates, a motley collection of Dutch and French sailors. When completed in 1577, the fort had already outlived its usefulness, as history had passed Puerto Plata by. Visiting the fort is, however, rather a spooky experience, given its idyllic setting, the coral-encrusted moat, and the historical whispers that seem almost audible. Many visitors to Puerto Plata head straight for the beaches and discos, and the fort seems rather lonely.

General Gregorio Luperón Statue

Just up from the fort is a large statue of General Gregorio Luperón on horseback. Luperón led the resistance to Spanish colonial rule from 1860–65, and when it came time for him to rule,

RESERVA CIENTÍFICA ISABEL DE TORRES

Perhaps the most popular, and invigorating, place to visit outside Puerto Plata is the **Reserva Científica Isabel de Torres,** located only about one kilometer outside the eastern city limits. You can't miss seeing **Loma Isabel de Torres,** a lofty mountain behind the city. Perhaps it is this mountain which caused Columbus to name the city as he did, after the silver mist which accumulates on its 800-meter (2,595-foot) peak. In the past, the peak had a tower and a fort, built under Trujillo, but now the entire mountain is a scientific reserve and botanical garden, and the fort and outbuildings are souvenir shops and a café. A statue of Christ the Redeemer, similar to the one in Rio de Janeiro, dominates the area. To reach the peak, follow Calle Colón at the western edge of Puerto Plata to the main Santo Domingo Highway going west. You can't miss the parking lot for the cable car *(teleférico),* a tingling seven-minute ascent up the mountain's nearly vertical slope that costs RD$20. In recent years, the cable-car system has been undergoing significant repairs and is often shut down. The cable car, botanical gardens, café, and shops are open Tuesday and Thursday–Sunday 8 A.M.–5 P.M. There are often long lines to make the ascent, so be prepared for waits, and for occasional breakdowns. This ride is not for the faint hearted. On last inspection, the road up Isabel de Torres was in terrible condition, a bone-shaker. In rain, big rocks tend to slide down the side walls and create a hazard to drivers. The north side of the mountain is now marked by a landslide scar.

Land, Flora, and Fauna
Geologically, Loma de Isabel de Torres is made of silt and marl. There are nearly 15 small brooks and streams rising in its area. From the steamy coast, temperatures are nearly 15°C (30°F) cooler on top, with average summit temperatures of 17°C, and fog and wind common. Often rain sweeps the mountain top, while the coast remains in full sun; in fact, the average yearly rainfall in the botanical garden is 1,800mm. The vegetation on top is mainly subtropical low mountain forest. Characteristic of the gardens are the sierra palm, tamarind, satinleaf, Jamaica nectandra, Hispaniolan mahogany, copey, catalpa, and mara. Birders have spotted 32 species in the area, including the palm chat, Hispaniolan woodpecker, honeycreeper, and more rarely, the common ground dove, the Hispaniolan parrot, plain pigeon, limpkin, and red-tailed hawk. Views from the mountain terraces are spectacular, and you can see down the coasts for many miles. In winter, the panorama is brightened by the emergence of the orange blossom of immortelle, or the red of amapola.

he made Puerto Plata briefly the capital of the newly integrated country. The fort area and its museum—displaying old cannonballs, coins, and weapons—as well as the grounds, the moat, and the statue of General Luperón can be seen in a very short time. Still, the area is truly unique, alive with color and passion.

The Malecón
Needless to say, the Malecón is a sight unto itself. Running directly along the oceanfront, the Malecón is the center of the town's social life. On its urban run, the Malecón strikes through the heart of the commercial part of Puerto Plata with a narrow walk on the ocean side of the street, a wall, and then the pounding surf. Going east, more hotels appear; palms and almond trees begin to pile up behind the street, and then there are more small hotels and open-air bars and cafes. The Malecón goes all the way to the Long Beach area, and it is easily walkable. Nowdays, the Malecón is a little dirty and rundown, but it is still an exciting place almost any night of the week, especially on weekends.

Brugal Rum Distillery
The Brugal Rum Distillery is located less than a kilometer east of the town limits on the main

Sosúa-Playa Dorada highway, or from town on Avenida Luis Ginebra, which cuts away from John Kennedy. The distillery is open every day of the week except Saturday and Sunday, from 9 A.M.–noon and 2 P.M.–5 P.M. There is no admission charge, and you will be met in a reception area by a pleasant guide who will escort you inside the huge distillery which produces about a million and a half liters of white and dark rum each year. Almost all the Brugal production is consumed in the Dominican Republic, the rest consumed on nearby Caribbean islands. There isn't much to do on the tour, as actual distillation isn't done on site. The plant is strictly a bottling operation. Nevertheless, the guides are pleasant, and the reception area will serve you *great* drinks at the end, all in an open-air and breezy tile-floored room. Of course, you can buy slightly discounted rum by the liter, and expensive souvenirs.

Area Tours

Many major tour companies have main or branch offices in or near Puerto Plata. Some of them can even take you as far as the Samaná peninsula, and will organize boat trips to Parque Nacional Los Haitises, though it is a long way off. The **tourist information office** is on the Malecón #25, and you can call the private **Association of Tour Guides** at 809/586-2866. The offices are located at Av. J.F. Kennedy #5 and they may answer questions and lead you to the proper tour company. Private guides can be good for groups wanting to visit secluded or less-developed beaches west of Puerto Plata, like Punta Rucia and Playa Guzman. Major tour companies include **Go Caribic** (Ave. Luis Ginebra, Plaza Turisol 55, tel 809/586-4075), **Apolo Tours** (J.F. Kennedy 15, tel. 809/586-2751), and **Prieto Tours** branch (tel. 809/685-0102 in Santo Domingo for information) or in Puerto Plata at **Calle Marginal** (tel. 809/586-3988). Others include **Agencia de Viajes Cafembra** (Calle Separación 12, tel. 809/586-2177), the small **Agencia de Viajes Victoria** (Calle Duarte 59, tel. 809/586-3744), and **Vimenea Tours** (tel. 809/586-3833). All of these can arrange extensive north coast trips, national park tours, and water sports. The local Yellow Pages, or *Páginas Amarillas,* are very helpful and up to date.

The influx of tourists to Playa Dorada has hurt Puerto Plata in some ways. Package tourists on all-inclusive hotels rarely leave their cages long enough to spend any money in the town. Some do, however, go on tours, which has led to the recent establishment of new groups on the north coast like Iguana Mama. In town, **Rum Runners** (Plaza Isabela, tel. 809/586-6155) runs interesting jeep tours into the mountains both west and east along the coast. **Freestyle Catamarans** (tel. 809/586-1239) can set up sailing trips to Sosúa and back for about US$50. The aforementioned Go Caribic is less formal but can arrange just about any kind of tour or adventure.

Puerto Plata abounds in "local guides," usually young men who porter tourists. They're a hassle and not worth the trouble. Refuse firmly and move on.

ACCOMMODATIONS

There are three ways to go when you're staying in or near Puerto Plata. First, you can stay downtown, where you'll be close to the real Puerto Plata. From downtown, you can walk to the tourist attractions and the Malecón, or take one of the ubiquitous cheap taxis and *motoconchos* to the many beaches for swimming. The hotels of Puerto Plata, save for two, are moderate or inexpensive in price and offer solid value. The second lodging option in the Puerto Plata area is to stay in Long Beach. Long Beach used to be a center for tourist activity, but with the building of so many rooms at Playa Dorada, Sosúa, Cofresí, and Costambar resorts, it seems a bit faded. Still, there are some fine hotels on Long Beach, which leaves the visitor with a short stroll into town for shopping and sight-seeing. Finally, there is the all-inclusive resort option, where the experience you'll have will be similar to those available at Punta Cana, Juan Dolio, or Villas del Mar.

Inexpensive

There are many inexpensive places to stay in downtown Puerto Plata and out on Long Beach. Some are good, some not. Choices downtown include the **Hotel El Condado** (Av. Circunvalación Sur, M.T. Juto 45, tel. 809/586-3255) and the central **Hotel Castilla** (J.F. Kennedy 36, tel. 809/586-3736). Out on Long Beach, try

Hotel Beach (tel. 809/586-3736). It's inexpensive, but some rooms have air-conditioning, and there are a few bungalows; it's a fave with backpackers. You can walk to the beach, just across the street. It has been, off and on, a bordello. The cautious traveler might want to check before making any commitments.

There are some really cheap places to stay in town, including **Hotel Atlántico** (Av. 12 de Julio, near Caribe Tours), which includes basic rooms for US$10 with a fan and bath, or air-conditioned rooms for slightly more. Call them at 809/586-6108. Also for budget travelers is the rather run-down **Hotel Dilone** (Calle 30 de Marzo, next to Beach Hotel). Other inexpensive spots include the **Hotel Ilra** (Villanueva 25, tel. 809/586-2337), **Hotel Dona Julia** (San Felipe 11, tel. 809/586-6440), **Hotel Martin** (30 de Marzo 40, tel. 809/586-4616), **Hotel Guaronia** (12 de Julio 76, tel. 809/586-2109), and **Hotel Comedor Glenn** (Ortega 5, near Calle Beller, tel. 809/586-4644). Finally, there is the low-budget **Hotel Alfa** at Calle Padre Castellanos 20, tel. 809/586-2648. Most of these low-budget hotels have no more than 25 rooms. Many have shared baths, mosquito nets, fans, and quite a bit of noise.

A contender for best-buy is the **Hotel Victoriano** (San Felipe 33, tel. 809/586-9752). Its 25 rooms are large and clean, and each has cable TV and hot bathrooms. Rooms are either fan cooled or air conditioned, and there is a generator. Doubles are US$13–18. Slightly higher up the scale are the **Portofino Guest House** (Av. Hermanas Mirabal, tel. 809/506-2858) and the **Aparta-Hotel Lomar** on the Malecón.

Moderate

Probably the queen of downtown hotels is the **Hotel Jimessón** (Av. John F. Kennedy 41, tel. 809/586-5131, fax 809/586-6313), which has 22 rooms close to the central park in town. This hotel looks like an old colonial home and is furnished with antiques in the lobby. Many of the rooms are in a modern building in back and are air-conditioned and clean, with cable TV. Word has it that the old queen has slipped quite a bit recently and is experiencing both water and power problems. A good alternative on the Malecón near the Puerto Plata Beach resort is the **Apart-Hotel Lomar** where there seems to be plenty of hot water, a generator, and rooms

with balconies overlooking a pool. Rates are around US$45 in season, half that in the summer. There is no restaurant. In the same price category, but different in atmosphere, is the **Hotel Puerto Plata Latin Quarter** (Malecón, tel. 809/586-2770, fax 809/586-1828), which has very comfortable rooms, a pool, and a decent restaurant for US$35 single, US$45 double. In the same moderately priced category, but slightly outside of town, are the **Mountain View Hotel** (Av. J.E. Kundhardt, tel. 809/586-5757), with 22 air-conditioned rooms, a pool, piano bar, and restaurant, and the new **Hotel Marapica** (Santo Domingo Highway Km 21, tel. 809/541-1796, fax 809/549-5943), with 126 rooms, pool, and air-conditioning. For an unusual stay, the moderately priced **Hotel Restaurante El Indio** (on Plaza Anacaona, 30 de Marzo 94–98, tel. 809/586-1201), is a bargain at about US$35. This German-owned hotel is just the place to relax in town, and the owners can provide you with information on travel and tours, especially about scuba diving and snorkeling adventures. There is a patio and garden, occasional live guitar music, and a good restaurant for quiet breakfasts and seafood dinners. On the Malecón, the **Hotel Carocol** (tel. 809/586-2588) is a modestly priced resort-type hotel with about 50 air-conditioned rooms, cable TV, terrace, pool, piano bar, and disco-nightclub. You can walk to the beach. **Sofy's Bed and Breakfast** (Las Rosas 3, tel. 809/586-6411) is located in a private home with only two rooms rented to travelers. You get a large room, an excellent breakfast, and laundry service, all for about US$40.

Expensive

The **Hotel Montemar** (Hermanas Mirabeal, P.O. Box 382, tel. 809/586-2800, fax 809/586-2009, tlx. 809/346-2019), on Long Beach, has 95 rooms, suites, and bungalows, and a special bus to Playa Mara Pica, where you can swim. If you stay here, you'll be offered a package of three meals and all beverages, which can boost the rates to more than US$80. The hotel offers bus service to Playa Dorada and local casinos. Directly across the street from Long Beach, this hotel has some unusual and attractive features. First of all, it has a very distinctive lobby, with bamboo chandeliers and an impressive wall-wide mural behind the desk. Secondly, the hotel is home to a regional hotel management school, so you are served by students who are very, very eager to please you. There are two tennis courts, and the bar/disco has live merengue every night under illuminated palms, a pretty cool scene, all in all. This pioneer resort is a good value, especially as an alternative to Occidental Playa Dorada.

Probably the nicest resort-type hotel in Puerto Plata is the **Puerto Plata Beach Resort and Casino** (Los Piños 7, tel. 809/586-2423). It's actually on the Malecón and has beautiful gardens, a casino, swimming pools, and over 200 balconied rooms, suites, and deluxe Victorian Club Suites in several small, pastel buildings. The restaurants are good, and there is plenty to do, from two restaurants to a disco, jazz bar, cafe, planned water sports, and tours. Puerto Plata Beach Resort and Casino is managed by AMHSA and is a well-run, friendly alternative to Occidental Playa Dorada. Besides being on Long Beach, the resort is within easy walking distance of local nightclubs and restaurants, and unlike Occidental Playa Dorada, does not have that imprisoned feeling. From anywhere in the Dominican Republic, call 800/752-9326, fax 800/320-4858. From the United States call 800/472-3985. All-inclusive rooms are generally in the US$110 range, but you should consult a travel agent to nail down the exact rate before you reserve. Rates vary here and you might be able to negotiate a special deal on the spot. Give it a try for half price or less!

FOOD

As time passes, Puerto Plata fills with quick and inexpensive sandwich shops, pizza and ice cream joints, and international quick shops geared to specific national tastes. You can find both a New York Deli–style sandwich and a "Quebec menu" at the **Restaurant 26** (tel. 809/586-3876) at the Puerto Plata Rotonda. "Quebec menu" means that Moosehead Beer is served, and the satellite dish is aimed at some hockey game or another. Many mini-markets, *colmados,* and *supermercados* also cater to those wanting snacks and fresh food for their kitchenettes. All of the luxury beach resorts have

restaurants, some more than one, which cater to international tastes. Nevertheless, several good restaurants, cafes, and cafeterias in Puerto Plata still retain some individuality and flair.

Inexpensive

Naturally, you'll find many cafes and cafeterias here where you can get the quick Cuban sandwich. The **No Name Pub** on Calle Colón is good, and there are numerous stalls and vendors at Long Beach for empanadas and sandwiches. The **Pepe Postre** is the name of a pastry chain (Av. Colón 24), and the **El Burrito** on the Malecón serves quick-style Mexican food. There are some beachside restaurants and cafes at Long Beach, including **La Paella, El Cable, Swiss Garden,** and **Tex-Mex.** Just stroll down the Malecón and you can't miss finding a cafe or terrace bar worth a short visit. For special sweet treats and fresh bread, try **El Dorado** at Duarte and San Felipe. For a splash of Europe, visitors to Long Beach should try **Don Pedro, Restaurant Mozart,** and **Marie Andres,** all of which serve good food at moderate prices, mostly regional European cuisines.

Finally, there are two places serving "international" modern cuisine. Set at the Playa Dorada Plaza, **Hemingway's Cafe** serves burgers, nachos, steaks, pasta, and ribs, as well as pitchers of cold beer from all over the world. The place opens at noon and quickly fills with an international tourist set. Call them at 809/320-2230. The **Mi Bohio** steak house (with seafood), at Av. Mando Tavárez Justo (tel. 809/586-8042), has a thatched atmosphere, with outside dining for dinner.

Moderate

Should the desire for middle-European food come over you, try **Hansi's Wienerwald,** a beachside cafe good for quick food from a place near the beach with a few tables and some stools. Located on Long Beach (tel. 809/586-2551), you can get omelettes and real strawberry jam. A good local place for Italian is the **Pizzeria Roma II,** near the Parque Central. You can get both pizza and paella, and the pizzas are excellent. It's located on Calle Beller (tel. 809/586-3904). For good and less-expensive local food, try the **Plaza Los Mesones** (corner Separación and Beller, across from Parque Central), where you can get Dominican *pica-pollo* and seafood. Good basic Dominican food is also available at the **Plaza Cafe** (Calle 30 de Marzo, near Beller), the **Star Cafe** (Calle Beller 87), and **La Canasta** (two blocks north of Parque Central), all of which serve both lunch and dinner. The **El Español,** on Av. Circunvalación Sur (tel. 809/586-1655), has Spanish and international dishes moderate in price, yet served in good surroundings. The **Portofino** in the hotel district on Avenida Mirabal also serves good pizza and Italian dishes on an outdoor terrace. On the Malecón near Calle Separación, **Oceanico** serves Italian-style seafood. Also on or near Calle Separación is **La Carreta,** the **Victorian Pub,** and the **Roma II** (this last near Calle Beller at Prud'Homme), all serving seafood and *comida criolla* at moderate prices. The restaurant **Camacho** on the east central part of the Malecón is an unpretentious place serving good *comida criolla.* You can get a view of the slightly decrepit statue of Neptune from its windows.

Expats and people-watching are featured at several Puerto Plata spots. **Sams Bar and Grill** (Ariza 34) is the official American hangout, with strictly a Chuck Berry atmosphere, Philly cheesesteak and burrito menu, and pancake breakfasts. Lunch is about US$4. **Anna's Bar and Grill** (Ave. Colón 59) is an English-style sports bar with ribs and good beer. The **Café del Sandwich** (Calle Kennedy at Ariza) serves the best Cuban sandwiches in town. The nearby **Palanco** serves quality budget Dominican food all day, with appetizing breakfasts too.

Expensive

For me, an expensive meal is anything US$10–25. Probably the cream of the crop in expensive (and good) restaurants in Puerto Plata is **De Armando** (Av. Antera Mota 23, tel. 809/586-3418), which serves a variety of international dishes in a pleasant setting where soft, live music is often playing. The specialty is seafood, *comida criolla,* and homemade desserts. This is the place to spend some money on great lobster, and on desserts like majarete, cocoyuca, and flán with coconut. Near the central park, De Armando is a good one to walk to. **Valter's** (Av. Las Hermanas Mirabel, tel. 809/586-2329) serves pasta dishes and "surf and turf" in a Victorian house painted lime green.

It's in the center of town and you can hang out on the low-slung Victorian porch. De Armando is open every day until 11 P.M., while Valter's is open for lunch Tue.–Sun., and for dinner until 11 P.M. every day except Monday. At the hotels, try **La Isabela** in the Hotel Montemar on the Malecón (tel. 809/586-2800) for seafood and steak and a good selection of desserts. The **Neptune Bar and Grill** in the Puerto Plata Beach Resort is also good for seafood and meat dishes and is open for lunch. **Los Piños** (Av. Hermanas Mirabal, tel. 809/586-3222) has good steak, lobster, and *comida criolla.* In all of these restaurants, it is advisable to make reservations in advance, if possible.

Several newer restaurants are also quite good. In particular, the **Acurarela** (Professor Certos 3, tel. 809/586-5314) is in an elegant setting and serves things like lobster and rack of lamb. The **Otro Mundo** (Carratera 5) is east of Playa Dorada in an old Victorian mansion and serves wild dishes like tempura frog legs. The owner lets wild animals run the fenced grounds! Call and a taxi will pick you up at your hotel for the ride out to dinner. Less expensive, but a great spot, is the popular **Cafe Cito,** at San Felipe 23. Here you get a quiet courtyard, jazzy and great food. Expensive but worth it.

ENTERTAINMENT AND EVENTS

Like so many places dominated by tourism, Puerto Plata tends to have a frenetic nightlife. So many people come to party that it can wear you down, unless partying is your specific goal, as well. As always, the luxury tourist complexes at Occidental Playa Dorada, Cofresí, and Costambar have their own self-contained discos, nightclubs, and piano bars that cater to all-inclusive guests of those particular resorts.

As usual, local sports and recreation are focused in the tourist complexes, which specialize in water sports, golf, and tennis. Do-it-yourselfers are not, however, without considerable resources. Deep-sea fishing isn't as good on the north coast as it is in the southeast and southwest, but the diving, snorkeling, and windsurfing are terrific here. To the west of Puerto Plata in particular, you'll find many shallow water reef systems, some not much frequented by visitors.

statue of Christ the Redeemer, Isabel de Torres, Puerto Plata

LEO DE WYS

Nightlife

I have to admit that international disco makes me a bit woozy, especially the kind that blends a watered-down, over-produced Michael Jackson style with psycho-cybernetic synthetic rhythms. Unfortunately, there's a lot of that going around in Puerto Plata. It's like the Bee Gees on serious psychedelics. However, the beat goes on and on at the infamously popular **Vivaldi's** (Av. Las Hermanas Mirabal at the Malecón, tel. 809/586-3753), where the ground floor disco (there's a small restaurant above) is composed of neon wrap and heavy-duty sparklies. There is an admission charge of RD$20, and drinks cost from RD$25 for beer to RD$100 for rum mixes. It's wall to wall and moving all the time, especially late. The disco opens at 9 P.M. A suitable competitor to Vivaldi's is **La Lechuza** (The Owl), located in the Puerto Plata Beach Resort. Down the street from Vivaldi's is the bar and club in **Los Piños,** which has a nice atmosphere.

An air of heavy-duty machismo pervades the **Rock Cafe,** where sunburned northerners hang out (Av. Circunvalación), and on the same road with the same machismo is **Willy's Sports Center Restaurant.** The **Orion** is a more deliberately paced nightclub with some live music and a cover charge that varies with the type of band appearing that night. The Orion is on Av. 16 de Julio at 30 de Marzo. You can sometimes find real merengue or salsa on weekends at **Cafetería Los Bonilla** at Las Javillas. At other times this spot features canned disco.

Bars are a dime a dozen in Puerto Plata. There is a knock-off **Hard Rock Cafe** downtown, and on the Malecón is **Paco's Bananas** near Avenida Hermanas Mirabal, west of Long Beach.

The **Heavens Hotel** has a quiet disco (imagine that), while outside of town the **Mermaid** plays disco loud all night. The **El Príncipe** has live shows, near Cofresí on the highway.

Although Puerto Plata isn't exactly Kathmandu, the counterculture—as it currently exists—is represented at the **Yellow Beard Pub** on 30 de Marzo. Here the walls are grafitti-ridden, and sometimes quite humorous.

Gambling

You'll find a **casino** in Puerto Plata at the Puerto Plata Beach Hotel (there are others at Playa Dorada), which features all the standard games,—blackjack, craps, roulette, and poker, as well as slot machines, some of which only take U.S. dollars.

Festivals

The town's patron saint festival for San Felipe takes place on July 5, and Puerto Plata hosts a well-known **Merengue Festival** in late October with a mix of live merengue, open-air food stalls, parades, and dances.

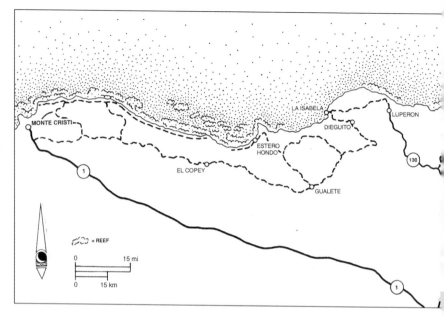

SHOPPING

Arts and Crafts

A must stop for local crafts and arts is the **Centro Artesanal** (Calle J.F. Kennedy 3, tel. 809/586-3724), a nonprofit school that trains Dominicans in the arts of jewelry making, carpentry, carving, and related studies. The local crafts are on sale Mon–Sat, 8 A.M.–noon and 2 P.M.–5 P.M. Drop by and see if you like something, because a purchase will really help a local student. Take a special look at the dolls, chess sets, and wood creations. Other places for good crafts and Dominican-manufactured goods are the **Rancier Boutique** and the **Rainbow Gift Shop,** both on Calle Duarte. Handmade jewelry, ceramics, and fashionable clothing are on display at **The Mine** on Calle San Felipe 32, near Calle Duarte. Needless to say, **El Museo del Ámbar** gift shop features amber jewelry of all kinds, but the area also boasts the **Tourist Bazaar Boutique** (Calle Duarte 61, tel. 809/586-2848), which is a densely packed seven-shop affair featuring carved mahogany, amber, and larimar, in addition to Haitian paintings and fashionable clothes. When you wear yourself out, you can sit down on the patio bar for a drink. The ubiquitous rocking chairs (and other crafts) are on sale at the **Macaluso** shop (Calle Duarte 32), and the **Grand Factory Gift Shop** has jewelry (Calle Duarte 23). In the same general area is the **Liberia Fénix,** which has some English books and English-language newspapers for those needing news from home.

On Calle Separación, **Casa Nelson** has a jumble of interesting merchandise, while the nearby **Casa Colón** is mostly for T-shirts and tourist souvenirs.

Jewelry

The big-daddy jewelry store is **Harrison's** (Plaza Isabel, Playa Dorada, tel. 809/586-3933). If you're staying in Puerto Plata, you'll have to take the five-minute taxi ride over to the complex to shop. And not only is Harrison's a big daddy in Puerto Plata, but there are 30 stores across the island, principally in major hotels, but also in Punta Cuna/Bavaro. Check out its fledgling website: www.harrisons.com. For jewelry right in

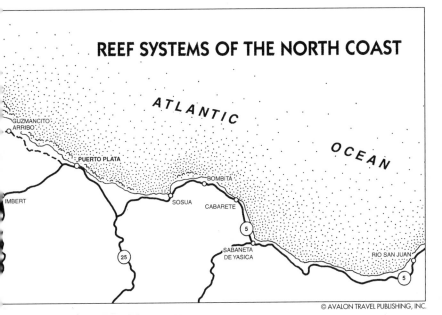

REEF SYSTEMS OF THE NORTH COAST

ATLANTIC

OCEAN

GUZMANCITO
ARRIBO
PUERTO PLATA
IMBERT
BOMBITA
SOSUA
CABARETE
5
SABANETA
DE YASICA
RIO SAN JUAN
25
5

© AVALON TRAVEL PUBLISHING, INC.

town, there is the **Fine Gift Center Cibao** (Calle 12 de Julio, tel. 809/586-6467). In these stores, all major charge cards are accepted.

Music
For a wide selection of merengue and salsa records, tapes, and discs, try the **Dominicana Record Shop** on Separación 65 (tel. 809/586-1244). This record and disc chain also has shops in Sosúa on Pedro Clisante, and in Costambar at Plaza San Marcos, as well as a big store in the Playa Dorada Plaza.

Malls
The shopping mall has made its appearance on the north coast—with a vengeance. The original recipe was the Playa Dorada Mall, now known as the **Plaza Turisol Complex,** located about halfway between Puerto Plata and the gate of Occidental Playa Dorada resort. It's on the main highway from town and you can't miss this huge multicolored "plaza" containing about 80 stores (and growing). Like all malls everywhere, it is stylized according to a uniform concept, and to my mind, quite cheesy.

However, it is always unbelievably busy. Just about 500 yards from the entrance to Playa Dorada itself is the **Plaza Isabela,** a more subdued mall of specialty shops constructed in Victorian faux-gingerbread style. Some of the shops are, admittedly, rather interesting.

Souvenirs
Down on the beach, or almost anywhere in Puerto Plata, you can buy inexpensive souvenirs. On Plaza 26 the Mini Market has the **Journal de Montréal** (tel. 809/586-6313).

PRACTICALITIES

Orientation
Orienting yourself to Puerto Plata is relatively easy. Driving from Santiago or Santo Domingo, you'll come toward town from the west. At the first roundabout, turn left and you'll be on Calle Colón, which forms the western boundary of the city. To the south of the city is Avenida Circunvalación Sur, while Circunvalación Norte (which is the Malecón) fronts the beach. In the far east,

Avenida Mirabal in the hotel district forms a rough boundary to the city, thus enclosing Puerto Plata in a kind of lopsided rectangle. Puerto Plata is laid out in fairly understandable ways, though driving through the city these days is quite a chore, given the narrow streets and the extreme congestion, along with the relative lack of parking space. It really is best to walk. Take inexpensive taxis, or *motoconchos* if you must.

Getting There
Three main bus lines serve Puerto Plata, making it one of the easiest of Dominican cities to reach by public transport, right behind Santo Domingo in that category. Between the main cities of Santiago and Santo Domingo, **Metro Bus** (Celle Beller, tel. 809/586-6063) has regular departures on streamlined, air-conditioned, comfortable buses that make the trip all the way to Santo Domingo in about four hours. There are about six departures and arrivals every day, but most are express to the destination. **Caribe Tours** (Calle 12 de Julio, tel. 809/586-0282) makes the central run to Santo Domingo but also heads to cities like Sosúa, Mao, Dajabón, and others. The central runs stop at towns like Bonao and La Vega as well, filling in the Metro Bus gap. **Transportes de Cibao** (tel. 809/586-9408) departs from a lot across from the Hotel Atlantico, and runs up and down the valley. Hence, the transport situation on major lines to and from Puerto Plata is quite good.

By Taxi or *Motoconcho:* Taxis to and from the airport to Puerto Plata are about US$15, to and from Sosúa about US$10, and to and from Cabarete about US$20. Before you hop in, be sure to nail down the price.

By Plane: Flying into Puerto Plata has been made easier by the addition of numerous international flights into the airport, about 18km west of town.

Getting Around
Getting around inside Puerto Plata is easy. Go on foot for most things. If you're tired, hire a taxi for a negotiated ride, or hop on one of the many *carreras,* which can be chartered on the spot for rides to Playa Dorada, Sosúa, and local beaches. Again, nail down the price. Little *motoconchos* flit around town as well, and they are cheap and will take you anywhere you want to go in

a noisy cloud of choking dust. For inter-city travel, and cheaper than local *guaguas* or Metro and Caribe, are minivans that leave from the central park, the hospital, and La Javilla. You'll have to speak Spanish to negotiate the destination and the price, be nimble enough to ride in a packed van, and alert enough to hop out when you arrive.

SPORTS AND RECREATION

The north coast is a major water sports center. Many of the activities available are operated by major resorts in Playa Dorada, and by luxury and tourist hotels in Costambar, Cofresí, Sosúa, and Cabarete.

Diving and Snorkeling
For diving and snorkeling, you can't beat some of the reefs. Specialists on the north coast are **Gri-Gri Divers** (Gaston Delinge 4, tel./fax 809/589-2672), who can certify and outfit divers, help with snorkeling plans, and conduct expeditions to the nearby Gri-Gri lagoon, all out of their headquarters in Río San Juan, just east of Puerto Plata along the coast. Otherwise, a diving shop in the Playa Dorada Plaza helps hotel guests and others with outfitting and trips. All of the larger hotels in Puerto Plata are able to help with diving and snorkeling. As to deep-sea fishing, the best place to fish is in Luperón Bay, and trips can be organized out of the **Luperón Beach Resort.** Sosúa is the western center for fishing, diving, and snorkeling.

Windsurfing
One of the biggest sports on the north coast is windsurfing. The major windsurfing spot is Cabarete, and there are more than a dozen specialty shops renting boards, with prices being about the same in each. The cost is about US$15 per hour, or about US$50 per day, with lessons available. These establishments also offer equipment storage for a set fee.

Tennis and Golf
Of course, the major hotels in Playa Dorada have many tennis courts, and Playa Dorada is home to the justly famous 18-hole **Robert Trent Jones Golf Course,** where hotel guests are welcome. Tennis is in short supply on the north coast, though the major hotels all have courts. In

Cabarete, the **Las Orquídeas Hotel** has the best courts, with lessons available. Horseback riding is best at the Luperón Beach Resort, in the small town of Luperón, about an hour west of Puerto Plata by car.

Because sport is so much the province at hotels and resorts on the north coast, I'll discuss various opportunities below in sections on each resort.

Transportation Rentals

All the major car rental agencies, and then some, are located at the Puerto Plata International Airport: **Avis** (tel. 809/586-4436), **National** (tel. 809/586-0285), **Hertz** (tel. 809/586-0200), **Thrifty** (tel. 809/586-0242), and **Nelly** (tel. 809/586-0505). In town, contact **Budget,** (Av. L. Ginebra, tel. 809/586-4433), **Puerto Plata Rent Car** (tel. 809/586-0215), **Rentauto Puerto Plata** (Av. Kennedy, tel. 809/586-0240), or **Abby** (tel. 809/586-2516). If you feel lucky, rent motorcycles and motor scooters from any of a dozen agencies in Puerto Plata. **Trixy** rents scooters and cycles at a reasonable cost, as does **Yuyo** (tel. 809/585-5440) on 12 de Julio. Be sure your insurance is up to date, and watch out for theft; stealing motorscooters and cycles is a popular pastime in the area.

INFORMATION AND SERVICES

There are three **Codetel** offices in the Puerto Plata area for those calls back home. The main office downtown is at Beller 58, another is at Plaza Turisol, and a third is at the airport. The competing **Tricom** is on Calle San Felipe at Beller, while the new **All America** phone company is at J.F. Kennedy 40. All the hotels handle mailing of postcards and letters. The main **post office** is at Separación and 12 de Julio. The post office is open 8 A.M.–5 P.M.

There is a **U.S. consulate** office at 12 de Julio 55 (tel. 809/686-3143), and a Canadian consul as well (tel. 809/586-5761), while the British can call 809/586-4244. The British and Canadian numbers are for a *charge d'affaires.*

PLAYA DORADA

Playa Dorada, just a few kilometers east of Puerto Plata, is probably the most popular package-tour destination in the country. What was once rolling hills of sugarcane and wild grass is now an extremely organized group of more than a dozen hotels, grouped around the golf course and the beach. All of the hotels are in the luxury, expensive class, and each offers similar activities. Of course, the rooms in the hotels are nicely furnished (some studios and apartments), with air-conditioning, phone, TV, bath, and some terraces. In the complex are dozens of restaurants, bars, cafes, and discos. Many of the hotels operate on a "Club Package" arrangement, which means that the guest will book his or her vacation through a travel agent back home, and upon arrival be provided with all meals, drinks, and entertainment at a set price.

Playa Dorada is also all inclusive when it comes to sports. Every hotel can organize horseback riding, tennis, golf, diving, snorkeling, swimming, and windsurfing. All of the hotels have health spas and swimming pools. It's entirely possible to spend a week at the Occidental Playa Dorada resort and never know you've been to the Dominican Republic at all.

Occidental Playa Dorada usually books solid during the winter. Sometimes you can show up and get a room, but it costs a lot.

ACCOMMODATIONS

If Playa Dorada is your destination, it is far better to plan well in advance, study the price-plan brochures, and pay in advance for the program that suits your needs. With the exception of the Jack Tar Village, which is the most expensive hotel in the area, the hotels at Playa Dorada offer rooms in the US$100–140 single range, slightly less in the off-season. Some hotels specialize in all-inclusive vacations, others combine inclusive vacations with partial meal programs. Be sure to check with your travel agent for specific details.

Victoria Beach Resort

Near the golf course, and a short walk from the

PLAYA DORADA

ATLANTIC OCEAN

PARADISE BEACH CLUB AND CASINO

VICTORIA BEACH RESORT

DORADO NACO I

PLAYA NACO

DORADO NACO II

JACK TAR VILLAGE

HEAVENS HOTEL

VILLAS DORADAS BEACH RESORT

ROBERT TRENT JONES GOLF COURSE

PLAYA DORADA HOTEL AND CASINO

PUERTO PLATA VILLAGE RESORT AND SPA

CARIBBEAN VILLAGE FUN TROPICALE AND VILLAGE FUN ROYAL

RIO   SOSUA

PLAYA DORADA

CARIBBEAN VILLAGE CLUB ON THE GREEN

= TEE

= FAIRWAY

= GREEN

MOON

© AVALON TRAVEL PUBLISHING, INC.

NOT TO SCALE

beach, is the Victoria Beach Resort (tel. 809/320-1200, fax 809/320-4862). Its 190 rooms and suites are comfortable, and the resort has pools, deck lounges, buffet lunches, and a good restaurant called El Jardín.

Heavens Hotel

Along with the Victoria, the Heavens Hotel (tel. 809/320-5250, fax 809/320-4733) has the lowest prices at Playa Dorada, probably because the Heavens is kind of a jumble of styles. Even if Heavens isn't quite as stylish as other resorts, its 192 rooms are OK, and it has all the amenities and sports of the other resorts.

Paradise Beach Club and Casino

Formerly the Eurotel, the Paradise Beach Club

and Casino (tel. 809/320-3663, fax 809/320-4858) has 436 rooms, restaurants, bars, two tennis courts, a shopping center, horseback riding, and water sports. The several buildings of Paradise Beach Club and Casino feature attractive woodwork, impressive grounds with gardens and waterfalls, open water, swimming pools in bizarre shapes, and a very beautiful gourmet restaurant. The casino was the first in Puerto Plata and has all the games 4 P.M.–4 A.M. in European-style surroundings.

Caribbean Village Club on the Green

The Caribbean Village Club on the Green (Playa Dorada, tel. 809/320-1111) is owned by an outfit that also owns other hotels in the Dominican Republic and Mexico. Offering 336 rooms, all of which are tasteful and simple, the hotel is all inclusive. There are seven tennis courts, a gym, a swimming pool, and three restaurants, including El Pilón, Firenze, and Miranda's, offering a variety of Italian, steak, and seafood, along with a bar and nightclub.

Hotetur Dorado
The Hotetur Dorado (Apdo. Postal 162, tel. 809/320-2019, U.S. tel. 800/322-2388, fax 809/586-3608) and its 196 units was the second hotel built in the Playa Dorada complex. Here, each unit has a kitchen, and there are some two-bedroom suites and larger penthouses. Close to every unit is a beach bar and grill. There is a nightly buffet near the pool, and the Flamingo Gourmet Restaurant and Valentino's serve excellent food. The hotel features live entertainment every night of the week, and specialty shows twice a week. It also has a water sports center, which specializes in scuba diving, snorkeling, and sailing.

lily pond near Playa Dorada

LEO DE WYS

Occidental Playa Dorada
The hotel with the best beachfront is probably Occidental Playa Dorada (Apdo. Postal 272, tel. 809/586-3988 or U.S. tel. 800/423-6902, fax 809/230-4448). Here you can get modified meal plans and a sports package. Most of the 500 rooms are set on shaded corridors right on the beachfront. The La Palma is the chief gourmet restaurant, but there are two others as well: the Mar Azul and Las Brisas. You'll find plenty of live entertainment here, as well as three lighted tennis courts, golf, water sports, baby-sitting, laundry, and valet service. Of course, there is a plush casino. This is one hotel that is almost always full.

Villas Doradas Beach Resort
The Villas Doradas Beach Resort (Apdo. Postal 1370, tel. 809/586-3000, fax 809/586-4790) has 244 rooms and 32 suites, with both modified and full plans available. This hotel features town houses, barbecues around the pool, and a very popular thatched-roof pool bar. **El Pescador** serves good seafood dishes; **Pancho's** dishes up Mexican food. This is a cozy place, but there is no direct beachfront. One nice thing about this resort is its **Jardín de Jade,** where you can get excellent Chinese food and good value for your money. The specialties include Peking duck, sliced chicken in chili sauce, and fried crab claws.

The sister institution of Villas Doradas Beach Resort is the larger **Flamenco Beach Resort** (282 rooms). Their phone number is 809/320-5084, and fax at 809/320-6319. The accommodations include doubles, junior suites, and suites, with all the amenities. Sports are emphasized here.

Caribbean Village Fun Tropical and Caribbean Village Fun Royal
Containing a total of 352 rooms combined, both the Caribbean Village Fun Tropical (tel. 809/320-4054, fax 809/320-6120) and Caribbean Village Fun Royal (tel. 809/320-4054) offer similarly comfortable rooms and all the amenities, with the village concept in mind.

Playa Naco
The 418-room Playa Naco touts itself as the most beautiful resort in Playa Dorada, and it has

a case. There are many types of rooms here, from singles to suites, and the resort concentrates on golf and tennis, as the name would indicate. It was opened in 1993 with newly remodeled rooms. Call them at 809/320-6226; toll free in the United States, 800/223-6510; and toll free in Canada, 800/424-5500. In addition to all the basic sporting activities offered by Playa Naco, it has the most completely outfitted fitness center at the complex.

Puerto Plata Village Resort and Spa

Also geared to health and fitness is the Puerto Plata Village Resort and Spa (tel. 809/320-4012, fax 809/320-5113), which has 386 rooms, additional apartments, and villas all done up in Victorian style. It has a small mall with shops, two pools, a disco, restaurants, five tennis courts, horseback riding, a big spa, and, of course, many bars.

Jack Tar Village

The oldest and most expensive hotel at Playa Dorada is the Jack Tar Village (Apdo. Postal 368, Puerto Plata, tel. 809/320-3800 or U.S. tel. 800/999-9182, fax 809/320-4161). Rates for this 350-room (some suites) hotel start at about US$170–200 single, US$300–340 double, for an all-inclusive package stay. Suites are extra, off season about 30% less. This "village" is clustered around two swimming pools, all situated close to the beach. The Jack Tar prides itself on having everything in the way of dining, entertainment, and sports, which it does, in spades. It also has an exclusive **casino,** and you can arrange horseback riding, sauna, and health club activities. There is little left to chance here, and the service is excellent.

Grand Ventana Beach Resort

This deluxe resort features 500 rooms (tel. 809/320-2111, fax 809/320-2112) on the beach. Touting a combination of Victorian and Caribbean design these mustard-colored three-story buildings face a large pond. Everything here is "five star" as they say, including a buffet restaurant, a gourmet à la carte restaurant, an ocean grill and Italian restaurant. There is music nightly, including some good live shows. Rates are US $150–300 double.

Occidental Flamenco Beach Resort

This large 582-room deluxe resort consists of three-story brown and white buildings surrounding a couple of swank pools (tel. 809/221-2121, fax 809/532-4494). Everything is here—shopping, beach, whirlpool, two buffets, six restaurants, four bars, and a disco. It's a bit like a cruise ship on the beach. There is a kids' club and every leisure activity known to man.

FOOD

Dining and shopping are featured activities at Playa Dorada. I've already mentioned some of the restaurants in the hotels, but in addition are **El Cupey** and the **Guananico Steak House** in Puerto Plata Village resort; **Elaine's,** which has good lamb chops, at Jack Tar Village; and **La Condesa,** at Club on the Green. Occidental Playa Dorada has **La Palma.** At many of these restaurants, a jacket is required, and reservations are recommended. Check the brochures and price guide for further information.

If extra-deluxe dining is your specialty, then the best and most expensive restaurants at Playa Dorada are **La Condesa** in Club on the Green, which is ultra elegant and serves fresh fish and great local steaks. It has a great wine list. Also, the **Flamingo** at the Hotetur Dorado is great for beef, veal, and chicken. In both spots, reservations and jackets are required.

RECREATION AND ENTERTAINMENT

In addition to the countless sports and recreation activities at the various resorts, at the Playa Dorada Plaza, you'll find **Lorilar Fine Horses,** (tel. 809/320-0498) where you can arrange horse trips on the beach or in the mountains. There is also a sports center at the Plaza, but it features mostly teenage rollerblading.

Nightlife is a main feature at Playa Dorada. There are bars, pool bars, discos, and nightclubs in every resort. In particular, the **Crazy Moon Disco** at the Paradise Beach Club and Casino is very wild and crazy, while Jack Tar has **Charlie's Disco** and Playa Dorada Village has the **Disco Village.** Well, you get the idea.

If you are a relatively adventuresome sort, or just a normal person wanting a break from Plaza Dorada's frenetic pace, try walking east down the beach from the major resorts. In a short way you'll reach a small fishing village called **Playa Bergantín**. Some enterprising souls from the village have set up tables and sunshades on the beach and there you can pick out fresh lobster or fish from the day's catch. It will be cooked in front of you. This is a cheap and delicious way to eat. Plenty of cold beer and soda is on hand.

COSTAMBAR AND COFRESÍ

INTRODUCTION

Costambar (Amber Coast) is the first beach west of Puerto Plata. Only about three km from the city and located near the entrance to the cable car ride up Loma Isabel de Torres, the long stretch of white beach used to be relatively undeveloped, a place where wealthy Dominicans and a few foreigners made their winter homes. Now, the villas are still owned by wealthy Dominicans and foreigners, but the beach locale is becoming heavily developed. A nine-hole golf course called Los Mangos has been built, and the area is getting a complement of restaurants, motorcycle rental shops, and boutiques. The main attractions are still the beach, water sports, and exclusive luxury resorts. You can rent vacation homes in the area by consulting local realtors.

Just a few kilometers west of Costambar is Playa Cofresí, on a well-marked road that branches off the Santiago Highway. Like Costambar it has a long white beach and has not developed much identity as a place. You can get a taxi to Playa Cofresí for a nominal cost, or catch a local bus heading west toward Luperón, which will let you off at the entrance to the beach. It is a 10-minute walk from the highway to the beach. Playa Cofresí is nice, with some good hotels, markets, shops, and a slowly developing tourism infrastructure. As everywhere along the north coast, hotels rent water sports equipment and arrange tours of the countryside. Playa Cofresí is quieter than Puerto Plata, and quieter than Costambar, without all the hustle and bustle of Playa Dorada.

ACCOMMODATIONS

When you shop for a resort at Cofresí and Costambar, be sure to consult with your travel agent in detail. For example, the rooms at the Cofresí Hotel and Club don't have air-conditioning. Set on a hill, the resort catches a steady, pleasant ocean breeze, but if air-conditioning matters to you, then pick something else. The same is true for the Apart-Hotel Marlena. It is also possible for non-guests to buy a daily pass at the Cofresí to visit the beach, take meals, and use some facilities. Should you wish to stay cheaply at Puerto Plata, you can save money with one of the daily passes. The Cofresí, and other such beach resorts tend to fill up with package tourists quite early, so be lively if you wish to visit.

In truth, both Cofresí and Costambar have little identity as places. They tend to be convoluted mixtures of condos and timeshares, some apartments and hotels, all of which seem to shuffle names and regimens regularly. One thing to do is simply to drive the circuitous roads looking for "For Rent" signs, then stop and ask when you see one. One change of pace, but expensive, is **Villas Olas Tropical** (Duarte 53, tel. 809/970-7132), a luxurious bed-and-breakfast on the Costambar beach. There are, quite literally, dozens of villa-style accommodations from which to choose, all quite pricey and all very similar.

Costambar Ocean Village
The Costambar Ocean Village (tel. 809/553-2844, fax 809/553-5041) is served by Tropical Resorts Marketing, so make reservations through them. This hotel offers one-bedroom suites in a series of hexagonal two-story buildings, kitchens, golf, tennis, and cable TV. Rooms are not all-inclusive and start at around US$80 per night for a single.

Apart-Hotel Marlena
Less expensive is Apart-Hotel Marlena (tel. 809/586-3692), which has 33 units and some

studios available. As yet, Costambar has not developed a significant downtown, so there aren't any commercial hotels or low-budget accommodations. For inexpensive stays at this beach, make your home in Puerto Plata and take a taxi to the beach, or ride the local buses.

Club Hacienda Elisabeth

Moderate in price is the Club Hacienda Elisabeth, an all-inclusive resort with 160 rooms, located very near the beach. The Club Hacienda is marketed by Connex Caribe, and you can contact them for reservations at 809/586-1227, fax 809/586-3300. The Club Hacienda is a large, three-story modern hotel, with nice grounds, a large swimming pool, a thatched outdoor bar, horseback riding, water sports, a minimart, and live entertainment in the nightclub.

Cofresí Cove Hideaway

Cofresí Cove Hideaway (tel. 809/586-6881, fax 809/586-6882, in Canada 514/292-5835) is a resort featuring 12 one- and two-bedroom condos with ocean and mountain views. This Spanish-style place is built near the beach, and covers the field with plenty of horseback riding, golf, windsurfing, and swimming in the big hotel pool. At both of these hotels, expect to pay more than US$100 per night for a single; rates depend upon the time of year and the plan adopted.

Club Paradise

Also in Cofresí is an intimate inn with only 18 rooms. Called Club Paradise (tel. 809/586-5551, fax 809/586-5552), it offers gardens, a pool, and a restaurant. This little hideaway also has some significant charm.

Club Las Rocas

About five minutes by car from Cofresí and Costambar is Club Las Rocas (tel. 809/586-5303, fax 809/586-8533, in Canada 514/922-3252), a 52-unit resort equipped with fans, cable TV, a refrigerator, balconies, pools, a restaurant, bars, water sports, and horseback riding.

Cofresí Hotel and Club

At Playa Cofresí, the most exclusive and dramatic-looking hotel is the Cofresí Hotel and

COFRESÍ THE PIRATE

The names of pirates have become watchwords of the Caribbean: Henry Morgan, Blackbeard, Hawkins, Drake, and Leclerc (nicknamed Wooden Leg). When people think of pirates, they probably think of Errol Flynn types, loners who sweep the seas in search of plunder. In fact, many pirates operated in huge gangs, which would attack and then sack towns, sometimes several times. For example, Drake attacked San Juan, Puerto Rico, in 1594 with 25 ships. Pirate gangs as large as 2,000 men regularly attacked towns in Panama, Mexico, and Venezuela. Usually, the towns would pay ransoms, and the pirates would sail away.

Hispaniola's most famous pirate, and one of the last to make regular raids, was Roberto Cofresí, whose name is still spoken in Puerto Plata. Born in Cabo Rojo on the southeastern tip of Puerto Rico, Cofresí was the son of a German-Jewish immigrant. He and his gang hid in caves on Mona and Saona Islands and in the coconut groves along Samaná, preying on ships plying the North and South American trade routes via the Virgin Islands. For years, authorities tried to trap him. Finally in 1825, they caught him in a Puerto Rican bay and took him to San Juan for trial. After a very brief trial, Cofresí and his men were found guilty and executed. A bay west of Puerto Plata is named after Cofresí—some say because some of his treasure is buried there.

Find a shovel and get to work.

Club (tel. 809/586-2898, fax 809/586-8064). Located on a quiet cove and set on a spectacular hillside, the Cofresí offers great views from its hotel terraces and balconies. You can see the lights of Puerto Plata in the distance at night, and the hotel is noted for its awesome sunset vistas. The hotel has 281 rooms, as well as restaurants, bars, pools, a game room, a gym, a sauna, a minimart, a beauty salon, and a gift shop. You can get an all-inclusive package deal here. The pool has a scuba clinic, and there is a wide array of winter sports including windsurfing, snorkeling, sailing, and swimming. Of course, there is a disco and daytime tennis. The Cofresí is in the US$120 s range, though you must check the price brochures carefully before booking.

Apart-Hotel Atlantis
For equally exclusive and expensive apartments and villas, try Apart-Hotel Atlantis (tel. 809/586-3828), which has 63 units.

Bayside Hill Resort and Beach Club
The premium luxury tourist hotel at Costambar is Bayside Hill Resort and Beach Club (tel. 809/586-5260, fax 809/586-5545), a swanky place with 150 all-inclusive rooms, two pools, a restaurant, tennis, and golf. If you wish to book from the United States, call toll free 800/223-6510, from Canada 800/424-5500. The Bayside is located at Calle Guyacanes, at the corner of Bermejo. All-inclusive packages cost around US$120 per person single. As always,

consult the price brochures carefully before booking. Bayside has horseback riding and tennis as well. Bayside is on Puerto Plata Bay, which is nearly three miles long. It offers several different types of units, including two- and three-bedroom cottages and apartments, with living and dining areas and fully equipped kitchens. Each building houses six units and a pool.

L'Oase
Just west of Costambar along a secluded and beautiful stretch of beach sits the wonderful L'Oase, a small seven-room hotel set in tropical gardens. The hotel is run by Ton and Willy, a Dutch couple, who work hard to present a clean and hospitable place. And at US$30–50 with breakfast for a double, it is reasonably priced. There is no noise or entertainment, just peace and quiet (tel. 809/471-1321, fax. 809/970-7362).

WEST FROM PUERTO PLATA

Not many people visit the country west of Puerto Plata. There are only a couple of real tourist complexes along the whole coast, at Luperón and Punta Rucia. The rest of the coast, an extensive rolling coastal plain nearly 150km long, stretches all the way to the Haitian border and includes several good beaches, and the country's most articulated and extensive area of coral reefs. Here, the roads tend to be a little rougher and less traveled, the villages very small, and the services less available. Beyond Luperón, which can be reached by good road from Puerto Plata, the roads are very primitive, and you'll need to pay attention to your directions.

It is certainly possible to make day trips to the area from either Puerto Plata or Monte Cristi. The **Cayos Siete Hermanos,** a series of keys off Monte Cristi, is a diver's paradise, and a visit to the low marshlands and the **Parque Nacional Monte Cristi** is worthwhile for marine and birdlife.

Most of the people in the western parts of the north coast make their living from fishing and small-scale agriculture, not tourism. As one goes farther west, the climate becomes more arid, the facilities more rudimentary. For travelers and adventurers, the area can be a real challenge, especially in seeking out rarely visited reefs and small, isolated beaches.

LUPERÓN

Luperón is a small town of about 20,000, located on a lovely, wide bay of the same name. Luperón is a lovely spot, perfect for travelers who wish to dive and snorkel in relative isolation. Down near the port, you'll find fishermen who make their living from the sea. Luperón itself is a quiet, provincial town, without much wild nightlife. For many, this could be what makes their visit to Luperón a happy one.

The focus of tourism in Luperón is the **Luperón Beach Resort** (809/581-4153, fax 809/581-6262), a 150-room luxury beach resort. All-inclusive packages in this hotel cost around US$180 per day single. As always, if you wish to stay at this resort, check with a reputable travel agent about the various packages available. The Luperón Beach Resort offers air-conditioned rooms near a luxurious beach of golden sand, pools for children and adults, a golf course, horseback riding, jogging paths, and car and motorbike rentals. Most importantly, the hotel is completely rigged with water sports, especially diving.

Inexpensive hotels in the town of Luperón are **Hotel Luperón** (Calle Independencia, tel. 809/571-8125) and **La Morena** (Calle Duarte, near the **Codetel**). These hotels are strictly commercial ones with rates in the US$12 range. You'll likely get a fan, but you'll share a bath and should be prepared for frequent electricity failures and sometimes going without water. For those desiring water sports without luxury, stay in one of the commercial hotels and head for the beach at Luperón Beach Resort.

Getting There
Luperón is about 45km from Puerto Plata, an easy day trip along the coast, though I wouldn't advise taking this road at night. If you like, the bay can also be reached by a twisty road from Imbert.

Some people hire motorcycles and scooters to make the trek. One or two *públicos* drive over from Puerto Plata for about US$3. If you have no car, the best way to go to Luperón is with a private tour organized by any of the good tour companies in Puerto Plata.

The tour agencies can make arrangements for a day trip to the bay of Luperón, a swing by La Isabela, and a return. The roads past Luperón, even to Punta Ricia, but especially beyond, are very difficult to manage unless your Spanish is good and you've time to burn getting directions.

LA ISABELA

The National Parks Department is trying to develop La Isabela, the town founded by Columbus so long ago, for tourists. The site of La Isabela, however, isn't much to see and is somewhat oversold from a traveler's standpoint. The locale of the ruins are officially a national park, and archaeological excavation has been seriously undertaken since 1987. The outlines of principal structures have appeared, including what some say were a church, guard stations, a channel through a coral reef, and a cemetery. A complete skeleton has been found on the site, as well as many shards of pottery. Unfortunately, scientific excavation hasn't proven totally satisfactory because over many years the site, which was known by locals, has been plundered for profit and pleasure.

LA ISABELA

To tell the truth, the site of La Isabela on the north coast of Hispaniola was hardly suitable for a major Spanish settlement. The bay was shallow and the weather perilous at best. There was, however, a rocky cliff where building could be done, and plenty of wood in the nearby forests. Besides, the 1,200 men who had just spent 100 days crammed into 17 ships on the second voyage of discovery were eager to get started searching for their fortunes in gold. After spending a month prospecting in the Cibao valley, Columbus sailed away from La Isabela, leaving 56 soldiers to continue the search under the command of Pedro Margarit.

Things went downhill fast in La Isabela during Columbus's absence. The Indians were a big disappointment to the Spanish—they didn't work hard enough. Communication was a problem, and disease took its toll. The Spanish took out their anger on the Taínos.

Three months later, Columbus returned. Fire had destroyed much of La Isabela, and there had been a terrible storm, sinking some ships. Columbus restored order by hanging several troublemakers and appointing his brother, Bartolome, as mayor. A wall was built around the settlement, and on March 10, 1496, Columbus sailed back to Spain on his beloved *Niña*. Bartolome went to Puerto Plata, with instructions to proceed south and look for gold along the coast. In 1497, a fleet from Spain returned, carrying the first 30 Spanish women to settle in the New World. Most of them were prostitutes from Seville and were taking an "honorable" opportunity to start over. Most residents of La Isabela had moved west, to be greeted by famous cacique Guacanagarix and his tribe. Less than 10 years later, La Isabela was completely uninhabited, almost forgotten.

During the 1950s, Trujillo was expecting an important visitor who wished to see the site of La Isabela. Trujillo gave orders by telegram to clean up the ruins of La Isabela, and these orders were followed to the letter: a bulldozer shoved every piece of debris over the cliffs and into the sea. Fortunately, recent excavations have revealed many surviving foundations and grave sites.

History

The history of La Isabela is probably more interesting than the site itself. As Columbus coasted Hispaniola on his first voyage in 1492, he deposited 39 unfortunate souls at a place in Haiti called La Navidad, now En Bas Saline in Haiti. When Columbus returned a year later, he brought with him 1,500 settlers in 17 boats to continue the settlement of La Navidad, but the town had been burned down, and the inhabitants were missing, perhaps killed and dispersed by Taínos.

Columbus moved his flotilla east along the coast, probably to approach the supposedly gold-rich Cibao valley. He was in a hurry to put down his settlers and get on with the real business of finding wealth, and so he dropped them at a point of land near the present town of Luperón, which he called La Isabela, after his Spanish queen. The 1,500 settlers he left near the coast were mostly farmers and tradesmen from the extremely dry region of Spain called Estremadura. Like most immigrants, these farmers were lured by promises and hope. The first settlement at La Isabela was set up near the coast on a river called Río Bajabonico. Some months later, a second and more secure location was chosen just a short distance away from the coast. Epidemic, famine, and agricultural disappointment led to the abandonment of La Isabela in 1496. The choice of the site was a big mistake: infertile soil, disease, and bad water all contributed to La Isabela's demise.

Both the first and second settlement sites make up present-day La Isabela. Unfortunately, scientific excavation hasn't proven totally satisfactory because over many years La Isabela has been plundered for profit and pleasure. Once, during the 1940s, Trujillo ordered the provincial governor to clean up the site in anticipation of a visit by a group of foreign historians. This the governor did with a vengeance, with the help of heavy tractors which "rolled out" the site. Even in the 1960s, more "cleanup" disguised much destruction of delicate strata.

In the fall of 1991, the Spanish government, through its official agency AEMA, helped to create a broad plan of action in cooperation with the archaeologist in charge, José María Cruxent, of Coro University in Argentina. The ruins have now been surrounded by a wooden structure and covered.

Getting There

Probably the best way to see La Isabela, or what passes for its ruins, is to take an organized bus tour from Puerto Plata. Contact any travel agent in Puerto Plata for information on tours, many of which run daily. The only alternative for those without transport is to take the *público* to Luperón, then hire a *motoconcho* or taxi in Luperón. The trip by *motoconcho* is very cheap, no more than US$5 round trip, though as always, you should arrange the price in advance.

The main highway from Luperón leads to a small village named **El Castillo.** Thirteen km from Luperón, this little village sits on a lonely bay and is fronted by a long chain of living reefs which offer terrific snorkeling and diving opportunities, something of a rarity on the island. Nearby the highway (Carretera de Las Américas) is the entrance to **Parque Nacional La Isabela,** which is open 9 A.M.–5:30 P.M. every day but Sunday. There is a RD$30 entry fee.

The park contains the ruins, some freshly constructed cabins whose purpose is uncertain, and the contemporary **Templo de Las Américas,** a neocolonial church built in 1992 when Pope John Paul II visited the site. The Playa Isabela, a beach close by, is perfect. Near El Castillo is **Rancho del Sol** (tel. 809/543-8172), which offers duplexes with kitchen and bath for about US$30 including breakfast. On the grounds are tennis courts and a swimming pool.

PUNTA RUCIA

Punta Rucia is a small fishing village with several nice beaches. Believe me, the place is isolated, accessible only by rough gravel road from Luperón (beyond La Isabela), so you should be sure to ask for directions as you negotiate the coast road. An easier way to reach Punta Rucia by car is to go back from Puerto Plata to the Duarte Highway and drive northwest until you reach Villa Elisa. A decent road north from Villa Elisa heads toward Punta Rucia, and the main town nearby the point, Estero Hondo.

The great thing about Punta Rucia is that the headlands are completely surrounded by reef, making the diving and snorkeling very good. Only the **Punta Rucia Sol** is operating as a hotel there.

There are good seafood shacks on the beach. Beware of mosquitoes. The orchids are lovely.

MONTE CRISTI AND VICINITY

Monte Cristi is a dry and dusty desert town located at the head of the Valle de Norte, home to about 22,000 people, most of whom live from fishing and cattle ranching. Along the coast from Punta Rucia to Monte Cristi, roads are either non-existent, or little more than dirt tracks across rolling coastal bush. This area is, however, a prime one for good reefs.

History
Monte Cristi is—even by Dominican standards— a very old city, having been founded in the early part of the 16th century. Originally, the town was supposed to be a port and entrepôt for goods coming out of the upper Cibao valley, but pirates changed all that. Due to buccaneering nearby, the inhabitants of Monte Cristi were ordered to abandon the city in 1605–06. Most of them moved south.

In the middle of the 18th century, Monte Cristi was nourished by a wave of foreign immigration, this time from English, German, and Italian sources, all of whom made the town a center of export. Later, Cubans influenced the town, as they did the entire Valle de Norte region, establishing cattle ranches and sugarcane plantations. The national hero of the Cuban struggle, Máximo Gómez, made his home in Monte Cristi and later went on to become something of a hero in the second struggle for liberation from Spain during the period 1860–65.

Sights and Recreation
Monte Cristi is dominated by the flat-topped mesa called **El Morro,** a promontory on the edge of a rocky seashore where you can often spot turtles. Reaching the ocean and El Morro from Monte Cristi is easy. Follow a gravel road through town. You'll pass a salt facility near the port, and then travel along the bay to the right (or north), where you'll hear some beach cafes and bars belching loud merengue. The road leads to El Morro, and there is a trail up the steep, nearly 200-meter slopes. From the top, you can get an excellent view of the countryside.

In town, the **house of Máximo Gómez** has become a small museum, and there is an unusual clocktower on the square. Other than this, the town of Monte Cristi is dusty, and somewhat forlorn. In general, there is little to do or see in Monte Cristi, and the few nightspots are loud and drab and generally empty. This is a part of the Dominican Republic that few tourists ever visit.

Festivals
Cristianos hold an interesting celebration for their patron saint on May 30, and the **Carnaval** in Monte Cristi is particularly authentic.

Diving
Getting at the very isolated and sometimes distant reefs is a chore best accomplished with the help of professional divers, especially those in Puerto Plata, Río San Juan, or even Santo Domingo. If you are a do-it-yourself diver or snorkeler, remember to never dive alone and always practice the ultimate in safety techniques. Better yet, get someone to organize a diving tour for you to these areas. They're dangerous.

The waterfront of Monte Cristi is very rough for tourists, but it is there that you can arrange boat trips to **Siete Hermanos,** the seven keys that lie several kilometers off the Monte Cristi coast. These cays, and the **Laguna de Saladillo,** and several other coastal lagoons stretching southward from Monte Cristi and in the valley of the Río Dajabon, form the Parque Nacional Monte Cristi. A dive shop called **North Caribbean Adventures** (U.S. tel. 800/653-7447, fax 809/954-6237, email info@oldship.com) is now operating out of the Hotel Las Caravelas.

Accommodations
There is not a lot to choose in Monte Cristi by way of hotels. On the road to El Morro is **Las Caravelas,** near the Playa Paroli (tel. 809/579-2682), which has 19 rustic rooms and some cabanas. Most of the guests will be Dominican. The price per room is about US$20 with breakfast. In town, the **Hotel El Chic** (tel. 809/579-2316) is centrally located at Calle Monción 44. On Playa Bolaños there is **Hotel Roalex** and **Hotel Montechico,** both quite inexpensive. Similarly reasonable is **Mike's Hotel** (Colón 86, tel.597-3095) which has spacious and clean rooms for about US$15 for a double. Mike's is a

THE PIPE WRECK OF MONTE CRISTI

As soon as Europeans experienced the Taíno custom of smoking tobacco, they took to it in droves. During the 17th century, the Dutch developed their own twist on the smoking convention, using small clay pipes that they themselves invented, then marketed to the rest of the world. One Dutch ship loaded with these fragile pipes ran aground on a sandbank off the Dominican town of Monte Cristi, just beside a salt cay. For years, locals have dived for the clay pipes, though nobody ever knew where the ship came from, or when it went down. All that has now changed, thanks to a researcher named Jerome Lynn Hall.

Hall is director of the Monte Cristi shipwreck project and president of the Pan-American Institute of Maritime Archaeology. With the help of Earthwatch, a nonprofit based in Massachusetts, Hall has excavated 40 feet of the 100-foot wreck, located in only 15 feet of water. Hall says he now knows where the ship came from because he can tell by way of tree-ring analysis that it was built from wood forested in England in 1642 and 1643. He also says that the clay pipes were made by a man named Edward Bird, an Englishman living in Amsterdam. Hall suspects that the ship was involved in illegal trade between European merchants and buccaneers on Tortuga and Hispaniola's north coast. So far, Hall has recovered 13,400 pipes, gold objects, coins, and ceramics. Some of the silver coins were from the famous Potosí mine in Bolivia, while other coins are dated 1651 at the Bogota mint in Colombia. Hall has even recovered special apothecary weights manufactured in Germany around 1650.

One local fisherman claims to have taken more than 1,000 people to the site of the wreck over a period of 20 years. Visitors can still see the wreck site, though artifacts are off limits.

---

good spot for information gathering.

The most expensive, and best, accommodations in town are at Playa Bolaños. The **Cayo Arena** (tel. 809/579-3145, fax 809/579-2096) offers superior apartments on the beach, security, a pool, and a bar. At US$30–50 for a single/double, it is a good buy.

Food

Most of the restaurants in town are located at or near Calle Duarte. **Heladería and Pizzeria Kendy** is at Calle Duarte 92, and **Taberna de Rafua** is just down the street. South of town, the **Restaurant Rabel** is on the main road to Dajabón.

On the beach, the restaurant **Cocomar** is a good choice for seafood, especially crab. In town the **Don Gaspar** has good traditional Spanish food, including paella.

Phones

In Monte Cristi the **Codetel** is at Calle Duarte 85.

Getting There

Monte Cristi is 270km (167 miles) from Santo Domingo along the Duarte Highway. From Santo Domingo, Puerto Plata, and Luperón it is very difficult to make one's way by public transportation to Monte Cristi. About the best you can do is to go by Metro to Santiago, then catch *guaguas* toward the town of Jose Bisonó, continuing on by a series of *guaguas* and *públicos* to Monte Cristi. It can be an exhausting journey, taking most of the day if you're lucky. Plan to start quite early. By car, the journey is very easy, along the Duarte Highway, which passes through the newly established **Reserva Científica Natural de Villa Elisa,** a scientific reserve in Guayubín, near the village of Villa Elisa, the turnoff for Punta Ricia. There are no facilities in the reserve, nor any station. The reserve is a small stretch of subtropical forest, where there are no maps and no trails.

On the way to Monte Cristi, you'll pass the town of **Villa Vásquez,** a small truck transport way station where there are a few cafes. The country hereabouts is very dry, and scrub cactus and dry grass are the prominent vegetation.

PARQUE NACIONAL EL MORRO

The Parque Nacional El Morro is composed of both land and sea portions, though the most prominent feature is the huge mesa called El Morro, rising expansively out of the sea. The wind blows in this corner of the Dominican Republic, and the mesa El Morro, and its associated hill called La Granja (the farm) are covered by windblown shrubs and cactus, with some trees on the ocean side and a near-desert in the rain shadow of the mesa. The views from the side of the El Morro, reached by a gravel road north of town from Monte Cristi, are quite spectacular.

Walks

There are no marked trails on the El Morro mesa. However, it is possible to walk the mesa following goat trails. The mesa walks are not particularly dangerous, but be sure to take water.

Diving

You'll find double reefs on this stretch of coast. The inner reef generally stands in just 2–3 m (7–10 feet) of water, while the outer reef is deeper, in the 3–12 meter (12–40 foot) range. There are many wrecks in and around Monte Cristi, at least one of which you can visit from the port at Monte Cristi.

You can arrange a ride to the Los Siete Hermanos Islands at the port. The islands themselves are generally flat and covered with tropical thorn scrub, but the waters surrounding them are reefed like crazy, providing wonderful diving and snorkeling. You'll need most of your own equipment. The very *best* way to dive and snorkel in this area of the Dominican Republic is with an organized tour out of Santo Domingo, Puerto Plata, or Río San Juan. If you do it yourself, exercise extreme caution: dive with at least one buddy, and be experienced.

Birdlife

El Morro is known for its birdlife. The wood stork and the American oystercatcher frequent these waters. Here, too, you might spot the huge frigate bird, osprey, American kestrel, plovers, ruddy turnstone, willet, gulls, brown tody, and many terns.

Getting Around

A road at the base of El Morro continues east through dry woodland to other beaches and bathing areas. Between El Morro and Punta Ricia there are many fine reefs, most within swimming distance of the beaches. Some of the beach is rocky (and a mess); some is nice sand. The grav-

el and dirt road that leads from El Morro gets a bit sticky at times, and you'll have to have your own transportation unless you run into a particularly knowledgeable taxi driver in Monte Cristi.

PARQUE NACIONAL MONTE CRISTI

Situated on the far northwestern coast of the Dominican Republic, between the mouths of the rivers Yaque del Norte and Dajabón, the Parque Nacional Monte Cristi includes coastal mangroves, salt- and freshwater lagoons, and offshore keys. The area of the park is mostly flat, dry (average rainfall is only 600mm per year), and somewhat hot, with an average temperature of 28.5°C. The vegetation in the park is predominantly dry subtropical forest. There is an abundance of wild frangipani, poisonwood, sage, croton, West Indian boxwood, sweet acacia, holywood, mesquite, and both red and button mangrove in certain areas.

Fauna

The animals in the park are either birds or reptiles, though there are some amphibians and mollusks. Birds lead the way with at least 163 species represented in the park, including brown pelican, frigate birds, great egret, yellow-crowned night heron, glossy ibis, northern jacana, red-footed booby, willet, and burrowing owls. There are also American crocodiles in the area.

Getting In

It isn't easy to arrange a visit to the national park. One of the best ways is to join an organized tour with **Ecoturisa,** or another professional guiding service. You can bargain with fishermen at the port to take you into the windy and thick lagoons and mangroves of the coastal areas. If you do so, be certain to fix the price in advance, pack plenty of supplies—including food, water, and emergency medical equipment—and be home before dark. Some of the park is close to the Haitian border, and with smuggling and illegal immigration in the area, tensions run high. However, the park is a haven for bird and marinelife and can be quite lovely, if sometimes hot and mosquito-choked.

Crossing into Haiti

A single, flat, dusty road leads south from Monte

PARQUE NACIONAL MONTE CRISTI
AND VICINITY

TERRERO

MONTE GRANDE

RATOS

CAYOS SIETE HERMANOS

MONTE CHICO

MUERTOS

TORORU

CORAL

CORAL

PUNTA DE LA GRANJA

ISLA CABRA

BAHIA DES ICAQUITOS

LAGUNA DE LA PIEDRA

ISABEL DE TORRE

LAGUNA QUEYMADA DEL COJO

CAYO AHOGADO

BAHIA DE
MONTE CRISTI

MONTE CRISTI

LA CAÑADA

DUARTE HIGHWAY

LAGUNA VERDE

1

PUNTA LUNA

LAGUNA DE MARIGO

RIO YAQUE DEL NORTE

BATEY JULIANA

PUNTA POZA

PUNTA PRESIDENTE

PUNTA CANGREJO

LAND

SUBJECT

TO

INUNDATION

BATEY ISABEL

LA JUDEA

CARRETERA PRESIDENTE VINCENT

BAHIA DE MANZANILLO

LOS CONUCOS

45

LAGUNA LA SALINA

PEPILLO SALCEDO

RIO CHAUCUEY

COPEY

SANITA

H A I T I

LAGUNA SALADILLA

0   2 mi

0   2 km

SANTA MARIA

© AVALON TRAVEL PUBLISHING, INC.

Cristi to the border town of **Dajabon**. It is one of two major crossing points for vehicular traffic from the Dominican Republic. If you wish to go to Haiti, check with the Haitian and Dominican immigration authorities in Santo Domingo, and do not attempt to cross at Dajabon without proper identification and permissions. The region of Haiti on the other side of the border from Dajabon is a welter of dirt tracks without rhyme or reason. You should only cross if you absolutely know what you're doing.

SOSÚA

As you proceed east along the north coast, you'll find wider choices in accommodation, more authentic provincial towns, and smaller, less-crowded beaches. Even so, Sosúa and Cabarete are part of the international tourist scene and all that implies, both good and bad. It's a fascinating stretch of country.

HISTORY

Sosúa was once a little banana-growing town about 25km (16 miles) east of Puerto Plata. It was located on a nicely sheltered bay on a fine stretch of white-sand beach about one kilometer long. The people who lived there fished for a living and worked in local banana plantations. At the end of the 19th century there was a wave of foreign immigration, mostly Germans and Italians and Cubans, and boat building became something of a local industry. The only roads were dirt tracks winding between banana trees and through the rough savannah bush.

Jewish Refugees
Then, in 1938, suffering from a terrible international reputation as a fascist, the dictator Trujillo publicized an offer to settle 100,000 European Jews in the Dominican Republic. The move to admit refugee Jews went slowly, rather understandably—by 1939, when the war broke out, sea lanes and available shipping were almost unavailable. Still, Trujillo organized the Dominican Settlement Association and donated 26,000 acres of fertile land to the effort, wilderness territory on the edges of the little banana town of Sosúa. The settlement organization was provided with funds to help set up refugee families in farming, and in May 1940, the first two shiploads of 54 settlers arrived to take up their new lives. With the Japanese attack on Pearl Harbor, it became increasingly difficult for refugees to flee Europe. Finally, when the Allies conquered the sea lanes, several thousand Jews were able to come to the Dominican Republic, many of them with papers for their onward journey to the United States.

However, about 800 refugees settled in Sosúa, although some of them could not adapt to farming and isolation and eventually left the small colony. The settlement organization made some preliminary estimations about what it would take to settle around Sosúa and decided to give each refugee at least five acres (30 hectares), 10 head of cattle, and special inducements to raise pork and poultry. Grants were made to begin community projects like a hospital, a school, and sanitation and antimalarial measures. Most of the immigrants were professional people and soon adapted, forming cooperatives, food-processing plants, and dairy industries. They improved cattle-raising techniques, made the first cheeses and butters in the country, and created a new cultural community, including the building of a synagogue which still functions. In the 1940s and 1950s, Sosúa hams, sausages, butters, and cheeses sold at a premium in Santo Domingo.

During the 1970s, many wealthy retirees bought property and erected beach homes in Sosúa. Then, in a stunning reversal, Sosúa nearly succumbed to a wave of sex tourism, which turned nearly every bar into a makeshift brothel. By 1996, the police had stopped the sex tourism, but at the same time, Sosúa suffered an economic downturn.

Tourism and Homogenization
These days there isn't much evidence of the old thriving Jewish community left. For one thing, the community of Sosúa as it was in the late 1940s no longer exists, having been swept under by the rising tide of international tourism and homogenization. The old synagogue on Calle Martínez still stands, and many of the

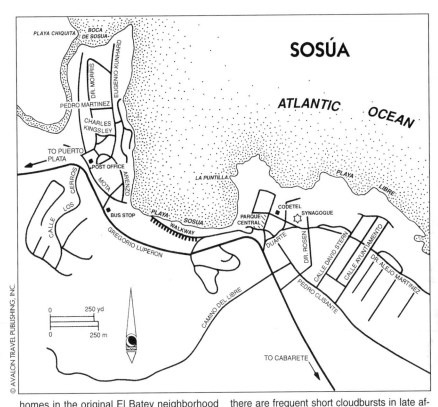

homes in the original El Batey neighborhood have a European feel, but like the historic central sections of Puerto Plata, Sosúa has just about gone under. What can you expect in a town with over 2,000 hotel rooms housing a floating, somewhat vagrant population of sunworshipers, service workers, and international vagabonds?

But even if you're for the lost Sosúa, it's possible to enjoy yourself in modern Sosúa, where there is always a lovely breeze, blue water, and a kilometer of white beach.

CLIMATE

In this part of the country, winds are high, due to the constant presence of the northeast trades. Rain tends to come more in late winter, and

there are frequent short cloudbursts in late afternoons. At Cabo Francés Viejo, the land juts sharply out into the Atlantic Ocean, and the continental shelf narrows considerably. In this ocean region, the water is very deep near shore, increasing both tidal and wave action. Here, the water is a little colder due to its depth, which makes for even greater contrasts in temperature between water and land. Thus, the town of Cabarete on the west side of the cape has become known as "the windsurfing capital of the world" because of its steady high winds.

ORIENTATION

You can orient yourself in Sosúa with relative ease. The main highway runs right by the two neighborhoods distinctive to Sosúa. The **El**

Batey neighborhood is 18th century in origin and is now the site of most of the major hotels, Codetel, the post office, and central park. The other neighborhood, **Los Charamicos,** is poor and separated from El Batey by the long Sosúa beach. A roadway connects the two neighborhoods but is set far behind the beach, so the ocean isn't competing with all the traffic. However, hundreds of shops, stores, and markets are located along this major avenue. Here you can get your T-shirts, scuba lessons, and guided tours.

If you're coming from Puerto Plata and trying to reach El Batey from the main highway, find Calle Duarte and turn left, and then bear right at the fork in the road and look for Calle Alejo Martínez after you pass a triangular park. In this area are many modestly priced hotels. The synagogue is also in that area, next door to the Industria Lechería, the prosperous milk cooperative established by the original Jewish refugees.

Avenida Luperón connects El Batey to Los Charamicos. Near the beach at Los Charamicos is the boat club where yachts are moored.

SPORTS AND RECREATION

Beaches
There are three beaches in Sosúa. First, of course, is the kilometer-long **Playa Sosúa,** which is the main attraction, reachable by public walkway in between El Batey and Los Charmicos. The small **Playa Libre** is in front of El Batey, while **Playa Chiquita** is northwest of Los Charmicos. Although Playa Chiquito is about a kilometer from the main Sosúa beach, it is quite superb, and the area is dominated by Sand Castle Hotel, set on a hill above the water.

Water Sports
Sosúa is probably the most popular location on the whole north coast for deep-sea fishing, snorkeling, and scuba diving. All the resorts organize very good junkets, and keep in mind that there is a marina in Los Charamicos where fishing boats can be hired by the day and half-day. **North Coast Aquasports,** in the Hotel Los Almendros (tel. 809/571-1028), can conduct diving and snorkeling tours, give lessons, and rent equipment. **Dive with Hans** operates a dive shop out of the Hotel Larimar (tel. 809/571-2858), and good old Hans can take you out to the reefs anytime. In the nearby town of Río Juan is **Gri-Gri Divers,** who also handle tours to the Sosúa vicinity. Although there are many dive schools in Sosúa (they come and go regularly), of particular note is **Big Blue,** run by a pair of Swiss divers and their employees. The shop is 50 meters from the main beach. There is a rep in the Sol-de-Plata hotel as well (tel. 809/571-2916). A basic four-day certification course is about US$300. Day trips to caves can be arranged, as well as other super diving trips.

More Recreation
Local travel agents like **Paradise Safaris** and **Melissa Tours** offer excursions that include **hiking.** Hotels in the hills offer **horseback riding,** but you must be a guest.

Because of windy conditions, **tennis** is not the preferred sport in Sosúa, but the main hotels do have tennis courts. Go down to Cabarete to the Las Orquídeas Hotel for the best courts. **Casino gambling** is available in Sosúa only at the Playa Chiquito Beach Resort.

ACCOMMODATIONS

With 2,000 rooms from which to choose, surely you can't go wrong? Well, yes and no. The important thing to remember about Sosúa is that the town is completely given over to tourism. There are a few remaining hotels downtown where you can get affordable, meaning cheap, rooms. For the most part, the area has gone to seed with luxury resorts or expensive tourist hotels. The good news is that competition seems to have kept prices somewhat in line, so that tourist hotels, at least most of them, are in the moderate price range, charging anywhere from US$50–80 per night single.

Apart-Hotels
One way to try to save some money in Sosúa, and still have an excellent vacation on the beach, is to put up in an apart-hotel and cook some of your own food. Of course, some apart-hotels are modestly expensive, but most are very reasonably priced. With a very good location in El Batey, one of the best choices is **Apart Hotel**

One Ocean Place (tel. 809/571-3131, fax 809/571-3144). The One Ocean Place has 55 units with kitchenettes, cable TV, phone, pool and children's pool. It is on the upper end of the price scale, at around US$45 per night. You can decrease your costs by engaging the hotels for long-term stays. One higher end apart-hotel is the **El Neptuno** (La Puntila, El Batey, tel. 809/571-2664), with 18 deluxe two-bedroom apartments. This isn't a way to go budget at all, but long-term, it can save money over a luxury resort. El Neptuno has pool, whirlpool, and snack bar, all overlooking the ocean. Much less expensive is **Apart Hotel Alcázar** (tel. 809/571-2321) and the **Dominicanos Apart-Hotel** (tel. 809/571-2504), which has 12 studio apartments, some with one and some two bedrooms, no pool. To the east, on Pedro Clisante, the **Club Residential** (tel. 809/571-3675, fax 571-1143) rents nice units by the week or month.

Inexpensive
There are a number of decent tourist hotels for good value in downtown Sosúa (i.e., the El Batey neighborhood). Most offer clean rooms, a bar, and sometimes a small restaurant. They usually have pleasant service, but no big pools, free drinks, game rooms, water sports, or chocolates on the pillow in the morning. You can be happy at these hotels, however. One excellent choice, for small but comfortable cabins and studios, is the **Sosúa Sol** (tel. 809/571-2334, fax 809/571-2416), located a 10-minute walk from El Batey. Some of the 16 units have kitchens, and there are fans, a pool, billiards, a bar and restaurant, all for around US$25 double. Equally pleasant is the small **Hotel Tropix** (Camino El Mirador, tel. 809/571-2291) which has 10 cabanas on garden-like grounds with a pool. Some cabanas have air-conditioning, some only fans, and there are no phones orTVs. The Tropix, though, has special appeal for its down-home atmosphere, and the communal eating arrangements from December to August, which allow people to see the cooks making a set-menu dinner each evening for guests and non-guests alike. The beach isn't too far away, either.

Less expensive yet, but still much raved about, is the **Auberge Village Inn** (Calle Dr. Rosen, tel. 809/571-2569, fax 809/571-2865), a small American-owned inn with only eight rooms, a small pool, and facilities for breakfast. You can get drinks and watch TV in the restaurant, and walk to all three Sosúa beaches in a matter of a few minutes. The Auberge is very near the Tiburón Blanco. Note, though, that the Auberge is somewhat dirty and dark, reported to be on a slide downhill. Nearby, on Calle Pedro Clisante, is the **Hotel Yaroa** (tel. 809/571-2578), which features a rooftop deck, French restaurant, and swimming pool. There are several very modest hotels in the El Batey area, including **La Posada** (Av. Kunhardt, tel. 809/571-2235), **Hotel Solimar** (Av. Kunhardt, tel. 809/571-3303), and the **Hotel Atlantic,** (Calle Martínez, tel. 809/571-2707).

On the El Batey side of Sosúa, try the inexpensive 53-room **Hotel Montana** (Calle Libre, tel. 809/571-2255). Check it out first and see if you can handle the simple rooms. Other reasonable accommodation is found mostly in Los Charamicos. In the US$15 range is **Pensión Gómez** (Calle Carmen, tel. 809/571-5159) and **Hotel El Bambú** (tel. 809/571-2379). Both the **Pensión La Cancilleria** (tel. 809/571-3594) and the **Pensión Tata** (Calle Kinder 15) are true budget accommodations.

And finally, the situation in Sosúa has grown so overwhelming that some hotels are spreading out on the roadway between the airport and Sosúa, and then beyond Sosúa toward Cabarete. For example, right near the airport is the **Hotel Colina Sol y Mar** (tel. 809/571-3250, fax 809/571-3540), which has 72 rooms and features a pool, restaurant, disco, and 18-hole miniature golf course, and provides shuttles to the various beaches. New is the **Sol de Plata Beach Resort** on the road to Cabarete (tel. 809/571-3600, fax 809/571-3389), a luxury resort with everything a luxury resort should have, of course.

The pleasant, German-owned **El Paraíso** (tel. 809/571-2906) charges US$30 double, US$20 double off-season, which includes breakfast and the use of a courtyard pool.

Among the oldest and most famous of the modest tourist hotels is **Koch's Ocean Front Guest House** (Calle Martínez, tel. 809/571-2284), owned by one of the original refugees. The guest house has nine cabanas and four rooms, two with ocean views. In the same price range, US$25–35 per night single, are the **Apart Hotel Neuvosol** (Clisante 11, tel./fax 809/571-

2124), with basic rooms, and the **Pensión Anneliese** (Calle Dr. Rosen, El Batey, tel. 809/571-2208), which can house about 12 people who are all served a good breakfast.

Moderate

Sosúa is also blessed by a large number of relatively small tourist hotels, modest in price, most within easy walking distance of the main Sosúa beach on the bay. You should consider a price between US$35–60 single in the moderate range during the high season. Most have pools, air-conditioning, small restaurants, and outdoor bars.

In the moderate price range is the **Hotel Sosúa,** located right in El Batey (Calle Martínez, tel. 809/571-2683, fax 809/571-2180). This small hotel has only 40 rooms and advertises that it is 106 meters from the beach. Some of the accommodations are apartments, and there are some studios, some with fans, some with air-conditioning. There are, however, tennis courts, a laundry, massage room, bar, Italian restaurant, and swimming pool. This hotel is reported to have gone considerably downhill lately. It would be best to check and see what's up.

Villas Carolina (tel. 809/571-3626) in El Batey has junior and senior suites, two pools, air-conditioning, and cable TV. Very nice is the **Hotel Jardín del Sol,** Canadian-run and quite restful, located in El Batey too. Call them at 809/571-3553 or fax at 809/571-3485, about their one- and two-bedroom villas and some studios. They have a restaurant, bar, and pool. The **Hotel Sea Breeze** offers good value in El Batey, and is much like the Hotel Sosúa. The Sea Breeze (tel. 809/571-3858, fax 809/571-2129) has 31 air-conditioned rooms with private balcony, either ocean or garden views, kitchenettes, the Rose Garden restaurant, aquatic sports, cable TV in the game room, a swimming pool, and medical and security service. You can also walk to the beach. Just up the hill, 400m from the beach, is the reasonably priced **Hotel Vistamar** (tel. 809/571-3308, fax 809/571-2900), which is quite intimate and has a nice pool area, a terrace bar and restaurant, and shuttle service to downtown Sosúa and to Cabarete.

A condo-style hotel is the **Palm Village/Palm Resort** (tel. 809/571-3315, fax 809/571-3240), which is upper moderate in price but has two swimming pools, air-conditioned rooms, and cable TV. There are 69 units at the Palm Resort. Also in the upper bracket of moderate prices is the brand new **Marco Polo Club,** featuring luxury apartments, private whirlpool, and a view of the bay. Telephone them at 809/571-3128, fax at 809/571-3233. The Marco Polo has two gourmet restaurants, one French, one Italian, a cafe bar with live music, and the Banana, a breakfast buffet and bar above the ocean. Its style is Victorian gazebo. In Puerto Chiquito, the **Hotel Tropicana Sur** (tel. 809/571-1170, fax 809/571-1169) has 49 rooms.

Farther away from the beach, at the the main highway turnoff for El Batey, is the old fixture **Los Almendros Hotel** (tel. 809/571-3530), which has nice, air-conditioned rooms. It is a fully equipped apart-hotel. Newer, but somewhat expensive is the **Hostal de Lora** (Calle Martínez, tel. 809/571-3939), with 32 suites, either junior or executive, a pool, and lots of stained glass and artwork. Also in El Batey is the expensive **Woody's Hotel** (Calle Dr. Rosen, next to the Village Inn), which has 66 rooms and a nice pool. Also on Calle Dr. Rosen is the **Tiburón Blanco Hotel Restaurante** (tel. 809/571-3471).

Expensive

Probably the most elegant and exclusive tourist hotel in Sosúa is located right on Calle Martínez, not far from the main Sosúa beach. Called the **Hotel Corralillo** (Av. Martínez 1, tel. 809/571-2645, fax 809/571-2095), this Spanish-style hotel overlooks Sosúa Bay and has 52 guest rooms including five deluxe cabanas, all set in gardens that are lovely. There aren't any phones in the rooms, and only the cabanas have TV sets. The hotel has a nice pool, an outdoor dining terrace, and a gourmet restaurant. In the same price range, and also in El Batey above Sosúa Bay, is the 32-room inn called **Club Marina** (Calle Martínez, tel. 809/571-3939, fax 809/571-3110), prettied up with spiral staircases and stained-glass windows. Not quite as expensive as the Corralillo, Club Marina does not have a restaurant, but has a small pool, a whirlpool, a bar, and very lush gardens. Both of these exclusive tourist hotels are in the US$70–90 per night range.

In Puerto Chiquito, down the hill from the Sand Castle, is the Victorian-design **Coral Beach Re-**

sort (tel. 809/571-2577, fax 809/571-2197), which has 63 rooms in a split-level design, some suites, and all the amenities. In the same price range (US$80–100 per night) is the nearby **Playa Chiquita Beach Resort** (tel. 809/571-2800 or 809/571-3222, fax 809/571-2470), which has 90 rooms with kitchen facilities near the beach, along with a pool and restaurant.

Also located in El Batey is the quiet **Larimar Beach Resort** (Calle Bruno Phillipp, tel. 809/571-2868, fax 809/571-3382). Right on the beach, you can step from the swimming pool onto the sand here. There are 135 total rooms, standard with air-conditioning, superior with fan and ocean view, junior suites with fan, two balconies, and ocean view, all with double beds. Also available are a gymnasium, sports activities, mini-store, and beauty salon. Rates are around US$90–110 per day.

Luxury

The **La Esplanada Sosúa Resort** is also located in Pedro Clisante (tel. 809/571-3333 or U.S. tel. 800/423-6902, fax 809/571-3922). The 210 rooms come with all the amenities, and half of them are called "junior suites." Available sports include windsurfing, tennis, and volleyball. It's a bit more spread out than most resorts and therefore less crowded. Still, the cost is about US$100 per day, though you must check the plan before making a reservation.

Perhaps the most traditional of the luxury resorts is the old stand-by, **Sosúa By the Sea** (tel. 809/571-3222 or U.S. tel. 800/531-7043, fax 809/571-3020), with 81 studios and apartments, all done in rattan, featuring views of the ocean and a restaurant on Sosúa Bay. Another luxury resort is the **Charamicos Beach Resort** (tel. 809/571-2675). A nontraditional luxury resort is the **Sosúa Sun Bay Club** (tel. 809/571-0704), a 68-room resort for singles, with three bars, restaurant, disco, pool, and sports. Good access to the Playa Libre beach is the advantage of the luxury resort **Casa Marina Beach Club** (tel. 809/571-3690, fax 809/571-3110), a chain-operated 116-room resort with a large pool, three restaurants, health club, and all the sports you could want, including scuba and windsurfing. The rooms are spread among five three-story buildings surrounding the pool.

The **Piergiorgio Palace Hotel** (La Puntilla 2,

tel. 809/571-2215, fax 809/571-2786) is a new all-inclusive resort overlooking Playa Sosúa. Two meals at the excellent La Puntilla restaurant terrace are included in the US$150 price for a double. Slightly less expensive is the **Waterfront** (Dr. Rosen 1, tel. 809/571-2760), which has bungalos with sea views and a great ocean-view pool on a terrace.

The **Sand Castle Beach Resort** (tel. 809/571-2420, fax 809/571-2000) is located on a cliff above Puerto Chiquito and has a great view from its terraces and balconies. This is an all-inclusive resort, and average prices run about US$140 per night single for one of its 240 rooms in pink Moorish style. For that price you also get two pools, two tennis courts, a fitness center, four restaurants, five bars, a disco, and a shopping center. As at all the big resorts in the Dominican Republic, the Sand Castle has plenty of organized water sports, including snorkeling, scuba, and deep-sea fishing.

On the other side of town, the **LTI Sol de Plata Beach Resort** (tel. 809/571-3600, fax 809/571-3389) is spread out over two million square feet of land and has its own beach. This place threatens to become another Playa Dorada. There are 216 rooms in six three-story buildings, 134 rooms and 20 suites in 29 villas, and all have the normal stuff—TV, mini-bar, and telephone. There is a lot of landscaping here and two pools, including one with sea water, four tennis courts, archery, volleyball, and a sports center for surfing and diving. At this resort you get privileges at the Playa Dorada golf course and can play at a 9-hole course nearby. Here you can rent a car, get your hair done, exchange money and go horseback riding and deep-sea fishing. Although prices vary with the plan and the number of persons, you can expect to pay US$150 per day all-inclusive.

The LTI is also home to the **Sea Horse Ranch** (tel. 809/571-3880, fax 809/571-2374), a secluded area of homes, pasture, and woods, with tennis courts and a riding center. Here you can rent a private vacation home for an arm and a leg. Back away from the beach in the hills is the exclusive and expensive, all-inclusive **Club Escapade** (tel. 809/571-5852), which has several restaurants, a big pool, tennis courts, and a shuttle to the beach every 30 minutes. The 209 rooms come with booze and entertainment. Also in the hills are the **Villas Baleares** (tel. 809/562-7461).

Bear in mind that not all these luxury resorts are all-inclusive, and that rates tend to vary depending upon the type of room and the season. Be sure you include taxes in your calculations. The resorts in Sosúa tend to be less expensive than those in Playa Dorada, although the resorts in the hills are more expensive yet.

FOOD

There are two or three ways to think about eating and drinking in Sosúa. In the first place, food stalls and small outdoor bars are the norm along the Sosúa beach. These stalls serve fried chicken, sandwiches, and empanadas, along with all kinds of fresh fruit drinks and cold beer. There are also cafes and cafeterias spread throughout the town where you can get inexpensive sitdown food, much of it in the *comida criolla* vein, and much of it tricked up by international-style outfits offering pizza, burgers, and other fast food. Likewise, eating expensively and well is easy in Sosúa. All of the best hotels and resorts sport one or more gourmet restaurants where you can dine on the finest steaks, seafood, and Caribbean cuisine. Finally, there are a large number of modestly priced restaurants, and a few expensive ones as well, along the Calle Pedro Clisante.

Inexpensive

You'll find the truly inexpensive food in local cafeterias, many of which are in Los Charamicos. It doesn't take much to cross the walkway in front of Sosúa beach. Among several other cafeteria-style eating places is **La Deportiva. Restaurant Tortuga** is a sit-down cafe with *comida criolla,* as is **El Oasis.**

For fresh-baked goods, try **Alemán Panadería** (German Bakery) on Calle Ayuntamiento in El Batey, or **Molinos Dominicanos** in Los Charamicos. Fresh bakery goods and fruit can go a long way toward cutting food costs in Sosúa.

Moderate

Highly recommended is **On the Waterfront** (Calle Dr. Rosen, tel. 809/571-3024), connected to Charlie's Cabañas. This funky restaurant

serves a little bit of everything on its menu, and you might get live music, folk bands, or a spectacular view of the ocean too. They serve up breakfast, lunch, and dinner; dinners cost about US$10, not including drinks. Calle Clisante is really the place for moderately priced meals if you're not going for burgers, fries, or cardboard pizza. There are strings of restaurants big and small, all pretty good, including **Don Juan's Restaurant, Restaurante Amigos, Pollo Rico, PJ's, International,** and **Casablanca Bar and Grill.** One of the local favorites of note is **Restaurant Spaguetti House** (Calle Clisante 28, tel. 809/571-3301), which serves delicious, wood-baked oven pizzas.

The Larimar offers both the **Pancho Bar and Grill** and **The Larimar Restaurant.** For reasonably priced organic food try **Caribe** (tel. 809/571-3138), located near the Club Escapade Hotel. Also on Pedro Clisante is **Lorenzo's,** which serves both Italian and Dominican food. There are many other small, nook-and-cranny places in Sosúa to find a decent meal and not spend a bundle. They are, literally, everywhere. For example, **Restaurant Mamma Mia** (tel. 809/571-3394) has Italian quick food, and in El Batey, the **Guajiros Café** (tel. 809/571-2161) serves Caribbean food and claims to have a German bar. Moderately priced German food is also the specialty of **La Carve** in El Batey.

Expensive

Many say that **El Coral** is the best restaurant in town (El Batey, tel. 809/571-2645). Located in the Hotel Corralillo, this gourmet restaurant is set in a Spanish-style building with white walls, lots of wood, and much terra-cotta. The menu features octopus, grilled shrimp, and pork chops, among many other things. As is the case in all the expensive restaurants in Sosúa, meals, with appetizers, wine, and dessert could run as much as US$25 per person. The general appetizer is US$3–4, while main courses average US$8–20. This is more or less average for gourmet restaurants in the area. Two other hotel restaurants are excellent. **Sunset Place Restaurant** in Sosúa by the Sea (tel. 809/571-3222) serves both lunch and dinner in a rooftop dining area. You can watch the sun go down and later eat special pâté, seafood pastry, or a selection of fresh fish like tuna. The restaurant is also open for early breakfast. Another fine hotel restaurant is the **Restaurant Verena** in the Hotel Yaroa (El Batey, tel. 809/571-2651), which serves daily lunch and evening dinner until late. The menu is Dominican International, so there is a wide variety represented.

The **Morua Mai** (Pedro Clisante 5, tel. 809/571-2503) is on a popular intersection in town. This place is a cross between European sidewalk cafe and sophisticated evening grill. You can eat sandwiches and have drinks under a thatched roof in the afternoon, or eat in elegant surroundings at night. The Morua Mai serves lobster and shrimp, seafood platters, and grilled steaks. Lunch is more like oven-fresh pizza and light pasta dishes.

The **Restaurant del Atlántico** (Los Charmicos, tel. 809/571-2878) has gourmet steak and seafood. You can dine right over the water. On the other side of the bay is the famous **La Puntilla de Pierfiorgo** (Calle La Puntilla 1, tel. 809/571-2215), an expensive restaurant on a terrace overlooking Sosúa Bay. This place was formerly the home of an American diplomat but now specializes in seafood and Italian dishes. This is probably *the* spot to enjoy an expensive sunset. At the lower end of the expensive scale is **De Armando** (Calle Clisante, tel. 809/571-3022), which, like its sister in Puerto Plata, serves Italian food.

The Larimar has the gourmet **Don Thomas.** Of the remaining gourmet restaurants, those of note are in the **Sand Castle Beach Resort,** the **Playa Chiquito Beach Resort,** and the **Marco Polo Club.** Up in the hills, try the **Club Escapade** to get away from the city.

Markets

If you're staying in an apart-hotel, you can save money by cooking for yourself. **Playero** (tel. 809/571-2554) is a well-stocked supermarket right in the middle of El Batey. You can find everything at **Supermercado El Batey** on the Calle Clisante or **Super** on Calle Ayuntamiento. Cheap booze is at **Mesón Liquor Store** on Pedro Clisante. There are mini-markets galore.

ENTERTAINMENT AND EVENTS

Nightclubs

Unfortunately, a lot of the nightlife in Sosúa is geared strictly to tourist traffic. For example, the **Central Connection** in Sosúa, on Pedro Clisante, is a kind of entertainment mall, themed with thatched roofs and cream-colored stucco walls where there are 15 restaurants and clubs, along with three dance clubs, including **Under the Mango Tree,** which bills itself as a "typical Caribbean dancing bar." Funny, I didn't know bars could dance—but so be it. Inside this entertainment mall are a few themed restaurants including the **Devil's Pavilion,** a beer bar, and **Pinocchio** featuring Austrian and Italian food in a "south Tyrol" atmosphere. Other patently tourist enterprises include the **Schwaben Hütte Bistro,** which bills itself as an international pub but caters to northern Europeans, and other uncompelling spots like **Dr. Quax,** which calls itself a cruising bar and offers special rooms for rent. The unfortunate truth is that Sosúa has a bit of a prostitution problem, and steering among and between the cute girls and guys can be entertaining. A big part of the Sosúa scene is the loud beer and rum bars where young people with sunburns swill alcohol.

For a big night on the town, some people enjoy the quackery at the **Copacabana Club** (El Batey, tel. 809/571-3949), where huge stage shows are the focus of attention. The building is set in a white mock-Moorish castle and is stricken with neon. Despite its garishness and camp libido atmosphere, it is kind of fun. At certain times during the week, you can catch displays of Dominican folk-dancing at the second floor of the **Plaza Marinero.**

There are dozens of bars along Calle Martínez and Pedro Clisante.

Bars

For quieter times, all the luxury resorts have pleasant bars, some poolside, some with live music. Check out the live jazz at **Charlie's Cabañas,** and the Dominican guitar music at the **Merengue Bar** across from Moby Dick's. A great place for quiet drinks, games of backgammon, and soft music is the **Tree Top Lounge** (Calle Pedro Clisante, tel. 809/571-2141), where the decor is tropical and the drinks all have little umbrellas in them. There is a good pizzeria downstairs that is open every day from 4 P.M. until the wee hours of the morning. The

Casablanca Bar and Grill, also on Pedro Clisante at #12, plays lively Caribbean and American music, and just before you hit the beach is **La Roca,** one of the oldest spots in Sosúa, with great atmosphere and good food and music, especially the "gourmet" pizzas. Also try **The Britannia** on Calle P. Clisante, where dive masters and English-speakers hang out and drink beer.

Discos

Perhaps the best disco is **Moby Dick's** at Pedro Clisante and Calle Dr. Rosen. Other good discos include **La Pirámide** and **Barrock,** also in the hotel district. Bear in mind that discos are sometimes frequented by prostitutes. It is part of the scene. If something can be recommended it is **High Caribbean,** on the outskirts of town on the road to Cabarete, which features an indoor swimming pool.

SHOPPING

Sosúa isn't the greatest shopping town in the Dominican Republic. Of course, there are lots of souvenir shops and small hole-in-the-wall markets where you can buy standard amber and larimar. The **Viva Galería de Arte** (next to the Banco Popular, tel. 809/571-2581) has a selection of Dominican ceramics and jewelry, along with giftware of many kinds. The **Dominicana Record Shop** is on Pedro Clisante (tel. 809/571-2778). Also on Pedro Clisante is **Toe Rings,** which features gems, fossils, and various New Age rigmarole, and down the street on the landside are several boutiques. For special leather work, including hand-tooled saddles, try the workshop of **Juan Francisco de los Santos** on the main highway out of Sosúa, near the Gran Parada.

INFORMATION AND SERVICES

There are two **Codetel** offices in Sosúa, the main one being on Calle Dr. Rosen at Martínez, and another on the main street of Los Charmicos. **Comet Couriers** (Calle Dr. Rosen #2, tel. 809/571-3030) is well known for its message, fax, mail, typing, and photocopying services.

Honda Rent a Car has a desk at the Hotel Los Almendros (tel. 809/571-3280), and there are numerous places to rent motorcycles and motorscooters, including **Rubio Rent a Motor** (El Batey, tel. 809/571-3698) and **Elba Rent-a-Bicycle** (tel. 809/517-2050). The best place to rent a car is at the Sosúa Airport before you hit town. Remember, renting a motorcycle, motorbike, or scooter in Sosúa carries certain risks, not the least of which is theft. Make sure you know what you're doing, and be insured.

In case of emergencies there are several good pharmacies in the Sosúa area, including **Farmacia San Rafael** (tel. 809/571-2515).

TRANSPORTATION

Probably the best way to enjoy this part of the coast is by car. However, public buses are very common, and it is easy to catch them at each town heading in your direction, or to bargain for a *motoconcho* or local taxi between cities and resorts, most of which tend to be quite close together in absolute terms.

Getting There

If you arrive at the Puerto Plata International Airport, a taxi to Sosúa should cost you as little as US$10 with tip. From Puerto Plata, a taxi to Sosúa should run you about US$15 with tip. *Públicos* leave quite often from the main square, or even more often from the hospital on Circunvalación Sur. **Caribe Tours** goes east along the coast; the cost to Puerto Plata is about US$3. Caribe tours also runs eight buses a day to Santo Domingo, a trip of 4–5 hours for RD$85. There is a variety of public transport heading out of Puerto Plata, going along the east coast, including the ubiquitous *guaguas,* minivans, and even *motoconchos.* They are very cheap and always crowded. These minivans and *guaguas* also leave every so often (you can't tell when) from the main square when the van is full. You can get to Sosúa for about US$1.50.

Getting Around

The chosen form of transportation in Sosúa is the *motoconcho,* a motorcycle taxi. They will take you anywhere you want to go for a negotiated price. Taxis congregate everywhere as well and are a bargain, though you must be firm about your price.

Area Tours

There are fewer tour agencies headquartered in Sosúa than in Puerto Plata. If your desire is a complete tour of the north coast area, it would be good to shop around in Puerto Plata before heading to Sosúa. However, there are several good operators with offices in town. **Melissa** is a large outfit (Calle Duarte, tel. 809/571-2567), as is **Turinter** (Edificio Bommarito, tel. 809/571-2635, fax 809/571-2402). Specialty trips are offered by **Camping Tours** (Calle Martínez, tel. 809/571-2810), though none is about camping. But you can go to the Cabarete Caves or Los Haitises, along with some other journeys. **Servitur Travel** (Calle Clisante 2, tel. 809/571-3500) has similar trips. **Paradise Safaris** (Jardín del Sol Hotel, tel. 809/571-3090) can give you a ride through the back country on excellent trips with jeeps. Should you desire a real Dominican experience, check out what they have to offer.

The **Caribe Tours** (tel. 809/571-3808) office is in Los Charmicos, just as you enter the neighborhood. They have buses back to Puerto Plata, and from there to Santo Domingo. Fares are cheap. *Guaguas* and vans ply the highway east and west. Stand on the roadside and flag down one going in the proper direction.

CABARETE

INTRODUCTION

Before its present incarnation, Cabarete was a fishing village and nothing else. Fate, however, placed it on three km of pure white sand and endowed it with brisk, year-round trade winds. Because the coast at Cabarete lays north and west, the water is pushed into the land, and at times, huge waves result. Consequently, in the 1970s a few Canadian and European windsurfers and surfers began coming to Cabarete. Today, Cabarete is the windsurfing capital of the Dominican Republic. The region has hosted the Wind Surfing World Championships, and international competitions are held here annually in June.

The main highway splits the town of Cabarete in half. Near the beaches are dozens of tourist hotels, apart-hotels, cabanas, and bars catering to a mostly young, mostly athletic clientele.

ACCOMMODATIONS

When the windsurf boom started a couple of decades ago, Cabarete held a number of small hotels catering to young surfers. They were basic and inexpensive. Today, however, tourism is creeping up on Cabarete. Already you'll find one all-inclusive resort and a large number of moderately priced tourist hotels in Cabarete. Not surprisingly, the inexpensive apart-hotels and tourist hotels have raised their prices considerably. Hence, Cabarete is not so cheap as it once was. Cabarete used to be all about windsurfing, but now there is a seemingly bewildering array of bars and discos on the main drag, and more and more tourists and travelers are "hanging out," adding to the already substantial number of windsurfers. Cabarete is most crowded in February, when Cabarete Algería is held every weekend. During this time, local businesses hold a series of athletic events, capped by the Dominican national surfing championships. In June, the Encuentero Classic is held, a world-class windsurfing championship. If you want to go to Cabarete during winter, the best thing to do, even if it goes against the grain, is book hotels ahead.

Inexpensive

It would be nice to report that Cabarete is crawling with inexpensive places to stay. It is not. Many who come here to windsurf wind up sharing rooms and facilities with other surfers. There are some individual rooms for rent, so you can check out the scene and see what's available.

Probably the pick of the litter among "budget" hotels is the **Laguna Blu** (tel. 809/571-0659), near the town center. It has 26 rooms, each with a private hot-water bathroom, and is fairly quiet.

There's also a pool; at US$25, it is best to book ahead. Other less-expensive hotels include the **Gigi Beach Hotel** (tel. 809/571-0722) and the **Hotel El Magnífico** (tel. 809/571-0686). For doubling up there is the **Windsurf Apartment Hotel** (tel. 809/571-0710).

Moderate

Most of the tourist hotels in Cabarete average about US$60–80 per night, depending upon the number of people in occupancy and the time of year. Many people who come to Cabarete double-up, triple-up, or quadruple-up in rooms—keep that in mind as a possibility.

Not too expensive is the **Banana Boat Hotel** (tel. 809/571-0690), which has rooms in the US$35 range and is quiet and centrally located with a laundry and some kitchens.

Tourist hotels include the **Ocean Breeze Inn** a lovely hotel in a quiet setting at the edge of town. A double room in the high season is priced at about US$55 a night. You can make a reservation from the United States at 800/524-7610. **Teddy's Caribe Surf Hotel** (tel. 809/571-0788, fax. 809/571-3346), at US$50, is an overpriced flop. Windsurfing is king at the older **Auberge du Roi Tropical** (tel. 809/571-0770). Located right on the windsurf beach, the Auberge caters to the surfing crowd. Here you can rent boards or bicycles, or swim in the pool, but you should be prepared to share the hotel with dedicated surfers, many of whom cram their rooms with three or four people each night. On the beach, the **Camino del Sol** (tel. 809/571-2858) has a whirlpool and tennis court, while the similarly named **Cita del Sol** (tel. 809/571-0720, fax 809/571-0795) has 48 rooms with kitchenette, pool, restaurant, and bar. One interesting smaller hotel is the **Hotel Ka-O-Ba** (tel. 809/571-0837), which has 30 thatched-roof bungalows spread over lush gardens, most with fan only. There is a good pool here, a restaurant and bar, and you can get reductions for lengthy stays. This would be a good spot for one of those month-long getaways to clean out the spirit.

Among the newer establishments

are the **Seagrape Beach Club** (tel./fax 809/571-0651) and the **Caracol** (tel. 809/571-0680, fax 809/571-0665), both of which offer deluxe air-conditioned rooms with pool, bar, and restaurant. One of the deluxe tourist hotels in Cabarete is the **Hotel Playa de Oro** (tel. 809/571-0880, fax 809/571-0871). Another is located just out of town, reachable by shuttle. Called the **Hotel Bella Vista** (tel. 809/571-0759), it has 36 rooms, a cafeteria, a pool, and a focus on water sports.

In the *ultra* luxury league is the **Coconut Palms** (tel. 809/571-1625, fax 809/571-1725), which has large rooms, some two-bedroom apartments with kitchens, a bar, a tennis court, and a big pool. The Coconut Palms is very near the heart of a windsurfing beach.

Probably the most expensive of them all is the nice **Cabarete Beach Hotel** (tel. 809/571-0755, fax 809/571-0831). This hotel sits right on the beach and, with only 24 rooms (some with air-conditioning, some with fan), has the virtue of being small and intimate; there are two restaurants, a disco, and a gift shop. The restaurant is called the Mariposa and serves nice seafood and Caribbean dishes. The best room here goes for about US$90 in winter, and you can get a room for under US$40 in the off-season.

Expensive

For hip-chic, you can't beat the trendy **El Magnífico** (Curratera 5, tel. 809/571-0868), an adobe structure with great rooms, a pool, a private beach, and unique architecture. At US$80–100 per night it is not cheap, but it is generally booked solid months in advance. Also on Carratera 5 is the **Windsurf Apart-Hotel** (tel. 809/571-0718), a clean and efficient place to stay with a pool and good service. Rooms are US$80 or thereabouts.

The most exclusive and expensive luxury resort in the Cabarete area is the **Punta Goleta Beach Resort** (tel. 809/571-0700, fax 809/571-0707). Actually, this resort and its 160 air-conditioned rooms are located about two kilometers from the center of Cabarete, on a beach called

brown pelican

BOB RACE

Punta Goleta, which is just an extension of Cabarete beach. The property is located on 100 acres of lush vegetation, and the rooms feature one king or two double beds. There are two tennis courts, two whirlpools, a sauna, a small gym, a pool bar, a beach bar, a disco, horseback riding, and bicycle rentals. The hotel also has a restaurant and offers windsurfing, snorkeling, and scuba diving concessions as well. There is even a billiard room and golfing privileges at the nearby Costa Azul course (nine holes). The resort is only 18km from the Puerto Plata International Airport.

Also in the luxury category is the **Royal Larimar Beach Resort** (tel./fax 809/571-0940), which has a very secluded location and 72 rooms, each with air-conditioning, color TV, phones, and a terrace balcony. Both of these luxury resorts are expensive by any standards, with the all-inclusive rate of US$120 at Punta Goleta, and US$100 at the Royal Larimar. These prices are significantly less in the off-season.

Luxury Condos

European-style luxury condos seem to be the latest thing on the Cabarete beach scene. Usually a collection of studio and one- and two-bedroom apartments grouped around a pool, most of these condo hotels also feature a whirlpool or sauna. A good example of these kinds of hotels is the **Palm Beach Condominiums** (tel. 809/571-0758, fax 809/571-0752), with 16 units for rent, a pool, maid service, complete kitchens, and patios. Each has two bedrooms and two baths. At an average of about US$160 per night, these condos are made to be shared in order to be affordable. More elaborate yet is the **Villas del Atlántico** (tel. 809/571-0730, fax 809/571-0740). Here there are 41 one- and two-bedroom units with pool, restaurant, BBQ, bar, and the ubiquitous whirlpool. The same kind of thing is offered at Bahía de Arena in the **Hotel Condos Albatrós** (tel. 809/571-0841, fax 809/571-0704), which has 21 units, a pool, a restaurant, and baby-sitters. New is the **Terrazas Las Palmas Condo Hotel** (tel. 809/571-0780, fax 809/571-0781), located very near the ocean with 78 units, 39 of which are studios, and offering a small pool, manicured grounds, a whirlpool, and an emphasis on wind and water sports.

It used to be that the best place for tennis in Cabarete was the **Las Orquídeas de Cabarete** (tel. 809/571-0787, fax 809/571-0853), with its 24 large one- and two-bedroom apartments. This established condo hotel has a nice restaurant, gardens, a bar, and a large pool and is set away from the main street for quiet, down a 500-meter road at the east end of town. The hotel was up for sale, so check and see what's happening; it has always been good value, and the tennis courts are the best on the north coast. The **Tropic Breeze Apartments** (tel. 809/571-0748, fax 809/571-3346) also offers luxury condos with one-, two-, and three-bedroom places. On the beach is the **Cabarete Beach Studio Apartments** (tel. 809/571-0772, fax 809/571-3346), which has rooms with kitchens and a German restaurant attached to the hotel. Sort of in the middle is the **Casa Laguna Hotel and Resort** (tel. 809/571-0725), which has some straight hotel rooms and some two-bedroom units (all with air-conditioning), a pool, a bar, and a restaurant. Keep in mind that all these luxury condo units are in the US$80–120 range, depending upon the number of rooms, length of stay, time of year, and so on. The rates can be even higher at some condo hotels, so be sure to check with travel agents before you book.

A new addition to the condo estate concept is the **First Class Resort Hotel** (tel. 809/571-0911) on the main street in Cabarete, with 17 units, each with kitchen and bar-quipped living room. Other amenities include a pool, breakfast room, maid service, boutique, and Codetel center for telephones. Call for information on price. Also luxurious in concept and price is the **Nanny Estate** (tel. 809/571-0744, fax 809/571-0655), which offers 20 units with a pool, whirlpool, and restaurant. The units are in two-story condo-style apartments and they are all two-bedroom apartments.

FOOD

Inexpensive

The bad news in Cabarete is the fact that there are so few stalls, vendors, and stands serving quick food for cheap prices. The place hasn't the space to accommodate many of these kinds of pleasant food vendors, which can make eating so cheap in other parts of the country. The good news is that Europeans have brought a dash of the flair and international adventure to Carabete's dining scene. Good new restaurants seem to pop up all the time.

Moderate

For reasonable prices, the place to go is **Las Brisas,** which doubles as a disco at night. Here you will find reasonably priced Dominican food, a happy hour every evening, and sometimes, though not often, live music at night. Still, you can dance after dinner. **El Pirata,** on the main road facing the ocean, has decent steaks and crepes, with good desserts. New to the beach is the **New Wave Cafe,** which features lighter foods, fresh-squeezed fruit juices, ice cream, and music. The setting here is very pleasant.

Another nice place right on the beach (you can see the waves crashing in) is **Julio's Fish-n-Chips** (tel. 809/571-0668). Julio's not only serves fish and chips, but good steaks and a selection of seafood dishes as well. Also on the main road is **Leandro's,** one place you can get authentic *comida criolla* in a town that caters mostly to foreign tastes.

For Italian food try the lunches, dinners, and Friday buffets at **L'Italiano.** Also with good pizza is **La Pizzeria de Cabarete** and **Island Pizzeria Restaurant.**

Also good is **Mariposa's** at the Cabarete Beach Hotel, a good place to try the breakfast buffet that features pancakes, crepes, and omelettes. For slicker fare at higher prices, good bets are **La Casita** and **Miro's,** both upscale spots for dinner in the RD$150 range. Both feature seafood, but La Casita specializes in lobster. For a quick but delicious snack, try down the Carratera at **Panadería Repostería Dick,** a French bakery with delicious croissants and cappuccino. For casual Italian, the **Vento** is good.

Expensive

All the resorts have restaurants. In the exclusive Coconut Palms is the **Palm Room,** featuring international food at gourmet prices. Las Orquidias de Cabarete features **Basilic Café,** and at Villas del Atlántico, **El Taíno** serves a wide variety of gourmet dishes. Along with **Le Jasmín** set in the Casa Laguna Hotel, there are enough gourmet restaurants in town to keep your pocketbook empty for a while. Independent of any hotel but still quite expensive is the **Casa del Pescador,** with a beachside location. It's a great restaurant by any standards. New and trendy is **Basilic** (tel. 809/571-0959), a French restaurant compelte with chamber music. If you can afford it, this is a real treat.

Markets

There are two supermarkets in town, the **La Casa Rosada** and **Albertico.** If you're staying at a hotel, apart-hotel, or condo with a kitchen or kitchenette, you can save money by cooking a few meals for yourself.

SPORTS AND RECREATION

There are, quite literally, no sights in Cabarete in the normal sense. Relaxed fun, sun, and windsurfing make Cabarete go.

Windsurfing

Windsurfers say the best months are February and March, with November and December being less good, but still OK. Conditions in summer are somewhat flat, and in winter there are days when the waves are just too big. It tends to rain a bit more during February and March than in most places in the Dominican Republic, but most rain is confined to short, pleasant showers.

Unless by some miracle you can bring your own board to Cabarete, the windsurfing habit is not cheap, even in the Dominican Republic. There are literally dozens of places to rent boards, to get lessons, and to store equipment, but most charge about US$40 per day, or about US$170 per week for board rental. During most of the late winter and early spring, the pressure on the windsurfing beaches is high, so be prepared for some crowds. Naturally, the luxury resorts have extensive water-sports facilities, offering boards and lessons as part of the package.

In Cabarete there are a number of "high wind" centers. These include **Spin-Out-Vela** (tel. 809/671-0805, fax 809/571-0805 or 809/571-0856), the **Windsurfing Club** (tel. 809/571-0848), and the **Carib Bic Center** (tel. 809/571-0540, fax 809/571-0649). Most of these places cater to the high-tech windsurf fanatics, but they can outfit anyone. Connected with the Auberge du Roi is the **MB Funboard Center** (tel./fax

809/571-0957). Also on the beach is **Happy Surf and Ski Tours** (tel. 809/571-0784).

Carbarete is a hedonist paradise. So, as you might expect, operators catering to windsurfing can come and go rather quickly. Opened in 1998, **The Mistral Center** (El Refugugio Hotel, tel. 809/671-0770) looks as if it might stick, if only because of its connection to the company that manufactures equipment. They offer group classes (US$35/hr) and rent high-tech equipment (US$180 for 10 hours). **Fanatic** (tel. 809/571-0861) is relatively new as well, has competitive rates, and caters to students. There is also a nice bar on the premises. For instruction in French only, try **Club Nathalie** (tel. 809/571-0848), an outfitter designed for French Canadians and French, connected to Pura Vida, a rafting tour group for French speakers.

More Recreation

Although windsurfing is the primary sport at Cabarete, there are a few other opportunities avail-

BOB RACE

able as well. More will pop up as Cabarete grows, I'm sure. Located facing the Coconut Palms Resort is a place called **Gipsy Ranch,** which rents horses for nice rides along the beach. **Iguana Mama** (tel. 809/571-0908, fax 809/571-0842) rents mountain bikes, leads river rafting and trekking tours, and rents and repairs bikes of all kinds.

More horseback riding is available at **Rancho Montana** (tel. 809/571-0990), which offers beach rides for US$25. Up in the hills is a large ranch called **Rancho Al Norte** (tel. 809/223-0660). Conducting all-day rides on beautiful trails, they charge about US$50.

New pastimes are offered by **Tropical Wakeboard Center** (tel. 809/707-0048, fax 809/571-0890). These folks will teach you how to waterski the Río Yasica on a miniature surfboard, as well as to wakeboard. All day sessions are US$120. The **Dolphin Dive Center** (tel. 809/571-0842) is the best scuba center, offering PADI courses for about US$270. They go to reefs and a shipwreck.

Tours

Down the road in Río San Juan, the **Cabarete Adventure Park and Caves** gives tours of area caves, grottoes, and lagoons, as well as arranging trips and treks of various kinds.

PRACTICALITIES

Information and Services

So far, there are no banks in Cabarete, but you can bank in Sosúa. There is a moneychanger in town, and most luxury resorts and major tourist hotels will change money for you. There is a small magazine at the hotels called *Cabarete Winds,* where you can find information on surfing, hotels, tours, etc.

The Cabarete **Codetel** is located on the main highway, about one km in the direction of Sosúa. The Cyber Café offers Internet services and the town now sports a couple of ATM machines. You won't find a post office but there are a number of mailboxes. Good luck with that. American Express is at Tricom Plaza.

Vehicle Rentals

Operators in town are relatively new and tend to come and go. Try **Arcar** (tel. 809/511-1282) or

Tropicar (tel. 809/571-0991). There are a couple of others, so it's best to shop and compare.

Getting There
Once you're out of Sosúa, heading east, the traffic tends to thin out. The elegant east-bound highway actually runs almost due south, about 13km along the coast, to Cabarete. It's about 15 minutes by taxi, which should cost about US$12. *Públicos* run from Puerto Plata and Sosúa and will let you off right on the main highway in town. Be sure to settle on a price first.

RÍO SAN JUAN AND VICINITY

The road from Cabarete through Gaspar Hernández, which ultimately connects Río San Juan to Cabera, Nagua, and finally the lovely Samaná peninsula, runs very near the ocean and through lush savannah countryside and thick coconut palm groves.

Only 10km from Cabarete, the little town of **Gaspar Hernández** has missed out on tourist development, having only a few banks and commercial hotels, and some small restaurants. Gaspar Hernández will probably remain a quiet little town because there are no beaches in the nearby regions. The townspeople make their living mostly from agriculture and fishing.

Río San Juan is a dairy farming and fishing town located about 64km (40 miles) east of Sosúa. The main highway passes the outskirts of town, and you'll need to find Calle Duarte to turn off toward the main commercial areas and hotels. Much of the town has retained its pastel Caribbean ambience, especially the neighborhood known as **El Barrio Acapulco,** which is near the ocean on the west side of Calle Duarte. It is in this area that the only economic activity beyond farming and fishing takes place: boat-building.

Río San Juan is just now experiencing growth from tourism and can be expected to change in character over the next decade or so. Right now it is pleasantly small and serviced just enough to be fun without being crowded.

RECREATION

Beaches
Beaches in the area include the two small beaches making up the Río San Juan urban beach. These beaches lie on either side of the Hotel Bahía Blanca property. Down the coast to the east is **Playa Caletón,** while just farther on is **Playa Grande,** accessible to visitors even if they're not staying at one of the luxury hotels nearby. On the Cabo Francés Viejo there is **Playa El Bretón,** while **Playa La Entrada, Playa Diamante,** and **Playa Boba** are all farther east along the coast. Certainly the beaches along the wide bays around Nagua are worth stopping at for a dip. They are not developed, however, and have no facilities.

Gri-Gri Lagoon
Those coming to Río San Juan come for the quiet beaches and relaxed atmosphere. There is, however, a wonderful, large lagoon. The Gri-Gri Lagoon is known for its clear water, lush vegetation, including huge mangroves, and unusual rock formations. To get to the lagoon from the main highway, turn north on Calle Duarte and go through town straight to the end of the main road. There you'll find boat-rental areas where tourists may rent small boats for the trip to the lagoon. Individuals can rent boats for RD$200, extra if you wish to stop and swim. Excursions can be organized through the Bahía Blanca Hotel and through Cabarete Adventure Park and Caves as well.

Altogether the boat trip lasts about 90 minutes. You'll cruise the extensive mangroves, go past the *gri-gri* trees, and see seabirds and bizarre rock formations. The boat traverses the open ocean in order to view the **Cueva de Las Golandrinas,** which is situated just beyond the mouth of the river San Juan. Swimmers can practice their strokes at Playa Caleton.

Diving
For diving, **Gri-Gri Divers** is located near the Bahía Blanca Hotel. Telephone them at 809/589-2671, or stop by and ask for Sandria or Mark. They know the entire north coast, put together wonderful dive packages, and give lessons. Warm, friendly people.

ACCOMMODATIONS

There are only a few choices for accommodations in Río San Juan. Fortunately, they are good ones, and good bargains at that.

Inexpensive

There are several inexpensive hotels in town, including the 14-room **Hotel Santa Clara** (Calle Bellini, tel. 809/589-2286), which is about US$15 a night. The hotels **San Martín** and **Caridad** are very cheap, but you should check them out before you decide to plunk down the US$8.

Moderate

The project of Quebecquois Lise Pineau, the **Bahía Blanca Hotel** (tel. 809/589-2562 or 809/589-2563, fax 809/589-2528) is located on Gaston Delinge. To get there take Calle Duarte to the end, turn left, and then bear right when you see the signs for the hotel. The rooms are great, the ocean views marvelous, and the staff of the hotel are able to organize horseback rides and cave visits. Average room prices cost around US$32 per night, much less off-season. This hotel is one of the gems of the coast.

On Calle Duarte, the **Hotel Río San Juan** (tel. 809/589-2211, fax 809/589-2379) has 38 rooms in a two-story country inn–style hotel. All rooms have air-conditioning, and there is a piano bar, a disco, and a good restaurant. From the hotel, it is only a short walk to the Gri-Gri Lagoon, and the hotel organizes excursions. The average room rate is about US$80 per night single, much less in the off-season. You can swim in the nice pool, as well.

RÍO SAN JUAN

ATLANTIC OCEAN

PLAYA RÍO SAN JUAN
HOTEL BAHIA BLANCA
GRI-GRI DIVERS
SANCHEZ
LAGUNA GRI-GRI
CALLE SAN JUAN
16 DE AGOSTO
CAPOTILLO
DURTE
HOTEL RIO SAN JUAN
5
TO CABO FRANCES VIEJO AND NAGUA
5 COASTAL HIGHWAY
TO LOS CACAOS AND NAGUA

NOT TO SCALE

© AVALON TRAVEL PUBLISHING, INC.

FOOD AND ENTERTAINMENT

For eating, you'll find a number of pizzerias locally, as well as the restaurants in the two major hotels. All are good. One appetizing choice is the **La Casona** for Creole and fish. The Hotel Bahía Blanca restaurant is especially recommended, both for the quality food and the great view from the terrace. Finally, downtown on Calle Duarte is the **Brigandina,** an inexpensive place for decent seafood. You can eat outside on a small terrace, if you like.

Río San Juan is not a loud party or disco town. Not yet, anyway. In town, there is one small disco, and the piano bar of the Hotel Río San Juan is especially nice in the evenings.

One option for entertainment involves a 10km 4WD adventure. Río San Juan's Calle Duarte becomes a dirt road south of the main highway. Bearing right at a fork in the road, you'll see **Adventure Riding Park** (tel. 809/571-0890), a ranch that offers horseback riding on obscure mountain trails. On-site are 40 horses and a guest house appropriately called the **Bush Hotel.** For about US$150, you can stay the night, eat three meals, and ride to your heart's content.

Near town, at **Playa Caletón,** there is a small fishing village. On the beach try the freshly caught lobster, cooked before your eyes. Cheap and delicious.

EAST OF RÍO SAN JUAN

Playa Grande

Continuing east beyond Río San Juan about nine km (six miles) is Playa Grande beach. At the headlands of the Cabo Francés Viejo, Playa Grande is a beach just now in the middle stages of development. Soon, this lovely beach and headland with lighthouse will turn into another Playa Dorada. It's too bad, because the whole cape area, with its high cliffs, big surf, and stretch of white beach, is quite spectacular.

In the stretch just past Río San Juan, you'll begin to go out onto the Cabo Francés Viejo and toward Puerto Escondido, a small, hidden beach just off the highway. Continuing on around the cape, there is Punta Preciosa (Precious Point), then the lighthouse on the cape itself, and finally the town of Cabrera and Laguna Grande beach.

Just outside town is the **Caribbean Village Playa Grande** (tel. 809/563-5565 or 800/858-2258, fax 809/422-5152), which has 300 luxury rooms and is built near a golf course. It claims to possess one of the most beautiful beaches in the country.

Of the three new all-inclusive resorts east of Río San Juan, **Bahía Príncipe** (tel. 809/226-1590, fax 809/226-1994) is the most massive, with an almost unbelievable 940 rooms including several hundred private villas, all set on stunning grounds. Guests have access to a casino, a private beach, shopping, and tour operators. All this luxury is something new to the area, and it is bound to have an effect on the town itself. Rates average around US$150 for a double. Nearby is the new **Costa Verde** (tel. 809/248-5287, fax 809/248-5286), also an all-inclusive, but smaller and less dominant, with a nice pool area. This whole area is keyed to the existence of an 18-hole golf course designed by Robert Trent Jones. Rich retirees are building mansions too.

A nudist resort called **Club Paradise** operates just beyond Playa Grande (U.S. tel. 813/949-9327, fax 813/949-1008). For written inquires, write P.O. Box 750, Land O'Lakes, Florida 34639.

Cabrera

Beyond Playa Grande, the little town of Cabrera is away from the road and on clifflands over deep blue seas.

There are no good hotels in Cabrera, but there are some nice beaches close by. You'll need good directions to find them. Check with a local.

Nagua

Down the road, Nagua serves as the gateway along the coast to the Samaná peninsula.

This middle-sized town is the capital of the province of María Trinidad Sánchez. The whole coast is studded with coconut palm trees, in some places quite thick, providing both beauty and shade from the sun. This stretch of coast is a preview of the coconut palm environment of Samaná peninsula, just a few more miles down the coast road toward Sánchez.

An unattractive fishing village, Nagua is not geared to tourists, so there are no particular sights or facilities. The town has only a few inexpensive hotels. The 16-unit **Caban-Carib** (tel. 809/543-6420, fax 809/584-3145) is on the main road toward Samaná. Its cabins vary in rate, though none is expensive. An on-site restaurant serves good food. On the highway toward Río San Juan are the **Las Brisas** and **Casa Blanca** hotels. In downtown Nagua you can stay at the basic **Hotel Familiar,** which has rooms with fan and private bath, or the **Hotel San Carlos,** both for about US$10. Nagua has a few cafes and cafeterias that serve basic *comida criolla.* **La Escocesa** serves seafood and is said to be the best.

Bahía Escocesa

South of Nagua, you'll find the lovely beach of Bahía Escocesa, which looks like a place that could be developed any day.

BOB RACE

THE SAMANÁ PENINSULA
INTRODUCTION

THE LAND

The Samaná peninsula is one of the most wild and beautiful spots in the whole of the Dominican Republic. Located about 210km from Puerto Plata along the coast highway, or about 200km northeast from Santo Domingo, this 48km-long peninsula is one of the most remote areas a traveler can encounter. Here there is abundant rainfall, perhaps the most rainfall on the island, rain that contributes to the thick vegetation which covers the rolling limestone countryside. The backbone of the peninsula is the rounded Cordillera Samaná. Its slopes drop off into the very shallow shelf surrounding the peninsula: shallow Atlantic waters, which make for excellent fishing. Given the limestone constitution of the terrain, numerous small lakes dot the countryside. As any geologist knows, limestone under great pressure metamorphoses into marble. Today, a number of marble quarries operate on the peninsula, providing white, pink, green, and gray marble for industry in Santo Domingo, as well as for export. The Cordillera rarely reaches heights of more than 500 meters. In its nearly 1,000 square km of territory, there are few good roads on the peninsula, though the luscious white beaches of the north and south coasts have during recent years lured tourists in droves.

HISTORY

Maguá
The history of the peninsula begins well before the arrival of Columbus. This whole fruitful territory belonged to the chieftainship of Maguá, which, during the time just preceding the arrival of the Spanish, was ruled by the Ciguayo Indian Guarionex. These Maguá Indians, living as they did near the fierce Caribes, had learned early on to defend themselves with vigor.

Columbus
And so it was that when Columbus appeared off the coast of Samaná on January 12, 1493, the Indians were in no mood to welcome unwanted guests. A fierce battle took place, and Columbus was forced to flee, forever after referring to the bay as the Golfo de las Flechas (Gulf of the Arrows).

The peninsula remained a backwater, though its shallow coastal waters are a graveyard of

© AVALON TRAVEL PUBLISHING, INC.

THE MERCURY WRECKS OF SAMANÁ

In 1724, two ships—*Conde de Tolosa* and *Nuestra Señora de Guadeloupe*—set sail for Mexico from Cadiz, Spain. The ships were laden with mercury—used in silver and gold refining—and 144 cannons destined for forts along the way. From Aguada on the western tip of Puerto Rico, the ships tried, in August, to cross the Mona Passage but were overtaken by a hurricane that blew them helplessly toward Samaná Bay, where each foundered and sank. Of the 1,250 passengers on both vessels, nearly half died. Some of the survivors found their way to Haiti, while others were forced to walk all the way over the mountains to Santo Domingo.

In 1976 American archaeologist Tracy Bowden gained the right to search for relics of the wrecks. Using sophisticated magnetometers, Bowden picked up signals from the ocean bottom, where items from the wrecks had been languishing for 250 years. The tedious process of recovering artifacts took years, but ultimately the searchers found diamond jewelry, pearls, brass instruments, glassware, and multitudes of implements. The scientists were also successful in recovering a quantity of mercury, which had leaked from cases. The archaeological treasures from both the *Guadeloupe* and the *Tolosa* are on exhibit in Santo Domingo today.

Meanwhile, Bowden's search ship, the *Hickory,* was sunk near Santo Domingo as part of a man-made reef known as Punta Caleta National Underwater Park.

Spanish vessels that ran aground in bad weather. Finally, the town of Santa Bárbara de Samaná was founded in 1756 by the Spanish Brigadier Governor of the island, Francisco Rubio Peñaranda. Most of the original inhabitants of the town were emigrants from the Canary Islands. However, commencing in the early 19th century, a whole new group of immigrants came to Samaná, mainly from the United States.

American Immigrants
The story of the black American immigrants starts with the capture of the Samaná peninsula

in 1822 by the Haitian General, Jean Pierre Boyer, also president of Haiti. President Boyer, wanting to people his newly conquered peninsula with English-speaking farmers, sent representatives to Philadelphia and New York to speak with abolitionist groups. Soon thereafter, a group of refugees found shelter on the peninsula, though they were wracked by typhoid fever. Of the several thousand that ultimately went to Samaná, about 2,000 stayed on and became the backbone of a thriving community.

These former slaves had all escaped from Southern plantations and brought to Samaná their Protestant faith, a sharp contrast to the Catholic natives. The refugees, however, felt somewhat abandoned by their church elders in the United States, and they soon were sent to England where Wesleyan pastors responded. Ultimately, both American and British Methodists gave the refugees help. Over the years, the descendants of these original English-speaking black slaves prospered, founded Protestant churches, and became citizens. During the Trujillo years, they were persecuted for their language, customs, and religion.

American Imperialism
During the imperialist period 1850–1880, the United States actively attempted to colonize the Samaná Bay region. In 1854 an American naval officer steamed into the bay looking for good coaling stations for the Caribbean fleet, all without asking permission from the Dominican government. Numerous schemes were hatched by European powers to dominate the Samaná peninsula as part of the debt problems facing the Dominican government. Then President Baéz, having been called back from exile, encouraged the corrupt Grant administration to sign a treaty annexing the Dominican Republic. Grant signed, primarily to get at Samaná's good port and plantations. In this audacious move, the annexed country was to receive 1.5 billion dollars, a huge sum for the time, and all Dominicans were to be U.S. citizens. Unfortunately for the plan's supporters, the treaty required Congressional approval to take effect. Republican senators overwhelmingly opposed this move, partly because of the money involved, partly through reluctance to become hand-maiden to a

patently bankrupt country, and partly because the era of blatant United States imperialism was still 30 years away.

Today

Today the descendants of American blacks on Samaná are rapidly dwindling in number; their rich cultural heritage, including folk tales, folk music, and rich religious practice, is fading away. They currently make up only about five percent of the population of the peninsula, and many successful descendants are departing for large cities, or even other countries. They leave behind their distinctive Protestant church in downtown Samaná, nicknamed La Churcha, characterized by its simple style and the red and white corrugated iron roof.

The Samaná peninsula's economy is defined by fishing, coconuts, bananas, and tourism. The great, beautiful humpbacked whales that live in cold Arctic waters return every year to the Silver Banks and the bay to calve and spend December, January, and February (some extend their holiday into March). Given the return of the whales, the beauties of the Bahía del Rincón, the white beaches, and the proximity of Parque Nacional Los Haitises, Samaná Peninsula is truly unique.

SANTA BÁRBARA DE SAMANÁ AND VICINITY

SIGHTS

The main town on the peninsula is Santa Bárbara de Samaná, home mostly to tiny villages and huge plantations, with a population of about 50,000. The town itself is in grassland with a background of mountains, fronted by a sparklingly blue bay dotted with tiny islands, some of which can be visited by boat. In the good old days, Samaná was a cluttered village of narrow streets and pastel-colored wooden houses. It had real aesthetic feel, a Caribbean ardor, and the back-alley charm of, say, New Orleans or Key West in their heydays. Back then, the main cuisine was based on coconut and bananas, and locals still remember their grandmas' original recipes for gingerbread, johnnycakes, and coconut fish. Samaná is still home to the dance called *chivo florete,* which is characterized by "obscene movements" and by the *oli-oli* performed by the men of Samaná during the town's colorful Carnaval.

Unfortunately, the town burned in 1946. Plans were drawn up for its rebuilding, but there was precious little money available. Even so, the town retained some of its original charm and tone. The true bad fortune of Samaná was to be hometown of the politician and Trujillo right-hand man, Balaguer. During Balaguer's first 12-year stint as president, he decided to level the town and replace its narrow streets and charming houses with wrought-iron balconies with wide avenues and concrete buildings. These efforts were most likely disguised efforts by Balaguer to erase his own ethnic past and to destroy his connection with black, Protestant natives. Whatever the motive behind it, the demolition and reconstruction was called redevelopment, with the supposed goal of attracting tourists.

All of which leaves Samaná a pretty ugly place. The **Malecón** is now a four-lane highway that runs along the bay. This broad street is used mostly by pedestrians and equestrians, and it is along this road that most of the present hotels and restaurants in the town are situated.

An odd thing called the **Nowhere Bridge** now connects a couple of offshore islands with the Malecón, but ultimately there is no destination. Originally, a restaurant was planned for one of the islands, but nothing came of it. Today, you can walk out on the bridge, look over the bay, and walk back, all in about an hour. There is a small waterfall at the seven-km mark beyond Sánchez on the road to Samaná, though you must hike about 15 minutes away from the road, and you'll need some directions.

The simple truth is that there aren't any likely or comely beaches in Samaná. The beach by the Cayacoa Hotel is small. Most visitors to Samaná

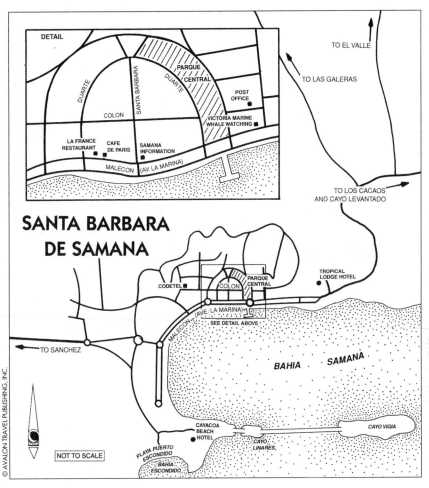

SANTA BARBARA DE SAMANA

head for **Cayo Levantado,** the largest and most popular of the offshore islands in the bay, and home to Cayo Levantado Beach Hotel. Public boats hired at the Samaná dock on the Malecón take visitors to the Cayo Levantado beach. Planned visits cost about US$40 per day round trip, more with lunch. Another alternative is to take a *público* from the Malecón to a spot eight km east of town where Transportes José and Simi Báez run boats to the island. Boat excursions from there cost about US$15 roundtrip.

Also, the two tourist hotels in Samaná can organize your trips to Cayo Levantado, as can some of the whale-watching outfits.

If you wish to go to Cayo Levantado, be forewarned. Though fresh breezes blow over the lush, beautiful island, and though you can get a good view from the stretch of white beach facing the peninsula, the crowds are horrendous on weekends, the vendors aggressive, and the food stalls overpriced. In addition, water is scarce, so try to bring your own.

WHALE-WATCHING

Samaná is now the most popular whale-watching destination in the whole Caribbean. The government estimates that 15,000 people watched whales in Samaná Bay in 1993, and all of the all-inclusive luxury hotels offer excursion visits there. **Whale Samaná** is the oldest tour operator in the Samaná area, and you can contact them at any of the major hotels. **Victoria Marine Whale-watching,** operated by the Canadian Kim Beddell (tel. 809/538-2588, fax 809/538-2545, Box 53-2, Samaná, DR), is an ecologically responsible tour operator in the bay. Her rate is US$35 per person for a four-hour tour, and she has pledged to conduct herself according to the new Whale Watch Regulations.

For more information on Silver Bank or Samaná whales, contact the **National Parks Office** in Santo Domingo (tel. 809/682-7628), the **Centro de Investigaciones de Biología Marina** (CIBINA) at the University of Santo Domingo (tel. 809/668-8633), or the **Fundacion Dominicana Pro-Investigacion y Conservacion de los Recursos Marinos** (MAMMA) at Av. Anacaona #77, Apdo. C-4, Santo Domingo. Kim Beddell knows officials of MAMMA and can put you in contact with them and get you some official literature on whale conservation; she may be reached at tel. 809/538-2588, fax 809/538-2494. (For more on this subject, see "Whale-watching" under "Outdoor Activities" in the On The Road chapter.)

ACCOMMODATIONS

Inexpensive
Budget back-
p a c k e r s
often head
for the ab-
solute rock-
bottom **Plaza
Taína** (Av. Rosario
Sánchez at La Loba), which offers rough accommodations for
about US$10. Other low-budget ho-
tels include **King's** (tel. 809/538-2352) and
Nilka (tel. 809/538-2245).

Moderate
Perhaps the best hotel in town is the **Tropical Lodge Hotel** (Malecón, tel. 809/538-2480), which offers a bay view in a quiet area shaded by coconut palms. They have a generator for those electricity interruptions in town, and plenty of hot water. The hotel also offers fishing excursions. Call and ask for Brigitte. Prices at the Tropical Lodge are in the US$40 range. Even so, this hotel can be buggy and hot, so beware. Less expensive are the **Hotel Kiko** (tel. 809/538-2565), in the Calle La Logia, the **Hotel Doria,** in Calle Santa Bárbara, and **Cotubanama** (Malecón and Santa Bárbara, tel. 809/538-2557), which is overpriced at US $30.

Luxury
There are three all-inclusive luxury resorts in Santa Bárbara de Samaná area. At the western edge of town, with a fine bay view, is the expensive **Cayacoa Beach Hotel** (tel. 809/538-3111, fax 809/538-2985), which is reached by taking the first roundabout and going up the hill until you see the hotel complex on the left. This complex and its 82 rooms are managed by Occidental Hotels and were remodeled in 1992. The complex boasts a good restaurant, pool, and nice rooms with air-conditioning. Continuing down the hill and slightly right brings you to the Puerto Escondido Beach, where guests of the hotel can go to swim and walk. The Cayacoa is relatively expensive for its all-inclusive ways, averaging about US$160 per night, though the hotel provides all meals and can arrange sports and excursions. Just behind the hotel is the notorious Nowhere Bridge, which extends a long way out into the bay, and ends at the small island of Cayo Vigia. The bay is popular for yachters and is usually dotted with vessels from all over the world.

The two other all-inclusive resorts are east of town. Also run by Occidental Hotels is the ex-
p e n s i v e

Humpback whale

BOB RACE

Hotel Gran Bahía (Los Cacaos, Samaná, tel. 809/538-3111, fax 809/538-2764). Set on a small beach opposite Cayo Levantado, this resort has a total of 106 all-inclusive rooms, a pool, a tennis court, air-conditioning, excursions to Cayo Levantado, and in the appropriate months, whale-watching excursions. To make arrangements for stays, call toll free from the United States at 800/221-4542, in Germany 06196-48-38-18, or in Santo Domingo 809/562-6271, fax 809/562-5232. Again, prices are in the US$160 range, all-inclusive.

For a few years now, Occidental Hotels has operated the luxury **Cayo Levantado Beach Hotel** (tel. 809/538-2988 or in Santo Domingo 809/223-8704, fax 809/223-8705). This expensive, all-inclusive resort has 44 rooms, and a good restaurant where you can eat fresh lobster and fish. Before you check in, consult with a travel agent about precise package costs, and review the brochures on the amenities of the hotel. The beach here can be crowded on weekends with hosts of tourists out for sun, and the vendors and food stall–hawkers can be outrageously forward. If you have no problem with walking, then secluded areas can be found on the opposite side of the island, and in certain sheltered areas down the beach from the main stretch.

MORE PRACTICALITIES

Food

For years, the basic foodstuff of the Samaná peninsula was the banana, coconut, and fish. It still is. Consequently, you can get good seafood at the big hotels. The restaurant at the **Gran Bahía** and the **Cayacoa Beach Hotel** are fine in the expensive range. For moderately priced French food try **La France** along the Malecón. Also on the Malecón are the **Típico El Coco** and **La Hacienda,** both of which offer *comida criolla* and good seafood at reasonable prices. **La Mata Rosada,** near the central park, is somewhat expensive but has good food and features local dishes. There are numerous other small basic cafes and cafeterias in town, and a couple of *supermercados* for do-it-yourselfers.

Nightlife

In the evenings, the place to be is definitely the Malecón. The knowledgeable locals and hip whale enthusiasts like to gather at the **Café de Paris** or **Grant's Café** for *cubas libres.* There are happy hours there, and wonderful sunsets on the water.

If you want to dance, look for **El Coco** and **Naomi Nightclub** on the waterfront, though there are half a dozen other discos.

Information and Services

The Samaná **Codetel** is located at Calle Santa Bárbara 6, while the **post office** is just off the Parque Central. There is a visitor information service called **Samaná Information** on Avenida La Marina, but it is closed during the off-season.

Rental cars didn't used to be available in Samaná, but now they are, thanks to the establishment of three new agencies in town. **J.A. Rent-Car** (on the Malecón, tel. 809/538-2229, fax 809/538-2049) has seven jeeps and three sedans for rent. Charges are RD$750 per day or RD$4,500 per week. Insurance is included in the price. Second-driver insurance is optional and extra. Visa is accepted, but you'll need a credit card voucher as security. Also on the Malecón is **Estilo Rent-a-Car** (tel. 809/538-2555 or 809/538-2100, fax 809/538-2545). This company has jeeps that cost RD$850 per day or RD$5,250 per week, including full insurance on car and driver. Visa is encouraged, but you must leave your passport as added security. Both are open 8 A.M.–6 P.M. every day but Sunday. **Xamaná Rent a Motor** on the Malecón (tel. 809/538-2556) also has cars for rent.

GETTING THERE AND GETTING AROUND

By Car

By car, it is a long 4.5-hour trip from Santo Domingo to Samaná. The road north is the Duarte Highway. Take the marked turnoff south of La Vega about seven km for San Francisco de Macorís, then the road east out of San Francisco to Nagua. A second road, albeit mostly unmarked, leads from the small town of Piedra Blanca on the Duarte Highway, to Cotui, then Pimentel, and finally to Nagua. This route is distinctly shorter, but the possibility of getting lost is enormous unless you speak good Spanish and you are not shy about being in provincial countryside.

a typical house on the Samaná Peninsula

LEO DE WYS

From Puerto Plata or any other city along the north coast, getting to the Samaná peninsula is a snap. Just follow the coast highway, which is gorgeous, well paved, and lightly traveled. The trip takes about four hours from Puerto Plata. Leave time for plenty of stops to get *coco frío.*

The roads around the peninsula to Las Terrenas are good, as is the road to Las Galeras. The inland road from Los Galeras to El Portillo is good, but overland to Limón and Samaná is bad and should not be attempted except in serious 4WD, high-clearance vehicles.

The reach the Samaná peninsula you'll need to go through the old port town of **Sánchez.** After passing through Sánchez, the road heads straight for Samaná, passing through coconut groves and along stretches of beach and cliffs. To reach Las Terrenas on the north coast, turn left just past Sánchez. The road heading north is newly paved and quite good. The road from Sánchez to Samaná leads you directly into the center of the city where you can see the Malecón, the walkway along the beach. To reach the other resort area on the peninsula called Las Galeras, just continue through town and follow the highway. It ends at Las Galeras on the Bahía del Rincón.

By Bus

By bus, the simplest route is Metro direct to Samaná with several trips daily, or **Caribe Tours,** which runs along the north coast and also departs three times a day from Santo Domingo. Bus stops in Samaná are on the Malecón. Cheap *públicos* do run along the north coast highway, and you can catch them on the edge of the road. These publicós usually run town to town, so you may have to go to Sosúa, hop off, catch another to Gaspar Hernández, and so on. This kind of travel, while cheap, can be exhausting and can also leave you stranded.

Another route is possible as well. If you desire adventure, head for the Parque Independencia in Santo Domingo and hop a public bus going to San Pedro de Macorís. Then get on another bound for the coastal town of Sabana de la Mar (right across the bay from Santa Bárbara de Samaná).

By Ferry

Three ferries each day cross the bay headed for Samaná, though they don't carry cars. If you choose to go this way, beware that sometimes scalpers buy up the tickets put on sale for the public, then sell them to motorcyclists and pedestrians at highly inflated prices.

By Plane

There is a small airport between Sánchez and Samaná called **Arroyo Barril.** It is situated outside Sánchez about 18km (11 miles) and 29km (18 miles) from Samaná. Its 5,000-foot runway is designed to handle domestic flights from Herrera Airport in Santo Domingo. For those in a hurry, the domestic flights take about 25 minutes.

SÁNCHEZ: GATEWAY TO SAMANÁ

By car, taxi, *público,* or *guagua,* the road to the Samaná peninsula leads through the old port town of Sánchez, located on a stretch of unimpressive beach along the bay. Once a thriving banana port and the terminus of the late-19th-century Cibao railway from La Vega, the town itself is not particularly exciting, though it does have a few sections with older houses painted in traditional pastel shades, a couple of commercial hotels, and a Codetel office. If you wish to visit the city, just turn left.

If you stay in Sánchez, try the **Hotel Restaurant La Costa** (Calle Libertad 44, tel. 809/552-7275) or the **Hotel La Gran Parada,** neither of which is expensive.

LAS TERRENAS AND VICINITY

INTRODUCTION

Las Terrenas is the only town of any size on the whole north coast of the Samaná peninsula. In fact, as you progress east along the coast, you'll find no developments, no roads, and almost impenetrable mountain and forest all the way around to Cabo Cabrón and the Bahía del Rincón. Las Terrenas itself has about 8,000 permanent inhabitants. On the oceanside roads east and west lie many small seafront hotels, cabanas, and restaurants, with a fair share of cafes and vendors.

As years go by, the village of Las Terrenas is becoming a tourist destination—with all that designation implies. Still, the organization of Las Terrenas remains fairly simple. One main road heads into town. Turning left leads you off to Playa Bonita; continuing straight ahead takes you to El Portillo. It isn't hard to find the sandy roads along the beach where the bulk of the hotels and cabanas are situated.

SIGHTS

The area immediately surrounding Las Terrenas has some of the country's finest stretches of beach. At times, the tide takes the water out so far you can walk to great reefs. The secluded beach directly west of the Las Terrenas headland is called Playa Bonita, while to the east is the vast and secluded El Portillo beach. Sand roads run east and west from Las Terrenas, the one east eventually reaching Limón, where you can find the starting point for a four-km hike to the superb **Salto de Caloda** waterfall. If you're going to make this walk, you'll need a good 4WD vehicle to Limón, or a motorcycle rented from one of the stalls in Las Terrenas.

All in all, there are approximately 10km of white beach along the Las Terrenas coast. Toward the west, for example, is a stretch called Cozón Beach, located in front of Cayo Ballena (Whale Key), where many wealthy Dominicans have built vacation homes, and from which it is sometimes possible to see humpback whales as they migrate.

SPORTS AND RECREATION

Water Sports
Water sports, sunning, and diving are the main entertainment at Las Terrenas. For diving, look for **Divebold** in town, or the German-run **Stellina Dive Center** (tel. 809/240-6000, fax 809/240-6020) on Cacao beach. Here you can rent a dive boat or take a tour in a glass-bottom boat. There are several places along the beach to rent catamarans and sailboards.

Even if you're not staying at the Cacao Beach or El Portillo resorts, these are still the places to check out scuba and water sports rentals.

Horseback Riding
Rent horses at **Ranchito** (tel. 809/240-6060), or at the El Portillo Beach Club.

ACCOMMODATIONS

The hotels in Las Terrenas are surprisingly moderate in price, save for those in the luxury category. At the end of the village toward the beach on either side of the town lie perhaps a dozen

modest tourist hotels that offer good a/c rooms, decent food, and access to the miles of white beach that make Las Terrenas so inviting. Many of these hotels have a selection of rooms or cabanas, thus making their prices range rather widely, anywhere from US$60 all the way down to US$20.

Inexpensive

The budget hotels are located mostly near Las Terrenas or in town. You can stay at **Mami** (tel. 809/240-6074) or at **Dinnys** in town, both for around US$10. The **Hotel Villa Caracol** has some rooms without bath and with a fan for about US$10. If you're traveling with several people, you can always rent cabañas and sleep three or four. On Punta Bonita, try the **Apartamentos El Atlántico,** which has sleeping rooms for up to four people for about US$35 per night. Finally, the **Finchen Restaurant** has a few rooms above the cafe that are cheap, but noisy until very late. For dormitory-style rooms for US$10, try **Los Piños** (see below) right on Calle El Portillo.

It is also possible to find modest accommodations heading east out of town on the El Portillo Road. On this four-km stretch there are many hotels and pensions with rooms to rent. Some are quite cheap and dirty, some less cheap and less dirty. The **Villa Vieja** faces the ocean and has some furnished two-bedroom apartments with kitchen, available for about US$30 per night.

Right on the El Portillo road is **El Papagayo** (tel. 809/240-6095), which features a restaurant and bar. The rooms are passable and go for about US$25 per night. Also in the same category is the less-costly **Cabañas Esmeralda,** where you can get a room with a shower, fan, and mosquito net for about US$25. With a wide range of accommodations from simple rooms in a dorm-like setting for about US$10 to large rooms and bungalows in the US$40 range, the **Los Piños** (Calle El Portillo, tel. 809/240-6168) is a bargain.

Moderate

The small but good **L'Aubergine** (tel. 809/240-6167, fax 809/240-6070) charges about US$35 for the rooms, and both **La Louisiane** and **Las Habitaciones** are small guest-house type hotels with good rooms in the same modest price range, the restaurant at L'Aubergine is a moderately priced find. Run by a trained chef from French-Canada who keeps her kitchen spotlessly clean. The *snapper al coco* is marvelous.

To the west of Las Terrenas is Punta Bonita, where you'll find a selection of moderately priced hotels and cabañas as well. The priciest is the **Hotel Atlantis** (Punta Bonita, tel. 809/682-4730, fax 809/687-5535), where the 19 rooms could use some fixing up. Also on Playa Bonita are the **Acaya** (tel. 809/240-6161, fax 809/240-6166) an excellent small hotel that cultivates its inn-style image. The service here is good; a small **dive center** gives tours and instructions. The **Punta Bonita Cabañas** (tel. 809/240-6082) and the **Isla Bonita Beach Hotel** (near the Tropic Banana) have rooms priced around US$60 per night.

On the main road, slightly away from the beach, the **Palococo** (tel. 809/240-6080, fax 809/240-6151) has nice rooms, a pool, and the ubiquitous whirlpool for about US$50 per night, in season. Down by the beach, the moderately priced **Hotel Tropic Banana** (tel. 809/240-

6110, fax 809/240-6112) has good rooms and a pool for about US$40. The Tropic Banana is a favorite with Canadians. On the beach is the **Kanesh Beach Hotel** (tel. 809/240-6187, fax 809/240-6070) with rooms for about US$30 with fan.

Of particular interest in the modest price range is the strangely appealing **Las Cayenas Hotel,** run by a Swiss-French lady of exquisite taste. She has put a hotel in a Caribbean great house, and it works. The rooms in the house go for about US$50–60, which includes a decent breakfast.

Luxury

By way of all-inclusive resorts, right in Las Terrenas on the beach is the attractive **Cacao Beach Hotel** (tel. 809/240-6000 or in Santo Domingo 809/565-2097, fax 809/240-5020). This large hotel has 130 air-conditioned rooms and all the amenities you'd expect, in the US$110 range. One has to admit that the Cacao Beach is pretty spectacular with its huge and elaborate pool, three restaurants and bars, deck bar, lighted tennis courts, sailing, horse rental, fishing excursions, scuba school, bike and motorcycle rentals, and even archery.

Heading out the Punta Bonita way (west) is the very expensive and lush **Plantation Club** (tel. 809/240-6008) for high rollers. In the other direction (east) about four km on a rough road is the very nice **El Portillo Beach Club** (tel. 809/240-6100, fax 809/240-6104), which has 170 rooms and cabañas, a pool, two tennis courts, scuba clinics, horses for rent, and other water sports, including catamarans. Many package tours come down each winter from Europe, and you should check with a travel agent about prices, though most average about US$110 per night. The local tour agent in the Dominican Republic for El Portillo Beach is Prieto Tours (tel. 809/685-0102, fax 809/685-0457). The El Portillo Beach Club has two restaurants, a disco, a whirlpool, live music and entertainment, and bicycles for rent for those long rides on hard wet sand. The pool is the size of a football field—or so it seems. If you're on your own and not staying at the Cacao Beach or El Portillo resorts, these are still the places to check out for scuba and water sports rentals.

FOOD

Inexpensive

In town you'll find a market where you can wander and shop, eating your choice of fried fish, plantains, or rice and beans. Budget diners will like the **Finchen Restaurant** downtown, which serves German and Dominican food, or the restaurants at **Kanesh** or **Las Cayenas Hotel,** which are good but not expensive. An excellent downtown bakery called **Panadería Francesa** makes wonderful bread, pastries, and the like.

Moderate

The restaurant **Rincón de Fleur** and the French-run **La Orquídea** are both near the water and serve moderately priced meals. On the road to El Portillo you'll find several moderately priced restaurants, including the locally famous **El 28** (you'll have to guess what the name means), serving fish and paella at the beginning of the road, and lower-priced restaurants at Los Piños. Numerous stalls, cafeterias, and cafes serve basic overcooked and overfried fish. You'll also come across many open-air bars where you can get snacks. Probably one of the best is **Casablanca.** Also near the beach is the restaurant **La Chicha,** which serves inexpensive *comida criolla.*

Expensive

You'll find Las Terrenas's best and most expensive restaurants at the Cacao Beach Resort, El Portillo Beach Club, and Plantation Club. The finest restaurant in town is at the Palococo Hotel, serving Spanish and local dishes. At the Hotel Atlantis, a good restaurant offers German food and local dishes, and sometimes live music. You'll always find good drinks and ambience here. **El Colibrí** restaurant next to the Cacao Beach Hotel serves good German food as well. Along the main road is the **Posada Chez Paco** for seafood and French cuisine.

ENTERTAINMENT

Due to Las Terrenas's remoteness, you won't find a lot of live entertainment in town. The big resorts have **discos** and **piano bars,** some of them not unpleasant, though they tend to be rather expensive. The beach is lined by **outdoor thatched-roof type bars** where you can relax for a pleasant drink Jimmy Buffet–style.

In town, after wandering, eating, and shopping your way through the market, you can repair to the several discos that line the street, including **Mambo, El Tiempo** (rather surreal in tone), and the **Disco Terraza Nuevo Mundo.** Also downtown is the **Rock Café,** which stays open late for drinkers and dancers.

PRACTICALITIES

Services
For phone or fax service, the **Codetel** office is on the main street—you can't miss it. There are several small supermarkets in town, and a couple will change your money, though not at good rates. Your best bet is to come to Las Terrenas with plenty of Dominican pesos.

Information
You will find a **Green Tours** office near the Tropic Banana Hotel, and a tourist information service on the main road.

Getting There
There are two ways to get to the isolated fishing village of Las Terrenas. The first is to drive your car on the road that runs from just outside (east) of Sánchez into the Cordillera Samaná, up and over the mountains, to the coast which has beautiful coconut palm–lined beaches. This road, which is slow driving but well maintained, provides incredible views of the bay and ocean. The 17-km trip takes at least an hour.

If you must take public transportation, the only way in and out of Las Terrenas is by *carrera,* which usually means a rusty pickup truck. The *carreras* are cheap, but they wait in the center of Sánchez until they have full loads, which can take some time. If you are in Samaná, you must take a *público* back to Sánchez to make the trip.

A dirt and gravel road takes off cross country from Samaná to Sánchez, going through Limón. The government threatens to improve the road, which currently goes through rough brush, crosses several rivers, and plunges through coconut and banana forest before emerging along the coast outside El Portillo. Ordinarily, the drive requires 4WD and high-clearance vehicles, but you might check with locals. You can reach Las Galeras on the south side of the Bahía de Rincón by good paved road north from Santa Bárbara de Samaná.

Getting Around
On the main road, **Caribbean Rent-a-Motor** rents cars at expensive rates. You can walk or hire a cheap *motoconcho* to almost everywhere you need to go in Las Terrenas, so why bother? You won't find much in the way of transportation to Limón and then cross country to Samaná—the road is very tough going.

On the main street you can hire *motoconchos* to El Portillo or Limón, if you dare. A *motoconcho* will also run you out to the beaches, west to Playa Cosón, or east to El Portillo, for about US$1.

NORTH OF SAMANÁ TOWN

LAS GALERAS/BAHÍA DEL RINCÓN

Some 26km north of Samaná, toward the eastern end of Rincón Bay, you'll find a lovely spot on a peninsula. It's not wired for electricity, so the hotels and restaurants generate their own. There are no distractions way out here, though the place is ripe for money-ripping development any day. The beach, the bay, and the cliffs all are beautiful and impressive, and a good breeze is always blowing.

Keep in mind that on the beach at Las Galeras is the same kind of *al fresco* cooking available in many places in the Dominican Republic. Friendly people too.

Beach

Located about 10km along the shore from Las Galeras is the isolated **Playa Rincón.** Back of the beach stand cliffs 660 meters (2,000 feet) high. You can swim on this isolated beach if you hire a boat in the village, or take a jeep over rutted, bumpy sand and gravel roads. It's a rough 20-minute trip, but worth it. Snorkeling all along this coast is marvelous.

Accommodations

There are about a dozen small pensions on the beach in Las Galeras. The 12-room, French-owned **Moorea Beach Hotel** (fax 809/538-0007) is quiet and contains a good patio and restaurant. The owner is a long-time resident and knows the area well.

The **Hotel Villa Serena** (tel. 809/696-0065), owned by hoteliers Natasha Despotovic and Kresimir Zovko, is a remote, colonial-style villa with 11 rooms, each with a private terrace and special "theme" decoration (such as the "Laura Ashley" room, with flowers and lace). The hotel folks can arrange snorkeling in world-class waters. There is a thatched-roof bar and pleasant pool, right near the beach. Price is US$80 double.

The other choices at Las Galeras include **Paradiso Bungalos** (tel. 809/538-0210), with gardens and direct access to the beach at about US$50 a night. Both **Dilas** and **Cas Lotus** are about US $80 and need to be booked in advance. Call Dilas at 809/538-0108 and Lotus at 809/538-2545.

More informal choices include **Club Bonita,** with 14 rooms (tel. 809/696-0082). It is located right at the beach and has a pretty good Italian restaurant. A double room during the high season is about US$90 a night. One may also try **Paradise,** a group of four huts owned by a German family who also runs Dive Samana. The huts are only 50 meters from the beach. Call ahead at 809/538-0001.

The newest hotel in the village is the all-inclusive luxury resort **Club Bonito** (tel. 809/538-0203), which has 100 deluxe rooms, approximately 50 of them "junior suites" with two beds, a bar, a kitchen, and an upstairs bunkroom. The motif is wood and fan, and everything is quite well kept and ritzy. The rooms have a large terrace, and the complex is close to the beach. There is a restaurant, several bars, and a new disco.

Getting There

To get to Las Galeras you'll need to hire a *concho* or taxi, or take a car there on the good road along the coast, then north across the mountains to the bay. To get to the road, go straight through Samaná town along the waterfront, past the Yacht Club, then out of town past the Baez pier (eight km), on the Gran Bahía Hotel (10.5km), just across from Cayo Levantado. The road curves north, is paved, and is well marked to Las Galeras. The road ends in the village.

Though there is a naval station in Las Galeras, it doesn't intrude on the solitude. The village itself is quiet and dignified but has no special services for tourists. The beach stretches out along the bay, which is perfect for shallow-water snorkeling and wading. In some ways, the beaches at Las Galeras have a Gallic flavor. Perhaps it's the topless bathing that lends a European tone to the proceedings.

PARQUE NACIONAL LOS HAITISES AND POINTS EAST

PARQUE NACIONAL LOS HAITISES

The Land

The Parque Nacional Los Haitises is located on the southern side of Samaná bay. Its nearly 1,435-square-km area is bounded on the east by the community of Sabana de la Mar, and on the northwest by Sánchez. All total, there are about 160km (100 miles) of mangrove-studded coastline with plenty of estuaries, coves, and bays on its length. This is rugged country. The rainfall is very heavy here, more than 230cm (90 inches) per year, which means that there is frequent cloud cover and there are lots of mosquitoes. This national park is very remote. There are no roads into its territory, and the one short interior trail constructed by the park service goes in and out of service due to rain and mud. Many visitors stick to the littoral routes, examining the rocky, cliff-bound shoreline with several caves along its length.

On the shoreline of the park are numerous reefs, cays, islands, and rock outcrops, all of which produce an astounding variety of birdlife and marine animals. The weather in the park and on the coast is very humid and hot, with an average daily temperature of 26°C year-round. When the land heats up during the early morning, humidity increases, and by afternoon, the wind begins to blow, increasing chances of rain by evening.

The topography of the park is very rugged. For one thing, the whole area is raised limestone shelf consisting of Miocene (40 million years ago) rock that has been subjected to eons of rain erosion. The water table is very shallow, and there are numerous karstic formations including caves, hummocks, and dolines. Many of the littoral caves have petroglyphs or pictographs. Typical, too, of the coastline are dense mangroves that line the lower beaches. The mainland sections of the park consist mainly of limestone knolls and corresponding valleys, with some of the knolls reaching 300 meters (1,000

feet) in height. The series of knolls and valleys, along with rain and heat, make for difficult walking terrain.

The soil on the mainland is thin and reddish in color, with an upper white layer. There is almost no surface freshwater in the whole area of the park, because the coral and limestone soak up almost immediately whatever rainfall comes.

Flora and Fauna

The valleys are densely covered by trees ranging from montane plants like mountain palms to lowland forest species like balata, copey, almacigo, and hosts of ferns, bromeliads, lianas, and begonias. In addition to these varieties, you can also see silk-cotton trees, Hispaniolan mahogany, and American muskwood along with the littoral red and white mangroves. If you visit the park, take care to identify (with the help of a guide) the ever present pringamoza plant, which, if touched, can produce an annoying rash.

Near the ocean the predominant fauna are the birds, including the brown pelicans, snowy egrets, and roseate terns. Inland are Ridgeway's hawk, narrow-billed tody, least grebe, white-checked pintain, and ruddy duck. Probably the most dense biomass in all the Dominican Republic can be found along the coast from Boca de Inferno, near the Isla de los Pájaros (Bird Island). Nearly 24km (15 miles) west to the mouth of the Río Barracote where the coast turns north, there are some 208 square km (78 square miles) of mangrove forest and swamp. In this dense environment, one can see oysters, mussels, and many crustaceans on the mangrove roots. Where rivers come down to the ocean, or where there are small estuaries and coves, there are plenty of blue herons, coots, northern jacanas, ibis, and even a cormorant or two.

Cave Routes

Inland, the limestone terrace of Los Haitises is a great example of intertropical mogote karst. Mogotes—limestone hills—dominate the park's landscape. Mogotes that have been isolated by the ocean are called keys, while inland mogotes are called dolines (deep rock-pools). Dolines are sinkholes that lead to passageways, which lead to caves, which lead to who knows?

You'll find three posted cave routes in Los Haitises. The caves are all located on the coast of the park, two of them quite close to the Bay of San Lorenzo, reached either by boat from Samaná or Sabana de la Mar. The three caves available for tours are called **Willy's Cave** (Cueva de Willy), **Sand Cave** (Cueva de la Arena), and **Railroad Cave** (Cueva del Ferrocarril).

The route along the coast, accessible only by boat, is called the Arrozal Path. You can pick it up at the specially built Bambú Pier in Caño Hondo near San Lorenzo Bay, only about 10 minutes by boat from Sabana de la Mar (much farther from Samaná town. Nearby you'll find Willy's Cave. Sand Cave lies just down the coast from Willy's Cave, near its own specially constructed pier and a small, covered interpretive area. The cave itself has access stairways, handrails, and about 80m of trails, posted with information signs and rules. Railroad Cave, even farther down the coast, has no such development.

All three of these extensive caves are excellent examples of karstic limestone sink, and all three show evidence of Taíno habitation. Filled with petroglyphs and shards of ceramics, the caves have recently been the subject of investigation by Spanish anthropological teams working in cooperation with the University of Santo Domingo.

The Inland Trail

The only inland trail starts at the entrance of Caño Salado, about a 15-minute boat ride around the mangroves from Sabana de la Mar. Marked with 17 interpretive stations, the trail takes you from the coast into abandoned cacao plantations thick with secondary forest growth, on through humid forest, savannah meadows, and into deeply forested valleys. You can actually choose to hike a shorter loop trail, which takes about 25 minutes to walk and returns you to Caño Salado. The other alternative is to walk about two hours all the way to Caño Hondo dock and be picked up there by a waiting boat.

The two-hour walk along the inland trail can be difficult if the weather doesn't cooperate. Be sure to bring plenty of insect repellent, drinking water, your camera, binoculars, long pants and a long-sleeve shirt, a sun hat, and good hiking boots. If you choose to wear tennis shoes, you might be sorry, because there are muddy patches. However, even though the inland trail is difficult, it is the best, indeed the *only,* way to get a close look at the mogote country.

Noted here are the easiest caves to reach, as well as the only inland trail route so far established. Keep in mind that there are other caves along the coast west of San Lorenzo. Included in these are the caves at San Gabriel and La Línea, both of which contain pictographs and petrographs.

Practicalities

Most people think the time to go to Los Haitises is January or February, when the rainfall is lowest. These things are relative, however. One good bet is to combine a whale-watching expedition with a trip to Los Haitises. Because there are no extensive systems of trails in the park, and because camping isn't a terribly rational choice, most visits to the park can be handled in one long day, starting early in the morning when the bay is calm.

Travel agencies in Puerto Plata, Sosúa, and Cabarete can arrange visits to Los Haitises. So can the often-mentioned Ecoturisa. In Samaná, any tourist hotel can help with excursions to the national park. Down by the pier, many boat owners try to offer their services for the trip across the bay to visit the caves. For a price, you can go with one of them, though you'd best check the safety equipment, be certain of your price, and try to determine if the guide has experience in the area. Many kids who head out into the bay don't have the slightest idea what they're doing.

For information about Los Haitises trips, contact the **National Parks Administration,** Av. Independencia #359 (corner Cervantes), or call them, if you speak Spanish, at 809/221-5340. **Prieto Tours** in Samaná is an old hand at these trips. For information on the anthropological investigations of the caves, contact the **Spanish Agency for International Cooperation,** Av. Pedro Henriquez Urena #171 (corner Av. Lincoln), or call them at 809/565-1870, fax 809/544-0331.

SABANA DE LA MAR

Another interesting approach to Los Haitises is to go to the town closest by on the coast, the village of Sabana de la Mar. By car, head to San Pedro de Macorís from Santo Domingo, take the second roundabout north to Hato Mayor, then head north (past the cathedral) out of Hato Mayor on a good paved road for Sabana de la Mar. The road twists and turns but never gets terrible, so don't give up. The road to Sabana passes a military zone, and then you'll see a sign for the national parks office. Officially, the national parks office is located at Avenida Los Heróes #54, Sabana de la Mar (tel. 809/556-7333). There you'll find some good wall maps of the park and the cave routes. In addition, the park office personnel seem helpful and concerned, and they occasionally provide tours of the park trails. Otherwise, you'll have to head for the pier or the city's biggest hotel for boats and guides.

Sabana de la Mar is small and built around a central park where the sea breeze scatters the trash and cools the air. There is a basic restaurant on the square, and there are a couple of cheap commercial hotels that aren't too nice. However, also in town is the **Complejo Turístico Villa Suiza** (tel. 809/556-7609, fax 809/532-8164), located on the Calle Monción on the shore of the bay to the east of town. It has 14 rooms with fans, and a view of the bay, and its owners will help you with everything to do with Los Haitises trips, boats, and guides. There is a restaurant and pool, but the big attraction is the park.

Although Sabana de la Mar is remote and difficult to reach, in some ways it is a most satisfying jumping-off point from which to visit Los Haitises, at least for adventurers.

RESERVA CIENTÍFICA NATURAL LAGUNAS REDONDA Y LIMÓN

East of Sabana de la Mar, two large, muddy lagoons have been made part of the scientific reserve system of the Dominican National Parks Administration. Fortunately for the extensive bird and marine species that make these lagoons their home, the area is one of the most remote and unpeopled places in the whole Dominican Republic. There are only two roads in and out of the place, and it is rather far down the east coast to be readily reachable by day boat-trip from anywhere along the bay of Samaná. The lagoon of Redonda is about 17km from the isolated town of Miches, while the Limón is another 10km down the coast.

The Land and Flora

These two lagoons are very shallow. The Redonda lagoon averages only 1.5 meters in depth, while its sister lagoon Limón is somewhat deeper, averaging 2.1 meters. The bottom of each lagoon is a thick sediment of mud, and each lagoon is surrounded by thick mangrove. The lagoons are about the same size, but Redonda is connected to the sea by the narrow Caño Celedonio. The lagoon Limón is entirely landlocked and surrounded by rather thick tropical bush.

Fauna

Birders are the most likely visitors to the lagoons. It is hot and damp in the vicinity of the lagoons, and mosquitoes are a constant annoyance. However, visitors can see pied-billed grebes, great egrets, black-crowned night herons, roseate spoonbills, northern pintails, and dozens of other species of birds.

Getting There

Do-it-yourselfers are going to have a terrible time with the two lagoons. They are isolated, swampy, shallow, hot, and inconveniently situated between a coast and heavy bush country. The coast road from Sabana de la Mar does reach to **Miches,** a very isolated town near the lagoons, and from there past the lagoons themselves. Near Miches, the Swiss-run **Hotel Punta El Rey** can get you to the lagoons. In fact, the Punta El Rey is a bit of an adventure in itself. Owned and operated by "Leo," this resort consists of six cabins on a secluded beach about nine km outside of Miches. The price is about US$30 a night for a double and includes a huge breakfast and dinner. Contact Leo at 809/248-5888 and he will arrange for transport from Miches by motorbike or boat, welcoming you with open arms. Remember that this is not a fancy resort—but it is a wonderful place for adventure.

You can hike to Laguna Limón from the village

of Los Guineos, but to hike to either you should have a guide. Try the nearby villages if you speak Spanish and are equipped with water and first-aid equipment for a hot day. Horses and guides would be a good idea.

Organized Trips: My recommendation for serious birders and wildlife aficionados is to plan ahead with an organization that specializes in wild trips. You might contact the National Parks Office in Sabana, but the best bet is a private hotel called **Complejo Turístico Villa Suiza** on Calle Monción, probably the best hotel in town. Call them at 809/566-7609 or fax 809/532-8164. An alternative phone number is 809/547-2278. The hotel's staff is known for its arranged trips to Los Haitises, and they can help you plan a trip to the lagoons. Another of the best is **Ecoturisa** (tel. 809/221-4104, fax 809/685-1544), located at Calle Santiago No. 23B, Gazcue, Santo Domingo. Several other tour operators offer excursions in the Samaná Bay vicinity, including tourist hotels in and around the town of Samaná. The same hotels in Samaná that offer tours to Parque Nacional Los Haitises on the south shore of the Samaná Bay can also help arrange tours to the lagoons.

SPANISH PHRASEBOOK

PRONUNCIATION GUIDE

Consonants

c - as 'c' in "cat," before 'a', 'o', or 'u'; like 's' before 'e' or 'i'
d - as 'd' in "dog," except between vowels, then like 'th' in "that"
g - before 'e' or 'i,' like the 'ch' in Scottish "loch"; elsewhere like 'g' in "get"
h - always silent
j - like the English 'h' in "hotel," but stronger
ll - like the 'y' in "yellow"
ñ - like the 'ni' in "onion"
r - always pronounced as strong 'r'
rr - trilled 'r'
v - similar to the 'b' in "boy" (not as English 'v')
y - similar to English, but with a slight 'j' sound. When y stands alone it is pronounced like the 'e' in "me".
z - like 's' in "same"
b, f, k, l, m, n, p, q, s, t, w, x, as in English

Vowels

a - as in "father," but shorter
e - as in "hen"
i - as in "machine"
o - as in "phone"
u - usually as in "rule"; when it follows a 'q' the 'u' is silent; when it follows an 'h' or 'g' it's pronounced like 'w,' except when it comes between 'g' and 'e' or 'i', when it's also silent

NUMBERS

0 - *cero*	17 - *diecisiete*
1 (masculine) - *uno*, 1 (feminine) - *una*	18 - *dieciocho*
2 - *dos*	19 - *diecinueve*
3 - *tres*	20 - *veinte*
4 - *cuatro*	21 - *vientiuno*
5 - *cinco*	30 - *treinta*
6 - *seis*	40 - *cuarenta*
7 - *siete*	50 - *cincuenta*
8 - *ocho*	60 - *sesenta*
9 - *nueve*	70 - *setenta*
10 - *diez*	80 - *ochenta*
11 - *once*	90 - *noventa*
12 - *doce*	100 - *cien*
13 - *trece*	101 - *cientouno*
14 - *catorce*	200 - *doscientos*
15 - *quince*	1,000 - *mil*
16 - *dieciseis*	10,000 - *diez mil*

DAYS OF THE WEEK

Sunday - *domingo*
Monday - *lunes*

Tuesday - *martes*
Wednesday - *miércoles*
Thursday - *jueves*
Friday - *viernes*
Saturday - *sábado*

TIME

What time is it? - *¿Qué hora es?*
one o'clock - *la una*
two o'clock - *las dos*
at two o'clock - *a las dos*
ten past three - *las tres y diez*
six A.M. - *las seis de la mañana*
six P.M. - *las seis de la tarde*
today - *hoy*
tomorrow, morning - *mañana, la mañana*
yesterday - *ayer*
week - *semana*
month - *mes*
year - *año*
last night - *anoche*
next day - *el próximo día* or *al día siguiente*

USEFUL WORDS AND PHRASES

Hello. - *Hola.*
Good morning. - *Buenos días.*
Good afternoon. - *Buenas tardes.*
Good evening. - *Buenas noches.*
How are you? - *¿Cómo está?*
Fine. - *Muy bien.*
And you? - *¿Y usted?* (formal) or *¿Y tú?* (familiar)
So-so. - *Así así.*
Thank you. - *Gracias.*
Thank you very much. - *Muchas gracias.*
You're very kind. - *Usted es muy amable.*
You're welcome; literally, "It's nothing." - *De nada.*
yes - *sí*
no - *no*
I don't know - *no sé* or *no lo sé*
it's fine; okay - *está bien*
good; okay - *bueno*
please - *por favor*
Pleased to meet you. - *Mucho gusto.*
excuse me (physical) - *perdóneme*
excuse me (speech) - *discúlpeme*
I'm sorry. - *Lo siento.*
Goodbye. - *Adiós.*
see you later; literally, "until later" - *hasta luego*
more - *más*
less - *menos*
better - *mejor*
much - *mucho*
a little - *un poco*
large - *grande*
small - *pequeño*
quick - *rápido*

slowly - *despacio*
bad - *malo*
difficult - *difícil*
easy - *fácil*
He/She/It is gone; as in "She left," "He's gone" - *Ya se fue.*
I don't speak Spanish well. - *No hablo bien español.*
I don't understand. - *No entiendo.*
How do you say . . . in Spanish? - *¿Cómo se dice . . . en español?*
Do you understand English? - *¿Entiende el inglés?*
Is English spoken here? (Does anyone here speak English?) - *¿Se habla inglés aquí?*
I'm sorry. - *Lo siento.*
Goodbye. - *Adiós.*
see you later; literally, "until later" - *hasta luego*
more - *más*
less - *menos*
better - *mejor*
much - *mucho*
a little - *un poco*
large - *grande*
small - *pequeño*
quick - *rápido*
slowly - *despacio*
bad - *malo*
difficult - *difícil*
easy - *fácil*
He/She/It is gone; as in "She left," "He's gone" - *Ya se fue.*
I don't speak Spanish well. - *No hablo bien español.*
I don't understand. - *No entiendo.*
How do you say . . . in Spanish? - *¿Cómo se dice . . . en español?*
Do you understand English? - *¿Entiende el inglés?*
Is English spoken here? (Does anyone here speak English?) - *¿Se habla inglés aquí?*

TERMS OF ADDRESS

I - *yo*
you (formal) - *usted*
you (familiar) - *tú*
he/him - *él*
she/her - *ella*
we/us - *nosotros*
you (plural) - *ustedes*
they/them (all males or mixed gender) - *ellos*
they/them (all females) - *ellas*
Mr., sir - *señor*
Mrs., madam - *señora*
Miss, young lady - *señorita*
wife - *esposa*
husband - *marido or esposo*
friend - *amigo (male), amiga (female)*
sweetheart - *novio (male), novia (female)*
son, daughter - *hijo, hija*
brother, sister - *hermano, hermana*
father, mother - *padre, madre*

GETTING AROUND

Where is . . . ? - *¿Dónde está . . . ?*
How far is it to . . .? - *¿Qué tan lejos está a . . . ?*

from . . . to . . . - *de . . . a . . .*
highway - *la carretera*
road - *el camino*
street - *la calle*
block - *la cuadra*
kilometer - *kilómetro*
north - *el norte*
south - *el sur*
west - *el oeste*
east - *el este*
straight ahead - *derecho or adelante*
to the right - *a la derecha*
to the left - *a la izquierda*

ACCOMMODATIONS

Can I (we) see a room? -
¿Puedo (podemos) ver una habitación?
What is the rate? - *¿Cuál es el precio?*
a single room - *una habitación sencilla*
a double room - *una habitación doble*
key - *llave*
bathroom - *retrete or lavabo*
bath - *baño*
hot water - *agua caliente*
cold water - *agua fría*
towel - *toalla*
soap - *jabón*
toilet paper - *papel higiénico*
air conditioning - *aire
acondicionado*
fan - *abanico, ventilador*
blanket - *cubierta or manta*

PUBLIC TRANSPORT

bus stop - *la parada de la guagua*
main bus terminal - *la central camionera*
airport - *el aeropuerto*
ferry terminal - *la terminal del transbordador*
I want a ticket to . . .- *Quiero un tiqué a . . .*
I want to get off at . . .- *Quiero bajar en . . .*
Here, please. - *Aquí, por favor.*
Where is this bus going? - *¿Dónde va este guagua?*
roundtrip - *ida y vuelta*
What do I owe? - *¿Cuánto le debo?*

FOOD

menu - *carta, menú*
glass - *taza*
fork - *tenedor*
knife - *cuchillo*
spoon - *cuchara, cucharita*
napkin - *servilleta*
soft drink - *refresco*
coffee, cream - *café, crema*
tea - *té*

sugar - *azúcar*
drinking water - *agua pura, agua potable*
bottled carbonated water - *club soda*
bottled uncarbonated water - *agua sin gas*
beer - *cerveza*
wine - *vino*
milk - *leche*
juice - *jugo*
eggs - *huevos*
bread - *pan*
watermelon - *patilla*
banana - *plátano, guineo*
apple - *manzana*
orange - *naranja, china*
meat (without) - *carne (sin)*
beef - *carne de res*
chicken - *pollo*
fish - *pescado*
shellfish - *camarones, mariscos*
fried - *frito*
roasted - *asado*
barbecue, barbecued - *barbacoa, al carbón, or a la parilla*
breakfast - *desayuno*
lunch - *almuerzo*
dinner (often eaten in late afternoon) - *comida*
dinner, or a late night snack - *cena*
the check - *la cuenta*

MAKING PURCHASES

I need . . . - *Necesito . . .*
I want . . . - *Deseo . . .* or *Quiero . . .*
I would like . . . (more polite) - *Quisiera . . .*
How much does it cost? - *¿Cuánto cuesta?*
What's the exchange rate? - *¿Cuál es el tipo de cambio?*
Can I see . . . ? - *¿Puedo ver . . . ?*
this one - *ésta/ésto*
expensive - *caro*
cheap - *barato*
cheaper - *más barato*
too much - *demasiado*

HEALTH

Help me please. - *Ayúdeme por favor.*
I am ill. - *Estoy enfermo.*
pain - *dolor*
fever - *fiebre*
stomache ache - *dolor de estómago*
vomiting - *vómitos*
diarrhea - *diarrea*
drugstore - *farmacia*
medicine - *medicina*
pill, tablet - *pastilla*
birth control pills - *pastillas contraceptivas, la píldora*
condoms - *condones, preservativas*

BOOKLIST

GOVERNMENT GUIDES

Background Notes: The Dominican Republic. Washington, D.C.: Bureau of Public Affairs, 1987.

Haggerty, Michael A., ed. *Dominican Republic and Haiti: Country Studies.* Washington, D.C.: Federal Research Division, Library of Congress, 1991.

GENERAL

Athiens, G. *Arms and Politics in the Dominican Republic.* Boulder, CO: Westview Press, 1981.

Bell, Ian. *The Dominican Republic.* Boulder, CO: Westview Press, 1991.

Black, Jan Knippers. *The Dominican Republic: Politics and Development in an Unsovereign State.* Boston, MA: Allen and Unwin, 1986.

Cooper, Page. *Sambumbia: A Discovery of the Dominican Republic—the Modern Hispaniola.* New York: Caribbean Library, 1947.

Crahan, Margaret E. and Franklin W. Knight, eds. *Africa and the Caribbean.* Baltimore, MD: John Hopkins University Press, 1979.

Cripps, Louise L. *The Spanish Caribbean, from Columbus to Castro.* Boston, MA: G.K. Hall, 1979.

Georges, Eugenia. *The Making of a Transnational Community: Migration, Development, and Cultural Change in the Dominican Republic.* New York: Columbia University Press, 1989.

Haniff, Nesha Z. *Blaze a Fire: Significant Contributions of Caribbean Women.* Toronto, Canada: Sister Vision Press, 1988.

Hazard, Samuel. *Santo Domingo, Past and Present, with a Glance at Hayti.* New York: Harper and Brothers, 1873.

Hoetink, H. *The Dominican People 1850–1900: Notes for a Historical Sociology.* Baltimore, MD: Johns Hopkins University Press, 1982.

Jacobs, Francine. *The Taínos: People Who Welcomed Columbus.* New York: G.P. Putnam, Patrick Collins Imprint, 1992.

Klein, Alan. *Sugarball, the American Game, the Dominican Dream.* New Haven, CT: Yale University Press, 1991.

Lowenthal, Abraham. *The Dominican Intervention,* 2nd ed. Baltimore, MD: Johns Hopkins University Press, 1995. (Complete bibliography.)

Martin, John B. *Overtaken by Events: The Dominican Crisis from the Fall of Trujillo to the Civil War.* Garden City, NY: Doubleday and Co., 1966.

Mintz, Sidney and Sally Price. *Caribbean Contours.* Baltimore, MD: Johns Hopkins University Press, 1985.

Nelson, W.J. *Almost a Territory: America's Attempt to Annex the Dominican Republic.* New York: St. Martin's Press, 1986.

Olsen, Fred. *On the Trail of the Arawaks.* Norman, OK: University of Oklahoma Press.

Ruck, Rob. *The Tropic of Baseball: Baseball in the Dominican Republic.* New York, NY: Carrol and Graf, 1991.

Vedovato, Claudio. *Politics, Foreign Trade, and Economic Development: A Study of the Dominican Republic.* New York: St. Martin's Press, 1986.

Wiarda, Howard and Michael Kyzanek, eds. *The Dominican Republic: A Caribbean Crucible.* Boulder, CO: Westview Press, 1992.

Wucker, Michelle. *Why the Cocks Fight: Do-*

minicans, Haitians, and the Struggle for Hispaniola. New York, NY: Hill and Wang, 1996.

FICTION AND TRAVEL

Alvarez, Julia. In the Time of the Butterflies. Chapel Hill, NC: Algonquin Books, 1994.

Danticat, Edwidge. The Farming of Bones. New York, NY: Soho, 1999.

Díaz, Junot. Drown. New York, NY: Penguin Putnam, 2000.

Kurlansky, Mark. A Continent of Islands: Searching for the Caribbean Destiny. New York: Addison Wesley, 1992.

Morrison, Samuel E. The Caribbean as Columbus Saw It. Boston, MA: Little and Co, 1964

Severin, Timothy. The Golden Antilles. New York: Alfred A. Knopf, 1970.

Shukman, Henry. Travels with my Trombone: A Caribbean Journey. New York: Crown Publications, 1992.

Willes, Sumner. Naboth's Vineyard: The Dominican Republic 1844-1924. New York: Payson and Clarke, 1928.

PIRACY

This is one of the great topics in history, and there are thousands of books on the subject. Just a sampling is offered here.

Defoe, Daniel. A General History of the Pyrates. Columbia, SC: University of South Carolina Press, 1972. Reprint of the original 18th-century work.

Naipaul, V.S. The Loss of El Dorado. New York: Alfred E. Knopf, 1970 (Vintage reprint).

Naipaul, V.S. The Overcrowded Barracoon. New York: Alfred E. Knopf, 1973 (Vintage reprint).

Sauer, Carl O. The Early Spanish Main. Berkeley, CA: University of California Press, 1969.

Woodbury, George. Great Days of Piracy in the West Indies. New York: W.W. Norton, 1951.

NATURAL HISTORY AND ART

Austerlitz, Paul. Merengue: Dominican Music and Dominican Identity. Philadelphia, PA: Temple U. Press, 1998.

Bond, James. Birds of the West Indies, 3rd edition. Boston, MA: Houghton-Mifflin, 1971.

Fishes of the Caribbean Reefs. London: Macmillan Caribbean, 1978.

Flowers of the Caribbean. London: Macmillan Caribbean, 1978.

Honeychurch, Penelope. Caribbean Wild Plants and Their Uses. London: Macmillan Caribbean, 1986.

Islands and the Sea: Five Centuries of Nature Writing from the Caribbean. New York: Oxford University Press, 1991.

Jones, Alick and Nancy Sefton. Marine Life in the Caribbean. London: Macmillan Caribbean, 1978.

Kaplan, Eugene. Peterson Field Guide to Coral Reefs. Boston, MA: Houghton-Mifflin, 1999

Riley, Norman D. Butterflies of the West Indies. London: William Collins Sons and Co., 1975.

Roessler, Carl. Coral Kingdoms. New York: Abrams, 1986.

Slater, Mary. Cooking the Caribbean Way. London: Hippocrene Books, 1998.

Stockton de Dod, Annabelle, ed. Aves de la República Dominicana. Santo Domingo, Dominican Republic: Museo Nacional de Historia Natural, 1978.

Stratton, Suzanne. Modern and Contemporary

Art of the Dominican Republic, Americas Society and the Spanish Institute. Washington, D.C.

Trees of the Caribbean. London: Macmillan Caribbean, 1980.

Warmke and Abbott. *Caribbean Seashells.* New York: Dover Publications, Inc., 1961.

Wood, Beryl. *Caribbean Fruits and Vegetables: Selected Recipes.* White Plains, NY: Longman Caribbean, 1973.

INDEX

ABOUT THE AUTHOR

Gaylord Dold was born in Kansas and raised in rural Southern California during the good old days. He has also lived in Florida and London, England, where he attended the London School of Economics. Over the years he has published twelve novels as well as many articles and book reviews. He has traveled widely in the Caribbean, Europe, and Africa. These days, he's back on the prairie of southern Kansas, where he lives with his wife, Megumi, and their dog, Aki. Fly-fishing in the Rockies is his passion, and writing his profession. He is currently at work on a new novel and is planning a book about fishing the Continental Divide.

U.S.~METRIC CONVERSION

1 inch = 2.54 centimeters (cm)
1 foot = .304 meters (m)
1 yard = 0.914 meters
1 mile = 1.6093 kilometers (km)
1 km = .6214 miles
1 fathom = 1.8288 m
1 chain = 20.1168 m
1 furlong = 201.168 m
1 acre = .4047 hectares
1 sq km = 100 hectares
1 sq mile = 2.59 square km
1 ounce = 28.35 grams
1 pound = .4536 kilograms
1 short ton = .90718 metric ton
1 short ton = 2000 pounds
1 long ton = 1.016 metric tons
1 long ton = 2240 pounds
1 metric ton = 1000 kilograms
1 quart = .94635 liters
1 US gallon = 3.7854 liters
1 Imperial gallon = 4.5459 liters
1 nautical mile = 1.852 km

To compute celsius temperatures, subtract 32 from Fahrenheit and divide by 1.8. To go the other way, multiply celsius by 1.8 and add 32.

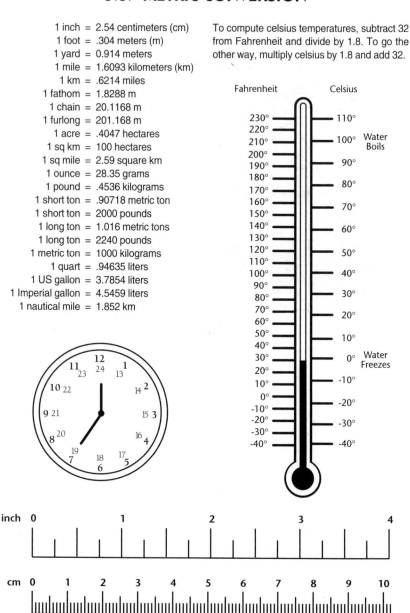

AVALON
TRAVEL
publishing

How far will our travel guides take you? As far as you want.

Discover a rhumba-fueled nightspot in Old Havana, explore prehistoric tombs in Ireland, hike beneath California's centuries-old redwoods, or embark on a classic road trip along Route 66. Our guidebooks deliver solidly researched, trip-tested information—minus any generic froth—to help globetrotters or weekend warriors create an adventure uniquely their own.

And we're not just about the printed page. Public television viewers are tuning in to Rick Steves' new travel series, *Rick Steves' Europe*. On the Web, readers can cruise the virtual black top with *Road Trip USA* author Jamie Jensen and learn travel industry secrets from Edward Hasbrouck of *The Practical Nomad*.

In print. On TV. On the Internet.

We supply the information. The rest is up to you.

Avalon Travel Publishing

Something for everyone

www.travelmatters.com

Avalon Travel Publishing guides are available at your favorite book or travel store.

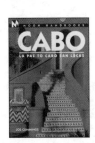

Will you have enough stories to tell your grandchildren?